A Political Companion to Ralph Waldo Emerson

POLITICAL COMPANIONS TO GREAT AMERICAN AUTHORS

Series Editor: Patrick J. Deneen, Georgetown University

The Political Companions to Great American Authors series illuminates the complex political thought of the nation's most celebrated writers from the founding era to the present. The goals of the series are to demonstrate how American political thought is understood and represented by great American writers and to describe how our polity's understanding of fundamental principles such as democracy, equality, freedom, toleration, and fraternity has been influenced by these canonical authors.

The series features a broad spectrum of political theorists, philosophers, and literary critics and scholars whose work examines classic authors and seeks to explain their continuing influence on American political, social, intellectual, and cultural life. This series reappraises esteemed American authors and evaluates their writings as lasting works of art that continue to inform and guide the American democratic experiment.

A POLITICAL COMPANION TO
Ralph Waldo Emerson

Edited by
Alan M. Levine and
Daniel S. Malachuk

THE UNIVERSITY PRESS OF KENTUCKY

Copyright © 2011 by The University Press of Kentucky
Paperback edition 2014

Scholarly publisher for the Commonwealth,
serving Bellarmine University, Berea College, Centre
College of Kentucky, Eastern Kentucky University,
The Filson Historical Society, Georgetown College,
Kentucky Historical Society, Kentucky State University,
Morehead State University, Murray State University,
Northern Kentucky University, Transylvania University,
University of Kentucky, University of Louisville,
and Western Kentucky University.
All rights reserved.

Editorial and Sales Offices: The University Press of Kentucky
663 South Limestone Street, Lexington, Kentucky 40508-4008
www.kentuckypress.com

The Library of Congress has cataloged the hardcover edition as follows:

A political companion to Ralph Waldo Emerson / edited by Alan M. Levine and Daniel S. Malachuk.
   p.   cm.
  Includes bibliographical references and index.
  ISBN 978-0-8131-3430-7 (hardcover : alk. paper) —
  ISBN 978-0-8131-3432-1 (ebook)
  1. Emerson, Ralph Waldo, 1803–1882—Political and social views. 2. United States—Intellectual life—19th century. 3. Democracy—United States—History—19th century. 4. Democracy in literature. I. Levine, Alan, 1961– II. Malachuk, Daniel S.
  PS1642.P64P65 2011
  814'.3—dc23
                         2011021731

(ISBN 978-0-8131-4740-6 (pbk. : alk. paper)

This book is printed on acid-free paper meeting
the requirements of the American National Standard
for Permanence in Paper for Printed Library Materials.

Manufactured in the United States of America.

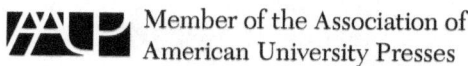

Member of the Association of
American University Presses

Contents

Series Foreword vii

Acknowledgments ix

Abbreviations xi

Introduction: The New History of Emerson's Politics and His Philosophy of Self-Reliance 1
 Alan M. Levine and Daniel S. Malachuk

PART I. CLASSICS ON EMERSON'S POLITICS

1. Emerson: The All and the One 43
 Wilson Carey McWilliams

2. Emerson and the Inhibitions of Democracy 53
 Judith N. Shklar

3. Self-Reliance, Politics, and Society 69
 George Kateb

4. Aversive Thinking: Emersonian Representations in Heidegger and Nietzsche 91
 Stanley Cavell

PART II. EMERSON'S SELF-RELIANCE PROPERLY UNDERSTOOD

5. Self-Reliance and Complicity: Emerson's Ethics of Citizenship 125
 Jack Turner

6. The Limits of Self-Reliance: Emerson, Slavery, and Abolition   152
   James H. Read

7. Emerson, Self-Reliance, and the Politics of Democracy   185
   Len Gougeon

PART III. THE STUBBORN REALITY OF EMERSON'S TRANSCENDENTALISM

8. Skeptical Triangle? A Comparison of the Political Thought of Emerson, Nietzsche, and Montaigne   223
   Alan M. Levine

9. Emerson's Politics, Retranscendentalized   265
   Daniel S. Malachuk

10. Emerson's Transcendental Gaze and the "Disagreeable Particulars" of Slavery: Vision and the Costs of Idealism   305
    Shannon L. Mariotti

PART IV. EMERSON AND LIBERAL DEMOCRACY

11. Property in Being: Liberalism and the Language of Ownership in Emerson's Writing   343
    Neal Dolan

12. Standing for Others: Reform and Representation in Emerson's Political Thought   383
    Jason Frank

13. Emerson's Democratic Platonism in *Representative Men*   415
    G. Borden Flanagan

Selected Bibliography   451

List of Contributors   463

Index   467

Series Foreword

THOSE WHO UNDERTAKE A study of American political thought must attend to the great theorists, philosophers, and essayists. Such a study is incomplete, however, if it neglects American literature, one of the greatest repositories of the nation's political thought and teachings.

America's literature is distinctive because it is, above all, intended for a democratic citizenry. In contrast to eras when an author would aim to inform or influence a select aristocratic audience, in democratic times, public influence and education must resonate with a more expansive, less leisured, and diverse audience to be effective. The great works of America's literary tradition are the natural locus of democratic political teaching. Invoking the interest and attention of citizens through the pleasures afforded by the literary form, many of America's great thinkers sought to forge a democratic public philosophy with subtle and often challenging teachings that unfolded in narrative, plot, and character development. Perhaps more than any other nation's literary tradition, American literature is ineluctably political—shaped by democracy as much as it has in turn shaped democracy.

The Political Companions to Great American Authors series highlights the teachings of the great authors in America's literary and belletristic tradition. An astute political interpretation of America's literary tradition requires careful, patient, and attentive readers who approach the text with a view to understanding its underlying messages about citizenship and democracy. Essayists in this series approach the classic texts not with a "hermeneutics of suspicion" but with the curiosity of fellow citizens who believe that the great authors have something of value to teach their readers. The series brings together essays from varied approaches and viewpoints for the common purpose of elucidating the political teachings of the nation's greatest authors for those seeking a better understanding of American democracy.

Patrick J. Deneen
Series Editor

Acknowledgments

OUR THANKS GO FIRST to Patrick Deneen, the series editor, and Stephen Wrinn, Allison Webster, Susan Murray, and the rest of the UPK staff for making this volume possible. With everyone else today who takes Emerson's politics seriously, we are deeply indebted to the authors of this volume's four "classic" essays, Wilson Carey McWilliams, Judith Shklar, George Kateb, and Stanley Cavell. Others have since refined the history of Emerson's politics, and we offer our introduction as tribute to those fine scholars of what we call the "new history." Our seven contributors of new essays made editing this volume a rewarding intellectual experience: our thanks to all of you for lively discussions in Toronto, Atlanta, and D.C., not to mention the countless emails and conversations in the margins.

We each have our own acknowledgments to make, too. Dan wishes to thank two more scholars particularly. I am very lucky to have been introduced to Emerson by the late Richard Poirier, who taught me to pay attention not only to what Emerson thinks but to how he writes. And, for a couple decades now, I have fundamentally relied upon the scholarship of Len Gougeon; it's a pleasure to thank him here for his work. Finally, my thanks and love to my wife, Katie, and our son, Paul, for giving me the time to work on this book.

Alan wishes to thank some individuals and organizations without whose help this volume might never have been conceived or come to fruition. The idea for this volume occurred while I was a visiting fellow at the James Madison Program in American Ideals and Institutions at Princeton University. I am grateful to everyone at JMP, especially Robert P. George and Bradford P. Wilson, for the leisure to think. It took me in this unforeseen direction. I am grateful to Susan Spagna for a Spagna School of Public Affairs Faculty Research Award that helped me during the last stages of pulling this book together. Finally, my thanks and love to Lynn for intellectually and emotionally supporting my work on this book.

We have worked together on this project since the start of 2007, a nearly half-decade collaboration that has been completely rewarding in and of itself. That a book came out of it along the way is nice, too. It tangibly documents our intellectual partnership and provides us with this opportunity to thank one another publicly. Dan dedicates this book to Alan Levine, who brought to our work together the qualities Emerson identified as the essence of friendship, "a total magnanimity and trust." Alan dedicates the book to Daniel Malachuk, Emersonian extraordinaire.

Abbreviations

AW   *Emerson's Antislavery Writings.* Edited by Len Gougeon and Joel Myerson. New Haven: Yale University Press, 1995.

CW   *The Collected Works of Ralph Waldo Emerson.* Edited by Robert E. Spiller, Alfred R. Ferguson, Joseph Slater, Jean Ferguson Carr, Wallace E. Williams, and Douglas Emory Wilson. 5 vols. to date. Cambridge: Harvard University Press, 1971–.

E&L   *Essays and Lectures.* Edited by Joel Porte. New York: Library of America, 1983.

EL   *The Early Lectures of Ralph Waldo Emerson.* Edited by Robert E. Spiller, Stephen E. Whicher, and Wallace E. Williams. 3 vols. Cambridge: Harvard University Press, 1959–1972.

JMN   *The Journals and Miscellaneous Notebooks of Ralph Waldo Emerson.* Edited by William H. Gilman et al. 16 vols. Cambridge: Harvard University Press, 1960–1982.

Letters   *The Letters of Ralph Waldo Emerson.* 1939. Edited by Ralph L. Rusk and Eleanor M. Tilton. 10 vols. New York: Columbia University Press, 1990–1995.

LL   *The Later Lectures of Ralph Waldo Emerson: 1843–1871.* Edited by Ronald Bosco and Joel Myerson. 2 vols. Athens: University of Georgia Press, 2001.

S   *Complete Sermons of Ralph Waldo Emerson.* Edited by Albert J. von Frank et al. 4 vols. Columbia: University of Missouri Press, 1989–1992.

W   *The Complete Works of Ralph Waldo Emerson.* Edited by Edward Waldo Emerson. 12 vols. Boston: Houghton Mifflin, 1903–1904.

Introduction: The New History of Emerson's Politics and His Philosophy of Self-Reliance

Alan M. Levine and Daniel S. Malachuk

IF MELVILLE, THOREAU, AND other major American authors have suffered significant periods of neglect, Ralph Waldo Emerson (1803–1882) has never wanted for commentators. And yet from *The Centenary of the Birth of Ralph Waldo Emerson* (1903) forward, none of the many collections of essays dedicated to Emerson has focused exclusively on his political thought until *A Political Companion to Emerson*.[1] It is an auspicious moment for this volume. Not since the Civil War, when Emerson was adored in the North and reviled in the South, has there been such interest in Emerson's politics. This new interest has been building since the last quarter of the twentieth century, when two things happened. First, political theorists and philosophers began to take Emerson seriously as a political thinker. Second, literary historians began to recover Emerson's political writings and activities. This book reassesses Emerson as a political theorist in light of these two developments.

This introduction has three sections. Section 1 reviews the highlights of Emerson's political writings and activities as recovered in what we call here the "new history." The new history is the result of painstakingly careful research and has opened up to scholars a set of political writings and activities by Emerson that thoroughly debunk the old myth that Emerson's project is exhibit one of the phenomenon Tocqueville most famously labeled "individualism": that is, "a reflective and peaceable sentiment that disposes each citizen to isolate himself from the mass of those like him and to withdraw to one side with his family and his friends, so that after having thus created a little society for his own use, he willingly abandons society at large to itself."[2] Individualism, according to Tocqueville, derives from feelings of isolation, alienation, and a sense of impotence to affect one's larger society. Emerson never advocated or succumbed to individualism in this sense. Like Tocqueville, he laments such withdrawal from society. Instead, also like Tocqueville, John Stuart Mill, and other liberals, Emerson advocated a strong, healthy, independent-mindedness that we shall distinguish from individual*ism* and call "individual*ity*."[3] Emerson's advocacy of individuality occurs via a philosophy he called "self-reliance," which entails individuality but far more than this, too. As Emerson used the term, self-reliance entails not a narrow selfishness or even just cultivation of one's self but an empathy with all selves. That is, self-reliance for Emerson entails not only an ethical commitment to the active "reform" or "cultivation" of one's self but also a political commitment to a democracy where all other individuals are able to do the same. While Emerson always believed "souls are not saved in bundles," as he memorably puts it in the 1860 "Worship" (*E&L*, 1062), he also always believed that democracy is the best setting to actively promote self-reliant souls.[4] Insofar as self-reliance is his central concern, Emerson is thus also concerned with democratic politics and not merely the fate of isolated individuals. These mutually reinforcing commitments to self-reliance and democracy were lifelong for Emerson, and he expressed them in political activities and writings that have been the intense focus of the new history, which we summarize here.

Section 2 considers how, in the century after Emerson's death, most readers forgot about his political activities and writings. This neglect would not be important except that what filled the vacuum was a pernicious myth about Emerson's apolitical individualism. Because this myth endures as the most significant obstacle to a better appreciation of Emerson's political thought, we take the time here to debunk it.

Section 3 introduces the essays in this volume. Part 1 of this book consists of four classic essays that are the best and most influential previously published writings on Emerson's political thought. Any serious encounter with Emerson's political thought must consider them. Still, mainly as a result of focusing on what we follow one scholar in calling the "small canon" of Emerson's writings—mainly writings from 1836 to 1844 that have been the mainstay of Emerson scholarship until very recently[5]—these classic texts do not fully comprehend how Emerson's emphasis on self-reliance led to more than individuality: that Emerson's self-reliance entailed political commitments, too. By dealing with the complete range of Emerson's writings as recovered by the new history, however, our original contributors offer nine new essays on what we consider the three fundamental concerns of Emerson's political philosophy: self-reliance as a political practice; the implications of transcendentalism for politics; and key elements of democracy beyond self-reliance, especially representation and property. The essays on each of these three concerns form parts 2–4 of this volume.

The New History

Thanks to a set of scholars in the 1990s, we now study a very different Emerson from the one studied from the 1880s through the 1980s. Where Emerson prior to 1990 was generally and wrongly understood to be advocating "individualism" (a word we use throughout the introduction only in Tocqueville's sense of a "reflective and peaceable . . . withdraw[ing]" from society), after 1990 scholars began to recover the history of his social and political engagements, particularly his abolitionism. Our contributor Len Gougeon's 1990 *Virtue's Hero: Emerson, Antislavery, and Reform* is universally regarded as the book that initiated this new era in Emerson scholarship. The other key books usually mentioned in this wave of scholarship are David M. Robinson's *Emerson and the Conduct of Life: Pragmatism and Ethical Purpose in the Later Work* (1993); Robert D. Richardson's *Emerson: The Mind on Fire* (1995); and Albert J. von Frank's *The Trials of Anthony Burns: Freedom and Slavery in Emerson's Boston* (1998); as well as T. Gregory Garvey's valuable 2001 collection, *The Emerson Dilemma*.[6] No fewer than three anthologies of Emerson's once forgotten political writings have since been published, too, part of a more general expansion of the Emerson corpus (ongoing since the 1960s) through the publication of authoritative editions of Emerson's published essays and books, sermons, lectures, correspondence, and journals.[7] Finally and most recently, a few books have begun to reinterpret Emerson's liberalism in light of the scholarship of Gougeon and others; most notable among these is our contributor Neal Dolan's *Emerson's Liberalism* (2009), the first comprehensive and historically informed exposition of Emerson's political thought.[8] Together, these anthologies, authoritative editions, and monographs since 1990 comprise the new history of Emerson, a history we now sketch.

The old "historical" portraits of Emerson are very familiar: the dreamy seer wandering in the woods, the alienated naysayer sitting primly in his study; they also are very wrong. Throughout his public career, Emerson tirelessly advocated for his philosophy of self-reliance, which meant that he also tirelessly advocated for a democracy that would inspire not conformity but reflective, ethical, and engaged citizenship: that is, self-reliance as Emerson defined it. Emerson believed that no message was more important than self-reliance for a nation still in the midst of inventing the world's first representative democracy. His political activity as a "democratic intellectual" comprises the "very marrow of his biography," as the historian Peter Field aptly puts it.[9] In the 1820s, Emerson became a minister to preach religious self-reliance but left his church when it seemed to breed spiritual and intellectual conformity instead. In the 1830s, to reach a broader, more diverse audience, he effectively invented the career of public lecturer: his message was the reform of the self—and reform of society, too, so long as it did not jeopardize a democracy of self-reliant individuals. In the 1840s, now "the spokesman for American idealism," he joined the cause of abolition, redefining slavery as the negation of self-reliance for master, slave, and complicit citizen.[10] By the 1850s, he became not only one of the nation's most prominent voices for ending slavery but a democratic visionary who commanded the attention of every major political figure in that turbulent period from John Brown to Abraham Lincoln. In the 1860s, following the Civil War, he was recognized as the nation's sage, lecturing huge audiences from coast to coast about his vision of an American democracy of self-reliant individuals. A consistent, active, and public commitment to self-reliance and democracy is the theme of this new history of Emerson. It demolishes the pernicious myth of Emerson's indifference to politics.

Based on the new history, we divide Emerson's career into four periods: 1826–1835, 1836–1844, 1844–1863, and 1864–1872. About the earliest stage of Emerson's public career, from 1826 to 1835, the new history teaches us three important things about his politics: the core relationship between his ethics and his politics, what Emerson meant by the "self" in his philosophy of "self-reliance," and his roots in a mode of political advocacy known then as "moral suasion." First, beginning as a liberal Protestant minister in 1826, Emerson understood democratic politics as the practical application of ethics, and ethics to be a matter of self-reform. This view was common among liberal Protestants of Emerson's day, and throughout his career Emerson never really strayed from it. He rejected the traditional Calvinist premise of innate human depravity, contending instead that the most effective political change begins with an ethical change in one's self. This conviction continues to find expression in modern democratic thought, such as in the slogan, derived from a famous quote of Gandhi's, "Be the change." Social reform thus must begin with individual initiative, not collective action. As Gougeon describes Emerson's views at the time: "Social reformation that comes as a result of the forceful imposition of change upon individuals or institutions from without is not true reformation because it deals with symptoms and not causes, sins but not sinners."[11] Besides the duty of reforming himself, which every individual has, Emerson believed the public intellectual has the additional duty to encourage others to undertake self-reform—but to do no more than this. In his youth, Emerson thought this was sufficient. It led Emerson to promote a vision of America as a democratic nation of self-motivated self-reformers. If each citizen promoted self-reliance, then and only then could justice be achieved for all. Emerson advocated this strenuously, as in this 1832 sermon: "We ought never to lose sight of the truth that national offences are private offences carried out and represented at full length. . . . It becomes every reflecting American to consider [that] his vote and his influence [are] a measured share in the government, [and that he] is really responsible, in that proportion, to God and to men for the acts of government. . . . Let every man say then to himself—the cause of the Indian, it is mine; the cause of the slave, it is mine; the cause of the union, it is mine; the cause of public honesty, of education, of religion, they are mine" (S, 4:114–15). As Wesley Mott summarizes this philosophy: "In a democracy, Emerson declares, the burden is on the *individual* to maintain righteous government."[12]

The second important political aspect of Emerson's early period is the development of his view of the self. The epistemological aspect of Emerson's self has long been understood, but the new history also draws out its ethical and political significance.[13] Like others of his generation, Emerson rejected the established Lockean view of the mind as a tabula rasa. Instead, drawing on the Scottish Enlightenment, German Romanticism, neo-Platonism, and radical Protestantism, he developed an intuitional philosophy of how we know the world. Emerson called our power of intuition "Reason." And because he deemed this faculty granted to us by and as partaking in the divine, he also variously called it "the Soul" or our "moral sense" or "Intuition," among other things. "Your reason is God," Emerson explained in an

1826 sermon, his first (*S*, 1:57). To know what is true, but also to do what is right, we must rely upon our divine Reason, and not upon what he called our "Understanding," his name for our merely worldly, calculating abilities that are divorced from deeper truth.[14] Once this reliance upon Reason is embraced, "self-reliance" (as Emerson began to call this ethic around 1830) can be pursued productively and safely. As he put it in an 1831 sermon:"To a man who sees that he has no other existence than that which he derives every moment from a power not his own, that is from God, the doctrine may be safely preached of a boundless reliance on himself because that is a reliance on God" (*S*, 3:203). The self-reliant individual intuits that all selves have this potential; therein lies the politics of self-reliance. As Emerson explains in an 1830 sermon: "It is important to observe that this self-reliance which grows out of the Scripture doctrine of the value of the soul is not inconsistent either with our duties to our fellow men or to God. . . . In listening more intently to our soul [that is, our intuitional faculty], we are not becoming in the ordinary sense more selfish, but are departing farther from what is low and falling back upon truth and upon God" (*S*, 2:266–67). What exactly Emerson means by God is not entirely clear. It is neither the traditional God of Christian revelation that directly intervenes in human affairs nor the personal God of Protestantism. Rather, Emerson variously equates God with notions like "the Soul," "the Over-Soul," the "Creator," and the "Divine," among other things. But whatever Emerson means by God, the new history indicates that it underlies his moral and political vision.[15] Ethically, all selves—all bearers of God's imprint—have a duty to help one another. Politically, only democracy makes sense, for we are all of equal moral worth. "Democracy/Freedom has its roots in the Sacred truth that every man hath in him the Divine Reason," Emerson writes in an 1834 journal. While he acknowledges that "few men since the creation of the world live according to the dictates of Reason," he nonetheless insists that "all men are created capable of so doing. That is the equality and the only equality of all men" (*JMN*, 4:356–57).

The third important political aspect of Emerson's early period is his belief that the best way for self-reliant individuals to encourage others to become self-reliant is by "moral suasion." Through attention to this particular aspect of Emerson's early period, the new history has helped dispel the old myth of Emerson's individualism not just in his theoretical writings but also in his deeds. Far from retreating from the world, Emerson energetically pursued its reform by way of moral suasion. As developed by abolitionists in the early 1830s, moral suasion meant trying to persuade people using the full range of activities that we today associate with both civil society and most social activism, including speaking out, collaborating to sponsor public lectures, publishing pamphlets and newspapers, organizing clubs, associations, and societies, and petitioning the federal, state, and local governments.[16] Emerson—seeking to promote self-reliance—not only sermonized and lectured as an individual about self-reliance, but he also collaborated with others in all these ways. That is, he collaborated with others to publish addresses and books, to edit a journal (the *Dial*, dedicated to self-reliance, among other ideas), to try to transform the Unitarian church into an agent for promoting self-reliance before leaving it to organize looser associations like the "Transcendental Club," and to petition local, state, and, most famously, the federal government (in 1838, as discussed momentarily) regarding controversies he understood to be related to self-reliance.[17] In short, by collaboratively using moral suasion in this period to advocate self-reliance, Emerson was hardly withdrawing from democratic society; on the contrary, he was deliberately pioneering new ways for self-reliant individuals to work together to encourage all individuals to become more self-reliant.

By the mid-1830s, then, Emerson had developed a vision of participatory democracy where self-reliant individuals unite to encourage others to become self-reliant, too. Perhaps the most compelling public expression of this symbiotic relationship between self-reliance and democracy in Emerson's early thought is his "Historical Discourse at Concord" (1835). On the occasion of the two-hundredth anniversary of the town's founding, Emerson admired how, with those first settlements, "the nature of man and his condition in the world, for the first time within the period of certain [i.e., recorded] history, controlled the formation of the State." Just as Tocqueville famously praises the self-governance of New England towns in volume 1 of *Democracy in America* (1835, see especially vol. 1, pt. 1, chap. 5), Emerson in the same year praises the early Massachusetts settlers for forming a new kind of state that emphasized individual and collective growth. According to Emerson, the engine of that new democratic state of self-reliant individuals was the town meeting. "In a town-meeting, the great secret of political science was uncovered," he wrote (meaning that the great secret *was* the town meeting), "and the problem solved, how to give every individual his fair weight in the government, without any disorder from numbers. In a town-meeting, the roots of society were reached" (*W*, 11:40, 43, 46).[18] Ancient theorists of democracy like Plato and modern theorists such as Montesquieu and Publius were, of course, more skeptical about such a democratic "solution"; Emerson at this stage in his career shows little concern about demagoguery or related problems in the public sphere. Instead, Emerson imagines an America of democratic deliberation (that is, using the many modes of moral suasion) in town meetings leading to more and more individuals pursuing more and more self-reliance.

The new history generally presents what we call Emerson's second period, 1836–1844, as a transitional time. During this period, the relationship between self-reliance and democracy increasingly seemed to Emerson less like a symbiosis than a "dilemma," as T. Gregory Garvey felicitously puts it (*The Emerson Dilemma*, xii). Again and again in this period's writings, Emerson calls into question his early optimistic vision of the town meeting ideal.[19] His doubts were typical of many reformers at the time. Moral suasion came to seem no match against the mob rage that led to the 1837 murder of the abolitionist publisher Elijah Lovejoy or the racist nationalism that led to the forced removal of the Cherokee in 1838. Working with others, Emerson employed moral suasion to object to both events. "The soul of man, the justice, the mercy, that is the heart's heart in all men . . . does abhor this business," Emerson wrote to President Van Buren in protest of the Cherokee's removal (*AW*, 3). It was all for naught: these were instead sobering lessons about the limits of political speech to all reformers. In this period's writings—which dominate the "small canon," including *Nature* (1836), late 1830s addresses such as "The American Scholar" (1837) and "Divinity School Address" (1838), and the 1841 and 1844 *Essays* including "Self-Reliance," "Circles," and "Experience"—Emerson critiqued the town meeting in many different ways, most powerfully as the engine no longer of self-reliance but of social conformity. And, as Emerson explained in "Self-Reliance," social conformity "was the virtue most in request. Self-reliance is its aversion" (*E&L*, 261).

In just a few years, then, Emerson completely changed his mind about democratic society: far from the ally of self-reliance, it had become the enemy. Extreme rhetoric, dark irony, and wild hyperbole enter his writing. For example, to emphasize that human laws promote not self-reliance but conformity, Emerson declares early in "Self-Reliance," "No law can be sacred to me but that of my own nature" (*E&L*, 262). Of course, close attention to the essay soon reveals that this is indeed hyperbole; Emerson soon clarifies that the law of one's own nature is granted us by God, and thus Emerson's "lawlessness" is really only an instance of complaint against human-made law, because "the relations of the soul to the divine spirit are so pure, that it is profane to seek to interpose helps" (E&L, 269). Still, Emerson's objection to such "helps," or what he often calls "forms," seems to become more extreme in this period—akin to Tocqueville's criticism that people living in democracies come to see all "forms" as hindrances instead of as helps.[20] In the earlier period, Emerson was more moderate on the subject. For example, in the 1832 sermon announcing his departure from his ministry in objection to the formal rite of the Eucharist, Emerson explained that the "dead forms" of sectarian religion had become hindrances to him; they were no longer "helps" to his self-reliance. Still, he was careful to explain that "forms are as essential as bodies. It would be foolish to declaim against them," even if he immediately adds that "to adhere to one form a moment after it is outgrown is foolish" (S, 4:192–93). In 1836–1844, however, Emerson often declaims against forms with gusto. In the most obvious case, in "Circles" (1841), Emerson notes that, as thoughts form themselves into "circular wave[s] of circumstance,—as, for instance, an empire, rules of an art, a local usage, a religious rite," subsequent thoughts then tend "to heap [themselves] on that ridge, and . . . hem in the life. But," he continues, "if the soul is quick and strong, it bursts over that boundary on all sides. . . . [T]he heart refuses to be imprisoned" (E&L, 404). In short, during this second period Emerson recognizes the limits of democratic politics: how its collaboratively built forms can in turn thwart individual growth. Emerson couples a pragmatic sobriety about these limits to a deep desire to shatter them.

In such moments in the writings from 1836 to 1844, we see a tension emerging in Emerson's thought between what we call Emerson's sober liberalism and a more ecstatic one. The new history has emphasized Emerson's sober, reforming liberalism, but the ecstatic liberalism needs more attention. Beginning in this period, these two threads in Emerson's thought jostle one another in an uneasy tension, a tension that influences his politics, too. For example, Emerson in this period seems at once enthralled by nature's example for human beings—"a universe of ends . . . a work of *ecstasy*," he marvels in "The Method of Nature" (1841)—and broodingly troubled that his ecstatic vision will never gain widespread traction among us: we know, he observes in "Man the Reformer" from the same year, that "the community in which we live will hardly bear to be told that every man should be open to ecstasy or a divine illumination" (*E&L*, 120, 135). Some of his essays convey this tension perfectly, as in the concluding sentences of "The American Scholar" (1837). Concerned that conformity threatens self-reliance, Emerson there famously urges everyone to "be an unit" rather than "reckoned in the gross." But Emerson then describes this self-reliance as entailing both a sober respect for the liberty of others ("the dread of man") and an ecstatic union of all individuals ("the love of man"). That is, self-reliance requires from us both a pragmatic respect for the liberty of others (as recommended by other liberals like Tocqueville and Mill) *and* an agapic love of all humankind. "The dread of man and the love of man shall be a defence and a wreath of joy around all," Emerson writes; "a nation of men will for the first time exist, because each believes himself inspired by the Divine Soul which also inspires all men" (*E&L*, 71). Careful to gesture to both his sober and ecstatic concerns, Emerson's vision includes fiercely independent individuals somehow lovingly united in universal brotherhood.

Emerson continues to develop both the "dread of man" and the "love of man" in the third stage of his political life, 1844–1863, though the new history has focused on the former aspect of Emerson's thought. The new history has correctly taught us to read this period as Emerson's greatest moment of consistent, effective reform activity: activity that proves his commitment to liberal democracy rested upon an absolute respect for—that is, a "dread of"—each individual's liberty, especially the liberty of those persons currently enslaved. Beginning with Emerson's first significant abolitionist address in 1844 ("Address on the Emancipation") and culminating in his 1863 statement about the United States after the Emancipation Proclamation ("Fortune of the Republic"), this is indeed Emerson's great period of reform liberalism. At the heart of this reform liberalism is his abolitionism. As documented in the 1995 collection *Emerson's Antislavery Writings,* between 1844 and 1863 Emerson wrote a new denunciation of slavery almost every year, and delivered these in public forums dozens and dozens of times. Slavery effectively replaces conformity in Emerson's thought as the great enemy of self-reliance: the enemy of the self-reliance of the enslaved person, most obviously, but also of the master and the consumer of goods produced by slaves.[21] Correspondingly, self-reliance emerges in Emerson's thought as standing for, in Field's words, "a theory of human rights and capacities that engendered respect of others as unique, dignified human beings" (*Ralph Waldo Emerson*, 221–22). As Emerson wrote in an 1851 letter shortly after the enactment of the 1850 Fugitive Slave Law: "At this moment, it seems imperative that every lover of human rights should, in every manner, singly or socially, in private and in public, by voice and by pen—and, first of all, by substantial help and hospitality to the [fugitive] slave, and defending him against his hunters,—enter his protest for humanity against the detestable statute of the last Congress" (*AW*, 51). Emerson argued that the United States must be reformed to live up to its liberal principles. "The theory of our government is Liberty," he announces in 1855, and "all the mind of America was possessed by that idea," including (as he lists) the Declaration of Independence, the Constitution, the newspapers, and even the national anthem (*AW*, 104). In his defense of John Brown in the November 1859 "Speech at a Meeting to Aid John Brown's Family," Emerson explains his support for Brown this way: Brown "believes in the union of the United States [and] conceives that the only obstruction to the union is slavery, and for that reason as a patriot, he works for its abolition" (*AW*, 118). (In a draft of his 1838 letter to President Van Buren, Emerson had similarly written, "The one thing that means & makes union [of the states], is justice" [*AW*, 159]). Emerson and Emerson's Brown are for the Union here, seeking only to reform it until it is consistent with its original liberal principles in the Declaration. Pointing to statements such as these, Gougeon persuasively concludes that "Emerson emerged in the 1850s and 1860s as the spokesperson for liberal democracy in America."[22]

At the same time, though, Emerson's ecstatic liberalism—the liberalism driven by the "love of man" rather than the "dread of man"—is also prominent in the third period, 1844–1863. Rather than merely reform the state in pursuit of justice, Emerson in this mode also imagines a stateless world dedicated to love. Consider what happens if we treat not the 1844 "Address on the Emancipation" as the inaugural text of this period but the 1844 essay "Politics." Preoccupied with conformity as he was in so many of the great essays from the early 1840s, Emerson tells us in "Politics" that "we ought to remember that [the state's] institutions are not aboriginal, though they existed before we were born: that they are not superior to the citizen" (*E&L*, 559). As with the state of nature theorists, Emerson avers that the individual comes before the state; self-reliance is not born in symbiosis with the town meeting and other institutions of democracy but rather is entirely prior to these institutions. And so we must remember that "our [democratic] institutions . . . have not any exemption from the practical defects which have discredited other forms": our democratic institutions were made by people just like other forms, and, just as Emerson once radically dismissed what he believed to be the discredited forms of established religion, so he becomes radically dismissive of even the most basic of democratic institutions, including the rule of law. Echoing Montaigne, Emerson adds: "Every actual State is corrupt. Good men must not obey the laws too well" (*E&L*, 563).[23] Both of these points—that individuals precede the state and that because of human imperfection all institutions that humans create are also imperfect—are standard arguments in traditional liberal thought. But Emerson goes further, inflecting these arguments with utopian optimism. Since he can conceive of a time when humans existed without a state, Emerson—like Marx around the same time—fantasizes about a future when the state will simply be unnecessary. But whereas Marx argued that a state would be rendered universally unnecessary by relying upon *public ownership* of the means of production, Emerson, noting how states tend to proliferate laws and thus limit our self-reliance, contends that "the antidote to this abuse of formal Government, is, the influence of *private character*, the growth of the Individual." Emerson is thus less utopian than Marx insofar as the appearance of one "Individual" for Emerson does not necessarily imply the concurrent attainment of economic, social, and political conditions that will make everyone else true individuals also, as it does for Marx. Emerson describes this "private character" or self-reliant "Individual" as the "wise man," governing himself, and thus making the state, so far as that particular wise man is concerned, utterly unnecessary: "The appearance of the wise man, of whom the existing government, is, it must be owned, but a shabby imitation. . . . To educate the wise man, the State exists; and with the appearance of the wise man, the State expires. The appearance of character makes the State unnecessary. The wise man is the State" (*E&L*, 568). On the one hand, the idea that the wise do not need the state for morality is an old one. It is the idea behind Plato's philosopher-king being the living law, religious prophets, and Publius's notion that if men were angels, no state would be necessary. But, on the other hand, like Marx and unlike Plato and Publius, Emerson also imagines a future where *all* humans are wise, self-reliant. "The power of love, as the basis of a State," he coyly notes, "has never been tried" (*E&L*, 569). "Could not a nation of friends even devise better ways" than the traditional state? (*E&L*, 570). While clearly fighting for liberalism and the universal rights on which it is based, Emerson's imagination simultaneously flirts with the idea of a utopian community consisting entirely of self-reliant wise men held together by agapic love. This optimistic, radical egalitarianism is Emerson's ecstatic liberalism.

At moments in the 1850s, Emerson's ecstatic liberalism led him to radical politics. Appealing both to the moral principles articulated in the Declaration of Independence and to his vision of agapic love, Emerson repeatedly cast doubt on the legitimacy of the U.S. government. For Emerson, the 1850 Fugitive Slave Act (which required northern officials to actively seek out and capture fugitive slaves) exposed the U.S. government itself as a dead form. "Let us respect the Union to all honest ends," he announced in his 1851 "Address to the Citizens of Concord," "but also respect an older and wider union, the law of nature and rectitude" (*AW*, 71). Indeed, throughout the 1850s, Emerson was one of the fiercest advocates of "the law of nature and rectitude," or what was more commonly called "higher law," as more legitimate than the Constitution of the United States. As the nation moved to the verge of civil war and politicians prevaricated, Emerson boldly appealed to "higher law" over the Constitution. The most extreme example of this is Emerson's defense of John Brown's raid on Harpers Ferry.[24] "Beware when the great God lets loose a thinker on this planet. Then all things are at risk," Emerson had written in "Circles" (*E&L*, 407). Emerson deemed Brown just such a thinker. In his 1859 "Speech," he announced that Brown was "the rarest of heroes, a pure idealist" (*AW*, 118). "He saw how deceptive the forms are," Emerson explained, referring to the U.S. government and its laws. "We fancy, in Massachusetts, that we are free; yet it seems the Government is quite unreliable. . . . Why? Because the judges rely on the forms, and do not, like John Brown, use their eyes to see the fact behind the forms" (*AW*, 119). What Brown saw behind the forms was the "higher law" of the equal worth of all individuals. In "John Brown," a January 1860 address delivered just after Brown's execution, Emerson explained Brown's deed as an expression of agapic love: "And [yet] our blind statesmen go up and down, with committees of vigilance and safety, hunting for the origin of this new heresy [abolitionism]. They will need a very vigilant committee indeed to find its birthplace, and a very strong force to root it out. For the arch-Abolitionist, older than Brown, and older than the Shenandoah Mountains, is Love, whose other name is Justice, which was before Alfred, before Lycurgus, before Slavery, and will be after it" (*AW*,

123–24). Not only did Emerson sometimes deem the U.S. government illegitimate and agree with John Brown's vision of Love and Justice, but he also seemingly approved of Brown's violent methods to bring about their shared moral goal. In the course of explaining Brown's belief in "two instruments . . . The Golden Rule, and the Declaration of Independence," Emerson reminded his Massachusetts audience—and in what seems an approving manner—that Brown had said that it is "[b]etter that a whole generation of men, women and children should pass away by a violent death, than that one word of either [the Golden Rule or the Declaration] should be violated in this country." "There is a Unionist—there is a strict constructionist for you," Emerson added to "applause and laughter" (*AW*, 118). Slavery was truly horrible, and one must praise the unblinking clarity Emerson developed on this point, but it is nonetheless chilling to see Emerson's joke about a whole generation of violent death and to have the room laugh. This is the frightening enthusiasm that can result from ecstatic moral absolutism.

Emerson's liberalism is alternately sober and ecstatic during the Civil War. The new history makes clear that Emerson did not support the war until Lincoln explicitly dedicated it to emancipation, an aim Emerson demanded in a January 1862 address in Washington, D.C.[25] Immediately following Lincoln's Emancipation Proclamation in September 1862, though, Emerson wrote in his journal that there can now be "no durable peace, no sound Constitution, until we have fought this battle, & the rights of man are vindicated" (*JMN*, 15:293). Publicly, in an October address, "The President's Proclamation," Emerson announced: "The aim of the war on our part is indicated by the aim of the President's Proclamation, namely . . . to destroy the piratic feature in [southern society] which makes it our enemy only as it is the enemy of the human race" (*AW*, 134). In Emerson's view, the North fought not for the Union but for the human race and against all "piratic" crimes against humanity.[26] In his December 1863 address, "Fortune of the Republic," Emerson announced: "The end of all political struggle, is, to establish morality as the basis of all legislation. 'Tis not free institutions, 'tis not a republic, 'tis not a democracy, that is the end,—no, but only the means: morality is the object of government. We want a state of things in which crime will not pay. A state of things which allows every man the largest liberty compatible with the liberty of every other man" (*AW*, 153). Love and Justice will now find expression in our national forms: "The height of Reason, the noblest affection, the purest religion will find their house in our institutions, and write our laws for the benefit of men" (*AW*, 154).

Following the Emancipation Proclamation, in what we call his last period, 1864–1872, Emerson continued to imagine the "reinvention of democracy," as Gougeon puts it in a recent essay, including the extension of political rights to women. Emerson cheered the three Reconstruction amendments to the Constitution, celebrating in his journal in 1871 that "the Constitution [was] not only amended, but construed in a new spirit."[27] That spirit was the spirit of self-reliance, which motivated Emerson's politics from the 1820s to the end of his public career in the early 1870s.

The Myth of Emerson's Apolitical Individualism

This new history of Emerson is still not widely known, however, due to the stubborn persistence of a myth about Emerson's apolitical individualism, a myth that has endured (in Gougeon's words) "almost solely on the basis of historical reiteration rather than historical fact" (*Virtue's Hero*, 4). In this section, we briefly review this reiterated myth, explaining its genealogy so as to debunk it.

In the regional culture war that followed the Civil War, there was no room for Emerson's philosophy of self-reliance, either in the South or the North. Beginning in the 1850s, many southern intellectuals traced northern aggression to transcendentalism, which they interpreted as just the new face of New England Puritanism. According to this interpretation, as one southern essayist astutely but uncharitably put it just before the war, northern intellectuals and politicians shared a fanatical devotion to "the *higher* or moral law, . . . which . . . in their literature, constitutes that element recognized as *transcendentalism*." In another southern essay from just after the war, nothing had really changed. The Radical Republicans, the essayist opined, relying upon "their tools, the German infidels" (meaning the Transcendentalists) "rule this nation, and if undisturbed in power, will soon ruin it."[28] But the North, too, was anxious to leave transcendentalism behind. The generational shift from transcendentalism to pragmatism is well known. As Louis Menand puts it: "The Civil War swept away the slave civilization of the South, but it swept away almost the whole intellectual culture of the North along with it."[29] A classic example is Oliver Wendell

Holmes Jr., the son of Emerson's good friend Oliver Wendell Holmes Sr. The younger Holmes left for a war he called "a crusade in the cause of the whole civilized world," but returned to announce, "I do not know what is true."[30] Higher law lost its allure among the young men who fought a bloody war on its behalf; after experiencing the horrors of war, truth was judged by them not based on its transcendence but by its "cash value," as William James put it in *Pragmatism*.[31]

As a number of critics have shown, following Emerson's death, his champions responded to this challenging postbellum, post-transcendentalist world by depoliticizing Emerson.[32] For example, the 1884 and 1887 biographies by his friends Holmes Sr. and James Elliot Cabot, respectively, avoided mentioning Emerson's abolitionism or presented it as exceptional, quixotic, and, most of all, decorous. One contemporary admirer and supporter of Emerson's antislavery activity, Thomas Wentworth Higginson, explained these biographies' omissions of Emerson's politics by observing that "Dr. Holmes saw him but little on that [political] side, and Mr. J. E. Cabot . . . was, as he frankly admitted to me, constitutionally reticent" (qtd. in Gougeon, *Virtue's Hero*, 14). But in eliminating Emerson's sharp political edges, these "genteel critics," as they have since come to be called, sought to do more than depoliticize Emerson. They additionally hoped to make Emerson acceptable not only to a new generation of pragmatic Americans but also to new arrivals to America. Noting the wave of new immigrants from eastern and southern Europe, Holmes, Cabot, and others remade Emerson as the nation's sage, a detached, civilizing guide for generations of Americans to come. To accomplish this, their sanitizing effort reduced Emerson's writing to a "repository of elevating thoughts and cleansing emotions" (Mitchell, *Individualism and Its Discontents*, 35). Another of these "genteel" critics, Charles Eliot, the president of Harvard University, put together the fifty-one-volume *Harvard Classics* (colloquially known as "Dr. Eliot's Five-Foot Shelf") that was designed for the general reader and promised them a liberal education if perused for just fifteen minutes a day. In introducing a selection of Emerson's writings that made up volume 5, effectively defining the "small canon" for the next century, Eliot, like the other genteel critics, asserted that Emerson's real value lies not in his ideas but in his "tact and reasonableness."[33] As Charles Mitchell explains, "the genteel critics diverted attention from Emerson's [political] writings while enshrining him as a cultural icon, leaving the impression that he was someone who demanded reverence but not necessarily a careful reading" (*Individualism and Its Discontents*, 5). By 1900, Emerson's corpus was so defanged that even astute readers, such as George Santayana, began concluding that Emerson "had no doctrine at all," political or otherwise.[34] Indeed, the pattern of Emerson scholarship was now set for the next one hundred years. From then until recently, scholars agreed that Emerson had no political teaching other than his apolitical individualism.

Beginning in the second decade of the twentieth century, liberals on the left as well as the New Humanists on the right agreed that Emerson was America's central author—the genteel critics were successful to this extent—but they also agreed that Emerson's seeming lack of political conviction deserved censure.[35] Troubled by a perceived escalation of American materialism, liberals championed a more socially engaged literature, and, unsurprisingly, could not find it in the genteel version of Emerson. In his *America's Coming-of-Age* (1915), the liberal Van Wyck Brooks bemoaned that "since the day of Emerson's address on 'The American Scholar' the whole of American literature [has only been] addressed to the private virtues of young men."[36] Brooks viewed Emerson as offering the United States only a "thorough-going self-reliant individualism" (79), "presid[ing] over and [giving] its tone to this world of infinite social fragmentation and unlimited free will" (81). "Essentially passive," Emerson was (to Brooks) clearly "incapable of an effective social ideal" (81, 82). In his *Our America* (1919), fellow liberal Waldo Frank agreed that Emerson "had the genius of aspiration," but, disengaged from the world as he was, "the *motif* of Emerson is an hysterical plea." "Implicitly he leaves the world—the actual world, New England's world—to the low enemy. 'Beauty and Spirit are lonely fellows,' he seems to shrill. 'Come with me and I will show them to you.'"[37] On the right, the New Humanists were more concerned by American culture's excessive emotionalism and impulsiveness, and sought a literature that cultivated the readers' "inner check." In 1912, Irving Babbitt was drawn to the lingering aura of authority granted Emerson by the genteel critics, but their depiction of Emerson as a naïve sage of uplift led Babbitt to worry that Emerson "gave undue encouragement to the ordinary man, to the man who is undisciplined and unselective and untraditional."[38]

In the 1930s, as more extreme ideologies came to dominate American thought, readers on both the far left and far right became much harsher in their assessments of Emerson's apolitical individualism.[39] To the far left, Emerson's self-reliance exemplified the predatory selfishness that was destroying America. When the Marxist critic V. F. Calverton diagnosed in 1932 America's rapacious "frontier mentality," Emerson was his prime culprit. "Eternally," Calverton thundered, "Emerson's stress is upon the self, the individual self, the personal ego. Society can take care of itself, or go hang, as the frontiersman would have put it."[40] Calverton's book, along with Granville Hicks's 1935 *The Great Tradition*, found overwhelming evidence in Emerson's small canon of a poisonously apolitical individualism, or what Calverton called the "petty bourgeois individualist" as opposed to the favored "proletarian collectivist" (480).[41] Critics on the far right held a similar view of Emerson's apolitical individualism. In 1932, the Southern Agrarian Allen Tate echoed older southern views in damning "Emerson man" as a radical Puritan who "gave an heroic proportion and a tragic mode to the experience of the individual." Even more wrongheaded for Tate was Emerson's proclamation that each individual, "being himself the Over-Soul, is innately perfect."[42] Yvor Winters, a conservative from the Midwest, expanded upon this point in 1937. Winters explained how Emerson's trust in intuitions leads, invariably, to insanity. "Immediate inspiration amounts to the same thing as unrevised reactions to stimuli," Winters explained, and "unrevised reactions are mechanical; man in a state of perfection is an automaton; an automatic man is insane. Hence, Emerson's perfect man is a madman."[43] In another essay written ten years later, Winters concluded confidently that "the doctrine of Emerson[,] if really put into practice, should naturally lead to suicide."[44]

In the postwar period, Emerson scholars began "the great work of redemption," as Buell puts it, but not by challenging the myth of Emerson's apolitical individualism.[45] As Sarah Wider astutely notes, "the first forty years [of Emerson scholarship in the twentieth century] shaped the next sixty" (*The Critical Reception of Emerson*, 91). All that the postwar critics did differently was to propose that Emerson's withdrawal from society now be read not as a political failure but a spiritual success: evidence, that is, of his impressive religious commitment to "his master term, 'the Soul'" (Buell, "The Emerson Industry in the 1980s," 117). These postwar decades saw the invention of Emerson as a religious iconoclast, mystic, and seer.[46] Works like Perry Miller's 1940 essay "From Edwards to Emerson" (revised for inclusion in the 1956 *Errand into the Wilderness*), F. O. Matthiessen's 1941 *American Renaissance*, and Stephen Whicher's 1953 *Freedom and Fate:*

An Inner Life of Ralph Waldo Emerson redesigned Emerson's apolitical individualism as the religious antinomianism of a spiritual seeker who put the integrity of his conscientious faith journey before all else.[47] Doing little to expand the small canon (Whicher's 1957 *Selections from Ralph Waldo Emerson* only matched the usual texts with related journal entries, and Miller's 1950 anthology *The Transcendentalists* only solidified the focus on religion [Capper, "A Little Beyond," 22–23]), these readers found in "Self-Reliance" not evidence of a frontier mentality or insanity but rather a brave but private dedication to spiritual truth (Garvey, *Emerson Dilemma*, xix).[48]

This positive spin on apolitical individualism, however, did not persuade everyone. On the contrary, as historians began to take more interest in the abolitionist movement especially, Emerson and the rest of the Transcendentalists—now pared down to just a literary-religious movement—seemed to have "no close commitment to any of society's institutions," as Stanley Elkins put it in his 1959 *Slavery*; these were "truly men without responsibility."[49] For the Left, particularly in the wake of the Vietnam War, Emerson continued to stand as the embodiment of the irresponsible frontier mentality, now called the "imperial self." In his 1971 book of that title, Quentin Anderson denounced Emerson's individualism as the origin of this fateful turn: in Emerson's writings, for "the first time since Aristotle[,] the habitudes that accompanied the belief that we are social animals were effectively denied."[50] "In Emerson," Anderson raged, "society was not spurned; it was judged irrelevant to human purposes" (5). His "infantile fantasy" was to replace the "associated life" stressed by the Founders with "projections of the self" (54, 57), which is "something . . . distinct from a psychotic, even though it sounds very much the same" (55). The Left continued this assault through the remaining decades of the twentieth century. Emerson's "atomistic individualism" makes impossible "anything like a social praxis or politics of solidarity," the literary critic Cary Wolfe argued in 1994, echoing what Calverton wrote in 1932, Elkins in 1959, and Anderson in 1971.[51] In 1989, the communitarian political philosopher Charles Taylor argued that Emerson recklessly promotes a "Romantic expressivism" that values the fulfillment of the self—the pursuit of "authenticity"—above all else.[52]

Conservatives made similar accusations, especially as the culture wars heated up in the 1980s. In 1984, John Patrick Diggins argued that Emerson brazenly rejected civic virtue, the fruit of centuries of political philosophy, and thus left Americans without any sense of purpose.[53] Emerson and some others had "lost [the] soul of American politics," Diggins concluded, and "today when America seems to be awash in a 'culture of narcissism' and Emerson's doctrine of 'self-reliance' has dropped from the 'Oversoul' to the underbelly, Tocqueville's fears of 'the passionate and exaggerated love of self' have made the demands of the 'Me' the first priority of politics" (*The Lost Soul of American Politics*, 336). Like Babbitt in 1912 and Tate in 1932 and Winters in 1937, Diggins particularly emphasized the spiritual depravity of Emerson's apolitical individualism: "Did Emerson . . . ever consider that the doctrine of 'self-reliance' could be either completely illusory or . . . the source of sin as well as virtue? That same proud doctrine, in making the self obedient only to itself, also spelled death to the very meaning of authority, the individual's obligation to obey something other than himself" (228).[54] In 1981, disturbed by that same disobedience, and determined that at least one graduating class that year would be, too, Yale president A. Bartlett Giamatti traced it to the same source. For Giamatti, Emerson's apolitical individualism was the root of both the antigovernment fervor of the Reagan Revolution as well as the general cultural "insist[ence] that whatever willful impulse sat in the throne of the heart holds legitimate sway. In another creed," Giamatti darkly observed, "his self-reliance would be the sin of pride."[55] The baleful influence of Emerson—this "brazen adolescent" (177)—was everywhere, a despairing Giamatti concluded, a thesis John Updike took up himself in his 1983 address "Emersonianism" (reprinted in a 1984 issue of the *New Yorker*). Updike summarized Emerson's philosophy as "righteous selfishness," and found evidence of it in the rapacious hedonism of both the yippies and the captains of industry, in racism and in slavery, in urban sprawl, and even in the extermination camps: "The totalitarian leader is a study in self-reliance gone amok."[56] It is difficult to imagine a reading of Emerson more distant from the truth, but such has been the hypnotic power of the myth of Emerson's apolitical individualism.

At the end of the twentieth century, one final group of critics refashioned and celebrated Emerson's antinomianism as an American pragmatist version of European postmodernism. In the work of Richard Poirier and Harold Bloom, especially, Emerson as a private seeker became the American Nietzsche, champion of an aristocratic self-fashioning and despiser of metaphysics as well as meliorism. For these postmodern readers, Emerson derided society not in a quest for spiritual truth (or as a selfish narcissist) but out of a dedication to humanity, a humanity that, with the death of

God, stood in desperate need of courageous secular models of individual self-fashioning, what Poirier called "the performative self."[57] The great accomplishment of these postmodern readers of Emerson was to take him seriously as a thinker, particularly a thinker about power.[58] But their Emerson remained an apolitical thinker, and, when Poirier wrote in 1992 that Emerson's pragmatism "is not essentially addressed to—indeed it shies away from—historical crises," he echoed what a century of readers, left and right, had concluded before him: Emerson advocated apolitical individualism.

In short, in order to secure a place for Emerson in the pantheon of American thinkers, his "friends" in the materialistic, post–Civil War era stripped him of his political and transcendental threads. They achieved their goal, but at the price of passing down a rump Emerson, a part passed off as the whole. This apolitical Emerson of the small canon is what scholars have discussed for more than a hundred years. Until now. It is our aim in this volume to build on the new history's recovery of Emerson's politics and to examine Emerson's political thought almost, as it were, for the first time.

The Contents of This Volume

The main exception to the twentieth-century trend of depoliticizing Emerson is the handful of political theorists and a philosopher who almost alone grappled with the political implications of Emerson's writings. Part 1 of this book, "Classics on Emerson's Politics," includes the work of four of these scholars: the political theorists Wilson Carey McWilliams, Judith N. Shklar, and George Kateb, and the philosopher Stanley Cavell. These essays were originally published between 1973 and 1995, mostly before the new history. These thinkers all write about what they call Emerson's self-reliance, but drawing upon the small canon, they either still subscribe to some extent to the myth of Emerson's individualism or focus on what we have called individuality, not fully appreciating the array of political implications of Emerson's self-reliance properly understood. Focused on individuality rather than self-reliance, these thinkers nonetheless differ importantly from that century-long consensus in taking Emerson's calls for individuality to be more than just pleas for privacy. Emerson, in their work, emerges instead as a great political theorist of individuality—the explicator of the political value of the disengaged individual.

In the excerpt included here from his magisterial *The Idea of Frater-*

nity in America (1973), Wilson Carey McWilliams contends that Emerson's belief in progress drifted into a passive faith, leading Emerson to neglect politics. As an example, McWilliams, working with only the small canon, notes that Emerson believed that "history was moving to abolish slavery (hence, abolitionism was needless and possibly imprudent)." Despite this criticism of what he deems Emerson's misplaced faith in progress and disdain for politics, McWilliams admires Emerson's vision of a final brotherhood of man, what Emerson called (and McWilliams cites) a "nation of friends" and a "political brotherhood." The problem according to McWilliams is that, because Emerson believed in the inevitability of this nation of friends, he saw no reason to work for its realization. Not caring much about how a nation of friends might work politically, Emerson did not subject his own practice of friendship to much scrutiny. If he had, McWilliams implies, he might have recognized that friendships "premised on a radical individualism and privatism" cannot last. In this way, Emerson offered "a [theoretical] sense of 'union' . . . at the price of [actual] separation from individual men."

One of the reasons McWilliams's interpretation is different from contemporaneous assaults upon Emerson's "radical individualism" and "privatism" is that McWilliams senses a political goal to Emerson's individuality, even if he deems it unfeasible. In McWilliams's view, Emerson's ambition for each individual—to make "each man a state," as Emerson wrote in "Politics"—leaves the actual political state "only the task of designing ways for his assertive individuals to live in reasonable concord." McWilliams does not object to Emerson's vision of a minimalist state assisting private characters; in the antebellum United States, McWilliams argues, this might have worked. What is objectionable to McWilliams is Emerson's notion of character. Drawing on Paul Elmer More, one of the New Humanists who, with Irving Babbitt, were convinced that Emerson's version of character was too easygoing and lacked that "inner check," McWilliams saw in Emerson's version of character only "a near-cult of 'spontaneity,' or unreflective and instinctual response to situations." Such individualism—worshipping privacy and instinct—could never replace the state or lead to enduring friendships as Emerson proposed. For McWilliams, Emerson's nation of friends is an exciting vision, but Emerson lacked the political savvy and the conception of character necessary to make it practicable.

The other classic texts find more positive political features in Emerson's individuality. Like McWilliams, Judith Shklar, in her 1990 "Emerson and the Inhibitions of Democracy," considers Emerson's preoccupation with the individual to be at odds with his occasional forays into real political thought, but, much more than McWilliams, Shklar finds subtle virtues in Emerson's arguments for private skepticism about public actions. "Emerson may not have been what is conventionally called a political philosopher," she writes, "but political considerations played a more subtle part in his thinking" than previously recognized. Shklar presents Emerson's individuality as akin to Madison's fear of majority tyranny, which proves to be a more flattering context for Emerson than the proto-communitarian one in McWilliams's study of American strains of fraternity. When Shklar looks at the central text of the small canon, "Self-Reliance," she actually reads what Emerson writes there, bucking a century-long practice of just assuming Emerson is for apolitical individualism. While at first glance she notes, "Emerson seems quite prepared to flout the democratic creed in his enthusiasm for the self-reliant individual," a more careful reading of the essay reveals that "in fact, he avoids a full assault [on democracy] and backs off from it." Shklar points out that Emerson's deliberately shocking seventh paragraph in "Self-Reliance" is "softened . . . by irony"; after all, Emerson "confesses with shame and regret that, in fact, he is too weak to refuse a dollar to the poor." Emerson "has not withdrawn himself from fellowship after all. It is easy to turn one's back on parties, churches, and a 'dead Bible society,' but on the poor? That is only to be proclaimed; it cannot be done." With close attention to Emerson's writing, Shklar shows how Emerson cares about both individuality and democracy.

Shklar makes another major contribution to the recovery of Emerson's political thought by drawing our attention to his interest in representation, which she sees Emerson relying on to navigate between his commitments to individuality and democracy. For all his attention to what makes individuals great, she explains, Emerson "could not get himself to say . . . that the great are absolutely different and better within their sphere. That was the inhibition of democracy." What Emerson could get himself to say was that great individuals are important to democracy but only because they represent something to the rest of us. Unlike Carlyle or Nietzsche, Emerson, in *Representative Men* especially, insists that while we must believe in great people, our belief must be critical; we should especially understand that the greatness of great men is partially dependent upon our own recognition of their worth. Shklar describes Emerson's writing in *Representative Men* as "a zig-zag," tacking back and forth between praise for and resistance to individual greatness. A commitment to democratic equality thus inhibits us from hero worship and, further, teaches us to be skeptical of the grander aspirations of others as well as our selves. (Shklar's ability to cherish Emerson's skepticism as a political virtue is yet another strength of this essay.) Emerson, for Shklar, redefines representation in order to teach us how to value both individualism and democracy as checks on one another.

In an earlier book (1992) than the 1995 one we excerpt here, George Kateb, our third classic theorist, distinguishes Emerson's "democratic individuality" from other forms of individualism, not only Tocqueville's but Byron's, Nietzsche's, Napoleon's, and the solipsist's.[59] Kateb continued to build on this distinction in his 1995 *Emerson and Self-Reliance,* the last chapter of which, "Self-Reliance, Politics, and Society," is included here. Attending closely to Emerson's language (like Shklar), and venturing beyond the small canon (unlike Shklar), Kateb presents us with an Emerson committed—in stark contrast to the myth of apolitical individualism—to a rambunctious democracy of individual opinions, exemplified not in withdrawal but in town meetings. Kateb's Emerson certainly recognizes the iniquity of some political institutions, but through the 1840s, Kateb contends, Emerson still believed the individual might work through these institutions, rather than through associational reform, a mode of reform that Emerson rejects not as a "brazen adolescent" (as Giamatti and dozens of others charged throughout the twentieth century) but as a shrewd critic of associations. Like Shklar, Kateb sees Emerson finding ways to balance a commitment to individuality (or what Kateb calls self-reliance) and a commitment to democracy, but Kateb's contention remains that these are projects in tension, not symbiosis.

That tension is especially clear in Kateb's response to Emerson's abolitionist activities. Unlike McWilliams and Shklar, who wrote earlier, Kateb wrote his book just as the new history was beginning to make an impact, and he takes into consideration Emerson's abolition activity in the 1850s. In Kateb's view, however, Emerson's involvement in abolition deviated from his theory of self-reliance, for he realized that if all (including the currently enslaved) are to enjoy self-reliance, then some people must temporarily surrender their own self-reliance in order to help others achieve theirs. In Kateb's reading, Emerson understood democracy to involve these kinds of trade-offs. Democracy is a gamble worth taking for Emerson, for it is the only moral political system. Practiced well, as in New England town meetings, it thrives on individual diversity, disputatious speeches, and unembarrassed frankness. Individuality makes democracy stronger. But individuality and democracy remain in fundamental tension, a tension that only intensifies as democratic culture becomes "massified."

Like Kateb, Stanley Cavell also defended Emerson's individuality as central to his politics, nowhere more than in "Aversive Thinking: Emersonian Representations in Heidegger and Nietzsche," a chapter from his 1990 *Conditions Handsome and Unhandsome* that is included in this volume. Here Cavell describes Emerson's ideal society as a tool for the mutual improvement of individuals; individuals model for one another the aversion to social conformity that the project of individual perfection requires. One of the strengths of Cavell's essay is that he makes explicit what Shklar implies in her essay: that Emerson's writing matters. Even more than in Shklar's and Kateb's essays, Emerson emerges in Cavell's essay as much more than the iconic sage of the genteel critics. Instead, Cavell describes Emerson's main rhetorical operation as "transfiguration," by which he means the way Emerson illustrates through the play of language how a strong writer engages in "an incessant conversion or refiguration of society's incessant demands for his consent." Cavell thus shows how Emerson's political individuality occurs not just in the actions he describes—his inhibition before democracy, his praise for town meetings, and so forth—but in the very way he writes about those actions.

In the selection included here, Cavell raises the question (more pointedly than in the other classic essays) of Emerson's importance to not just the history of political ideas but to normative liberal theory. Cavell argues strenuously that Emerson's emphasis upon self-culture, or what Cavell follows John Rawls in calling "perfectionism," is not elitist and antidemocratic as Rawls worried in his 1973 *A Theory of Justice*. Drawing on Nietzsche for his portrait of extreme perfectionism, Rawls had rejected any focus on (in Nietzsche's words) "produc[ing] individual great human beings" as inappropriate for liberal democratic societies. Instead, Rawls argued for the kind of balance among competing values (such as the individual and democracy) that Shklar finds in Emerson's writings. In contrast, Cavell boldly argues that "the particular disdain for official culture taken in Emerson and in Nietzsche" is not an aristocratic disdain for democracy but on the contrary "an expression of democracy and commitment to it. . . . This may well produce personal tastes and private choices that are, let us say, exclusive, even esoteric. Then," Cavell continues, "my question is whether this exclusiveness might be not just tolerated but treasured by the friends of democracy." Emerson and Nietzsche are just such friends of democracy, in Cavell's view, for they model for all of us a perfectionist individuality that does indeed entail nonconformity but in so doing vigorously reminds us that we are each to be valued as ends in ourselves, not as means to a better society. In this way, Emerson's unchecked perfectionist individuality is a great boon to democracy, for such individuality compels democracy to value its exclusive and even esoteric individual members as ends in themselves, rather than means.

As interpreters of Emerson's politics, our classics have many more strengths than we have room to review here, but one shared narrowness is their preoccupation with Emerson's writing about individuality, which has been typical, we have seen, of those readers of Emerson prior to the new history of the 1990s. That is, our classic authors more or less share the assumption common to twentieth-century readers that Emerson simply cared little for conventional political activity, viewing the engagement with democracy as valuable only to others, not to oneself. Rather than noting how Emerson combined an interest in self-reliant perfectionism *and* abolition, for example, Cavell, working with only the small canon, simply concedes that perfectionism might indeed have the "vice [of] shirking participation in democracy." Similarly, Kateb worries that Emerson's "mental self-reliance . . . may go too far in the direction of heedlessness."[60] Moments like these reveal our classic theorists to still believe that Emerson didn't really care about conventional politics: that Emerson's "self-reliance" was more selfish than we would like. This is the result, we believe, of knowing only the small canon and not the new history.[61]

Significantly influenced by the four classic texts, our new contributors are equally if not more indebted to the new history; the result is nine new essays that draw upon *all* of Emerson's significant political writings to reach three general conclusions about Emerson's political thought. The authors in part 2 show that Emerson's philosophy of self-reliance entails major moral commitments and specific political practices. The authors in part 3 argue that Emerson's political thought is stubbornly transcendental; this may be good or bad, but it cannot be denied. Each of the authors in part 4 analyzes an important but neglected characteristic of Emerson's liberal democracy: property, representation, and finding a place for human excellence. By explicating the requirements of self-reliance, showing its transcendental underpinnings, and exploring key liberal features of its practice, these nine new essays together shine needed light on Emerson's political thought.

Part 2, "Emerson's Self-Reliance Properly Understood," is conceived in the spirit of Tocqueville's "Self-Interest Properly Understood," the famous proposition in *Democracy in America* that Americans have a generous, long-term, and enlightened understanding of self-interest. Emerson's concept of "self-reliance" has been construed too narrowly by many readers, as examined above. The three essays in this section show how Emerson's self-reliance has broader, deeper implications in dealing with others. They illuminate the fundamental relationship between Emerson's political activity—particularly his abolitionism—and his philosophy of self-reliance. Since 1990, the new history has contended that Emerson's philosophy of self-reliance entails political activism, but many scholars remain skeptical. George Kateb argues, for example, that in the 1850s Emerson "suspends" his theory of self-reliance in order to combat slavery: "Emerson's moral commitments silence his existential passions."[62] Our new contributors disagree, each contending that Emerson's "existential passion" for self-reliance and moral commitments were integrally related: to be self-reliant means to be political. These contributors differ, though, on what exactly Emerson's politics of self-reliance were.

Jack Turner argues that for Emerson self-reliance entails not only avoiding complicity in wrongdoing but actively seeking to end that wrongdoing. Turner shows that Emerson consistently advocates that citizens avoid complicity in activities that restrict others from practicing self-reliance, and that Emerson even urges us to end such activities, especially slavery. Drawing on the relatively neglected 1841 address "Man the Reformer" as well as a number of Emerson's major antislavery addresses, Turner shows that, for Emerson, "self-assertive though self-reliance is, truly self-reliant individuals realize themselves while respecting the rights of others."

James H. Read agrees with Turner that Emerson sought to square his philosophy of self-reliance with political action against slavery. However, Read contends that Emerson's efforts were less successful. Emerson persuasively shows how self-reliance requires individuals to support other self-reliant individuals, such as fugitive slaves in search of freedom, but beyond this Emerson "vibrated" among different solutions to the sectional crisis, revealing the limits of self-reliance in the process. In urging contradictory strategies—the North's peaceful secession from the Union, the gradual and compensated emancipation of slaves, and the violent liberation of enslaved people as led by John Brown—Emerson inadvertently shows the limits of self-reliance as a political ethics. These are limits, however, that Read believes to be instructive for citizens of imperfect—that is, all—democracies. Emerson's struggle to make self-reliance solve the sectional crisis teaches us to consider more closely the spirit of one's times, the complex causality of political events, and the enduring importance of critically reflecting upon one's duties.

Focused like Read and Turner on Emerson's abolitionism, Len Gougeon finds neither an instructive vibration among positions nor a subtle insistence on eliminating complicity but instead an explicit commitment to self-reliance based on "the divinity of the individual and the moral efficacy of a democracy that relied upon the collective conscience of individual citizens." In making this argument, Gougeon builds upon his unparalleled contributions to the new history of Emerson's politics. Gougeon argues that Emerson believed the collective conscience to be articulated by representative individuals relying upon the intuitions of Reason rather than self-interested understanding. Reason teaches the equal worth of all individuals, a conviction that drove Emerson to become not only one of the nation's foremost abolitionists but also an advocate after the war for black male suffrage and women's rights. Throughout his life, Gougeon shows, Emerson acted on the belief that individuals of conscience must constantly enter the public sphere to teach their fellow citizens the equal worth of all individuals. That is what "self-reliance" requires.

The three essays in Part 3, "The Stubborn Reality of Emerson's Transcendentalism," all contend that this aspect of his philosophy is not only undeniable but of political importance. While Emerson, thanks to the classic texts and the new history, has been "repoliticized," he has yet to be "retranscendentalized." On the contrary, as Lawrence Buell noted in an important 1984 essay, Emerson has been detranscendentalized by historians and theorists alike ("The Emerson Industry in the 1980s," 120). Historians, including those involved in writing the new history, have emphasized how Emerson's politics were inspired both by the activism of his family and colleagues and by political developments on the national stage. This has enriched our understanding of the contexts of Emerson's thought, but often at the price of a deeper understanding of that thought itself as a motivation:

how transcendentalist concepts like the divinity of the self or "higher law" drove Emerson's politics. Thinkers, including several of our classic theorists as well as Poirier and Bloom as described above, have downplayed Emerson's reliance on terms like "soul" and "God" and instead emphasized Emerson's affiliations with modern Continental philosophy, especially Nietzsche. In our secular age, this detranscendentalizing urge has been hard to resist. In 1995, Kateb even recommended overlooking Emerson's "religiousness . . . even if we lose Emerson in the process" (*Emerson and Self-Reliance*, 65). Agreeing with the historians that Emerson's political motivations were complex, and with the theorists that Emerson's philosophy deserves to be read alongside of the most important modern political philosophers, the three contributors to this section disagree that this requires overlooking Emerson's stubbornly religious conviction that "Truth exists," as Emerson proclaimed in the 1855 "Lecture on Slavery," "though all men should deny it" (*AW*, 102). The contributors in this section propose that what may matter most in Emerson's political thought is his conception of the transcendental nature of moral "truth." "Our faith comes in moments," Emerson wrote in his 1841 "The Over-Soul," while "our vice is habitual. Yet there is a depth in those brief moments, which constrains us to ascribe more reality to them than to all other experience" (*E&L*, 385). Just as Emerson emphasized the reality of transcendental truth "though all men should deny it," so these contributors emphasize its essential importance to Emerson's politics though many scholars have ignored it or wished it away.

Alan M. Levine contends that Emerson's skepticism is much more limited than that of both the skeptic Emerson most admired, Montaigne, and the skeptic to whom he is today most often compared, Nietzsche. In so doing, he challenges a major initiative of scholars in the last three decades to read Emerson through a Nietzschean lens.[63] Focusing on "Self-Reliance," "Fate," and "Experience"—widely recognized as Emerson's most Nietzschean and most skeptical essays—Levine argues that Emerson's skepticism is fundamentally bounded by his deep and abiding conception of transcendent truth and that his vision of this truth shapes his moral concerns for others. This bounded skepticism may make Emerson's epistemological thought less deep than Nietzsche's or Montaigne's, Levine allows, but it makes his political theory more politically useful to us today than Nietzsche's.

The other two essays in this section explore that usefulness. Daniel S. Malachuk shows how those critics he calls "detranscendentalists" have obscured Emerson's commitment to the equality of all human beings as "part of God"—what he calls "transcendentalist equality"—for several decades. Malachuk then examines a number of Emerson's writings that demonstrate this commitment to transcendental equality, some texts beyond the small canon as well as three from that canon that are traditionally cited as evidence of Emerson's skepticism (as also discussed in Levine's essay): "Self-Reliance," "Fate," and "Experience." Malachuk argues that Emerson's transcendental liberalism represents an important alternative to contemporary political liberalism, especially today as we reconsider the totalizing secularism of recent generations.

Shannon L. Mariotti reaches a different conclusion about Emerson's transcendentalism or idealism. Other critics have noted the importance of sight to Emerson, and particularly how he (in his own words) believed himself "created [as] a seeing eye and not a useful hand."[64] Mariotti questions Emerson's ability to really see, noting how often his "transcendental gaze" takes him beyond the very particulars he wishes to see changed. However, from 1844 forward, Emerson seems to question his own practice of "focal distancing," as Mariotti calls it, offering glimpses of a political theory that reconciles transcendental idealism with attention to the particulars necessary for successful reform. Mariotti concludes that "Emerson can teach us about the importance of focusing our eyes in a way that takes in the material world without losing sight of ideals."

Finally, in Part 4, "Emerson and Liberal Democracy," three contributors consider important aspects of liberal democracy emphasized by Emerson, qualities generally overshadowed by our enduring interest in how Emerson squares democracy with self-reliance: property, representation, and concern for human excellence.

Neal Dolan illuminates the sophisticated roles of property in Emerson's vision of democracy. Building on his recent, groundbreaking account of Emerson's theories of commerce in *Emerson's Liberalism,* Dolan teases out here the dual importance of property in Emerson's vision of the future of liberal democracy.[65] Emerson, Dolan shows, was committed not only to the material power of commerce but to its aesthetic or existential power, too. At crucial moments throughout his major writings, Emerson uses the language and imagery of property to perform a dual political-cultural task. He both seeks to symbolically fortify the emerging liberal-capitalist civilization, at the base of which stand property rights, and proposes to correct liberal civilization's tendency to understand property in merely instrumental terms by elucidating property's existential and aesthetic values. Where Matthew Arnold and John Stuart Mill had urged culture as a response to democratic materialism, Emerson, in Dolan's rendering, proposes a similar cultural role for property.

Jason Frank discovers new significance in Emerson's idea of representation in democracy. Like Shklar and Cavell before him, Frank contends that Emerson successfully navigated the tension between self and society through a theory of representation. However, Frank shows that Emerson advocates neither a "mandate" nor an "independence" theory of democratic representation but a "transformational" one, wherein representative and represented engage in an ongoing dynamic encounter with "the new." Frank argues that Emerson understood representatives as those who help others in a democracy to transcend their particular partialities in order to pursue aspirational ideals, oriented by terms like "Spirit" and "Over Soul" but never fixed by moral teleologies. Emerson's vision of representation should not be "domesticated by the prevailing concerns of contemporary democratic theory." We should instead look carefully, as Frank does in closing, at Emerson's admiration for John Brown as a representative man urging a nation to "rise above itself."

G. Borden Flanagan illuminates another neglected quality of Emerson's vision of liberal democracy, the pursuit of excellence. Focusing on *Representative Men*, Flanagan shows how Emerson defends the possibility of excellence in democracy against Carlyle's attacks by demonstrating how democracy not only tolerates but encourages self-reliant, wisdom-seeking citizens to flourish. Emphasizing Emerson's debt to Plato and Aristotle, Flanagan shows how Emerson marries an ancient concern for the cultivation of virtue to a modern interest in the growth of all citizens. In Flanagan's account, Emerson defends democracy before the bar of excellence, and excellence before the bar of democracy.

Thanks both to the classic theorists and the new history, we are for the first time in a position to appreciate Emerson's many contributions to political theory. In ridding ourselves once and for all of the myth of Emerson's apolitical individualism, it remains important to focus on Emerson's adamant liberal vision of universal moral and political rights.[66] Emerson made his political intentions known in his public activities and public writings, and, thanks to the new history, that public record is more comprehensive and accessible than ever before. That record must remain the focus of our assessments of Emerson's political thought: Emerson is too important a figure to suffer another century of misreading.

Notes

1. Boston: Riverside Press, 1903. A very important contribution to what we call "the new history" of Emerson's politics, T. Gregory Garvey's 2001 edited volume, *The Emerson Dilemma: Essays on Emerson and Social Reform* (Athens: University of Georgia Press, 2001), put the "familiar 'Emerson the Transcendentalist' face to face with a now recognizable 'Emerson the reformer'" (xxi, hereafter cited parenthetically); this volume does include a few essays specifically on Emerson's political thought.

2. Alexis de Tocqueville, *Democracy in America*, trans. Harvey C. Mansfield and Delba Winthrop (Chicago: University of Chicago Press, 2000), vol. 2, pt. 2, chap. 2, "On Individualism in Democratic Countries," 482.

3. For an important earlier discussion of Emerson's individuality versus individualism, though one much more skeptical about the differentiation, see Sacvan Bercovitch's "Emerson, Individualism, and the Ambiguities of Dissent" (1989), included as a chapter in *The Rites of Assent: Transformations in the Symbolic Construction of America* (New York: Routledge, 1993), 307–52.

4. Lawrence Buell has admirably crystallized the new history's major lesson that Emerson, Thoreau, and all the Transcendentalists balanced individual and communal goals: while there were "disagreements among Transcendentalists as to the relative importance of the elevation of single individuals versus the elevation of society as a whole[,] virtually all of them cared about both, but . . . differed over the prioritization. Emerson and Thoreau staunchly believed that the key to social transformation lay through individual transformation" (introduction to *The American Transcendentalists: Essential Writings* [New York: Modern Library, 2006], xxiv–xxv).

5. Sarah Ann Wider, *The Critical Reception of Emerson: Unsettling All Things* (Rochester, N.Y.: Camden House, 2000), 44, hereafter cited parenthetically.

6. Len Gougeon, *Virtue's Hero: Emerson, Antislavery, and Reform* (Athens: University of Georgia Press, 1990), hereafter cited parenthetically; David M. Robinson, *Emerson and the Conduct of Life: Pragmatism and Ethical Purpose in the Later Work* (New York: Cambridge University Press, 1993); Robert D. Richardson, *Emerson: The Mind on Fire* (Berkeley and Los Angeles: University of California Press, 1995); Albert J. von Frank, *The Trials of Anthony Burns: Freedom and Slavery in Emerson's Boston* (Cambridge: Harvard University Press, 1998).

7. Len Gougeon and Joel Myerson, eds., *Emerson's Antislavery Writings* (New Haven: Yale University Press, 1995), hereafter cited as *AW*; David Robinson, ed., *The Political Emerson: Essential Writings on Politics and Social Reform* (Boston: Beacon Press, 2004); Kenneth Sacks, ed., *Emerson: Political Writings* (Cambridge: Cambridge University Press, 2008). Authoritative editions used in this book are listed on the abbreviations page.

8. Neal Dolan, *Emerson's Liberalism* (Madison: University of Wisconsin Press, 2009). In addition to his contribution to this volume, we are grateful to Dolan for his comments on this essay. Other recent interpretations of Emerson's liberalism that rely on the new history are Daniel S. Malachuk, *Perfection, the State, and Victorian Liberalism* (New York: Palgrave Macmillan, 2005); and Alex Zakaras, *Individuality and Mass Democracy: Mill, Emerson, and the Burdens of Citizenship* (New York: Oxford University Press, 2009).

9. Peter Field, *Ralph Waldo Emerson: The Making of a Democratic Intellectual* (Lanham, Md.: Rowman and Littlefield, 2002), 3, hereafter cited parenthetically.

10. Gary Collison, "Emerson and Antislavery," in *A Historical Guide to Ralph Waldo Emerson*, ed. Joel Myerson (New York: Oxford University Press, 2000), 189. See Jack Turner's essay in this volume on Emerson's critique of complicity.

11. Gougeon, *Virtue's Hero*, 35. On Emerson's early view of ethics and politics, see also the work of David M. Robinson, especially "Introduction: Emerson as a Political Thinker," in *The Political Emerson*, 1–6, and "Emerson and Religion," in *A Historical Guide to Ralph Waldo Emerson*, 151–58. See also Dolan, *Emerson's Liberalism*, chap. 6.

12. Wesley T. Mott, "Emerson, Second Church, and 'The Real Priesthood,'" UUA Emerson Bicentennial Program, Boston, 7 March 2003, http://archive.uua.org/aboutuu/emerson200/mott.html.

13. On the development of Emerson's epistemology, see Barbara Packer, *The Transcendentalists* (Athens: University of Georgia Press, 2007), chap. 2, "The Assault on Locke," 20–31. On the importance of various traditions to Emerson's view of the self, see Dolan, *Emerson's Liberalism*, 12–16; and Kenneth S. Sacks, introduction to *Emerson: Political Writings*, xv–xvii. On the radical Protestant (particularly Quaker) influence, see Field, *Ralph Waldo Emerson*, 111–13.

14. For a fuller account of Emerson's distinction between Reason and Understanding, see Gougeon's essay in this volume, 186–87.

15. Among the original authors of the new history, see especially Richardson on the influence of Quakerism on Emerson's ethical vision in *Emerson*, 157–63; and von Frank on the nature of higher law for Emerson in *The Trials of Anthony Burns*, 96–106. A good overview of Emerson's developing conception of God in his early work is the chapter "The Theist" in David Robinson, *Apostle of Culture:*

Emerson as Preacher and Lecturer (Philadelphia: University of Pennsylvania Press, 1982), 112–37. For a review of more recent scholarship on Emerson's transcendentalist politics, see Malachuk's essay in this volume.

16. On the American Anti-Slavery Society's influential model of moral suasion, see C. Bradley Thompson, introduction to *Antislavery Political Writings, 1833–1860: A Reader*, ed. Thompson (Armonk, N.Y.: M. E. Sharpe, 2004), xvi. Emerson did not support civil disobedience at this time. On Emerson's commitment to civil society as part of his political theory, see Daniel S. Malachuk, "The Republican Philosophy of Emerson's Early Lectures," *New England Quarterly* 71, no. 3 (September 1998): 404–28; Malachuk, *Perfection, the State, and Victorian Liberalism*, chap. 4; and especially Dolan, *Emerson's Liberalism*, chap. 7.

17. Emerson's practice of moral suasion prior to 1844 is described in many places. On his struggles with the Unitarian church, see Field, *Ralph Waldo Emerson*, chaps. 3 and 4. On his early reform activities, see esp. Gougeon, *Virtue's Hero*, 24–85; Gougeon and Myerson, AW, xi–xxvii; and Collison, "Emerson and Antislavery," 179–92.

18. See also Field, *Ralph Waldo Emerson*, 114–16.

19. On Emerson's reassessment of the relationship of self-reliance to democracy in 1837–1838, see Robinson, "Introduction," *The Political Emerson*, 7–8; Gougeon, *Virtue's Hero*, 35–40; AW, xvii–xix; Garvey, *The Emerson Dilemma*, xiii–xv; and Field, *Ralph Waldo Emerson*, 177–85. The abolition movement also reconsidered moral suasion in this period, eventually splintering over the subject (see Thompson, introduction to *Antislavery Political Writings*, xvii–xx).

20. Tocqueville, *Democracy in America*, vol. 2, pt. 4, chap. 7, "Continuation of the Preceding Chapters," 669–70.

21. The 1844 "Address on the Emancipation of the Negroes in the British West Indies" offers this critique (see AW, 7–33). Montesquieu had previously argued the same point that slavery undercut the master's self-reliance. The point of his *Persian Letters* is to make the reader empathize with the oppressed and to show the dependence, anxieties, and fears that necessarily come with mastership.

22. Len Gougeon, "Emerson and the Reinvention of Democracy: A Lesson for the Twenty-first Century," in *New Morning: Emerson in the Twenty-first Century*, ed. Arthur S. Lothstein and Michael Brodrick (Albany: State University of New York Press, 2008), 162.

23. Like Emerson, Montaigne views all human beings as imperfect and thus deems human creations also to be imperfect: "Our structure, both public and private, is full of imperfection" (III.1, 767 [599]); "men, vain and irresolute authors," create laws that are nothing but "a singular testimony of human infirmity" (III.13, 1049 [821]; III.12, 1026 [803]); "there is nothing so grossly and widely and ordinarily faulty as the laws," he says, so: "Whoever obeys them because they are just, does not

obey them for just the reason he should" (III.13, 1049 [821]); "we should conform to the best rules, but not enslave ourselves to them" (III.13, 1063 [831]). For an explanation of these citations, please see note 34 of Levine's essay in this volume.

24. Emerson was among the first and certainly the most prominent American to take Brown's side following the failed raid on the Harpers Ferry Arsenal in late 1859 (see David S. Reynolds, *John Brown, Abolitionist* [New York: Vintage, 2005]).

25. Cited in Gougeon, *Virtue's Hero*, 280. On Emerson's concern that the war be fought for emancipation, see ibid., 261–90. As Dolan observes, Emerson believed Emancipation and the Civil War "not only . . . legally ended the moral blight of slavery but in doing so began to initiate the entire American public into precisely the new kind of liberal culture he had spent his life promoting. For Emerson, this is the special greatness of Lincoln: he seems not only to be successfully pursuing the war but also to have correctly interpreted its largest cultural meaning" (*Emerson's Liberalism*, 300).

26. As Philip Butcher recognized a half century ago, "[Emerson] was primarily an idealist, not a partisan social critic; his concern was principles rather than people. His attitude toward the South was the result of his observation that it, more than any other section of the nation, fell short of the ideal" (see "Emerson and the South," *Phylon* 17, no. 3 [1956]: 285).

27. Gougeon, "Emerson and the Reinvention of Democracy: A Lesson for the Twenty-first Century," 171. See Armida Gilbert's assessment of Emerson's feminism in "Emerson in the Context of the Woman's Rights Movement," in *A Historical Guide to Ralph Waldo Emerson*, 211–49. On Emerson's postbellum support of liberal immigration policies and the franchise for black men, see Reynolds, *John Brown, Abolitionist*, 482–84; and Richard F. Teichgraeber III, "'Our National Glory': Emerson in American Culture," in *Transient and Permanent: The Transcendentalist Movement and Its Contexts*, ed. Charles Capper and Conrad Edick Wright (Boston: Massachusetts Historical Society, 1999).

28. Cited in Reynolds, *John Brown, Abolitionist*, 482, 480.

29. Louis Menand, *The Metaphysical Club: A Story of Ideas in America* (New York: Farrar, Straus and Giroux, 2001), x.

30. Cited respectively in Gregg D. Crane, *Race, Citizenship, and Law in American Literature* (New York: Cambridge University Press, 2002), 158; and George M. Frederickson, *The Inner Civil War: Northern Intellectuals and the Crisis of the Union* (New York: Harper and Row, 1965), 220.

31. William James, *Writings 1902–1910* (New York: Library of America, 1987), 573.

32. See especially Gougeon, *Virtue's Hero*, chap. 1, "Abolition and the Biographer," 1–23; Charles Mitchell, *Individualism and Its Discontents: Appropriations*

of Emerson, 1880–1950 (Amherst: University of Massachusetts Press, 1997), hereafter cited parenthetically; and Garvey's introduction to *The Emerson Dilemma*, xv–xix. Robert D. Habich's *Building Their Own Waldos: Emerson's First Biographers and the Politics of Life-Writing in the Gilded Age* (Iowa City: University of Iowa Press, 2011) illuminates more complex motives of Holmes and Cabot than we can cover here; we are grateful for his comments on this essay.

33. Charles Eliot, ed., *Harvard Classics*, vol. 5, *Ralph Waldo Emerson, Essays and English Traits* (New York: Collier and Son, 1909–1914), 3–4. A few notables from the "small canon" are missing (*Nature*, "Experience," *Representative Men*, "Fate,"), but otherwise Eliot's focus on just a few of the early addresses, the 1841 and 1844 *Essays*, and *The Conduct of Life* was the norm until the 1995 publication of *Emerson's Antislavery Writings*.

34. George Santayana, *Interpretations of Poetry and Religion* (Cambridge: MIT Press, 1989), 131.

35. Charles Capper, "'A Little Beyond': Transcendentalism in American History," in *Transient and Permanent*, ed. Capper and Wright, 12, hereafter cited parenthetically. For additional analysis of this period, see especially Mitchell, *Individualism and Its Discontents*, 37–72.

36. Van Wyck Brooks, *America's Coming-of-Age* (New York: Huebsch, 1915), 84, hereafter cited parenthetically.

37. Waldo Frank, *Our America* (New York: Boni and Liveright, 1919), 69–70.

38. Irving Babbitt, *The Masters of Modern French Criticism* (Boston: Houghton Mifflin, 1912), 354.

39. Capper rightly describes scholarship in the 1930s as a "backwater" with the exception of Vernon Louis Parrington's work ("A Little Beyond," 15, 13). In his 1927–1930 *Main Currents in American Thought: An Interpretation of American Literature from the Beginnings to 1920* (New York: Harcourt, Brace and World, 1954), Parrington, still limited as all twentieth-century readers were to the "small canon," nonetheless mounts a persuasive reading of Emerson as a transcendentalist Jeffersonian (2:378–92).

40. V. F. Calverton, *The Liberation of American Literature* (New York: Scribners, 1932), 249, hereafter cited parenthetically.

41. For several other contemporaneous texts associating Emerson with the frontiersmen, see Wider, *The Critical Reception of Emerson*, 116–17.

42. Allen Tate, "Four American Poets," in *Reactionary Essays in Poetry and Ideas* (New York: Scribners, 1936), 6, 8.

43. Yvor Winters, "The Experimental School in American Poetry," in *In Defense of Reason* (Denver: Alan Swallow, 1947), 54–55.

44. Yvor Winters, "The Significance of 'The Bridge' by Hart Crane, or What

Are We to Think of Professor X?" in *In Defense of Reason* (Athens, Ohio: Swallow Press, 1987), 589.

45. Lawrence Buell, "The Emerson Industry in the 1980s: A Survey of Trends and Achievements," *ESQ: A Journal of the American Renaissance* 30, no. 2 (1984): 117, hereafter cited parenthetically. An important exception to this trend is Daniel Aaron, *Men of Good Hope: A Story of American Progressives* (New York: Oxford University Press, 1951), a book that reads Emerson's politics along the Jeffersonian lines laid out by Parrington. Capper notes another "Parringtonian" exception later in this period ("A Little Beyond," 22–23), Staughton Lynd's *Intellectual Origins of American Radicalism* (New York: Pantheon, 1968), which locates the dissenting Protestant, neo-Lockean, and radical republican roots of Thoreau's politics but not Emerson's, the oversight likely due to the dominance of the small canon at that time.

46. See also Garvey, *The Emerson Dilemma*, xix–xx.

47. Perry Miller, "From Edwards to Emerson," *New England Quarterly* 13 (December 1940): 589–617; F. O. Matthiessen, *American Renaissance: Art and Expression in the Age of Emerson and Whitman* (Oxford: Oxford University Press, 1941); Stephen Whicher, *Freedom and Fate: An Inner Life of Ralph Waldo Emerson* (Philadelphia: University of Pennsylvania Press, 1953). Wider explains that these critics used "mysticism as a way around the difficulties posed by aligning Emerson with idealism" (*The Critical Reception of Emerson*, 32). Cf. Capper and (to a lesser degree) Garvey, who defend these critics as deftly reinterpreting Emerson's politics in terms acceptable to the postwar period (see Capper, "A Little Beyond," 19–24; and Garvey, *The Emerson Dilemma*, xix–xx).

48. Stephen Whicher, ed., *Selections from Ralph Waldo Emerson* (Boston: Houghton Mifflin, 1957); Perry Miller, ed., *The Transcendentalists: An Anthology* (Cambridge: Harvard University Press, 1950).

49. Stanley Elkins, *Slavery: A Problem in American Institutional and Intellectual Life* (Chicago: University of Chicago Press, 1959), 18, hereafter cited parenthetically. In 1945, Arthur Schlesinger described the Transcendentalists "in their book-lined studies or their shady walks in cool Concord woods" and apart from "the hullabaloo of party politics." Perhaps they sought to make their "flinching from politics . . . into a virtue," "le[aving] responsibility far behind for a magic domain where the mystic sentiment and gnomic utterance exorcised the rude intrusions of the world" (see *The Age of Jackson* [Boston: Little, Brown, 1945], 382). See also *AW*, liii–liv; and Capper, "A Little Beyond," 18–19.

50. Quentin Anderson, *The Imperial Self: An Essay in Literary and Cultural History* (New York: Knopf, 1971), 4, hereafter cited parenthetically. Capper is rightly critical of this book ("A Little Beyond," 24).

51. Cary Wolfe, "Alone in America: Cavell, Emerson, and the Politics of Indi-

vidualism," *New Literary History* 25 (1994): 153, 144. In this vein, see also Taylor Stoehr, *Nay-Saying in Concord: Emerson, Alcott, and Thoreau* (Hamden, Conn.: Archon, 1979); David Marr, *American Worlds since Emerson* (Amherst: University of Massachusetts Press, 1988), 4–7; and Christopher Newfield, *The Emerson Effect: Individualism and Submission in America* (Chicago: University of Chicago Press, 1996), 2–4. Wolfe sympathetically summarizes these late contributions to the myth of apolitical individualism ("Alone in America," 154n); Wider provides a more critical account (*The Critical Reception of Emerson*, 142–44).

52. Charles Taylor, *Sources of the Self: The Making of Modern Identity* (Cambridge: Harvard University Press, 1989), 506–7. Buell rightly criticizes Taylor's caricature of Emerson's philosophy of self-reliance (see *Emerson* [Cambridge: Harvard University Press, 2003], 99).

53. John Patrick Diggins, *The Lost Soul of American Politics: Virtue, Self-Interest, and the Foundations of Liberalism* (Chicago: University of Chicago Press, 1984), 197–201, 224–29, hereafter cited parenthetically.

54. Wilfred M. McClay has pursued this line of attack in a more measured way (see "Mr. Emerson's Tombstone," *First Things* 83 (May 1998): 16–22; and *The Masterless: Self and Society in Modern America* [Chapel Hill: University of North Carolina Press, 1994]).

55. A. Bartlett Giamatti, "Power, Politics, and a Sense of History," in *The University and the Public Interest* (New York: Atheneum, 1981), 171–72, 176.

56. John Updike, *Odd Jobs: Essays and Criticism* (New York: Knopf, 1991), 159, 160, 161, 163. For excellent summations of the myth of Emerson's apolitical individualism in this period, see Wesley T. Mott, "'The Age of the First Person Singular': Emerson and Individualism," in *A Historical Guide to Ralph Waldo Emerson*, 67–68; and Mitchell, *Individualism and Its Discontents*, 188–89. Two exceptional critics who rejected the myth of Emerson's apolitical individualism without the benefit of the new history were Irving Howe, *The American Newness: Culture and Politics in the Age of Emerson* (Cambridge: Harvard University Press, 1986); and Christopher Lasch, *The True and Only Heaven: Progress and Its Critics* (New York: Norton, 1991).

57. Richard Poirier, *The Renewal of Literature: Emersonian Reflections* (New Haven: Yale University Press, 1987); Richard Poirier, *Poetry and Pragmatism* (Cambridge: Harvard University Press, 1992); Harold Bloom, *Agon: Toward a Theory of Revisionism* (Oxford: Oxford University Press, 1982). See the introduction to Dolan's *Emerson's Liberalism* for a similar critique of these critics' "starkly anachronistic" approach (9). Malachuk examines these critics in his essay in this volume.

58. Particularly representative of the next generation of postmodern interpreters of Emerson is Michael Lopez, *Emerson and Power: Creative Antagonism*

in the Nineteenth Century (DeKalb: Northern Illinois University Press, 1996). Levine examines this interpretation (particularly its linking Emerson with Nietzsche) in detail in his essay in this volume.

59. *The Inner Ocean: Individualism and Democratic Culture* (Ithaca: Cornell University Press, 1992), 31.

60. Stanley Cavell, "Aversive Thinking: Emersonian Representations in Heidegger and Nietzsche," 108 in the current volume; Kateb, *Emerson and Self-Reliance* (1995; new ed., Lanham, Md.: Rowman and Littlefield, 2002), 201.

61. McWilliams and Shklar had only the small canon to work with. Kateb does venture beyond the small canon, but his major points about Emerson are made with it. An online citation index accompanying Cavell's 2003 book on Emerson reveals that, while he cites a wide range of Emerson's writings, Cavell focuses on just a few texts from the small canon: "The American Scholar," "Self-Reliance," "Circles," "Experience," and "Fate" (see Stanley Cavell, *Emerson's Transcendental Etudes*, ed. David Justin Hodge [Stanford: Stanford University Press, 2003]; and "Citation Index for *Emerson's Transcendental Etudes* by Stanley Cavell," www.sup.org/cavell_index/Citations.pdf).

62. For other reviews of this tendency to conclude that Emerson's self-reliance and antislavery politics are opposed, see Michel Strysick, "Emerson, Slavery, and the Evolution of the Principle of Self-Reliance," in Garvey, *The Emerson Dilemma*, 139–42; and Robinson, "Introduction," *The Political Emerson*, 1–22.

63. On the central role of Nietzsche in the recuperation of Emerson by theorists in recent years, see Wider, *The Critical Reception of Emerson*, 180–82. Dolan also seriously questions the equation of Emerson and Nietzsche (*Emerson's Liberalism*, 10–16).

64. *Letters*, 7:79. On the long tradition of writing about Emerson's use of the eye, see Wider, *The Critical Reception of Emerson*, 128.

65. On Emerson's interest in commerce see, in addition to Dolan's book, Field, *Ralph Waldo Emerson*, 155–57.

66. That Emerson may have written about race in some of his journals, for example, should not inspire us, in pursuit of our own ideological preoccupations, to once again—as in the early twentieth century—blithely look past Emerson's own moral and political intentions as a public intellectual. Cf. Nell Irvin Painter's reliance upon journal entries and her misreading of Emerson's use of the word "race" in *English Traits* to conclude that he was "the philosopher king of American white race theory," in *The History of White People* (New York: Norton 2010), 151.

PART I

Classics on Emerson's Politics

CHAPTER 1

Emerson: The All and the One

Wilson Carey McWilliams

When the conditions of society are becoming more equal and each individual man . . . more like all the rest, a habit grows up . . . of overlooking individuals to think only of their kind. . . . The idea of unity so possesses a man . . . that if he thinks he has found it, he readily yields himself up to repose. Nor is he content with the discovery that there is nothing in this world but creation and Creator; still embarrassed by this primary division . . . he seeks to . . . simplify his conception by including God and the Universe in one great Whole.
—De Tocqueville, *Democracy in America*

America's Philosopher

AMERICANS OF THE nineteenth century acclaimed Ralph Waldo Emerson with an impressive unanimity. They lavished on him all the accolades that the schoolmen had reserved for Aristotle; he was nonpareil, the sage, the philosopher, the metaphysician. Even Julian Hawthorne, carrying on a family tradition of distaste for the seer of Concord, felt obliged to call Emerson's work "enlightening"—though, he hastened to insist, Emerson was at best only a collector of truths.[1]

Prophets, however, are not honored in their own houses, and the genius who is praised in his own time is frequently no genius at all. He is likely to see too much as his own contemporaries see: parochiality is more often than not the price of applause. This is not to imply that Emerson engaged in fulsome flattery of America and Americans. He was often a critic, sometimes a powerful one, of American life and conduct. Flatterers win laurels as rarely as prophets; men at any time have doubts about their own conduct and even more about that of their fellows. The popular sage may be a critic, but he will see the virtues and vices of a people as it sees them, ascribe them to causes it finds persuasive, and prescribe remedies congenial to the public mind.

"I love a prophet of the soul," Emerson wrote, and he came at a time when America needed just such a prophet. Like most New Englanders, he was troubled by the industrial order he saw emerging, distressed by its impersonality, doubtful of its aesthetics and morality. In that, as Parrington realized, he reflected the "submerged idealism" of his region. In thought, however, he stayed close to the surface; he "came out" of the Unitarian church, but he retained the Enlightenment liberalism which was the basis of its doctrine.[2]

As Santayana (and others) saw, Emerson's philosophy was decisively influenced by Locke and the theorists of the eighteenth century. German thought in the nineteenth century influenced him less than critics like Frothingham imagined; the European authorities were added as footnotes to a doctrine already developed and articulated. His political prescriptions show if anything an even greater dependence on eighteenth-century ideas. The Enlightenment was the source of all his key premises: existence of a deity in and not outside nature, the rejection of authority, and a belief in individualism and the creed of progress.[3]

In his attitude toward personal morality and conduct, Emerson never doubted the precepts of traditional religion. (Small wonder that Whitman, otherwise boundlessly admiring, thought him "bloodless.")[4] Yet he did not see his own moral attitudes as the result of culture and institutions. Himself undoubting, tutored in the doctrines of individualism, he was satisfied that the morality he accepted was founded in individual "instinct" and that self-honesty would suffice to produce it.

In the same spirit, he accepted the theory of progress. Rejecting any authority beyond the individual, he was led to reject a God beyond nature. Emerson changed the angle of man's vision: where once man had sought right by trying to steal a glimpse of what lay behind the veil of human things, Emerson insisted that the good was to be found in the scrutinizing of this-worldly process. In that sense, Emerson was not "transcendental" at all. His vision remained bound to the immanent world; his conceptions were not those of the great prophets of the soul, but the beliefs of a typical if talented American intellectual.

Living in the All

Chance was absent from Emerson's universe; all things were part of the great design. Man, however, could not see the aim or the plan; he could only observe motion. Faith in the "oneness" of the universe, which the Enlightenment had believed it could demonstrate by reason, Emerson derived from intuition; the critical doctrines of Hume and Kant (not to say Jonathan Edwards) had bitten deeply into the crust of eighteenth-century rationalism. Emerson carried that critical tradition to its logical conclusion: since man could not discern nature's logic, neither could he discern nature's laws. The scientism of the Enlightenment—its belief that the laws of motion could be learned and then directed—had now to be rejected. For Emerson, man was limited, so far as reason was concerned, to the knowledge of motion itself, ignorantly adrift in the currents of nature and history.

It was a fatalistic but optimistic doctrine. Emerson argued that man's intuition of the wholeness of things should lead him to a faith or realization that all the movement of history worked for the good, that present ills, if seen truly, were part of the process which tended toward unity and harmony. His panglossism was stern and unyielding; he set it as a dogma to rule against all the dark perceptions of men, including his own, and he established sunniness as a test of reason and poetry alike.

His optimism, moreover, was naturalistic. Hence he rejected any idea that there were limits to the goods for which men might hope or any natural restrictions of human desire. He censured the great orthodoxies, Calvinism and Catholicism, because they insisted on the seemingly rational proposition that men were "born to die." Emerson never accepted death as a natural end, even though he doubted the existence of a future life. There were at least two possibilities for this-worldly immortality: the historical immortality of the "success of that to which we belong" and, more importantly, immortality through the "oneness of nature itself." Men, Emerson counseled, should "accept the tide of being which floats us into the secret of nature." The Mother who was Emerson's Nature reabsorbs, and all dilemmas and choices, values and qualities, disappear.

> If the red slayer think he slays
> Or if the slain think he is slain,
> They know not well the subtle ways

> I keep, and pass, and turn again.
> Far or forgot to me is near;
> Shadow and sunlight are the same;
> The vanquished gods to me appear;
> And one to me are shame and fame.[5]

On a less exalted level, Emerson did not disdain fame and success "of that to which we belong." Indeed, although the "natural" soul, with its physical and involuntary needs, was lower than the "transcendent" soul which saw something of the nature of the cosmos, Emerson conceded that man must first develop his "practical" faculties. The lesser immortality of success might be a necessary stage to the attainment of the higher.

Emerson transferred that permissive, naturalistic optimism to his analysis of history. He never lost his conviction of progress, even in the gloomier reflections of old age. The task of philosophy, he wrote, is to "console" men who suffer "under evils whose end they cannot see," which, when rightly understood, will prove not evils at all but only stages to some unseen good.

Consequently, Emerson could never bring himself to participate in politics. Even when the issues of the day seemed to involve questions of great moral import, they were not truly serious. History was moving to abolish slavery (hence, abolitionism was needless and possibly imprudent), to establish peace (hence pacifism was ill-timed and shortsighted), and to create conditions of equality. Reformers and utopians should realize that their advocacy merely described "that which is really being done."[6]

In this sense, Emerson was a "progressive" and might, as Daniel Aaron argues, be considered some sort of forerunner of the movement which took that name. He did formulate many of the relativistic doctrines that later reformers used to challenge the "steel chain of ideas" of late-nineteenth-century liberal orthodoxy. American institutions were suited to their historical period, he commented, but will someday have to pass away; the doctrine that "property writes its own laws" will have to yield to a more equitable standard. Emerson, however, firmly believed that progress did not require a movement; it was written in the motion of nature, and would come of itself.

At the end of history, Emerson was certain, he could discern man's ultimate destiny. His political ideal was a "nation of friends," a "political brotherhood" based on inward unity of spirit and the power of love. Beyond that ideal lay the final city, the brotherhood of man. The issues that divide men, their wars and conflicts and agonies, he wrote, are merely "the melting pot," just as the calamities of the Dark Ages brought forth a new Europe. One day "all men will be lovers," pain and catastrophe will cease, and all mankind will stand "in the universal sunshine."[7]

It is tempting simply to classify Emerson's doctrines as only the most noxious example of the meliorism of the nineteenth century. Yet Emerson could also write of fraternity in eloquent language. Friendship, he said, was man's ultimate ideal, but because it is, men are tempted to romanticize—to believe that the other is "tantamount" to the self and not separate, or to "idolatrize" the other to the detriment of vision. The "ultimate friend" is a "dream and fable," Emerson counseled; men are always separate and imperfect, though the ideal remains valid. Actual friends must be honored, not resented, for their independence. Anticipating Nietzsche, Emerson insisted that a friend must be a "beautiful enemy" and not merely a "trivial conveniency."[8]

Emerson drew much of this wisdom from the traditional doctrine whose moral precepts he always followed. His concept of fraternity, however, was placed in a context which subtracted almost all its content from that teaching. Wisdom taught by a fool can become folly.

First, Emerson distrusted personal friendships, not from a concern for the common values which should be the basis of a "common soul," but in the name of universal fraternity. Fraternity itself is the ultimate ideal, not a means to it. Each friend is the "harbinger of a greater friend" in the sense that the circle of friendship gradually grows wider. The "transcendental friend" is the "other me" which unites me not only to humanity, but to all of nature. Friendship, Emerson believed, was the great leveler, which strode over all barriers of age, sex, religion, circumstance, and character. Friendship abrogates, in other words, all personal judgment of value and quality. Hence, personal friendships based on qualities of personality hamper men in their efforts to "merge" with the all.[9]

Second, Emerson's universal fraternity was premised on a radical individualism and privatism. Indeed, his was a doctrine so extreme that despite his own practice it could serve to moralize disloyalty and self-seeking. For Emerson, Ralph Barton Perry observed, "humanity" often seems an "automatic by-product of selfishness." Emerson might and did denounce "egotism," but he insisted that the "universal soul" was to be found in the individual. Moreover, he felt that this "higher" soul could best be sought in the "spirit of infancy," the erotic sense of "oneness." Friendship, he warned, is never as "large as one man" if he truly understands himself; all society is a "descent" into parochial and "animal spirits" for one of vision. The good man must separate himself from class or party; he must regard all association as only "natural," "momentary" and hence suspect. "All private sympathy," Emerson intoned, "is partial." The individual should reject the "material limitations" which unite him to particular human beings and places; Emerson went so far as to argue that an impoverished environment which holds no temptations is peculiarly conducive to the growth of thought. The path of greatness, Emerson declared, is the road that will most swiftly unite the individual with the race. In effect, Emerson's was a teaching of sublimation, offering a sense of "union" with the race at the price of a separation from individual men.[10]

> Give all to love;
> Obey thy heart;
> Friends, kindred, days,
> Estate, good fame,
> Plans, credit and the Muse—
> Nothing refuse. . . .
>
> Leave all for love;
> Yet hear me, yet,
> One word more thy heart behoved,
> One pulse more of firm endeavor—
> Keep thee today
> Tomorrow, forever
> Free as an Arab
> Of thy beloved.[11]

Each Man a State

Many have been misled by Emerson's rhetorical use of the symbols of fraternity. More than one critic has argued that Emerson was, in some sense, a philosopher of democracy. But the divinity which Emerson saw in man was a deified self, independent of other individuals and the democratic public alike. Government and politics moved him only to disdain. While Emerson valued success in the human attempt at "making the world," he traced it to the "spiritual impulse" of a man who "trusts himself" and seeks to make the world in the image of his own will. The world, Emerson held, is "realized will," emanating from the One of which man is a part. The individual, in Emerson's view, can be said to have self-knowledge when he wills what must be; but it is also a valid demonstration of that exalted state that what he wills, must be. Since Emerson's was a doctrine of activity, individualistic romanticism, not democracy, was the logical result of his teaching. He hoped to make "each man a state," not all men equal citizens of a democratic polity.[12]

Emerson left to the state only the task of designing ways for his assertive individuals to live in reasonable concord. Even so, the state exists to minimize itself; coercion and compulsion, which Emerson identified with politics, are evil because they violate the autonomy of the individual will, and the task of political wisdom is to decrease them. The state has a passive role; believing that only education could change men's "hearts," Emerson saw education as something separate from politics. Political life was merely a negative, almost accidental, factor in man's life, not a part of his nature.[13]

Valuing an expanded sociability, Emerson saw the growth of the city as part of the development toward universal fraternity. In the hectic streets he saw the meeting and mingling of all classes and peoples. He was aware of the isolating effect which urban life could have, and at times it troubled him. His greater fear, however, was characteristic: he worried that the city might be too collective, too social, too political. "He who should inspire . . . his race," he warned, "must be defended from travelling with the souls of other men."[14]

Private character, not public virtue, formed the core of Emerson's ethics, and the theme of his political teaching is that the second must be shaped in the image of the first. That doctrine, stated abstractly, always seems defensible; doubtless it seemed even more reasonable in the early industrial age, when private morals rooted in smaller, stabler communities and in the religious tradition were contrasted with the amorality and rapacity that often characterized public life. Emerson's own standards for private character, however, were far from exacting. He did denounce "self-oriented" action, insisting that the individual act for the "good of man." Yet what Emerson was demanding was an intention, a mental attitude, not a type of conduct; provided the intention was pure, he could and did justify many private derelictions. It is too extreme to say, as did Paul Elmer More, that Emerson was indifferent to personal responsibilities, but it is close to the truth.[15] Emerson had one test for intention in action, one measure of ethics and conduct: the standard of success. This was, of course, the logical result of Emerson's faith in individual will and in the morality immanent in historical process, but it can hardly be argued that such a standard made many demands on the conscience of the individual.

Even when Emerson defended the intellectual against the deprecations of practical men of action, he did so on the grounds that "the most abstract truths are the most practical." Men of practice are misled by what is temporary and transient, while philosophers have a sense of movement and of the impermanence of existing institutions, an insight into nature's processes and goal. (This includes the fact that philosophers sense, as practical men may not, the relativity of standards of ethics.) Intellectuality was necessary to genuine *virtu*; Emerson offered a philosophy of action which purported to be a guide superior to the practical knowledge of men who do not see the philosophy in their own action, the moral meaning of events.[16]

Emerson made a near-cult of "spontaneity," of unreflective and instinctual response to situations resulting from the "simple" and "original" talents of man, which he found superior to the "external refinements" of education and culture. Yet knowledge of the superiority of unreflective spontaneity is a wisdom which, for Emerson, was not an "external refinement" but a true philosophy and insight into human things. Those who possessed only the spontaneity could not appreciate or use it rightly.

Hence, though Emerson trusted the moral direction of the people (and of the Democratic Party), he did not trust their judgment of means. The United States was a young and "barbaric" country, and its instincts were "rough," deficient in true "grandeur of character." The barbarian people lacked the long view, the vision of history; they were too prone to demand immediate goods and fulfillments, too sensitive to merely apparent evils. The need of the land was for a great man who would not "obey the laws too well," who would obey the law of movement, not the statutes of a moment—and who, overcoming the rough public instincts, could guarantee America's destiny.

The "openness" and "opportunity" which Emerson saw in the United States would, if allowed free competitive play, guarantee "success to the best." This is turn would lead to progress in trade and commerce and in "science and computation," and through such material advances lay the path to the final goal of history. Groups, localities, and even fraternal relations might encourage men to follow a by-road which would delay the course of things. True statecraft would give these concrete groups scant and hostile attention; it would seek to make it easier for "events born out of prolific time" to enter and shape American life.[17]

Restating the Enlightenment ideal in the language of will and intuition, Emerson retained the essential prescriptions of that ideal, especially its hostility to fraternity among men in the name of the fraternity of mankind. Certainly his doctrine helped to ease the conscience of industrializing America, and the ebullience of American development, aided or not by the teaching, was such that even Emerson in the end had momentary doubts. Yet only for a moment: Emerson at length retained the curious mental glasses that blinded him to cruelty, stupidity, and sordidness and convinced him that what he saw was in truth the dawning of the "universal sunshine."

Notes

Originally published as Wilson Carey McWilliams, "Emerson and Thoreau: The All and the One," in *The Idea of Fraternity of America* (Berkeley and Los Angeles: University of California Press, 1973), 280–89. Reprinted by permission of the University of California Press.

1. Julian Hawthorne, "Ralph Waldo Emerson," *Harper's* 65 (1882): 278–81.
2. *The Complete Works of Ralph Waldo Emerson* (Boston: Houghton Mifflin, 1883), 9:15–17; Parrington, *Main Currents in American Thought: An Interpretation of American Literature from the Beginnings to 1920* (New York: Harcourt, Brace and World, 1954), 2:372.
3. *The Journals of Ralph Waldo Emerson*, ed. E. W. Emerson and W. S. Forbes (Boston: Houghton Mifflin, 1909–1914), 10:195.
4. Edmund Wilson, *The Shock of Recognition: The Development of Literature in the United States Recorded by the Men Who Made It* (New York: Farrar, Strauss and Cudahy, 1955), 277–78, 286–87.
5. *Works*, 9:170; see also 1:87, 96; 6:43, 100, 306; 10:130, 149, 189; and *Essays* (New York: Hurst, n.d.), 1:42–46; 2:108–11.
6. *Journals*, 4: 430–31; 5:288; 8:449; *Works*, 6:306; *The Early Lectures of Ralph Waldo Emerson*, ed. S. E. Whicker ad R. E. Spiller (Cambridge: Harvard University Press, 1959), 22; and *The American Transcendentalists*, ed. Perry Miller (New York: Doubleday, 1957), 5–20.

7. *Journals,* 3:235; 5:380; 6:336; 7:115–16; 8:456; *Works,* 1:242; *Essays,* 2:116–17, 142.

8. *Essays,* 1:104–14; 2:140–41.

9. *Works,* 1:96; 2:304; 10:136.

10. Ibid., 1:9, 272; 3:276; 9:11; *Essays,* 2:78, 116, 140–41; *Journals,* 5:310–11; Wilson, *Shock of Recognition,* 626.

11. *Works,* 9:84–86.

12. *Journals,* 3:369; 4:95; 5:302, 307; *Works,* 1:46, 102, 323, 328; 6:44, 295, 302.

13. *Works,* 1:115, 347–48; 3:253–54; *Essays,* 2:107–8, 114–15; *Journals,* 7:220; 10:144.

14. *Works,* ed. E. W. Emerson (Boston: Houghton Mifflin, 1903–1904), 6:56–57, 148–49, 153–56; 7:10–11, 153–54, 244, 424–25; *The Correspondence of Thomas Carlyle and Ralph Waldo Emerson* (Boston: Houghton Mifflin, 1883), 1:269–70.

15. Paul Elmer More, "Emerson," *Cambridge History of American Literature* (New York: Macmillan, 1946), 1:354, 360–61.

16. *Works,* 1:10; Wilson, *Shock of Recognition,* 654; Henry Nash Smith, "Emerson's Problem of Vocation," *New England Quarterly* 12 (1939): 52–67.

17. *Essays,* 2:109–11, 115; *Works,* 1:150, 221–22; 10:132, 149, 153; 12:60; *Journals,* 8:449.

CHAPTER 2

Emerson and the Inhibitions of Democracy

Judith N. Shklar

Editors' Note: This essay was published twice by Shklar. We reprint the *Political Theory* version since that is what Shklar chose for the widest audience. The other text has minor differences and begins with one additional paragraph: "Many years ago it was said to me: 'But he is not Nietzsche!' We know that he is not, but there are reasons to wonder why, especially after reading *Self-Reliance*. The exploratory essay, the possibility of unlimited self-creation, and the same ex-protestant tension between the equal impossibilities of solitude and society and the irony that it evokes, all these are surely not trivial similarities. Nevertheless there is a great distance between them, and I shall argue that it is political. And with that I am also saying that politics, or at least democracy, which is what is at stake here, is not irrelevant to the way we read some of the most significant philosophical texts" (Ted Cohen, Paul Guyer, and Hilary Putnam, eds., *Pursuits of Reason: Essays in Honor of Stanley Cavell* [Lubbock: Texas Tech University Press, 1993], 121).

EMERSON MAY NOT HAVE been what is conventionally called a political philosopher, but political considerations played a more subtle part in his thinking than mere expressions of opinion on public affairs would suggest. For Emerson, the beliefs and practices of American representative democracy constituted an integral moral barrier which he could neither ignore nor cross. It brought him up short, like a stop sign at a junction. This inhibition was not, however, something externally imposed on him against his will or better judgment. He was not giving in to something he could not overcome. Not only did democratic political experiences offer him an ample source of illustration but quite often gave his essays their intellectual purpose and direction. That could never be said of Nietzsche, and it is a great part of the difference in the very substance of what they wrote. What are the democratic convictions and habits that are so relevant to Emerson's writings? They are the most obvious ones. The most important is that we are "created equal" and that the qualities that truly distinguish us are not those that are available to only exceptional individuals but those which we can all potentially achieve. Neither inherited nor accidentally acquired advantages can have any moral standing. Last, the consent of the governed is one of the necessary, though not the only, mark of the just powers of governments. With that, there is, most important of all, an intuitive respect for one's fellow citizens, felt not as an obligation but as a given. At a more reflective level, democratic government also entails its own genre of political criticism, and this was also part of Emerson's system of complaints. Since Madison, the tyranny of the majority has been seen as a major threat to the republican liberty. And since Tocqueville, no one has forgotten the dangerous pressure of public opinion on free individual expression and development. Mill may have been right to regard timidity and social conformity as the burdens of middle-class civilization rather than of democratic government, but that hardly improves America's prospects. In either case, to fret about equality is an enduring act of democratic American self-criticism as well as to lament that democratic class society is more hostile to individuality than a society of castes. It was certainly part of Emerson's democratic inheritance to accept these democratic discontents. To these he added a no less usual suspiciousness of the probity of all parties and elected officials.

It is not simply the presence of some or all of these political dispositions in Emerson's various essays that is, in itself, interesting but the way in which they control the flow of his thought generally. That is particularly revealing in those cases where politics is not the overt topic, as in "Self-Reliance."[1] It is, in any event, not an essay one can ignore, but is also one in which the boundaries of democracy would appear to be crossed by the call to each of us to create our own world and to acknowledge our isolation. Here, Emerson seems quite prepared to flout the democratic creed in his enthusiasm for the self-reliant individual, but, in fact, he avoids a full assault and backs off from it. Early on in "Self-Reliance" we are told very firmly that "society everywhere is in conspiracy against the manhood of every one of its members" (261). One does not, therefore, given the danger, have to offer reasons for refusing any association or acts of convention. "I shun father and mother and wife and brother, when my genius calls me." Why should he be generous to the needy? *"Are they my poor?"* He will go to prison for a cause that is his, but not for Christianity's poor. And not a dime will he give to ordinary socially, democratically approved charities. There must be some "spiritual affinity" to move him to act for another. Dissociation could hardly go further. He certainly means to shock his readers. He also does so in order to demonstrate his indifference to any obligation that is not self-made. The impact is, however, softened at once by irony. He confesses with shame and regret that, in fact, he is too weak to refuse a dollar to the poor. The principle remains intact, the joke is on him, but he has not withdrawn himself from fellowship after all. It is easy to turn one's back on parties, churches, and a "dead Bible society," but on the poor? That is only to be proclaimed; it cannot be done (262–63). As for genius, we hear the names of all the greatest men and the misunderstanding that society has always vented on them. Greatness, however, radiated its bounty in spite of that. And again we retreat. Greatness is a genuine quality that is not really a matter of extraordinary talent and rare acts. We can all be great when we are called to it, and so Emerson ends with the fable of the poor sot who was dressed up and treated like a duke in his sleep, and who, on awakening, used his wits and behaved like a true prince (267). This is not the genius as destroyer-creator, second Prometheus, or the superman of a more desperate imagination. Self-creation without the signposts of normality needs to be asserted, but not at the expense of every person.

What, then, is self-reliance to achieve? It is not a call to reject the usual bonds of family life but to take them on as one's own discovery. Making one's own rules is a new life and, indeed, the only remaining possibility for constructing a law out of that transforming experience of nature. Nature, to be sure, might be a universal territory of exploration. Supposing that it were, then there is no reason to exclude anyone who did not turn one's back on self-reliance as an adventure, at the very least. This would be possible even if "it demands something godlike in him who has cast off the common motives of humanity" (274). Most people are simply too timid and too dependent to try, especially in the big cities. The godlike qualities are not, however, a matter of locality or class or genius in a vulgar sense. The model of self-reliance is the Yankee farmer. There are untutored yeomen in Vermont and in New Hampshire who were for Emerson, no less than for Jefferson before him, the embodiment of democratic ideals. The Yankee lad moves from social role to social role with no difficulty. He always lands on his feet. He farms, peddles, teaches school, gets elected to Congress, and then tries something else. He is always competent, and, above all, he never *is* his job or social definition. Clearly, "greater self-reliance must work a revolution in all the offices and relations of men," if this is what it would mean in daily terms (275). This man has no past and, indeed, no social baggage to encumber him at all. No aggregate can contain him. And "is not a man better than a town?" (282). That allows Emerson to leave democratic man on his pinnacle, without having to make any compromises with those features of democratic life that were not compatible with self-reliance. He could scorn the parties and their members, indeed membership as such, without falling into the cant of a quasi-aristocratic individualism.

There remains, nevertheless, a real difficulty. "Self-Reliance" is a veritable roll call of great men. Explorers, scientists, poets, and even philosophers are invoked to show what a self-reliant, unimitating character can be and do. They are not great, surely, either because they were first scorned and later copied by other men. Yet Emerson cannot face them directly. He notes depths and energies but swerves off to worry about the impact of greatness on the rest of us. All disciples infuriate Emerson, but he cannot simply look away and let the great man be. The genius, whose light, after all, does illuminate those intimations of unmediated contact with pure nature, cannot be left to his greatness. "The great genius returns to essential man" (280). That is not entirely what that extraordinary litany of names, each one the creator of a new religion, the discoverer of a continent, or an incomparable artist, means. It may well be that society does not improve, thanks to their deeds. It may even be true that lesser men fall into passive admiration when they contemplate them. They may not invigorate people who resist vitality, but that is not and cannot be the whole purpose of recalling the great, who were each and every one of them original to a superlative degree. It is as if Emerson could not bring himself to decide openly whether the difference between them and the Yankee lad either does or does not exist. Is it a matter of scale, or does genius constitute an unbridgeable gulf? In fact, he meant both. There is a space between all self-reliant men. Their awareness of that uncrossable division is what renders them self-relying persons in the first place. What Emerson could not get himself to say was that the great are absolutely different and better within their sphere. That was the inhibition of democracy. The great speak to us without barriers of time or class or space. The Yankee lad may or may not hear them. As long as he also is in his every act and feeling dissociated in that same way, he is not an inferior.

Emerson's great neither destroy nor re-create worlds. They do not eliminate human obstacles to do their will. That is very comforting, but are we to avoid admiring them as well? We may ask: What use are they at all? It is, indeed, the very question Emerson was forced to ask himself. *Representative Men* is Emerson's effort to answer the question about human greatness which he had posed for himself most of all. That was not, however, the only incentive to return to the matter. There was also his friend Carlyle's *Heroes and Hero-Worship* to confront him with a way of thinking about the relations between great and small men that he could not ignore. Carlyle had few problems. He only recorded the already well-worn themes of conventional romanticism. The hero was indeed a force of Nature, who created universal history. That there might be a vast gap between the energies of nature and the course of human history did not appear to occur to Carlyle. That thought was left to Marx, although a quick reading of Rousseau might have given even Carlyle pause. In any event, "they are the leaders of men, these great ones in a wide sense creators of whatever the wide mass of mankind do or attain." To worship such heroes is the only path to any sort of spiritual life open to all other persons. Indeed, the failure to do so is the cause of the degeneracy of the age. Emerson's own account of the mind's passage to oneness with Nature made such a scenario quite plausible, though not inevitable. It was certainly important for him to avoid Carlyle's summons to fall humbly silent as we listen to the single heroic voice of the nation, just as if it were the call of the universe, addressing us in poetry, prose, and military orders. Emerson would not obey, but what was he to do instead?

Emerson's first move was simply to refuse to talk about heroes or great men at all. Plato, Swedenborg, Montaigne, Shakespeare, Napoleon, and Goethe are *representative men,* not, by definition, therefore, objects of worship. Even this was not enough, and he remained uneasy:

> Many after thoughts, as usual, and my book seems to lose all the value from their omission. Plainly one is the justice that should have been done to the unexpressed greatness of the common farmer and laborer. A hundred times have I felt the superiority of George and Edmund Barrows, and yet I continue the parrot echoes of the names of literary notabilities and mediocrities.[2]

This piece of self-criticism, put into his *Journal,* can come as no surprise to readers of "Self-Reliance," but it is important nonetheless. For it reveals that Emerson completely understood the divisions within the essay, his own convictions, and that the impulses of democracy were not something he merely had to take into account but were a part of himself. The evident difficulty was that they were not without rivals in his mind. Who was he to deny that the great men on his roster were, indeed, great? If most political great men were charlatans, destroyers, and certainly a deadly threat to any of the more decent forms of government, what of the other greats? Was he to accept that they had names, while all the rest of his neighbors were to be known only as statistics? What became of "created equal" in that case? Even the universal accessibility of Nature might be threatened. But to deny that Shakespeare or Mozart was not wholly apart, wholly superior? Emerson was acutely aware of the decisions that he would have to make. And so, in his effort to navigate between these conflicts, he resorted to a very political metaphor, the representative, the central figure of American political practice, the elected spokesperson of one's constituency.

The whole movement of "Uses of Great Men," the essay which opens *Representative Men*, is a zig-zag. Nature exists for excellence (up), but anyone who is good among us qualifies (down). Do the great raise our sights? Yes, they do (up), but they are a part of all humanity, else they could not reach us (down). If they see things more quickly and before others do (up), we all can see eventually (down). To be sure, they are so absorbed in and by Nature that they can interpret it for us and make it intelligible to us. That is what great scientists do for us (up), but this power is not to be construed as a personal quality. These men are vessels of an idea, conveyors as it were (down). Even as messengers, however, do the great not alter mankind significantly (up)? And do we not gain encouragement from reading the biographies of great people (up)? Maybe. A wise man in our village would do more for us on all counts (down). And the deepest encouragement that can ever come to us is from a true friend (down). Genius does guide us to a "supersensible region" and takes us out of the pettiness and monotony of everyday life (up). That is also the source of its dangers. It tempts us to passivity and idolatry (down). The antidote to that is supplied by the fact that great people replace their predecessors and so reveal the relativity of all greatness, its passing character. It is all time-bound, as every successor puts one's predecessor in the shadow and so keeps things alive and moving (down and up). The trouble with this last remark is that it is so obviously untrue that it must have been a prescription for how to treat greatness rather than an even remotely plausible statement about it. Just who, after all, has put Plato, Montaigne, and, say, Mozart, in a shadow? The notion is ridiculous. Emerson's best and preferred argument is that without an audience, there is effectually no genius, and that while knowledge is revealed to us, no one can know it for us. We, small men and women, also must act. Without Plato, we would not have known that rational discourse was possible (up). Without it, all would have been complacency and self-satisfaction. However, were we not able to respond to him, he would not have been great (down). Indeed, Emerson distrusted even his own occasional paternalism, his care for the independence of ordinary people. They will not be lost forever in an excess of admiration for great people. Sooner or later they will regain their balance.

We need others to know ourselves and great people, especially, are measures, but we can eventually attain a true sense of our being and dispense with that overpowering otherness. Only moral grandeur endures, and that is not a socially recognized form of greatness. The moral genius abolishes oneself and leaves a lasting resonance. The acts survive the person, and refresh us. Even so, let us be bold. If we must remember famous names, let us learn to say from time to time, "Damn George Washington." This roller coaster of weights and measures is less a revelation of a mind's discomfort than a proof of Emerson's unswerving determination to reject the political implications of a romanticism which, in most other respects, was his own. He was not going to replace God with genius. He would not permit any person to say, "I am that I am" and to be wholly unaccountable to humanity for one's oppressive power. Nevertheless, he would not simply pretend that greatness did not matter at all. The very possibility of a supersensible sphere, of transcendence, is more accessible to great individuals' eyes and more open to the rest of us because genius brings its intimations to us. That admits not only a vast gap between the two kinds of people but offers all possible grounds for admiring the great and their works. The absolute necessity of great men for revealing the possibilities of reason, imagination, discovery and beauty is implicit in everything Emerson said about them. He had no way around that. Nevertheless, he grudged the great their glory, not because he was small-minded but because an uncritical belief in great people was not compatible with his democratic convictions. The way he coped with it was nothing if not ingenious. The masses of humanity certainly do not exist in order to allow a great person to emerge from their depth to lead and mould them. The great person serves them. And that service is described in the language of democratic politics. The way out of the tension between the sense of the apartness of the great and the claims of humanity was, as in constitutional states, to resort to representation. It is the only way out of the seesaw between anarchy and oppression. Nothing could illustrate more vividly the hold that democratic norms had on Emerson's intellectual imagination.

In what way do great people act as representatives? They may serve us directly by giving us something, be it material or metaphysical, but that is not representation. They also do something for us that is "pictorial," that is, they make something present that is absent. In this representation, a great person puts before our eyes some part of nature that is peculiarly one's own and makes us aware of it, makes it present to us. Dalton's atoms are "his" and he pictures them for us, so that we can eventually say, "Now I see it" (618). It is easier for him than for us, but we are not altogether passive. It is not a matter of some neo-Platonic overflowing of spiritual energy from a pinnacle downward. Moreover, Emerson quickly drops the pictorial analogy and turns to political representation. That is not a matter of aristocratic generosity:

> The constituency decides the vote of the representative. He is not only representative, but participant. Like can only be known by like. The reason he knows about them is, that he is of them; he has just come out of nature, or from being a part of that thing. (619)

As he is chosen by nature to be great, he represents it to us. For one always represents to someone. The congressperson speaks on behalf of one's district (nature) to Congress, the nation's assembled representatives (the world of others, of humanity at large, lesser people, ourselves). And as such, we are not consumers of their activity. Assemblies are deliberative bodies, and we become vigorous as we talk to the other delegates. "We are entitled to these enlargements." They save us from domesticity through multiplied extended relations and to be a delegate is to inspire trust, not subservience, moreover. We are drawn out, not bullied. Certainly, nature's attorney is no demonic force. The imagery, if not political, is nautical. The great person is a "mapmaker," easily the most useful, practical form of pictorial representation. Still, the point is for us to actively use that map and take to the road ourselves. The way by which the great individual liberates us is that this person does not stay around forever. Like all public servants, one's term comes to an end—and none too soon. What is important is the process of "rotation," again a word from the vocabulary of democracy. In fact, rotation in office was *the* great watchword of Jacksonian democracy; it meant that, since anyone could perform the modest tasks of the civil servant, no one should occupy an office for too long or monopolize it or think that one had some sort of proprietary right to it. When Emerson said that "rotation is the law of nature" (623), he was clearly speaking of the social no less than of the physical laws of change. Each great person is a separate class and can have no clones. Jefferson and Franklin will be succeeded by a "great salesman; then a road-contractor, then a student of fishes." Clearly, Emerson was no culture snob. What unites these disparate types is that they are all servants of an idea. And though they alone glow with it, they share the light with the rest of us. Theirs is not the vulgarity that exploits our imbecility to dazzle us. "If a wise man should appear in our village, he would create, in those who conversed with him, a new consciousness of wealth, by opening their eyes to unobserved advantages; he would establish a sense of immovable equality." He would defend us against our worst impulse, the passion for worshipping great people. He would, in short, liberate us.

The great one who introduces us to the "qualities of primary nature" (624) may also rescue us from the tedium and futility of political contests, the normal process of democratic politics. A stranger to parties who, coming from a higher sphere, gets to the heart of "the equity" of any policy also liberates us. In politics, the great person is not the winner but the self-liquidating hero, who leaves not a name but a just law behind. Public opinion devoid of intellect was also in need of service from the great (625). They put a drop of acid on complacency and sentimentality, "on maudlin agglutinations" and on the insanity of our frenzied cities. It is their "foreign" quality, their distance from us, after all, that is the source of their gifts (626–27). Emerson could not, however, leave it at that. He must immediately warn us against the dangers of submission to the great, lest we become "underlings and intellectual suicides." The constitutional, free state depends on a "seesaw" between radicals who defy the past and its great men and those who will go right on admiring George Washington and the rest of their ancestors (627–28). It is no disgrace. As individuals, we might afford a degree of trust in the old great men, because ultimately we too will regain the balance of an independent, critical state. No sooner said than Emerson's irony asserts itself, and the rug is pulled out from the reader who might have been lulled into self-satisfaction. "But *great men:* the word is injurious" (629). Great people are not good for us, because we are small. We are unstable in our moods, moving haltlessly "from dignity to dependence." We do not allow rotation to occur. We are *not* democratic enough. Instead, we talk meanly of masses and common people; "there are no common men. All men are of a size" (630). If we mean business with "created equal," we will have to change our entire way of thinking about history. Is it just as he is warning or is he teetering back and forth himself—drawn by his two poles? In a dismissive moment, we leave the great behind us.

Heroes are relative to their time and place. Great today and gone tomorrow. Only humanity goes on. "The genius of humanity" should be the subject of biography. The spirit of the genius is absorbed in the flow of humanity's passage through time. We ought to think of great people in social and impersonal terms, as messengers from an idea that they represent to us, or really to all humanity. Then, they should get lost as fast as possible. "We have never come to the true and best benefit of genius, so long as we believe him an original force" (631). There could not be a more complete rejection of the romantic notion of genius than that. Great individuals have only one claim on our attention: to help us grow up and to do without them, except that there are many reasons to believe that this is not the whole story.

It would be wrong to think that Emerson was just dispensing wholesome milk and cookies to his fellow citizens. First of all, he spends most of his energy on excoriating their social pettiness and competitiveness and their mental torpor. Moreover, not all the incoherence of the essay is due to democratic pathos. Emerson is illuminating the two very different and incompatible faces of human greatness. Along with the rest of us, he knew that great people were in touch with the forces that transform the realms of experience; let us again say, Mozart. It is not we who elect them, they are delegated to us, to unite us with the powers that have chosen them. They *are* the elect. That is not all, however. Great people are historical figures. Without their followers, their disciples, and their audiences, they would remain unknown and unrecognized. It is as absurd to speak of a hidden great person as of an ungifted genius. That is, surely, Emerson's chief point. To assert all its implications against Carlyle and the politically obtuse longing for hero-leaders and to reassert his loyalty to democratic men and women, however, required more, far more, than an account of the dual nature of human greatness. It required a choice between the two sides, and Emerson, in the language of democratic politics, came down heavily on the side of the democratic ethos. What is needed, once the choice has been made, is a more generous sense of appreciation, a larger vision of human worth and achievement, so that there will be more honor for uncommon, but universally possible, acts of ordinary decency.

It cannot be said that Emerson really tells us how to think about Plato and his other representative men. He does give us an idea of what he thought about them. And as one might expect, he is very carping. Only Montaigne comes off fairly well. We are told in *Montaigne; or the Skeptic* that he was gross in the way that he talked about sex, but that was in keeping with the manners of his time. He was the "prince of egotists" and an "admirable gossip" (697–98). These sentiments do not do Emerson much honor, but they are not grounded in spite or envy. It was really a mild form of self-criticism. For he also tells us that when he first read Cotton's translation of the *Essays*, he felt that he had written them himself (697). He had become, and in many ways remained, Montaigne. What was the skepticism that Montaigne represented like? It was not the skepticism of the *Apology for Raimond Sebond* but that of *Of Cannibals*, social rather than philosophical. And its audience is defined psychologically. Most people find skepticism intolerable. They cannot endure it. It is a matter of temperament (706–7). Some people do take to it spontaneously, however, as did Montaigne and he speaks for them and for their great truth: *There are doubts.*

One cannot easily imagine Emerson accepting the religion of his country simply because it was there and the alternatives were not really any better, possibly worse, as novelties are likely to be. Montaigne's resignation to religious custom was not compatible with the agonies of Protestantism. So deep an indifference to the content, to the specifics of religious belief, or unbelief for that matter, was not within Emerson's range of possibilities. His skepticism was limited to the social world where it was enhanced rather than constrained by democracy. The social case for skepticism was overwhelming. On one side, there is the arrogance of the intellectuals, who look on the rest of humankind as rats and mice (691–93). Between the pretensions of the intellectuals and the cynicism of the business person, the skeptic is a breath of fresh air who blows the dogmatizers away. He is not going to affirm or deny; one can survive without proclamations or judgments. Emerson did not think that this implied complete unbelief or "scoffing and profligate jeering at all that is stable and good." The genuine skeptic is a spectator whom one can trust, for aloofness is not incompatible with conventional probity. Far from it (695–96). Montaigne who represents this skepticism was the most honest and frank and sincere man who ever lived. Honesty, fastidious and self-contained, is the skeptic's virtue, and Emerson did not grudge it his admiration (698–700). We may find such honesty repulsive, for we are all natural believers, but one cannot overlook its results. Not only is skepticism the scourge of bigots and blockheads, the skeptic has the strength to be a very bad citizen and is just the dose of salts that democracy needs. The skeptic is neither a conservative nor a reformer and is not a joiner of any sort. No club, party, or cause can claim the skeptic as its own (702–3). This person is just the cure for both the crude materialism and the cloying religiosity that democratic societies seem to encourage. The conventional case against skepticism, therefore, leaves Emerson cold. Only a childish religiosity will suffer from it: nothing to regret in that. As for asserting the instability of human opinion, who can deny the record of history? What is permanent except human selfishness? We cannot blame skepticism for the facts of life. They may upset us, but that is not the skeptic's fault. Will we feel defeated in our pursuits if we suspect that all is illusion? Why should we react that way? Doubt is more likely to inspire courage and determination than credulity (703–6). And Montaigne and the skepticism he represented were not wholly without belief, however tentative. He held onto, or at least practices, honesty. The difficulty is that honesty puts one at odds with the world. But what is skepticism without its claim to that state of mind which we call honest?

Having said so much on behalf of his one and only hero, Emerson did, in the end, feel compelled to withdraw. "The final solution in which skepticism is lost is in the moral sentiment, which never forfeits its supremacy." Dissolving or resolving, in our time, "the final solution" is a phrase that evokes other resonances. It makes a mockery of Emerson's pieties. They were needed even then only to reconcile him to the chasm between hope and experience. Did he really believe that sentimentality? At the social level, there is some reason to believe that this was a quiet acceptance of conventional belief, not unlike Montaigne's peace with public manners, rituals, and conventions, but more creedal and less provisional. The moral sense assures "that appearance is immoral; the result is moral." The whole absorbs and purified its parts. The public religion of Emerson's America was the faith in progress, real moral and political advance. Democracy depended on it. Emerson could not dismiss that faith. And so we are told that every successive government may only be a parade of knaves and fools, but in the end, "a great and beneficent tendency irresistibly streams." Having just poured scorn on Charles Fourier, who really did believe that sort of thing, Emerson was not in the best position to endorse a historical myth against which his entire essay rebelled. To have rejected it out of honesty might, however, have removed him from his community to an intolerable degree. So like Montaigne, he respected the prevailing religion, but unlike the great skeptic he did not do so openly. It was not democratically possible, and then he *did* believe in something more, in an Eternal Cause, a supersensible Nature, an intimation of another World.

Whatever the limits of Emerson's skepticism were, whether they were political or mystical, he gave his doubts a free rein when he thought about social reformers. Neither "Self-Reliance" nor *Representative Men* is about politics, which is why the constant intrusion of political language, illustrations, and preoccupations is so striking. In "New England Reformers," Emerson is talking about the political conduct of his friends, and as he says "we," one must suppose his own as well. In one sense, Emerson thought that we were all reformers, because we all want to improve ourselves in some way. That is not, however, what he means in this, his most ironic and self-deprecating essay. Here, he is defending democratic people against the moral-reform societies that were the most conspicuous feature of Jacksonian New England: utopian communities, temperance, prison reform, educational experiments, and, of course, more seriously, abolitionism. Most of the young men and women who undertook to devote their lives to these causes had been moved by Emerson, a point of which he was aware. His responsibility was obvious; therefore, it is "we," not "you." Moreover, the scorn does not have to be softened in that case. One need not spare oneself for the sake of tact or prudence. It is here that we can find out why skepticism and democracy were jointed in Emerson's mind. To be mindful of the people of one's town, to respect their opinions may well force "us" to doubt our most cherished political dreams. We may have to give up utopian enterprises, because our neighbors think that they are ridiculous and the townspeople just may be right. So there *are* doubts. The pursuit of the perfect city is an insult to the actual town, and that is a very questionable political action. To look at the reform of the other people from their point of view, to consider their consent, is democratic, and it must introduce doubts of the most severe sort into the mind of the reforming agent. Skepticism about reform was what Emerson thought he owed his town. It was a debt to be paid to democracy, not only as something out there but as it existed in half of his own mind and as part of his own moral sense for which he, as part of "we," had to apologize.

The Church, that is, the truly religious party, is leaving the "church nominal." That is the way of Protestant piety, of course. The quest for perfect purity means sectarianism. The established congregation has again been rejected in "a spirit of protest and detachment." That sounds pretty serious and dignified, but before we are fooled for too long, irony removes our blinkers. "What a fertility of projects for the salvation of the world! [A] society for the protection of ground worms, slugs and mosquitoes was to be incorporated without delay" (591–92). It was a replay of the antinomianism of "the elder puritans." As an assertion of the independence of private citizens, this is fine, but it loses all value when it is copied, when it is a matter of group life. There is, moreover, something inherently absurd about the projection of the purity of conscience into the public glare. "Hands off! Let there be no control and no interference in the administration of this kingdom of me." The verbal imbecility reflects the confusion of intentions. The result is predictable. The independence of conscience once it enters the public domain is exploited by less scrupulous political agents. So freedom quickly is translated into free trade, as reformers and regular politicians soon are engaged in a ritual dance. Groups are all alike. Emerson had no intention of whitewashing the established institutions. Education, especially, was futile, cynical, and indifferent to the development of individual children. He did not support slavery but did not choose to act until the passage of the Fugitive Slave Law. He thought that the efforts of reformers who were not themselves reformed were no better than their awful adversaries. They were, indeed, particularly obtuse. When their domestic life was a mess, they thought that everything could be solved by joining a utopian commune on the assumption that collective activity was the equivalent of a psychological self-transformation. In fact, the tax levied by radical conformity was no less heavy than that extracted by official associations. The ardent do-gooders were not for "my poor" after all. Emerson was not going to allow philanthropy to pressure him nor to deflect him from his will to act only on his grounds. No part of society was really better than any other. And the radical "groupie" was just a rebellious conformist in his view. The only way to reform is to begin with oneself and then to deal only with others as discrete individuals, not "causes."

There is, to begin with, far less inequality between individuals than we pretend, so we may not need to reform each other. Everyone is good at something. Moreover, they are as keen to do their best for their town as one could wish. So we might refrain from preaching to them. When they vote, they try to choose the better candidate, and all prefer the company of people whom they regard as their superiors. The desire to improve is universal. It is thoughtless and also cynical to see pure malignity among those with whom we disagree or who may indeed be utterly wrong. To organize others is to demote them in advance. The town is better than it may seem, and it is ready to alter when it is approached patiently and appreciatively—democratically, in fact. The alternative is a deserved failure:

> We wish to escape from subjection, and a sense of inferiority, and we make self-denying ordinances, we drink water, we eat grass, we refuse the laws, we go to jail, it is all in vain. (608)

All this public display of virtue neither liberates the reformer nor impresses the town. If you want to do something about education, teach a child. If you want to change the local laws, talk to the citizens. Everyone can be free, and no one can rise to any height by stepping on the Yankee lad.

Emerson did not claim that he had the key to public or private success: "Every discourse is an approximate answer." To the end, however, there were simply two immovable propositions from which he never departed. The first was that the approach to truth could be made only in complete solitude. If it is unspoken, it is, after all, beyond doubt and dogma. The second was that if there was a moral law, it was democratic. He might choose to be alone, but he would not look down on the ploughboy. He would scorn the New England reformers, the great men, and even his own impulse to antinomian assertion because he could not, and would not, turn his back on the townspeople. And in the end, it was for their sake that he chose only bearable doubts and to be a skeptical bad citizen, who would resist both the enthusiasms of radicalism and the matey thuggery of all established parties. He was just not going to talk that way. We are all better than we think and a lot better than we are usually told we are. In its way, this wry affirmation is deeply democratic. And it inspired Emerson's philosophy, as often as it inhibited him from following his mind's impulse to explore those darkest moments of contempt from which one cannot redeem oneself or others.

Notes

Originally published as Judith N. Shklar, "Emerson and the Inhibitions of Democracy," *Political Theory* 18, no. 4 (November 1990): 601–14. Reprinted by permission of Sage Publications.

    1. All references are to Ralph Waldo Emerson, *Essays and Lectures* (New York: Library of America, 1983).
    2. *Emerson in His Journals,* ed. Joel Porte (Cambridge: Harvard University Press, 1982), 40.

CHAPTER 3

Self-Reliance, Politics, and Society

George Kateb

AT THIS POINT, a reasonable question may arise. What provision does Emerson make for a self-reliant individual to work with others, to cooperate and collaborate? No doubt the very idea of association disturbs self-reliant people when association moves out of a small circle of friends and includes numbers of people, many of them strangers or only acquaintances. When association is extended even more to one's numerous fellow citizens, the condition of self-reliance becomes all the more uncertain. Unfolding one's powers, becoming and staying what one is, living a life that one defines for oneself—all these conceptualizations fit uneasily with associative activity, if they fit at all. Systematic association is a disfigurement, a loss of integrity.

> People wrap themselves up in disguises, and the sincere man is hard to reach. A man is concealed in his nation, concealed in his party, concealed in his fortune, and estate, concealed in his office, in his profession, concealed in his body at last, and it is hard to find out his pure nature and will. They speak and act in each of these relations after the use and wont of those conditions. They talk as Americans, as Republicans . . . each cunningly hiding under these wearisome commonplaces the character and flavor which is all that can really make him interesting and valuable to us. Of course, he only half acts,—talks with his lips and not his heart. (Notes to "Courage," *Society and Solitude*, W, 7:431)

At the same time, working with others may mean that each person in the group aims to make a direct contribution to the well-being of the group, oneself included. Yet Emerson is wary of the organized effort to compel or even elicit continuous benevolence from individuals. Both the prudential motive and the moral motive have a necessary place in every individual life and in the psychological economy of every complex society. Nevertheless, active self-reliance, as Emerson conceptualizes it, is not, for the most part, motivated morally or prudentially, though it must be framed by both morality and prudence. The motives of individualism are, so to speak, existential.

There are obstacles, then, to reconciling active self-reliance and working with others. How does Emerson deal with these obstacles?

Before attempting an answer to this question, we should notice that in one essay, "Manners" (*Essays: Second Series*), where Emerson impersonates aspects of the idea of worldliness—fashion, manner, decorum—he makes a fine case for suppressing active self-reliance and, instead, encouraging conformity to codes or styles for the sake of cooperating to maintain the fabric of elegance in being. Emerson eventually allows, even in this essay, the reassertion of creative individuality as sanely disruptive, but for a time he lets the idea of worldliness appear attractively. But I believe this essay is aberrant. The system of exquisite manners has no general significance in Emerson's thought; it is not a model for other activity. In any case, taking part in a system of manners (ordinary politeness is not at issue) is, or should be, more like playing a game by the rules or performing a ritual correctly than living a life. As long as games and rituals are seen for what they are, they bring only a little benefit or a little harm to self-reliance.

A passage from "New England Reformers" (*Essays: Second Series*) contains the gist of Emerson's usual disposition:

> These new associations are composed of men and women of superior talents and sentiments; yet it may be easily questioned whether . . . the members will not necessarily be fractions of men, because each finds that he cannot enter it without some compromise. Friendship and association are very fine things, and a grand phalanx of the best of the human race, banded for some catholic object: yes, excellent; but remember that no society can ever be so large as one man. He, in his friendship, in his natural and momentary associations, doubles or multiplies himself: but in the hour in which he mortgages himself to two or ten or twenty, he dwarfs himself below the stature of one. (*E&L*, 598)

Emerson passes this judgment in the course of considering small, communal societies started in Massachusetts on the principles of Saint-Simon or Fourier or Robert Owen. (It is surprising that Emerson briefly flirted with the idea of living in the Fourierist Brook Farm community.) He intends to apply what he says about these societies to all associations beyond those of intimate friendship, love, and plain good-neighborliness. I think that the key consideration is that by mortgaging or pledging oneself to others, by committing oneself to defer to the preponderant will and judgment of others for the sake of some common purpose, by embarking on the relationship of solidarity, one may dwarf oneself. Movements for reform fall under the same individualist skepticism as experiments in communal living. Emerson insists:

> The union is only perfect when all the uniters are isolated. It is the union of friends who live in different streets or towns. Each man, if he attempts to join himself to others, is on all sides cramped and diminished of his proportion; and the stricter the union the smaller and the more pitiful he is. (*E&L*, 599)

Emerson preaches "the distrust of numbers" when numbers are zealous to improve society ("Lectures on the Times," *E&L*, 162).

It could be asked, Does not the urgency of reform—to leave aside communal experiments—override concern for the individualistic independence of the reformers? Indeed, can't reformers find realization of their individuality, employment for their active self-reliance, in lending—giving—themselves to movements of reform? Can't reformers discover new energies and unsuspected talents in themselves? Emerson gives little to the good effects of reformist participation on the individual's unfolding. He does not find in the average reformer the apparent selflessness that is actually a commitment to his or her own integrity. There is shrinkage into monomania, and then into reaction.

> To every reform, in proportion to its energy, early disgusts are incident, so that the disciple is surprised at the very hour of his first triumphs, with chagrins, and sickness, and a general distrust: so that he shuns his associates, hates the enterprise which lately seemed so fair, and meditates to cast himself into the arms of that society and manner of life which he had newly abandoned with so much pride and hope. ("The Method of Nature," *E&L*, 127)

If the reform is to be genuine, the reformer must first be self-reformed. It is not clear, however, that Emerson thinks that a self-reformed person will find it sensible to devote himself or herself to projects of reform, which often appear to be projects for the reform of the character of others as much as for the reform of practices and institutions. The unreformed cannot reform the unreformed; all must reform themselves. He says:

> The criticism and attack on institutions which we have witnessed, has made one thing plain, that society gains nothing whilst a man, not himself renovated, attempts to renovate things around him: he has become tediously good in some particular, but negligent or narrow in the rest; and hypocrisy and vanity are often the disgusting result. ("New England Reformers," E&L, 596)

Emerson provides the sketch of a sociology of formal associations for reform:

> A society of 20,000 members is formed for the introduction of Christianity into India or the South Sea. This is not the same thing as if twenty thousand persons without formal cooperation, had conceived a vehement desire for the instruction of those foreign parts. In that case, each had turned the whole attention of the Reason, that is, the quite infinite force of one man, to the matter, and sought by what means he, in his place, could work with most avail on this point. ("Society," EL, 2:106)

The end is compromised or lost in regard for the organization.

> But in our formal association, how much machinery! How much friction! The material integument is so much that the spiritual child is overlaid and lost . . . the least streamlet of the vast contributions of the public trickles down at last to the healing of the evil. (EL, 2:106)

And the pressure exerted by an organization on nonmembers to sign pledges or join up is "using numbers, that is, mobs and bodies, and disusing principles" ("Society," EL, 2:107). Emerson would hate himself for going along: "If I yield to this force, I degrade myself and have only exchanged one vice for another, self-indulgence for fear, which it is to be presumed was not the intention of the society" (EL, 2:106).

But the question persists: Are there not institutions so dreadful that what matters is their reform or abolition, not any other consideration? Emerson pays tribute to the spirit of dissent and to the conscientious protest against the ingrained abuses of American society. "Man the Reformer" (1841) is a powerful indictment of prevailing practices, centered in the maldistribution of property: "Of course, whilst another man has no land, my title to mine, your title to yours, is at once vitiated" (E&L, 138–39). But Emerson, throughout the 1840s, looks for remedy to individual exertions, to personal reform or material improvement, to self-help or the practice of "economy" (in the full sense later elaborated by Thoreau) (E&L, 144). Emerson also tries to establish so great a need of reform as to make efforts to achieve it quixotic. In addressing those who harp on one deficiency, he says:

> Do not be so vain of your one objection. Do you think there is only one? Alas! my good friend, there is no part of society or of life better than any part. All our things are right and wrong together. The wave of evil washes all our institutions alike. ("New England Reformers," E&L, 596)

The wave of evil does not wash over, it washes.

With the passage of the Fugitive Slave Law of 1850, Emerson embarks on a lengthy episode of agitation for one reform: the containment or abolition of slavery. This spreading of evil—this evil which is truly evil, not only apparently so—forces him to change his attitude on the subject of associating for reform. He does his share by speaking his mind and trying to persuade others to a common antislavery cause. What is remarkable is not that Emerson frequently makes public speeches against slavery and even campaigns in 1851 for a particular antislavery candidate, John Gorham Palfrey. (Even in the denunciation of slavery he can be philosophically respectful of the fateful and as it were helpless enmeshment of slave-owners in their evil.) The aberration is that he urges solidarity—indeed mobilization—on others, and, when the occasion arises, does not shrink from advocating violence in the effort to destroy slavery. That profound change is a deviation from his theory of self-reliance, not its transformation. Or, we can say that Emerson accepts the sacrifices of every sort—including the abandonment of aspirations of free persons to self-reliance—which are needed to give all Americans, not just some, the chance for self reliance. Perhaps a society has no self-reliance anywhere in it if there are slaves anywhere in it. But before this change in, or suspension of, Emerson's teaching takes place, he discountenances association as solidarity.

There must be association, but proper terms are needed so that no dwarfing results and practical self-reliance remains intact. Are proper terms ever really possible? I would concentrate my discussion of this question by exploring Emerson's thinking about citizenship and political life. I will then return to the issue of slavery.

Can you be politically active and still be self-reliant? Citizenship is enacted in a political system or in defiance of it. Emerson's acts of citizenship as well as his reflections on the meaning of citizenship take place in and are framed by American democracy. That the democracy is radically incomplete, that it is stained by slavery, exclusions, and territorial rapacity, is precisely what leads Emerson to produce most of his political writings. But protest is not the totality of his political thought. He also thinks about what an unstained democracy would be, and does so as an adherent. He may not say explicitly enough or often enough that his doctrine of self-reliance in all its kinds, mental and active, is a democratically-inspired doctrine, a doctrine unthinkable outside democracy and that also signifies the culmination and the spiritual reason for the being of democracy. But that thought is there, sometimes on the surface of his work, and the rest of the time not far beneath it.

It must be conceded that before the slavery crisis in the 1850s permanently changes Emerson's political sensibility, he can speak with a certain lightness of his commitment to democracy. In "Politics," which is not an impersonation of the dignity of politics, but of the sentiments of antipolitics, he makes democracy into something merely congenial, not something morally imperative:

> In this country, we are very vain of our political institutions, which are singular in this, that they spring, within the memory of living men, from the character and condition of the people, which they still express with sufficient fidelity,—and we ostentatiously prefer them to any other in history. They are not better, but only fitter for us. We may be wise in asserting the advantage in modern times of the democratic form, but to other states of society, in which religion consecrated the monarchical, that and not this was expedient. Democracy is better for us, because the religious sentiment of the present time accords better with it. Born democrats, we are nowise qualified to judge of monarchy, which, to our fathers living in the monarchical idea, was also relatively right. (E&L, 563)

These words culminate in the stern reminder that "every actual State is corrupt. Good men must not obey the laws too well" (E&L, 563). Corruption, however, does not prevent Emerson from being magnanimous to political parties in their "benign necessity" to represent "some real and lasting relation," but he is harsh to party leaders who "reap the rewards of the docility and zeal of the masses which they direct." The defense of interests is good; the defense of principle much better; but a party is "perpetually corrupted by personality" (E&L, 564).

Despite his complex bemusement with democratic politics, however, Emerson's work is soaked in democratic spirit. Emerson's guiding sense is that society is a means for the ends of individuals, who are themselves ends. Only modern democracy, among societies, is devoted to this precept. Democracy is the set of political arrangements that provide the protections and encouragements for individuals to become individuals, rather than the servants of society. This is an Emersonian theme. Emerson says:

> The modern mind teaches (in extremes) that the nation exists for the individual; for the guardianship and education of every man. The Reformation contained the new thought. The English Revolution is its expansion. The American Declaration of Independence is a formal announcement, though a very limited expression. ("Introductory," "Human Culture," *EL*, 2:213–14)

The passion in Emerson for democracy is strong, and is made poignant when he adds:

> The furious democracy which in this country from the beginning of its history, has shown a wish, as the royal governors complained, to leave out men of mark and send illiterate and low persons as deputies,—a practice not unknown at this day—is only a perverse or yet obstructed operation of the same instinct,—a stammering and stuttering out of impatience to articulate the awful words *I am*. (*EL*, 2:214)

Democracy is the unfinished rescue of ordinary humanity from ignominy. But does democracy as a practice of citizenship fulfill self-reliant individuals or does it impede their self-reliance? Before I explore this question, I would like to mention how Emerson praises democracy.

Democracy, for Emerson, is emancipation ("Boston," *Natural History of Intellect*, *W*, 12:87). This word appears in his work at the beginning of the Civil War, but its sense dominates his political thinking from the start. Democracy is emancipation from aristocracy, especially. No real aristocracy has ever reflected the natural aristocracy of a society, but had had, instead, an enforced and artificial hierarchy ("Aristocracy," *Lectures and Sketches*, *W*, 10:33). In England and elsewhere, the aristocracy "incorporated by law and education, degrades life for the unprivileged classes" ("The Young American," 1844, *CW*, 1:243). In the same lecture, Emerson says:

> The unsupportable burdens under which Europe staggers, and almost every month mutters "A Revolution! a Revolution!" we have escaped from as by one

> bound. No thanks to us; but in the blessed course of events it did happen that this country was not open to the Puritans until they had felt the burden of the feudal system, and until the commercial era in modern Europe had dawned, so that without knowing what they did, they left the whole curse behind, and put the storms of the Atlantic between them and this antiquity. (*CW*, 1:242)

It is a matter of luck that America has been spared aristocratic degradation, but it is the kind of luck that has been commendably exploited. In his lecture about the city of Boston, Emerson says:

> European critics regret the detachment of the Puritans to this country without aristocracy; which a little reminds one of the pity of the Swiss mountaineers when shown a handsome Englishman: "What a pity he has no goitre!" The future historian will regard the detachment of the Puritans without aristocracy the supreme fortune of the colony; as great a gain to mankind as the opening of this continent. ("Boston," *Natural History of Intellect*, W, 12:201)

"We began well," Emerson says, because "America was opened after the feudal mischief was spent and so the people made a good start" ("The Fortune of the Republic," *Miscellanies*, W, 11:528).

For Emerson, democracy is a gamble, but it is one worth taking:

> We wish to put the ideal rules into practice, to offer liberty instead of chains, and see whether liberty will not disclose its proper checks; believing that a free press will prove safer than the censorship; to ordain free trade, and believe that it will not bankrupt us; universal suffrage, believing it will not carry us to mobs, or back to kings again. I believe that the checks are as sure as the springs. ("Progress of Culture," *Letters and Social Aims*, W, 8:231)

More positively, Emerson affirms democracy because it is the only political system that pays homage to the idea that all human beings, just by the fact that they are human beings, are morally equal, morally identical; they share "radical identity." In the most important respects, one is "more like and not less like other men" ("The Over-Soul," *E&L*, 396). Monarchy is a romantic system because, like romantic art, it is full of chance and caprice; democracy is classic, and like classic art, it grows out of necessity and is organic ("Art and Criticism," *Natural History of Intellect*, W, 12.304). In 1863, in the middle of a terrible and uncertain war, Emerson writes:

> There is in this country this immense difference from Europe, that, whereas all their systems of government and society are historical, our politics are

almost ideal. We wish to treat man as man, without regard to rank, wealth, race, color, or caste, simply as human souls. We lie near to nature, we are pensioners on Nature, draw on inexhaustible resources, and we interfere the least possible with individual freedom. ("The Fortune of the Republic," Notes, *Miscellanies*, W, 11.644)

Democracy is a moral system; it is the only moral political system. In the American democracy, the only democracy in the world at that time, the human race is "poured out over the continent to do itself justice" by hard work. The poor climb out of poverty and into a dignified equality. The country is constantly full of "exclamations of impatience and indignation at what is short-coming or is unbecoming in the government,—at the want of humanity, or morality." American protest is universalist, not driven by narrow class feeling. This fact, Emerson says, demonstrates that the United States is "a nation of individuals" ("The Fortune of the Republic," W, 11:526, 529). After the Civil War, he offers this judgment: "I will not say that American institutions have given a new enlargement to our idea of a finished man, but they have added important features to the sketch" ("Progress of Culture," *Letters and Social Aims*, W, 8:208).

Respect for democracy as an ideal is Emerson's positive political theory. Let us now return to the question of whether the practice of citizenship can be an expression of active self-reliance. Emerson's fullest answer comes out in an address he gave in 1835, before he began publishing those books that established his reputation. The "Historical Discourse" was occasioned by the 200th anniversary of the incorporation of the town of Concord. Emerson reflects on the character of New England, and the essence of the address lies in the way the people of the various towns created a society by agreement and maintained it through constant attention and involvement. He fixes his attention also on the Massachusetts Bay colony and praises the consensual relation that tied the overall political authority and the people. Boston did not monopolize power, but left the towns to govern themselves in most respects. Power was tolerable because it was decentralized, and in each lesser unit—that is, in each town—popular self-government existed in the form of the town meeting. Emerson says:

> In a town-meeting, the great secret of political science was uncovered, and the problem solved, how to give every individual his fair weight in the government, without any disorder from numbers. In a town-meeting, the roots

of society were reached. Here the rich gave counsel, but the poor also; and moreover, the just and the unjust. (*Miscellanies, W*, 11:46–47)

The right to speak and hence exercise some power was given to all as God makes rain to fall on the just and the unjust. Such is primary democracy.

Emerson builds a picture of a band of individuals working together for a common purpose, and that purpose often a directly moral one. Where is the individual in all this? Did he submerge himself in a unitary cause, or was he conscripted into making a moral contribution? If so, then the town meeting can be praised as true group self-government, but group self-government is not the same as an individual's active self-reliance. Can the latter be politically expressed? Does Emerson avoid the theoretical move made by Rousseau, by which social uniformity effaces the distinction between the individual and the general, and one's will ideally tends to the general will? The proposition that I obey myself by obeying the same law everybody else does, and which we have made together to bind us all, is not truly individualist. Emerson does not reach for it. To be sure, self-reliant individuals demand popular self-government, and each demands inclusion for himself ("The Fortune of the Republic," *Miscellanies, W*, 11:528). But Emerson's approach is not Rousseau's.

If, from one perspective, the town meeting is collaboration and cooperation, from another and equally valid perspective, it is an opportunity for individuals to speak their minds, and just by doing that, remain individuals. Their wills are to be bound by the laws and decisions that no one individual can make for oneself. But before the will is bound, the mind of each may disclose itself. Indeed, active self-reliance sublimates itself into mental activity by becoming speech for the sake of speech. The content, of course, is practical, not philosophical. Still, equal citizenship provides an excellent opportunity for everyone's practical sense to be used in a group without compromising anyone's self-reliance. The politics of the cooperation of equals is also the politics of individual self-expression. And self-expression occurs in conditions of unembarrassed and indeed encouraged frankness. Democracy becomes, in its political process, the register of diversity, of *individual* diversity, perhaps even of individual uniqueness. Emerson makes it clear that without diversity of voice, of speech, of articulated attitude, there is no democracy. He finds that both the humdrum and the urgent lend themselves as subjects that can elicit the self in its political appearances. He says:

Self-Reliance, Politics, and Society

> In these assemblies, the public weal, the call of interest, duty, religion, were heard; and every local feeling, every private grudge, every suggestion of petulance and ignorance, were not less faithfully produced. Wrath and love came up to town-meeting in company. ("Historical Discourse," *Miscellanies*, W, 11:47)

Emerson mixes moral motives together with nonmoral and even immoral or impure ones, and indulges the articulation of the latter sorts and even their influence. For him, unlike Rousseau, the jury is not the best model of deliberative politics. His extraordinarily democratic inclusiveness shows more wisdom than any theorist of civic virtue can ever hope to show:

> I shall be excused for confessing that I have set a value upon any symptom of meanness and private pique which I have met with in these antique books [the Town Records], as proof that justice was done; that if the results of our history are approved as wise and good, it was yet a free strife; if the good counsel prevailed, the sneaking counsel did not fail to be suggested; freedom and virtue, if they triumphed, triumphed in a fair field. (W, 11:48–49)

In Emerson's hands, the town meeting becomes a miniature world in which the observer can take the sort of high pleasure that he or she can take in the contrasting and antagonistic elements of the whole world. As for the participants, they show the proper spirit when they see themselves as individuals joined in a common enterprise of speech that thrives to the extent that they remain individuals. They uphold the structure that is rooted in everyday necessities, but that needs them to be or become individuals. The better each person speaks, the better the life: "an example of a perfect society is in the effect of eloquence" ("Society," *EL*, 2:109). Primary democracy is the best worldliness.

Where politics is speech, and the choir of voices is disputatious, then Emerson is prepared to square citizenship and active self-reliance. Even at the national level he has the same sympathy. He approvingly calls Congress "a standing insurrection" ("The Fortune of the Republic," *Miscellanies*, W, 11:529). Are there other occasions than deliberative ones that Emerson sees as individualist exercises of citizenship? There is, first, the politics of individual resistance. He is initially unattracted by the refusals of Alcott and Thoreau to pay taxes as protest against war, and slavery, and religious establishment, but passage of the Fugitive Slave Law in 1850 changed his mind. In his speech of 1851 on the law, he says:

> An immoral law makes it a man's duty to break it, at every hazard. For virtue is the very self of every man. It is therefore a principle of law that an immoral contract is void. For, as laws do not make right, and are simply declarative of a right which already existed, it is not to be presumed that they can so stultify themselves as to command injustice. . . . If our resistance to this law is not right, there is no right. (*Miscellanies, W,* 11:186–87)

His journals record his horror at the thought of enlisting people in the legal duty to help catch and return runaway slaves. He lent himself to one or another attempt to help runaways; he quietly broke the law, I suppose. But it is really Thoreau who, before the Fugitive Slave Law and after, best epitomizes Emerson's defense of individualist politics as resistance in behalf of others. It may not be inconsistent for Emerson to speak twice in admiration of John Brown, but the advocacy of violence *is* inconsistent with the theory of self-reliant activity.

Emerson's own characteristic citizenship was giving speeches at meetings or writing public letters rather than claiming a part in the give-and-take of debate in assembly. He lectured on many occasions, especially about slavery. This was the only public matter that ever really engaged him, except for the displacement of the Cherokee Indians, on which he wrote a passionate public letter of protest to President Martin van Buren in 1838.

In another way Emerson pays tribute to the self-reliant possibilities of political involvement. These possibilities, however, pertain to the eminent man, the one whose political self-reliance is shown in creative initiative and in command. The primary example is Napoleon, about whom Emerson writes an ambivalent essay in *Representative Men*. What Emerson admires about Napoleon was his uncanny ability to match means with ends and thus effect his will. The events of Europe became the effluence of Napoleon's genius. But Emerson does not admire merely; in fact, by the time the essay ends, Emerson expresses disgust and horror at the costs of Napoleon's individualism, among them the destruction of the individuality of thousands who obeyed him or lent him their force.

> And what was the result of this vast talent and power, of these immense armies, burned cities, squandered treasures, immolated millions of men, of this demoralized Europe? It came to no result . . . this exorbitant egotist narrowed, impoverished, and absorbed the power and existence of those who served him. (*E&L,* 744–45)

Emerson also came to revere Lincoln, whom he speaks about movingly after the assassination. But the war leader does not fit into the conceptualization of active self-reliance in a democratic society.

Given Emerson's individualist political ideas, what follows when cooperation is desperately needed? Slavery energizes Emerson's own citizenship, but the truth is that evil, this evil, cannot be handled by his theorization of what counts as admirable in political life. Even his appreciation of the virtues that war can inspire and employ only goes so far. In war he sees barbarism above all, while a barbarous war was needed to abolish slavery. The institution that denied every hope for millions of people that they could ever aspire to self-reliance had to be destroyed by the ready abandonment of self-reliance through mobilization, military discipline, obedience, and eventually by a conscripted self-sacrifice. The potential individualism of black slaves required the suspension of the individualism of free Northern whites. The politics and then the war of abolition became all-devouring. The Fugitive Slave Law of 1850 leads Emerson to a wholly uncharacteristic praise of mobilized human beings. He finds it delicious to act with great masses to great aims. "We shall one day bring the States shoulder to shoulder and the citizens man to man to exterminate slavery" ("The Fugitive Slave Law," 1851, *Miscellanies, W,* 11.208). At another point he says in his journal:

> 'Tis high time the people came together. I know the objections commonly urged by the best against popular meetings. . . . This has ceased to be a Representative Government. . . . nothing remains but to begin at the beginning to call every man in America to counsel, Representatives do not represent, we must (now) take new order and see how to make representatives represent us. (*JMN,* 14:420, 421, 423)

A stupendous moral emergency existed beyond the reach of self-reliance. But, of course, slavery and the Civil War shattered all conceptual frameworks, not only Emerson's, and replaced a positive idealism with the negative one of abolishing evil.

In the decade before the Civil War, Emerson repeatedly expresses a sense of the desperation which slavery created on all sides. A committed abolitionist, he develops no settled opinion on the policies needed to contain, weaken, or end slavery. His only counsel is noncompliance with the Fugitive Slave Law. His fondest hope is for a compensated emancipation:

> Why not end this dangerous dispute on some ground of fair compensation on one side, and satisfaction on the other to the conscience of free states? . . . I say buy,—never conceding the right of the planter to own, but that we may acknowledge the calamity of his position, and bear a country-man's share in relieving him; and because it is the only practicable course and is innocent. ("The Fugitive Slave Law," 1851, *Miscellanies*, W, 11:208)

He estimates the cost at $2 billion (*JMN*, 14:400). But he never indicates that compensated emancipation has much of a chance. He does not demonize slaveholders: he knows how easy it is to persist in custom, whatever conscience says. What, if not the universal persistence in custom, has irritated him into his philosophy of self-reliance? He only knows that if slavery is not wrong, nothing is wrong. "The case is so bad, that all the right is on one side" (*JMN*, 14:385). His capacity to embrace phenomena that go against his grain simply will not allow itself to be enlisted by slavery. At moments his sorrow is bitter:

> If by opposing slavery I undermine institutions, I own I do not wish to live in a nation where slavery exists. The life of this world has but a limited worth in my eyes, and really it is not worth such a price as the toleration of slavery. (*JMN*, 14:383)

Emerson does not flinch. He suspends his theory, just as the war against slavery suspended many positive projects. Emerson urges the war on. "America, the most prosperous country in the Universe, has the greatest calamity in the Universe, negro slavery" ("The Fugitive Slave Law," 1851, *Miscellanies*, W, 11:186). The lesser calamity of war must be endured to end the greater calamity. Emerson's moral commitments silence his existential passions. Just after the war ends, he addresses a Harvard commemoration, and accepts for himself a thought he had attributed to John Brown on the eve of the war:

> We see—we thank you for it—a new era, worth to mankind all the treasure and all the lives it has cost; yes, worth to the world the lives of all this generation of American men, if they had been demanded. (*Miscellanies*, W, 11:345)

What Emerson hates most about politics—its violent suppression and destruction of individuals—he now confesses he had eagerly accepted. That the occasion demanded a certain rhetoric does not reduce the shock that the rhetoric is Emerson's.

Slavery causes a tremendous strain in Emerson's thinking, which was far advanced along its own lines before he felt he had to worry about slavery. The strain shows itself as a clash between Emerson's passionate desire to end slavery by all means, on the one hand, and his characteristically low view of most politics, on the other hand. This point emerges more starkly when we consider his hatred of slavery against the background of his general political teaching in the essay of 1844, "Politics" (*Essays: Second Series*), published before he allowed the issue of slavery to dominate him.

We have seen that he admires the primary democracy of the town meeting, but admiration is ungrudging only because his emphasis is on the talk that goes on. I do not deny that he has an eye for the good decisions that sometimes were made and hence the projects of common good that the people themselves authorized and benefitted from ("Historical Discourse," *Miscellanies*, W, 11:49). But when politics leaves the face-to-face situation, Emerson finds abstractness, alienation, unreality; he also finds gross distortions of the political person's character that indicate various kinds of egotistical self-loss. Further, enterprises of power are often wicked. If he does not define self-reliant activity as morally driven, he certainly insists that it be morally enclosed. The regular immorality of political life—even when democratic—appalls him. The inveterate nature of political life—even when democratic—appalls him. As Emerson says in his speech of 1856 on the troubles in Kansas:

> I own I have little esteem for governments. I esteem them only good in the moment when they are established. I set the private man first. He only who is able to stand alone is qualified to be a citizen. Next to the private man, I value the primary assembly, met to watch the government and to correct it. That is the story of the American State, that it exists to execute the will of the citizens, is always responsible to them, and is always to be changed when it does not. First, the private citizen, then the primary assembly, and the government last. (*Miscellanies*, W, 11:258)

These words distill Emerson's political sense and they obviously suspect the grandeur of politics and locate its individualist excellence in talk, but not in command or administration or discretionary judgment or in heroic initiative that subordinates large numbers of people. The unfortunate essence of government is the executive power, and the democratic assembly scarcely restrains it from becoming dictatorial, and often does not restrain it at all, but encourages it.

Emerson would be an anarchist if he could. "The appearance of character makes the state unnecessary" ("Politics," *E&L*, 568). In an earlier and perhaps better formulation, he says: "The appearance of character rebukes the state. It makes the state unnecessary" ("Politics," *EL*, 2:243). As the Federal Union is close to breaking up, Emerson says:

> I am glad to see that the terror at disunion and anarchy is disappearing. Massachusetts, in its heroic day, had no government—was an anarchy. Every man stood on his own feet, was his own governor; and there was no breach of peace from Cape Cod to Mount Hoosac. ("Speech" [Kansas Relief Meeting], *Miscellanies, W*, 11:261–62)

Emerson goes on to talk about the unadministered justice of California in its gold rush days, and even attributes to "Saxon man" a natural social tendency very much like that of harmoniously ungoverned social insects. This expression of mood is interesting only because it tells us that Emerson is sincere when he records, as he regularly does, his aversion to political life. Town meetings are marginal, almost merely incidental.

Politics is a machine that exists to create "friction" ("Politics," *EL*, 2:69). The search for power corrupts character, and so does its exercise. The association of politics with force and violence, and with deceit and charlatanry, is incurable and dismaying. Of all worldly pursuits, politics is the most likely to be immoral, and that is in part the case because it joins the most real means to the most unreal ends. Equally important, the very idea of political order—namely, that each of us is to be bound by innumerable political enactments—is offensive. Political discussion is a lovely thing, but no matter how lovely, discussion has an upshot: regulation. I am being told what I must do, well beyond the minimum of respecting the claims of others. Even though I may be a participant in the assembly that makes a decision, I revert to the status of subject insofar as I now must obey. But more typically, politics is not all deciding for each, but some deciding for others, when it would be better if no decision were made. And when the law commands me to do what I know I must do without being told, the insult is deep. What Emerson thinks Jesus perceived about the law of Moses is present also in Emerson's opinion about the state's codification of the moral minimum: "Having seen that the law in us is commanding, he would not suffer it to be commanded" ("Divinity School Address," *E&L*, 80).

Emerson is faithful to the original democratic idea as recorded by Aristotle (whom he read but does not cite). According to Aristotle, democrats want to live as they like, which is the source of the "claim of men to be ruled by none, if possible" (*The Politics*, trans. B. Jowett, bk. 6, chap. 2, 1317b). The alternative principle that all should take turns in ruling and being ruled is only second-best and should be put into practice if nonrule is impossible. As Thoreau puts the Athenian and Emersonian point in "Civil Disobedience": "For government is an expedient by which men would fain succeed in letting one another alone" (*Thoreau: The Major Essays*, ed. Jeffrey L. Duncan [New York: Dutton, 1972], 107). For Emerson, it is a horror that democracy should be continuously active, even if it were a primary democracy. Democracy is a device to limit rule, to neutralize legislation as well as to chasten administration. To think otherwise is to attribute individuality to a fictitious entity, whether it be a people or a society or a state, and proceed to find the value of group expressiveness or group self-realization in its activity. Emerson is ill-disposed to such abstractness. In "Politics," he says:

> This undertaking for another is the blunder which stands in colossal ugliness in the governments of the world. It is the same thing in numbers, as in a pair, only not quite so intelligible. I can see well enough a great difference between my setting myself down to a self-control, and my going to make somebody else act after my views; but when a quarter of the human race assume to tell me what I must do, I may be too much disturbed by the circumstances to see so clearly the absurdity of their command. Therefore all public ends look vague and quixotic beside private ones. . . . A man who cannot be acquainted with me, taxes me; looking from afar at me ordains that a part of my labor shall go to this or that whimsical end—not as I, but as he happens to fancy. . . . Hence the less government we have the better—the fewer laws, and the less confided power. (*E&L*, 567)

The machine of politics, however, must and will find work to do. It will induce dependence on it. At the same time, the growth in scale, numbers, and wealth of American society makes the state ever more important and hence ever more distant. Emerson is keenly aware that the old American days of semianarchy are gone forever:

> But now, vast property, gigantic interests, family connections, webs of party, cover the land with a network that immensely multiplies the danger of war. ("Speech" [Kansas Relief Meeting], *Miscellanies*, W, 11:263)

Thus the grim fatality by which a more complex politics interweaves itself with a more complex society threatens to undo Emerson's thinking on the possibilities of all forms of active self-reliance, not only primary citizenship.

The evil of expanding slavery and the lesser evil of violent mobilization in order to end it shake the theory of self-reliance. But there is the problem of the growth of society, and this problem will outlive slavery and civil war. In Emerson's view, the combination of social underdevelopment and intellectual refinement that was once definitive of America was receding. The urgency with which Emerson teaches the doctrine of the individual does not increase with time. It was urgent at the beginning. Society itself, whatever its size or complexity, is the inevitable adversary of active self-reliance because it is the indispensable setting. But the "massification" of society, if I may call it that, can make the defense of self-reliance more interesting or more poignant. Of course it may turn out that the only self-reliance possible in a huge society is mental self-reliance in the manner of the late Stoics living in the Roman empire, with practical activity subjected to disciplines and constraints that render it less and less self-reliant. But it would be wrong to think that Emerson ever gives up on self-reliant activity.

In the lecture, "The Individual," 1837, he says:

> All philosophy, all theory, all hope are defeated when applied to society. There is in it an incontrovertible brute force and it is not for the society of any actual present moment that is now or ever shall be, that we can hope or argue well. Progress is not for society. Progress belongs to the Individual. (*EL*, 2:176)

He puts his point more mildly later in "Self-Reliance":

> Society never advances. It recedes as fast on one side as it gains on the other. (*E&L*, 279)

But his real passion is in the first statement. It is consoling that in a few societies the very idea of the individual does get started. Emerson knows that fact well. The trouble is that individuality—perhaps more in the form of active self-reliance than mental self-reliance—is an easily blocked aspiration. We have already explored his concern with conformity and lack of courage: they account for both "the brute force" that is in society, that *is* society, and the reluctance to controvert it. The sense of this force increases in Emerson with the sense of massification. I now want to take up some of Emerson's thoughts about masses, about the growth of society, and the relation to the possibilities of active self-reliance.

Emerson hates the word "masses," but uses it, especially in the work published in 1860, *The Conduct of Life* (his last great book and a book as great as any he wrote). Masses are large crowds of undifferentiated people. They seem to resist individualization. Emerson tries to avoid adopting the reactionary perspective from which large numbers of people simply look like a mass and therefore must be a mass. He tries to judge honestly. He finds that at all times people lend themselves to being massed, heaped up:

> Why are the masses, from the dawn of history down, food for knives and powder? The idea [of the hero] dignifies a few leaders, who have sentiment, opinion, love, self-devotion; and they make war and death sacred;—but what for the wretches whom they hire and kill. The cheapness of man's life is every day's tragedy. It is as real a loss that others should be low, as that we should be low; for we must have society. ("Uses of Great Men," *E&L*, 629)

Common susceptibility to social illusions makes people into masses waiting for a sacrificial use. A use will always be found. He reports Plutarch's judgment without taking exception to it:

> He thinks that the inhabitants of Asia came to be vassals to one, only for not having been able to pronounce one syllable; which is No. ("Plutarch," *Lectures and Biographical Sketches*, W, 10:314)

The struggle for self-reliance is a struggle against being used. But the struggle is frequently a failure. It is easier to be silent than to say No.

Emerson articulates one of the main sentiments which dispose the few to use the many, especially in the modern age. In "Fate," the first section of *The Conduct of Life*, he says:

> The opinion of the million was the terror of the world, and it was attempted, either to dissipate it, by amusing nations, or to pile it over with strata of society.... The Fultons and Watts of politics, believing in unity, saw that it was a power, and, by satisfying it (as justice satisfies everybody), through a different disposition of society—grouping it on a level, instead of piling it into a mountain—they have contrived to make of this terror the most harmless and energetic form of a State. (*E&L*, 959–60)

Emerson seems to be saying, and without regret, that modern democracy is the regime of docility. He seems to dislike people when they are numerous. His misanthropy thrives amid multitudes. "If I see nothing to admire in the unit, shall I admire a million units?" ("The Method of Nature," *E&L*, 116). The charity present in the passage on the sacrificial susceptibilities of people that benefit the one or the few tends to be occasionally compromised. For example, Emerson says, in a passage reminiscent of the darkest page of Plato's *Gorgias*:

> A person seldom falls sick, but the bystanders are animated with a faint hope that he will die:—quantities of poor lives; of distressing invalids; of cases for a gun. ("Considerations by the Way," *The Conduct of Life*, *E&L*, 1080–81)

(In *Gorgias*, the ship's pilot "knows enough to reason that it's not clear which passengers he has benefitted by not letting them drown, and which ones he has harmed" [trans. T. Irwin, 511e–512a]). Emerson here looks at humanity with an unsparing sense of beauty, a sense that seeks not to uncover beauty but to condemn ugliness, a sense that is undemocratized aestheticism. He can say:

> The man is physically as well as metaphysically a thing of shreds and patches, borrowed unequally from good and bad ancestors, and a misfit from the start. ("Beauty," *E&L*, 1108)

"The man" is anyone at all. But masses darken Emerson's vision even more. And toward the end of *The Conduct of Life*, when he is impersonating the thesis that life is sustained and saturated with illusions, he gives words on the failure to become individual that sounds all the more harsh when massification is present to mind:

> Like sick men in hospitals, we change only from bed to bed, from one folly to another; and it cannot signify much what becomes of such castaways,—wailing, stupid, comatose creatures,—lifted from bed to bed, from the nothing of life to the nothing of death. ("Illusions," *E&L*, 1122)

But Emerson does not yield to despair or to his misanthropy. It is of course characteristic of him that he tries not to allow his most disturbing thoughts merely to disturb. Masses are one of his hardest tests. In one passage on "hypocritical prating about the masses," there is a strenuous mixture of anger and hope:

> Masses are rude, lame, unmade, pernicious in their demands and influence, and need not to be flattered but to be schooled. I wish not to concede anything to them, but to tamp, drill, divide, and break them up, and draw individuals out of them. The worst of charity is, that the lives you are asked to preserve are not worth preserving. Masses! the calamity is the masses. I do not wish any mass at all, but honest men only, sweet, accomplished women only, and no shovel-handed, arrow-brained, gin-drinking million stockingers or lazzaroni at all. If government knew how, I should like to see it check, not multiply, the population. When it reaches its true law of action, every man that is born will be hailed as essential. ("Considerations by the Way," *E&L*, 1081)

It is as if the mere presence of numbers, apart from any human susceptibility to invite being used, is intrinsically degrading. But Emerson wants hope to triumph; he wants to give hope. He therefore abates his anger:

> Meantime, this spawning productivity is not noxious or needless. You would say, this rabble of nations might be spared. But no, they are all counted and dependent on. Fate keeps everything alive so long as the smallest thread of public necessity holds it on the tree. The coxcomb and bully and thief class are allowed as proletaries, every one of their vices being the excess of acridity of a virtue. . . . The rule is, we are used as brute atoms, until we think: then we use all the rest. . . . To say then, the majority are wicked means no malice, no bad heart in the observer, but, simply, that the majority are unripe, and have not yet come to themselves, do not yet know their opinion. (*E&L*, 1082–83)

Emerson, then, will try to break up the mass, break up the masses, by both the method of his perception and the substance of his teaching, thus teasing out individuals. He desires to discredit a condition in which "most men and most women are merely one couple more" ("Fate," *E&L*, 947).

His final insistence is that not by means of politics and not in spite of politics will people become self-reliant individuals, at least some of the time and to some degree, both philosophically and practically. In a paragraph in which he grants that public necessity may be a standard of judgment, he once again affirms the ultimacy of the individual:

> No sane man at last distrusts himself. His existence is a perfect answer to all sentimental cavils. If he is, he is wanted, and has the precise properties that are required. That we are here, is proof we ought to be here. We have as good right, and the same sort of right to be here, as Cape Cod or Sandy Hook have to be there. ("Considerations by the Way," *E&L*, 1082)

Every person must be inspired to have moments when he or she passes outside society in thought and deed. Emerson says, "Speak as you think, be what you are, pay your debts of all kinds" ("Illusions," *E&L*, 1122). He endorses the view he attributes to the Hindus: "the beatitude of man they hold to lie in being freed from fascination" (*E&L*, 1123). That is to say, the only affirmation of life that is defensible comes from an opening to reality and is as unillusioned as possible. What elevates democracy above aristocracy, after all, is the possibility that individuals may take themselves seriously as separate beings. Individualism must battle massification, more and more.

More than twenty years before his death, Emerson produces his valedictory in the words that close *The Conduct of Life*. He tells a parable of a young mortal who suddenly finds himself in the company of the gods. On this creature "fall snow-storms of illusion." But illusions can be resisted, provided one holds to oneself—against oneself, against the state, against society, against masses, against the gods. The aim is to heal oneself. Emerson ends his parable in this way:

> He fancies himself in a vast crowd which sways this way and that, and whose movement and doings he must obey: he fancies himself poor, orphaned, insignificant. The mad crowd drives hither and thither, now furiously commanding this thing to be done, now that. What is he that he should resist their will, and think and act for himself? Every moment, new changes, and new showers of deceptions, to baffle and distract him. And when, by-and-by, for an instant, the air clears, and the cloud lifts a little, there are the gods still sitting around him on their thrones,—they alone with him alone. ("Illusions," *E&L*, 1123–24)

Alone, one is like a god because only when one is withdrawn can reality present itself by presenting itself as beauty. This life of illusions is transformed by self-reliance into the sublime spectacle of appearances.

Note

Published as George Kateb, "Self-Reliance, Politics, and Society," in *Emerson and Self Reliance* (1995. New ed., Lanham, Md.: Rowman and Littlefield, 2002), 173–96. Reprinted by permission of Rowman and Littlefield.

CHAPTER 4

Aversive Thinking: Emersonian Representations in Heidegger and Nietzsche

Stanley Cavell

IN TAKING THE PERSPECTIVE of the Carus Lectures as an opportunity to recommend Emerson, despite all, to the closer attention of the American philosophical community, I hope I may be trusted to recognize how generally impertinent his teachings, in style and in material, can sound to philosophical ears—including still, from time to time, despite all, my own. But what else should one expect? My recommendation is bound to be based—unless it is to multiply impertinence—on something as yet unfamiliar in Emerson, as if I am claiming him to remain a stranger. In that case to soften his strangeness would be pointless—which is no excuse, I do realize, for hardening it. About my own sound it may help to say that while I may often leave ideas in what seems a more literary state, sometimes in a more psychoanalytic state, than a philosopher might wish—that is, that a philosopher might prefer a further philosophical derivation of the ideas—I mean to leave everything I will say, or have, I guess, ever said, as in a sense provisional, the sense that it is to be gone on from. If to a further derivation in philosophical form, so much the better; but I would not lose the intuitions in the meantime—among them the intuition that philosophy should sometimes distrust its defenses of philosophical form.

It is common knowledge that Emerson's "The American Scholar" is a call for Man Thinking, something Emerson contrasts with thinking in "the divided or social state," thinking, let us say, as a specialty. I do not know of any commentary on this text that finds Emerson to be *thinking* about the idea of thinking. Uniformly, rather, it seems to be taken that he and his readers understand well enough what it is he is calling for, that it is something like thinking with the whole man; and I suppose this can be taken so for granted because there has been, since Emerson's time, or the time he speaks for, a widespread dissatisfaction with thinking as represented in Western philosophy since the Enlightenment, a dissatisfaction vaguely and often impatiently associated, I believe, with an idea of romanticism. And of course there has been, in turn, a reactive impatience with this dissatisfaction. Emerson is, in his way, locating himself within this struggle when he calls upon American thinkers to rely on and to cheer themselves: "For this self-trust, the reason is deeper than can be fathomed—darker than can be enlightened."[1] As if he anticipates that a reader might suppose him accordingly to be opposed to the Enlightenment, he will famously also say, "I ask not for the great, the remote, the romantic; . . . I embrace the common, I sit at the feet of the familiar, the low," a claim I have taken as underwriting ordinary language philosophy's devotion to the ordinary, surely one inheritance of the Enlightenment.

Existentialism—in the years in which it seemed that every mode of thinking antagonistic to analytical philosophy was called Existentialism—was famous for some such dissatisfaction with philosophical reason, expressed, for example, by Karl Jaspers in his book on Nietzsche, originally published in 1935:

> That the source of philosophical knowledge is not to be found in thinking about mere objects or in investigating mere facts but rather *in the unity of thought and life,* so that thinking grows out of the provocation and agitation of the whole man—all this constitutes for Nietzsche's self-consciousness the real character of his truth: "I have always composed my writings with my whole body and life"; "All truths are bloody truths to me."[2]

("Cut these sentences and they bleed.") Philosophy, as institutionalized in the English-speaking world, has not much felt attacked by nor vulnerable to such criticism, partly because the style and animus of the criticism is so foreign as to suggest simply other subjects, but partly, and sufficiently, because surely since Frege and the early Russell, analytical philosophy can see what thinking is, or should be, namely reasoning, expressed in a certain style of argumentation.

In taking on Emerson's view of thinking I will not be interested to advocate his view over, nor much to characterize it against, views more familiar to us (say a view of reason as rationality) but rather to ask attention to an attitude or investment in words that Emerson's view seems to depend upon, an attitude allegorical of an investment in our lives that I believe those trained in professional philosophy are trained to disapprove of. The disapproval of the attitude interests me as much as the attitude itself. If, as professional philosophers, we were asked whether philosophizing demands of us anything we would think of as a style of writing, our answer, I guess, would waver, perhaps because our philosophical motivation in writing is less to defend a style than to repress style or allow it only in ornamental doses. In speaking of disapproval, accordingly, I am not raising a question of taste, of something merely not for us, but a question of intellectual seriousness and illicitness. However glad we may be to think of ourselves as intellectually fastidious, I do not suppose we relish the idea of ourselves as intellectual police.

I should perhaps confess that an ulterior stake of mine in speaking of Emerson's attitude to words is that—to begin specifying a suggestion already made—I find J. L. Austin and the later Wittgenstein to participate in a region of the attitude, the region that places an investment in the words of a natural language so heavy as to seem quite antithetical to sensible philosophizing. It was half a lifetime ago that I began writing philosophy by preparing a paper ("Must We Mean What We Say?") for this division of our philosophy association defending J. L. Austin's practice with ordinary language against criticisms of it articulated by Benson Mates, criticisms notably of Austin's apparently insufficient empirical basis for his claims to know what we say and mean when. I did not really answer Mates's criticisms because I could not account for all that investment in the ordinary. I still cannot. This failure pairs with my inability to answer Barry Stroud's question to me twenty years later, at another Association meeting, about whether my *Claim of Reason* didn't amount to a claim to find a general solution to skepticism. I wanted to answer by saying that by the end of the first two parts of that book I had convinced myself not only that there is no such solution, that to think otherwise is skepticism's own self-interpretation, but that it seemed to me, on the contrary, work for an ambitious philosophy to attempt to keep philosophy open to the threat or temptation to skepticism. This left me what I named as Nowhere, and it led me, in the fourth part of my book, to particular territories customarily associated with literature—especially to aspects of Shakespearean and of certain romantic texts—in which I seemed to find comic and tragic and lyric obsessions with the ordinary that were the equivalent of something (not everything) philosophy knows as skepticism.

Emerson became more and more prominent an inhabitant of these regions. His investment in the ordinary is so constant and so explicit that, perhaps because of the very strangeness and extravagance of his manner, it may indicate afresh why a philosopher interested in the manner might spend a reasonable lifetime looking for an account of it.

The first half of this lecture takes its bearing from pertinences Emerson's "American Scholar" address bears to Heidegger's sequence of lectures translated as *What Is Called Thinking?* (all citations of Heidegger are from this text);[3] the second half continues the discussion broached in my Introduction of that moral perfectionism for which Emerson's writing is definitive, particularly in connection with its dominating influence on, among others, Nietzsche.

Emerson's sense of thinking is, generally, of a double process, or a single process with two names: transfiguration and conversion. For instance (still in "The American Scholar"), "A strange process, . . . this by which experience is converted into thought, as a mulberry leaf is converted into satin. The manufacture goes forward at all hours" (70). And again:

> The actions and events of our childhood and youth are now matters of calmest observation. . . . Not so with our recent actions,—with the business which we now have in hand. Our affections as yet circulate through it. . . . The new deed . . . remains for a time immersed in our unconscious life. In some contemplative hour it detaches itself . . . to become a thought of the mind. Instantly it is raised, transfigured; the corruptible has put on incorruption. (70–71)

Transfiguration is to be taken as a rhetorical operation, Emerson's figure for a figure of speech—not necessarily for what rhetoricians name a known figure of speech, but for whatever it is that he will name the conversion of words. In "Self-Reliance," he calls the process that of passing from Intuition to Tuition, so it is fitting that those who find Emerson incapable of thought style him a philosopher of Intuition, occluding the teacher of Tuition. Tuition is what Emerson's writing presents itself to be throughout; hence, of course, to be articulating Intuition. It is when Emerson thinks of thinking, or conversion, as oppositional, or critical, that he calls it aversion. This bears relation not alone to Emerson's continuous critique of religion but to Kant's speaking of Reason, in his always astonishing "Conjectural Beginning of Human History," as requiring and enabling "violence" (to the voice of nature) and "refusal" (to desire), refusal being a "feat which brought about the passage from merely sensual to spiritual attractions," uncovering "the first hint at development of man as a moral being."[4] And Emerson's aversion bears relation to Heidegger's discussion of why thinking in his investigation of it "is from the start tuned in a negative key" (*What Is Called Thinking?* 29).

Accordingly, a guiding thought in directing myself to Emerson's way of thinking is his outcry in the sixth paragraph of "Self-Reliance": "The virtue in most request is conformity. Self-reliance is its aversion." I gather him there to be characterizing his writing, hence to mean that he writes in aversion to society's demand for conformity, specifically that his writing expresses his self-consciousness, his thinking as the imperative to an incessant conversion or refiguration of society's incessant demands for his consent—his conforming himself—to its doings; and at the same time to mean that his writing must accordingly be the object of aversion to society's consciousness, to what it might read in him. His imperative is registered in the outcry a few paragraphs later, "Every word they say chagrins us." Emerson is not, then, as the context might imply, expressing merely his general disappointment at some failure in the capacity of language to represent the world but also expressing, at the same time, his response to a general attitude toward words that is causing his all but complete sense of intellectual isolation. It is his perfectionism's cue.

The isolation is enacted in "The American Scholar," whose occasion is enviably if not frighteningly distinctive. Whoever Emerson invokes as belonging to the class of scholars that commencement day at Harvard in the summer of 1837—himself, his audience (whether as poets, preachers, or philosophers)—the principal fact about the class is that it is empty, the American Scholar does not exist. Then who is Emerson? Suppose we say that what motivates Emerson's thinking, or what causes this call for the American Scholar, is Emerson's vision of our not yet thinking. Is this plain fact of American history—that we are, we still find ourselves, looking for the commencement of our own culture—worth setting beside the intricate formulation whose recurrences generate Heidegger's *What Is Called Thinking?*: "Most thought-provoking in our thought-provoking times is that we are still not thinking" (6) (*Das Bedenklichste in unserer bedenklichen Zeit ist, dass wir noch nicht denken*). It probably does not matter that the translation cannot capture the direct force in the relation of *bedenklich* to *denken* and the senses of *bedenklich* as doubtful, serious, risky, scrupulous—it would mean capturing the idea of the thing most critically provoking in our riskily provocative time to be that we are still not really provoked, that nothing serious matters to us, or nothing seriously, that our thoughts are unscrupulous, private. (Emerson's remark in his "Divinity School Address" echoes for me: "Truly speaking, it is not instruction, but provocation, that I can receive from another soul." What translation will capture the idea of provocation here as calling forth, challenging?) Nor hence capture the surrealistic inversion of the Cartesian thought that if I am thinking then I cannot be thinking that perhaps I do not think. In Heidegger, if I am thinking, then precisely I must be thinking that I am (still) not thinking. I say the translation may not matter because one who is not inclined, as I am, at least intermittently to take Heidegger's text as a masterpiece of philosophy will not be encouraged—on the contrary—to place confidence in a mode of argumentation which invests itself in what is apt to seem at best the child's play of language and at worst the wild variation and excesses of linguistic form that have always interfered with rationality. For someone who has not experienced this play in Heidegger, or in Emerson, the extent of it can from time to time appear as a kind of philosophical folly.

I summarize two instances from the essay "Experience" to suggest the kind of practice that has convinced me that Emerson's thought is, on a certain way of turning it, a direct anticipation of Heidegger's. Emerson writes: "I take this evanescence and lubricity of all objects, which lets them slip through our fingers then when we clutch hardest, to be the most unhandsome part of our condition." You may either dismiss, or savor, the relation between the clutching fingers and the hand in handsome as a developed taste for linguistic oddity, or you might further relate it to Emerson's recurring interest in the hand (as in speaking of what is at hand, by which, whatever else he means, he means the writing taking shape under his hand and now in ours) and thence to Heidegger's sudden remark, "Thinking is a handicraft," by which he means both that thinking requires training and makes something happen, but equally that it makes something happen in a particular way since the hand is a uniquely human possession: "The hand is infinitely different from all grasping organs—paws, claws, fangs" (Heidegger, *What Is Called Thinking?* 16). (It matters to me in various ways to recall a seminar of C. I. Lewis's on "The Nature of the Right," given at Harvard in the academic year 1951–1952—the year Heidegger delivered the lectures constituting *What Is Called Thinking?*—in which Lewis emphasized the hand as a trait of the human, the tool-using trait, hence one establishing a human relation to the world, a realm of practice that expands the reaches of the self. The idea seemed to me in my greenness not to get very far, but it evidently left me with various impressions, among others one of intellectual isolation. Lewis's material was published posthumously under the title "The Individual and the Social Order.") Emerson's image of clutching and Heidegger's of grasping, emblematize their interpretation of Western conceptualizing as a kind of sublimized violence. (Heidegger's word is *greifen*; it is readily translatable as "clutching.") Heidegger is famous here for his thematization of this violence as expressed in the world dominion of technology, but Emerson is no less explicit about it as a mode of thinking. The overcoming of this conceptualizing will require the achievement of a form of knowledge both Emerson and Heidegger call reception, alluding to the Kantian idea that knowledge is active, and sensuous intuition alone passive or receptive. (Overcoming Kant's idea of thinking as conceptualizing—say analyzing and synthesizing concepts—is coded into Emerson's idea that our most unhandsome part belongs to our condition. I have argued elsewhere [in "Emerson, Coleridge, Kant"] that Emerson is transfiguring Kant's key term "condition" so that it speaks not alone of deducing twelve categories of the understanding but of deriving—say schematizing—every word in which we speak together [speaking together is what the word condition says]; so that the conditions or terms of every term in our language stand to be derived philosophically, deduced.)

Now reception, or something received, if it is welcome, implies thanks, and Heidegger, in passages as if designed to divide readers into those thrilled and those offended, harps on the derivation of the word "thinking" from a root for "thanking" and interprets this particularly as giving thanks for the gifts of thinking, which is what should become of philosophy. Does it take this thematization to direct attention to one of Emerson's throwaway sentences that, as can be said of essentially every Emersonian sentence, can be taken as the topic of the essay in which it finds itself, in this case "Experience"? : "I am thankful for small mercies." To see that this describes the thinking that goes on in an Emersonian sentence you would have to see the joking tautology in linking his thankfulness with a *mercy*, that is to say a *merci*; and to recognize "small mercy" as designating the small son whose death is announced at the beginning of "Experience," an announcement every critic of the essay comments on, a child never named in the essay but whose death and birth constitute the lines of the father's investigation of experience—and it is the philosopher's term "experience" Emerson is (also) exploring, as in Kant and Hume, an effort to counteract the role of experience as removing us from, instead of securing us to, the world. The idea, again argued elsewhere (in "Finding as Founding"), is that Emerson's essay "Experience" enacts the father's giving birth to Waldo—the son that bears Emerson's name for himself, hence declares this birth (as of himself) as his work of writing generally, or generously. The clearer the intricacies become of the identification of the child Waldo with the world as such, the deeper one's wonder that Emerson could bring himself to voice it socially, to subject himself either to not being understood or to being understood—yet another wonder about intellectual isolation. I am for myself convinced that Emerson knew that such devices as the pun on "thankful" and "mercy" were offensive to philosophical reason. So the question is why he felt himself bound to give offense. (An opening and recurrent target of Dewey's *Experience and Nature* is thinkers who take experience to "veil and screen" us from nature. Its dissonance with Emerson is interesting in view of Dewey's being the major American philosopher who, without reservation, declared Emerson to be a philosopher—without evidently finding any use for him. For Dewey the philosophical interpretation of experience was cause for taking up scientific measures against old dualisms, refusing separation. For Emerson the philosophical interpretation of experience makes it a cause for mourning, assigning to philosophy the work of accepting the separation of the world, as of a child.)

It is in Nietzsche, wherever else, that some explanation must be sought for the inner connection between a writer (such as Heidegger) who calls for thinking knowing the completed presence of European philosophy or, say, facing its aftermath, as if needing to disinherit it, and a writer (such as Emerson) who calls for thinking not knowing whether the absence of the philosophical edifice for America means that it is too late for a certain form of thinking here or whether his errand just is to inherit remains of the edifice. Nietzsche is the pivot because of his early and late devotion to Emerson's writing together with his decisive presence in Heidegger's *What Is Called Thinking?* But no matter how often this connection of Nietzsche to Emerson is stated, no matter how obvious to anyone who cares to verify it, it stays incredible, it is always in a forgotten state. This interests me almost as much as the connection itself does, since the incredibility must be grounded in a fixed conviction that Emerson is not a philosopher, that he cannot be up to the pitch of reason in European philosophy. The conviction is variously useful to American as well as to European philosophers as well as to literary theorists. When one mind finds itself or loses itself in another, time and place seem to fall away—not as if history is transcended but as if it has not begun.

The reverse of the unhandsome in our condition, of Emerson's clutching, and Heidegger's grasping—call the reverse the handsome part—is what Emerson calls being drawn and what Heidegger calls getting in the draw, or the draft, of thinking. Emerson speaks of this in saying that thinking is partial, Heidegger in speaking of thinking as something toward which the human is inclined. Heidegger's opening paragraphs work inclination into a set of inflections on *mögen, vermögen,* and *Möglichkeit*: inclination, capability, and possibility. Emerson's "partiality" of thinking is, or accounts for, the inflections of partial as "not whole," together with partial as "favoring or biassed toward" something or someone. Here is Emerson weaving some of this together:

> Character is higher than intellect. Thinking is the function. Living is the functionary.... A great soul will be strong to live, as well as strong to think. Does he lack organ or medium to impart his truths? He can still fall back on this elemental force of living them. This is a total act. Thinking is a partial act. Let the grandeur of justice shine in his affairs. Let the beauty of affection cheer his lowly roof. Those "far from fame," who dwell and act with him, will feel the force of his constitution. ("The American Scholar," 72)

("Affairs," "lowly roof," and "constitution" are each names Emerson is giving to functions of his writings.) A number of clichés, or moments of myth, are synthesized here, opening with a kind of denial that virtue is knowledge, continuing with the existentialist tag that living is not thinking, picking up a romantic sound ("lowly roof") to note that strong thoughts are imparted otherwise than in educated or expert forms, and hitting on the term "partial" to epitomize what he calls at the beginning of his address "the old fable" "that the gods, in the beginning, divided Man into men, as the hand was divided into fingers, the better to answer its end" (thus implying that Man has an end, but that to say so requires a myth).

When Emerson goes on to claim to have "shown the ground of his hope in adverting to the doctrine that man is one" (75), the apparent slightness of this, even piousness, in turning toward a doctrine, as if his hopes are well known, and well worn, may help disguise the enormity of the essay's immediate claim for its practice, that is, for its manner of writing. The passage (citing thinking as partial) proposes nothing *more*—say something total—for thinking to be; it declares that *living* is total, and if the living is strong it shows its ground, which is not to say that it is *more* than thinking, as if thinking might leave it out. Thinking *is*—at its most complete, as it were—a partial act; if it lacks something, leaves something out, it is its own partiality, what Kant calls (and Freud more or less calls) its incentive and interest (*Triebfeder*).

Since the lives of this people, Emerson's people, do not yet contain thinking, he cannot, or will not, sharing this life, quite claim to be thinking. But he makes a prior claim, the enormous one I just alluded to, namely to be providing this incentive of thinking, laying the conditions for thinking, becoming its "source," calling for it, attracting it to its partiality, by what he calls living his thoughts, which is pertinent to us so far as his writing is this life; which means, so far as "the grandeur of justice shine(s)" in the writing and "affection cheer(s)" it. Then this lowly roof, in which the anonymous will dwell with him, will provide them with the force of his constitution—there is no further fact, or no other way, of adopting it. (To follow out the idea of Emerson as (re)writing the constitution of the nation, or amending it, in the system of his prose, is a tale I do not get to here.) This provisionality of his writing—envisioning its adoption, awaiting its appropriation in certain ways (it cannot *make* this happen, work as it may)—is the importance of his having said, or implied, that since in the business we now have in hand, through which our affections as yet circulate, we do not know it, is it not yet transfigured, but remains in "our unconscious life," the corruptible has not yet put on incorruption. But what is this corruptible life, this pretransfigurative existence of his prose, unconscious of itself, unconscious to us? It is, on the line I am taking, one in which Tuition is to find its Intuition, or in which Emerson's thinking finds its "material" (as psychoanalysis puts it). In the opening two paragraphs of "The American Scholar," it "accepts" its topics in hope, and understands hope as a sign, in particular of "an indestructible instinct," yet an instinct that thinking must realize as "something else." I suppose this to mean that thinking is replacing, by transfiguring, instinct (as Nietzsche and as Freud again will say).

The opening reluctance and indefiniteness of Emerson's definition of his topic in "The American Scholar," his notation of this anniversary event as the "sign of the survival of the love of letters amongst a people too busy to give to letters any more" (than love and hope and instinct), suggest to me that Emerson means that his topics are our everyday letters and words, as signs of our instincts; they are to become thought. Then thinking is a kind of reading. But thought about what? Reading for what?

Sign suggests representation. How can "The American Scholar" represent the incentive of thinking—constitute a sign of its event—without at the same time presenting thinking, showing it? If thinking were solving problems, the incentive would be the problems or could be attached to the solutions. But Emerson's crack about our being "too busy to give to letters any more" exactly suggests that we are precisely busy solving things. When he opens by defining the anniversary on which he is speaking as one of hope and perhaps not enough of labor, he means of course that our labors (including those of what *we* call thinking) are largely devoted elsewhere than to letters—which is what everyone who cared was saying in explanation of the failure of America to found its own letters, its own writing, and its own art. But Emerson also means that founding letters demands its own labor and that we do not know what this (other) labor (the one that produces letters) is, that it is also a mode of thinking. Labor—as a characterization of thinking—suggests brooding. An interplay between laboring as reproductive and as productive (say as the feminine and the masculine in human thought) suggests Emerson's relentlessness concerning the interplay of the active and the receptive, or passive, in our relating to the world. (Thinking as melancholy reproduction characterizes Hamlet.) The other labor of thinking—devoted to letters—is, accordingly, one that requires a break with what we know as thinking. (Wittgenstein says our investigation has to be turned around; Heidegger says we have to take a step back from our thinking.) The incentive to this other mode will presumably consist in recognizing that we are not engaged in it, not doing something we nevertheless recognize a love for, an instinct for. Then Emerson's task is to show to that desire its satisfaction, which is to say: This writing must illustrate thinking. This means at the least that it must contain thought about what illustration is, what an example is.

In "The American Scholar" Emerson's transfiguration of illustration is his use of the word "illustrious." For example: "[The scholar] is one who raises himself from private considerations ["innermost" he sometimes says] and breathes and lives on public ["outermost"] and illustrious thoughts"

(73). In Emerson's way of talking, this is a kind of tautology. It is a favorite idea of Emerson's that the passage from private to public ideas is something open to each individual, as if there is in the intellectual life the equivalent of the Moral Law in the moral life, an imperative to objectivity. In "Self-Reliance," he imagines a man who is able to reachieve a certain perspective that society talks us (almost all of us) out of, as one whose opinions would be "seen to be not private but necessary" (149), and in "The American Scholar" he phrases what he will call the ground of his hope that man is one by saying "the deeper [the scholar] dives into his privatest, secretest presentiment, to his wonder he finds this is the most acceptable, most public, and universally true" (74). The contrast to the superficially private, which the *most* private can reach, Emerson characterizes sometimes as necessary, sometimes as universal, thus exactly according to the characteristics Kant assigns to the a priori. I suppose Emerson knows this. But why would Emerson speak of illustrating the a priori conditions of thinking as illustrious? Surely for no reason separate from the fact that the illustration of thinking as attaining to the necessary and universal illustrates the conditions shared by humanity as such; such thoughts are illustrious exactly because they are completely unexceptional, in this way representative.

This thought produces some of Emerson's most urgent rhetoric, some of the most famous. In the opening paragraph of "Self-Reliance": "To believe your own thought, to believe that what is true for you in your private heart is true for all men,—that is genius." "In every work of genius we recognize our own rejected thoughts; they come back to us with a certain alienated majesty." Self-evidently no one is in a position to know more about this than any other, hence in no position to *tell* anyone of it, to offer information concerning it (this is the Ancient Mariner's mistake, and his curse). So pretty clearly Emerson is not talking about science and mathematics. Then what is he talking about? Whatever it is, he properly—conveniently, you might think—describes himself as *showing* his ground. But if his ground, or anyone's, will prove to be unexceptional (except for the endlessly specifiable fact that it is one's own life on that ground), why the tone of moral urgency in showing it, declaring it? Is thinking—something to be called thinking—something whose partiality or incentive is essentially moral and perhaps political?

Let us confirm Emerson's transfiguration of the illustrative in its other occurrence in "The American Scholar": "The private life of one man shall be a more illustrious monarchy, more formidable to its enemy, more sweet and serene in its influence to its friend, than any kingdom in history" (76). The idea is that the illustrious is not, or shall not be, merely a particular result of monarchy but monarchy's universal cause, and the paradox alerts us to consider that while of course monarchy is derived as the rule of one (for whoever is still interested in that possibility), it may also come to be seen to speak of the *beginning or origin* of one, of what Emerson calls "one man," the thing two sentences earlier he had called "the upbuilding of a man," that is, of his famous "individual." (Hence the paradox of a private life as an illustrious monarchy is to be paired with the argument, as between Jefferson and Adams, of the natural aristocrat. Both knew that *that* was a paradoxical idea—as if democracy has its own paradox to match that of the philosopher-king. The Adams-Jefferson exchange is invoked in a complementary context in my *Pursuits of Happiness*).[5] When this process of upbuilding, or origination, is achieved, then, as the final sentence of "The American Scholar" puts it, "A nation of men will for the first time exist"—or as Marx put the thought half a dozen years after Emerson's address, human history will begin. For Emerson you could say both that this requires a constitution of the public and at the same time an institution of the private, a new obligation to think for ourselves, to make ourselves intelligible, in every word. What goes on inside us now is merely obedience to the law and the voices of others—the business Emerson calls conformity, a rewriting of what Kant calls heteronomy. That no thought is our own is what Emerson signals by interpreting the opening fable of his essay, concerning the gods' original division of Man into men, to mean that "Man is thus metamorphosed into a thing" (64). That we are already (always already) metamorphosed sets, I suppose, the possibility and necessity of our transfiguration. Then what were we before we were metamorphosed? (Emerson speaks not only of our conversion, which is to say, rebirth; he also says that we are unborn. This is worth brooding over.)

If we are things, we do not belong to Kant's Realm of Ends, we do not regard ourselves as human, with human others. For Kant the Realm of Ends might be seen as the realization of the eventual human city. As for Kant, for Emerson this vision is an inception of the moral life. What is the entrance to the city?

Here we cross to the second part of this lecture, to follow out a little the questionable tone of moral urgency in Emerson's descriptions of thinking. My thought is that a certain relation to words (as an allegory of my relation to my life) is inseparable from a certain moral-like relation to thinking, and that the morality and the thinking that are inseparable are of specific strains—the morality is neither teleological (basing itself on a conception of the good to be maximized in society) nor deontological (basing itself on an independent conception of the right), and the thinking is some as yet unknown distance from what we think of as reasoning. An obvious moral interpretation of the image of figuring from the innermost to the outermost is that of moral perfectionism (on a current understanding) at its most objectionable, the desire to impose the maximization of one's most private conception of good on all others, regardless of their talents or tastes or visions of the good.

I remarked that moral perfectionism has not found a secure home in modern philosophy. There are various reasons for this homelessness, and, as I have said, the title "perfectionism" covers more than a single view. Taking Emerson and Nietzsche as my focal examples here, and thinking of them, I surmise that the causes for the disapproval of perfectionism will orbit around two features or themes of their outlook: (1) A hatred of moralism—of what Emerson calls "conformity"—so passionate and ceaseless as to seem sometimes to amount to a hatred of morality altogether (Nietzsche calls himself the first antimoralist; Emerson knows that he will seem antinomian, a refuser of any law, including the moral law). (2) An expression of disgust with or a disdain for the present state of things so complete as to require not merely reform, but a call for a transformation of things, and before all a transformation of the self—a call that seems so self-absorbed and obscure as to make morality impossible: What is the moral life apart from acting beyond the self and making oneself intelligible to those beyond it?

A thought to hold on to is that what Emerson means by conformity is to be heard against Kant's idea that moral worth is a function of acting not merely in conformity with the moral law but for the sake of the law. Kant famously, scandalously, says that a mother who cares for her child out of affection rather than for the sake of the moral law exhibits no moral worth. Kant does not say that this woman exhibits no excellence of any kind, just not of the highest kind, the kind the makes the public life of mutual freedom possible, that attests to the realm of ends. Emerson's perception can be said to be that we exhibit neither the value of affection nor the worth of morality (neither, as it were, feminine nor masculine virtues), but that our conformity exhibits merely the fear of others' opinions, which Emerson puts as a fear of others' eyes, which claps us in a jail of shame.

This in turn is to be heard against John Rawls's impressive interpretation of Kant's moral philosophy in which he presents Kant's "main aim as deepening and justifying Rousseau's idea that liberty is acting in accordance with a law that we give to ourselves" and emphasizes that "Kant speaks of the failure to act on the moral law as giving rise to shame and not to feelings of guilt."[6] A text such as Emerson's "Self-Reliance" is virtually a study of shame, and perceives what we now call human society as one in which the moral law is nowhere (or almost nowhere) in existence. His perception presents itself to him as a vision of us as "bugs, spawn," as a "mob"; Nietzsche will say (something Emerson also says) "herd." It is a violent perception of a circumstance of violence. How do we, as Emerson puts it, "come out" of that? How do we become self-reliant? The worst thing we could do is rely on ourselves as we stand—this is simply to be the slaves of our slavishness: it is what makes us spawn. We must become averse to this conformity, which means convert from it, which means transform our conformity, as if we are to be born (again). How does our self-consciousness—which now expresses itself as shame, or let us say embarrassment—make us something other than human? I have elsewhere (in "Being Odd, Getting Even") tried to show that Emerson is taking on philosophy's interpretation of self-consciousness in its versions in both Descartes and Kant.

In Descartes, self-consciousness, in the form of thinking that I think, must prove my existence, human existence. When in "Self-Reliance" Emerson says that we dare not (as if we are ashamed to) say "I think," "I am," as if barred from the saying of the *cogito ergo sum,* his implication is that we do not exist (as human), we as if haunt the world. And I find this pattern in Emerson (of discovering our failing of philosophy as a failure of our humanity) also to be interpreting Kant's idea of freedom as imposing the moral law upon oneself. It is for Emerson not so much that we are ashamed because we do not give ourselves the moral law—which is true enough—but that we do not give ourselves the moral law because we are already ashamed, a state surely in need of definition, as if we lack the right to be right. Again, it is not that we are ashamed of our immorality; we are exactly incapable of being ashamed of *that*; in that sense we are shameless. Our moralized shame is debarring us from the conditions of the moral life, from the possibility of responsibility over our lives, from responding to our lives rather than bearing them dumbly or justifying them automatonically. That debarment or embarrassment is for Emerson, as for Kant, a state other than the human, since it lacks the humanly defining fact of freedom. That we are perceived as "bugs" says this and more. Bugs are not human, but they are not monsters either; bugs in human guise are inhuman, monstrous.

How does Emerson understand a way out, out of wrongdoing ourselves, which is to ask: How does Emerson find the "almost lost . . . light that can lead [us] back to [our] prerogatives?" ("The American Scholar," 75)—which for Emerson would mean something like answering for ourselves. Here is where Emerson's writing, with its enactment of transfigurations, comes in. Its mechanism may be seen in (even as) Emersonian Perfectionism.

Perfectionism makes its appearance in Rawls's *A Theory of Justice* (sec. 50) as a teleological theory and as having two versions, moderate and extreme. In the moderate version its principle is one among others and "[directs] society to arrange institutions and to define the duties and obligations of individuals so as to maximize the achievement of human excellence, in art, in science, and culture." Then how shall we understand Emerson's and Nietzsche's disdain for the cultural institutions, or institutionalized culture, of the day (including universities and religions and whatever would be supported by what Rawls describes as "public funds for the arts and sciences"), a disdain sometimes passionate to the point of disgust? The distribution of nothing of high culture as it is now institutionalized is to be maximized in Emersonian Perfectionism, which is in that sense not a teleological theory at all. What Nietzsche calls "the pomp of culture" and "misemployed and appropriated culture" is, on the contrary, to be scorned. It makes no obvious sense to ask for some given thing to be maximized in what this perfectionism craves as the realm of culture, the realm to which, as Nietzsche put it, we are to consecrate ourselves, the path on which, as Emerson puts it, we are to find "the conversion of the world" ("The American Scholar," concluding paragraph). There is, before finding this, nothing to be maximized. One can also say that the good of the culture to be found is already universally distributed or else it is nothing—which is to say, it is part of a conception of what it is to be a moral person. Emerson calls it genius; we might call this the capacity for self-criticism, the capacity to consecrate the attained to the unattained self, on the basis of the axiom that each is a moral person.

The irrelevance of maximization (as a particular teleological principle) should be clearer still in what Rawls calls the extreme version of perfectionism, in which the maximization of excellence is the sole principle of institutions and obligations. As I noted earlier, *A Theory of Justice* epitomizes this extreme version by a selection of sentences from Nietzsche. They are from the third Untimely Meditation, *Schopenhauer as Educator:*

> Mankind must work continually to produce individual great human beings—this and nothing else is the task. . . . For the question is this: how can your life, the individual life, retain the highest value, the deepest significance? . . . Only by your living for the good of the rarest and most valuable specimens. (As in *A Theory of Justice*, 325 n. 51)

This sounds bad. Rawls takes it straightforwardly to imply that there is a separate class of great men (to be) for whose good, and conception of good, the rest of society is to live. Rawls is surely right to reject this as a principle of justice pertinent to the life of democracy (see *A Theory of Justice*, 328). But as I also noted, if Nietzsche is to be dismissed as a thinker pertinent to the founding of the democratic life, then so, it should seem, is Emerson, since Nietzsche's meditation on Schopenhauer is, to an as yet undisclosed extent, a transcription and elaboration of Emersonian passages. Emerson's dismissal here would pain me more than I can say, and if that is indeed the implication of *A Theory of Justice*, I want the book, because of my admiration for it, to be wrong in drawing this implication from itself.

In Nietzsche's meditation, the sentence, "Only by your living for the good of the rarest and most valuable specimens," continues with the words "and not for the good of the majority."[7] However, the majority is then characterized still further in that sentence; it is not part of constitutional democracy that one is to live for the good of the majority—something Rawls's book is the demonstration of for those committed to democracy. If not for the good of the majority, then is one to live for the good of each (for each societal "position")? I suppose this is not captured in the idea of making rational choices that have justifiably unequal benefits for all (measured by the Difference Principle, Rawls's second principle of justice), but it may yet be a life taken within the commitment to democracy. There will doubtless be perfectionisms that place themselves above democracy or that are taken in the absence of the conditions of democracy. The former might describe a timarchy, an oligarchy, or a dictatorship. These are not my business, which is, rather, to see whether perfectionism is necessarily undemocratic. I might put my thought this way: the particular disdain for official culture taken in

Emerson and in Nietzsche (and surely in half the writers and artists in the 150 years since "The American Scholar," or say since romanticism) is itself an expression of democracy and commitment to it. Timocrats do not produce, oligarchs do not commission, dictators do not enforce, art and culture that disgust them. Only within the possibility of democracy is one committed to *living* with, or against, such culture. This may well produce personal tastes and private choices that are, let us say, exclusive, even esoteric. Then my question is whether this exclusiveness might be not just tolerated but treasured by the friends of democracy.

There are two further problems with the final sentence among those Rawls quotes from Nietzsche concerning living for rare specimens and not for the majority. First, Nietzsche's word translated as "specimens" is *Exemplare* (faithfully translated as "exemplars" later in *Untimely Meditations* [1983 ed.] by the same translator from whom Rawls takes his Nietzsche sentences [R. J. Hollingdale, in his earlier *Nietzsche: The Man and His Philosophy*]). The biological association of "specimens" suggests that the grounds for identifying them (hence for assessing their value) are specifiable independently of the instance in view, of its effect on you; its value depends upon this independence; specimens are samples, as of a class, genus, or whole; one either is or is not a specimen. Whereas the acceptance of an exemplar, as access to another realm (call it the realm of culture; Nietzsche says, echoing a favorite image of Emerson's, that it generates "a new circle of duties"), is not grounded in the relation between the instance and a class of instances it stands for but in the relation between the instance and the individual other—for example, myself—for whom it does the standing, for whom it is a sign, upon whom I delegate something. ("Archetype," translatable as "exemplar," is the word Kant associates with the Son of God in *Religion within the Bounds of Reason Alone*, [e.g., 109].) Second, when Nietzsche goes on, in the sentences following the one about exemplars, to begin characterizing the life of culture, it must in a sense be understood as a life lived for the good of the one living it. It accordingly demands a certain exclusiveness, its good is inherently not maximizable (transportable to other lives). But it is not inherently unjust, requiring favored shares in the distribution of good. Its characteristic vice would not be envy (a vice methodologically significant for *A Theory of Justice*) but perhaps shirking participation in democracy. Then the question becomes, If it is not shirking, then *what* is its participation? Nietzsche continues, after the sentence Rawls quotes, as follows:

> The young person should be taught to regard himself as a failed work of nature but at the same time as a witness to the grandiose and marvelous intention of this artist.... By coming to this resolve he places himself within the circle of *culture*; for culture is the child of each individual's self-knowledge and dissatisfaction with himself. Anyone who believes in culture is thereby saying: "I see above me something higher and more human than I am; let everyone help me to attain it, as I will help everyone who knows and suffers as I do." (*Schopenhauer as Educator*, 162)

In the next sentence the "something higher," the desire for which is created in self-dissatisfaction, is marked as "a higher self as yet still concealed from it." It is my own, unsettlingly unattained.

Maximization is roughly the last thing on the mind of the suffering individual in this state of self-dissatisfaction, the state of perceiving oneself as failing to follow oneself in one's higher and happier aspirations, failing perhaps to have found the right to one's own aspirations—not to the deliverances of rare revelations but to the significance of one's everyday impressions, to the right to make them one's ideas. It is a crucial moment of the attained self, a crossroads; it may be creative or crushing. To look then for the maximization of a given state of culture is to give up looking for the reality of one's own. To be overly impatient philosophically with this crisis is to be overly impatient with the exploration of what we call adolescence. Emerson and Nietzsche notably and recurrently direct their words to "youth" as words against despair, showing that they themselves have survived the incessant calls to give over their youthful aspirations. For youth to be overly impatient with these calls is to be overly impatient with the adults who voice them; it is a deflection of the interest of the contest with adulthood, of the crisis in giving consent to adulthood, say with the arrogation of one's voice in the moral life, the law. Since democracy is the middle or civil world of political possibilities—not ceding its demands for itself either to possibilities defined courteously or violently (neither to diplomacy nor to rebellion), it may be taken as the public manifestation of the individual situation of adolescence, the time of possibilities under pressure to consent to actualities. The promise of Emerson and of Nietzsche is that youth is not alone a phase of individual development but—like childhood for the earlier romantics—a dimension of human existence as such.

When Nietzsche says, in the words of his passage last quoted, describing the young person as a failed work of nature and as a witness, "for culture is the child of each individual," and imagines one who seeks this child to pray that everyone will help him or her to attain it, could it be clearer that the "something higher and more human" in question is not—not necessarily and in a sense not ever—that of someone else, but a further or eventual position of the self now dissatisfied with itself? (The quantification is old-fashioned. Not, "there is a genius such that every self is to live for it," but, "for each self there is a genius." I am thinking particularly of the passage in "Self-Reliance" where Emerson reports that his genius calls him; it calls him, it turns out, to his own work, which, it happens, is writing. I do not imagine this to be some other person calling him.) Nietzsche goes on: "Thus only he who has attached his heart to some great man is by that act *consecrated to culture*; the sign of that consecration is that one is ashamed of oneself without any accompanying feeling of distress, that one comes to hate one's own narrowness and shriveled nature" (*Schopenhauer as Educator*, 163). The perfectionist idea of culture is projected in contrast to this idea of "one's own nature." The sense is that the move from the state of nature to the contract of society does not, after all, sufficiently sustain human life. If the idea of unshriveling our nature is that of transforming our needs, not satisfying them as they stand, the moral danger that is run may seem to be that of idealistic moralism, forgetting the needs of others as they stand. Since the task for each is his or her own self-transformation, the representativeness implied in that life may seem not to establish a recognition of others in different positions, so to be disqualified as a moral position altogether. "Representativeness" invokes one of Emerson's "master-tones," both as characterized in his writing and as exemplified by his writing. And I think we can say: Emerson's writing works out the conditions for my recognizing my difference from others as a function of my recognizing my difference from myself.

Nietzsche's idea of "attaching one's heart," here to some great man, is, let us say, acting toward him in love, as illustrated by Nietzsche's writing of his text on Schopenhauer. But the author of that text is not consecrating himself to Schopenhauer—Schopenhauer, as everyone notes, is scarcely present in the text. If what you consecrate yourself to is what you live for, then Nietzsche is not living for Schopenhauer. It is not Schopenhauer's self that is still concealed from the writer of this text. The love of the great is, or is the cause of, the hate of one's meanness, the hate that constitutes the sign of consecration. ("The fundamental idea of culture, insofar as it sets for each one of us but one task [is]: to promote the production of the philosopher, the artist and the saint *within us* and without us and thereby to work at the perfecting of nature" (163, my emphasis). This is said to set one in the midst of "a mighty community." Obviously it is not a present but an eventual human community, so everything depends on how it is to be reached.)

Many, with Rawls, have taken Nietzsche otherwise than as calling for the further or higher self of each, each consecrating himself/herself to self-transformation, accepting one's own genius, which is precisely not, it is the negation of, accepting one's present state and its present consecrations to someone fixed, as such, "beyond" one. Perhaps it was necessary for Nietzsche to have left himself unguarded on this desperate point.

Emerson provides an explanation and name for this necessary ambiguity in the passage of "The American Scholar" of which Nietzsche's passage on the relation to greatness is a reasonably overt transcription (with sensible differences):

> The main enterprise of the world for splendor, for extent, is the upbuilding of a man (76) . . . in a century, in a millennium, one or two men; that is to say, one or two approximations to the right state of every man. All the rest behold in the hero of the poet their own green and crude being—ripened; yes, and are content to be less, so *that* may attain to its full stature. (75)

But Emerson does not say that this contentment is the best or necessary state of things. For him, rather, it shows "what a testimony, full of grandeur [in view of what we might become], full of pity [in view of what we are], is borne to the demands of his own nature [by the poor and the low. The poor and the low are] to be brushed like flies from the path of a great person, so that justice shall be done by him to that common nature which it is the dearest desire of all to see enlarged. . . . He lives for us, and we live in him" (76). (Emerson is unguarded; we are unguarded.) As we stand we are apt to overrate or misconstrue this identification. Emerson continues:

> Men, such as they are, very naturally seek money or power. . . . And why not? for they aspire to the highest, and this in their sleep-walking they dream is highest. Wake them and they shall quit the false good and leap to the true,

and leave governments to clerks and desks. This revolution is to be wrought by the gradual domestication of the idea of Culture. . . . Each philosopher, each bard, each actor has only done for me, as by a delegate, what one day I can do for myself. (76)

Here there simply seems no room for doubt that the intuition of a higher or further self is one to be arrived at in person, in the person of the one who gives his heart to it, this one who just said that the great have been his delegates and who declares that "I" can one day, so to say, be that delegate. I forerun myself, a sign, an exemplar.

In the so-called "Divinity School Address," delivered the year after "The American Scholar," Emerson will in effect provide the originating case of our repressing our delegation and attributing our potentialities to the actualities of others, the case of "Historical Christianity['s] dwell[ing], with noxious exaggeration about the *person* of Jesus," whereas "the soul knows no persons." Evidently Emerson is treating this form of worship or consecration, even if in the name of the highest spirituality, as idolatry. (Here is a site for investigating the sense that perfectionism is an attempt to take over, or mask, or say secularize, a religious responsibility, something Matthew Arnold is explicit in claiming for his perfectionism in *Culture and Anarchy*, something Henry Sidgwick criticizes Arnold for in "The Prophet of Culture.")

In Emerson's way of speaking, "one day" ("Each philosopher . . . has only done, as by a delegate, what one day I can do for myself") always also means today; the life he urgently speaks for is one he forever says is not to be postponed. It is today that you are to take the self on; today that you are to awaken and to consecrate yourself to culture, specifically, to domesticate it gradually, which means bring it home, as part, now, of your everyday life. This is Perfectionism's moral urgency; why, we might say, the results of its moral thinking are not the results of moral reasoning, neither of a calculation of consequences issuing in a judgment of value or preference, nor of a testing of a given intention, call it, against a universalizing law issuing in a judgment of right. The urgency is expressed in Emerson's sense of fighting chagrin in every word, with every breath. If calculation and judgment are to answer the question Which way?, perfectionist thinking is a response to the way's being lost. So thinking may present itself as stopping, and as finding a way *back*, as if thinking is remembering something. (This is a kind of summary of the way I have read Emerson's "Experience" in my "Finding as Founding.")

The urgency about today is the cause of Emerson's characteristic allusions to the gospels. In "The American Scholar" it is rather more than an allusion: "For the ease and pleasure of treading the old road . . . [the scholar instead] takes the cross of making his own"—a road Emerson characterizes in the passage as one of poverty, solitude, stammering, self-accusation, and "the state of virtual hostility in which he seems to stand to society, and especially to educated society" (73). In "Self-Reliance" the parody is as plain as the allusion: "I shun father and mother and wife and brother when my genius calls me. I would write on the lintels of the doorpost, *Whim*" (150). The shunning reference is to the call to enter the kingdom of heaven at once, today, to follow me, to let the dead bury the dead (Matthew 8:22). Emerson's parody mocks his own preachiness, and while it acknowledges that the domestication of culture is not going to be entered on today, yet it insists that there is no reason it is postponed; that is, no one has the reason for this revolution if each of us has not. It is why he perceives us as "[bearing] testimony, full of grandeur, full of pity . . . to the demands of [our] own nature," a remark transcribed in Nietzsche as "[regarding oneself] as a failed work of nature but at the same time as a witness to the grandiose and marvelous intentions of their artist." Bearing testimony and witnessing are functions of martyrdom. In moral perfectionism, as represented in Emerson and in Nietzsche, we are invited to a position that is structurally one of martyrdom; not, however, in view of an idea of the divine but in aspiration to an idea of the human.

What can this mean? (Whatever it means it suggests why I cannot accede to the recent proposal, interesting as it is in its own terms, of taking Perfectionism to be exemplified by the well-rounded life. See the essay by Thomas Hurka.)[8] And how does thinking as transfiguration bear on it? Which is to ask, How does Emerson's way of writing, his relation to his reader, bear on it? Which in turn means, How does his writing represent, by presenting, the aspiration to the human?

Before going on to sketch an answer to this pack of questions, it may be well to pause to say another word about my sense that the view Emerson and Nietzsche share, or my interest in it, is not simply to show that it is tolerable to the life of justice in a constitutional democracy but to show how it is essential to that life. What is the pertinence, for example, of perfectionism's emphasis, common from Plato and Aristotle to Emerson and Thoreau and Nietzsche, on education and character and friendship for a democratic existence? That emphasis of perfectionism, as I have said, may be taken to serve an effort to escape the mediocrity or leveling, say vulgarity, of equal existence, for oneself and perhaps for a select circle of like-minded others. There are undeniably aristocratic or aesthetic perfectionisms. But in Emerson it should, I would like to say, be taken as part of the training for democracy. Not the part that must internalize the principles of justice and practice the role of the democratic citizen—that is clearly required, so obviously that the Emersonian may take offense at the idea that this aspect of things is even difficult, evince a disdain for ordinary temptations to cut corners over the law. I understand the training and character and friendship Emerson requires for democracy as preparation to withstand not its rigors but its failures, character to keep the democratic hope alive in the face of disappointment with it. (Emerson is forever turning aside to say, especially to the young, not to despair of the world, and he says this as if he is speaking not to a subject but to a monarch.) That we will be disappointed in democracy, in its failure by the light of its own principles of justice, is implied in Rawls's concept of the original position in which those principles are accepted, a perspective from which we know that justice, in actual societies, will be departed from, and that the distance of any actual society from justice is a matter for each of us to access for ourselves. I will speak of this as our being compromised by the democratic demand for consent, so that the human individual meant to be created and preserved in democracy is apt to be undone by it.

Now I go on to my sketch in answer to how Emerson's writing (re)presents the aspiration to the human, beginning from a famous early sentence of "Self-Reliance" I have already had occasion to cite: "In every work of genius we recognize our own rejected thoughts. They come back to us with a certain alienated majesty." The idea of a majesty alienated from us is a transcription of the idea of the sublime as Kant characterizes it. Then the sublime, as has been discussed in recent literary theory, bears the structure of Freudian transference. (See, e.g., Weiskell; Harold Bloom; Hertz; and my "Psychoanalysis and Cinema.")[9] The direction of transference—of mine to the text, or the text's to me in a prior countertransference (or defense against being read)—seems to me an open question. In either case reading, as such, is taken by Emerson as of the sublime.

This comes out in Emerson's (and Thoreau's) delirious denunciation of books, in the spectacle of writing their own books that dare us to read them and dare us not to; that ask us to conceive that they do not want us to read them, to see that they are teaching us how—how *not* to read, that they are creating the taste not to be read, the capacity to leave them. Think of it in this way: If the thoughts of a text such as Emerson's (say the brief text on rejected thoughts) are yours, then you do not need them. If its thoughts are *not* yours, they will not do you good. The problem is that the text's thoughts are neither exactly mine nor not mine. In their sublimity as my rejected—say repressed—thoughts, they represent my further, next, unattained but attainable, self. To think otherwise, to attribute the origin of my thoughts simply to the other, thoughts which are then, as it were, implanted in me—some would say caused—by let us say some Emerson, is idolatry. (What in "Politics of Interpretation" I call the theology of reading is pertinent here.)

In becoming conscious of what in the text is (in Emerson's word) unconscious, the familiar is invaded by another familiar—the structure Freud calls the uncanny, and the reason he calls the psychoanalytic process itself uncanny. Emerson's process of transfiguring is such a structure, a necessity of his placing his work in the position of our rejected and further self, our "beyond." One of his ways of saying this is to say "I will stand here for humanity" as if he is waiting for us to catch up or catch on. When this is unpacked it turns out to be the transfiguration of a Kantian task. To say how, I track for a moment Emerson's play, pivotally and repeatedly in "Self-Reliance," on inflections of standing up and understanding in relation to standing for and in relation to standards.

"Standing for humanity," radiating in various directions as *representing* humanity and as *bearing* it (as bearing the pain of it) links across the essay with its recurrent notation of postures and of gaits (leaning and skulking among them—postures of shame) of which *standing* or uprightness, is the correction or conversion that Emerson seeks, his representative prose. This opens into Emerson's description of our being drawn by the true man, as being "constrained to his standard." (Emerson says he will make "this" true—I assume he is speaking of his prose—and describes the true man as "measuring" us.) Now *constraint*, especially in conjunction with *conformity*, is a Kantian term, specifically noting the operation of the moral law upon us—of the fact that it applies only to (is the mark of) the human, that is, only to a being subject to temptation, a being not unmixed in nature, as beasts and angels are unmixed. If you entertain this thought, then the idea of "standard" links further with the Kantian idea that man lives in two worlds, that is, is capable of viewing himself from two "standpoints" (in Kant's term). It is this possibility that gives us access to the intelligible world—the realm of ends, the realm of reason, of the human—"beyond" the world of sense. If Emerson assigns his pages as standards (flags and measures) and if this is an allusion to, an acceptance of, the Kantian task of disclosing the realm of ends, the realm of the human, then what is its point?

The point of contesting the Kantian tasks is presumably to be taken in the face of its present failure, or parody, its reduction to conformity. In picking up its standard—and transfiguring it—Emerson finds the intelligible world, the realm of ends, closed to us as a standpoint from which to view ourselves individually (our relation to the law no longer has *this* power for us). But at the same time he shows the intelligible world to be entered into whenever another represents for us our rejected self, our beyond; causes that aversion to ourselves in our conformity that will constitute our becoming, as it were, ashamed of our shame. Some solution. Well, some problem.

Kant describes the "constraint" of the law as an imperative expressed by an ought (*Foundations*, second section). For Emerson, we either *are* drawn beyond ourselves, as we stand, or we are *not*; we recognize our reversals or we do not; there is no ought about it. It remains true that being drawn by the standard of another, like being impelled by the imperative of a law, is the prerogative of the mixed or split being we call the human. But for Emerson we are divided not alone between intellect and sense, for we can say that each of these halves is itself split. We are halved not only horizontally but vertically—as that other myth of the original dividing of the human pictures it—as in Plato's *Symposium*, the form of it picked up in Freud, each of us seeking that of which we were originally half, with which we were partial.

Here, in this constraint by recognition and negation, is the place of the high role assigned in moral perfectionism to friendship. Aristotle speaks of a friend as "another myself." To see Emerson's philosophical authorship as taking up the ancient position of the friend, we have to include the inflection (more brazen in Nietzsche but no less explicit in Emerson) of my friend as my enemy (contesting my present attainments). If the position of that loved one were not also feared and hated, why would the thoughts from that place remain rejected? If one does not recognize Emerson in his version of such a position, his writing will seem, to its admirers, misty or foggy; to its detractors, ridiculous. (*Almost* everyone gets around to condescending to Emerson.)

How can philosophy have, in such a fashion, worked itself into the position of having to be accepted on intimate terms *before* it has proven itself? It seems the negation of philosophy.

If Emerson is wrong in his treatment of the state of conformity and of despair in what has become of the democratic aspiration, he seems harmless enough—he asks for no relief he cannot provide for himself—whatever other claims other perfectionisms might exert. But if Emerson is right, his aversion provides for the democratic aspiration the only internal measure of its truth to itself—a voice only this aspiration could have inspired, and, if it is lucky, must inspire. Since his aversion is a *continual turning away* from society, it is thereby a continual turning *toward* it. Toward and away; it is a motion of seduction—such as philosophy will contain. It is in response to this seduction from our seductions (conformities, heteronomies) that the friend (discovered or constructed) represents the standpoint of perfection.

The idea of the self as always to be furthered is not expressed by familiar fantasies of a noumenal self, nor of the self as entelechy, either final or initial. May one imagine Emerson to have known that the word "scholar" is related in derivation to "entelechy" (through the idea of holding near or holding back, as if stopping to think)—so that by the American Scholar he means the American self? Then, since by Cartesian and by Kantian measures the self in America does not exist, America does not exist—or to speak in proper predicates, is still not discovered as a new, another, world.

And the question might well arise: Why does Emerson take on the Cartesian and Kantian measures? Why does he put English on the terms of philosophy? Instead of transfiguring these terms, why not take the opportunity of America as one of sidestepping philosophy, as one more European edifice well lost? Why does Emerson care, why ought we to care, whether he is a philosopher? Why care when we come to his page, his standard, whether the encounter with our further self, the encounter of reading, the access to an intelligible world is a *philosophical* one? Evidently because the gradual domestication of culture he calls for—what he names his revolution—is a philosophical one. How?

How is this domestication—call it finding a home for humanity; Emerson and Thoreau picture it as building a house, another edification—how is this a task for philosophy? We may take for granted Plato's description of his task in the *Republic* as creating a "city of words," hence accept it that philosophy in the Western world unfolds its prose in a depicted conversation concerning the just city. Emerson's house of words is essentially less than a city; and while its word is not that of hope, its majesty is not to despair, but to let the "grandeur of justice shine" in it, and "affection cheer" it. Kant had asked, What can I hope for? Emerson in effect answers, For nothing. You do not know what there is hope for. "Patience—patience [suffering, reception]"; "abide on your instincts" (cf. "The American Scholar," 79)—presumably because that is the way of thinking. For him who abides this way, "the huge world will come round to him" (ibid.)—presumably in the form in which it comes to Emerson, one person at a time, a world whose turning constitutes the world's coming around—the form in which you come to your (further) self.

In coming to Emerson's text from a certain alienated majesty, we (each of us as Emerson's reader) form an illustrious monarchy with a population of two. It illustrates that possibility of recognizing my finitude, or separateness, as the question of realizing my partiality. Is the displacement of the idea of the whole man by an idea of the partial man worth philosophy?

I see it this way. Emerson's perception of the dispossession of our humanity, the loss of ground, the loss of nature as our security, or property, is thought in modern philosophy as the problem of skepticism. The overcoming or overtaking of skepticism must constitute a revolution that is a domestication for philosophy (or redomestication) because, let us say, neither science nor religion nor morality has overcome it. On the contrary, they as much as anything cause skepticism, the withdrawal of the world. *Is* philosophy left to us, even transformed? Well, that is my question. I think it is philosophy's question, which accordingly now comes into its own—as if purified of religion and of science.

I can formulate my interest in Emerson's situation in the following way. Domestication in Emerson is the issue, or urgency, of the *day*, today, one among others, an achievement of the everyday, the ordinary, now, here, again, never again. In Wittgenstein's *Philosophical Investigations* the issue of the everyday is the issue of the siting of skepticism, not as something to be overcome, as if to be refuted, as if it is a *conclusion* about human knowledge (which is skepticism's self-interpretation), but to be placed as a mark of what Emerson calls "human condition," a further interpretation of finitude, a mode, as said, of inhabiting our investment in words, in the world. This argument of the ordinary—as what skepticism attacks, hence creates, and as what counters, or recounts, skepticism—is engaged oppositely in a work such as Heidegger's *What Is Called Thinking?*; hence the argument of the ordinary is engaged between these visions of Wittgenstein and of Heidegger. (It may present itself as an argument between skepticism and sublimity, between transfiguration down and transfiguration up.) It is why I am pleased to find Emerson and his transfigurations of the ordinary to stand back of both Wittgenstein and Heidegger. They are the two major philosophers of this century for whom the issue of the ordinary, hence the skepticism, remains alive for philosophy, whose burden is philosophy's burden; it is, to my mind, utterly significant that in them—as in Emerson—what strikes their readers as a tone of continual moral urgency or religious or artistic pathos is not expressed as a *separate* study to be called moral philosophy, or religious philosophy, or aesthetics. The moral of which—or the aesthetics of which—I draw as follows: what they write is nothing *else* than these topics or places of philosophy, but is always nothing but philosophy itself. Nothing less, nothing separate, can lead us from, or break us of, our shameful condition. Philosophy presents itself as a (an untaken) way of life. This is what perfectionists will find ways to say.

Then, needless to say, in calling for philosophy Emerson is not comprehensible as asking for guardianship by a particular profession within what we call universities. I assume what will become "philosophy itself" may not be distinguishable from literature—that is to say, from what literature will become. Then that assumption, or presumption, is, I guess, my romanticism.

I come back to earth, concluding by locating what I have been saying in relation to a passage from John Stuart Mill's *On Liberty* that should be common ground among professional philosophers. I adduce it with the thought that what I have been saying suggests to me that Perfectionism, as I perceive the thing that interests me, is not a competing moral theory but a dimension of any moral thinking. Kant found an essential place for perfection in his view of it at the end, as it were, of his theory, as an unreachable ideal relation to be striven for to the moral law; in Emerson this place of the ideal occurs at the beginning of moral thinking, as a condition, let us say, or moral imagination, as preparation or sign of the moral life. And if the precondition of morality is to be established in personal encounter, we exist otherwise in a premoral state, morally voiceless. Mill's passage, while no doubt not as eager to court the derangement of intellect as Emerson's prose has to be, is no less urgent and eloquent in the face of human dispossession and voicelessness:

> In our times, from the highest class of society down to the lowest, every one lives as under the eye of a hostile and dreaded censorship. Not only in what concerns others, but in what concerns themselves, the individual, or the family, do not ask themselves—what do I prefer? . . . or, what would allow the best and highest in me to have fair play, and enable it to grow and thrive? They ask themselves, . . . what is usually done? I do not mean that they choose what is customary in preference to what suits their own inclination. It does not occur to them to have any inclination except for what is customary. Thus the mind itself is bowed to the yoke: even in what people do for pleasure, conformity is the first thing thought of; they like in crowds; they exercise choice only among things commonly done; peculiarity of taste, eccentricity of conduct, are shunned equally with crimes: until by dint of not following their own nature, they have no nature to follow: their human capacities are withered and starved; they become incapable of any strong wishes or native pleasures, and are generally without either opinions or feelings or home growth, or properly their own. Now is this, or is it not, the desirable condition of human nature? (chap. 3, par. 6)

I call attention to the toll of that Millian word "desirable." In a passage in *Utilitarianism*, Mill famously conceives the claim that anything is desirable —on analogy with the claim that anything is visible or audible—to rest finally on the fact that people do, or presumably under specifiable circumstances will, actually desire it. Philosophers in the years I was in graduate school never used to tire of making fun of that passage from *Utilitarianism*. Yet the drift of it still strikes me as sound. According to it, the question at the conclusion of the quotation from *On Liberty* becomes: Do you, or would you his reader, under any circumstances, desire this censored condition of mankind? It is Perfectionism's question, its reading of the cry of freedom, for a life of one's own, of one's choice, that one consents to with one's own voice. The eloquence of Mill's passage is to awaken its friend to the question, to show that it is a question. The implication seems to be that until we each give our answers to the question, one by one, one on one, we will not know what it is to which—long before we begin our calculations of pleasure and of pain—we are giving our consent.

Notes

Originally published as Stanley Cavell, "Aversive Thinking: Emersonian Representation in Heidegger and Nietzsche," in *Conditions Handsome and Unhandsome: The Constitution of Emersonian Perfectionism: The Carus Lectures, 1988* (Chicago: University of Chicago Press, 1990), 33–63. Reprinted by permission of the University of Chicago Press.

1. "The American Scholar," *Selections from Ralph Waldo Emerson*, ed. Stephen E. Whicher (Boston: Houghton Mifflin, 1957), 75, hereafter cited in the text.
2. Karl Jaspers, *Nietzsche: An Introduction to the Understanding of His Philosophical Activity*, trans. Charles F. Wallraff and Frederick J. Schmitz (Baltimore: Johns Hopkins University Press, 1997), 386.
3. Martin Heidegger, *What Is Called Thinking?* trans. J. Glenn Gray (New York: Harper and Row, 1968), hereafter cited in the text.
4. Immanuel Kant, "Conjectural Beginning of Human History," trans. Emil Fackenheim, in *Kant: On History*, 56-57, ed. Lewis White Beck (Indianapolis: Bobbs-Merrill, 1981), 56–57.
5. Stanley Cavell, *Pursuits of Happiness: The Hollywood Comedy of Remarriage* (Cambridge: Harvard University Press, 1981), 155.
6. John Rawls, *A Theory of Justice* (Cambridge: Belknap Press of Harvard University Press, 1971), 256.
7. Friedrich Nietzsche, *Schopenhauer as Educator*, trans. James Hillesheim and Malcolm Simpson (South Bend, Ind.: Regnery/Gateway, 1965), 162.
8. Thomas Hurka, "The Well-Rounded Life," *Journal of Philosophy* 84 (December 1987): 727–46.
9. Thomas Weiskell, *The Romantic Sublime* (Baltimore: Johns Hopkins University Press, 1986); Harold Bloom, "Mr. America," *New York Review of Books* (November 22, 1984); Neil Hertz, *The End of the Line* (New York: Columbia University Press, 1985); Stanley Cavell, "Psychoanalysis and Cinema: The Melodrama of the Unknown Woman," in *The Trial(s) of Psychoanalysis*, ed. Francoise Meltzer (Chicago: University of Chicago, 1988), 257–58 n. 29.

PART II

Emerson's Self-Reliance Properly Understood

CHAPTER 5

Self-Reliance and Complicity: Emerson's Ethics of Citizenship

Jack Turner

EMERSON IS NOT KNOWN as a voice of social or civic responsibility. Wilson Carey McWilliams lambastes him as antipolitical: "Emerson saw in man . . . a deified self, independent of other individuals and the democratic public alike. . . . [I]ndividualistic romanticism, not democracy, was the logical result of his teaching."[1]

Defenders of Emerson emphasize the intrinsically political nature of his vocation. In the words of Stanley Cavell, "The endlessly repeated idea that Emerson was only interested in finding the individual should give way to or make way for the idea that this quest was his way of founding a nation, writing its constitution, constituting its citizens."[2] Emerson works to inspire democratic selves for whom "thinking is of the essence, as a man whose wholeness, say whose autonomy, is in command of the autonomy of thinking."[3]

Neither of these views takes seriously the possibility that Emerson has a full-fledged ethics of liberal democratic citizenship. While the first view dismisses Emerson's political potential altogether, the second view reduces Emerson's political significance to self-cultivation. Yet Emerson addresses a straightforwardly political challenge in liberal democracy—civic motivation. Why should well-off individuals sacrifice private goods for the cause of justice? Emerson answers this question, though not in any single essay. The answer is spread over two decades of writings and speeches in response to the major issue of his time: racial slavery. A careful reading of this work reveals Emerson's ethics of citizenship.

Emerson's ethics of citizenship arises out of the complex interplay of two ideas: self-reliance and complicity. Self-reliance is Emerson's name for positive freedom, for personal autonomy. George Kateb divides Emersonian self-reliance into mental and active components. Mental self-reliance, he says, "is the steady effort of thinking one's thoughts and thinking them through. It is intellectual independence." Active self-reliance is "being oneself by realizing oneself"; it is the spirit of vocation, of "doing one's own work."[4] Emerson's idea of complicity receives far less attention than self-reliance,[5] but its role in his ethics is great. Complicity is collaboration with wrongdoing. One becomes complicit in injustice by either explicitly authorizing it or tacitly supporting it through one's civic, social, and economic actions (and inactions).[6] Self-reliance and complicity are inversely proportionate: the greater one's complicity, the lesser one's self-reliance.

The antagonism between self-reliance and complicity is multidimensional. When individuals politically, socially, or economically enable the violation of others' rights, they undermine the principles of moral equality and moral reciprocity underwriting self-reliance.[7] The ground of Emerson's commitment to moral equality is not necessarily Christian or even metaphysical. It is, rather, a practical axiom derived from (1) Emerson's fallibilism and (2) his sense that all individuals are inwardly infinite and therefore inestimably worthy.[8] Human perception is imperfect. No individual is qualified to rank order human beings. At the same time, each individual is "new in nature" and therefore "an inscrutable possibility":[9] "I never know, in addressing myself to a new individual, what may befall me."[10] Emerson's combined sense of the limits of human perception and the "infinitude" of individuals leads him to embrace moral equality as the most responsible operating assumption. Adhering to this assumption will keep him attentive to the novelty and inestimable worth of each individual, even when that novelty and worth are not immediately apparent. It will save him from the erroneous overconfidence of heroic individualist immoralism, which justifies exploitation by presuming that one's own flourishing is more important than the flourishing of others.

Self-assertive though self-reliance is, truly self-reliant individuals realize themselves while respecting the rights of others. Through egalitarian moral respect, the self-reliant register their commitment to human equality and signal their transcendence of the base desire to establish one's dignity through others' degradation. Conditioning one's dignity on the subjection of others is not strength but weakness, an exposure of the spiritually slavish need to dominate, and an admission of a lack of self-trust: "It is only as a man puts off all foreign support, and stands alone, that I see him to be strong and to prevail."[11]

Complicity also militates against the intellectual wakefulness required by self-reliance. Almost always complicity involves self-deception—the rationalization of actions (or inactions) we suspect to be unjust. Willful and repeated moral rationalization corrupts our ability to see and think clearly, and so habituates us to dishonesty that we come to mistake mental and moral slumber for mental and moral wakefulness.

Complicity, finally, is often a form of conformity: we fail to question prevailing political, social, and economic arrangements because we fear social ostracism. Insofar as complicity constitutes conformity, the aversion of complicity constitutes the aversion of conformity. And since the aversion of conformity defines self-reliance,[12] the aversion of complicity enacts self-reliance.

Emerson never wrote a sustained treatise on the relationship between self-reliance and complicity, but his antislavery writings and activities demonstrate his belief in their incompatibility. Throughout the antebellum era, Emerson struggled to live self-reliantly within a polity that sponsored slavery. His first love was his intellectual calling—his effort to think original thoughts all the way through. At the same time, the entrenchment of New World slavery made him wonder whether he could really be self-reliant—could do work that was truly his own—so long as he participated in a constitutional and economic order in which racial slavery played so crucial a role. Ultimately, Emerson concluded that he was bound by the strictures of his own doctrine to take action against slavery. Though he began giving antislavery speeches in the 1830s and 1840s, his antislavery activism climaxed in the 1850s, when he encouraged massive resistance to the Fugitive Slave Law and advocated compensated emancipation.[13] To be self-reliant, Emerson believed, individuals had to help secure freedom—the precondition of self-reliance—for all Americans.

The presence of a coherent ethics of citizenship within Emerson's antislavery writings challenges prevailing political philosophical interpretations of Emerson. Christopher Newfield sees Emerson as the consummate philosophical patron of democratic docility.[14] Judith Shklar thought Emerson's only valuable contribution to democracy was intellectual honesty and skepticism.[15] Kateb recognizes the significance of Emerson's antislavery activity, but characterizes it as a departure from rather than an enactment of self-reliance.[16] In addition to elaborating the ethics of citizenship implicit in Emerson's antislavery lectures and activism, I argue that Emerson understood these civic actions to be required by self-reliance. What emerges from my interpretation is a far more political Emerson than Newfield, Shklar, or Kateb allow. Emersonian self-reliance becomes a politically dynamic ethical ideal, one that can motivate and energize democratic political action. Insofar as citizens are interested in being self-reliant, Emerson's example can help us address the problem of civic motivation in the United States—for Emerson illustrates how moral self-examination, avoiding complicity, and political action are essential to self-reliance.

The Idea of Complicity

Emerson never explained the concept of complicity in a sustained philosophical way, but it hovers in the background of his work. While the idea appears in his public writings as early as 1841, he does not begin to use the word "complicity" frequently until the 1855 "Lecture on Slavery."[17] In that lecture, Emerson uses the word to refer to and condemn Massachusetts' compliance with the Fugitive Slave Law of 1850—a law whose morally horrific consequences had become vivid to Emerson when Boston officials arrested the fugitive slave Anthony Burns and returned him to his Virginia owner.[18] The Fugitive Slave Law, Emerson claims, brought slavery "home to New England, and made it impossible to avoid complicity."[19] Complicity is unavoidable since, as citizens of Massachusetts, Emerson and his neighbors authorize the commonwealth's actions, and the commonwealth now acts to return fugitive slaves.

In his 1860 essay "Fate," Emerson uses the word "complicity" in a startling manner. In a paragraph arguing that "Nature is no sentimentalist" and "the way of Providence is a little rude," Emerson writes, "You have just dined, and, however scrupulously the slaughter-house is concealed in the graceful distance of miles, there is complicity,—expensive races,—race living at the expense of race."[20] The statement refers literally to the human race's destruction of nonhuman races for consumption. Whenever we eat meat, we partake in the work of the slaughterhouse. But because the word "race" refers not only to different species of animals, but also to different "races" of humans, Emerson's characterization of "complicity" as "race living at the expense of race" also signifies humans living at each other's expense. "Fate" divides American humanity into seven "races": English, French, German, Irish, Jew, Indian, and Negro.[21] Emerson documents how some of these races live at others' expense: "The German and Irish millions, like the Negro, have a great deal of guano in their destiny. They are ferried over the Atlantic, and carted over America, to ditch and to drudge, to make corn cheap, and then to lie down prematurely to make a spot of green grass on the prairie."[22] Just as Americans partake in the slaughter of animals whenever they eat meat, Americans participate in the exploitation of German and Irish labor whenever they buy corn. German and Irish sweat and death nourish the native born.

Because Emerson sees "race" as "natural" and defines complicity as "race living at the expense of race," should we infer that he thinks some races are destined to serve the needs of others?[23] While Emerson initially invites this inference, he ultimately negates it. As Eduardo Cadava and Michael Magee have previously demonstrated, Emerson subverts the discourse of biological racism even as he employs it.[24] While Emerson sees race as a naturally constitutive fact of human being, an aspect of fate, a form of natural organization "tyrannizing over character,"[25] he also insists that "though Fate is immense, so is power, which is the other fact in the dual world, immense."[26] Emerson argues that "if we must accept Fate, we are not less compelled to affirm liberty, the significance of the individual . . . the power of character."[27] "To hazard the contradiction," Emerson continues, "freedom is necessary. . . . [A] part of Fate is the freedom of man."[28] Emerson's emphasis on individual power—independent of race—signals that he does not see "race living at the expense of race" as humanity's inevitable condition.

Emerson means to critique complicity as a social phenomenon, not resign us to it as a natural one. "Man the Reformer" (1841), a lecture read by Emerson nineteen years before the publication of "Fate," provides good evidence for this. Though "Man the Reformer" does not use the word "complicity," it gives a social account of "race living at the expense of race" whose substantive parallel with "Fate" is remarkable. One of the central concerns of "Man the Reformer" is the rule of trade over New England life and the interpenetration between the region's commerce and Atlantic slavery. The key passage is worth quoting at length:

> The ways of trade are grown selfish to the borders of theft, and supple to the borders (if not beyond the borders) of fraud. . . . We are all implicated, of course, in this charge; it is only necessary to ask a few questions as to the progress of the articles of commerce from the fields where they grew, to our houses, to become aware that we eat and drink and wear perjury and fraud in a hundred commodities. How many articles of daily consumption are furnished us from the West Indies; yet it is said, that, in the Spanish islands . . . no article passes into our ships which has not been fraudulently cheapened. . . . The abolitionist has shown us our dreadful debt to the southern negro. In the island of Cuba, in addition to the ordinary abominations of slavery, it appears, only men are bought for the plantations, and one dies in ten every year, of these miserable bachelors, to yield us sugar.[29]

We New Englanders participate in slavery every time we add sugar to our coffee.[30] Emerson arrives at this conclusion by analyzing his everyday transactions. Examining the sugar that sits on his breakfast table, he tracks its genealogy from the store where he bought it, to the wholesaler where his merchant procured it, to the plantations in the Spanish West Indies where African slaves produced it. Through commerce and consumption, New Englanders subsidize the Caribbean slave system.[31]

Emerson's account of the relationship between New England consumption and slave exploitation is an account precisely of "race living at the expense of race." It is fair to view it as an elaboration of his idea of complicity. "Fate" and "Man the Reformer" both suggest that the modern division of labor conceals the economic relationships that constitute complicity. While "Fate" insinuates this cryptically through the images of the dining table and slaughterhouse, "Man the Reformer" exposes in detail the subtle and unsubtle methods by which commerce and consumption create and cover over complicity.[32] At its worst, modern trade "is a system of selfishness . . . of distrust, of concealment, of superior keenness, not of giving but of taking advantage."[33] It peddles its goods by putting their origins "out of sight, only showing the brilliant result, and atoning for the manner of acquiring, by the manner of expending."[34] Emerson is careful not to spare himself from this accusation: "I do not charge the merchant or the manufacturer. The sins of our trade belong to no class, to no individual. One plucks, one distributes, one eats. Every body partakes, every body confesses . . . yet none feels himself accountable."[35] By dividing the tasks of plucking, distributing, and eating, modern trade disperses responsibility for the wrongs it creates. It not only cheapens the price of luxury items, but also allows consumers to enjoy them with a sense of innocence.[36]

Emerson fleshes out this line of analysis in "An Address . . . on . . . the Emancipation of the Negroes in the British West Indies" (1844). The analysis turns on his description of Anglo-American civility as "shopkeeping civility."[37] Shopkeeping civility transforms human relationships into commercial ones; humanity is divided into customers, suppliers, and laborers. When visualizing Emerson's image of the Anglo-American shopkeeper, envision the barriers that separate the "back of the store" from the "front of the store." Walls and counters conceal the middle passages of trade. Seldom does the customer see beyond the display area. Rarely does he view the receiving area where the supplier brings his wares. Hardly ever does the customer observe the supplier's route to market from the factories and plantations that produce the goods. Never does the customer see the conditions of production in their entirety. Even if the shopkeeper knows something about how his wares are made, he can keep the knowledge to himself and minimize its significance in his mind. As Emerson impersonates him in the "West Indian Emancipation Address":

> What if it cost a few unpleasant scenes on the coast of Africa? That was a great way off; and the scenes could be endured by some sturdy, unscrupulous fellows, who could go for high wages and bring us the men, and need not trouble our ears with the disagreeable particulars. If any mention was made of homicide, madness, adultery, and intolerable tortures, we would let the church-bells ring louder, the church organ swell its peal, and drown the hideous sound. The sugar they raised was excellent: nobody tasted blood in it. The coffee was fragrant; the tobacco was incense; the brandy made nations happy; the cotton clothed the world. What! all raised by these men, and no wages? Excellent! What a convenience! They seemed created by providence to bear the heat and the whipping, and make these fine articles.[38]

The division of labor shields consumers from the moral claims of producers. The sugar ought to taste of blood, Emerson insists, but a trick is played on our moral senses. The division of labor allows us to ask innocently, who are we but private persons getting our bread?[39] Yet through moral self-scrutiny, Emerson shows the public valence of our private consumption.

Self-Reliance and Complicity

Self-reliance and complicity are antagonistic because self-reliance requires that individuals not benefit from exploitation. Exploitation confers ill-gotten, unearned benefits;[40] receiving such benefits undermines self-reliance's moral foundations and violates self-reliance's requirement that the self's gains mirror the self's labors: the self-reliant individual "hates what he has, if he sees that it is accidental,—came to him by inheritance, gift, or crime; then he feels that it is not having; it does not belong to him, has no root in him."[41] Self-reliance and complicity are also antagonistic in the states of mind they each require: while the mental hallmark of self-reliance is moral and intellectual honesty, the mental hallmark of complicity is moral and intellectual evasion. Emerson never systematically argues that self-reliance and complicity are antagonistic, but we can infer their antagonism by closely examining his analysis of American slavery, which, as the ultimate form of "race living at the expense of race," instantiates complicity.

Because it precludes personal independence and disallows intellectual awakening, slaveholding is the antithesis of self-reliance. "A man who steals another man's labor," Emerson declared in his 1854 address "The Fugitive Slave Law," "steals away his own faculties. . . . The habit of oppression cuts out the moral eyes, and though the intellect goes on simulating the moral as before, its sanity is invaded, and gradually destroyed."[42] By stealing away his own faculties, the slaveholder diminishes himself; forgoing the self-realization that comes with work, he abandons the possibility of active self-reliance. The habit of oppression also requires him to engage in strenuous moral rationalization. Defenders of slavery must obscure the obvious—namely, the slave's humanity and moral equality with the slaveholder; they must dress iniquity in a cloak of respectability. If the process of moral rationalization does not work on others, it eventually plays a trick on the slaveholder himself: he becomes convinced of slavery's permissibility, even its positive goodness.[43] This transformation marks the degeneration of his intellect. Mental self-reliance becomes impossible, for mental self-reliance demands that one think in good faith, that one stand militantly against self-deception.

Slavery enervates not only the slaveholder, Emerson claims, but the entire society that sponsors it. What first drew Emerson to the antislavery cause, in fact, was the antagonism he saw between slavery and free inquiry.

The catalyzing events were the 1835 mob attack on the abolitionist speaker Harriet Martineau in Boston and the 1837 murder of the abolitionist publisher Elijah P. Lovejoy by an anti-abolitionist throng.[44] The triumph of mob rule over free speech told Emerson that "slavery is no scholar, no improver . . . it does not love the newspaper, the mailbag, a college, a book, or a preacher who has the absurd whim of saying what he thinks."[45] Congress's institution of a gag rule on antislavery petitions between 1837 and 1844 confirmed Emerson's sense that slavery undermined free exchange.[46] Slavery encourages bad faith—willful self-deception—in moral justification and public debate: "It is remarkable how rare in the history of tyrants is an immoral law. Some color, some indirection [is] always used."[47] Slavery's natural affinity is not with philosophy but with sophistry.

Slavery also signifies the eclipse of moral by material life. How this eclipse manifests itself on the southern plantation is obvious, but Emerson is just as critical of its occurrence in his native New England. Emerson mourns the fact that so many northern leaders let their eagerness to do business with the South silence whatever moral doubts they have about slavery: "The truth is, the Northerners . . . are old traders, and make it a rule rarely to shoot their customers, and never until the bill is paid. . . . [T]hough slaveholders are apt to have a bad temper, and vicious politics,—a strong desire to keep the peace . . . is felt not only by the financial authorities in State street and Wall street, but also by the cotton-spinners, the freighters, the shoe-dealers, the cabinet-makers, the printers, the booksellers, and by every description of Northern salesmen."[48] Slave traders, slaveholders, investors in slave-driven industry, and sellers of slave-produced wares all share blame for slavery's wrongs. While direct exploitation is the ultimate form of complicity, indirect exploitation is a lesser but still considerable form. All parties involved must stifle their conscience and deform their judgment to justify the way they make their living. In this manner, America's engagement in and accommodation of slavery portend badly for "American Scholarship"—Emerson's ideal for intellectually and morally wakeful American citizenship.[49]

True opposition to slavery, for Emerson, requires intellectual and moral wakefulness. Social reform begins with self-reform, and self-reform begins with critical self-awareness. Emerson scorns what he sees as the shallow kind of abolitionism that revels in morally self-satisfied finger-pointing.[50] Too many antislavery activists spend their time blaming slavery on someone else, somewhere else.[51] In Emerson's eyes, these activists aim not at social improvement, but rather at buttressing their moral self-images and cultivating their reputations.[52] Their moral condemnations are social poses; they fume against slavery to purge their sense of responsibility at a cheap and easy rate. If Emerson's portrait of New England reformers is accurate, then his account of complicity in "Man the Reformer" must have greatly discomforted his audience. While some may have been sincere, serious, and dedicated antislavery activists, most were probably passive opponents of slavery—signers of antislavery petitions or subscribers to the *Liberator*. Emerson characterizes symbolic support for abolition as surface gesture meant to assuage guilty feelings. Emerson raises the cost of noncomplicity from expressive opposition to abstention from all the conveniences of life produced by slave labor. In so doing, Emerson assaults his audience's sense of innocence.

"Man the Reformer" models the kind of thinking necessary to overcome complicity. Beyond exposing the interconnections between our daily habits and extreme injustice, "Man the Reformer" impersonates a self-interrogating, and thus potentially self-reforming, sensibility. Emersonian self-interrogation is not, in the first instance, a moral imperative; above all, it is an intellectual imperative, an extension of what Emerson sees as our primary human duty: to know the self and the world. New Englanders' failure to acknowledge their complicity in the North Atlantic slave economy constitutes not only a moral failure, but also an intellectual failure—a failure to understand ourselves truly, to comprehend the full extent of our relations to others. At the same time, this intellectual failure is tied into a still deeper moral one. "Man the Reformer" hints that we are not innocently ignorant of our complicity in slavery, but willfully ignorant. This willful ignorance manifests itself not so much in blatant lies we tell ourselves, but in our failure to ask certain questions. Emerson emphasizes that "it is only necessary to ask a few questions as to the progress of the articles of commerce . . . to become aware that we eat and drink and wear perjury and fraud in a hundred commodities." This failure is not innocent, but evasive. Moral evasiveness diminishes us as moral agents. In an impersonation of innocence, Emerson asks rhetorically, "What is he? an obscure private person who must get his bread." He then replies caustically, "That is the vice,—that no one feels himself called to act for man, but only as a fraction of man."[53] Emerson's declaration that we act as "fractions of man" echoes the notorious "three-fifths clause" of the United States Constitution, subtly suggesting that we are the slaves.[54] Refusal to confront the interconnections between private consumption and public morality indicates our slavery to material desire, as well as to the ignorance that preserves our innocence.

Self-reliance, however, requires us to overcome our desire for cheap and easy innocence; it also requires us to overcome complicity itself. If the aim of mental self-reliance is, as Kateb argues, to "see and know, observe and trace the intricacy and complexity of the world,"[55] then the individual must be willing to confront candidly his place within that intricacy and complexity. Such confrontation may impart to him the uncomfortable knowledge of complicity in wrongdoing. Mental self-reliance nevertheless demands acquisition of this knowledge. Active self-reliance then requires that one eradicate, or at least reduce, one's complicity in injustice.[56] One cannot realize oneself, become one's own author, do one's own work, while exploiting others: exploitation indebts exploiter to exploited, compromising the exploiter's autonomy. Emerson suggests this in "Compensation" (1841) when he writes, "If you put a chain around the neck of a slave, the other end fastens itself around your own."[57] Thoreau reiterates the point in "Resistance to Civil Government" (1849). Arguing that "it is not a man's duty, as a matter of course, to devote himself to the eradication of any, even the most enormous wrong," he then stipulates, "but it is his duty, at least, to wash his hands of it, and if he gives it no thought longer, not to give it practically his support. If I devote myself to other pursuits and contemplations, I must first see, at least, that I do not pursue them sitting upon another man's shoulders. I must get off him first, that he may pursue his contemplations too."[58] While the self-reliant individual may ignore injustice in which he is no way concerned, he may not ignore injustice in which he somehow participates. One cannot be free and independent while living at the expense of others' freedom and independence. Help from others is inevitably necessary, but we liquidate our debts through reciprocity. Reciprocity transforms relations of temporary dependence into relations of mutually consensual interdependence: what one gives to others offsets what one receives from them.[59] Yet because exploitation violates reciprocity, it diminishes self-authorship. When injustice forms a significant part of the self-reliant individual's web of interdependencies, he must counteract it to maintain his self-reliance.

Action and Citizenship

What provision does Emerson make for the eradication of complicity through action? In "Man the Reformer," Emerson seems to be of two minds. Near the end, he calls on New Englanders to undo their complicity by renouncing slavery's fruits: "If the accumulated wealth of past generations is thus tainted,—no matter how much of it is offered to us,—we must begin to consider if it were not the nobler part to renounce it, and to put ourselves into primary relations with the soil and nature, and abstaining from whatever is dishonest and unclean, to take each of us bravely his part, with his own hands, in the manual labor of the world."[60] By rejecting modern commerce and "getting our living" through primary relations with the soil, we free ourselves of complicity, as well as from the violence wrought on human nature by the division of labor. Through the work of our hands, we achieve a more admirable sufficiency, a "self-sufficiency," wherein we earn "by use a right to [our] arms and feet."[61] This is Thoreau's strategy in *Walden*. Thoreau characterizes his sojourn to Walden as a quest to found a "true America," one where "you are at liberty to pursue such a mode of life as may enable you to do without . . . tea, and coffee, and meat . . . and where the state does not endeavor to compel you to sustain the slavery and war and other superfluous expenses which directly or indirectly result from the use of such things."[62] He adds, "I am convinced, that if all men were to live as simply as I . . . did, thieving and robbery would be unknown. These take place only in communities where some have got more than is sufficient while others have not enough."[63]

Yet Emerson did not follow Thoreau. He understood that there was no going back on commercial society and that modern trade interconnects societies, making the world interdependent.[64] At the very end of "Man the Reformer," Emerson withdraws his call to give up the conveniences of modern life:

> I do not wish to push my criticism on the state of things around me to that extravagant mark, that shall compel me to suicide, or to an absolute isolation from the advantages of civil society. If we suddenly plant our foot, and say,—I will neither eat nor drink nor wear nor touch any food or fabric which I do not know to be innocent, or deal with any person whose whole manner of life is not clear and rational, we shall stand still. Whose is so? Not mine; not thine;

not his. But I think we must clear ourselves each one by the interrogation whether we have earned our bread to-day by the hearty contribution of our energies to the common benefit? and we must not cease to *tend* to the correction of these flagrant wrongs, by laying one stone aright every day.[65]

At first it seems that Emerson abandons the possibility of recovered innocence. This is remarkable given the profound emphasis in his work on self-absolution.[66] Emerson, however, goes on to articulate a modest mode of recovering innocence: examination of oneself for complicity, followed by an honest attempt to reduce it, if not eliminate it. Emerson's articulated method in the passage for reducing complicity, however, does not rise above clichés: he calls on readers to contribute to "the common benefit . . . by laying one stone aright every day." Emerson's ethics of moral and political action seem unelaborated. But this is the case only if we focus exclusively on the canonical essays and lectures. If we give the antislavery lectures of the 1840s and 1850s their due,[67] Emerson's ethics of action come into visible relief.

How we read the antislavery lectures in relation to Emerson's main corpus is controversial; Emerson seemed to value his purely philosophical pursuits far more than his antislavery activities. In a letter to Thomas Carlyle written shortly after he gave a major antislavery address in 1844, Emerson said, "though I sometimes accept a popular call, & preach on . . . the Abolition of slavery, as lately on the First of August, I am sure to feel before I have done with it, what an intrusion it is into another sphere & so much loss of virtue in my own."[68] Partly for this reason, Kateb views Emerson's involvement in antislavery politics as an episodic abandonment rather than a self-conscious enactment of self-reliance.[69] Emerson's antislavery speeches "urge solidarity—indeed mobilization"—which Kateb sees as incompatible with self-reliance.[70] Kateb, however, goes too far in insulating Emerson's practice of self-reliance from the vagaries of democratic politics. A careful reading of Emerson's antislavery lectures shows that he saw antislavery protest as essential to his pursuit of self-reliance.[71]

Although Emerson delivered one antislavery address during the 1830s and four during the 1840s,[72] he did not find his voice as an antislavery advocate until 1851. Congress's passage of the Fugitive Slave Law as part of the Compromise of 1850 horrified Emerson, and only then did he begin to apply the full force of his eloquence and intellect to the fight against slavery. Outraged that he and his neighbors were now required to assist in the capture of fugitive slaves, he accepted an invitation from his fellow citizens in Concord to share his thoughts on the Fugitive Slave Law. Emerson's first speech on the subject—"An Address to the Citizens of Concord" (1851)—was such a success that he was invited to repeat the speech nine times to help elect the Free-Soiler John Gorham Palfrey to Congress.[73] Palfrey fell short of victory, but in 1854, Emerson took up the Fugitive Slave Law again in an address before New York City's Tabernacle.

Both of Emerson's speeches on the Fugitive Slave Law begin with a statement of reluctance to speak to political questions. In the 1854 address, he stipulated: "I do not often speak to public questions. They are odious and hurtful and it seems like meddling or leaving your work."[74] Emerson moves quickly, however, to a discussion of the ethical implications of recent political events. With the passage of the Fugitive Slave Law, he said in the 1851 address, "the value of life is reduced. Just now a friend came into my house and said, 'If this law shall be repealed, I shall be glad that I have lived; if not, I shall be sorry that I was born.'"[75] Laying bare his exasperation, Emerson underscores the crime of capturing "in our own state, on our own farms, a man who has taken the risk of being shot, or burned alive, or cast into the sea, or starved to death, or suffocated in a wooden box, to get away from his driver; and this man who has run the gauntlet of a thousand miles for his freedom, the statute says, you men of Massachusetts shall hunt, and catch, and send back again to the dog-hutch he fled from."[76] The Fugitive Slave Law's grim realities drove home to Emerson that "it is not possible to extricate oneself from the questions in which your age is involved."[77]

The Fugitive Slave Law also gave Emerson the occasion to elaborate his idea of complicity. In the first address, he said, "I have lived all my life in this State, and never had any experience of personal inconvenience from the laws, until now."[78] While at first it seems that Emerson is taking back his claim in "Man the Reformer" that the ways of trade implicate him in slavery on a daily basis, the passage's key phrase is "from the laws": Emerson focuses on political complicity. His suggestion that he had not been politically complicit in slavery before 1850 demands explanation. A weaker version of the Fugitive Slave Law had been on the books since 1793, and the Constitution from its inception had been a pact among the states to aid each other in the case of domestic insurrection, especially slave insurrection. As a citizen of Massachusetts, Emerson had always been party to a pact to protect slavery. Why did Emerson not feel political complicity before?

Part of the answer resides in the fact that—for most citizens in antebellum America—the state was the primary object of political allegiance.[79] The priority of state over national loyalty mitigated northerners' feelings of complicity, especially when their states refrained from active enforcement of slavery. Massachusetts, furthermore, had legislatively prohibited state officials from helping in the recapture of fugitive slaves.[80] Emerson's own statements indicate that he felt this prohibition cleared him and his fellow citizens of political complicity: "There was a fugitive law, but it had become, or was fast becoming, a dead letter; and, by the genius and laws of Massachusetts inoperative."[81] The new Fugitive Slave Law, however, "made it operative; required me to hunt slaves; and it found citizens in Massachusetts willing to act as judge and captors."[82] Political complicity was now undeniable. Moreover, it reminded Emerson and his neighbors of the less distinct forms of complicity they had been guilty of for years.

"What shall we do?" Emerson asks.[83] Echoing Thoreau's "Resistance,"[84] Emerson says, "First, abrogate this law; then proceed to confine slavery to slave states, and help them effectually to make an end of it."[85] Emerson calls for statewide defiance of the Fugitive Slave Law, mass opposition to slavery's expansion in the West, and wholesale abolition in South. "An immoral law makes it a man's duty to break," he insists. "If our resistance to this law is not right, there is no right."[86] In calling for massive resistance to the Fugitive Slave Law, Emerson takes a step toward mobilization. He gives no indication that he thinks this inconsistent with self-reliance. He believes, in fact, that aggregate civil disobedience will enhance the character of citizens, educate them in the moral meaning of democratic individuality, and habituate them to future acts of resistance. Because self-reliance is naturally allied with the idea that laws derive their authority from the consent of the governed, withholding consent instantiates self-reliance. When citizens exercise "original jurisdiction"[87] and evaluate whether positive law is worthy of their allegiance and obedience, they must rely on their own moral judgment; they must practice "self-trust."[88] Political agitation over the Fugitive Slave Law advances the moral education of the citizenry: "It has been like a university to the entire people. It has turned every dinner-table into a debating club, and made every citizen a student of natural law."[89]

Kateb might agree that all of this is consistent with self-reliance, but then argue that Emerson's encouragement of civil disobedience is not really a promotion of politics: civil disobedience is *negative* action, but politics—in its fullest sense—is *positive* action.[90] Yet Emerson's answer to the question, "What shall we do?" contains an unmistakably positive political element: his call to northerners to help southerners "effectually to make an end" of slavery.

Emerson's specific call is for compensated emancipation. In the 1851 address, Emerson asks: "Shall we call a new convention, or will any expert statesman furnish us a plan for the summary or gradual winding up of slavery, so far as the Republic is its patron? . . . Let us hear any project with candor and respect."[91] Several sentences later, Emerson indicates that a plan for compensated emancipation would win not just his endorsement, but also his labor on its behalf: "It is said, it will cost a thousand millions of dollars to buy the slaves,—which sounds like a fabulous price. But if a price were named in good faith,—with the other elements of a practicable treaty in readiness, and with the convictions of mankind on this mischief once well awake and conspiring, I do not think any amount that figures could tell, founded on an estimate, would be quite unmanageable. Every man in the world might give a week's work to sweep this mountain of calamities out of the earth."[92] Here is not only a positive political proposal, but a suggestion by Emerson of his willingness to give a week's work to help bring it into effect.[93] Notice also that he considers such an effort consistent with the mind-set of self-reliance: being "well awake." Emerson broached the idea of compensated emancipation again in his 1855 "Lecture on Slavery":

> Why in the name of common sense and the peace of mankind is not [the abolition of slavery] made the subject of instant negotiation and settlement? Why do not the men of administrative ability . . . join their heads and hearts to form some basis of negotiation to settle this dangerous dispute on some ground of fair compensation, on one side, and of satisfaction, on the other, to the conscience of the Free States. . . . It is really the great task fit for this country to accomplish, to buy that property of the planters, as the British nation bought the West Indian slaves. I say *buy*—never conceding the right of the planter to own, but that we may acknowledge the calamity of his position, and bear a countryman's share in relieving him, and because it is the only practicable course, and is innocent.[94]

Emerson is mistaken, of course, to say that compensated emancipation is innocent. Compensated emancipation dignifies the slaveholder's claim that slaves are legitimate property; furthermore, it showers wealth upon those who have been unjustly enriched, while not at all compensating those whose labor has been stolen.

After the Civil War began and hope for a bloodless revolution faded, Emerson repudiated his previous support for compensated emancipation. He even suggested that if compensation was due to anyone, it was due to the slaves. Emerson declared in "Boston Hymn," his 1863 poem commemorating the Emancipation Proclamation:

> Pay ransom to the owner
> And fill the bag to the brim.
> Who is the owner? The slave is owner
> And ever was. Pay him.[95]

Yet Emerson's prior support for compensated emancipation is still significant—for it shows that given the choice between war and compensated emancipation, Emerson would have chosen the latter.[96] Emerson supports group political action for compelling moral ends. Imagining a mass movement for compensated emancipation, he reflects, "It is so delicious to act with great masses to great aims."[97]

Emerson's quest for compensated emancipation proceeded from his quest for awakening; it did not violate self-reliance but enacted it. By comparing compensated emancipation to Britain's 1834 abolition of slavery in the West Indies, he suggested that compensated emancipation would strengthen the self-reliance of white citizens. Emerson saw West Indian Emancipation as "a moral revolution . . . achieved by plain means of plain men";[98] he characterized it as essentially "the repentance of the tyrant . . . the masters revolting from their mastery."[99] Though this interpretation may be historically naïve, it indicates that Emerson viewed compensated emancipation as an opportunity for white Americans to achieve self-mastery by giving up mastery over others. Relinquishing the desire to master others is essential to self-reliance: one must do one's own work while letting others do theirs.

Emerson's promotion of compensated emancipation was morally impure. Compensated emancipation legally recognized slaveholders' property interest in human beings; verbal disclaimer could not change this. But when we examine Emerson's social and political context and break down the options before him—the perpetuation of slavery, compensated emancipation in all its impurity, a war of liberation that would most likely result in the slaughter of the innocent as well as the guilty—we must conclude that the pursuit of liberty for all required moral impurity. In the face of slavery, and with the possibility of compensated emancipation before him, Emerson opted to act impurely rather than not act at all. His ethics of self-reliance entails a politics of self-reliance that allows for moral compromise. This is not to authorize any and all means of pursuing liberal democratic ideals. Prudence is mandatory, the obligation to uphold the life and basic rights of all remains unconditional,[100] and the doctrine of the lesser evil must reign. But the pursuit of noncomplicity required by self-reliance sometimes requires moral compromise. Such compromise has its own democratic quality. By forestalling the pursuit of the perfect city—to borrow a metaphor from Shklar—we pay respect to the imperfect one:[101] we pay respect, that is, to those we perceive as morally flawed.

Self-Reliance and Justice

Innocence is an aspiration we try to approximate, not an end state we ever permanently reach. If self-reliance required moral perfection, it would be an unlivable ethical ideal. Living in a fallen world sometimes requires us to choose the lesser of two wrongs.[102] Emerson did not counsel retreat in the face of such choices; he counseled action, and acted himself when he faced them. "Character is higher than intellect," Emerson wrote in "The American Scholar" (1837): "Thinking is the function. Living is the functionary.... A great soul will be strong to live, as well as strong to think."[103] Thinking and acting together compose character.[104] Because Emersonian self-reliance aims at the achievement of character, of a life in which thinking and acting enhance each other, moral compromise must be part of that life. The world we inherit is not innocent; we are born into complicity and remain complicit as we reach maturity. Inaction in the face of injustice is often worse than corrective measures that go only partway. Moral improvement requires us to temper our desire for moral perfection.

Emerson's ethics of citizenship is a promising model for meeting the contemporary challenge of civic disengagement. Civic republicans complain that American individualism has led to social injustice and the deterioration of the public sphere; they encourage citizens to view the quest for self-reliance as morally indefensible and politically self-defeating.[105] But Emerson demonstrates that the quest for self-reliance creates an impetus for moral and civic engagement. Because self-reliance requires its adherents to overcome complicity, it encourages action on justice's behalf. Insofar as the reduction of complicity requires the transformation of political and social structures, self-reliance demands political participation. An egoistic motive produces an altruistic outcome: the desire to be self-reliant engenders social concern and civic engagement. Would-be self-reliant citizens have good reason to give significant time and energy to the cause of justice—for only then can they truthfully credit themselves with self-reliance.[106]

Notes

An earlier version of this essay was published as Jack Turner, "Emerson, Slavery, and Citizenship," *Raritan* 28, no. 2 (2008): 127–46. Copyright 2008 by *Raritan*. Reprinted by permission. Since this essay's original publication, a new book has appeared that develops an account of Emerson's ethics of citizenship similar to mine: Alex Zakaras, *Individuality and Mass Democracy: Mill, Emerson, and the Burdens of Citizenship* (Oxford: Oxford University Press, 2009), esp. chaps. 6 and 10. The strength of Zakaras's account is its analytical detail. We have some differences in emphasis: I foreground the question of civic motivation more prominently, analyze Emerson's language of complicity more closely, and address the problem of moral compromise more directly. I have revised this essay with the benefit of hindsight and in light of new scholarship. Thanks to K. Anthony Appiah, Lawrie Balfour, Eric Beerbohm, Jillian Cutler, Patrick Deneen, Thomas Dumm, Eddie Glaude, George Kateb, Sharon Krause, Melissa Lane, Christopher Lebron, Isis Leslie, John Lowe, Stephen Macedo, Shannon Mariotti, Susan McWilliams, Sankar Muthu, Jennifer Pitts, Melvin Rogers, Amy Shuster, Cornel West, and Alex Zakaras for help, encouragement, and advice. Thanks especially to Eduardo Cadava for his inspired teaching and writing on complicity in Emerson. Thanks also to Alan Levine and Daniel Malachuk for inviting me to contribute to this volume and for incisive suggestions for revision.

1. Wilson Carey McWilliams, *The Idea of Fraternity in America* (Berkeley and Los Angeles: University of California Press, 1973), 286–87.
2. Stanley Cavell, "Finding as Founding: Taking Steps in Emerson's Experi-

ence," in *Emerson's Transcendental Etudes*, ed. David Justin Hodge (Stanford: Stanford University Press, 2003), 122.

3. Stanley Cavell, "Thinking of Emerson," in *Emerson's Transcendental Etudes*, 14. Cf. Stanley Cavell, *Cities of Words: Pedagogical Letters on a Register of the Moral Life* (Cambridge: Belknap Press of Harvard University Press, 2004), 139; and Hans von Rautenfeld, "Thinking for Thousands: Emerson's Theory of Political Representation in the Public Sphere," *American Journal of Political Science* 49, no. 1 (2005): 184.

4. George Kateb, *Emerson and Self-Reliance* (1995; new ed., Lanham, Md.: Rowman and Littlefield, 2002), 31, 26, 171.

5. The exceptions are Eduardo Cadava, *Emerson and the Climates of History* (Stanford: Stanford University Press, 1997), esp. 59–62; Cadava, "The Guano of History," in *Cities without Citizens*, ed. Cadava and Aaron Levy (Philadelphia: Slought Books, 2004), 137–65; and, most recently, Alex Zakaras, *Individuality and Mass Democracy: Mill, Emerson, and the Burdens of Citizenship* (Oxford: Oxford University Press, 2009), esp. 91–100.

6. Zakaras has an excellent analysis of how civic inaction in democracy often constitutes culpable negligence (*Individuality and Mass Democracy*, 92, 201–10).

7. See Emerson, "Self-Reliance," in *Essays: First Series* (1841), in *Emerson: Essays and Lectures*, ed. Joel Porte (New York: Library of America, 1983), 268, 272 (hereafter cited as *E&L*), where Emerson says that the proper moral orientation of individuals toward each other is "mutual reverence" and mutual awe. Cf. Emerson, "The American Scholar" (1837), in *E&L*, 70: "Every thing that tends to insulate the individual,—to surround him with barriers of natural respect, so that each man shall feel the world his, and man shall treat with man as a sovereign state with a sovereign state;—tends to true union as well as greatness." The words of George Kateb well capture the moral egalitarian spirit of self-reliance: "What one claims for oneself one must concede to the rest: to talk of rights at all is to talk of the same rights for all" ("Democratic Individuality and the Meaning of Rights," in *Liberalism and the Moral Life*, ed. Nancy Rosenblum [Cambridge: Harvard University Press, 1989], 188). See also Zakaras, *Individuality and Mass Democracy*, 99; and Len Gougeon, "Emerson, Self-Reliance, and the Politics of Democracy," in this volume.

8. For Emerson's fallibilism, see "Experience," in *Essays: Second Series* (1844), in *E&L*, 469–92; for his sense of individual infinitude, see "The American Scholar," 55, 57, 66, 71. Cf. George Kateb, "The Idea of Individual Infinitude," *Hedgehog Review* 7, no. 2: 42–54.

9. Emerson, "Self-Reliance," 259; Emerson, "Experience," 475.

10. Emerson, "Experience," 475; cf. 476.

11. Emerson, "Self-Reliance," 281.

12. Ibid., 261.

13. Emerson ultimately changed his mind and opposed compensated emancipation. I discuss this reversal later on. For general accounts of Emerson's antislavery activism, see *Emerson's Antislavery Writings*, ed. Len Gougeon and Joel Myerson (New Haven: Yale University Press, 1995), hereafter cited as *AW*; Len Gougeon, *Virtue's Hero: Emerson, Antislavery, and Reform* (Athens: University of Georgia Press, 1990); Albert J. Von Frank, *The Trial of Anthony Burns: Freedom and Slavery in Emerson's Boston* (Cambridge: Harvard University Press, 1998); Gary Collison, "Emerson and Antislavery," in *A Historical Guide to Ralph Waldo Emerson*, ed. Joel Myerson (New York: Oxford University Press, 2000), 179–209; and Peter S. Field, *Ralph Waldo Emerson: The Making of a Democratic Intellectual* (Lanham, Md.: Rowman and Littlefield, 2002), chap. 6.

14. Christopher Newfield, *The Emerson Effect: Individualism and Submission in America* (Chicago: University of Chicago Press, 1996).

15. Judith Shklar, "Emerson and the Inhibitions of Democracy" (1998), in this volume; Shklar, "Can We Be American Scholars?" in *Liberal Modernism and Democratic Individuality: George Kateb and the Practices of Politics*, ed. Austin Sarat and Dana R. Villa (Princeton: Princeton University Press, 1996), 64–77.

16. Kateb, *Emerson and Self-Reliance*, chap. 6 (republished in this volume).

17. Emerson, "Lecture on Slavery" (1855), in *AW*, 92, 93, 99.

18. Von Frank, *Trial of Anthony Burns*; Gougeon, *Virtue's Hero*, 200–206; Collison, "Emerson and Antislavery," 200–201. This was not the first time that the return of a fugitive slave energized Emerson to speak out against slavery. Emerson's anger over the capture and return of Thomas Sims to slavery in April 1851 invigorated his "Address to the Citizens of Concord," delivered just weeks after Sims's rendition (Gougeon, *Virtue's Hero*, 155–66; Collison, "Emerson and Antislavery," 198–99; Robert D. Richardson Jr., *Emerson: The Mind on Fire* [Berkeley and Los Angeles: University of California Press, 1995], 496–98).

19. Emerson, "Lecture on Slavery," 92.

20. Emerson, "Fate," in *The Conduct of Life* (1860), in *E&L*, 945.

21. Ibid., 950. Cf. Philip L. Nicoloff, *Emerson on Race and History: An Examination of "English Traits"* (New York: Columbia University Press, 1961).

22. Emerson, "Fate," 950.

23. This was Emerson's view when he was a student at Harvard (Field, *Ralph Waldo Emerson*, 170–72). Chapter 6 of Field's book is the most judicious account of Emerson's evolving views on race I have encountered. Five other important accounts are Nicoloff, *Emerson on Race and History*; Lawrence Buell, *Emerson* (Cambridge: Harvard University Press, 2003), 245–49, 258–77; Cornel West, *The American Evasion of Philosophy: A Genealogy of Pragmatism* (Madison: University of Wisconsin Press, 1989), 21–35; Anita Haya Patterson, *From Emerson to*

King: Democracy, Race, and the Politics of Protest (Oxford: Oxford University Press, 1997), chap. 6; and Nell Irvin Painter, *The History of White People* (New York: Norton, 2010), chaps.10–12.

24. Cadava, *Emerson and the Climates of History*, chap. 3; Cadava, "The Guano of History"; Michael Magee *Emancipating Pragmatism: Emerson, Jazz, and Experimental Writing* (Tuscaloosa: University of Alabama Press, 2004), chap. 2.

25. Emerson, "Fate," 946.

26. Ibid., 953.

27. Ibid., 943.

28. Ibid., 953.

29. Emerson, "Man the Reformer" (1841), in *E&L*, 136–37.

30. This rhetorical trope was a staple of British abolitionism. During the 1790s, more than three hundred thousand Britons boycotted slave-grown sugar to protest Parliament's refusal to abolish slavery (Adam Hochschild, *Bury the Chains: Prophets and Rebels in the Fight to Free an Empire's Slaves* [Boston: Houghton Mifflin, 2005], 7, 192–96).

31. For three valuable considerations of the interconnections between the New England economy and slavery in both the American South and the West Indies, see Ronald Bailey, "The Slave(ry) Trade and the Development of Capitalism in the United States: The Textile Industry in New England," *Social Science History* 14, no. 3 (1990): 373–414; Ronald Bailey, "'Those Valuable People, the Africans': The Economic Impact of the Slave(ry) Trade on Textile Industrialization in New England," in *The Meaning of Slavery in the North*, ed. David Roediger and Martin H. Blatt (New York: Garland, 1998), 3–31; and Anne Farrow, Joel Lang, and Jenifer Frank, *Complicity: How the North Promoted, Prolonged, and Profited from Slavery* (New York: Ballantine, 2005). For antebellum Bostonians' understandings of these interconnections, see Gougeon, *Virtue's Hero*, 42–43. For Emerson's evolving appreciation of the porous boundaries between local, national, and international affairs, see Magee, *Emancipating Pragmatism*, 70–76.

32. At the same time, Emerson thought that market capitalism was more good than bad, was—on balance—more conducive to freedom than any other economic system (see Neal Dolan, *Emerson's Liberalism* [Madison: University of Wisconsin Press, 2009], 111–20; and Neal Dolan, "Property in Being: Liberalism and the Language of Ownership in Emerson's Writing," in this volume).

33. Emerson, "Man the Reformer," 137–38.

34. Ibid., 138.

35. Ibid.

36. There is also a subversive quality to Emerson's mention that only bachelors are brought to Cuba to work the sugar plantations. Beyond calling to mind

images of a life deprived of the comforts of family (which are always vitiated under a chattel slave system), Emerson plants the thought that Cuba's slave population is not self-replenishing. When slaves die, as they do rapidly on sugar plantations, they can be replaced only by the importation of more slaves. Sugar consumption therefore supports not only the slave plantation, but also the very transatlantic slave trade that America thought it had left behind in 1808.

37. Emerson, "An Address . . . on . . . the Emancipation of the Negroes in the British West Indies" (1844), in *AW*, 20.

38. Ibid.

39. Emerson, "Man the Reformer," 138.

40. Exploitation is indirect robbery. According to Tommie Shelby: "X exploits Y only if: (a) Y is forced to make a sacrifice which results in a benefit for X and (b) X obtains this benefit by means of an advantage in power that X has over Y." This is structurally the same as robbery: when Y holds up X at gunpoint, and Y surrenders his wallet to X, Y is forced to make a sacrifice (his wallet) which results in a benefit for X, and X obtains this benefit by means of an advantage in power (the gun) that X has over Y. ("Parasites, Pimps, and Capitalists: A Naturalistic Conception of Exploitation," *Social Theory and Practice* 28, no. 3 [2002]: 393).

41. Emerson, "Self-Reliance," 281.

42. Emerson, "The Fugitive Slave Law" (1854), in *AW*, 84–85. Cf. Emerson, "Emancipation of the Negroes in the British West Indies," 21.

43. See, for example, John C. Calhoun, "Speech on the Reception of Abolition Petitions" (1837), in *Union and Liberty: The Political Philosophy of John C. Calhoun*, ed. Ross M. Lence (Indianapolis: Liberty Fund, 1992), 461–76.

44. Field, *Ralph Waldo Emerson*, 176–177; Gougeon, *Virtue's Hero*, 37–38; Richardson, *Mind on Fire*, 269.

45. Emerson, "Emancipation of the Negroes in the British West Indies," 21.

46. "Gag Rule," in *The Reader's Companion to American History*, ed. Eric Foner and John A. Garraty (Boston: Houghton Mifflin, 1991), 436–37.

47. Emerson, "Address to the Citizens of Concord" (1851), 57.

48. Emerson, "Antislavery Speech at Dedham" (1846), in *AW*, 42. Cf. Gougeon, *Virtue's Hero*, 187, 233, 310; Thoreau, "Resistance to Civil Government" (1849), in *The Higher Law: Thoreau on Civil Disobedience and Reform*, ed. Wendell Glick (Princeton: Princeton University Press, 2004), 68.

49. Emerson, "American Scholar," 51–71.

50. For Emerson's critique of reform movements—including but not limited to abolitionism—see "New England Reformers," in *Essays: Second Series* (1844), 591–609.

51. For an important analysis of the American tendency to locate wrongdo-

ing—especially racism—"somewhere else," see Lawrie Balfour, *The Evidence of Things Not Said: James Baldwin and the Promise of American Democracy* (Ithaca: Cornell University Press, 2001), chap. 4.

52. Cf. Emerson's famous passage in "Self-Reliance" in which he renounces his "obligation to put all poor men in good situations" with the shocking rejoinder, "Are they *my* poor?" (Emerson, "Self-Reliance," 262–63).

53. Emerson, "Man the Reformer," 138.

54. Emerson discusses the three-fifths clause explicitly in his "Lecture on Slavery," 99.

55. Kateb, *Emerson and Self-Reliance*, 28.

56. Insofar as both mental and active self-reliance are *aspirations* that can be approximated but never fully realized, the eradication of complicity is also an ideal to which self-reliant people aspire, even though the reduction of complicity is all that is achievable.

57. Emerson, "Compensation," in *Essays: First Series* (1841), 293. For a fascinating analysis of Emerson's doctrine of compensation, see Dolan, *Emerson's Liberalism*, 133–36.

58. Thoreau, "Resistance," 71.

59. Thoreau reflects in *Walden*, "It is difficult to begin without borrowing." The occasion for this reflection was his discovery that to start building his solitary abode on Walden Pond, he needed an ax. After borrowing an ax from his neighbor, thereby indebting himself, Thoreau liquidated the debt through an act of reciprocity. Referring to the ax, he noted, "I returned it sharper than I received it" (*Walden*, ed. J. Lyndon Shanley [Princeton: Princeton University Press, 2004], 40–41). Thanks to Thomas Dumm for pointing out the relevance of this passage to my argument.

60. Emerson, "Man the Reformer," 139.

61. Ibid., 140.

62. Thoreau, *Walden*, 205.

63. Ibid., 172.

64. As did, ultimately, Thoreau (ibid., 115).

65. Emerson, "Man the Reformer," 145.

66. Emerson, "Self-Reliance," 261: "Absolve you to yourself, and you shall have the suffrage of the world."

67. Emerson's one antislavery lecture from the 1830s has not survived. For a fascinating attempt to reconstruct its content from Emerson's journals, see Field, *Ralph Waldo Emerson*, 177–79.

68. Emerson to Carlyle, December 31, 1844, in *The Correspondence of Emerson and Carlyle*, ed. Joseph Slater (New York: Columbia University Press, 1964), 373.

69. Kateb, *Emerson and Self-Reliance*, 177–78, 186–89.

70. Ibid., 177–78.

71. For Zakaras's critique of Kateb on this score, see *Individuality and Mass Democracy*, 211–20.

72. See "Emancipation of the Negroes in the British West Indies," "Anniversary of West Indian Emancipation" (1845), "Antislavery Speech at Dedham," and "Antislavery Remarks at Worcester" (1849), in *AW*, 7–33, 35–38, 41–44, 47–50; Gougeon, *Virtue's Hero*, chap. 4; Field, *Ralph Waldo Emerson*, 178–90; Collison, "Emerson and Antislavery," 187–94.

73. "To the Citizens of Concord," in *AW*, 212 n. 1.

74. Emerson, "Fugitive Slave Law," 73.

75. Emerson, "To the Citizens of Concord," 55.

76. Ibid., 58.

77. Emerson, "Fugitive Slave Law," 88.

78. Emerson, "To the Citizens of Concord," 53.

79. Merle Curti, *The Roots of American Loyalty* (New York: Columbia University Press, 1946), 21–22.

80. Gougeon, *Virtue's Hero*, 153. Cf. Collison, "Emerson and Antislavery," 194–95.

81. Emerson, "Fugitive Slave Law," 80.

82. Ibid.

83. Emerson, "To the Citizens of Concord," 68.

84. Thoreau, "Resistance to Civil Government," 63–90.

85. Emerson, "To the Citizens of Concord," 68–69.

86. Ibid., 57. Cf. Lincoln's similar declaration that "if slavery is not wrong, nothing is wrong" (Lincoln to Albert G. Hodges, April 4, 1864, in *Lincoln: Speeches and Writings, 1859–1865*, ed. Don E. Fehrenbacher [New York: Library of America, 1989], 585).

87. Emerson, "To the Citizens of Concord," 56; "Fugitive Slave Law," 82.

88. Emerson, "American Scholar," 63.

89. Emerson, "To the Citizens of Concord," 64.

90. For his thesis that negative forms of politics—such as civil disobedience—are much more closely allied with the Emersonian tradition of democratic individuality than positive forms, see Kateb, *The Inner Ocean: Individualism: Individualism and Democratic Culture* (Ithaca: Cornell University Press, 1992), 30, 103.

91. Emerson, "To the Citizens of Concord," 69.

92. Ibid. In his journal, Emerson estimates the cost at $2 billion (*The Journals and Miscellaneous Notebooks of Ralph Waldo Emerson*, vol. 14, ed. Susan Sutton Smith and Harrison Hayford [Cambridge: Belknap Press of Harvard University Press, 1978], 400).

93. Emerson, of course, was hardly the first to advocate compensated emancipation. In 1790, Congressman Elbridge Gerry of Massachusetts proposed selling federal land to pay slaveholders to manumit their slaves. James Madison revived Gerry's proposal in 1819. In the 1850s, the radical abolitionist Gerrit Smith argued for the British model of compensated emancipation. During the Civil War, Lincoln encouraged the slave states still loyal to the Union to abolish slavery under a compensated emancipation program; Congress's abolition of slavery in the District of Columbia in 1862 also contained a compensation provision (Betty L. Fladeland, "Compensated Emancipation: A Rejected Alternative," *Journal of Southern History* 42, no. 2 [1976]: 169–86; John Hope Franklin and Alfred A. Moss Jr., *From Slavery to Freedom: A History of African Americans*, 7th ed. [New York: Knopf, 1994], 205–9).

94. Emerson, "Lecture on Slavery," 105–6.

95. Emerson, "Boston Hymn" (1863), in *Selected Writings of Emerson*, ed. Donald McQuade (New York: Modern Library, 1981), 895. For a beautiful reading of "Boston Hymn" as Emerson's repudiation of his prior support for compensated emancipation, see Cadava, *Emerson and the Climates of History*, 152–83.

96. That Emerson eventually recanted his support of compensated emancipation and hinted at support for slave reparations might be seen as making his previous advocacy of compensated emancipation insignificant. This would be a mistake. Emerson only recanted his support of compensated emancipation after the Civil War broke out and Lincoln effected emancipation by other means. Emerson's support for compensated emancipation hinged on its being the one course of action that would both effect emancipation and avoid war. Yet after war's outbreak and Lincoln's proclamation, the question of compensated emancipation became moot, freeing Emerson up to recant.

97. Emerson, "Lecture on Slavery," 105.

98. Emerson, "Emancipation of the Negroes in the British West Indies," 26.

99. Ibid.

100. See Jeffrey Stout, *Democracy and Tradition* (Princeton: Princeton University Press, 2004), chap. 8, for a sensitive discussion of unconditional obligations in democratic ethics and how to weigh them in cases of moral conflict.

101. Shklar, "Emerson and the Inhibitions of Democracy," 61.

102. See Michael Walzer, "Political Action: The Problem of Dirty Hands," *Philosophy & Public Affairs* 2, no. 2 (1973): 160–80.

103. Emerson, "American Scholar," 62. Cf. 60. Thanks again to Thomas Dumm for suggesting the importance of this passage for my argument.

104. See Thomas Augst, "Composing the Moral Senses: Emerson and the Politics of Character in Nineteenth-Century America," *Political Theory* 27, no. 1

(1999): 85–120; and Field, *Ralph Waldo Emerson*, 194: "For Emerson . . . ideas had to find validation in daily existence." Cf. Thoreau, *Walden*, 14–15.

105. See, for example, Michael Sandel, *Democracy's Discontent: America in Search of a Public Philosophy* (Cambridge: Belknap Press of Harvard University Press, 1996).

106. For a view more skeptical of the consistency between Emerson's philosophy of self-reliance and his antislavery activism, see James H. Read, "The Limits of Self-Reliance: Emerson, Slavery, and Abolition," in this volume.

CHAPTER 6

The Limits of Self-Reliance: Emerson, Slavery, and Abolition

James H. Read

"SELF-RELIANCE" IS CENTRAL to the philosophy of Ralph Waldo Emerson, his most famous and attractive idea. Emerson challenges the individual to "set at naught books and traditions," to "be a nonconformist," to recognize that ideas, books, religions, institutions, and occupations acquire life and value only when an individual enlivens them with his or her own experience and effort. "Though the wide universe is full of good, no kernel of nourishing corn can come to him but through his toil bestowed on that plot of ground which is given to him to till. The power which resides in him is new in nature, and none but he knows what that is which he can do, nor does he know until he has tried."[1]

From the beginning there have been critics who saw in Emerson's self-reliance a kind of "radical egoistic anarchism" that "vaporized the social world," pitting the individual against the community and its traditions and laws.[2] But Emerson never claimed that a self-reliant individual possessed unlimited freedom, or that self-reliance was inconsistent with fulfilling one's duties to others. The self-reliant human being recognizes his or her own limitations—must "take himself, for better or worse, as his portion"—but grasps that traditions, institutions, and received opinions are at least equally limited and imperfect. Self-reliant individuals recognize the call of justice and the obligation to fulfill duties toward others, but do so "in a new and unprecedented way": not after the customs of others, but as their own inward perception of truth prescribes.[3]

As many scholars have noted, there is an affinity between Emerson's idea of self-reliance and the conditions of a democratic society. Emerson clearly assumes a society of free, equal, and mobile individuals when, at the expense of the "city dolls" of Boston or New York who are lost if no one hands them a plum position, he praises the "sturdy lad from New Hampshire or Vermont, who in turn tries all the professions, who *teams it, farms it, peddles,* keeps a school, preaches, edits a newspaper, goes to Congress, buys a township, and so forth, in successive years, and always, like a cat, falls on his feet."[4] George Kateb describes Emerson's self-reliance as "a doctrine unthinkable outside democracy." Judith Shklar presents Emerson as a critic of majoritarian democracy but one for whom "democratic political experiences . . . quite often gave his essays their intellectual purpose and direction."[5]

But was the United States in Emerson's time a democracy? That depended on the color of one's skin. For an enslaved man or woman, the America of Emerson's time was a tyranny, not a democracy; and—as Emerson recognized—the institution of slavery radically negates the idea of self-reliance. If Emerson's philosophy of self-reliance is indeed closely connected with the conditions of a democratic society, then it follows, conversely, that it might *not* be especially suited to a slave society, or to one (like Emerson's antebellum United States) in which slavery and democracy live in troubled coexistence. That Emerson's philosophy of self-reliance condemns the practice of slavery is clear enough, but that is only the beginning of the problem. *How to take action* against slavery, without along the way compromising or suffocating one's own intellectual and practical self-reliance: that was the problem that increasingly preoccupied Emerson in the years leading up to the Civil War.

Recently scholars have begun revising the long-held image of Emerson as a thinker detached from practical politics and indifferent or downright hostile to abolitionism.[6] Emerson's antislavery commitments were genuine, publicly expressed on numerous occasions, and increasingly radical after the passage of the Fugitive Slave Law in 1850. In this essay, I reexamine Emerson's ideal of self-reliance by connecting it with elements typically treated as marginal to his philosophy: his antislavery addresses (especially his opposition to the Fugitive Slave Law); his ambivalent relation to organized abolitionism; his peculiar theories about race and human progress; and his own political choices during the deepening crisis over slavery.[7] The slavery crisis put the idea of self-reliance to the test, and Emerson knew it. The institution of slavery was both deeply unjust and radically incompatible with self-reliance, both for slave owner and slave. But how it was possible *to act* effectively against an evil as politically and morally voracious as slavery, without compromising self-reliance along the way, was another question.

Emerson's original vision of self-reliance (in the 1841 essay of that title) took free and equal individuals as its point of departure and did not consider the way in which American slavery challenged that vision. During the 1840s and 1850s, Emerson sought to reconcile his increasing commitment to the antislavery cause with his philosophy of self-reliance and his understanding of his own calling as a philosopher-poet concerned about the whole human condition. He applied the ideal of self-reliance, with varying degrees of success, to a number of slavery-related issues including resistance to the 1850 Fugitive Slave Law; the spread of slavery to new federal territories; the post-abolition prospects of the black race; and the darkening shadow of violence, disunion, and civil war.

The Fugitive Slave Law of 1850 radicalized Emerson's antislavery politics and at the same time conveniently harmonized his self-reliant philosophy with the fulfillment of his antislavery duties. Because the law required citizens of free states to cooperate in capturing fugitive slaves, slavery was no longer some abstract, far-off evil, but something personally and locally experienced and resisted in exactly the way most appropriate to Emerson's philosophy of self-reliance. Conservatives' insistence that the Constitution—including its fugitive slave clause—was sacred provoked Emerson to insist on a "higher law" than any traditionally received political text, just as he rejected the authority of religious texts in his famous "Divinity School Address" of 1838.[8] Because the Constitution itself (Article IV, section 2) explicitly provided for rendition of fugitive slaves, Emerson's advice in "Self-Reliance" to "set at naught books and traditions" here drew a direct political conclusion: a lifeless constitutional clause was entitled to no more respect from a self-reliant individual than a lifeless religion or custom or book. Emerson admired the self-reliance manifested by fugitive slaves— "this man who has run the gauntlet of a thousand miles for his freedom." He also saw the law as an assault on the self-reliance of free-state citizens whom it required to cooperate in capturing fugitive slaves, against their own judgment and consciences.[9]

But resisting the Fugitive Slave Law falls short of a comprehensive attack on the institution of slavery, and here Emerson's philosophy of self-reliance provided less clear guidance. Even as he engaged in it, Emerson saw antislavery activism draining time and energy away from his own proper work of freeing "imprisoned spirits, imprisoned thoughts, far back in the brain."[10] The obstacles to abolishing slavery in the United States were so great that, unless one committed oneself completely to its abolition (as did full-time abolitionists like William Lloyd Garrison, Wendell Phillips, and Frederick Douglass), one might not accomplish anything at all. Emerson simultaneously sensed the pull of total commitment against slavery and rebelled against its personal cost.

Emerson also found it difficult to settle on any coherent political strategy for addressing the problem of slavery during the sectional crisis that culminated in the Civil War. Though willing to risk disunion rather than obey the Fugitive Slave Law, he generally rejected the active secessionism of Garrison and Phillips. "I am an Unionist as we all are, or nearly all, and I strongly share the hope of mankind in the power, and therefore, in the duties of the Union," he said in 1851.[11] During the early 1850s, he endorsed a gradualist policy of stopping the expansion of slavery (the Free Soil and Republican Party platforms) combined with compensated emancipation over the long term—a policy that presupposed an intact Union and peaceful abolition. But later in the decade, he lent political and personal support to John Brown's violent antislavery efforts in Kansas and, after Brown's abortive 1859 Harpers Ferry raid, celebrated him as a hero and martyr. In early 1861, he initially greeted the southern secession with relief—"What is the use of a pretended tie!"—but soon afterward reversed course and became fully committed to the Union war effort.[12]

In *The Conduct of Life,* a book published on the eve of the Civil War, Emerson presents a more sober and politically engaged version of self-reliance that is in many respects richer and more persuasive than his 1841 examination of that theme. But self-reliance now becomes far more difficult to achieve, and Emerson arguably fell short of its demands himself by his vibrating political course and his less-than-complete comprehension of the sectional crisis through which he was living. Once we get beyond resistance to enforcement of the Fugitive Slave Law—where his ideal of self-reliance provided relatively clear guidance—Emerson's philosophy was limited in its capacity to ground effective action with respect to so politically complicated an evil as American slavery.

In noting the limits of Emerson's philosophy with respect to the greatest tragedy in American history, I am not characterizing his philosophy as a failure or denying its enormous value to thoughtful citizens of a democracy. No philosophy can speak to every human condition equally well. The crisis that culminated in the Civil War defied everyone's attempts to comprehend and resolve it. That Emerson's ideal of self-reliance here encountered its limits reveals as much about that incredibly difficult crisis as it does about his philosophy. Moreover, what limited Emerson's philosophy in addressing the crisis—his skepticism toward parties and movements, his search for reflective distance from politics without denying his political duties—is precisely what, under other circumstances, gives that philosophy enduring value for citizens of a democracy. Emerson's limitation in one respect may be his promise in another.

Self-Reliant Ideal in a Slaveholding Society

What is most attractive in Emerson's idea of self-reliance is simultaneously what is most problematic: that what individuals make of their lives depends above all on effective and courageous use of their own active mental and physical powers. External supports—economic, political, legal, intellectual, religious—are secondary. A self-reliant individual will find adequate external resources however challenging or primitive the social conditions; an individual lacking self-reliance will not achieve it through external assistance. "Nature suffers nothing to remain in her kingdoms which cannot help itself," Emerson observes—which shows that he does not limit the principle to any particular type of society or even to the human species alone.[13]

Emerson's idea of self-reliance is closely connected with his skepticism about societal progress, at least in his early writings. (The idea of progress, as we shall see, later becomes important to his diagnosis of the slavery problem.) To imagine that one's life would somehow be better, freer, and happier in some more advanced society than the one in which providence has placed one, is to fail at self-reliance. "All men plume themselves on the improvement of society; and no man improves. Society never advances. It recedes as fast on one side as it gains on the other." Progress is individual, not social. "No greater men are now than ever were." "Reformers summon conventions, and vote and resolve in multitude" to create a better world, but all in vain, because "it is only as a man puts off all foreign support, and stands alone, that I see him to be strong and to prevail."[14]

To illustrate the claim that self-reliance is independent of the advanced or backward state of society, Emerson contrasts the "well-clad, reading, writing, thinking American, with a watch, a pencil, and a bill of exchange in his pocket" with "a naked New Zealander, whose property is a club, a spear, a mat, and an undivided twentieth of a shed to sleep under." The civilized American is not necessarily an improvement on the "wild virtue" of the autonomous savage; as society advances, "for every thing that is given, something is taken."[15]

What is most revealing here, given Emerson's own time and place, is precisely the comparison he does *not* make. He does not compare either civilized man or savage man with the life circumstances of a chattel slave—who was far more intimately connected to Emerson's own social and political world than the savage New Zealander. Emerson's idealized savage has a hard life, but *he is free* and for that reason can be self-reliant. If instead Emerson had claimed that the slave on a southern plantation had just as much chance to achieve self-reliance under slavery, despite the whips, chains, and hounds, as the "well-clad, reading, writing, thinking [white] American," or that any slave truly capable of self-reliance will find his or her way to freedom, these would be hollow exhortations. He does not, of course, make such implausible claims. But neither does he in this essay examine the implications, for his philosophy of self-reliance, of the existence on American soil of a massive and entrenched system of plantation slavery.

Slavery does make an offstage appearance in "Self-Reliance" in one troubling passage. "If an angry bigot assumes this bountiful cause of Abolition, and comes to me with his last news from Barbadoes, why should I not say to him, 'Go love thy infant; love thy wood-chopper: be good-natured and modest: have that grace; and never varnish your hard, uncharitable ambition with this incredible tenderness for black folk a thousand miles off. Thy love afar is spite at home.'"[16] The passage is not necessarily directed against all abolitionists but arguably only the "angry bigots" among them—though bigoted about what, or toward whom, is not explained. He does refer to "Abolition" itself as a "bountiful cause" (an odd label). Nevertheless, the attack on abolitionism sweeps pretty broadly, and prefigures Emerson's later critical remarks about William Lloyd Garrison and Wendell Phillips even as Emerson was making common cause with them; Emerson called Garrison's newsletter the *Liberator* "a scold."[17]

More importantly, Emerson's attack here misfires: abolitionists had no alternative but to denounce evils "a thousand miles off" because not only were they prevented from carrying their views to the South (due to the infamous gag rule, slave state laws and slave codes, and the near-certainty of violent reprisal), but—as Emerson elsewhere realizes—New England was complicit in the fate of southern slaves. Moreover, Emerson's proposed alternative—at least in this passage—is not some less "bigoted" and more effective way of opposing slavery, but to urge the unnamed angry abolitionist to drop that activity altogether, and love his own children and neighbors instead of lavishing "incredible tenderness" on "black folk a thousand miles off." By that standard, a slaveholder who loved his own children and was decent to neighbors would be morally superior to the angry, graceless abolitionist.

This particular passage was by no means Emerson's only or final word on slavery and abolition. Nevertheless, it is worth asking why Emerson included it, and how it is connected with the problem of self-reliance.

The critique of abolitionists in "Self-Reliance" comes from a paragraph that begins, "Whoso would be a man must be a nonconformist." What seems to disturb Emerson is that someone would act, and urge others to act, on the basis of something abstract and distant rather than present and directly experienced. Citizens of Massachusetts who have (or believe they have) no personal connection to slavery, who never practice it, suffer it, or give it any thought whatsoever until a rhetorically persuasive abolitionist catches their ear, acquire their political opinions secondhand and in that respect fail at self-reliance. They are instead (as Emerson remarks in the preceding sentence) "capitulat[ing] to badges and names." To adopt opinions about slavery on authority, divorced from any lived experience of the institution, is in principle no different than uncritically accepting the dogmas of a church or the ideology of a party. A self-reliant individual "must learn to detect . . . that gleam of light which flashes across his mind from within,"[18] and this is no less essential for opinions about slavery than for opinions on other matters. The social reform efforts toward which Emerson was most sympathetic (he observes in "New England Reformers") were those directed to reshaping one's own community, and expressing "the dictate of a man's genius and constitution" rather than "adopted from another."[19]

In "Self-Reliance," abolitionist agitators seem to serve no useful purpose at all. By the 1850s, Emerson had become convinced that abolitionists and abolitionist rhetoric were essential weapons in the battle against slavery; in that respect, his position changed. What did not change was his suspicion that abolitionist orators do not exhibit self-reliant thinking of the kind Emerson considered it his own mission to practice and foster in others. In an 1853 journal entry (written during the peak of Emerson's public antislavery activity), Emerson observes:

> Of Phillips, Garrison, and others I have always the feeling that they may wake up some morning and find that they have made a capital mistake, and are not the persons they took themselves for. Very dangerous is this thoroughly social and related life, whether antagonistic or cooperative. In a lonely world, or a world with half a dozen inhabitants, these would find nothing to do.
>
> The first discovery I made of Phillips was, that while I admired his eloquence, I had not the faintest wish to meet the man. He had only a *platform* existence, and no personality. Mere mouthpieces of a party; take away the party and they shrivel and vanish.
>
> They are inestimable for workers on audiences; but for a private conversation, one to one, I must prefer to take my chance with that boy in the corner.[20]

Emerson here (fairly or unfairly) characterizes abolitionist orators as individuals who think and act entirely to create an effect on an audience, who have no authentic inner life, who do not "know themselves," and whose ideas are entirely reducible to the party or cause they represent. There is no "gleam of light" flashing across their mind "from within," which for Emerson is the essential ingredient of mental self-reliance. And yet Emerson concedes that their work is of "inestimable" value, which highlights a tension between self-reliance and effective political action that he never successfully resolved.

The criticism of abolitionists in "Self-Reliance" perfectly explains why it was the Fugitive Slave Law of 1850 (which gave teeth to a hitherto weakly enforced constitutional clause) that propelled Emerson into vigorous antislavery activity. Because the 1850 law obligated citizens of free states to assist in rendering fugitive slaves, it made the evil of slavery immediately and obviously something local and directly experienced—including for Emerson himself and his friends and family.[21] In his 1851 "Address to the Citizens of Concord," Emerson proclaimed: "If our resistance to this law is not right, there is no right. This is not meddling with other people's affairs: this is hindering other people from meddling with us. This is not going crusading into Virginia and Georgia after slaves . . . but this is befriending in our own state, on our own farms, a man who has taken the risk of being shot, or burned alive, or cast into the sea."[22]

So to assist a fugitive slave in Massachusetts, and to refuse to cooperate with legalized kidnapping, is precisely to exhibit self-reliance in one's opposition to slavery. No one needs an abolitionist to tell him or her that this law is wrong; Emerson believes one's own natural moral sense will show the way. This is to offer assistance to a flesh-and-blood human being whom one can see and meet "in our own state, on our own farms," not an abstract victim a thousand miles away. Between 1841 and 1851, Emerson's thinking evolved and changed in many ways, but there remains a direct line between his critique of abolitionism in "Self-Reliance" and his reasoning for urging resistance to the Fugitive Slave Law in 1851.

Thus Emerson's preference for acting from personal experience of the Fugitive Slave Law was consistent with his philosophy of self-reliance. But to full-time abolitionists like Garrison and Phillips, the Fugitive Slave Law was merely the most visible tip of an enormous slavery iceberg. They offered assistance to fugitive slaves, but never forgot the plight of the millions "a thousand miles off" for whom escape was not possible. Whether any effective, nationwide attack on slavery was possible, and what strategy to follow, was another question.

Moral Suasion, Free-State Secession, Republican Party, or John Brown?

To evaluate Emerson's troubled relation to organized abolitionism, it helps to survey the range of options—none of them good—available to citizens of free states who judged the institution of slavery radically unjust. Slavery was no ordinary political issue. It was the kind of evil for which, unless one threw all one's time and energy into the battle, one was unlikely to accomplish anything; one might throw oneself fully into the battle and still accomplish little. What in Emerson's case has sometimes been interpreted as indifference toward slavery appears in a different light once all the difficulties are taken into account. "I waked at night, & bemoaned myself, because I had not thrown myself into this deplorable question of Slavery, which seems to want nothing so much as a few assured voices," he wrote in an 1852 journal entry. But this would mean "my desertion of my post, which has none to guard it but me. I have quite other slaves to free than those negroes, to wit, imprisoned spirits, imprisoned thoughts, far back in the brain of man,—far retired in the heaven of invention, and which, important to the republic of Man, have no watchman, or lover, or defender, but I."[23] This passage reveals, not indifference toward slavery, but instead a fierce battle between two duties, both of which Emerson recognizes as legitimate, and which come into conflict because the time demands of fulfilling each duty are enormous. He was to remain divided between these two types of duties for the remainder of his active life as writer and thinker.

Citizens of free states found themselves in the peculiar position of being politically and morally implicated in *supporting* the institution of slavery, without having any constitutional right or power either to *abolish* the institution or to withdraw their support. Thus the usual reformist advice, to "work within the system" to effect change, rang hollow in this case. Even in the unlikely event of a congressional majority committed to abolition of slavery, the antebellum Constitution prohibited the federal government from interfering with slavery in the states where it existed. Any such action would have been unconstitutional, unenforceable, and greeted by immediate secession of most slave states from the Union. Yet this same antebellum Constitution positively obligated citizens of free states to return fugitive slaves. And the federal government was constitutionally obligated to "insure domestic tranquility," which included, if necessary, assisting slave states in suppressing slave insurrections. Thus there was little a slavery-hating citizen of Massachusetts could directly accomplish through regular political channels to fight slavery in South Carolina or Georgia. A natural reading of the Constitution would appear to give Congress the power to restrict or abolish slavery in federal territories not yet states (Article IV, section 3), and in the District of Columbia (Article I, section 8); and this narrow channel for federal action against slavery would become essential to the platform of the Republican Party at its birth in 1854. But southern leaders threatened to dissolve the Union rather than allow slavery to be subjected to future geographical confinement; this was not a bluff.[24]

Alternatively, one might decide to forgo political action and instead employ what was called "moral suasion" against slavery through books, speeches, petitions, and public information campaigns. The drawback of this strategy was not, as one might suppose, that it was too tame and safe— "mere words." On the contrary, it was a dangerous activity, and downright impossible where it mattered most: in the slave states themselves, where abolitionist mailings were confiscated by the local post office (with the complicity of the federal government), and any practicing abolitionist risked being lynched on sight. Slaveholders regarded abolitionist speech and writing as deliberate attempts to foment slave insurrections, and were ready to go to extreme lengths to prevent it from infecting their own communities. Antislavery petitions, no matter how respectfully phrased, and despite the First Amendment guarantee of the "right to petition the Government," were prohibited from Congress under the infamous "gag rule" (1836–1844), a bipartisan agreement to suppress public debate over slavery for the sake of national unity. Even in northern states it was dangerous to be an abolitionist; some were lynched and others (including Garrison and Phillips) physically assaulted. Emerson himself in his public antislavery addresses faced hostile and potentially violent crowds on more than one occasion.[25]

Thus to speak out publicly against slavery was not a safe or trivial act—not even in the North. This is worth emphasizing because Emerson's own antislavery efforts consisted almost entirely of public speeches and publicly circulated letters. Unlike Garrison and Phillips, he did not organize meetings or publish antislavery newsletters, though he sometimes spoke at their meetings and produced pieces for their publications. It would be wrong to downplay Emerson's public antislavery utterances as "mere words" because under the peculiar circumstances of antebellum America *to speak against slavery was to act against it,* in the only readily available way. The abolitionists as a movement were never more than marginal as a political party seeking votes; and some, like Garrison and Henry David Thoreau, forswore voting altogether because it legitimated a system corrupted by slavery. Abolitionists' power lay in their words, and in this respect Emerson made his contribution.

Nevertheless, the question remained: beyond words, what then? And here abolitionists were internally divided in ways that shed light on Emerson's own uncertain course. One option was for the free states themselves to secede from the Union. This was the position of William Lloyd Garrison and Wendell Phillips, among others. The rationale was that only in this way could citizens of free states end their moral complicity for supporting a Union that permitted slavery. The newly independent free states would then be absolved of their obligation to return fugitive slaves and could for the first time serve as a beacon of liberty to the oppressed slave. As Wendell Phillips put it in an 1845 letter to Frederick Douglass (who later adopted a very different view), "New England, cutting loose from a blood-stained Union, shall glory in being the house of refuge for the oppressed."[26]

The obvious objection to the secession of free states from the Union (which, despite its antislavery intention, would have been structurally identical to the southern proslavery secession of 1860–1861) is that it does little for the vast majority of southern slaves left to languish in a Union now unrestrained in its proslavery policies; and it squanders any future hope of employing the power of the federal government against slavery. That was the principal objection of Frederick Douglass, the escaped slave turned abolitionist, who at first accepted the Garrison/Phillips argument for free-state secession and later turned against it.[27]

Emerson himself was willing to risk disunion rather than capitulate on the Fugitive Slave Law, but during the 1850s he searched for some way of fighting slavery within the Union instead of resorting to secession. He also rejected the principled refusal to vote exemplified by Henry David Thoreau and William Lloyd Garrison. "Those who stay away from the election think that one vote will do no good," Emerson wrote in an 1854 journal entry. But they should "no more stay away from the election than from honesty or from affection."[28] Like Thoreau, Emerson advocated conscientious refusal to obey the Fugitive Slave Law. But Emerson was clearly unsatisfied with conscientious refusal alone; and in general (fairly or unfairly) he regarded Thoreau's political approach as too negative, a retreat from political responsibility.[29] Emerson himself sought other courses of action against slavery that included active involvement in electoral politics. Despite his discomfort with partisan politics, in 1851 Emerson actively campaigned for John Palfrey, a Free Soil Party candidate for Congress, and did the same in 1854 for Charles Sumner when Sumner was participating in creating the Republican Party.[30]

The Republican Party (like its predecessor, the Free Soil Party) condemned slavery as an evil, attempted to restrict its expansion, and sought to eventually abolish it according to some long and imprecise time frame. This at least allowed one to stake out a moral position against slavery while still remaining in the Union and working within the existing constitutional framework. It gave its supporters something positive and practical to organize for, vote for, and legislate upon. On the other hand, it arguably made one complicit in continuing to support slavery in the states where it existed. In this respect at least, Emerson was willing to make what he considered a principled compromise. Near the end of his 1851 "Address to the Citizens of Concord" (where he urges refusal to obey the Fugitive Slave Law), Emerson attempts to move beyond mere refusal. He identifies himself as a Unionist (which distinguishes him from Garrison and Phillips) and says, "I strongly share the hope of mankind in the power, and, therefore, in the duties of the Union." He proposes that we first abrogate the Fugitive Slave Law and then "proceed to confine slavery to slave states" (the Free Soil position); then he invites "any expert statesman" to "furnish us a plan for the summary or gradual winding up of slavery." He considers "a thousand millions of dollars to buy the slaves," an acceptable price to pay "to sweep this mountain of calamities out of the earth." He mentions in passing "the new importance of Liberia," which suggests support for the widely entertained (if morally questionable) idea of emancipation-with-removal of freed slaves to some other part of the world.[31] This aligns Emerson's thinking (at least in 1851) closer to what became the ideology of the Republican Party, than to the position of Garrison or Phillips.

But Emerson was always more attached to the philosophy of self-reliance than to the platform or strategy of any political party, and in one important respect this led him into commitments irreconcilable with the peaceful, gradualist, Unionist antislavery approach of the Republican Party.

In 1856, Emerson organized public efforts to provide assistance, including arms, to antislavery settlers in Kansas. The 1854 Kansas-Nebraska Act, which allowed territorial legislatures to decide whether slavery would be permitted or prohibited during the formative prestatehood phase, had produced a race between proslavery and antislavery settlers to gain control of unorganized western territories, and in Kansas a guerilla war between the two sides. In his speech at an 1856 Kansas Relief Meeting, Emerson proclaimed that "the people of Kansas" (meaning the antislavery settlers there) "ask for bread, clothes, arms, and men, to save them alive, and enable them to stand against these enemies of the human race." He asks his listeners to give "lavishly" to the cause, and makes explicit the connection to self-reliance: "They have a right to be helped for they have helped themselves. . . . He only who is able to stand alone is qualified to be a citizen."[32] So here self-reliance takes the form of individual, armed self-defense.

One might expect that Emerson would actively encourage the use of federal authority to prohibit slavery in Kansas; that goal was central to the national Republican strategy of restricting the spread of slavery. But instead

Emerson treats this as a low priority: "I own I have little esteem for governments. . . . Who doubts that Kansas would have been very well settled, if the United States had let it alone? . . . I am glad to see that the terror at disunion and anarchy is disappearing. Massachusetts, in its heroic day, had no government—was an anarchy." He supports this with the dubious claim that California in the early days of the gold rush, when no law or government existed anywhere near the gold fields, was characterized by "perfect security" because "Every man throughout the country was armed with knife and revolver, and it was known that instant justice would be administered to each offence, and perfect peace reigned."[33] Emerson here makes the questionable assumption that if the federal government simply refrained from acting one way or the other, slavery would never spread to the western territories. Thus despite his occasional convergence with the Republican agenda and active support for some of its candidates, Emerson's thinking drifted away from the Republican insistence on the constitutional right and moral duty of Congress affirmatively to outlaw slavery in the territories.

The most famous of the antislavery Kansas warriors was John Brown, whose use of violence against proslavery settlers on the Kansas frontier was far from merely defensive.[34] Brown stayed at Emerson's home at least twice during his trips to Massachusetts to raise money for his various armed antislavery initiatives, and Emerson raised money for Brown. Emerson's immediate reaction to Brown's 1859 raid on Harpers Ferry—that Brown was "a true hero, but he lost his head there"—indicates that Emerson was not informed in detail about Brown's activities and plans, and had no advance knowledge of Harpers Ferry.[35] But Emerson certainly knew that, in general, John Brown was willing to use violence against slavery. Emerson's praise of Brown implicitly criticizes other abolitionists for their sentimentality and impotence: "He believed in his ideas to that extent that he existed to put them all into action. He did not believe in moral suasion;—he believed in putting the thing through."[36]

Brown became for Emerson an instance of what the latter had called "Representative Men" in an 1850 book by that title.[37] Emerson calls Brown "a representative of the American public" and observes that "gentlemen find traits of relation readily between him and themselves"—which is precisely what defines a "representative man" in Emerson's thought. "Nothing can resist the sympathy which all elevated minds must feel with Brown, and through them the whole civilized world." As a representative American,

Brown naturally exhibits self-reliance, not only in action—in his armed individual courage—but also on the level of thought. In contrast to those who see only constitutional forms, Emerson observes, those only are free who "like John Brown, use their eyes to see the fact behind the forms."[38]

In becoming Emerson's representative American, Brown in effect takes the place of the disgraced Daniel Webster. Webster in Emerson's view forfeited that status when he "sold" himself to the slaveholders and supported the 1850 Fugitive Slave Law. A strikingly large percentage of Emerson's furious response to the Fugitive Slave Law is directed at Webster, who Emerson had once idealized as "the completest man," a true statesman, but who became "the victim of his ambition" and "to please the South betrayed the North."[39]

Brown's violent, extralegal antislavery efforts were irreconcilable with the Republican and Unionist antislavery agenda Emerson at other times supported, or with his own recommendation for peaceful, compensated emancipation. Brown's raid on Harpers Ferry was a nightmare for Republican leaders who sought (unsuccessfully) to reassure southerners that the Republican Party was not John Brown in disguise. Emerson's idealization of Brown makes little sense as coherent national policy toward slavery. But it exemplifies Emerson's search for the representative, self-reliant American man amid a crisis where previous idols had crumbled.

Race, Abolition, and Self-Reliance

Perhaps the most troubling element in Emerson's political thought is his view of race. Though Emerson fiercely opposed enforcement of the Fugitive Slave Law and condemned slavery as a violation of "higher law," he privately, and sometimes publicly, speculated about whether the Negro race was so uncivilized and inferior as to be fated to ultimate extinction in the evolutionary struggle of races.[40] On Emerson's supposed "scale of races," he considered the Anglo-Saxon race, at least among peoples of the nineteenth century, superior to all others; for that reason England was able to rule the far more populous and distant population of India. Emerson read seriously (if also skeptically) the writings of "racial scientists" like Samuel Morton and Robert Knox from whom antebellum slave owners drew for their racial defense of slavery.[41]

Yet Emerson genuinely admired and respected escaped slaves, who exhibited self-reliance in its purest form. He insisted that the State of Massachusetts had a duty to protect the rights of its black citizens against arbitrary treatment in southern ports. (The laws of South Carolina and several other slave states required the incarceration of free negro merchant seamen from other states or nations for the duration of their layover in the state.) In his 1844 "Address on the Emancipation of the Negroes in the British West Indies," he claimed that the peaceful and orderly result of emancipation had annihilated "the old indecent nonsense about the nature of the negro. . . . It now appears, that the negro race is, more than any other, susceptible of rapid civilization."[42] In 1845 he refused an invitation to speak at the New Bedford Lyceum because of its policy of excluding blacks from membership.[43]

There is already an enormous scholarly literature on Emerson and race.[44] I will not attempt here a comprehensive reexamination of Emerson's racial views, but will focus instead on the intersection between his racial speculations, his hope for the abolition of slavery, and his philosophy of self-reliance.

The most important conclusions Emerson drew about race were the following: first, that slavery equally brutalizes both master and slave—that *both* southern whites and their black slaves subsist as "inferior races"; second, that it is the duty of a "superior race" (England, or in the American context, New England) to display benevolence by abolishing a barbaric institution;[45] third, that after abolition the black race will be thrown on its own resources and either make an essential contribution to humanity, or fail as a people; and finally, that black fugitive slaves display self-reliance and thus merit assistance from self-reliant white citizens.

In his 1844 "Address on the Emancipation of the Negroes in the British West Indies," Emerson described how slavery deprives the slave owner of self-reliance and keeps him at a low level of civilization by suffocating the moral sense.[46] But in his journals, Emerson drew out what he considered the natural corollary: that if the slave owner is brutal and low, so is the slave and vice-versa. This directly challenged the tendency of many abolitionists to idealize the virtues of the suffering and abused slave.[47] Thus in Emerson's view, slave owner and slave equally participate in a brutal institution that stifles intellect and moral sense in both. Emerson predicted that the brutalizing effects of slavery on both slaves and white slaveholders would not immediately disappear with the abolition of slavery.[48]

Recall that in his original 1841 essay "Self-Reliance," Emerson had insisted that all progress was individual, not social; that self-reliant individuals thrive on whatever abundant or scarce resources their social environment provides. There Emerson had assumed free and mobile individuals and did not allow American slavery to complicate his democratic, egalitarian picture. In later writings describing the barbarizing effects of slavery on both master and slave, Emerson implicitly admits that the social and institutional obstacles to self-reliance are sometimes greater than individuals can overcome; *collective* moral and intellectual progress is necessary to remedy the poison of slavery.

But how was slavery to be abolished, and former slaveholders and slaves placed on the path to progress and superior civilization? Here Emerson offered two different answers: abolition "from above," by the privileged race itself, displaying its own increasingly refined sense of morality; and abolition "from below," by the slaves themselves, as an act of individual and collective self-liberation.

If, indeed (as Emerson claimed in "Self-Reliance"), "power is in nature the essential measure of right" and "Nature suffers nothing to remain in her kingdom which cannot help itself,"[49] then the ideal of self-reliance would appear to require *self*-liberation by slaves. *Individually* it was possible for a small percentage of slaves to liberate themselves through escape. But *collective* self-liberation, without outside support, was nearly impossible under the circumstances for black slaves in the American South. For non-slave-owning white Americans blithely to insist that it was "up to the slaves to free themselves" would mask the former's own complicity in upholding the institution of slavery. And if slaves in the American South did collectively liberate themselves entirely by their own efforts, this could be accomplished only by extreme violence; the ensuing race war would take both races several steps away from the civility Emerson valued and back into the reign of brute force. For all these reasons, Emerson could not claim that self-reliance required pure self-liberation by the slaves. All of his attempts to apply the philosophy of self-reliance to abolition of slavery include both benevolent action by free white citizens and black self-help in some form. There were tensions between these two paths to abolition which Emerson recognized but did not clearly resolve.

These tensions are already evident in Emerson's first important public abolitionist statement, his 1844 "Address on the Emancipation of the Negroes in the British West Indies." At first Emerson speaks as though liberation of West Indian slaves came entirely from above, reflecting the enlightened benevolence of England. Because England was in Emerson's view the most advanced and civilized of modern nations, its moral sense and enlightened self-interest mastered its love of sugar and strong drink; it freely decided to abolish slavery in its colonial dominions rather than having abolition forced from below. "Other revolutions have been under the insurrection of the oppressed; this was the repentance of the tyrant."[50] This top-down description of abolition captures one of Emerson's philosophical themes: that the mark of a more civilized people is "to defend the weak & redress the injured."[51] In the address, Emerson initially portrays the black race as a helpless victim: from the earliest historical records, he claims, "it appears, that one race [the Negro] was victim, and served the other races." Slavery commenced in America because "we had found a race who were less warlike, and less energetic shopkeepers than we." Emerson's formulations here simultaneously chastise the enslaving race, and suggest that the enslaved race lacked the self-reliance that would have prevented its servitude.[52]

Near the end of the address, Emerson himself recognizes the problem and attempts to resolve it: "I have said that this event interests us, because it came mainly from the concession of the whites; I add, that in part it is the earning of the blacks. They won the pity and respect they have received, by their powers and native endowments."[53] In this rather halfhearted praise, Emerson concedes the slaves a role, but clearly a subordinate role, in their own liberation from slavery in the British West Indies.

Emerson's praise of peaceful, regime-initiated abolition in the British West Indies contrasts with his admiration, elsewhere in the same address, for Toussaint L'Ouverture, who led the successful (and violent) 1790s slave uprising in the French colony of San Domingue, which became the republic of Haiti. "The arrival in the world of such men as Toussaint," Emerson remarks, "outweighs in good omen all the English and American humanity. The anti-slavery of the whole world, is dust in the balance before this. . . . The might and the right are here: here is the anti-slave: here is man: and if you have man, black or white is an insignificance."[54] Here Emerson appears to change course, now praising bottom-up, violent, antiregime acts of slave self-liberation instead of the peaceful top-down British model. He clearly admired both peaceful abolition from above (for exemplifying the morality of a higher civilization) and violent abolition from below (for displaying forceful self-reliance). Whether it was possible to combine both types of abolition, and which path to abolition was most likely for the United States, is a question Emerson leaves unresolved in this address.

Near the close of the 1844 address on abolition in the West Indies, Emerson speculates about the long-term future of the black race after its liberation from slavery. (What follows next must have been jarring to many abolitionists in the audience.) Emerson introduces his characteristic theme of history as a ceaseless struggle among races in which the strong flourish and the weak perish. Over the long run, Emerson claims, nature "will only save what is worth saving; and it saves not by compassion, but by power. It appoints no police to guard the lion, but his teeth and claws. . . . It deals with men after the same manner. If they are rude and foolish, down they must go. When at last in a race, a new principle appears, an idea,—*that* conserves it; ideas only save races. If the black man is feeble, and not important to the existing races, not on a parity with the best race, the black man must serve, and be exterminated. But if the black man carries in his bosom an indispensable element of a new and coming civilization, for the sake of that element, no wrong, nor strength, nor circumstance, can hurt him: he will survive and thrive."[55] Emerson here envisions the future of the black race in radically polar form: either the newly liberated black race takes the lead in the progress of civilization, or it perishes—as though nothing in between were possible. Emerson's chilling word "exterminated" remains unexplained: does he mean cultural assimilation or biological extinction? Nor does Emerson suggest that a chronically oppressed race merits continued assistance after abolition of slavery. Once slavery has disappeared, it seems, the formerly enslaved race is on its own and either survives or perishes on its own power. Emerson here echoes his original idea of self-reliance as success or failure in a more or less fair contest among free citizens; but now that idea has been transformed from *individual* self-reliance into a evolutionary contest among *collective* agents: peoples and races.

In this public 1844 address, Emerson spoke as though the black race was already showing itself capable of thriving in this demanding postabolition contest. In his private journals, at the time of that address and even during the peak of his antislavery activity in the 1850s, he expressed continued doubts.

In any case, Emerson's doubts about the black race in general did not prevent him from admiring and assisting fugitive slaves. Here again, Emerson's opposition to the Fugitive Slave Law best reconciled his ideal of self-reliance with his practical commitment to abolition. For fugitive slaves take upon themselves the first fateful and dangerous step toward freedom. This initial act of courage then entitles them to assistance by free citizens of the North, who in the process manifest their own moral self-reliance by refusing to act as cowardly pawns of the slave owners.[56] For the philosophy of self-reliance, assistance to fugitive slaves is a win-win scenario.

Emerson underscores the centrality of self-reliance when he claims that "it is a greater crime to re-enslave a man who has shown himself fit for freedom, than to enslave him at first."[57] This might be read as implying that slaves who do not escape to the North are not "fit for freedom." Emerson does *not* say this, though he unquestionably assigns fugitive slaves a higher rank than other slaves in the scale of self-reliance. What matters is that a fugitive slave has "shown himself" fit for freedom, that is, made that virtue *obvious* to northern citizens, who then must choose whether to support individual self-reliance or collaborate in suppressing it.

Despite his lengthy and tedious speculations about higher and lower races and civilizations, when Emerson condemns the Fugitive Slave Law from the escaped slave's point of view, he puts aside assumptions of superior and inferior races and instead denounces legalized "kidnapping" in terms of a violated, universal human nature: "A man's right to liberty is as inalienable as his right to life." The fugitive slave, he remarks elsewhere, "has certified, as distinctly as human nature could, his opinions. And to take him back is to steal."[58] This argument, which is in the end Emerson's strongest antislavery argument, does not depend on any theory of higher or lower civilizations or races.

Self-Reliance in Times of Crisis

Emerson's thinking altered in important ways between 1841, when "Self-Reliance" was published, and *The Conduct of Life* (1860), with its keynote essay "Fate." The precise character of the shift is debated, but clearly in later writings Emerson is more attentive to the limitations on individual self-reliance than he was in his youth. Emerson himself notes this shift in "Fate" where he observes: "Once we thought, positive power was all. Now we learn, that negative power, or circumstance, is half."[59] He never relinquished the fundamental ideal of self-reliance: setting aside books and traditions and thinking and acting according to one's own "positive power." Nor had he ignored the role of limitation in his earlier writings. In "Self-Reliance" he had spoken of accepting the circumstances in which providence has placed one, of confiding oneself to "the society of your contemporaries, the connection of events."[60] To do this is to accept constraints of a kind: self-reliance does not mean total independence of time and place. But limitations were here presented as resources for self-reliance rather than obstacles to it.

By the late 1850s, Emerson saw the individual as relatively less powerful, and circumstance or fate as relatively more powerful, than when he first issued his ringing call for self-reliance. Emerson begins the essay "Fate" by lamenting the "immovable limitations" that individuals encounter in their attempts to realize their wishes or to reform the world. He speaks of "torrents of tendency" against which individual resistance is "ridiculously inadequate . . . a protest made by a minority of one, under compulsion of millions." He demands that we recognize the "odious facts" of our own limited power: "A man's power is hooped in by a necessity, which, by many experiments, he touches on every side, until he learns its arc."[61] He had not described limitation as "odious" in 1841.

Emerson's preoccupation with limitation in "Fate" does not make him any less concerned with freedom and self-reliance. His aim instead is to preserve freedom and self-reliance by casting them in a form less vulnerable to the limitations and ravages of the world. Freedom means comprehending precisely the necessities that hem us in: "Intellect annuls Fate. So far as a man thinks, he is free." Sometimes in the essay Emerson speaks as though freedom were simply the recognition of necessity, a stoic embrace of circumstances one cannot change. At other times, Emerson's freedom-through-recognizing-necessity invokes the practice of natural scientists, inventors, and statesmen, who paradoxically acquire power over nature—and over other men—by subjecting nature's necessary laws to "fixed calculation."[62]

In "Fate" and its companion essay, "Power," from *The Conduct of Life*, Emerson appears more concerned with the possibilities and limitations of political action than he was in "Self-Reliance," where he had scoffed at those who depended for support from political parties, conventions, votes and resolutions: "It is only as a man puts off all foreign support, and stands alone, that I see him to be strong and prevail," he had written in "Self-Reliance."[63] In "Fate" Emerson still admires the human being who can stand alone, but "standing alone" with respect to politics has now come to mean something rather different. The opening paragraph of "Fate" asks the practical (and very Socratic) question, "How shall I live?" The answer is that individuals must learn how to reconcile their own "polarity"—their own individual uniqueness—with "the spirit of the times." Emerson admits that "we are incompetent to solve the times" and yet, instead of calling for detachment, urges individuals to enter into events and find their own "private solution" to "the riddle of the age."[64] In "Power," Emerson observes that "all power is of one kind, a sharing of the nature of the world," and then immediately applies this to politics. The self-reliant man is the one who "is made of the same stuff of which events are made," who "is in sympathy with the course of things; can predict it. Whatever befalls, befalls him first; so that he is equal to whatever shall happen."[65] In his original essay "Self-Reliance," Emerson favored the man detached from political foolishness. Now, in 1860, he admires the man who can best navigate a political torrent from which no one can escape. The publication date sufficiently indicates the events Emerson had in mind.

Scholars have attributed the new emphasis on constraint in Emerson's later writings to a variety of causes, among them the hard lessons of experience, private grief and loss, consciousness of his own advancing age and declining powers, disillusionment with reformist utopias like Brook Farm,[66] and receptiveness to contemporary developments in natural science. All of these are plausible factors. But it is also worth asking how the escalating sectional crisis over slavery, and Emerson's own active engagement in that crisis, might have shaped his thinking about fate, freedom, and self-reliance at a time in which political events increasingly spun out of anyone's control. The marks of the sectional crisis are abundantly evident in *The Conduct of Life*, beginning with Emerson's revealing lament that "we are incompetent to solve the times." His discussion of universal themes like fate, power, culture, religion, and wealth frequently allude to events of the 1850s. In "Fate," he talks about "strong natures" who were once "inevitable patriots . . . until their life ebbs and their defects and gout, palsy and money, warp them," and specifically mentions Daniel Webster (who betrayed Emerson's one-time admiration by supporting the Fugitive Slave Law).[67] In "Power," he refers to "sectional interests urged with a fury that shuts its eyes to consequences, with a mind made up to desperate extremities, ballot in one hand, and rifle in the other."[68]

Moreover, there is an affinity between the central problem addressed in "Fate" and "Power"—how to preserve individual freedom and capacity for action against "torrents of tendency"—and what must have been the anxious experience of American citizens during the 1850s. Many experiences acquaint one with "immovable limitations," but nothing underscores that point more clearly than the attempt to rid America of slavery. No doubt age and experience teach human beings that their powers are more limited than they once imagined. But the *political* powerlessness felt by many American citizens, young and old, during the escalating crisis of the 1850s is of a different order altogether.

Stephen Whicher's influential study of the shift in Emerson's thinking over time, *Freedom and Fate* (1953), nowhere suggests that the sectional crisis of the 1850s contributed to Emerson's growing preoccupation with fate and limitation—this despite Emerson's explicitly linking "fate" with "the spirit of the times." Whicher's thesis is that Emerson belatedly realized the emptiness of his earlier unbounded faith in individual freedom—the illusion that "he could set up the infinitude of the private man as counterpoise . . . to the imperatives of society and the power of fate." Time and experience, Whicher claims, taught Emerson that the world resisted his will, and he ultimately bid his "farewell to action," opting instead for purely personal liberation. Whicher does not discuss Emerson's antislavery activities at all (except briefly to note Emerson's moral zeal during the Civil War). In the end, Emerson (according to Whicher) "surrender[s] to fate," relinquishes his "evangelical attitude toward social change," and settles politically for a kind of patrician conservatism.[69]

No doubt Emerson learned through painful experience that individual self-reliance cannot easily overcome a resistant world. But Emerson's growing preoccupation with fate and limitation during the 1850s emphatically did *not* coincide with a "farewell to action"; on the contrary, he became far more politically engaged than before.[70] Rather than settling for genteel conservatism, he fiercely denounced precisely the comfortable Beacon Hill and Wall Street patricians who collaborated with the slave power. Whicher remains insightful on many points, but his conclusions become unconvincing once Emerson's antislavery engagements are taken seriously.

George Kateb in *Emerson and Self-Reliance* (2002) does take Emerson's antislavery activities seriously, but he sees them as the *abandonment* of self-reliance—a "suspension of individualism" in favor of "mobilization, military discipline, and eventually . . . conscripted self-sacrifice." For Kateb, what is essential in Emerson's philosophy is self-reliant *thinking:* a willingness to suspend all authorities and fixed intellectual positions and (anticipating Nietzsche) simultaneously to entertain multiple and conflicting moral perspectives without choosing among them. Kateb ranks self-reliant action lower than self-reliant thought because what can be achieved in action is always far more limited than what can be grasped in thought. "Self-reliant being and doing, whatever their worth, come up against tremendous obstacles in oneself and in the world, and approach impossibility." Kateb, in effect, saves Emersonian self-reliance from a recalcitrant world by privileging thought over action.[71]

Emerson's antislavery efforts exemplify Kateb's "tremendous obstacles" to self-reliant action. Kateb argues that, upon the passage of the Fugitive Slave Law in 1850, Emerson set aside his individualist principles and instead "urges solidarity—indeed mobilization—on others, and, when the occasion arises, does not shrink from advocating violence in the effort to destroy slavery. That profound change is a deviation from his theory of self-reliance, not its transformation." Kateb accepts Emerson's refusal to obey the Fugitive Slave Law as a genuine exercise of self-reliant citizenship, but sees Emerson's participation in organized abolition efforts, his association with John Brown, and his later support for the Union war effort as irreconcilable with Emerson's own philosophy: "The advocacy of violence *is* inconsistent with the theory of self-reliant activity." Kateb concedes that eradicating slavery may have justified the temporary sacrifice of self-reliance, but calls it sacrifice all the same.[72]

Kateb rightly emphasizes the enormous obstacles to individual self-reliant action, especially amid the contest over slavery. But his attempt to salvage Emersonian self-reliance in the face of a recalcitrant world by privileging thought over action runs counter to one of Emerson's central purposes in *The Conduct of Life*: to preserve the capacity for self-reliant *action* even under extraordinarily difficult circumstances. In "Fate" and "Power," Emerson seeks to maintain *both* individual thought and individual action amid the cruel necessities occasioned by "the spirit of the times." Whether Emerson effectively solved that problem, either in general or in his own case, is an open question. But Kateb's interpretation sidesteps that problem rather than pointing us toward Emerson's own attempts to resolve it.

Moreover, a crisis like the one Emerson (and the nation) faced in the 1850s—a crisis that demanded total commitment, and in the end left no one untouched—weakens the distinction between self-reliant thought and self-reliant action. If one cannot think clearly and effectively under such conditions, one cannot act clearly either; and conversely, a vacillating or confused course of action betrays unclear thinking. Here failure at self-reliant action and failure at self-reliant thought go hand in hand, so the stakes are high—as Emerson recognized.

Finally, Kateb's unsupported claim that Emersonian self-reliance requires pacifism confuses the issue by injecting a premise that Emerson himself did not accept. Emerson was never a pacifist, his writings frequently display admiration for military valor, and he never suggests that self-reliance is incompatible with sometimes resorting to violence. Emerson's support for John Brown does reveal something askew in Emerson's thinking—here I agree with Kateb—but that John Brown was not a pacifist is not the main problem.

When Emerson remarks in "Fate" that "the riddle of the age has for each a private solution,"[73] he does not mean by "private" a detached, apolitical stance—for by this time he recognized political detachment was not possible. He seems instead to mean that each individual has to navigate his or her own way through the crisis; only in that way can we preserve a measure of self-reliance, either in thought or action.

Self-reliance amid a political crisis would not necessarily mean the capacity to bend events to one's will, for the whole premise of "Fate" is that our power in this regard is extremely limited. Nor would it require self-reliant individuals to abstain from political and military organization (as Kateb claims). In a crisis that presses in from all sides, and for which inaction means complicity in injustice, one cannot preserve self-reliance simply by abstaining from political parties and armies.

What it would require, if we apply Emerson's own standard, is a clear understanding of the political causes of the crisis and some effective compass for guiding individual action through that political storm. In both "Fate" and "Power," Emerson places enormous importance on *understanding causes* as the key to self-reliance; only through the intellect is fate transformed into freedom. "All successful men have agreed in one thing,—they were *causationists*. They believed that things went not by luck, but by law."[74] A clear understanding of causes will not release one from necessity, but it makes one at least incrementally more self-reliant and free than someone who does not understand events at all. "He who sees through the design, presides over it, and must will that which must be. . . . Of two men, each obeying his own thought, he whose thought is deepest will be the strongest character." Clear understanding of causes in turn provides a clear course of action and thus makes self-reliance possible—at least for "strong characters" who resolve for themselves "the riddle of the age" even if they are not individually competent to "solve the times."[75]

Emerson's vision here of self-reliance in troubled times is thoughtful and persuasive, and in important respects an advance over his description of self-reliance in the original 1841 essay. The self-reliant individual of 1841 enjoyed a relative detachment from politics possible only with a peaceful, law-governed democracy as its foundation—and by suppressing the problem of slavery. Emerson's self-reliant individual in "Fate" and "Power" is swept up in an unpredictable crisis—now with slavery at the forefront—and can take nothing for granted.

On the plane of political philosophy, Emerson in *The Conduct of Life* thus presents (I would argue) a new, more politically engaged, more persuasive—but also more difficult and risky—vision of self-reliance than he had in 1841. Emerson's own success in living out this more politically demanding ideal of self-reliance during the 1850s was limited—not by lack of commitment on his part, but by the incredible difficulty of the political crisis itself. By the time he published *The Conduct of Life*, Emerson had sought for at least fifteen years to oppose slavery in his own way: to find a different philosophical outlook on the problem of slavery and race, and a different political strategy, than that represented by the most prominent abolitionists and antislavery organizations. He admired Garrison's and Phillips's passion for the cause and admitted the effectiveness of their efforts, but criticized what he considered their philosophical narrowness, their lack of self-reflection, and their addiction to the public platform. He also rejected their secessionism and, at least for a time, explored ways in which slavery might be peacefully abolished without sundering the Union. To this end, he overcame his distaste for partisan politics and actively campaigned for Free Soil and Republican candidates.

On the philosophical plane, he recognized that his time and energy were increasingly drawn into the slavery crisis, yet was reluctant to sacrifice his vocation to liberate "imprisoned thoughts, far back in the brain of man." He attempted to reconcile these two conflicting duties by placing the crisis over slavery and race into a much wider, more enduring philosophical and scientific perspective; this effort at synthesis is exemplified in *The Conduct of Life*. Recognizing that his earlier detachment from politics was no longer possible, he sought a new kind of balance for himself between political engagement and philosophical reflection—increasing the former without sacrificing the latter.

If we evaluate the aims behind Emerson's approach to slavery and abolition, we will find them consistent with Emerson's enduring vision of intellectual and practical self-reliance. The results, however, are a different matter. In his political approach to the slavery crisis, Emerson did not find any new path; instead he vibrated between at least three paths, each perhaps consistent on its own terms but irreconcilable with the others: the pro-Union, gradualist position of the Republicans; the free-state secessionism of Garrison and Phillips; and the violent agenda of John Brown. Achieving intellectual clarity and practical effectiveness amid this chaos of contradictory strategies would have required a more careful analysis of national politics than Emerson ever attempted.

Emerson's wider observations about the politics of the slavery crisis in *The Conduct of Life* are occasionally insightful but often woefully superficial. He tends to reduce complicated political and constitutional questions to simplified individual types, and even more dubiously, to physiological phenomena. "A good deal of our politics is physiological," he asserts in "Fate"; the difference between a future Whig and Free-Soiler is evident in an embryo's fourth day; "All conservatives are such from personal defects."[76] This view of politics leaves little room for debate or persuasion. Emerson's aim in assimilating politics to physiology was to place the political crisis of the day into a wider and longer-term evolutionary and scientific perspective. But the results are unpersuasive.

Emerson's attempts to reconcile political engagement with philosophical detachment frequently misfire. In "Power," immediately after vividly listing all the indicators of a coming crisis ("sectional interests urged with a fury which shuts its eyes to consequences"), and observing that everyone "hardens himself the best he can against the coming ruin," Emerson turns around and asserts that these fears are vastly exaggerated, that the solid exchange value of government bonds and the "personal power, freedom, and ... vigor" of individual American citizens reveal "the enormous elements of strength" that "make our politics unimportant."[77] It would be far more consistent with Emerson's new emphasis on clear-eyed comprehension of necessity to underscore the importance of carefully examining political causes and effects.

This tendency to downplay the importance of politics is reinforced philosophically by Emerson's faith in a benevolent Providence. The overall direction of Fate and the Universe, he assures us, "is toward benefit"; all the horrors of war and suffering are part of a higher plan that "pleases at a sufficient perspective."[78] This line of thought can easily lead *away* from clear comprehension of political causes and effects. However such passages are evaluated philosophically, they suggest that personally Emerson remained deeply ambivalent about sustained political engagement and sometimes, if only in imagination, wished to place himself a thousand miles above its wrenching dilemmas.[79]

Ralph Waldo Emerson's philosophy of self-reliance, as set forth in the original essay of that title, was best suited to a relatively peaceful, law-governed democracy characterized by free, equal, mobile individuals. The actual American social order that gave birth to Emerson and his philosophy did approximate that ideal for many of its white citizens. For slaves it was a different matter altogether. To what degree Emerson's philosophy of self-reliance could speak to the reality of slavery, and to the difficult challenges of abolishing it on American soil, remained an open question.

As Emerson became progressively more committed to abolition, he sought wherever possible to cast his opposition to slavery and his vision of its abolition in the language of self-reliance. In some respects, the application of self-reliance to slavery was straightforward: slavery denied self-reliance; fugitive slaves displayed it, as did white citizens who refused to become kidnappers. In other respects, Emerson's philosophy of self-reliance encountered greater challenges: in attempting to resolve the conflict between political engagement and political detachment, and in his broader speculations about peoples and races.

In his late writings, Emerson revised his ideal of self-reliance to take into account the limited power of human beings confronting a difficult and sometimes violent world. Emerson's call to turn fate into (limited) freedom by recognizing necessity and paying close attention to causality as well as "the spirit of the times" contains the seed of a more politically engaged version of self-reliance—and also one less preconditioned on a healthy democracy than the version Emerson set forth in 1841. But this new ideal of self-reliance is much more difficult to achieve. Emerson's own success in putting it into practice during the 1850s was mixed.

To observe that Emerson's philosophy of self-reliance could not fully address the sectional crisis over slavery and abolition is not to judge that philosophy a failure, but merely to acknowledge its limits. Nor should Emerson himself be judged harshly for failing to find a clear path through a crisis in which nearly every American was confused and internally divided. Emerson's determined efforts to do battle with slavery while remaining true to his philosophy of self-reliance remain instructive to everyone who has ever been torn between duty and reflection, and to anyone fortunate enough to experience an America closer to the one Emerson *hoped for* than the one in which he actually lived.

Notes

1. "Self-Reliance," in *Ralph Waldo Emerson: Essays and Lectures*, ed. Joel Porte (New York: Library of America, 1983), 259–61, hereafter cited as *E&L*.

2. Stephen E. Whicher, *Freedom and Fate: An Inner Life of Ralph Waldo Emerson* (Philadelphia: University of Pennsylvania Press, 1953), 28–40. Whicher here restates an objection raised during Emerson's lifetime and echoed by other critics over the years.

3. "Self-Reliance," 259, 273.

4. Ibid., 275.

5. George Kateb, "Self-Reliance, Politics, and Society" (1995), in this volume, 74; Judith N. Shklar, "Emerson and the Inhibitions of Democracy," 53–54.

6. This image was unfortunately reinforced by the (recently corrected) unavailability of many of Emerson's antislavery writings and speeches. See the "Historical Introduction," to Len Gougeon and Joel Myerson, eds., *Emerson's Antislavery Writings* (New Haven: Yale University Press, 1995), liii–lvi, hereafter cited as *AW*.

7. Shklar, in "Emerson and the Inhibitions of Democracy," does not mention Emerson's antislavery commitments. Kateb, in *Emerson and Self-Reliance*, sees Emerson's antislavery activity as an "aberration," a "deviation" from self-reliance. See the discussion below.

8. "An Address, Delivered before the Senior Class in Divinity College," July 15, 1838, in *E&L*, 73–92.

9. "Address to the Citizens of Concord," May 3, 1851, in *AW*, 58. I agree with Jack Turner that for Emerson, knowing complicity with injustice negated individual self-reliance (see Turner's essay in this volume).

10. Entry from 1852 in *The Journals of Ralph Waldo Emerson*, vol. 13, ed. Ralph H. Orth and Alfred R. Ferguson (Cambridge: Harvard University Press, 1977), 80.

11. "Address to the Citizens of Concord," 68.

12. "Attempted Speech," January 24, 1861, in *AW*, 127. Emerson had earlier speculated in his private journals about the possibility of forming a separate "Northern Union" after the brutal 1856 attack on the Massachusetts senator Charles Sumner by the South Carolina congressman Preston Brooks on the Senate floor in 1856. On Emerson's secessionist moments, see Len Gougeon, *Virtue's Hero: Emerson, Antislavery, and Reform* (Athens: University of Georgia Press, 1990), 222, 261–62.

13. "Self-Reliance," 272.

14. Ibid., 279–81.

15. Ibid., 279.

16. Ibid., 262.

17. *Journals*, 13:282.

18. "Self-Reliance," 259.

19. "New England Reformers" (1844), in *E&L*, 592–93.

20. *Journals*, 13:282.

21. For the fugitive slave battles in 1850s Massachusetts, including Emerson's role, see Albert J. Von Frank, *The Trials of Anthony Burns: Freedom and Slavery in Emerson's Boston* (Cambridge: Harvard University Press, 1998).

22. *AW*, 57–58.

23. *Journals*, 13:80.

24. For analysis of the southern perspective on slavery in the territories, see James H. Read, *Majority Rule versus Consensus: The Political Thought of John C. Calhoun* (Lawrence: University Press of Kansas, 2009), 95–106; and Mark A. Graber, *Dred Scott and the Problem of Constitutional Evil* (New York: Cambridge University Press, 2006), 135–44.

25. For the legal as well as illegal efforts to suppress abolitionist speech, see James B. Stewart, *Abolitionist Politics and the Coming of the Civil War* (Amherst: University of Massachusetts Press, 2008); and William Lee Miller, *Arguing about Slavery: The Great Battle in the United States Congress* (New York: Knopf, 1995). For Emerson's own encounters with hostile anti-abolitionist audiences, see Gougeon, *Virtue's Hero*, 169, 264–66.

26. Phillips to Frederick Douglass, April 22, 1845. The letter is included as

an introduction to *Frederick Douglass: The Narrative and Selected Writings*, ed. Michael Meyer (New York: Modern Library, 1984).

27. Frederick Douglass, *Autobiographies* (New York: Library of America, 1994), 705–6.

28. *Journals*, 13:304.

29. See Emerson's biographical sketch of Thoreau, where he observes that Thoreau "never voted" and was "unrepresented in actual politics" except in the person of John Brown; Thoreau "seemed born for great enterprise and for command" but chose to remain merely "the captain of a huckleberry party" (*Selections from Ralph Waldo Emerson*, ed. Stephen E. Whicher, [Boston: Houghton Mifflin, 1957], 379–95). Whether Thoreau's philosophy of political withdrawal was as negative as Emerson claims may be debated (see Shannon Mariotti, *Thoreau's Democratic Withdrawal: Alienation, Participation, and Modernity* [Madison: University of Wisconsin Press, 2010]). Emerson's personal commitment to voting is discussed in Len Gougeon's essay in this volume.

30. Gougeon, *Virtue's Hero*, 166–70, 204–6.

31. *AW*, 68–69.

32. Ibid., 112–13.

33. Ibid., 113–15.

34. In the Pottawatomie Massacre of May 24–25, 1856, John Brown led a group of antislavery raiders who entered the homes of proslavery Kansas settlers and killed five.

35. "Historical Introduction" to *AW*, xlvi–xlvii.

36. *AW*, 119.

37. Emerson's "representative men" are central to Shklar's "Emerson and the Inhibitions of Democracy." But Shklar mentions neither Emerson's opposition to slavery nor his admiration for John Brown. For insightful discussion of Brown as an Emersonian "representative man," see Jason Frank's essay in this volume.

38. *AW*, 118–19.

39. *Journals*, 13:111–12. See also the detailed critique of Webster in his March 7, 1854, speech on the Fugitive Slave Law (*AW*, 74–79).

40. See the 1840 and 1844 journal entries on race included in Kenneth S. Sacks, ed., *Emerson: Political Writings* (New York: Cambridge University Press, 2008), 127–29. See also Emerson, *Journals*, 11:385 (1851) and 13:35, 54, 198 (from the 1850s).

41. For Emerson's view of "Anglo-Saxons," see *Journals*, 13:216 and much of his 1856 book *English Traits*. For Emerson's interest in and criticism of "racial science" see *Journals*, 11:392 and 13:288.

42. "Address on the Emancipation of the Negroes in the British West Indies" (1844), in *AW*, 23, 29–30.

43. Gougeon, *Virtue's Hero*, 101–7.

44. For a very negative perspective on Emerson's racial views, see Nell Irvin Painter, *The History of White People* (New York: Norton, 2010), 151–89; for a more sympathetic assessment, see Gougeon, *Virtue's Hero*, 178–85, as well as Gougeon's essay in this volume. See also Philip Nicoloff, *Emerson on Race and History* (New York: Columbia University Press, 1961), who notes that for Emerson racial characteristics were not permanently fixed but susceptible to slow modification over time (120–23); Peter S. Field, *Ralph Waldo Emerson: The Making of a Democratic Individual* (Lanham, Md.: Rowman and Littlefield, 2002), who argues that Emerson's assumption of black inferiority diminished over time but persisted despite his abolitionist commitments (167–207); and Eduardo Cadava, *Emerson and the Climates of History* (Stanford: Stanford University Press, 1997), who argues that Emerson's racial utterances were inherently double-edged, simultaneously drawing from and destabilizing theories of racial science (57–62).

45. On England's status as a superior civilization because it took the lead on abolishing slavery, see Emerson, *Journals*, 13:153. For the parallel claim that New England represents a higher civilization compared to the white South, see the closing paragraph of his "Address to the Citizens of Concord" (May 1, 1851), in *AW*, 71. On benevolence toward the weak as the marker of superior civilization, see Emerson, *Journals*, 11:412–13.

46. *AW*, 19–22.

47. See Emerson, *Journals*, 13:35, 82. On the tendency of many abolitionists to idealize the suffering Negro as a "natural Christian," see George M. Fredrickson, *The Black Image in the White Mind: The Debate on Afro-American Character and Destiny, 1817–1914* (New York: Harper and Row, 1971), 97–129.

48. See Emerson, *Journals*, 13:35 (undated entry from the 1850s).

49. *E&L*, 272.

50. *AW*, 26.

51. Emerson, *Journals*, 11:412–13.

52. Emerson, "Address on the Emancipation" (1844), in *AW*, 8, 20.

53. *AW*, 30.

54. Ibid., 31.

55. Ibid.

56. On this theme, see Jack Turner's essay in this volume, which describes individual and collective resistance to unjust laws as instances of Emersonian self-reliance.

57. "Address to the Citizens of Concord," 62.

58. Ibid., 57; *Journals*, 11:411.

59. "Fate," in *E&L*, 949.

60. "Self-Reliance," 260.

61. "Fate," 943, 951–52.
62. Ibid., 950–53.
63. "Self-Reliance," 281.
64. "Fate," 943.
65. "Power," in *E&L*, 972.
66. See "Concerning Brook Farm," in Sacks, *Emerson: Political Writings*, 93–99.
67. "Fate," 948.
68. "Power," 975.
69. Whicher, *Freedom and Fate*, 25, 72–82, 116, 131, 163.
70. Here I agree with David Robinson in *Emerson and the Conduct of Life* (New York: Cambridge University Press, 1993) that Emerson's recognition of limits in "Fate" "was not a prescription for paralysis" (135) but presupposed continued political and ethical engagement.
71. George Kateb, *Emerson and Self-Reliance* (1995; new ed., Lanham, Md.: Rowman and Littlefield, 2002), 32, 37, 186.
72. Ibid., 177–78, 185.
73. "Fate," 943.
74. "Power," 971.
75. "Fate," 943, 956.
76. Ibid., 948.
77. "Power," 975.
78. Ibid., 960–61.
79. My observation here converges with Shannon Mariotti's analysis of Emerson's "focal distancing" in her essay in this volume.

CHAPTER 7

Emerson, Self-Reliance, and the Politics of Democracy

Len Gougeon

THERE WAS A TIME when most scholars assumed that Emerson's transcendental philosophy, with its emphasis on self-reliance, was antithetical to political activism. Even though Henry Steele Commager asserted in his *Era of Reform: 1830–1860* (1960) that "Emerson [was] the cow from which [reformers] all drew their milk," it was generally assumed that Transcendentalists as a group were nonpolitical and socially aloof.[1] Thus, Arthur M. Schlesinger Jr., in his influential study *The Age of Jackson* (1945), held that the Transcendentalists "from their book-lined studies, or their shady walks in cool Concord woods . . . found the hullabaloo of party politics unedifying and vulgar." For Schlesinger, this "flinching from politics" was indicative of the self-reliant reclusiveness of Transcendentalists that, in his view, was "a failure they were seeking to erect into a virtue." He was particularly critical of Emerson for this presumed aloofness and asserted that the bard had "failed himself, and ignored the responsibilities of his own moral position."[2]

In light of the established historical/biographical record that emerged in the 1990s, most scholars today acknowledge the fact that Emerson did engage in substantial political and social reform activities, especially antislavery, from the mid-1840s to the Civil War.[3] As a result of this development, a new line of critical argument has evolved. Instead of arguing whether Transcendentalists participated in social reform movements, scholars now debate whether this development was in keeping with transcendental philosophy or a contradiction of it. John Carlos Rowe, for example, in his study *At Emerson's Tomb: The Politics of Classic American Literature* (1997), holds that "Emersonian transcendentalism and Emerson's political commitments from 1844 to 1863 are fundamentally at odds with each other," and therefore "Emersonianism is ill suited to social and political reform."[4] For Rowe, any attempt to connect transcendentalism and social reform is doomed to failure because, "more often than not, Transcendentalism works to rationalize present wrongs rather than bring about actual social change."[5]

Other critics, however, have reached the opposite conclusion, especially regarding the impact of Emersonian self-reliance on his politics of reform. David Robinson, for example, asserts that "the internal logic of Emerson's program of self-culture inevitably dictated social justice as a means of willed enactment of the ideal." He goes on to note that "that logic was sharpened by the building movement of political dissent in the 1840s. By 1841, a political response was emerging in Emerson's work, which became an important ethical concern."[6] Also, T. Gregory Garvey insists that Emerson embraced democratic reform "as the essential link between liberal selfhood and authentic community." He further contends that "Emerson's theory of self-reliance is a model of liberal utopia because it makes autonomous and individualistic selfhood the necessary foundation of authentic community."[7]

The discussion that follows demonstrates how Emerson deployed his transcendental philosophy in the service of social reform. That philosophy was built upon the notion that every person participates in a divine and universal "Over-Soul." This "Over-Soul," whose influence is felt intuitively, provides the basis for both individual self-reliance and a collective social identity. In the period before the Civil War, Emerson repeatedly spoke out against slavery in both political and nonpolitical contexts. In his personal crusade against the institution, he attacked slavery as a moral abomination and a violation of the principle of equality upon which the nation was founded. With the coming of the war, Emerson emerged as an acknowledged moral voice of the Union cause, which he saw as the cause of universal freedom and social equality. In the aftermath of the Civil War, he continued to promote the principles of self-reliant freedom and equal opportunity for all Americans regardless of race or gender.

Emerson's Transcendental Philosophy

In order to understand Emerson's transcendental politics, it is first necessary to understand his transcendental philosophy. Emerson believed that human nature possesses a dual aspect, basically material and ethereal. Every person has the capacity to operate in both of these realms. In dealing with the practical world of everyday life, we use what Emerson called "the Understanding." But our actions in this world must be informed by universal moral laws that are intuitively perceived through what Emerson called, "the Reason." Like other Transcendentalists, Emerson borrowed these terms from the German philosopher Immanuel Kant, via his English interpreter, Samuel Taylor Coleridge.[8] In a letter to his younger brother Edward in May 1834, Emerson makes the distinction between the Understanding and the Reason explicit, and in the process he also indicates his sources. "Now that I have used the words," he says, "let me ask you to draw the distinction of Milton[,] Coleridge & the Germans between Reason & Understanding. . . . Reason is the highest faculty of the soul—what we mean often by the soul itself; it never *reasons*, never proves, it simply perceives; it is vision." On the other hand, "the Understanding toils all the time, compares, contrives, adds, argues, near sighted but strong-sighted, dwelling in the present the expedient the customary."[9] This important distinction is a hallmark of Emerson's transcendentalism. He goes on to further elaborate on these qualities. "Reason," he says, "is potentially perfect in every man—Understanding in different degrees of strength. The thoughts of youth, & 'first thoughts,' are the revelations of Reason. The love of the beautiful & of Goodness as the highest beauty the belief in the absolute & universal superiority of the Right & the True[.] But understanding[,] that wrinkled calculator[,] the steward of our house to whom is committed the support of our animal life[,] contradicts evermore these affirmations of Reason & points at Custom & Interest & persuades one man that the declarations of Reason are false & another that they are at least impracticable."[10] This dualism had an important impact on Emerson's understanding of politics, as well as his concept of self-reliance. According to the dichotomy described above, the most important values, those that inform our conduct of life, are derived through the function of the Reason. It is also through the intuitions of the Reason that we establish our individual identity as we simultaneously sense our oneness with the universal "Over-Soul," that spiritual dynamic that unites all things and brings meaning and harmony to our lives both personally and socially. In his classic essay "The Over-Soul" (1841), Emerson describes this entity as "that Unity, that Over-Soul, within which every man's particular being is contained and made one with all other" (*CW*, 2:160).

The important thing to note here is the expression of Emerson's belief in the ultimate unity and equality of humanity. Because he believed in the oneness of the human family, he also believed in the liberal democratic concept of universal human rights. As he notes in his essay "Politics" (1841): "Of persons, all have equal rights, in virtue of being identical in nature. This interest, of course, with its whole power demands a democracy" (*CW*, 3:118). Throughout his lifetime, Emerson's reform activities were consistently aimed at liberalizing American democracy. He believed that the universe was permeated with moral laws that provide a source of guidance in this quest. They are available to all individuals through intuition. He sometimes called this agency "moral sentiment."[11] Emerson believed that this force has been at work throughout history and is responsible for the liberal progress of civilization, a progress that will ultimately lead to universal democratic freedom and equality. As Neal Dolan observes, "For Emerson, the history of liberty was in part the history of a 'moral feeling.'"[12] Ideally, all civil laws should reflect this universal moral code because, as Emerson insists, just laws "do not make right, but are simply declaratory of a right that already existed."[13] Conversely, an unjust law or institution is a violation of this universal moral order and therefore cannot last. Thus, Emerson was able to declare with confidence that "the inconsistency of slavery with the principles on which the world is built guarantees its downfall" (*AW*, 86–87).

Emerson believed that American democracy represented a major step in the evolution of liberal democratic governance. Self-reliance, rather than being antithetical, was an essential element in this evolution. Like other Transcendentalists, Emerson admired the Declaration of Independence (which he once called "the greatest achievement of American literature") precisely because it articulated concepts of universal equality and universal human rights that are held to be "self-evident."[14] For Emerson, the essential truths of democracy, our very founding principles, were the intuitively perceived products of the Reason, that divine guiding force that is the birthright of all individuals. Gregg Crane rightly identifies this inner spiritual dynamic as the source of Emerson's concept of "Higher Law," a moral standard available to all individuals that overrides the authority of the Constitution, particularly where that document gives sanction to the institution of slavery. As Crane points out, "This indwelling and universal faculty of moral perception enables even an untutored child to intuit the wrongness of slavery."[15] Unfortunately, this aboriginal morality, which is the product of the Reason, is compromised in some by the dominance of the Understanding, which, as noted earlier, is focused on controlling material reality. In "Self-Reliance," Emerson asserts that this materialistic emphasis reflects a disconnection from the spiritual resources within. This, in turn, leads to a "reliance on Property, including the reliance on governments which protect it." Slavery is the ultimate expression of this dehumanizing materialism because it literally turns people into property. Such materialists naturally resist all efforts at reform "because they feel them to be assaults on property" (*CW*, 2:49).

Slavery was especially abominable in Emerson's eyes because it violated an essential principle of what might be called democratic morality, a morality based on our common human nature. For Emerson, the glue that holds society together derives from the universal sense of human rights and principles of justice that lie within us all.[16] Like other Transcendentalists, Emerson was convinced that blacks shared in the divinity that gives meaning and dignity to all human life and, therefore, were entitled to the same rights that are guaranteed to all citizens.[17] "Democracy/Freedom," he recorded in his journal in 1834, "has its root in the Sacred truth that every man hath in him the divine Reason," and therefore all men are capable of "liv[ing] according to the dictates of Reason." That is "the equality & the only equality of all men," and "because every man has within him some[thing] really divine therefore is slavery the unpardonable outrage it is."[18]

The political consequences of Emerson's commitment to the primal individual were unappreciated by most scholars before 1990. This seminal concept lies at the heart of his idea of liberal democracy. For him, the common moral nature shared by all individuals is the driving force behind social reform. Because of this, as T. Gregory Garvey has argued, "Emerson sought to promote a mode of reform that was premised on the possibility of infusing all of society with the same kind of insight that the individual gains at moments of inspiration." Garvey calls this, appropriately, Emerson's "political spirit."[19] This is why Emerson insists on emphasizing the importance of self-reliance as the key to collective efforts at social reform. For him, and for other Transcendentalists, social reform begins with the individual, but it does not end there. The Declaration of Independence is only efficacious as a social and political document if one personally feels an intuitive affirmation of the validity of its assertions. When such truth is felt and its implications comprehended, the individual becomes a living embodiment of it.[20] This feeling provides a natural motivation to join with others who also acknowledge this truth and, in the case of slavery, perceive the injustice that it illuminates. This perception, in turn, both demands and informs social action. As Emerson insists in his 1854 "Fugitive Slave Law" address, the moral obligation to extirpate the gross injustice of slavery is compelling and "seems to demand of us more than mere hoping," because "there is a Divine Providence in the world which will not save us but through our own co-operation" (*AW*, 87, 89). Emersonian self-reliance does not, therefore, remove the individual from society, as some critics maintain, but just the opposite. As Wesley Mott observes: "For Emerson . . . genuine individualism was not narcissism, monomania, or isolation. Indeed, it was the *answer* to these diseases of the self as well as the remedy for the 'existing evils' of institutional and social life."[21]

As the following analysis will show, Emerson's twenty-year campaign against the institution of slavery was the result of his belief in the divinity of the individual and the moral efficacy of a democracy that relied upon the collective conscience of individual citizens. The expression of this transcendental "political spirit," beginning in the 1840s, would culminate in his unwavering support for the principles of freedom, equality before the law, and universal male suffrage—key elements of a liberal democracy—as Union goals during the Civil War. Transcendental self-reliance was the primary weapon Emerson deployed in this long and ultimately successful struggle.

Emerson's Transcendental Politics before the Civil War

The relationship of Emerson's transcendental philosophy to his politics of reform is clear throughout his pre–Civil War writings. Emerson was fully aware that in a democracy "what great masses of men wish done, will be done" (*AW*, 28). But to be efficacious, this individual moral response must become part of a public discourse that ultimately shapes public policy. As T. Gregory Garvey observes, for Emerson, "self-reliance is a mode of public dialogue. It cannot exist in private, head-in-the-clouds communion with spirit."[22] Indeed, for Emerson the public articulation of what we think and feel is an essential element of our human nature. As he insists in "The Poet" (1844), "all men live by truth, and stand in need of expression. In love, in art, in avarice, in politics, in labor, in games, we study to utter our painful secret. The man is only half himself, the other half is his expression" (*CW*, 3:4).

Emerson's first efforts to address the slavery issue were indirect and relied on the efficacy of moral suasion directed at individuals. In lyceum lectures and public addresses, he sought to raise the consciousness of the American public regarding the need for self-reform that would lead, he believed, to social reform. He hoped through public discourse to stimulate moral insight. The process was highly individualistic, as moral reform must always be. But once the individual is awakened from moral lethargy, the perception of social evil becomes possible. This perception is then articulated in the context of civil discourse. The next step, ideally, would be a collective effort to extirpate the evil.[23] In his early public addresses, Emerson sought to awaken his audience from their complacency and to educate them on issues of social and personal importance. Because he believed that the moral laws of the universe could be intuitively perceived, Emerson was confident that through a combination of personal introspection and public dialogue, American society would inevitably identify and correct its moral flaws. A democracy is ideally suited to such a process, and he saw the beginnings of it already at work. In "Man the Reformer" (1841), Emerson observes that "in the history of the world the doctrine of Reform had never such scope as at the present hour" (*CW*, 1:146). In this lecture, he describes the kind of self-reform that he believed would ultimately lead to social reform. "Every man should assume his own vows," he insists, and "should call the institutions of society to account" (*CW*, 1:153). In Emerson's view, the freedom afforded citizens in a democracy results in a moral mandate for ongoing reform. As he states: "We are to revise the whole of our social structure, the state, the school, religion, marriage, trade, science, and explore their foundations in our own nature; . . . What is a man born for," he asks, "but to be a Reformer, a Re-maker of what man has made; a renouncer of lies; a restorer of truth and good" (*CW*, 1:156). The political implications of this notion are clear. As he states in a later address, in a democracy, Congress should be "a standing insurrection" that ensures "perpetual change."[24]

Meeting this mandate is both a moral imperative and a political and civic obligation. Emerson believed that democratic citizenship demands participation in the political process in order to ensure moral and social progress. In his lecture "The Transcendentalist" (1842), he expresses his growing displeasure with those young intellectuals and would-be reformers who failed to actively address the major social problems of the day. Emerson expected a new world from them, and they had failed so far to deliver. Instead they chose to remain passive and aloof from "the labors of the world; they are not good citizens, not good members of society; unwillingly they bear their part of the public and private burdens; they do not willingly share in the public charities, in the public religious rites, in the enterprizes of education, of missions foreign or domestic, in the abolition of the slave-trade, or in the temperance-society. They are inactive; they do not even like to vote" (*CW*, 1:210–11). Emerson reminds these young men and others that it is not enough to be passively good, but "the good and wise must learn to act, and carry salvation to the combatants and demagogues in the dusty arena below" (*CW*, 1:211). Political action is especially important in a democracy where the primary instrument for social reform is the ballot box.

Emerson always voted, and he always encouraged others to vote. He believed that voting was both an obligation and a privilege. In a democracy, to refuse to participate in the political life of the nation was to abandon one's obligation to address the pressing social problems of the day in a meaningful and constructive way. Also, as a Transcendentalist, Emerson believed in the basic goodness of humankind. In "New England Reformers" (1844), he states: "Nothing shall warp me from the belief, that every man is a lover of the truth. . . . The entertainment of the proposition of depravity is the last profligacy and profanation. There is no skepticism, no atheism but that. Could it be received into common belief, suicide would unpeople the planet." For Emerson, voting was one of the ways that humanity's basic decency might have its proper influence. "I remember standing at the polls one day," he recalls, "and a good man at my side looking on the people, remarked, 'I am satisfied that the largest part of these men, on either side, mean to vote right.' I suppose considerate observers, looking at the masses of men in their blameless and in their equivocal actions, will assent, that in spite of selfishness and frivolity, the general purpose in the great number of persons is fidelity" (*CW*, 3:163–64). Without such confidence, in Emerson's view, democracy itself would not be possible.

One of the problems that Emerson faced when engaging the specific issues of reform in the early 1840s concerned the role played by associations. Because of the emphasis he placed on the principle of self-reliance as the cornerstone of moral and social reform, he was concerned that membership in associations often compromised this principle. He did not feel that associations should dictate the actions of individuals. Each must find his/her own way. Thus, in his lecture "Reforms" (1840), he cautions against the loss of individuality that, in his view, associated efforts at reform often precipitate. "Accept the reforms," says Emerson, "but accept not the person of the reformer nor his law. Accept the reform but be thou thyself sacred, intact, inviolable, one whom leaders, one whom multitudes cannot drag from thy central seat." The danger is that "if you take the reform as the reformer brings it to you he transforms you into an instrument."[25] The lack of introspection and thoughtfulness leads to a loss of self-reliance because truth "cannot be received at second hand. Truly speaking, it is not instruction, but provocation, that I can receive from another soul. What he announces, I must find true in me, or wholly reject; and on his word, or as his second, be he who he may, I can accept nothing" (*CW*, 1:80). Speaking directly to reformers, Emerson makes his point with personal emphasis: "Though I sympathize with your sentiment and abhor the crime you assail yet I shall persist in wearing this robe, all loose and unbecoming as it is, of inaction, this wise passiveness until my hour comes when I can see how to act with truth as well as to refuse" (*EL*, 3:266). It is this same concern, in part at least, that informs his sharp and oft-noted criticism of abolitionists in "Self-Reliance."

Emerson's well-known wariness of reform associations is not because they are united, but because of how and why they unite. He describes some of these would-be reformers as "angry bigot[s]" who are both myopic and self-righteous. In his view, such moral busybodies with their "hard, uncharitable ambition" were merely self-serving egotists who were not interested in meaningful civil discourse or comprehensive moral reform (*CW*, 2:30). As such, they have no useful role to play in a democratic society where every issue must be subjected to sincere and open public discussion and not polarizing propaganda. Emerson's view of abolitionists at this time was based on limited personal experience.[26]

At the same time, Emerson expressed his confidence that reform can be accomplished without compromising the individuality of the reformers.

> I do not wonder at the interest these projects inspire. The world is awaking to the idea of union, and these experiments show what it is thinking of. It is and will be magic. Men will live and communicate, and plough, and reap, and govern, as by added ethereal power, when once they are united; . . . But this union must be inward, and not one of covenants, and is to be reached by a reverse of the methods they use. The union is only perfect when all the uniters are isolated. . . . Each man, if he attempts to join himself to others, is

on all sides cramped and diminished of his proportion; and the stricter the union the smaller and the more pitiful he is. But leave him alone, to recognize in every hour and place the secret soul; he will go up and down doing the works of a true member, and, to the astonishment of all, the work will be done with concert, though no man spoke. Government will be adamantine without any governor. *The union must be ideal in actual individualism.* (*CW*, 3:157; emphasis added)

Despite such criticisms of the pitfalls of associations, on August 1, 1844, just five months after his Amory Hall lecture, Emerson delivered his first major public statement on the subject of slavery in response to an invitation from the Concord Female Anti-Slavery Society. His "Address on the Emancipation of the Negroes in the British West Indies" marked a dramatic shift in his approach to the question of reform generally, and the antislavery movement in particular. He was now prepared to cooperate with organized reformers in their opposition to slavery. Over time, this cooperation would become a de facto alliance. While his basic philosophy of reform remained unchanged, this development indicates a significant shift in Emerson's tactics. What caused this change is not immediately clear.[27] One might point to the historical developments of the time, including the application of Texas for entry into the Union as a slaveholding state. Following its declaration of independence from Mexico, Texas first petitioned for statehood on August 4, 1837. Because it was clear that the entrance of Texas into the Union would result in a significant expansion of the slave power, the petition was hotly opposed by abolitionists everywhere. Like them, Emerson believed that Massachusetts should "resist the annexation tooth & nail" (*JMN*, 9:74). Despite such opposition, on April 12, 1844, under the direction of then secretary of state John C. Calhoun, a treaty was signed that provided for the annexation of Texas. President Tyler urged its approval in Congress and the passage of the measure appeared inevitable to many.[28] With it would come the end of the precarious balance of power that had obtained since 1820 and the Missouri Compromise. Following this, the possibilities for the continued expansion of slave territory, and slave power, were virtually unlimited.[29] It is safe to say that Emerson anticipated this situation by the summer of 1844, and this undoubtedly influenced his decision to become more active himself in opposing the increasingly aggressive evil of slavery. It should also be noted that by this time he had become personally acquainted with several major figures in the antislavery movement. As a result, in contrast to his earlier criticisms, he now felt a deep respect for them, especially William Lloyd Garrison and Wendell Phillips.[30]

While he was now willing to enter the abolitionist ranks, it is clear from the outset of his address that Emerson had no intention of putting aside his commitment to the principle of self-reliance and the need for reasonable civic discourse. Indeed, he wished to make a presentation that would encourage both thoughtfulness and insight. He continued to believe that the divine spirit residing in all people, when called upon, would lead individuals to the kind of collective action that would bring an end to slavery. His 1844 address emphasizes the role of individuals in the history of British emancipation, and how their work led to collective action. "On reviewing this history," Emerson notes, "I think the whole transaction reflects infinite honor on the people and parliament of England" (*AW*, 22). The process was one of extended public dialogue and political pressure informed and empowered by moral sentiment. Emerson hoped for something similar in the United States. "Whilst I have read of England, I have thought of New England" (23). If this kind of moral progress was possible in England with its limited democracy, then much more should be possible in America if the people and their representatives simply open their hearts and their minds to the moral force that would mandate such action. Unfortunately, this has not been the case. In part, the problem has been the lack of personal fortitude on the part of elected representatives from Massachusetts and the other free states. Emerson was particularly incensed at the practice of imprisoning black seamen, who were free citizens of these states, while their ships were in southern ports. Sometimes these free blacks were kidnapped when they were onshore and sold into slavery. But this outrageous practice brought no response from the elected representatives of the state of Massachusetts, and Emerson declares that he is "at a loss how to characterize the tameness and silence" of Massachusetts' elected representative at Washington. Indeed, it seems that "there is a disastrous want of *men* from New England" in the Congress just now (*AW*, 133). This lack of moral fortitude on the part of elected representatives is a significant factor in the perpetuation of slavery in America. As Emerson had noted three years earlier in his essay "Self-Reliance," "God will not have his work made manifest by cowards," and these failed representatives are an excellent example of the truth of that proposition (*CW*, 2:28). The alternative in this situation is a people's movement, such as that which took place in England, where common citizens were able to make their voices heard. Such a public "conversation" can lead to change if individual citizens are persistent in making their collective voices heard. Emerson assures his audience that it is through such "direct conversation" that a "man is to make himself felt by his proper force" (*AW*, 28–29).

For Emerson, the principle of self-reliance and resistance must also be applied to the black slaves themselves, a position that is in stark contrast to that of most abolitionists, who saw virtually no role for them to play in their own emancipation. Britain's emancipation day, Emerson asserts, "marks the entrance of a new element into modern politics, namely, the civilization of the Negro. A man is added to the human family. Not the least affecting part of this history of abolition is, the annihilation of the old indecent nonsense about the nature of the Negro" (*AW*, 29).[31] Emerson goes on to point out that the slaves in the West Indies contributed significantly to their own emancipation: "I have said that this event interests us because it came mainly from the concession of the whites; I add, that in part it is the earning of the blacks. They won the pity and respect which they have received, by their powers and native endowments. I think this is a circumstance of the highest import. Their whole future is in it" (*AW*, 30). Unlike most other abolitionists, Emerson emphasizes blacks' own agency in ending slavery.

The fact that the West Indian slaves participated in their own liberation is important because the power of nature is relentless. In words that shocked some abolitionists at the time, Emerson says of the force of nature: "It will only save what is worth saving; and it saves not by compassion, but by power. . . . If the black man is feeble and not important to the existing races not on a parity with the best race, the black man must serve, and be exterminated. But if the black man carries in his bosom an indispensable element of a new and coming civilization; for the sake of that element, no wrong, nor strength, nor circumstance can hurt him: he will survive and play his part" (*AW*, 31). Unlike many abolitionists who held a distinctly paternalistic attitude toward blacks, Emerson maintained a transcendental faith in universal equality. That faith assured him that oppressed blacks would inevitably arise from oppression and claim their proper place in the world. He envisioned a self-reliant "anti-slave," whom he saw embodied in the West Indian revolutionaries who led the fight for freedom there. He would see this vision fully realized in America almost twenty years later when the Union army eventually accepted and deployed nearly two hundred thousand Negro troops, many of whom were self-liberated former slaves. Here, he draws inspiration from the revolutionary struggles of blacks in the West Indies. "So now, the arrival in the world of such men as Toussaint, and the Haytian heroes, or of the leaders of their race in Barbadoes and Jamaica, outweighs in good omen all the English and American humanity. The anti-slavery of the whole world is dust in the balance before this,—is a poor squeamishness and nervousness: the might and the right are here: here is the anti-slave: here is man: and if you have man, black or white is an insignificance" (AW, 31). Emerson also insists that the emergence of this long-repressed race will be welcomed in the world because "their more moral genius is becoming indispensable and the quality of this race is to be honored for itself." But he also insists that as they emerge, they must be "clothed . . . in their own form" (AW, 32). This latter requirement is important and reflects Emerson's persistent emphasis on the importance of self-reliance. African Americans cannot merely seek to present a pale imitation of white civilization; they must be true to themselves.

Following this groundbreaking address in 1844, manifestations of Emerson's "political spirit" became more frequent as his commitment to the antislavery movement intensified. In the same year, he signed a petition, along with many of his Concord neighbors, calling on Massachusetts both to propose an amendment to the U.S. Constitution outlawing slavery and to eliminate all state laws and constitutional provisions "making any distinctions among citizens on account of color."[32] He reprised his August performance with emancipation addresses in 1845, 1846, and 1849. He gave an additional antislavery lecture at an event sponsored by the Massachusetts Antislavery Society on the Fourth of July in 1846. In his 1845 emancipation address, Emerson presented a bitter attack on the racism that reinforced the institution of slavery. As he well knew, there is nothing more injurious to a diverse democracy than the bigotry and bitterness of racism. Racism arbitrarily denies the individual self-worth of entire groups and seeks to deprive them of their natural and civil rights as people and citizens. As Emerson notes, this racism toward blacks was summarized in one word: "That word is *Niggers!*—a word which, cried by rowdy boys and rowdy men in the ear of this timid and sceptical generation, is reckoned stronger than heaven; it blows away with a jeer all the efforts of philanthropy, all the expostulations of pity, the cries of millions, now for hundreds of years—all are answered by this insulting appellation, 'Oh, the Niggers!' and the boys straightway sing Jim Crow and jump Jim Crow in the streets and taverns"

(*AW*, 36). For many, this noxious and thoughtless prejudice precludes the necessity, or even the possibility, of reform: "They who say it and they who hear it, think it the voice of nature and fate pronouncing against the Abolitionist and the Philanthropist." But Emerson will have none of it. He remains confident that moral law will prevail against such blind bigotry, and justice will ultimately be done. "The Universe is not bankrupt," he declares: "still stands the old heart firm in its seat, and knows that, come what will, the right is and shall be. Justice is for ever and ever" (*AW*, 36).

Emerson was fully prepared to put his antiracist creed into his deeds. Just months later, in November 1845, he boycotted the New Bedford Lyceum because of its recent exclusion of Negroes from regular membership.[33] In July 1846, with the Mexican War threatening a dramatic extension of the slave power, Emerson became increasingly irritated with the moral apathy of Massachusetts toward this unjust war. In his address to a large antislavery gathering at Dedham, Massachusetts, on the Fourth of July, the day that Americans celebrate their revolutionary beginnings, he called for the formation of a "revolutionary committee" to oppose the war with Mexico. He also castigated the citizens of the state for their cowardly "inaction and apathy," even referring to them at one point as "sniveling nobodies" who, by implication, failed the test of democratic citizenship. By contrast, he had nothing but praise for the abolitionists, "these brave men and brave women," who sought to prick the conscience of the people through public discourse and to stimulate them to a more active role in resisting the evil of the time (*AW*, 41, 43). Emerson's resistance to the encroachments of the slave power were obviously acquiring a more militant tone, and organized abolitionists were his natural allies.[34]

Later in 1846, following the forcible return from Boston to Louisiana of a fugitive slave who had stowed away on the cargo ship *Ottoman,* Emerson was presented with an example of the kind of vigilant resistance for which he had called. In the wake of this incident, a "Vigilance Committee" was formed to prevent such an outrage from happening again. Emerson sent a public letter of support to this committee in which he acknowledged the "irreparable shame to Boston of this abduction." He also applauded the committee's determination to cleanse the population "from the stain of this crime" by actively resisting all further efforts of this nature (*AW*, 47, 48). Many Boston abolitionists were coming to the realization at this time that physical resistance would be necessary to combat such outrages in the future, and Emerson supported their resolve.

Emerson's faith in revolutionary politics was buttressed during a ten-month lecture tour in England in 1847–1848. While there he attended sessions of the House of Lords and the House of Commons, as well as meetings of the radical Chartists, one of the earliest independent movements for the rights of the working class. Emerson witnessed their demonstrations and was positively impressed. He also traveled to revolutionary Paris in early May 1848. While there he observed meetings of the National Assembly and attended various radical gatherings at such places as the Free Trade Club and the Barbes Club. What he heard had a profound effect on his social consciousness.[35] In a long letter to his wife, Lidian, Emerson described the excitement of the place, where he witnessed "streets full of bayonets, and the furious driving of the horses dragging cannon towards the National Assembly," as an attempted coup d'état failed to gain popular support. He also noted the fierce resolve of the many participants, a stark contrast to the "sniveling nobodies" of his home state: "Though I have been to many places I find the clubs the most interesting—the men are in terrible earnest. The fire & fury of the people, when they are interrupted or thwarted, are inconceivable to New England. The costumes are formidable. All France is bearded like goats & lions, then most of Paris is in some kind of uniform red sash, red cap, blouse perhaps bound by red sash, brass helmet, & sword, and every body supposed to have a pistol in his pocket. But the deep sincerity of the speakers who are agitating social not political questions, and who are studying how to secure a fair share of bread to every man, and to get the God's justice done through the land, is very good to hear" (*Letters*, 4:73–74). While witnessing firsthand the popular uprisings against the entrenched ruling classes that were spreading across Europe in 1848, "The Year of Revolution," Emerson became more convinced than ever that the universal impulse for freedom and equality, emerging at the grassroots level among common people, would have a positive and lasting effect. Emerson saw these revolutions essentially as people's movements resulting from spontaneous and natural coalitions. As such they offered compelling evidence that the divine Over-Soul was stirring the hearts of people who were hungry for reform. This was Emerson's political spirit made manifest on a grand scale.[36]

When he returned to America, Emerson took the optimism of the Chartists and the French radicals with him. When called upon by William Lloyd Garrison to speak once again at an abolitionist rally celebrating emancipation in the British West Indies, he accepted. The gathering was held on August 3, 1849, in Worcester, Massachusetts. An estimated five thousand abolition supporters attended.[37] Emerson's mood was optimistic and his message upbeat. He felt that the spirit of liberty was on the march in the world and that America, too, would soon feel its natural effects. "The force of history is one everywhere," he told the crowd. "Revolutions, as we say, never move backwards." While there may be occasional setbacks, the arc of history is clear; democracy was on the rise. The desire for liberty, justice, and social equality was an irresistible, liberalizing force at work in the hearts of all people. The presence on this particular occasion of five thousand activists (undoubtedly the largest gathering that he had addressed to that point) must have reinforced his optimistic assumption that the movement was gaining momentum in America. "It should be praise enough for our friends who have carried forward this great work," he told them, "friends to whom it seems to me always, the country is more and more indebted." The reason for this indebtedness is that these individual reformers have touched the universal wellspring of reform in the hearts of many individuals. As he notes, "it is the glory of these preachers of freedom that they have strengthened the moral sense, that they have anticipated this triumph which I look upon as inevitable, and which it is not in man to retard" (AW, 48, 49).

Unfortunately, Emerson's optimism would soon suffer a major blow. When the Fugitive Slave Law was passed in September 1850, a law that punished with fine and imprisonment anyone found guilty of aiding a fugitive slave, even in a free state, he realized that an important threshold had been crossed. Now, more than ever, it would be up to common citizens, individuals possessed of both courage and conviction, to act in concert in resisting this outrageous and immoral act.

Emerson vowed to defy the law himself at every opportunity, and he was not alone in this resolve. After two failed attempts at returning self-emancipated slaves from Boston in October and February, a young fugitive named Thomas Sims was captured and successfully returned to slavery in the spring of 1851.[38] This happened despite protests, demonstrations, and legal pleading by abolitionists.[39] And it prompted Emerson to deliver the most acerbic presentation of his long career, his "Address to the Citizens of Concord on the Fugitive Slave Law." Emerson repeated this address, which he referred to as a "stump" speech, on several occasions throughout his Middlesex District in the spring of 1851 as part of a political campaign to elect a Free Soil candidate, John Gorham Palfrey, to Congress. This was the first time that Emerson participated directly in a political campaign. Obviously, he felt that the times demanded such commitment.

Emerson begins his address by observing that "the last year has forced us all into politics" (*AW*, 53). No longer, he insists, can citizens sit on the sidelines in "passive obedience" while the government falls more deeply under the pernicious control of the slave power (*AW*, 54). This parlous situation has developed, in part at least, because of the moral apathy of average citizens. This apathy has been encouraged by the influence of thoughtless, partisan politics. "Nothing proves the want of all thought, the absence of standard in men's minds," Emerson insists, "more than the dominion of party" (*AW*, 56). This situation must be reversed, first by turning away from the polarization of the party line and opening oneself to "the sentiment of duty" (*AW*, 57). This is that intuitive, moral sense that allows individual citizens to independently measure the conduct of government against a universal standard of justice. In this case, a law that demands that a man who has struggled for his freedom be returned to slavery is clearly immoral and a violation of the very standards that the Republic proclaims in its own foundational document. As Emerson reminds his audience, "A man's right to liberty is as inalienable as his right to life" (*AW*, 57). Because of this, abominations like the Fugitive Slave Law violate humanity's "primal sentiment of duty, and therefore all men that are born are, in proportion to their power of thought and their moral sensibility, found to be the natural enemies of this law." Indeed, "the resistance of all moral beings is secured to it" (*AW*, 58). Every individual citizen has a responsibility to respond to that "Higher Law," which is written in every heart (*AW*, 59).

For Emerson, "the only benefit that has accrued from the law" is the fact that it has stimulated the kind of thoughtful introspection and animated public discourse that are essential in a democratic republic. "It has been like a university to the entire people," he observes. "It has turned every dinner-table into a debating-club, and made every citizen a student of natural law. When a moral quality comes into politics, when a right is invaded, the discussion draws on deeper sources: general principles are laid bare, which cast light on the whole frame of society" (*AW*, 64). Even in the context of the present turmoil, Emerson remained hopeful that the animated discourse generated by informed and conscientious citizens would lead to a nonviolent solution to this problem. However, polarizing rhetoric and political propaganda must be put aside if this goal is to be achieved. In the meantime, morality must be served. "This law must be made inoperative. It must be abrogated and wiped out of the statute-book; but whilst it stands there, it must be disobeyed" (*AW*, 71). Such disobedience comes at considerable risk. It will require individual courage and self-reliant commitment. As Emerson reminds his audience, it is "not by the public, but by ourselves, [that] our safety must be bought" (*AW*, 71–72).

Emerson's emphasis on the necessity of self-reliance as the essential precursor to collective social action is made even more emphatic in his second "Fugitive Slave Law Address" (March 7, 1854). In the three years following his first public presentation on the topic, the national situation had only worsened. Recognizing the failure of previous legislation to even contain the growth of slavery, let alone abolish it, Emerson, in his 1854 "Fugitive Slave Law" address, points out the uselessness of relying on paper covenants rather than personal commitment to promote and sustain social justice. As in his earlier addresses and lectures, he insists that true reform can come only when individuals look within themselves for truth, and then act upon that truth in concert with others. To simply rely on lifeless legal codes rather than living acts is to invite the kind of abuse that was now happening. "I fear there is no reliance to be put on any kind or form of covenant," he says, "no, not on sacred forms,—none on churches, none on bibles." Recent developments "show that no forms, neither constitutions, nor laws, nor covenants, nor churches, nor bibles, are of any use in themselves. . . . There is no help but in the head and heart and hamstrings of a man" (*AW*, 83). Only individuals can make the moral sentiments of these acts mean something in the real world of human events. Emerson elaborates:

> Covenants are of no use without honest men to keep them; laws of none but with loyal citizens to keep them. . . . To interpret Christ, it needs Christ in the heart. The teachings of the Spirit can be apprehended only by the same spirit that gave them forth. To make good the cause of Freedom, you must draw off from all foolish trust on others. You must be citadels and warriors, yourselves Declarations of Independence, the charter, the battle, and the vic-

tory.... He only who is able to stand alone is qualified for society. And that I understand to be the end for which a soul exists in this world, to be himself the counterbalance of all falsehood and all wrong.... Why have the minority no influence? Because they have not a real minority of one. (*AW,* 83)

Emerson was fully aware of the importance of the masses in the politics of democracy, an appreciation that became more acute at this critical time. Thus, the following year in his "Lecture on Slavery" (1855), he explicitly states, "My political economy is very short, a man's capital must be in him." This is particularly true of those who seek to represent others. "'Tis a maxim in our politics," he says, "that a man cannot be formidable in Congress, unless he is strong at home. I am glad to hear that confession, but I say more,—that he must have his own support" (*AW,* 103). Emerson's point here is that the politician must sincerely believe in what he purports to stand for. It must come from within. If this is the case, he can be an effective leader because he will represent what every honest person feels to be just and true. This, in turn, makes collective action possible, and compelling. It also minimizes the possibility of demagoguery and Machiavellian manipulation. Emerson insisted that the actions of the democratic masses be informed by the thoughtfulness and sincerity of individual citizens who have developed positions independently. These beliefs, once shared, would lead to a natural coalition. The leader of such a group simply articulates—not dictates—the collective desires of the people. As noted earlier, this coalition would emerge through a democratic process of public discourse where issues are examined and debated openly and fully. It is with this idea in mind that Emerson goes on to state: "But whilst I insist on the doctrine of the independence and the inspiration of the individual, I do not cripple but exalt the social action. Patriotism, public opinion, have a real meaning, though there is so much counterfeit rag money abroad under it, that the name is apt to disgust. A wise man delights in the powers of many people" (*AW,* 103). Individual citizens have an important collective role to play. In a democracy the power for positive change ultimately resides with the people and because of this, Emerson observes, "It is ... delicious to act with great masses to great aims" (*AW,* 105).

For Emerson, the conspicuous inadequacy of most of the elected representatives from the free states continued to be a serious problem. He noted with chagrin in his 1844 emancipation address that they are routinely overmanned by their aggressive southern counterparts. Here he observes that the government once had noble leaders like "Washington, Adams, [and] Jefferson.... But now we put obscure persons into the chairs, without character or representative force of any kind" (AW, 103). The reason these men have failed so miserably is not their humble origins but their lack of sincerity. They are content to skate on the surface of life. Because they are oblique to the influence of "moral sentiment," they lack the courage of their convictions, or, worse yet, they simply lack convictions. In his 1854 "Fugitive Slave Law" address, Emerson indicates his belief that this deficiency was a critical factor in the passing of that heinous law. Weak-willed senators and representatives simply followed their leaders. Among these was the formidable but perfidious Daniel Webster, a man that Emerson finally concluded was utterly lacking in moral substance: "There were all sorts of what are called brilliant men, accomplished men, men of high office, a President of the United States, senators, men of eloquent speech, but men without self-respect, without character, and it was droll to see that office, age, fame, talent, even a repute for honesty, all count for nothing. They had no opinions, they had no memory for what they had been saying like the Lord's Prayer, all their lifetime; they were only looking to what their great Captain did, and if he jumped, they jumped,—if he stood on his head, they did" (AW, 74). In contrast to the existing corrupt representatives, Emerson believed that true leaders are representative, and therefore effective, only when they act upon universal moral principles. The ideal leader inspires others by example to have confidence in themselves and the power each possesses: "I find [a representative] greater when he can abolish himself and all heroes, by letting in this element of reason, irrespective of persons, this subtilizer, and irresistible upward force, into our thought, destroying individualism,—the power so great, that the potentate is nothing. Then he is a monarch who gives a constitution to his people; a pontiff who preaches the equality of souls, and releases his servants from their barbarous homages; an emperor who can spare his empire" (CW, 4:14). The difference between people is one of degree, not kind. Some form of power is the birthright of every person. The representative man (or woman) is thus one that brings a message of self-liberation that validates the integrity of each individual as it simultaneously reflects the spiritual unity of the human family. The political result of such representation is a democracy where all enjoy equal rights. As Emerson insists, "there are no common men. All men are at last of a size....

Fair play and an open field and freshest laurels to all who have won them! But heaven reserves an equal scope for every creature" (*CW*, 4:18).

Events of the 1850s would precipitate in Emerson another significant change in tactics in his pursuit of democratic reform. After shifting in 1844 from an emphasis on individual reform effected through moral suasion to associated efforts, the 1850s would witness yet another distinct shift, this one toward militant resistance and even violence. This shift would climax in 1859 with Emerson's strong endorsement of John Brown, a man whom he describes as "an idealist . . . [who] believed in his ideas to that extent, that he existed to put them all into action. He did not believe in moral suasion;—he believed in putting the thing through" (*AW*, 119). This change in tactic was likely due, in part at least, to the fact that public discourse on the slavery issue was largely limited to those parts of the country where slavery did not exist, thus negating reformers' efforts to appeal to the minds and hearts of those most in need of reform.

In the face of a growing challenge to the morality of slavery in the North, southern leaders sought to prevent all public discussion of the issue. Emerson and other Transcendentalists were well aware of this reality. Partially in response to the 1836 "gag rule," the October 1840 issue of the *Dial* (which Emerson was editing at the time) carried an account of the bitter and frightening experience of a New England Unitarian minister, George Simmons, who had had the temerity to preach on emancipation as a moral necessity while visiting Mobile, Alabama. The response to this exhortation was so furious that he had to flee the city, and the South, out of fear for his life.[40] Four years later, Emerson's Concord neighbor Samuel Hoar and his daughter Elizabeth had a similar experience. They were driven out of Charleston, South Carolina, by an angry mob after locals learned that Hoar had been sent by the Massachusetts legislature to investigate the mistreatment of black Massachusetts citizens there. Throughout the tumultuous 1850s, which witnessed open warfare between proslavery and antislavery forces in "Bleeding Kansas," the situation only worsened.[41] The utter collapse of rational political discourse reached a climax of sorts in May 1856, when Massachusetts senator Charles Sumner was nearly beaten to death on the floor of the United States Senate by a representative from South Carolina who was upset by Sumner's recent speech on affairs in Kansas.[42] Emerson was appalled by this barbaric act. In a public meeting called to protest the outrage, he spoke of the increasingly aggressive and violent nature of southern society and questioned "how a barbarous community and a civilized community can constitute one state" (*AW*, 107). They could not. Civil war came on April 12, 1861, with the firing on Fort Sumter.

Emerson's Transcendental Politics during the Civil War

Throughout the long and bloody Civil War, Emerson, who remained the de facto leader of the Transcendentalists, saw his reputation reach its zenith.[43] Robert Richardson notes that "Emerson had become by 1863 an inescapable part—a fixture—of American public life."[44] And Lawrence Buell points out that during the war, "for moderates as well as for progressives, [Emerson] seemed to personify the union's highest ideals."[45] From this position, Emerson articulated in a number of addresses and lectures a moral vision of the war and its ultimate purpose. In all of these, he would stress the importance of individuals collectively embracing the ideals that would lead to the moral regeneration of American society and a virtual reinvention of American democracy.

At the very outset of the conflict, in an address to the students at Tufts College titled "Celebration of the Intellect" (July 1861), Emerson observed that the war must be properly understood as a revolutionary application of moral power in the struggle for universal human liberty. "The brute noise of the cannon," he noted, "has . . . a most poetic echo in these days, when it is an instrument of freedom and the primal sentiment of humanity." This "primal sentiment," of course, is the voice of the Divinity that abides in the heart of all people. As Emerson well knew, the young men before him were being called upon to decide what their individual roles should be at this time of national crisis. In keeping with his transcendental philosophy, he encouraged each to look within himself for the answer. He "who looks with his own eyes," Emerson declares, "will find that there is somebody within him that knows more than he does." Those who would serve the good must "enthrone the Instinct. There, must be the perpetual rallying and self-recovery."[46] Emerson remained more convinced than ever that essential, life-sustaining truth was available to all if they would but open themselves to it. For him, during this time of national crisis when the very survival of the nation was at stake, that truth demanded not only the restoration of the Union but also the further advancement of the Republic. This would be wrought by ensuring freedom and equality for all citizens.

In America, a nation "conceived in liberty and dedicated to the proposition that all men are created equal," as Lincoln would soon express it at Gettysburg, that promise might now become a reality at last. Later, in a lecture appropriately titled "Moral Forces," delivered in the spring of 1862, Emerson articulated a grand vision of a nation united by love and dedicated to justice. Those individuals who have opened themselves to the power of the moral sentiment now find themselves spontaneously joined in a great "ring," or circle of "brotherhood." They are now united in a just and noble cause: "By the magic of a shout, and the unfurling of a flag, he who was alone, caring for nobody, and for whom none cared, is surprised with the delight of feeling himself one in the ring of a vast brotherhood, across the mountains, across the state border, from the Atlantic to the Pacific: that he and they all have one will, that this grand territory confided to them by the hand of God shall remain one, and shall remain for the benefit and not for the nuisance of mankind, for a country, and not for a slave-pen. This thought uplifts him: he has grown wise and elevated in a few hours more than in years before" (*LL*, 2:282). Later, in the fall of 1862, in a controversial lecture titled "Perpetual Forces," Emerson insisted that the universal principle of freedom be acknowledged as the key element in the reconstruction of America that the war has made possible. In this address, he argued not only for the emancipation of *all* slaves (the Emancipation Proclamation, announced by Lincoln in September, applied only to some) but also for their enfranchisement. This was an extremely radical position at the time, but one that was perfectly consistent with the liberal politics of transcendentalism. In his vision of the new America, Emerson insisted that we must "leave slavery out. Since nothing satisfies all men but justice, let us have that, and let us stifle our prejudices against commonsense and humanity, and agree that every man shall have what he honestly earns, and, if he is a sane and innocent man, have an equal vote in the state, and a fair chance in society" (*LL*, 2:300). For Emerson, all Americans should have an equal opportunity to participate fully in civic life, regardless of race or former condition of servitude.[47]

As noted earlier, Emerson's political philosophy was driven by his philosophical idealism, and nowhere is this more clearly expressed than in "Fortune of the Republic," arguably the most important political address of his career. On November 26, 1863, Emerson was invited to speak on the topic of "American Politics" (*Letters*, 5:340). The title that he eventually gave to his lecture was "Fortune of the Republic." He delivered this philosophical and practical piece several times in a relatively short period (fourteen engagements from December 1863 to February 1864), which suggests that he felt a sense of urgency at the time.

This lengthy lecture came at a time of deep crisis for the North when war weariness had caused spirits to flag and Copperhead accommodationists were demanding a cessation of hostilities and a restoration of the Union as it was, with slavery intact. Fear of British intervention was also high, and Lincoln's reelection was in jeopardy due to dissatisfaction with his policies, especially on emancipation.[48] In his presentation, Emerson sought to reassure the nation that the cause was just and that their steadfastness would be rewarded with victory in the end. In the process, he addressed several issues of major importance to American society at this defining moment in the history of the Republic. He also affirmed the need for the kind of high-minded idealism that the president had articulated so well just two months earlier at Gettysburg.[49] Additionally, he specifically attacked Copperhead backsliders like Clement L. Vallandigham, former representative from Ohio, and Fernando Wood, Democratic mayor of New York City, who would lead the nation to cast aside this unique opportunity to improve itself in what Emerson considered to be a second Revolution.

On the positive side, Emerson presents a glorious view of the new American republic that he believed would emerge from the turmoil of the war. This new nation would guarantee the freedom and equality of all citizens. The representatives of the people would rule with equity and fairness by enacting the will of the people. Aristocratic privilege, a hallmark of southern culture, would be unknown. Finally, in his lecture Emerson encouraged his listeners to support universal freedom and equal rights, to stay the course, and to make any sacrifice to bring the Republic to its ultimate fulfillment. In both content and context, as well as its potential impact on the nation's destiny, this address is one of the most significant of Emerson's long political career.

In this address, as in all his previous ones, Emerson again makes it clear that his democratic politics follow from his transcendentalism: "It is a rule that holds in economy, as well as in hydraulics, that you must have a source higher than your tap" (AW, 137). Ultimately, this principle can be seen in all areas of human endeavor and "if this is true in all the useful, and in the fine arts, that the direction must be drawn from a superior source, or there will be no good work,—does it hold less in our social and civil life?" (*AW*, 138). As he had suggested in *Representative Men*, Emerson here asserts that a true leader is an individual first, one who follows his ideal instincts, regardless of party politics or other considerations: "It is by no means by obeying the vulgar weathercock of his party, the resentments, the fears and whims of it, that real power is gained, but that he must often face and resist the party, and abide by his resistance, and put them in fear: that the only title to their permanent respect and to a larger following, is, to see for himself what is the real public interest, and stand for that;—that is a principle,—and all the cheering and hissing of the crowd must by and by accommodate itself to that" (*AW*, 138–39). For Emerson, Lincoln's consistent commitment to principle, shown in announcing and then implementing his controversial emancipation policy, not only marked Lincoln as a great leader, but it also would lead to the finest and most fortunate outcome of the present struggle. Indeed, because of this leadership, none will doubt, says Emerson, that at the present time America represents more truly than any other nation on earth, "the future of mankind" (*AW*, 139). However, echoing the sentiments expressed by Lincoln at Gettysburg, he also notes that the nation is now passing through a "great crisis," the outcome of which will determine the final destiny of the nation and "will make the peace and prosperity, or the calamity of the next ages" (*AW*, 139). Emerson warns that at the present juncture in the war, when victory is in sight if the forces of goodness and justice persist, the greatest danger is self-destruction through the loss of heart, which would mean the triumph of skepticism and the failure of idealism. With Lincoln's reelection on the horizon, what individual citizens think and feel about the war will ultimately determine its outcome.

In mulling the problems of a great leader who needs to be (re)elected, Emerson confronts a fundamental tension inherent in all democracies. On the one hand, a true leader must not simply capitulate to the self-interest of party politics or the uninformed demands of the masses. On the other hand, a leader cannot move forward without the support and consent of the masses. Because of this tension, the ideal leader must stand on principles and at the same time persuade the people of the efficacy of those principles and the policies that are dictated by them. This could be accomplished only through the effective use of rhetoric. For Emerson, as noted earlier, positive, constructive rhetoric requires that the speaker articulate positions that resonate with the inner core of universal truths that exist in the hearts of all of humanity. This resonance at one signifies the moral validity of the policies and persuades the masses to acknowledge and accept them. It is through this means that the ideal can be realized in policies that are both just and practical. Historically, Lincoln was able to achieve this through a powerful rhetoric that appealed to what he once appropriately called "the better angles of our nature."[50] It was Emerson's goal here to both ratify and reinforce Lincoln's agenda. History suggests that both succeeded.

Emerson always understood the importance of practical idealism. "A man for success must not be *pure* idealist," he insists, "then he will practically fail: but he must have ideas, must obey ideas, or he might as well be the horse he rides on." In the current crisis, individuals without ideas or ideals will fail to appreciate the moral principles at issue in the war and thus be tempted to accept a "short and hasty peace, on any terms" (*AW*, 140). Emerson emphasizes the importance of continuing the struggle to its ideal ends, those ends that were originally expressed in the Declaration of Independence and that were also recently reiterated by President Lincoln at Gettysburg. "It is the young men of the land, who must save it," Emerson insists; "it is they to whom this wonderful hour, after so many weary ages, dawns, the Second Declaration of Independence, the proclaiming of liberty, land, justice, and a career for all men: and honest dealings with other nations" (*AW*, 140). It is time for these young men to put their creed into their deed and to fulfill themselves by rising to the defense of principles that affirm the dignity and worth of every human being. Clearly, for Emerson this is a war of ideas and ideals, in short, it is a transcendental war that will unite individuals whose common cause is universal justice and equality. "When the canon is aimed by ideas," Emerson asserts, "then gods join in the combat, then poets are born. . . . When men die for what they live for, and the mainspring that works daily urges them to hazard all, then the cannon articulates its explosions with the voice of a man. Then the rifle seconds the cannon, and the fowling-piece the rifle, and the women make cartridges, and all shoot at one mark, and the better code of laws at last records the victory." The present revolution is "the chieftest of these" noble efforts and represents the "culmination of these triumphs of humanity" (*AW*, 142–43).[51]

While many believed that the emancipation of black slaves could only result in second-class citizenship for them at best, Emerson disagreed. American democracy is inclusive, he insists, and "can reach the highest and the lowest degrees. And it is possible that here we shall have the happiness of lifting the low." This process necessarily involves providing the resources necessary to support and promote the self-culture of former slaves. "The steps already taken to teach the freedman his letters, and the decencies of life, are not worth much if they stop there. They teach the teacher,—open his eyes to new methods. They give him manliness and breadth he had not; and accustom him to a courage and poise" (AW, 149).[52] The result of such efforts will be that which "the earth waits for,—exalted manhood, the new man, whom plainly this country must furnish" (AW, 151). The "new man" that Emerson here envisions will be a unique and dynamic national type that results from what he would later call the "fusion of races" in America, a place where the talents and abilities of all people can be developed and utilized to their fullest (W, 8:207).

It should be abundantly clear at this point that Emerson's transcendental philosophy neither encouraged nor condoned withdrawal from the world, but rather demanded a commitment to action. In this case, that commitment included a willingness to fight and die, if necessary, in a just war. Echoing the words of John Brown, Emerson here states that "slavery is broken, and, if we use our advantage, irretrievably. For such a gain,—to end once for all that pest of all free institutions,—one generation might well be sacrificed,—perhaps it will be,—that this continent be purged, and a new era of equal rights dawn on the universe" (AW, 153).[53]

Emerson was confident that African Americans would have an active role to play in this development, a role that the present struggle had opened for them. In keeping with his vision of the "anti-slave," which he had articulated almost twenty years earlier, Emerson was now in the forefront in the fight to allow the enlistment of black soldiers. He personally and publicly supported the formation of the Massachusetts Fifty-fourth, the first black regiment in the regular Union army.[54] Their current role in the struggle for freedom is but one step in a process of socialization that was made possible by the war. As Emerson would assure his audience in a later lecture, because of the war "we have grown internally—have begun to feel the strength of our strength. While European genius is symbolized by some majestic Corinne crowned in the capitol at Rome, American genius finds its true type—if I dare tell you—in the poor negro soldier lying in the trenches by the Potomac, with his spelling book in one hand and his musket in the other."[55] Clearly, for Emerson the greatness of America, (unlike aristocratic Europe or, until now, the American South), lies in the opportunity for advancement that is the natural birthright of *all* citizens, no matter how lowly their origins.

Emerson continues in "Fortune of the Republic" by assuring his listeners that America will emerge from the war a more just society that will "work for honest humanity, for the poor, for justice, genius, and the public good. I wish to see that this country, the last found, is the great charity of God to the human race" (*AW*, 152). Rapid social and material progress will come when the collective powers of all the people are released through the general promulgation of the transcendental values of equality, freedom, and justice. Emerson recognized that there can be no self-reliance, no self-culture, no uplifting of human kind without freedom. Individuality depended on a collective commitment to universal freedom.

In his address, Emerson goes on to indicate his confidence that those citizens who have embraced this war for justice by supporting Lincoln's policies will continue to do so. "In each new threat of faction," he observes, "the ballot of the people has been beyond expectation right and decisive" (*AW*, 152). Undoubtedly with Lincoln's reelection in mind, Emerson closes his address with a reminder to his audience of the power of their individual votes. "You will stand there for vast interests, North and South, East and West will be present to your mind, and your vote will be as if they voted. And you well know that your vote secures the foundations of the state, goodwill, liberty, and security of traffic and of production, and mutual increase of goodwill in the great interests, for no monopoly has been foisted in, no weak party or nationality has been, sacrificed, no coward compromise has been conceded to a strong partner" (*AW*, 153–54). Ultimately, it is the will of the people that will determine the future of the Republic.

In many ways, the Union victory in the Civil War could be looked upon as the climax of the transcendental movement, at least as far as its political agenda was concerned. Virtually all of the Transcendentalists were committed abolitionists, and all of them enthusiastically embraced and promoted the cause of emancipation. Several Transcendentalists had been key supporters of John Brown, and four of the "Secret Six," Brown's closest associates, were connected to transcendentalism. At the outset of the war, several young Transcendentalists took up arms as both foot soldiers and officers in the Union army, which they saw as an army of liberation. One, Thomas Wentworth Higginson, rose to the rank of colonel and commanded a regiment of black contraband troops in South Carolina.[56] Still others, like

Emerson, helped to provide the intellectual and moral underpinnings of a new, more liberal democracy that the war would bring about.

After the Civil War

In the postwar years, Emerson continued to promote the principles of self-reliant freedom and equal opportunity for all Americans, including women. In his address at Harvard in July 1867, appropriately titled "Progress of Culture," he applauded "the new claim of woman to a political status." Emerson saw the woman's suffrage movement as "an honorable testimony to the civilization which has given her a civil status new in history" (*W*, 8:208). He became a strong supporter of women's rights and lent his considerable influence to that cause. In the spring of 1869, he accepted the vice presidency of the New England Woman's Suffrage Association.[57] By this time, Emerson had become "an icon of the suffragist leaders."[58] He was also pleased to see the liberties that had been so dearly won in the war enacted into law in the passage of the Thirteenth Amendment (1865) that ended slavery forever; the Fourteenth Amendment (1866) that guaranteed equal protection to all citizens; and the Fifteenth Amendment (1870) that guaranteed suffrage to all adult males "without regard to race, color, or previous conditions of servitude."

In 1878, Emerson returned again to the topic of the "Fortune of the Republic" in what would be one of his last public lectures. In this presentation, he expressed succinctly the essence of the Transcendentalists' political vision. "The genius of the country has marked out our true policy," he notes, "opportunity. Opportunity of civil rights, of education, of personal power, and not less of wealth; doors wide open. If I could have it,—free trade with all the world without toll or custom-houses, invitation as we now make every nation, to every race and skin, white men, red men, yellow men, black men; hospitality of fair field and equal laws to all" (*W*, 11:541). Convinced of the inherent goodness and divinity of every human being, Emerson sought to stimulate improvement in society by encouraging every individual to follow the voice within. By doing so, they would find themselves joining in a natural coalition of like-minded idealists who would act collectively in a democratic environment for the greater good of all.

In conclusion, in his role as a public intellectual, Emerson sought to educate the American people on the responsibilities of citizenship in a democratic republic.[59] He understood that human beings, especially in a democracy, must maintain the ability to carry on a meaningful civic discourse or suffer dire consequences. The failure to achieve this goal in Emerson's time contributed to the outbreak of the Civil War. While I do not anticipate that this history will repeat itself anytime soon, it is nevertheless clear that at the present moment the Republic faces many significant challenges to the tradition of democratic dialogue. Polarization, alienation, and mindless animosity have often displaced public discourse with public discord. Traditional "town hall meetings," once a mainstay of grassroots democracy, have become in many instances little more than rhetorical food fights with insults, aspersions, and catcalls displacing rational conversation. Radio talk-show hosts and their cable news cohorts, instead of encouraging meaningful dialogue, routinely seek to amplify this polarization (and their ratings) by inciting mindless and self-proclaimed "ditto heads" with bumper-sticker sloganeering and misinformation. Many citizens, as well as their elected representatives, seem unwilling to look objectively and thoughtfully at the important issues of the day. Some appear to consider extremism a virtue and toleration a vice. As in Emerson's day, blind adherence to the party line makes reasonable compromise, the lifeblood of democratic polity, nearly impossible. Clearly, there is a great need at the present moment for meaningful self-education, independent thoughtfulness, and Emersonian self-reliance. It is imperative that conscientious citizens assume an active public role, that they embrace the principles of the Declarations of Independence by rejecting alienating and self-serving political rhetoric and demanding informed and rational discourse as well as an attitude of mutual respect. Those who seek to lead should be in the forefront of this effort. Then, and only then, will this nation continue its march toward becoming the liberal republic that Emerson once so clearly envisioned.

Notes

1. Henry Steele Commager, *The Era of Reform: 1830–1860* (Princeton: D. Van Nostrand, 1960), 7.

2. Arthur M. Schlesinger Jr. *The Age of Jackson* (New York: Little, Brown, 1945), 382, 385.

3. These studies include monographs on the topic such as Albert von Frank's *The Trials of Anthony Burns: Freedom and Slavery in Emerson's Boston* (1998);

David Robinson's *Emerson and the Conduct of Life: Pragmatism and Ethical Purpose in the Later Works* (1993); and my own *Virtue's Hero: Emerson, Antislavery, and Reform* (1990, 2010), as well as new collections of critical writings like *The Emerson Dilemma: Essays on Emerson and Social Reform* (2001), and a major biography, Robert Richardson's, *Emerson: The Mind on Fire* (1995). Also, new additions to the Emerson canon such as *Emerson's Antislavery Writings* (1995, 2001), three additional volumes of *Letters* (1990–1995), and *The Later Lectures of Ralph Waldo Emerson*, ed. Bosco and Myerson (2001), all provide evidence of Emerson's active social engagement.

The Collected Works of Ralph Waldo Emerson, ed. Albert R. Ferguson and Joseph Slater, et al., 7 vols. to date. (Cambridge: Belknap Press of Harvard University Press, 1971–), 1:141, 143. All subsequent references to this edition appear in the text as *CW*.

4. John Carlos Rowe, *At Emerson's Tomb: The Politics of Classic American Literature* (New York: Columbia University Press, 1997), 25.

5. Ibid., 40.

6. David Robinson, *Emerson and the Conduct of Life: Pragmatism and Ethical Purpose in the Later Works* (Cambridge: Cambridge University Press, 1993), 40.

7. T. Gregory Garvey, *Creating the Culture of Reform in Antebellum America* (Athens: University of Georgia Press, 2006), 163.

8. Barbara Packer. *The Transcendentalists* (Athens: University of Georgia Press, 2007), 25–26.

9. *The Letters of Ralph Waldo Emerson*, ed. Ralph L. Rusk and Eleanor M. Tilton, 10 vols. (1939; New York: Columbia University Press, 1990–1995), 1:412–13, hereafter cited as *Letters*. Emerson includes Milton, one of his favorites, with Coleridge and "the Germans" (Kant and Goethe) because of his strong emphasis on the inner light. As Basil Willey points out, in *Paradise Lost*, "Milton argues that the moral sense, which is the law of God written upon the heart, is the final tribunal—superior even to Scripture itself" (*The Seventeenth-Century Background: Studies in the Thought of the Age in Relation to Poetry and Religion* [New York: Doubleday,1953], 77).

10. *Letters*, 1:413. For an informed discussion of the importance of this seminal concept to all Transcendentalists, see Paul Boller, *American Transcendentalism, 1830–1860: An Intellectual Inquiry* (New York: Putnam's Sons, 1974), 46–51; and Philip F. Gura, *American Transcendentalism, A History* (New York: Hill and Wang, 2007), 53–56. For Emerson's particular rendering of the concept, see Gougeon, *Emerson and Eros: The Making of a Cultural Hero* (Albany: State University of New York Press, 2007), 88–90.

11. Emerson states in his "Divinity School Address": "The intuition of the moral sentiment is an insight of the perfection of the laws of the soul. These laws execute themselves. They are out of time, out of space, and not subject to circumstance" (*CW*, 1:77).

12. *Emerson's Liberalism* (Madison: University of Wisconsin Press, 2009), 46.

13. *Emerson's Antislavery Writings*, ed. Len Gougeon and Joel Myerson (New Haven: Yale University Press, 1995), 57, hereafter cited as *AW*.

14. Not surprisingly, because of its insistence on the "self-evident" nature of essential truths, truths that are literally heartfelt or intuitively perceived, the Declaration has been described by one scholar as a "semi-Transcendental document" (see Boller, *American Transcendentalism*, 137). Indeed, most, if not all transcendental reformers, Emerson among them, saw the Declaration exactly this way. For a discussion of Transcendentalists' frequent references to the Declaration, see Gougeon, "'Fortune of the Republic': Emerson, Lincoln, and Transcendental Warfare," *ESQ: A Journal of the American Renaissance* 65 (1999): 263–78.

15. Gregg Crane, *Race, Citizenship, and Law in American Literature* (Cambridge: Cambridge University Press, 2002), 113. This belief in the cognitive validity of intuition was undoubtedly a factor in Emerson's strong support for voting rights for emancipated slaves at the time of the Civil War.

16. For the importance of this concept to Transcendentalists generally, see Gura, *American Transcendentalism*, 187–88.

17. Boller, *American Transcendentalism*, 137.

18. *The Journals and Miscellaneous Notebooks of Ralph Waldo Emerson*, ed. William H. Gilman, Ralph Orth et al., 16 vols. (Cambridge: Harvard University Press, 1960–1982), 4:357, hereafter cited as *JMN*.

19. T. Gregory Garvey, "Emerson's Political Spirit and the Problem of Language," in *The Emerson Dilemma: Essays on Emerson and Social Reform*, ed. Garvey (Athens: University of Georgia Press, 2001), 15.

20. As Emerson noted in his 1854 "Fugitive Slave Law" address, "You must be citadels and warriors, yourselves Declarations of Independence, the charter, the battle, and the victory" (*AW*, 83).

21. Wesley Mott, "The Age of the First Person Singular: Emerson and Individualism," in *Historical Guide to Ralph Waldo Emerson*, ed. Joel Myerson (New York: Oxford University Press, 2000), 91.

22. Garvey, *Culture*, 163.

23. Gregg Crane argues that Emerson and other transcendental reformers believed that "in a republic devoted to making its laws and political behavior conform with universal ethical norms, . . . those norms are determined by a dialogue among the varying ethical perspectives of a diverse citizenry" (*Race, Citizenship, and Law*, 88).

24. "Fortune of the Republic," in *The Complete Works of Ralph Waldo Emerson,* ed. Edward Waldo Emerson, 12 vols. (Boston: Houghton, Mifflin, 1903–1904), 11:528–29, hereafter cited as W. This address should not be confused with an earlier address by the same name, discussed extensively here, that was delivered in the context of the Civil War.

25. *The Early Lectures of Ralph Waldo Emerson,* ed. Robert E. Spiller, Stephen E. Whicher, and Wallace E. Williams, 3 vols. (Cambridge: Harvard University Press, 1959–1972), 3:260, hereafter cited as *EL.*

26. In 1835, the British abolitionist George Thompson visited Concord while on a lecture tour. Emerson invited him to his home, where he attempted to engage him in an open discussion. In his journal, Emerson records his frustration with the failed result (*JMN,* 5:90–91).

27. For a comprehensive discussion of the circumstances leading up to this development, see Gougeon, "Emerson's Abolition Conversion."

28. The Senate rejected the treaty in June. In March 1845, following the election of John Polk to the presidency, the issue was again brought forward in the Congress. After substantial debate and political maneuvering, Texas was admitted to the Union as a state on December 29, 1845.

29. As Martin Duberman has observed, referring to the growth of active opposition to slavery: "The real watershed came in 1845, when Texas was annexed to the Union, and war with Mexico followed. The prospect now loomed of a whole series of new slave states. It finally seemed clear that the mere passage of time would not bring a solution; if slavery was ever to be destroyed, more active resistance would be necessary" ("The Northern Response to Slavery," in *The Antislavery Vanguard: New Essays on the Abolitionists,* ed. Duberman [Princeton: Princeton University Press, 1965], 397).

30. See Gougeon, *Virtue's Hero,* 66–67.

31. The "indecent nonsense" referred to here is undoubtedly the common belief at the time that blacks belonged to a "feminized race" and were "unwilling" to fight for their freedom and were "therefore deserving of enslavement" (Maggie Sale, "Critiques from Within: Antebellum Projects of Resistance," *American Literature* 34, no. 4 [1999]: 700).

32. Introduction to *Emerson's Antislavery Writings,* xxix. This was one of several such petitions, to both the state and federal government, that Emerson and members of his family signed in the 1840s.

33. For more information on this incident, see Gougeon, "Emerson and the New Bedford Affair," *Studies in the American Renaissance, 1981,* ed. Joel Myerson (Charlottesville: University of Virginia Press, 1981), 257–64.

34. Following his 1844 emancipation address, the abolitionists were quick to claim Emerson as one of their own. John Greenleaf Whittier, the poetic voice of

the movement, praised Emerson's performance in the *Middlesex Standard* (September 12) and noted that the bard's philosophy had apparently passed from the passive to the active stage. And the conservative *Boston Courier* noted, somewhat in dismay, "Before we saw notice of this celebration, we were not aware that Mr. Emerson had sufficiently identified himself with the abolitionists, as a party, to receive such a distinguished token of their confidence" (reprinted in the *Liberator*, August 23, 1844).

35. Larry J. Reynolds, *European Revolutions and the American Literary Renaissance* (New Haven: Yale University Press, 1988), 33ff. For a detailed discussion of this experience and its impact on Emerson, see Gougeon, "Emerson and Great Britain: Challenging the Limits of Liberty," in "Liberty Ltd.: Civil Rights, Civil Liberties, and Literature," ed. Brook Thomas, special issue of *REAL—Yearbook of Research in English and American Literature* (Tübingen: Gunter Narr Verlag, 2006), 179–213.

36. Emerson was especially impressed with the Chartists. He would celebrate them in his poem "The Chartist's Complaint" published in 1857 in the very first issue of the *Atlantic Monthly*. Later, he would reference their "Six Demands" for reform in his historic "Fortune of the Republic" address, discussed at length later here.

37. Gougeon, *Virtue's Hero*, 135.

38. Prior to Sims's rendition, William and Ellen Craft and Shadrach Minkins had been saved from capture by the efforts of the Boston Vigilance Committee, a group that was organized by the transcendental activist Theodore Parker (see Henry Steele Commager, *Theodore Parker: Yankee Crusader* [Boston: Beacon Press, 1947], 214–20).

39. Gougeon, *Virtue's Hero*, 155.

40. George Ripley, "Record," *Dial* 1(1840–1841): 246–47.

41. Gougeon, *Virtue's Hero*, 92, 217–18.

42. David Herbert Donald. *Charles Sumner.* 2 vols. in one (New York: Da Capo Press, 1996), 294–96.

43. Gura, *American Transcendentalism*, 265.

44. Richardson, *Mind*, 551.

45. Buell, Lawrence. *Emerson* (Cambridge: Harvard University Press, 2003), 34.

46. *The Later Lectures of Ralph Waldo Emerson: 1843–1871*, ed. Ronald Bosco and Joel Myerson, 2 vols. (Athens: University of Georgia Press, 2001), 2:246, 247; hereafter cited as *LL*.

47. When Emerson expressed these views on the matter, they were not always well received. After delivering the lecture in Albany, New York, an article printed in the *Albany Atlas-Argus* on December 26, 1862, noted that "when he [Emerson]

insisted that the negro should have 'an equal chance in society with the white man,'" the audience was "indignantly silent" (quoted in *LL*, 2:288).

48. Doris Kearns Goodwin, *Team of Rivals: The Political Genius of Abraham Lincoln* (New York: Simon and Schuster, 2005), 648.

49. Garry Wills, in his *Lincoln at Gettysburg: The Words That Remade America* (New York: Simon and Schuster, 1992), describes at length a distinct transcendental influence in Lincoln's thinking, and the ultimate expression of that transcendentalism in his most famous speech, "The Gettysburg Address." According to Wills, the address itself sets up a "dialectic of the ideal with the real" where "a nation conceived in liberty by its dedication to the Declaration's critical proposition (human equality) must test that proposition's survivability in the real world of struggle." Wills goes on to note—correctly, I think—that Lincoln's "dialectic of ideals struggling for their realization in history owes a great deal to the primary intellectual fashion of his period, Transcendentalism." In fact, he later describes Lincoln as "a Transcendentalist without the fuzziness" (174).

50. *The Collected Works of Abraham Lincoln*, ed. Roy P. Basler, 10 vols. (New Brunswick, N.J.: Rutgers University Press, 1953), 4:271.

51. In his message to Congress in July 1861, Lincoln himself had described the conflict in ideal terms. The war, he told the Congress, "is essentially a People's contest. On the side of the Union, it is a struggle for maintaining in the world, that form, and substance of government, whose leading object is, to elevate the condition of men—to lift artificial weights from all shoulders—to clear the paths of laudable pursuit for all—to afford all, an unfettered start, and a fair chance, in the race of life." It is clear that Emerson shared this vision. (Lincoln, *Works*, 4:438).

52. Emerson had for some time been aware of the success of the Port Royal experiment where, early in the war, freed slaves in Port Royal, South Carolina, were organized and educated. Emerson's wife and daughters, as members of the Female Anti-Slavery Society in Concord, provided clothing and other support to the group (see Gougeon, *Virtue's Hero*, 277–78). Emerson also made a cash contribution to the enterprise in which many of his friends were active (see Albert J. von Frank, *An Emerson Chronology* [New York: G. K. Hall, 1994], 325; and *Trials of Anthony Burns*, 372–73 n. 19).

53. For a comprehensive discussion of the militant aspects of transcendental philosophy, see Gougeon, "'Only Justice Satisfies All': Emerson's Militant Transcendentalism," in *Emerson for the Twenty-first Century: Global Perspectives on an American Icon*, ed. Barry Tharaud (Wilmington: University of Delaware Press, 2010).

54. Gougeon, "Fortune of the Republic," 289.

55. *Uncollected Lectures by Ralph Waldo Emerson*, ed. Clarence Gohdes Jr. (New York: William Edwin Rudge, 1932), 41–42.

56. For Transcendentalists and the Civil War, see Gura, *American Transcendentalism*, 263–66. David Reynolds reports that "the Harpers Ferry raid would not have come off without the support of the Secret Six, four of whom were connected to Transcendentalism, and since Transcendentalists would later take the lead in establishing Brown's reputation, the Concord philosophy must be recognized as a force behind events that led to the Civil War" (see Reynolds, *John Brown: Abolitionist: The Man Who Killed Slavery, Sparked the Civil War, and Seeded Civil Rights* [New York: Knopf, 2005], 215). For Higginson and other transcendentalist soldiers, see Gougeon, "Transcendental Politics and Economics," in *The Oxford Handbook to Transcendentalism,"* ed. Joel Myerson, Sandra Petrulionis, and Laura Dassow-Walls (Oxford: Oxford University Press, 2010).

57. Gougeon, "Emerson and the Woman Question: The Evolution of His Thought," *New England Quarterly* 71, no. 4 (December 1998): 590.

58. Armida Gilbert, "'Pierced by the Thorns of Reform': Emerson on Womanhood," in *The Emerson Dilemma: Essays on Emerson and Social Reform*, ed. T. Gregory Garvey (Athens: University of Georgia Press, 2001), 103.

59. Lawrence Buell refers to Emerson as "the first modern American public intellectual" (*Emerson*, 9).

PART III

The Stubborn Reality of Emerson's Transcendentalism

CHAPTER 8

Skeptical Triangle? A Comparison of the Political Thought of Emerson, Nietzsche, and Montaigne

Alan M. Levine

THIS ESSAY SHARPENS OUR understanding of the exact nature and consequences of Emerson's political thought by contrasting it to the thought of the skeptic Emerson most admired, Montaigne, and the skeptic with whom he is today most often compared, Nietzsche. In contradistinction to almost all scholars who have written on these connections in the past two decades, I show that Emerson is considerably less skeptical than both Montaigne and Nietzsche. It is important to correct these mistaken views because it is precisely the limits of Emerson's skepticism that account for his unique moral and political vision.

There is a well-established connection between these three thinkers. It has been noted that "Montaigne is one of the literary and philosophical figures for whom Nietzsche has practically no criticism."[1] Indeed, Nietzsche cites Montaigne as one of only eight figures from whom he will accept judgment and with whom he must come to terms.[2] He favorably compares Montaigne to Schopenhauer, Shakespeare, and Socrates.[3] Nietzsche praises Montaigne as "this freest and mightiest of souls," as a "true thinker," for his "honesty," for "a cheerfulness that really cheers," and for successfully "making [himself] at home in the world."[4] "That such a man wrote," Nietzsche avows, "has truly augmented the joy of living on this earth."[5] It is, therefore, unsurprising that shortly before his breakdown, Nietzsche confessed that he was reading Montaigne "to lift himself out of a gloomy mood."[6] In short, it is with justification that one scholar concludes that "the Frenchman had achieved Nietzsche's ideals of harmonious self-possession, absolute integrity, and joyful affirmation of the worth of existence," while another scholar,

Robert Pippen, concludes that Montaigne is Nietzsche's "hero," "standard," "a model for Nietzsche's enterprise," and that he "inspired [Nietzsche's] *ideal*."[7]

The connection between Emerson and Montaigne is similarly well established. Emerson read and loved Montaigne, writing, "I took such delight in Montaigne, that I thought I should not need any other book"[8] and that "no book before or since was ever so much to me as that."[9] And just as Nietzsche cites Montaigne as one of the eight to whom he must answer, Emerson cites Montaigne as one of his six "Representative Men."[10] Few, if any, scholars have doubted Emerson's intellectual kinship to Montaigne. Indeed, Judith Shklar calls Montaigne Emerson's "one and only hero," and the most systematic study of their connection concludes that Emerson is "the American in whom an instinctive sympathy with the *Essays*, or understanding of their author, was most articulate." The study continues: "Emerson knew him so well because he was enough like Montaigne to divine, through the more or less imperfect medium [of writing], the original quality of the man and writer," achieving "a fusion at last with the object of interest," that is, with Montaigne.[11]

The final leg of the triangle, the connection between Emerson and Nietzsche, has in recent decades gotten much more scholarly attention than the connection of either of them to Montaigne. This link, too, has been made with good reason. It is well established that Nietzsche read and enjoyed Emerson, especially in his early years. Walter Kaufmann fairly summarized scholarly findings on this connection in writing that Nietzsche "not only read him but also copied dozens of passages into notebooks and wrote extensively on the margins of flyleaves of his copy of [Emerson's] essays."[12] Indeed, Nietzsche describes Emerson as "a glorious, great nature, rich in soul and spirit," cites him as one of only four authors in his century that may justly be called "masters of prose," and praises him as "the author who has been richest in ideas in this century so far."[13] The first edition of *The Gay Science* began with an epigraph quotation from Emerson, and Nietzsche writes, "*Emerson.*—Never have I felt so much at home in a book, and in *my* home, as—I may not praise it, it is too close to me."[14] Taking their cue from such statements (among other reasons), the most important philosophers and political theorists who have written on Emerson in the last two decades have insisted on linking him to Nietzsche.[15] For example, Stanley Cavell considers Emerson and Nietzsche to be the two great exemplars, "my focal examples," of the moral perfectionism he advocates.[16] George Kateb agrees on the fundamental importance of this connection, arguing that "Nietzsche was Emerson's best reader." Indeed, Kateb goes further, arguing that "it may be wise to approach Emerson after one has been immersed in Nietzsche."[17] Judith Shklar finds many similarities between Emerson and Nietzsche excepting only Emerson's fundamental commitment to "democracy."[18]

For modern readers, however, these three authors are not merely connected by lines of acknowledged influence; they are said to share a philosophy of skepticism. Indeed, they do have several skeptical features in common. All three thinkers share the same enemies—habit, convention, and received opinion—and all three resist custom, tradition, and established ethical norms. All three aim to fight through what they deem to be the moral nonsense of their times, and all three place their primary emphasis on uncovering and securing what they deem to be the primordial good of the self. Accordingly, Emerson's most famous Nietzschean moment is his claim in his most famous essay, "Self-Reliance," that he "lives wholly from within." "If I am the Devil's child," Emerson there writes, "I will live then from the Devil. No law can be sacred to me but that of my nature. Good and bad are but names very transferable to that or this; the only right is what is after my constitution, the only wrong what is against it" (262). Citing this passage, Russell Goodman notes that "so central is self-development to Emerson's philosophy that . . . he assigns it a value not only beyond the customs or traditions of society but, as Nietzsche would say, 'beyond good and evil.'"[19] Similarly, Emerson and Nietzsche explicitly praise Montaigne's skepticism to a much greater extent than either praises Hume or any other modern skeptic.[20] And, of course, for Emerson, as the title of his essay makes clear, Montaigne is "The Skeptic."[21]

However, while these three thinkers have marked each other as a uniquely interrelated skeptical triangle, this essay contends that recent scholars' equation of these three authors' skepticisms goes too far. Despite flashes of deep similarity, when taken as a whole, Emerson's skepticism is neither Nietzschean nor Montaignean. My argument about the limited nature of Emerson's skepticism is the part of this essay that most challenges current scholarship, and it requires directly confronting the consensus view that Emerson's skepticism is equivalent to Montaigne's and Nietzsche's. The Emerson-Nietzsche connection, particularly, has been advanced by many major Emerson scholars from at least the 1980s forward, including not only Cavell and Kateb (mentioned above) but also Harold Bloom, Richard Poirier, and scores of scholars influenced by them. This consensus view has been most systematically articulated and defended by Michael Lopez and his contributors in a special issue of *ESQ* entitled "Emerson/Nietzsche," in which Lopez argues that the missing link between Emerson and Nietzsche "represents one of the major lacunae of modern scholarship."[22] Lopez's extraordinary claim is argued as follows. Nietzsche is the womb from which the main currents of twentieth-century philosophy have been born, and if Nietzsche was fundamentally influenced by Emerson, then Emerson is the true womb of twentieth-century thought. Lopez's excellent introduction reviews 150 years of the scholarship on the Emerson-Nietzsche connection, and his main claim reveals the depth of similarities he claims to find. Nonetheless, I argue that this recent consensus greatly exaggerates the similarities between Emerson and Nietzsche.

Using the recent scholars' claims about the similarities between Emerson and Nietzsche as its point of departure, this essay critically compares and analyzes the thought of Emerson, Nietzsche, and Montaigne. It divides these recent claims (especially as reported by Lopez) into three large categories, each discussed in its own section: style and language, the self in the world, and morality/politics. In each section, I begin with the main points of agreement between Emerson and Nietzsche, adding in Montaigne where he has been forgotten. I then turn to the three authors' main disagreements. Much good work has been done in the recent wave of Emerson scholarship; I seek only to correct its excessive claims. My aim in weighing these three thinkers' similarities and differences is to form a judgment of the unique aspects of each, intending in some cases to highlight forgotten aspects of their similarities but above all to show major differences obscured by the recent scholarly consensus.

Most importantly, I argue that the metaphysical difference in the three authors' respective philosophies leads to fundamental differences in their moral and political thoughts. Emerson's thought, correctly praised for its emphasis on the self and its sensitivity to the self's inner motion and fluidity, is always bounded by both a moral concern for others and what Emerson deems to be a higher universal reality. Emerson understands concern for others to be a component of one's own self-interest, and in this respect he resembles Montaigne but not Nietzsche. But Emerson's conception of the self and self-interest is integrally based on his conception of "Providence," "the

Over-Soul," and "higher law" (as well as the numerous other formulations Emerson gives to the universal divine), and in this respect Emerson proves considerably unlike both Montaigne and Nietzsche. Emerson emerges as a less thoroughgoing skeptic and with a much more optimistic and democratic moral vision than the ones advanced by Nietzsche and Montaigne.

Style and Language

The styles of Emerson and Nietzsche are said to have four main similarities, all of which are related to their skepticisms. First, they are described as sharing what is variously called an "exploratory essay style of writing" or a "discontinuous, aphoristic style."[23] This discontinuous style reflects their dubiousness of comprehensive narratives. Second, they are said to share doubts about the possibility of complete originality: "Original power is usually accompanied with assimilating power," writes Emerson; "there is no pure originality."[24] They thus are said to question or even break down the traditional distinctions between "originality" versus "borrowing" and "creation" versus "repetition."[25] Third, they both are heralded for raising doubts about the activity of reading itself. Reading is but a "return to themselves" since, as Nietzsche writes, "ultimately, nobody can get more out of things, including books, than he already knows" (*Ecce Homo*, 261). Finally, both are championed for seeing "all language" as "vehicular," meaning it is both necessary to and limiting of all thought.[26] It is for their profound understandings of the entangling, limiting (as well as liberating) power of language that Harold Bloom describes them as "twin titans of deconstruction."[27]

While the first three of the comparisons are accurate, and even more so for Montaigne, the fourth one is only qualifiedly correct about Emerson. First, all three authors do in fact have a discontinuous, "essay" style of writing and for the same skeptical reason. None thinks he has the capacity simply to announce truth. Instead, each very consciously struggles to be aware of the limits inherent in his subjective self, and each incorporates this into his style. Montaigne invented the essay both in name and substance. He coined the word from the French *essaier*, which means "to attempt" or "to try," and Montaigne's sole published work, entitled *Essais* in French and *Essays* in English, is the first book in the world to bear this title. Montaigne explicitly contrasts the essay to a treatise or a tract, the difference being that the latter claim to present truth, whereas Montaigne claims no such thing for his essay. He merely claims to "try" to "grapple" with issues. He explores his topics from every conceivable angle, exposing common opinions not only to contrary opinions and evidence, but also to humor, scorn, and wit. In the process, he frequently shifts perspectives without saying so.[28] Emerson uses the word "essay" and "essayed" in exactly Montaigne's sense. For example, in "Experience," Emerson declares that "every fine genius has essayed" the world (485), and in his "Literary Ethics" address he writes, "I also will essay to be" (98). Moreover, this explains Emerson's famous statement in "Self-Reliance" that "a foolish consistency is the hobgoblin of little minds" (265), because one must be true to one's ongoing attempts to understand, not to some fixed or permanent doctrine. The best that each thinks can be done is to articulate his perspective. Nietzsche states this most affirmatively, aiming to shift our mode from truth seeking to perspectivity. Everything is "perspective," he writes; "*perspective* [is] the basic condition of all life" (*BGE*, preface, 2, emphasis in original), and he wants to liberate his audience to embrace their own.[29] Emerson also describes every thinker's insight as a matter of perspective: "What can we see, read, acquire, but ourselves?" (*JMN*, 3:327), and he, too, urges the reader to embrace his or her perspective. Like Nietzsche, Emerson emphasizes that all geniuses have their perspectives on the truth, and he passionately calls for us to follow ourselves. The three thinkers' discontinuous writing styles are consciously crafted to reflect their views on the limits of what can be known.

As to the second quality, not just Emerson and Nietzsche but Montaigne, too, proves playful about originality and their relation to their sources. As a casual glance at Montaigne's pages make clear, his text is stuffed with quotations from numerous authors and texts, including ancient pagan Greek and Roman, Christian, contemporaneous, judicial, historical, folksy, and the imaginings of everyone from superstitious old maids to the most powerful humans who ever lived. He does not cite references for most of his quotations, but in the course of four hundred years, scholars have identified the sources and now include them in all contemporary editions of the *Essays*. Montaigne's original text is thus about as confused a scholarly jumble as imaginable, and Montaigne plays with his relations to his sources both more explicitly and implicitly than either Emerson or Nietzsche. He playfully and ironically cites pagans to support Christianity and the Bible to support pagan views. He regularly deconstructs the genealogy of an idea, undermining claims of originality throughout. He also writes that whatever he borrows he makes his own, and that in fact in taking from others he follows no one and no school of thought but only himself. In short, he uses others to make his own points, and he wrote his original text in a way that offered the reader no idea where Montaigne's sources end and he begins—unless the reader knows the various quotations himself. Hardly any author in the history of literature so consciously and brazenly plays with this theme, and Montaigne is the first to do it in the modern manner. Emerson and Nietzsche do the same things. They do not cite texts as authorities, but pick and choose and make the texts their own. So on the stylistic points of blending, blurring, merging, and playing with sources, Montaigne is emblematic of the skeptical trio.

The third similarity—their doubts about reading—explains the first two. All three thinkers have similar writing styles because they share a similar pedagogy. Their shared pedagogy includes both their ends and means. The point of studying others and the world for them is not to learn facts about phenomena different from oneself. On the contrary, it is to train the mind to return to oneself. This is the goal at which they all aim. They all doubt the ability of teaching others through rational discourse alone, so they think an oblique or indirect style is required to lead others to insight into themselves. Montaigne writes tentatively and from as many perspectives as he can summon so that the reader must engage the text and think along with Montaigne to follow the flow. To follow the text the reader must think, because Montaigne does not supply bridges from one perspective to another; the reader must supply the connections himself in his own mind's reading. This anticipates Nietzsche's claim that you need long legs to read him, because the reader must jump from aphorism to aphorism on his own, supplying the connections himself.[30] Richard Poirier finds the same qualities in Emerson, a writer who emphasizes the "transitive" over the "substantive" and thus promotes (as Poirier cites from Emerson's essay "Montaigne") a "philosophy . . . of fluxions and mobility."[31] All three thinkers write pedagogically and with performativity. You must re-create or perform their thoughts yourself, because they do not say all. The idea is not simply to persuade the reader about their truths. That is the aim of a dogmatist, someone with the certainty of his convictions. Rather, the aim of Montaigne's, Emerson's, and Nietzsche's writing is to move you to find your own truth, your own self. By leaving the connections between the parts of their arguments for the reader to create, these authors put readers in the position of having to forge and test a path of reflection for themselves. Readers must essay not only the text but themselves, too. Their texts aim to initiate a reflective thought process in the reader, with the latter being what proves the claim of the former. Pascal testifies eloquently to Montaigne's success in provoking introspection when he writes that "it is not in Montaigne, but in me, that I find all that I see there."[32] It is also what one scholar says Emerson found in Montaigne, declaring that "the secret" of Emerson's attraction is that from his first reading "he found Montaigne doing what, without knowing it yet, Emerson wanted himself to do."[33] It is also the reaction each hoped to engender in all his worthy readers. It is exactly what Lopez means when he says Emerson and Nietzsche aim to make readers "return to themselves." For all three authors, this is the best possible effect that a text can produce and so it is what they aim to accomplish with their writing styles.

While the recent scholars are thus basically correct in their first three claims, they are only partly correct in their fourth claim, the limits of language. Not only Emerson and Nietzsche but Montaigne, too, all refer to language as a mere symbol or sign that limits as well as liberates. Language, Montaigne writes, is but "this airy medium of words" (II.6, 359 [274]) and represents only a clumsy attempt at self-articulation.[34] It is neither subtle nor flexible enough to capture human thoughts and feelings. Not only is it overly rigid and insufficiently penetrating in its descriptions, but according to Montaigne it imprisons the self in the terms and analysis it uses and invents. Human beings use language to reveal, but it creates and conceals at the same time. Emerson and Nietzsche describe language as operating in exactly the same manner. Emerson describes language as a mere "vehicle or art by which [one's ideas are] conveyed to men" ("Intellect," 422), and he proclaims the limits of language: "if I speak, I define, I confine, and am less" ("Intellect," 426). Nietzsche also writes of the limiting nature of language, lamenting "the unconscious domination and guidance by . . . grammatical functions" (*BGE*, 20, 27). And in a limiting relationship that works both ways, Nietzsche writes: "the spell of certain grammatical functions is ultimately also the spell of *physiological* valuations" (*BGE*, 20, 28, emphasis in original). One's nature dictates and limits the language one invents, and that language then further limits all who use it.

However, Emerson still argues that language can reveal truth about reality, even if it does not do so in our deviant culture. In his essay entitled

"Language" in *Nature,* Emerson imagines the possibility of a "picturesque language" that would truly capture the essence of *what is:*

> But wise men pierce this rotten diction and fasten words again to visible things; so that picturesque language is at once a commanding certificate that he who employs it, is a man in alliance with truth and God. The moment our discourse rises above the ground line of familiar facts, and is inflamed with passion or exalted by thought, it clothes itself in images. A man conversing in earnest, if he watch his intellectual processes, will find that a material image, more or less luminous, arises in his mind, contemporaneous with every thought. Hence, good writing and brilliant discourse are perpetual allegories. This imagery is spontaneous. It is the blending of experience with the present action of the mind. It is proper creation. It is the working of the Original Cause through the instruments he has already made. (23)

If one focuses only on the thread here emphasizing that human productions are "perpetual allegories" based on "spontaneous" creation from within, Emerson's vision might sound Nietzschean. However, Emerson's emphasis on human creation has a totally different inflection from Nietzsche's or Montaigne's. For Emerson, while words and language are symbolic, they can reveal the truth about the world, because human creation "is the working of the Original Cause through the instruments [i.e., the people] he has already made." Indeed, "he who employs it [this picturesque language], is a man in alliance with truth and God." Emerson here is un-Nietzschean and un-Montaignean not only in asserting that language can convey truth but even more fundamentally in asserting the existence of truth itself. Emerson further asserts that the issues with language also hold for our understanding of material nature: "It is not words only that are emblematic. Every natural fact is a symbol of some spiritual fact" (20). If connecting language to reality remains but a longing for a typical individual, Emerson sees it as the very definition of what makes a great genius or artist. Above he attributes this ability to "wise men"; in his essay "The Poet," he writes: "For, as it is dislocation and detachment from the life of God, that makes things ugly, [it is] the poet, who re-attaches things to nature and the Whole,—re-attaching even artificial things, and violations of nature, to nature, by a deeper insight" (455). The poet rectifies the world on a level deeper than nature—on the level of "the Whole." Thus, we see that Emerson's skepticism about words and language, what the past two generations of Emerson scholars call Nietzschean, is only true for Emerson of a human life that has lost its way, lost its connection to what is.

In conclusion, while each thinker is generally skeptical about what can be known and communicated to another human being and writes accordingly, Emerson still trusts that language *can* portray the reality of the cosmos. To the extent of describing ordinary existing reality, Emerson is like Montaigne and Nietzsche. However, insofar as Emerson believes that both language (in the hands of "wise men" and "the poet") and the physical world itself reflect an underlying spiritual reality, he—unlike the other two skeptics—is profoundly more optimistic about the power of language. Emerson is more optimistic because, unlike the other two skeptics, he conceives of a true reality existing beyond linguistic constructs. In short, the reasons that Harold Bloom calls Emerson and Nietzsche "twin titans of deconstruction" are exaggerated about Emerson; the claim is truer of Nietzsche and Montaigne.[35] Moreover, far from being uncharacteristic, Emerson's discussion of an ideal language offers a glimpse into the major difference between him and the other two skeptics, a difference that is clarified and amplified by comparing their views on the self and the cosmos.

The Self in the Cosmos

The current consensus view of Emerson recognizes not only stylistic similarities to Nietzsche, but ontological and metaphysical similarities as well. Speaking for the consensus, Lopez argues that Emerson and Nietzsche have "a common ontological core"; they share a vision in which there is no being, only becoming.[36] Life in this realm of becoming is described as a "dynamic struggle of opposed forces,"[37] and an individual is thus, in Emerson's phrase, not a unitary whole but "a congress of nations" (*EL*, 3:251, cited in Lopez, 21). Emerson and Nietzsche are said to recognize no metaphysical reality that can or should constrain individuals. Indeed, Lopez characterizes Emerson's and Nietzsche's metaphysics as having a "shared 'pragmatic' (post-Christian and anti-absolutist) center."[38] The suggestion is that Emerson, like Nietzsche, was beyond absolutes, beyond truth, and especially beyond Christian truth claims. An individual living in this world is thus characterized by "the possibility of unlimited self-creation."[39] While these claims correctly describe Nietzsche and Montaigne, they do not accurately describe Emerson. The recent scholars are correct that Emerson and Nietzsche share a general ontology of becoming, but these scholars stop short of looking at the very different cores that each author attributes to the self, and they simply overlook the essential differences in the thinkers' metaphysics. Emerson situates his ontology of becoming in a metaphysics of being; the other thinkers do not.

Emerson, Nietzsche, and Montaigne do share two ontological similarities as the scholarly consensus holds. First, they all do see human beings as having an ontological core of becoming. For them, nothing in the material world is a fixed or permanent being. Instead, all living things are always changing, always becoming. Emerson identifies the whole process of life with becoming: "the soul *becomes*" (271, emphasis in original). And Nietzsche explicitly embraces this idea: "*becoming*, along with a radical repudiation of the very concept of *being*—all this is clearly more closely related to me than anything else thought to date" (*Ecce Homo,* 273, emphasis in original). And for Montaigne, "being consists in movement and action," not in anything fixed (II.8, 366 [279]). Second, they also understand the self as internally divided. Emerson speaks of individuals as being made up of many competing tendencies (773), and his phrase that each individual is a "congress of nations" aptly characterizes their formal similarities. Nietzsche writes: "our body is but a social structure," a "commonwealth," in which "the governing class identifies itself with the success of the commonwealth" (*BGE,* 19, 26–27). And Montaigne uses similar language to portray divisions within an individual, except he envisions the parts in an even looser federation: "We are all patchwork, and so shapeless and diverse in composition that each bit, each moment, plays its own game" (II.1, 321 [244]). So in the general sense that all three thinkers describe life as becoming and internally divided, the recent scholars are correct. However, here the similarities end.

While there are many overlaps between the thinkers' general ontologies and their views of the self, there are decisive differences in their conceptions of what the self is and, especially, the metaphysical reality in which each self exists. Nietzsche sees the self as inhabiting a godless universe from which the individual can gain no direction. He thus wants the individual to will his will without any reference to supposedly moral truths. Montaigne does not assert the nonexistence of God, but he says little about God, because he is skeptical about whether we can know even of

God's existence, let alone His will. Accordingly, he is dubious of all religious claims, and the essence of his thought is to turn humans away from what he considers to be unverifiable metaphysical claims in order to have us focus on what he thinks we can to some extent know: this world and especially the internal motions in ourselves. But unlike Nietzsche, Montaigne does not find a single ineluctable will at the core of the self that can and should take one into the world. Montaigne's self is more introspective and evanescent than Nietzsche's. In contrast to Nietzsche and Montaigne, Emerson has full confidence that there is a spiritual order to the cosmos that can and does guide individuals in proportion to their genius and self-development. Like Nietzsche and Montaigne, Emerson rejects obedience to external religious authorities and is indeed skeptical of authorities of every kind. But unlike the others and despite the occasional appearance of claims to the contrary, the self that Emerson describes is part of and should ultimately be guided by a higher providence. One can ignore Emerson's metaphysical ground and focus only on his ontology, as the recent scholars do, and one would learn much about oneself. But Emerson's advice to individual selves cannot be divorced from the spiritual structure that he sees as underlying, supporting, and constraining the world. Whereas Nietzsche and Montaigne think we must create a world on our own, alone, Emerson thinks that in doing so humans must aim at revealing its preexisting spiritual structure. Nietzsche and Montaigne dismiss such spiritual claims as fantasy and as fantastical self-deception.

To examine the claims of Emerson's recently alleged anti-absolutist metaphysics, this section is argued in two parts. I first analyze the conceptions of the self and metaphysics found in what are rightly deemed Emerson's most Nietzschean essays, "Self-Reliance" and "Fate," comparing and, more importantly, contrasting Emerson's vision to Nietzsche's. I then turn to Emerson's darkest and most skeptical essay, "Experience," where Emerson's skeptical doubting most parallels Montaigne's. I there show both great skeptical similarities between Emerson and Montaigne, and the ways in which Emerson ultimately proves to be much less skeptical. The premise of my argument is that if Emerson should ultimately prove to be un-Nietzschean and un-Montaignean in these essays, then it is unlikely he will be found to be Nietzschean or Montaignean anywhere.[40]

Emerson's Nietzscheanism and Its Limits in "Self-Reliance" and "Fate"

While Emerson and Nietzsche both see the self as divided and as becoming, they have radically different conceptions of what the self is that is divided and becomes. More importantly, they fundamentally differ in seeing the self as situated in radically different metaphysical situations. As a result, even in "Self-Reliance" and "Fate," Emerson emerges not as a Nietzschean but as a transcendental thinker.

For Nietzsche, all life is a struggle between wills because for him all life is nothing but will to power. He writes of "the essence of life, its *will to power*" (*GM*, II: 12, 79, emphasis in original).[41] This is no less true of plants and animals than for man. All life is essentially the same. When a plant bends toward the sun or a lion kills a deer, it is the exertion of a will to power. Moreover, for Nietzsche, this is all that life is. There is no "soul," "mind," "intellect," or "spirit" that has any self-subsistent reality. These are human constructs that falsely explain the true reality of will. Nietzsche conceives of will as simultaneously a physical and psychological force in a manner that collapses the traditional body-mind distinction. Ideas of the "soul," the "self," and the "subject" are false impressions, mere masks covering a jumble of competing wills. As Nietzsche writes: "L'effet c'est moi" (*BGE*, 19, 26). Each will attempts to will its will, and they all compete against each other for mastery of the individual. The strongest will dominates and creates the character or tendency of the individual (and the world). If the dominant will is particularly strong it can dominate, subsume, use, and sublimate the other wills. When one will marshals the lesser wills to its end, Nietzsche calls such a person strong-willed. Most people, however, according to Nietzsche, are weak-willed. They are an inchoate mass of competing wills and thus can never focus and apply their total strength. Such people experience their inner confusion as weakness, as spiritual suffering. For them, "everything is unrest, disturbance, doubt, attempt: the best forces have an inhibiting effect" (*BGE*, 208, 130). They can achieve nothing great. All great things, all human advances and innovations, according to Nietzsche, are the result of the strong-willed. In his view, history is nothing but the story of the few strongest-willed people. Everyone else follows—or is fodder.

Emerson also discusses the role of the will in human life such that if one examined his utterances on the will alone and out of context he might seem to describe the core of the self similarly to Nietzsche. Emerson states: "There can be no driving force, except through the conversion of the man into his will, making him the will, and the will him" (783); "The one serious and formidable thing in nature is a will" (783). Like Nietzsche, Emerson writes that "when a strong will appears, it usually results from a certain unity of organization, as if the whole energy of body and mind flowed in one direction. All great force is real and elemental. There is no manufacturing a strong will" (782). Moreover, Emerson's account of the internal motions in each individual has many elements that are later found in Nietzsche's account of will to power. Emerson sometimes describes the primal moving force of the individual as a subrational phenomenon, explaining how it "forever wells up the impulse of choosing and acting in the soul" (779). Like Nietzsche, he sometimes describes this key impulse as having an underlying physical or "organic power," and he variously links it to both thought and the will (782). He once locates this force in our atoms: "our atoms are as savage in resistance" (780). Another time he locates it in the cells: "The animal cell," he once writes, "makes itself;—then, what it wants. Every creature,—wren or dragon,—shall make its own lair. As soon as there is life, there is self-direction, and absorbing and using of material" (788). As a result of these forces, he writes of politics having a "physiological" basis (774; compare Nietzsche, *GM*, II: 12, 78–79). As Nietzsche equates the willing that is life with freedom (Nietzsche, *GM*, II: 2, 59–60), so Emerson writes, "Life is freedom" (788). Moreover, Emerson links the will not only with life and freedom but with "power": "power ceases in the instant of repose; it resides in the moment of transition from a past to a new state, in the shooting of the gulf, in the darting to an aim" (271). Insofar as Emerson links each of the above points to will, he seems to be very Nietzschean. Accordingly, one can interpret Emerson's famous willingness (cited above) to follow the devil if it was inside him as a Nietzschean statement of acceptance of the ineluctable physical reality that he is, whatever it is. This is what the Emerson scholars assert who want to make the case for the similarity between Emerson and Nietzsche. But to go only this far is fundamentally misleading in stating Emerson's overall conception of the self.

On each of the above points, Emerson has countervailing ideas (even staying only in "Self-Reliance" and "Fate") that inflect them as less Nietzschean and more transcendental than the above quotations make it seem. To start, for Emerson the human being is not just "will" as it is for Nietzsche. Unlike Nietzsche, Emerson distinguishes the "moral" from the "material" basis of human motivation (774) and roots human intentionality in the human psyche in places other than will, such as in "thought" (779, 780), "spirit" (779), "intellect" (779, 782), and the "moral sentiment" (782). Emerson explicates these terms elsewhere,[42] but even "Fate" highlights the importance of thought and the moral sentiment by explicitly enumerating them in the text:

1. But Fate against Fate is only parrying and defence: there are, also, the noble creative forces. The revelation of Thought takes man out of servitude into freedom. (780–81)

2. If thought makes free, so does the moral sentiment. . . . That affection is essential to will. (782)

Unlike Nietzsche, Emerson clearly recognizes parts of the self, here "Thought" and "moral sentiment," as fundamental and causal in addition to will. Emerson deems these two parts as so primordial that they are both described as necessary to "freedom" and the latter is also described as "essential to will." It cannot be identical to will if it is essential to it. Emerson continues to emphasize the limits of human will and its necessity of allying with the moral sentiment, Emerson's name for the faculty that intuits universal truth:[43]

> Where power is shown in will, it must rest on the universal force. Alaric and Bonaparte must believe they rest on truth, or their will can be bought or bent. There is a bribe possible for any finite will. But the pure sympathy with universal ends is an infinite force, and cannot be bribed or bent. Whoever has had experience of the moral sentiment cannot choose but believe in unlimited power. Each pulse from that heart is an oath from the Most High. I know not what the word *sublime* means, if it be not the intimations in this infant of a terrific force. (782–83, emphasis in original)

Unlike Nietzsche, for Emerson human will is both necessarily and fundamentally limited and gets its deepest strength by tapping into a universal will—"the universal force" that has "universal ends"—that exists outside of an individual's subjective will. In *Representative Men*, Emerson gives a more Machiavellian and psychologically astute account of Napoleon's motives, but Emerson emphasizes here that not only do strong-willed individuals need to believe in truth but also that such truth exists. It is thus clear that Emerson understands "will" not in the Nietzschean sense as the sole fundamental basis of life but in a more conventional sense; it is just one among several human faculties. Despite similarly emphasizing that humans inhabit the realm of becoming, their visions of what a human is are fundamentally different. Two huge differences between Emerson's and Nietzsche's conceptions of the self are that they mean radically different things by will and thus see the human essence as fundamentally different.

The fact that Emerson and Nietzsche see the fundamental essence of the self differently has two corollary differences worth making explicit. First, whereas Nietzsche sees the will to power as everything that is, and thus not bound by any external force, Emerson recognizes limits on the subjective will. For him, human power and fate are opposites. Will is only part of *what is* and by no means the most powerful or important part. Human will is only about choice in dealing with the fixed or unchosen parts of the cosmos, which Emerson variously defines as "Fate" or the "laws of the world" (769). Second, while Emerson ultimately brings power and fate together, he does so only by affirming the existence of a harmony in life, what he calls a "Blessed Unity," between us and what really is (793). For Emerson, life includes the material struggle of each organism, but underlying the material struggle is a deeper spiritual quest to tap into the essentially harmonious transcendent unity of the whole: "The indwelling necessity plants the rose of beauty on the brow of chaos, and discloses the central intention of Nature to be harmony and joy" (793). Nietzsche sees no essential harmony in life, underlying or otherwise. In fact, for him, "life operates *essentially,* that is in its basic functions, through injury, assault, exploitation, destruction, and simply cannot be thought of at all without this character" (*GM*, II: 11, 76, emphasis in original). Destruction and assault can only end according to Nietzsche if life ends, that is, if the will disappears.

The most important difference between Emerson and Nietzsche, however, is their fundamentally different metaphysics—and their different metaphysical visions totally alter the way they conceive that the self operates in the world. Whereas Nietzsche utterly rejects the existence of any normative or regulative truths outside the self, Emerson's whole corpus, including "Self-Reliance and "Fate," is inspired by the existence of such metaphysical truth. Nietzsche says that "truth" is merely the product of a human will to power, but Emerson repeatedly asserts that there is a reality to the world that grounds the human subjective will. Indeed, Emerson insists that it guides all great geniuses.

As with their conceptions of the will, so, too, are there many similarities between Emerson's and Nietzsche's conceptions of the self and its place in the cosmos that if taken alone, detached from their contexts, would make Emerson seem very Nietzschean. In "Self Reliance," Emerson, as Nietzsche does, councils "self-trust" (268). Emerson directly asks about the nature of the self: "What is the aboriginal Self, on which a universal reliance may be grounded" (268)? He begins his answer by grounding the self in such general terms as "Spontaneity or Instinct" or "Intuition," and "that deep force, the last fact behind which analysis cannot go" (269), all of which might be described as similar to aspects of Nietzsche's account of will to power. Moreover, like Nietzsche, Emerson describes the self as having to make its way in the cosmos devoid of help, assistance, or crutches from others: "We must go alone" (272). For a self to authentically be itself, it has to turn inward and become what it ultimately is, and, like Nietzsche, Emerson once describes this struggle for oneself as "enter[ing] into the state of war" (273). Emerson's conception of the authentic self-seeker and the political consequences of his struggle also have Nietzschean overtones: "And truly it demands something godlike in him who has cast off the common motives of humanity, and has ventured to trust himself for a taskmaster. High be his heart, faithful his will, clear his sight, that he may in good earnest be doctrine, society, law, to himself, that a simple purpose may be to him as strong as iron necessity is to others!" (274). The idea of a "taskmaster" whose "will" becomes "iron necessity" to others is indeed very Nietzschean. The recent scholars who see Emerson and Nietzsche as sharing the same fundamental ontological and metaphysical vision would be on solid ground if Emerson went only this far in describing the self in the cosmos. However, Emerson goes further in a way that overrides these similarities.

According to Emerson, self-reliance is not reliance on one's own inner will; self-reliance is, ultimately, God-reliance. Unlike Nietzsche, for Emerson the self is not radically alone in a metaphysically empty cosmos. When the self turns inward into itself and authentically digs down past all its encrusted layers, it finds the universal divine. Our interior journey must be made alone not so that we can authentically create (as Nietzsche would have it), but because "the relations of the soul to the divine spirit are so pure, that it is profane to seek to interpose helps" (269). Connecting with this divine spirit both illuminates the world and creates it, as it were, anew: "It must be that when God speaketh he should communicate, not one thing, but all things; should fill the world with his voice; scatter forth light, nature, time, souls, from the centre of the present thought; and new date and new create the whole" (269–70). It is not humans but God who authentically creates the world; humans can only dig down deep, seeking to "communicate" with the divine and to feel its indwelling presence. Thus, becoming oneself is not to define oneself by or to assert one's partial characteristics; it is to overcome these partialities in order to find oneself in the universal whole. Emerson writes:

> This is the ultimate fact which we so quickly reach on this, as on every topic, the resolution of all into the ever-blessed One. Self-existence is the attribute of the Supreme Cause, and it constitutes the measure of good by the degree in which it enters into all lower forms. All things real are so by so much virtue as they contain. (272)

Emerson's claims that we are but an "attribute" of the divine and that as part of the whole we can feel the divine reality running through us, are totally opposite of Nietzsche's metaphysical vision. Furthermore, Emerson's claims about the existence of a "Supreme Cause" and his idea that the "good" and "virtue" exist only insofar as we participate in them, is, to say the least, antithetical to Nietzsche's outlook.

In "Self-Reliance," Emerson states the fundamental connection between self-reliance and God-reliance over and over using many different metaphors and analogies. He employs the metaphor of going home: "Let us not rove; let us sit at home with the cause [i.e., the divine]. Let us stun and astonish the intruding rabble of men and books and institutions, by a simple declaration of the divine fact. Bid the invaders take the shoes from off their feet, for God is here within. Let our simplicity judge them, and our docility to our own law demonstrate the poverty of nature and fortune beside our native riches" (272). God "is here within." He dwells within in such a bounteous manner that Emerson calls his presence "our native riches." Our genius is thus urged to "stay at home, to put itself in communication with the internal ocean" (272), with the internal ocean representing the eternal divine. Emerson uses various other metaphors for trying to achieve unity with the eternal oneness, sometimes calling on people to go out: "Look out into the region of absolute truth" (274) and sometimes saying that God dwells within, exclaiming that spiritual power is "poured into the souls of all men" (782). In yet another place, he declares: "It is not in us, but we are in it" (781).[44] But whatever the directionality or spatiality of the metaphor, the connection between man and God is for Emerson what matters: "As soon as the man is at one with God, he will not beg" (276); "In the Will work and acquire" (282). The capitalized "Will" here is certainly not Nietzsche's will; rather it the universal Will, the creator of the cosmos, of which we are but an attribute. Emerson variously describes this higher power by a whole host of terms—all nonphysical, transcendent, and, I think, synonymous. In only the two essays in which the Nietzschean Emerson is most supposed to be found, "Self Reliance" and "Fate," Emerson describes this higher power as "God" (269, 270 [three times], 272, 276 [five times] 281, 282), the "Good" (271, 272), a "godhead" (782), "divine spirit" (269), "divine wisdom" (270), "the divine fact" (272), "the will of Divine Providence" (782), "universal miracle" (271), "eternal causation" (271), "the eternal law" (273), "the everblessed ONE" (272), "the will of all mind" (782), and "the region of absolute truth" (274). There is no such constellation of language in Nietzsche, because there is no such concept in Nietzsche. Nietzsche's self and Emerson's self thus in many ways inhabit opposite and contradictory universes. Where Nietzsche's self lives alone in a metaphysically void universe, Emerson's self lives in a universe where all its discrete and diverse elements are ultimately spiritually united as part of a larger cosmic whole. Their metaphysics are polar opposites.

Also opposite of Nietzsche, Emerson makes it clear that the divine reality of the cosmos trumps the merely human will. In "Self-Reliance," Emerson boldly asserts that an individual is only strong when "the God deign[s] to enter and inhabit you" (281). Similarly, in "Fate," Emerson describes this divine force in a most un-Nietzschean but very transcendental way: "I see, that when souls reach a certain clearness of perception, they accept a knowledge and motive above selfishness. A breath of will blows eternally through the universe of souls in the direction of the Right and Necessary. It is the air which all intellects inhale and exhale, and it is the wind which blows the worlds into order and orbit" (782). Not only does Emerson's idea of the existence of a higher reality fundamentally contradict Nietzsche's rejection of metaphysics, but his idea of that higher reality being a force for "Right" also fundamentally contradicts Nietzsche's conception that aside from our wills, the cosmos is devoid of morality. Nietzsche sees all morals as the product and embodiment of the selfish interest of a will to power, not as "seeing a light" or "receiving a wind" that somehow fulfills the self by subsuming it in the higher reality. Nietzsche's metaphysics is the opposite of Emerson's, who argues in the conclusion of "Fate" that the subjective will of each can be knit to the just, good, and beautiful order of the universal whole. Emerson sees everything in the cosmos as in a balance; every reward is offset and every suffering is compensated, often in this world but if not, in the next. This is the entire argument of his essay "Compensation," and it is restated in "Fate" thusly: "whatever lames or paralyzes you, draws in with it the divinity, in some form, to repay" (793). And so "Fate" concludes with repeated praise of the "Blessed Unity" and "Beautiful Necessity" (repeated three times) of the cosmos:[45] "Let us build altars to the Blessed Unity which holds nature and souls in perfect solution, and compels every atom to serve an universal end. I [wonder] . . . at the necessity of beauty under which the universe lies" (793). Emerson continues in this passage to dismiss the significance of looking at flowers and rainbows and all such merely physical manifestations of beauty that depend on the human senses. That is not the kind of beauty that Emerson ultimately seeks. Rather, the beauty Emerson seeks is "the indwelling necessity [that] plants the rose of beauty on the brow of chaos, and discloses the central intention of Nature to be harmony and joy" (793). Here we see the ecstatic Emerson, who repeatedly proclaims, "Let us build altars to the Beautiful Necessity" (793). If one cited only the ideas of an "indwelling necessity" that imposes order on chaos, it would sound Nietzschean. However, insofar as the order of which Emerson speaks is not the product of an individual's will to power but reflective of a higher order—his "Blessed Unity" and the harmony of the cosmos—and insofar as this higher order "compels every atom" of us "to serve an universal end," and insofar as Emerson conceives of that end to be the end of a harmonious cosmos, it is the opposite of Nietzsche. For Emerson, unlike Nietzsche (or Richard Rorty), "there are no contingencies" (794).[46]

At the conclusion of his supposedly Nietzschean "Fate," Emerson declares the cosmos to be the exact opposite of Nietzsche's conception: "Let us build altars to the Beautiful Necessity. If we thought men were free in the sense, that, in a single exception one fantastical will could prevail over the law of things, it were all one as if a child's hand could pull down the sun. If, in the least particular, one could derange the order of nature,—who would accept the gift of life?" (793). Whereas Nietzsche describes the world as a metaphysical void so that all life must impose its will, Emerson proclaims that all things are governed by a "law" and that it is impossible that any human "will" could ever "derange the order of nature" and upset the harmonious whole. If the cosmic order and unity could be altered, if the world was a human plaything in any sense—Emerson would rather die than live in such a Nietzschean universe.

Doubt and Its Limits in "Experience"

While "Self-Reliance" and "Fate" show that Emerson has a fundamentally transcendentalist difference from Nietzsche, to convincingly demonstrate this we must also examine "Experience," Emerson's darkest and most skeptical essay. In "Experience," Emerson shares many doubts that parallel Montaigne and Nietzsche. In particular, in "Experience," Emerson skeptically attacks several possible sources of guidance or knowledge: the human faculties, human institutions, and science. His skeptical critiques are powerful and echo Montaigne's; what he asserts beyond these critiques, however, is hardly skeptical and parallels the transcendentalist arguments of "Self-Reliance" and "Fate."

Like Montaigne, Emerson is skeptical about human capacities. Emerson discusses three different human phenomena that we cannot and should not trust: mood, senses, and our understanding. According to both thinkers, everything we know through any of these three things is distorted. Like Heidegger, Emerson pays much attention to mood. Our mood affects all our activities, it shrouds the world in "illusion" and "dream" (473). Emerson similarly asserts that our senses are inadequate at grasping the real: "we do not see directly, but mediately, and . . . we have no means of correcting these colored and distorting lenses" (487). Emerson also sneers at the human ability for rational understanding: "Life is not dialectics"; "Life is not intellectual or critical" (478). But Emerson rather asserts these limits than, as Montaigne does, systematically explore them. In "The Apology for Raymond Sebond," Montaigne's longest and most skeptical essay, he mounts a massively powerful and psychologically astute assault on reason (II.12, 543–71 [420–43]) and the sense organs (II.12, 571–86 [443–55]). What Montaigne means by reason is what Emerson means by understanding, our human calculating ability—as opposed to what Emerson often calls "Reason," by which he means the constellation of our moral intuitions, about which he is not skeptical.[47] Montaigne cites three internal factors, perception, body, and emotion, and two external ones, time and place, as affecting our reason and judgment.[48] According to Montaigne, human perceptions vary. Different people perceive the same thing differently and the same person does as well at different times. Bodily movements such as fevers and disease make us reason and judge differently. Everyone knows how emotions affect their souls and alter their thinking. These natural and ordinary changes limit our ability to reason and judge soundly. Additionally, testifying to the power of habit, one's time and place, which are not natural but conventional factors, also color the way one reasons and judges. According to Montaigne, peoples and epochs have a character. Some are more or less bellicose, just, temperate, or docile. Who is to say that this or that people, or all of them, have not been mistaken? "Reason," Montaigne concludes, is "that semblance of intellect that each man fabricates in himself" (II.12, 548 [425]). On the limits of the human senses, Montaigne argues that we may not have all the senses of nature and for that reason might be doing something very stupid. Of the ones we have, we know that we do not possess them in their perfection, as many animals smell, see, and hear better than we do. Our senses are limited by the mind. If our mind is occupied, we miss or misperceive data. Finally, different senses conflict with one another. Something might look smooth but feel rough. To get an objective measure we would need an adjudicative instrument, but to verify the instrument we would need a demonstration, but to verify the demonstration we would need an instrument. The circle never ends, and we are left to recognize our weak and fallible abilities, says Montaigne. Emerson does not as systematically make these critiques of our human faculties, but everything he writes is consistent with them. The comparison to Montaigne helps elaborate Emerson's skepticism on these points.

Like Montaigne, Emerson also derides the reliability of human institutions. As fallible creatures, everything we make is liable to the same problems. As Montaigne writes: "Our structure, both public and private, is full of imperfection" (III.1, 767 [599]); "men, vain and irresolute authors" create laws that are nothing but "a singular testimony of human infirmity" (III.13, 1049 [821]; III.12, 1026 [803]); "there is nothing so grossly and widely and ordinarily faulty as the laws" (III.13, 1049 [821]). Emerson makes the same point in "Experience" and explicitly applies his critique to the full range of human institutions.[49] Just as plays of children are "nonsense, but very educative nonsense," Emerson writes, so, too, are all human creations, even "the largest and solemnest things [such as] commerce, government, church, marriage" (477). Note that, like Montaigne, Emerson includes religion on his list of human institutions, and later in the chapter he labels the "Holy Ghost" as but a "quaint name" akin to Fortune, Minerva, and Muse for "the unbounded substance" that is the divine (485). Similarly, he treats Jesus' doctrine exactly as he treats the doctrines of ancient pagan thinkers: as a "metaphor" (485). So Emerson, like Montaigne, both deems Christianity to be a human creation and does not privilege it over any other human creation.[50] Emerson's praise of the transcendent, therefore, is no simple affirmation of Christianity, and the recent scholars are correct about this. In other writings such as "Culture," Emerson promotes culture as both an "antidote against . . . egotism" (1019) and as a way to "mount and meliorate" nature (1033), to "absorb" nature's power (1034), but in "Experience" he mocks "culture" and "party promises" as ending in nothing but "head-ache" (478). In short, by deeming the most important political, economic, religious, and familial institutions as nonsense and headache, Emerson shows the depth of his skepticism about human institutions.

Not only do both Emerson and Montaigne doubt human abilities and human institutions, but both also doubt science's ability to provide us with knowledge or guidance. Like Montaigne, Emerson lambastes junk science, such as the "so-called science" of phrenology (which Montaigne also explicitly attacked), and Emerson dismisses its practitioners as "theoretic kidnappers and slave-drivers" (475). He also lampoons a "witty physician who found theology in the biliary duct, and used to affirm that if there was disease in the liver, the man became a Calvinist, and if that organ was sound, he became a Unitarian" (474). But Emerson hardly has anything better to say about the empirical sciences. Whereas Montaigne, writing in the sixteenth century before science had fully triumphed, imagines the possibility of a science but ultimately rejects it as unachievable,[51] Emerson condemns empirical science on more fundamental grounds. Emerson's problem with science is that it reduces everything to materialism: "The physicians say, they are not materialists; but they are" (475). Emerson rejects materialistic determinism: "I distrust the facts and the inferences" (475). He rejects "the trap of [the] so-called sciences"—here meaning empirical science—because it is limited to "the chain of physical necessity" and the "sty of sensualism" (476). The consequence of bad science's materialism from Emerson's perspective seems to be that science cannot explain itself, that is, the scientist's own "creative power": "it is impossible that the creative power should exclude itself" (476). Pure materialism, Emerson avers, cannot explain the spark of genius or the deeper aspects of existence. He thus concludes that materialistic explanations are just "the thin and cold realm of pure geometry and lifeless science" (480). In short, like Montaigne, Emerson in "Experience" is skeptical of human abilities to know and the abilities of human creations, whether political, religious, economic, or scientific. "Experience" powerfully expresses skepticism toward all these things.[52]

The conclusion of Emerson's skepticism as expressed in "Experience" is that we exist and are limited, a condition Emerson equates with "the Fall of Man"—although unlike in the biblical account, Emerson never suggests the human condition was ever otherwise (487). We cannot see anything as it is but only subjectively: "The subject exists, the subject enlarges" (489); "As I am, so I see; use what language we will, we can never say anything but what we are" (489). As a result of our radical subjectivity, Emerson concludes that "life itself is a bubble and a skepticism, and a sleep within a sleep" (481). To describe the lack of real contact with the world, Emerson uses language later made famous by Nietzsche: we are each bounded by a "horizon" (487). The radical doubt and uncertainty of the human condition described in "Experience" so far is consistent with the radical doubt expressed by Montaigne and Nietzsche.

However, whereas Montaigne and Nietzsche accept this fundamental human subjectivity, Emerson does not. While Emerson acknowledges that we mostly experience becoming, he says human beings yearn for being: "our love of the real draws us to permanence" (476). But unlike Montaigne and Nietzsche, who try to dissuade their readers from pursuing (what they deem as) this fantasy, Emerson tries to move his readers in the other direction. We "wert [sic] born to a whole," that is, we are of the universal cosmic essence, he writes, but we are each also a "particular," that is, not identical to the whole from which we were torn and with which we seek union (477). We are but a mere part that always is and must be less than the whole that we seek. Every person, artwork, story, perception, friend, or human love is always of a mere particular and thus not ultimately the entirety of what we crave. No human creation or earthly thing can satisfy our deepest longing for the "ocean of thought and power" for which we yearn (477).

Emerson's answer to the incompleteness of our partial and subjective human condition is to seek metaphysical completion. All three thinkers share an ontology of becoming, but Emerson alone of the three situates it in a metaphysics of being. Montaigne and Nietzsche describe humans as beings that live *only* in this subjective realm of becoming. Nietzsche affirms that this is all there is. For Montaigne, since we cannot know whether there is any transcendent truth or not, we should not worry about it and act without regard to it. The effectual truth for both is a world of becoming only. They both see most humans as craving being, but they counsel their fellows to accept the world as flux and flow, and each in his own way seeks to come to terms with and make the best of it. By contrast, even in his most skeptical essay, "Experience," Emerson asserts that there is, happily for us, another realm with which we can make contact to attempt to satisfy our deepest longings for completion. In "Experience," Emerson councils relying on "the capital virtue of self-trust" (490)—exactly what he calls for in "Self-Reliance." By self-trust here he does not mean that we should trust our human calculating powers or that it is an intellectual matter of defining doctrine. Rather, he means what he also said in "Self-Reliance," that we should look into the deepest most primordial part of ourselves. Emerson means by self-trust here the same thing he meant in "Self-Reliance": self-reliance is God reliance.

The key to understanding the metaphysical completion that Emerson urges in "Experience" is recognizing that for him the divine spirit is not only outside us but also, most accessibly, inside us. This vision contrasts markedly with that of Nietzsche and Montaigne. Nietzsche has us turn inward to follow the core of the self, the will, and this leads him to a life of unlimited willing. For Montaigne, there is no single ineluctable reality, such as Nietzsche finds in the will. For Montaigne, we should turn inward and essay ourselves to see what we find and thus to order our lives accordingly, but what Montaigne finds in the self is everything and nothing. The seeds of every human virtue and vice, he posits, are found in all, but the exploration or essaying of our various traits lead them to dissolve under the analytical gaze. The more we look, the more and less we find. We find layer upon layer that seem to never end. This might not be the basis for anything great or heroic (as Nietzsche seeks), but according to Montaigne it is what we are, the best he thinks we can genuinely do, and it supplies a never-ending source of wonder and delight.[53] However, Emerson finds neither a strong will nor cosmic emptiness. "All I know is reception," he writes; "I am and I have: but I do not get" (491). But what is the ultimate "I" that receives, and what do "I" get, according to Emerson? Emerson's answer in "Experience" exactly parallels the answer he gives in "Self-Reliance" and "Fate": the universal divine that is in us all. He writes: "Nothing is of us or our works,—that all is of God" (483); "I can see nothing at last . . . [but] vital force supplied from the Eternal" (483). For Emerson, "The great and crescive self, rooted in absolute nature, supplants all relative existence" (487), so he recommends turning away from our partial, human concerns and instead trying to tap into the power of the absolute that dwells in us all. Emerson also describes this in erotic language: "The subject is the receiver of Godhead" (488); "The universe is the bride of the soul" (488). In addition to the citations of the universal divine cited above, "Experience" also repeatedly refers to and affirms the transcendental, including "God" (483 [two other times], 487, 490), "the First Cause" (485), the "one will" that is the "secret cause" of all (484), "this cause, which refuses to be named" (485), an underlying "musical perfection" (484), the "Divinity" (477), "the proper deity" (488), "the creator" (476), "the Ideal" (484), "the mighty Ideal" (486), and "Being" (486). "Experience" also speaks about some of the manifestations of this "Ideal," including "absolute truth" (476), "absolute good" (476), "absolute nature" (487), and "real nature" (473). All of these terms signify the same thing for Emerson: the transcendent realm of unchanging Being. Every human who is not in touch with the eternal oneness must be skeptical and unhappy.

Emerson explicitly recognizes the limits of his skepticism in "Experience" when he defines skepticism as the failure to find life's unity: the "skeptical" is being "without unity" (484). And Emerson equates lack of unity with an undesirable chaos: "Life will be imaged," Emerson writes, "but cannot be divided nor doubled. Any invasion of its unity would be chaos" (488). Emerson's advice to the reader of "Experience" is the exact opposite of persisting in skepticism. Rather, it is to find oneness:

> Obey one will. On that one will, on that secret cause, they nail our attention and hope. Life is hereby melted into an expectation or a religion. Underneath the inharmonious and trivial particulars, is a musical perfection, the Ideal journeying always with us, the heaven without rent or seam. (484)

Emerson's "Ideal" is not something to be ferreted out with our critical faculties, as Montaigne would have us use. Rather, "this region gives further sign of itself, as it were in flashes of light, in sudden discoveries of its profound beauty and repose" (484). Nor is it something made by human will and the product of our will to power as for Nietzsche: "I do not make it; I arrive there, and behold what was there already" (485). Emerson's metaphysics are profoundly different from these other two thinkers'.

The Self in the Cosmos: Conclusion

While all three of the essays considered in this section use a constellation of capitalized and interchangeable terms for the divine—God, Godhead, Being, the Ideal, among several others—it is not entirely clear what Emerson means by them. On the one hand, Emerson speaks very loosely about this eternal divine in giving it so many different names. On the other hand, Emerson believes he cannot be more precise. He believes that the power of being cannot be conceived or captured by the human mind. It can only be felt. You know it when you feel it, and it cannot be communicated: "The definition of *spiritual*," he writes in "Experience," "should be, *that which is its own evidence*" (475, emphasis in original). Emerson states, "In our more correct writing, we give to this generalization the name of Being, and thereby confess that we have arrived as far as we can go" (486). Whatever it is and by whatever appellation, it is clear that for Emerson subjectivity is a curse if that is all there is. Only by connecting with the universal divine do we overcome our incomplete, partial selves and can we be fulfilled and happy—a transcendental condition that both Montaigne and Nietzsche reject.

"Self-Reliance," "Fate," and "Experience"—Emerson's most skeptical and Nietzschean essays—reveal that Emerson's individual becomes an individual by following his own path, paradoxically, to what Emerson deems to be the higher, nonindividualistic, nonsubjective, universal, divine reality. For Emerson, each self finds itself, paradoxically, by complying with the higher law. As he writes in *Representative Men*, "The opaque self becomes transparent with the light of the First Cause" (631). Nothing could be further from Nietzsche's or Montaigne's outlooks.

In conclusion, the recent scholarly consensus on Emerson wrongly asserts that Emerson and Nietzsche share a categorical rejection of absolutist ideals in general and of Christianity in particular. This claim is true of Nietzsche. He is an enemy of both Platonism and Christianity, the latter of which he demeans as "Platonism for 'the people'" (*BGE*, preface, 3), insofar as both demand sacrifice of the self in the name of a higher, transcendent ideal. However, Emerson turns out to be the opposite of what the current scholarly consensus says he is; he is a transcendentalist thinker. While Emerson is not a Christian with respect to dogma or doctrine, he is an idealist who believes fundamentally in some noncorporeal reality in the Platonic-Christian mode. In fact, Emerson seems to synthesize the two, describing nature as "no other than 'philosophy and theology embodied'" (782). Emerson's view of a higher order that rules us and the cosmos, a higher order that transcends us, that we cannot create or change but merely appreciate, resonate with, and hence get power from, is a Platonic or Christian position—or embodies what Emerson deems to be the essence of both. According to Emerson, everything in the cosmos has its place and purpose even if we cannot divine it:

> There are no contingencies; the Law rules throughout existence, a Law which is not intelligent but intelligence,—not personal but impersonal,—it disdains words and passes understanding; it dissolves persons; it vivifies nature; yet solicits the pure in heart to draw on all its omnipotence. (794)

Insofar as Emerson's higher order is impersonal and not governed by a living, personal God, that is, insofar as it is "not intelligent but intelligence," it is not a Christianity of the willful, nominalist kind.[54] Insofar as he speaks of a universe governed by "intelligence" and "Law," it resembles a Platonic, Spinozistic, or deistic vision. Call it what you want, but it is all about absolute truth and it is the absolute antithesis of Nietzsche's view.

Morality and Politics

Where the recent scholarly consensus totally overlooks Emerson's transcendentalism but gets Nietzsche's metaphysics right, its account of the thinkers' moral and political projects is similarly spotty. The new scholars of Emerson cite two main moral similarities between Emerson and Nietzsche. First, they aver a shared "overcoming of Christian ethics," by which they mean other-regarding ethics. Related to this, they trumpet Emerson's idea of the "the good of evil."[55] This is a kind of Machiavellian or Nietzschean subversion of normal moral categories. Second, it is claimed that both authors advocate an "extreme individualism" to the point of anarchy.[56] When it comes to politics, the new scholars assert a fundamental commitment to democratic man in both authors, following especially Cavell and Kateb in lauding "the democratic possibilities in the 'moral perfectionism' of both."[57] These scholars' conception of Emerson's morality is not entirely accurate. The substance of Emerson's morality is uncannily Christian, even if it is not supported on traditional Christian grounds. Emerson's higher law prevents individuals from devolving to anarchy (assuming anarchy is akin to a Hobbesian state of war of all against all), and it leads Emerson to liberal democratic politics. Nietzsche does not recognize a higher power, and he does truly ditch Christian morality in favor of an anarchistic individuality. However, for Nietzsche, this does not lead him to democracy, as the new scholars claim, but to a harsh aristocracy. Montaigne splits the difference between Emerson and Nietzsche. Like Nietzsche, he does not see a metaphysical basis for morality, but, like Emerson, Montaigne argues for a more moderate, egalitarian moral vision. In short, the recent critics make huge mistakes in their moral and political interpretations.

No skeptic is skeptical of everything; otherwise he would be indifferent between eating or not and walking off a cliff or not. To choose these things presumes that doing them is better than the opposite. Thus, the key to understanding a skeptic's moral and political program is to find its starting point, the thing that he does not doubt. It is not their skepticism per se that colors their moral thought; it is what survives their skeptical doubting that matters. To understand the thinkers' moral and political visions, it is easiest to analyze each in turn.

Nietzsche's moral and political vision grows out of his fundamental distinction between the strong-willed and the weak-willed. As we have seen, according to Nietzsche there is no reality other than will, but there seems to be a sliding scale of the amount of will to power an individual has. In the end, however, Nietzsche speaks of the strong and the weak. Each, according to him, has an opposite viewpoint of value. The weak want to be taken care of and not dominated or to be allowed to dominate despite the shortcoming of their wills. The strong dominate, and they naturally do so with a clear conscience. They conquer, rape, and pillage as if it were nothing but a schoolboy prank, convinced that they have done great deeds for the poets to celebrate (*GM*, I: 11, 40). Each type has its own kind of morality that Nietzsche calls master and slave morality. He is not speaking literally of masters and slaves, but of psychological masters and psychological slaves.

Master morality, embodied in peoples like the Homeric Greeks, pagan Romans, Japanese nobility, Arabs, and Vikings, values strength, courage, aggression; the ability to exert one's will here-and-now on earth. In contrast, slave morality, embodied in Judaism, Christianity, and liberalism, is reactive and driven by resentment and hatred: "The slave revolt in morality begins when *ressentiment* itself becomes creative and gives birth to values: the *ressentiment* of natures that are denied the true reaction, that of deeds, and compensate themselves with an imaginary revenge. While every noble morality develops from a triumphant affirmation of itself, slave morality from the outset says No to what is 'outside,' what is 'different,' what is 'not itself'; and *this* No is its creative deed" (*GM*, I: 10, 36, emphasis in original). According to Nietzsche we must choose to promote the well-being of the weak or the well-being of the strong; both cannot simultaneously prosper. Nietzsche chooses—and he writes to urge us to choose—the well-being of the strong.[58] The strong have produced everything great and worthwhile, and only they will do so in the future. If we want to promote life, the will, and the future, we must choose the morality that promotes and unleashes them, not the one that enchains and eradicates them. Slave morality is so destructive of the will, according to Nietzsche, that he argues if we continue on a path of slave morality, eventually the will shall disappear altogether, what Nietzsche calls the path toward the "last man." If we want to evolve, as Nietzsche wants, the strong must be free to dominate the weak.

The political consequence of Nietzsche's view is aristocracy:

> Every enhancement of the type "man" has so far been the work of an aristocratic society—and it will be so again and again—a society that believes in the long ladder of an order of rank and differences in values between man and man, and that needs slavery in some sense or other. Without that *pathos of distance* which grows out of the ingrained difference between strata—when the ruling caste constantly looks afar and looks down upon subjects and instruments and just as constantly practices obedience and command, keeping down and keeping at a distance—that other, more mysterious pathos could not have grown up either—the craving for an ever new widening of distances within the soul itself, the development of ever higher, rarer, more remote, further-stretching, more comprehensive states—in brief, simply the enhancement of the type "man," the continual "self-overcoming of man," to use a moral formula in a supra-moral sense. (*BGE*, 257, 201, emphasis in original)

Greatness requires the "pathos of distance," the feeling of a gap between unequal things, so, according to Nietzsche, promoting greatness means promoting aristocracy, possibly even instituting slavery. Cruelty and suffering do not make Nietzsche blink. If these are required for progress, so be it. Indeed, he goes so far as to write: "Mankind in the mass sacrificed to the prosperity of a single *stronger* species of man—that *would* be an advance" (*GM*, II: 12, 78, emphasis in original). There is not a single egalitarian impulse in Nietzsche's entire corpus. The idea advanced by Cavell and his followers of democratic "perfectionism," which they choose to find in Nietzsche, is fundamentally un-Nietzschean.

Nietzsche hated democracy. He hated it both as an institution and as an ethos. He has nothing but contempt for "the democratic idiosyncracy which opposes everything that dominates and wants to dominate," because to be against domination is to be against greatness, life, and the prosperity of the species (*GM*, II: 12, 78). The idea of submitting to mass rule repulsed him because he deemed the many to be "weak" and "sick" and deemed it the main job of politics to keep the strong few away from the sick many so that they too do not become "infected": "That the sick should *not* make the healthy sick . . . should surely be our supreme concern on earth" (*GM*, III: 14,124). Nietzsche considers modern liberal democracy to be a secularized version of Christian slave morality. As Nietzsche sees it, Christianity restricts the will in the name of God; liberalism restricts it in the name of universal human rights. For Nietzsche, the impulse behind both democracy and Christianity is self denying and "other regarding." In the name of protecting others, both force a strong-willed individual to say "no" to his will to power and both thus say "no" to life. This is what Nietzsche means when he proclaims that "the democratic movement is heir of the Christian movement" (*BGE*, 202, 116). The recent Emerson scholars are right that Nietzsche rejects other-regarding morality, but in so doing Nietzsche establishes himself, contra their claims, as anti-egalitarian and antidemocratic.

Montaigne's fundamental starting point is not in a strong will but in his conception of an evanescent self. Like Nietzsche, he finds a metaphysically silent world and thus turns inward to the self. The key difference between Montaigne and Nietzsche concerns what they find at the self's core. Montaigne finds the self to be layer upon fascinating layer, with each moment playing its own delightful or odd game. Upon essaying himself, Montaigne finds a tendency for the self to be distracted and diverted from itself. Ordinary fears and anxieties and the desires for material goods, power, and glory lead people to flee into a socially constructed world in which appearance and acceptance from others is what matters most. The unlimited nature of the imagination and the unlimited conjuring of human vanity lead the self to construct and to pursue visions of the world and the good that have no basis in reality other than being in an individual's mind. Whereas Nietzsche celebrates these inner impulses as authentic and thus encourages the will to forge its own unity and to act on it—even if it means hurting others—Montaigne considers such forging to be forgery. Although Montaigne favors the kind of self-creation that results from self-exploration, he thinks that strong assertions of one impulse cut a self off from its natural multiplicity. Such a move, therefore, leads not to authenticity but to a distancing from oneself. Surrendering to the strong impulses that underlie such assertions leads to an internal imbalance or fraud. And since Montaigne doubts our ability to understand what these impulses mean and from whence they came—he suspects that they are but the manifestations of other things—he argues for moderation in exercising them and does not think they ever justify inflicting cruelty on others.

Montaigne warns against following these impulses outward and calls those who surrender to them insufficiently reflective, avaricious, and overly ambitious. He wants people to restrain themselves:

> The range of our desires should be circumscribed and restrained to a narrow limit of the nearest and most contiguous good things; and moreover their course should be directed not in a straight line that ends up elsewhere, but in a circle whose two extremities by a short sweep meet and terminate in ourselves. Actions that are performed without this reflexive movement, I mean a searching and genuine reflexive movement—the actions, for example, of the avaricious, the ambitious, and so many others who run in a straight line, whose course carries them ever forward—are erroneous and diseased actions. (III.10, 988–89 [773])

Montaigne judges harshly those who flee themselves. Instead, he wants people to come back to themselves, to return "home" (*chez soi*). The "home" analogy is central to Montaigne's conception of the self. A normative notion of "home" allows him to reconcile the existing reality, "We are never at home, we are always beyond" (I.3, 18 [8]), with the moral injunction, "You have quite enough to do at home; don't go away" (III.10, 981 [767]). To Montaigne, self-abandonment is responsible for most of the man-made ills. It is on this basis that he pleads for man to "break free from the violent clutches that engage us elsewhere and draw us away from ourselves" (I.39, 236 [178]) and condemns those who wander into other things as seeking "business only for busyness" (III.10, 981 [767]).

At the core of the self, Montaigne finds, paradoxically, everything and nothing. He sees a human being as an integral unity of body and mind, and he encourages individuals to explore both aspects of themselves. But he also finds the self to be a rich assortment of beautiful and horrifying wills, impulses, and desires. Being aware of the multiplicities in oneself creates the basis for a dialogue within oneself. When should one pursue one thing, when another? And what are these impulses that one finds in oneself and from where do they come? On the one hand, analysis reveals depth and never-ending layers. Wills and desires turn out to be derivative from and influenced by other wills and desires. And because these things are questionable, unsteady, and often dissolve under the analytical gaze, when we explore ourselves, "test [*essaye*] our common impressions," we find a "natural weakness" (II.12, 521 [403]; II.12, 486 [375]). This weakness is the self's uncertainty about itself. It is based on a kind of ultimate evanescence. If the self is bottomless, one can get immense and never-ending pleasure in the searches of oneself for oneself. This activity in itself, Montaigne argues, is the most enjoyable activity for a human being—and it is also the most real, because people have access to the phenomena of themselves more than they do to abstract questions about universal essences. However, not finding a final, ultimate self is also sometimes frustrating—and this partially explains why people flee themselves. But for Montaigne, this failure to stay in oneself, to stay "home," means to privilege one part of oneself and make that one's all. Montaigne is not against this on a temporary basis, for one must act on one's desires and wills in order to explore them, but one must never lose sight of the rest of oneself. To do that is to cheat oneself, to rob oneself of one's possibilities.

The political conclusion of Montaigne's vision is to call for one of liberalism's key tenets—toleration—and for one of its key political ideas—the separation of the public sphere from the private sphere. If the human good is the self-exploration of the essaying process, Montaigne wants the state merely to create the peace and stability that allows this process to take place. He is indifferent to regime type as long as the government allows a private sphere of free conscience, which was his most radical call. Moreover, unlike conceptions of the self that envision the good as the satisfaction of material desires or willing one's will, in Montaigne's conception, the self has no interest in violating others. And since what the self finds in itself is a kind of ultimate evanescence, the self has nothing to force. Finally, Montaigne argues that self-aware people feel others' pain. When individuals become aware of the weaknesses in themselves, Montaigne argues, this forms an identification, a mutual identification through empathy, with other equally vulnerable selves. This creates an affirmative desire for every self to be able to explore itself and form itself free from external violation. Toleration for Montaigne is grounded not on self-denial, as Nietzsche says, but on self-knowledge. Tolerating others and self-interest are united. Indeed, Montaigne's conception of self-interest is not only compatible with toleration, it demands it.[59]

Emerson's moral beginning point is his metaphysical conception of transcendent reality. While, as we have already seen, Emerson is not a conventional Christian, he nonetheless affirms the objective existence of transcendent truth that is morally regulative of individuals. Emerson does not conjure up images of Heaven and Hell or a God throwing lightning bolts to scare humans away from wrongdoing. Instead, Emerson argues for his transcendental morality based on, as do Nietzsche and Montaigne, self-interest. But he also says that self-interest compels us to equally respect all other selves, since we are all one. Emerson is morally and politically egalitarian because of his fundamentally metaphysical view of the world. For example, in "The American Scholar" he draws the moral consequences of his metaphysics:

> The one thing in the world, of value, is the active soul. This *every man* is entitled to; this *every man* contains within him, although, in almost all men, obstructed, and as yet unborn. The soul active sees absolute truth; and utters truth, or creates. In this action, it is genius; not the privilege of here and there a favorite, but the sound estate of *every man*. (57, emphasis added)

As this passage and Gougeon's and Malachuk's essays in this volume make clear, Emerson has a clear notion of human rights grounded in the inner divinity of each of us. We all participate in and are attributes of God, so we all must have our inner divinity respected. Our inner godliness requires respect. As this passage and the essays in this volume by Frank and Flanagan make clear, Emerson deems these rights to belong equally to everyone. And as the essays in this volume by Turner, Read, and Gougeon make clear, Emerson asserts that these rights exist even for those held as slaves.

Emerson would be repulsed by Nietzsche's anti-egalitarian moral impulses, although he might very well be attracted to the recent scholars' egalitarian misreading of Nietzsche, as Emerson himself is fundamentally democratic. Like Nietzsche, Emerson criticizes democratic political institutions and the rule of the majority, but for very different reasons. Emerson laments the alienation from truth and justice from which most people suffer, but he deems this due not to an inescapable reality but only to their alienation from being, because of some social conformity or for following a too-narrow natural impulse. But if they return home to themselves and God, they will feel and find, contra Montaigne, every moral sense necessary; Montaigne offers no such assurance. Indeed, for Emerson, not only does our divine spark endow everyone in human dignity, but everyone's potential is in theory unlimited. We are each potentially great, each potential geniuses. According to Emerson, the only difference between a genius and the rest of us is that the genius has realized his potential, has tapped into reality, whereas the rest of us have not yet done so. Human beings differ only in their different realizations of their equal potential.

All of Emerson's moral ideas are antithetical to Nietzsche's. It is for this reason, as Shklar's and Flanagan's essays show, that Emerson, unlike Nietzsche and Carlyle, refuses to worship great men. Emerson's great men are not labeled as heroes, gods, or demigods. They are not *Übermenschen*, who can do what they will with the rest of us. Emerson does not allow them or any men more rights than anyone else. No, Emerson's great men are merely "representative" men. They represent human potential. They represent what we all can be. They have no legitimate claims to use or to rule over us. The great moral difference between Emerson and Nietzsche is that Nietzsche promotes the few in what he considers their inescapable struggle with the many, whereas Emerson envisions all human beings blossoming together. Nietzsche sacrifices the mass of mankind to promote a new race of Over-men; Emerson wants everyone to tap into the eternal Over-soul.

In conclusion, Emerson is less skeptical than Montaigne or Nietzsche, despite the current scholarly consensus to the contrary. While it is beyond doubt that Nietzsche read Emerson seriously, I have shown not only that Emerson and Nietzsche are not identical, but also that on many points they are polar opposites. The relationship of Nietzsche to Emerson is something like a version of Marx's relationship to Hegel. Hegel set out certain ideas and parameters that Marx found useful, but, notwithstanding this, in the end Marx stood Hegel on his head. If Nietzsche got the idea of an Overman from Emerson's Over-Soul (as some scholars claim), then he did the same thing. Advocating that every human being tap into a transcendent Over-Soul to reach completion in harmony with the divine forces of the cosmos is the polar opposite of advocating a willful directed-from-within Over-man (or species of them). Emerson's and Nietzsche's conceptions of the self, their conceptions of the cosmos, their conceptions of the self's place in the cosmos, and the moral and political consequences they draw from them are almost fundamentally opposite. Nietzsche turns Emerson on his head.

The recent Emerson scholars cherry-pick the threads that they select from both Emerson and Nietzsche. They equally ignore Emerson's transcendentalism and Nietzsche's cruel aristocratic streak—and for the same reasons. They share the postmodern predilection of highlighting the aspects of a thinker's thought that they like and seek to promote while ignoring the threads that they dislike.[60] This is consistent with Nietzsche's vision of the world—that one should interpret it to suit oneself—and one might thus admire such actions as a bold political move. However, it is a shallow Nietzscheanism since for Nietzsche the only self-expression that escapes the delusions of metaphysics is that which affirms the will to power, not democratic norms and certainly not the widespread social and political norms of the society in which one happens to live or the scholarly community in which one happens to work. From Nietzsche's, Emerson's, and Montaigne's points of view, the reduction of any thinker to the ethos of one's own time is a wishful or willful conformity. Honesty demands that one acknowledge the threads one does not like rather than pretend they are not there. Selective reading, or what Harold Bloom calls "strong reading," enables us to pass along our view as another's or to use the text as an authority to support our own views.[61] And unless such selective interpretation is explicitly and carefully acknowledged (as the better of the recent scholars do), it is bad scholarship and shows bad faith with the reader. Moreover, selective reading is a fundamental contradiction to postmodern scholars' own stated desire to promote singularity and "difference," not sameness. Although in some sense it is inevitable that we read ourselves into a text, rather than doing it wholeheartedly, it is better to try to find the author's truth in order forthrightly to confront a different mind. Not doing so is to lose an opportunity to free our own minds from our own intellectual presuppositions and cultural fads. If these scholars are so self-certain of their single-minded desire to reproduce their current opinions, they might want to revisit Montaigne, who is more egalitarian than Nietzsche and less transcendental than Emerson. Is our egalitarianism so fragile that we need to minimize Nietzsche's critique of it? Is our rejection of metaphysics so complete that we do not want even to consider Emerson's ecstatic spirituality?

Notes

1. Brendan Donnellan, *Nietzsche and the French Moralists* (Bonn: Bouvier, 1982), 35. See also Robert B. Pippin, *Nietzsche, Psychology, & First Philosophy* (Chicago: University of Chicago Press, 2010), 11, who writes that Montaigne is an author "about whom [Nietzsche] had almost nothing critical to say." Nietzsche offers mild criticism of Montaigne in *Beyond Good and Evil*, aphorism 208. References to *Beyond Good and Evil* are henceforth included in the text as *BGE*, including the aphorism number followed by the page number in the English translation by Walter Kaufmann (New York: Random House, 1966).

2. Nietzsche, "Assorted Opinions and Maxims" in *Human, All Too Human*, trans. R. J. Hollingdale (Cambridge: Cambridge University Press, 1986), aphorism 408, 299.

3. Nietzsche, "Schopenhauer as Educator" in *Untimely Meditations*, trans. R. J. Hollingdale (Cambridge: Cambridge University Press, 1983), aphorism 2, 135; "From the Souls of Artists and Writers," in *Human, All Too Human*, aphorism 176, 91; "The Wanderer and His Shadow," in *Human, All Too Human*, aphorism 86, 332.

4. Nietzsche, "Schopenhauer as Educator," aphorism 2, 135. On Nietzsche's idea of Montaigne making himself at home in the world, see Pippen, *Nietzsche, Psychology, & First Philosophy*, esp. 11, 23.

5. Nietzsche, "Schopenhauer as Educator," aphorism 2, 135.

6. Donnellan, *Nietzsche and the French Moralists*, 23, paraphrased from Nietzsche's "Letter to Peter Gast," October 27, 1887. As late as *Ecce Homo*, Nietzsche also favorably writes of Montaigne: "I have in my spirit—who knows? perhaps also in my body—something of Montaigne's sportiveness" (*On the Genealogy of Morals and Ecce Homo*, trans. Walter Kaufmann [New York: Random House, 1967], 243). Hereafter *On the Genealogy of Morals* is cited in the text as *GM*, fol-

lowed by the essay number, aphorism number, and page number to this translation. Further references to *Ecce Homo* are cited in the text followed by the page number in this edition.

7. Donnellan, *Nietzsche and the French Moralists*, 36; Pippen, *Nietzsche, Psychology, & First Philosophy*, 123, 121, 20, 11 (emphasis in original). Pippen further argues that Nietzsche "so much admired" Montaigne's "perspective" (120) and refers to Montaigne as Nietzsche's "model" on two other occasions (23, 121).

8. Emerson, "Experience," 476. Unless noted otherwise, all citations to Emerson are to *Essays and Lectures*, ed. Joel Porte (New York: Library of America, 1983).

9. *Journals of Ralph Waldo Emerson*, ed. Edward Waldo Emerson and Waldo Emerson Forbes (Boston and New York: Houghton Mifflin, 1909–1914), 6:372. This statement comes from 1843, when Emerson was at the peak of his powers and many years after first having read Emerson. For a reconstruction of Emerson's first encounters with Montaigne, see Charles Lowell Young, *Emerson's Montaigne* (New York: Macmillan, 1941), 1–7.

10. Emerson, "Montaigne; Or, The Skeptic," in *Representative Men* (*E&L*, 690–709). Dudley Marchi, *Montaigne among the Moderns* (Providence: Berghahn, 1994), chap. 2, "Emerson and Nietzsche: Between Tradition and Innovation," is the most insightful on this connection.

11. Judith N. Shklar, "Emerson and the Inhibitions of Democracy," 64, in this volume. Shklar's assessment may reflect her own view of Montaigne more than Emerson's. For an analysis of Shklar on Montaigne, see Alan Levine, "Cruelty, Humanity, and the Liberalism of Fear: Judith Shklar's Montaigne" in *Montaigne Studies* 20 (2008): 157–70. Young, *Emerson's Montaigne*, 15, 13.

12. Walter Kaufmann, "Translator's Introduction" to Nietzsche, *The Gay Science* (New York: Random House, 1974), 7.

13. Nietzsche to Franz Overbeck, December 22, 1884, cited ibid., 7; Nietzsche, *The Gay Science*, aphorism 92, 146; Nietzsche, posthumously published note from volume 11 of the Musarion edition of Nietzsche's works, cited ibid., 11.

14. Ibid., 7; Nietzsche, posthumously published note from volume 11 of the Musarion edition of Nietzsche's works, cited ibid., 11. Nietzsche did qualify some of these remarks. In his letter to Overbeck, he laments that because of Emerson's lack of rigor, "we have lost a philosopher," and Nietzsche did remove the Emerson epigraph after the first edition.

I agree with Kaufmann's final judgments that the similarities between Emerson and Nietzsche "become[] much less striking as one reads on, and one would never mistake a whole page of Emerson for a page of Nietzsche," and that "on balance, however, it seems to me that most of those who have written on this subject have exaggerated the kinship of these men, and that the differences are far more striking" (ibid., 10, 11). Just as Kaufmann was criticizing the scholars who advanced this substantive connection between Emerson and Nietzsche before he wrote those words in 1974, so I am criticizing the recent scholarly consensus of the last two generations. For succinct accounts of this scholarly consensus, see note 15 below.

15. Two excellent recent accounts of this trend are Neal Dolan, *Emerson's Liberalism* (Madison: University of Wisconsin Press, 2009), especially the introduction, 3–27; and Michael Lopez, ed., "Emerson/Nietzsche," special issue of *ESQ: A Journal of the American Renaissance* 43, nos. 1–4 (1997). Dolan is critical of the Nietzschean interpretation of Emerson for reasons similar to those presented in this essay. Lopez advocates a Nietzschean interpretation, and he is much discussed below.

16. Stanley Cavell, *Emerson's Transcendental Etudes*, ed. David Justin Hodge (Stanford: Stanford University Press, 2003), 154. Cavell also writes, "It is rarely apparent to me initially what has taken me back, or on, to a text of Nietzsche; but for some years it has become familiar to me that, however I get there, what I find eventually takes me further back to Emerson" (224). He also deems Nietzsche to be the "pivot" in the movement from Emerson to Heidegger, whom he also reads as a perfectionist (148). Cavell argues that "Nietzsche is not 'influenced' by Emerson but is quite deliberately transfiguring Emerson, as for the instruction of the future" (213). See, generally, 148, 154–60, 224–33.

17. George Kateb, *Emerson and Self-Reliance* (1995; new ed., Lanham, Md.: Rowman and Littlefield, 2002), xliii (xxix in the 1995 and 2000 editions).

18. Shklar finds Emerson and Nietzsche to share "the exploratory essay, the possibility of unlimited self-creation, and the same ex-protestant tension between the equal impossibilities of solitude and society and the irony that it evokes" (Shklar, "Emerson and the Inhibitions of Democracy," Editors' Note, 53).

19. Russell B. Goodman, "Moral Perfectionism and Democracy: Emerson, Nietzsche, Cavell" in Lopez, ed., "Emerson/Nietzsche," special issue, *ESQ*, 166. Goodman further notes that this passage was "partly transcribed" by Nietzsche (166).

20. Emerson applauds Hume's writing style, but he criticizes materialistic conceptions of humanity as reducing us to mere "Reasoning Machines," and he attributes this view to thinkers "such as Locke and Clarke and David Hume" (Emerson, quoted in Oscar W. Firkins, *Ralph Waldo Emerson* [Boston: Houghton Mifflin, 1915], 24). For an informative and compelling comparison of Hume's and Emerson's skepticisms, see Dolan, *Emerson's Liberalism*, esp. chap. 5.

21. Emerson, *Representative Men*, chap. 4.

22. Lopez, ed., "Emerson/Nietzsche," 6.

23. This is Lopez's characterization of Shklar's view and his own (1, 17).

24. Emerson, *W*, 8:178, 190, cited in Lopez, "Emerson/Nietzsche," 21.

25. Lopez, "Emerson/Nietzsche," 21.

26. Emerson's phrases, *E&L*, 463, cited by Lopez, "Emerson/Nietzsche," 17.

27. Harold Bloom, *Map of Misreading* (Oxford: Oxford University Press, 2003), 174–75, cited in Lopez, "Emerson/Nietzsche," 17.

28. For a discussion of the meaning and history of both the word "essay" and the concept of essaying oneself, see Levine, *Sensual Philosophy: Toleration, Skepticism and Montaigne's Politics of the Self* (Lanham, Md.: Lexington, 2001), 26, 121–66.

29. "There is *only* perspective seeing, *only* a perspective 'knowing'" (emphasis in original). Since perspective is all that exists, Nietzsche cannot even write the word "knowing" without putting it in quotation marks (*GM*, III: 12, 119).

30. Nietzsche writes: "In the mountains the shortest way is peak to peak: but for that one must have long legs. Aphorisms should be peaks—and those who are addressed, tall and lofty" (*Thus Spoke Zarathustra*, "First Part," chap. 7, "On Reading and Writing," in *The Portable Nietzsche*, ed. Walter Kaufmann [New York: Penguin, 1984], 152).

31. Richard Poirier, *The Renewal of Literature: Emersonian Reflections* (New Haven: Yale University Press, 1987), 15. The phenomenon I discuss here is also discussed in Poirier, *The Performing Self* (New Brunswick, N.J.: Rutgers University Press, 1992).

32. Blaise Pascal, *Pensées*, number 689, in *Oeuvres Complètes*, ed. Louis Lafuma (Paris: Seuil, 1963), 591.

33. Young, *Emerson's Montaigne*, 6.

34. For textual citations to Montaigne's *Essais*, I give four numbers. The first Roman numeral and the following arabic numeral refer to the book and essay number, respectively (so II.6 thus means book 2, essay 6.) The third number is the page number in the French Pléiade edition, Montaigne, *Oeuvres complètes*, ed. Albert Thibaudet and Maurice Rat (Paris: Gallimard, 1962). The last number [in brackets] refers to the page number in Donald Frame's English translation, *The Complete Works of Montaigne* (Stanford: Stanford University Press, 1957).

35. It is for this reason that Montaigne became a darling of the deconstructionists and was called postmodern by one of postmodernity's leading lights (see Jean-François Lyotard, "Answering the Question: What Is Postmodern?" trans. Régis Durand, in *The Postmodern Condition*, by Lyotard [Minneapolis: University of Minnesota Press, 1984], 81). Derrida's most political writing not only uses Montaigne but borrows its title from him: Jacques Derrida, "The Force of Law: 'The Mystical Foundations of Authority,'" found in French and English in *Cardozo Law Review* 11, no. 5–6 (July–August 1990): 919–1045. For a postmodern overview of the postmodern interpretations of Montaigne, see Richard Regosin, "Recent Trends in Montaigne Scholarship: A Post-Structuralist Perspective," *Renaissance*

Quarterly 37 (1984): 37–54. For a nice nonpostmodern overview of the many postmodern uses of Montaigne, see Marchi, *Montaigne among the Moderns,* chap. 4.

36. Lopez, "Emerson/Nietzsche," 18, crediting this view to Cavell and George Stack especially.

37. Ibid., 9.

38. Ibid., 18, crediting this view to Poirier among others.

39. Ibid., 1, quoting Shklar.

40. In contrast, the supporters of the view that Emerson and Nietzsche are alike focus selectively only on his most Nietzschean moments. On what grounds can these scholars ignore the contrary "moments" or "utterances" in Emerson's thought? I make my argument citing only what are deemed to be the least favorable texts to my case. I omit mentioning texts such as "Love," "The Over-Soul," "Spiritual Laws," "Worship," *Nature,* and "The Transcendentalist," let alone Emerson's sermons and the explicit rejections of skepticism in the antislavery addresses analyzed by Malachuk in his essay.

41. In writing of the "essence" of life, however, Nietzsche does not mean to posit the truth of a metaphysical doctrine. Rather, he accepts that the will to power is the product of his own will to power, that it is his own creation. He advances this idea as the most plausible given what we know and as the most useful for us to believe in regardless of its validity.

42. For a fuller account of Emerson's moral psychology, see this volume's introduction and the essays by Malachuk and Gougeon.

43. For a fuller account of the moral sentiments and other faculties of the soul, see this volume's introduction and the essays by Malachuk and Gougeon.

44. Similarly, Emerson elsewhere calls this the "universal soul' and says that "it is not mine, or thine, or his, but we are its; we are its property and men" (*Nature,* 21).

45. For Nietzsche, one should act *as if* there is an eternal return, because this is an incentive to struggle most mightily and nobly now. Whereas Nietzsche's eternal return is a hypothetical to move us, Emerson has complete faith in the actual existence of a higher law that compensates us justly.

46. Consider the liberalized Nietzscheanism of Richard Rorty, *Contingency, Irony, and Solidarity* (Cambridge: Cambridge University Press, 1989).

47. For a fuller discussion of Emerson's "Reason," see the introduction to this volume.

48. For a full account of Montaigne's skeptical critiques, of which only the flavor can be given here, see Levine, *Sensual Philosophy,* chap. 1, esp. 64–79.

49. See the introduction of this volume for a fuller account of Emerson's views of "forms," including institutions, and his ecstatic dream of no state.

50. On Montaigne's critique of religion in general and Christianity in particular, see Levine, *Sensual Philosophy,* chap. 1, esp. 38–64.

51. Montaigne, *Essays* (II.12, 523 [405]). For a discussion of Montaigne on science, see Levine, *Sensual Philosophy*, 74–76. For an alternative view, David Schaefer argues that Montaigne did clearly and fully support modern science: "I argue that this new conception of science was fully, not just partly, in accordance with Montaigne's teaching" (Schaefer, *The Political Philosophy of Montaigne* [Ithaca: Cornell University Press, 1990], 118 n. 8; cf. 114–33).

52. Emerson's overall view of science is complex. While Emerson detests purely empirical and materialistic sciences, he is excited about a science that includes and explains the transcendental and spiritual realms (see "The American Scholar," 56; and "Prospects," in *Nature*, 43). For an enthusiastic account of Emerson's view of science, see Laura Dassow Walls, *Emerson's Life in Science* (Ithaca: Cornell University Press, 2003). Walls argues that "modern America owes largely to Emerson its faith in science as the bulwark of truth against the tides of history and the storms of war" (4). Dolan, *Emerson's Liberalism*, chap. 2, situates Emerson's view of science in the Enlightenment context.

53. See Levine, *Sensual Philosophy*, 121–66.

54. See Michael Gillespie, *The Theological Origins of Modernity* (Chicago: University of Chicago Press, 2008).

55. *E&L*, 1083, cited in Lopez, "Emerson/Nietzsche," 19.

56. Lopez, "Emerson/Nietzsche," 17.

57. Ibid., 18.

58. Master morality values in terms of good and bad, slave morality in terms of good and evil. Nietzsche writes: "What my *aim* is, what the aim of that dangerous slogan is that is inscribed at the head of my last book, *Beyond Good and Evil.*—At least this does *not* mean 'Beyond Good and Bad.'" (*GM*, I: 17, 55, emphasis in original).

59. For a fuller account of Montaigne's politics, see Levine, *Sensual Philosophy*, 167–240.

60. See Malachuk's essay in this volume for a compelling account of this selectivity in interpreting Emerson.

61. Harold Bloom, *Agon: Toward a Theory of Revisionism* (New York: Oxford University Press, 1982), 19–20. See Malachuk's essay in this volume for a fuller account of Bloom's (and similar) interpretative strategy.

CHAPTER 9

Emerson's Politics, Retranscendentalized

Daniel S. Malachuk

IN HIS FIRST BOOK, the 1836 *Nature*, Emerson famously proclaimed, "I am part or particle of God" (*E&L*, 10). For the next forty years, Emerson continued to express this conviction, not only about himself but about all human beings: "the doctrine," as he put it in the 1841 "Lecture on the Times," "of the indwelling of the Creator in man" (*E&L*, 167). All of Emerson's significant political positions stemmed from his fundamental belief that our equality as human beings is based upon our shared transcendental essence, a belief here called "transcendental equality."

Very few modern academic readers, however, have pursued the importance of Emerson's belief in transcendental equality to his political thought.[1] Why is this? This essay argues that an important but neglected reason is the influence of a group of academic readers of Emerson from the late twentieth century. These readers, here called "the detranscendentalists," pioneered a set of interpretive tactics that encourage us to look past Emerson's own intentions as a public intellectual. Their tactics are now habitual in academic work on Emerson. After scrutinizing these tactics to reveal how they obscure Emerson's own transcendentalist intentions, this essay illustrates how most of Emerson's political writings very clearly express his belief in transcendental equality. A third section then looks at a few famous essays where Emerson deliberately dramatizes his struggle to believe in transcendental equality, including "Self-Reliance," "Fate," and "Experience." In closing, the essay briefly contends that a "retranscendentalized" Emerson is not only factual but valuable.

Bad Habits

In a 1984 essay, Lawrence Buell described a new "Emerson industry" reviving interest in the author.[2] The industry involved diverse efforts: textual scholars publishing authoritative editions of Emerson's private and public writings (119–21), literary historians proving "Emerson [to be] the product of his social/intellectual subculture [and not] the antitraditionalist affirmer of the Self" (123), and theorists discovering a postmodern Emerson whose "Transcendental side [actually reveals] intimations of self-skepticism" (127). But Buell discerned a common objective: to "de-transcendentalize" Emerson (120), mainly by rejecting the earlier postwar consensus that Emerson's "master term [is] 'The Soul'" (117). The theorists led the charge, especially the literary critic Harold Bloom; he and a few others approached "Emerson's discourses as rhetorical constructs" that "double back upon [themselves]" (133) in order to question, not affirm, the existence of "the Soul," "the Self," "God"—virtually all of the concepts that the postwar consensus had emphasized, and that Emerson himself had originally seen fit to capitalize in his writings. Acknowledging his own training by some of the leading postwar scholars of the transcendentalist Emerson (117), Buell admitted to being impressed by this new detranscendentalizing movement, complimenting Bloom and his allies for "prov[ing] exceptionally astute at charting the elements of indeterminacy and discontinuousness in Emersonian rhetoric" (133).[3]

On the surface, detranscendentalism seemed to have relatively modest aims. The detranscendentalists rejected the old "master term" of "the Soul" but offered no new one in its place. They merely followed Emerson in questioning all master terms. Three years after Buell's essay, this was how the literary critic Richard Poirier presented the aims of this growing group coming "out of Concord" in his 1987 *The Renewal of Literature: Emersonian Reflections*. Poirier identified several "near contemporaries of mine"—including Bloom, the philosophers Stanley Cavell and Richard Rorty, and the political theorist George Kateb—as advocating "a way of reading things which Emerson induces in us, rather than . . . any ideas or attitudes abstracted from a reading of him."[4] Michael Lopez praised these same scholars as "a major, current trend in Emerson scholarship" in his 1988 "De-Transcendentalizing Emerson."[5] For Lopez, Poirier's book was the "watershed" text precisely because it humbly followed in Emerson's footsteps: Poirier explained (and Lopez cited, 104) that "within a given paragraph, [Emerson] tends not to develop an argument in the direction already laid down by a previous remark, but to veer away from it, as from some constraining influence" (*Renewal,* 70). Detranscendentalism sought only to do the same: it veered, like Emerson, away from all master terms. Emerson was "more a struggler than an affirmer," in the formulation of the literary critic Barbara Packer, applauded by both Buell (127) and Lopez (84). Or, if Emerson affirmed anything, it was not master terms but "the crisis of knowledge," in the words of Stanley Cavell echoed by Lopez (110). The detranscendentalists merely elaborated upon Emerson's struggle, his crisis.

On closer examination, though, detranscendentalism was doing more than this—a lot more. In the 1980s, European postmodernism was on the rise, and many American academics believed their nation needed its own version. The detranscendentalists pointed to Emerson, to whom most Americans unfortunately condescended. Such condescension, Cavell objected in 1985, "keeps our culture, unlike any other in the West, from possessing any founding thinker as a common basis for its considerations." Emerson needed to be "recanonized," Cavell and Rorty argued in 1987.[6] Emerson's "writing off the self," Poirier averred, could be the basis for a more pragmatic postmodernism than the apocalyptic version Nietzsche bequeathed Europe (*Renewal,* 191–92). The detranscendentalists pushed this agenda so strongly that some observers wondered if the detranscendentalists were indeed following the lead of Emerson or of European postmodernism. In his 1984 article, for example, Buell worried in passing if detranscendentalism might merely be the latest in "the succession of isms" (135). Lopez, too, acknowledged that the movement tended to be "present-minded" (98).[7]

The detranscendentalists were unfazed by these doubts, though. Indeed, their interpretive bravado still sounds startling several decades later. Bloom best described the overall spirit of detranscendentalism in his 1982 *Agon: Toward a Theory of Revisionism,* where he called it "strong reading": "American pragmatism, as Rorty advises, always asks of a text: what is it good for, what can I do with it, what can it do for me, what can I make it mean? I confess that I like these questions, and they are what I think strong reading is all about, because strong reading doesn't ever ask: Am I getting this poem right? Strong reading *knows* that what it does to the poem is right, because it knows what Emerson, its American inventor, taught it, which is that the true ship is the shipbuilder."[8] Bloom's explicit agenda, like Rorty's, was not getting texts right but making them work for him, an approach to "interpretation" Bloom traced to Emerson. Bloom didn't hesitate to turn this approach on its supposed author. In Bloom's strong reading of Emerson, Emerson's transcendentalism was a bother. And so Bloom decided that, if Emerson affirmed transcendental truths, he must have denied them, too. After all, "with so fervent a vision of transcendence [in Emerson's writings], there *must be* an implication of a radical dualism [that is, transcendentalism *and* detranscendentalism], *despite* Emerson's professed monistic desires, his declarations that he is a seer of unity" (9, emphasis added). Lopez cited this sentence of Bloom's "as a summary statement" of detranscendentalism (104). What Emerson "professed" as a Transcendentalist does not ultimately matter; Emerson must be "strongly read" as a detranscendentalist.

Another moment of candor—and one that leads to the three tactics to be scrutinized below—was offered by George Kateb, another of Poirier's "out of Concord" group, in his 1995 *Emerson and Self-Reliance*. Kateb referred to Emerson's transcendentalism or monism as "Emerson's religiousness," which, frankly, had to be "dealt with." Kateb advocated several tactics, two of which accurately conveyed what the detranscendentalists had been doing for some time already: mainly, "elicit[ing] a secular meaning from his religious conceptions" and "work[ing] with the inexhaustible abundance of detachable utterance his writings contain [thus] easing [Emerson] unencumbered by religiousness to us."[9] These tools of strong reading—secularizing and detaching—along with a focus on Emerson's private rather than public writings, are the three tactics of the detranscendentalists now to be scrutinized.

The first tactic is to secularize Emerson's concepts. Kateb defined secularism as being "unnervously disenchanted" and no longer requiring "divinity as the source of some kind of meaningfulness in the world" (81). Kateb recognized that, according to his definition, Emerson was not secular; Kateb understood that Emerson required divinity for a meaningful, including politically meaningful, world. But, like the other detranscendentalists, Kateb wanted a secular Emerson, and he defended secularizing Emerson's concepts this way: "We can elicit a secular meaning from his [Emerson's] religious conceptions just as he extricated his own religiousness from church religions. We can translate him, as he translated his traditions. We can push him in a more unreligious direction. In doing that, we would actually be far less coercive than he was: we would have much less to do than he did" (95). To secularize Emerson's concepts today, Kateb argued, is akin to Emerson's own extricating of religiousness from church religions. Just as Emerson removed his concepts from church, we can remove his concepts from religion.

Emerson, however, did not understand his extraction of religiousness from church as a secularizing operation, and neither should we. Emerson did indeed leave the ministry in 1832 in order to disentangle his religious beliefs from the "forms" of the Unitarian church, specifically its doctrine of the Eucharist. But, if he strenuously rejected formal church religions, he just as strenuously upheld the core religious beliefs he extracted from those church religions. As he explained in the sermon announcing his departure, "I am not engaged to Christianity by decent forms. . . . What I revere and obey in it is its reality" (S, 4.193). Emerson left the church in search of new forms with which to express that "reality," an important word for Emerson, as shown below. Where the forms may be transient, the religious belief or "reality" is permanent.[10] To secularize or disenchant that reality, as Kateb does, is not the same as giving that reality new form, as Emerson does. Disenchanting Emerson's reality means completely changing it into another reality; it means inventing an alternate reality in which Emerson did not actually believe. To his credit, Kateb was perfectly candid that in creating a new secular "Emerson" we may have to get rid of the real Emerson. As he bluntly puts it, "one finds the [religious] thought so persistent [in Emerson's writing] that it must be dealt with, *even if we lose Emerson in the process*" (65, emphasis added). By secularizing Emerson's concepts, Kateb and the other detranscendentalists effectively invented a new political theory. New political theories should be invented, of course. But understanding—and being challenged and inspired by—the actual theories of thinkers from the past is important intellectual work, too. It seems fair to conclude that if our main goal as Emerson scholars is *not* to invent a new secular "Emerson" but rather to illuminate the thought of the real Emerson, then we must not secularize Emerson's concepts.

A second detranscendentalist tactic is to treat Emerson's private writings as just as important as his published work.[11] Particularly attractive to the detranscendentalists were those journal entries that sounded skeptical about transcendentalism. For example, in order to create an American religion of "self-reliance," Bloom proposed a strong reading of Emerson's original idea, so that "self-reliance" now would mean strictly "*self*-reliance as opposed to God-reliance, though Emerson thought the two were the same" (145). To justify this invention of a new secular Emerson, Bloom pointed to a mere one-sentence 1866 journal entry, which concludes "for every seeing soul there are two absorbing facts,—*I and the Abyss.*" "This grand outflaring of negative theology," Bloom announced, "is a major text, however gnomic, of *the* American religion, Emersonianism" (146). Similarly, in a 1992 book, Poirier pointed to an 1835 journal entry as evidence that Emerson not only anticipated Nietzsche's phrase "the Death of God," but handled it in a far more "easygoing, even jocular" manner, the proof being Emerson's use of "&c" as in "the Death of God &c."[12]

Of course, the journals *are* important. As others have argued, they provide a glimpse of Emerson's thoughts prior to their public formulation. Additionally, at least some journal writings were quasi-public in that he shared them with others in his circle.[13] However, in search of Emerson's political philosophy, it is his public, not his private writings that matter most, for at least two reasons. First, as the greatest of Emerson's biographers, Robert D. Richardson, reminds us: "Much of Emerson's journal is not intended as finished work or public utterance, nor even as the record of private conviction. He is concerned to explore—and then to save—impulses, essays, hints, trials, spurts, exaggerations, the most fleeting and evanescent flowers of the mind."[14] In other words, what in the journals may *seem* to be Emerson's true personal position may just as easily be Emerson's intellectual floundering en route to the true thought he expressed in public. There is no way to settle this perennial question about the value of Emerson's private writing. For example, Emerson's use of "&c" in the 1835 entry noted above seems, pace Poirier, to signify not Emerson's insouciance about atheism but rather the intensity of his disdain for atheism, a disdain that, as shown below, was expressed throughout his public writings (*JMN*, 5:61). Secondly, and in contrast to Emerson's obscure motives as a journal writer, we now know Emerson's motives as a public writer far better than ever before: those motives—particularly the political ones—have been richly documented by "the new history" of Emerson's political thought and activity, as reviewed in the introduction to this volume. As another excellent biographer of Emerson, Peter Field, has shown, Emerson took his role as a "democratic intellectual" seriously; not his private musings but his "public life and career represent the very marrow of his biography."[15]

A third tactic, refined if not invented by the detranscendentalists, is to make arguments about Emerson based not on an entire essay or lecture by Emerson but only on the "detachable utterance" (to use Kateb's phrase) from an Emerson text. Emerson is partly responsible for encouraging such an approach. He mentioned in a few private writings that he struggled as a writer when it came to joining sentences to form paragraphs and essays. The most often cited such statement is from a May 10, 1838, letter to Carlyle, in which Emerson bemusedly describes his household, including his wife, mother, son, domestic help, and then finally himself: "Here I sit and read and write, with very little system, and, as far as regards composition, with the most fragmentary result: paragraphs incompressible, each sentence an infinitely repellent particle."[16]

In the context of the letter, Emerson's self-description is clearly intended to amuse Carlyle, a fellow writer who would certainly recognize the struggle Emerson depicted. However, since at least 1883 this one sentence by Emerson has instead been treated as a serious "confession" by Emerson that his writing is hopelessly fragmentary. That was the year that Matthew Arnold cited this sentence to justify his conclusion that Emerson was "not a great writer [because] his style has not the requisite wholeness of good tissue." Arnold's would prove to be the most influential essay about Emerson for the next eighty years, into the 1960s, and even today one still sees this "confession" being used to justify reading Emerson in parts rather than wholes.[17] This includes the detranscendentalists, who justified the third tactic (like the other two) as something that Emerson himself recommends. We should work with Emerson's "detachable utterance," Kateb explained, because Emerson himself once wrote that there is "a class of passages [in Shakespeare] which bear to be separated from their connexion as single gems do from a crown and choicely kept for their intrinsic worth" (95). Emerson's point here, though, is not to recommend a mode of reading but to praise the exceptional Shakespeare: only Shakespeare's writing (and only a certain portion of it) can actually survive such a destructive mode of reading.[18]

Some of the detranscendentalists themselves challenged this focus on the short utterance by encouraging us to look at longer ones they called "passages." In whole passages, not sentences, they argued, Emerson dramatizes the construction (and deconstruction) of his ideas before our eyes, a process Poirier called "troping" (*Renewal*, 13–14) and Cavell "transfiguration" (*Conditions Handsome*, 144). In a 2007 essay, Poirier rightly described

Emerson as "everywhere a dramatist of his own thought." For this reason, Poirier explained, we must look at more than the sentence, "It is only by coping with the words and phrases in the order in which he [Emerson] left them—not disrupted here and there by the substitution of dots and dashes for words—that we can adequately experience [Emerson's writing]."[19] This is true, but to focus *only* on the passage—rather than the entire essay or lecture—is still to ignore much of the drama. As the third section of this essay shows, this detranscendentalist focus on the utterance (whether it be a short phrase or a long passage) as opposed to the essay as a whole has led to enduring misinterpretations of the major essays.

All three of the tactics examined above—secularizing Emerson's concepts, privileging his gnomic journals, and detaching his utterances—are at odds with Emerson's own dedication to the public work of art, including political addresses and essays.[20] In his 1844 "The Poet," Emerson explains that the "true poet" conveys "a thought so passionate and alive that, like the spirit of a plant or an animal, it has an architecture of its own, and adorns nature with a new thing" (*E&L*, 450). Emerson thought of his essays like poems and other works of art, each with "an architecture of its own." The detranscendentalists' tactics do have at least one virtue; like the critic who looks closely at one column of the Parthenon, or a single motif in a piece by Mozart, these tactics teach us to value precise details about Emerson's texts, including the journals. But these tactics also have one major vice. Like the blind men and the elephant, who each conclude on the basis of different body parts that they are facing a pillar, a rope, a wall, or a pipe, the detranscendentalists found what they were looking for but "los[t] Emerson in the process." Emerson, in contrast, admired the whole elephant, and urged artists to seek a similar wholeness even if art can never rival nature. As he wrote in the late essay "Country Life": "When I look at natural structures, as at a tree, or the teeth of a shark, or the anatomy of an elephant, I know that I am seeing an architecture and carpentry which has no sham, is solid and conscientious, which perfectly answers its end, and has nothing to spare. But in all works of human art there is deduction to be made for blunder and falsehood." This inevitable "deduction" in any work of art was no reason for the artist to give up; on the contrary, Emerson writes, the artist must follow the example of "Goethe, whose whole life was a study of the theory of art, [and who] said, No man should be admitted to his Republic [of artists], who was not versed in Natural History" (*CW*, 12:160–61)—versed, that is, in knowledge of "natural structures," "solid and conscientious, . . . perfectly answer[ing their] end[s]."

Transcendental Equality

Contrary to what the detranscendentalists have implied, most of Emerson's public writings clearly affirm some aspect of his transcendentalism, particularly in the concluding paragraphs of those writings. In most of his public essays and lectures bearing on politics, the principle argued throughout each text and then finally affirmed is transcendental equality. There is a small group of essays in which Emerson intentionally dramatizes his struggle to believe in that principle; some of these will be examined in the next section. In this section of the essay, though, the focus will be on Emerson's usual style of public writing in all of the stages of his public career as described in the introduction (1826–1835, 1836–1844, 1844–1863, and 1864–1872), the first two stages being combined here. In each stage, Emerson clearly expresses his commitment to transcendental equality.

Before looking closely at Emerson's writings, it is necessary to explain briefly Emerson's transcendentalist vocabulary. While in his earliest writings Emerson generally restricts himself to words with clear transcendentalist connotations (e.g., God, the Divine, the Soul), by the 1830s he begins to use a wider variety of other words as well. There are three important reasons Emerson expanded his transcendentalist vocabulary this way. First, he uses different words in order to accurately describe different facets of our transcendental essence. There are two major facets of that essence in Emerson's view: a divine essence, which he called "the Over-Soul," "Being," "God," and so on, and a divine faculty within each person, which he called "Reason," "the Moral Sense," "Genius," "Intuition," and so on. Further, both of these major facets have different qualities that Emerson used different words to highlight. For example, Emerson might call the divine faculty within us "the moral sense" when explaining how we know goodness in the world, but "genius" when explaining how we perceive beauty. There are certainly no strict rules to Emerson's transcendentalist vocabulary, but there are consistencies in usage that deserve our careful attention. A second reason Emerson uses a variety of words to describe his transcendentalist commitments is to avoid sectarian controversy. Religious liberals like Emerson prided themselves on avoiding theological disputes; an expressive but loose way of describing matters of ultimate concern was very important to antebellum public intellectuals like Emerson, who sought to promote not only religious tolerance but democratic inclusiveness.[21] Emerson's own vocabulary was consequently loose. And, a third reason Emerson's transcendentalist vocabulary was large was because his greatest ambition was to show that transcendentalism—regardless of its name—was true for all times and all places. As he put it in "The Transcendentalist," transcendentalism is just "Idealism as it appears in 1842" (E&L, 193). Using a wide variety of words to express the "reality" of transcendental truths was Emerson's postsectarian attempt to persuade as many people as possible that transcendentalism lay at the basis of their beliefs; in a more recent work, Buell has nicely described this as Emerson's "lifetime of spiritual deparochialization."[22] One example of Emerson deparochializing is in the section of the 1844 essay "Experience" called (as explained below) "Reality," which was a word Emerson used often to designate permanent transcendental truth: "Fortune, Minerva, Muse, Holy Ghost,—these are quaint names too narrow to cover this unbounded substance. The baffled intellect must still kneel before this cause, which refuses to be named,—ineffable cause, which every fine genius has essayed to represent by some emphatic symbol, as, Thales by water, Anaximenes by air, Anaxagoras by (Nous) thought, Zoroaster by fire, Jesus and the moderns by love: the metaphor of each has become a national religion" (E&L, 485). Emerson is suggesting here that, beyond national or sectarian attachments to certain terms, there is a common reality, or (here) "substance." What ultimately matters is not the national metaphors but the universal truth these metaphors seek to describe. Emerson's keen desire to move past a partisan terminology to universal truths—and in this case, to the universal truth of transcendental equality—is evident in an 1851 lecture, discussed below, when he urges the nation, North and South, to recognize transcendental equality as justified by "morals, religion, or godhead, or what you will" (AW, 58). That insouciant "what you will" is not an invitation to make light of the concept—to secularize it—but, on the contrary, to recognize that, regardless of what we call it, the concept is a universal, permanent "reality."

The first two stages of Emerson's public career begin with his becoming a minister in 1826 and end with his becoming an abolitionist lecturer in 1844. Emerson's sermons provide many, many examples of his belief in transcendental equality, starting with the very first, "Pray without Ceasing," which argues God's omniscient knowledge of our thoughts is due to God's being "not so much the observer of your actions, as . . . the potent principle by which they are bound together" (*S*, 1:57). God is at once the divine essence informing the cosmos and a divine faculty within the individual. "Your reason is God, your virtue is God" (*S*, 1:57), Emerson explains. All human beings have God as a faculty within them this way. An 1830 sermon explicitly urges us to "honor . . . this image of God in human nature which has placed a standard of character in every human breast" (*S*, 2:266).

In 1832, as Field puts it, Emerson left the "smug exile" of the Unitarian establishment not because he was indifferent to religion but so that he could preach his transcendentalism—including his belief in transcendental equality—to broader audiences: he left in order to "do God's work in the world" (29, 30).[23] His early lectures thus initiate a lifelong effort to promote transcendentalism beyond the sect (liberal Unitarianism) that happened to sponsor it in Emerson's time. Some of the most important writings in this regard were the late 1830s addresses. In concluding his 1838 "Divinity School Address," Emerson urged his audience of theology students to turn from "the Church" to "the Soul" (*E&L*, 88). The politics of transcendentalism are mostly implicit here. "Dare to love God without mediator or veil," Emerson advised; "cast behind you all conformity [to old forms], and acquaint men at first hand with Deity." When you encounter men and women from your parish, Emerson urged these students, "be to them a divine man [and] let their timid aspirations find in you a friend. . . . By trusting your own heart you shall gain more confidence in other men" (*E&L*, 89). In other words, when you know that *you* are a part of God (as *Nature* announced), you will in turn recognize the godly in others and "gain more confidence in other men." The importance of recognizing other persons as godly is more clearly explained in the last paragraph of the 1837 "The American Scholar." Bemoaning the rise of "masses," Emerson urges his audience to recognize God within each person: "We will walk on our own feet; we will work with our own hands; we will speak our own minds. . . . The dread of man and the love of man shall be a wall of defence and a wreath of joy around all. A nation of men will for the first time exist, because each believes himself inspired by the Divine Soul which also inspires all men" (*E&L*, 71). That final sentence powerfully suggests how Emerson's belief in transcendental equality drives his political vision: once we learn that a Divine Soul inspires not only the individual but all men, we must recognize all other persons as godly—that is, that each person deserves both our dread respect and love. Only then will "a nation of men" exist for the first time.[24]

The 1841 "The Over-Soul" is perhaps Emerson's most compelling articulation of transcendental equality in this early stage of his public career.[25] The first paragraph states in no uncertain terms that, whatever doubts we may have about our own godliness, it is (once again) the "reality." "Our faith comes in moments," Emerson acknowledges, while "our vice is habitual. Yet there is a depth in those brief moments, which constrains us to ascribe more reality to them than to all other experience" (E&L, 385). "Constrain" is another important word for Emerson in this essay; he uses it five times to describe the nature of his belief in transcendent equality: he is "constrained every moment to acknowledge a higher origin for events than the will I call mine" (E&L, 385). In this essay, Emerson depicts how he has—and we should—accept this constraint, embrace it even; he uses metaphor after metaphor to convey the idea that we are all part of an "Over-Soul": that we lay in it "as the earth lies in the soft arms of the atmosphere" (E&L, 385); that "we live in succession, in division, in parts, in particles [but] within man is the soul of the whole . . . to which every part and particle is equally related: the eternal ONE" (E&L, 386); that "we see the world piece by piece, as the sun, the moon, the animal, the tree; but the whole of which these are the shining parts, is the soul" (E&L, 386); and that "from within or from behind, a light shines through us upon things, and makes us aware that we are nothing, but the light is all" (E&L, 387). This last metaphor is a favorite of Emerson's at this time: in the 1836 *Nature*, "Spirit" is revealed by "a great shadow pointing always to the sun behind us" (E&L, 40); in the 1841 "The Method of Nature," there is an "unseen pilot" who "governs all men" (E&L, 124); later, in "The Over-Soul," there is "the Maker of all things and all persons, [who] stands behind us, and casts his dread omniscience through us over things" (E&L, 392). What each of us must learn, Emerson repeatedly insists, is "that the Highest dwells with him" (E&L, 399). But what Emerson also emphasizes in the conclusion of "The Over-Soul," just as he did at the end of "The American Scholar," is that in learning our own godliness we also must recognize the godliness of others and thus begin to build a truly just nation. In the final paragraph, Emerson calls for a new, plain faith in "the Soul." He imagines a person—"the Lonely, Original, and Pure"—inhabited by a soul which addresses that person about its divine origins and the politics that this mandates: "Behold, it [the soul] saith, I am born into the great, the universal mind. I the imperfect [because within a person], adore my own Perfect. I am somehow receptive of the great soul, and thereby I do overlook the sun and the stars, and feel them to be the fair accidents and effects which change and pass. More and more the surges of everlasting nature enter into me, and I become public and human in my regards and actions. So come I to live in thoughts, and act with energies which are immortal" (E&L, 400). When my soul is "receptive of the great soul," I "become public and human in my regards and actions." Emerson's transcendentalism—his belief that we all have the Over-Soul within us—is fundamentally political: our individual godliness, once recognized, will make us more public and human in our regards and actions, because we will know that all other people are godly too.

A new stage in Emerson's public career begins with his joining the abolitionist movement in 1844 and ends when slavery was abolished with the Emancipation Proclamation in 1863. Without question, this 1844–1863 portion of Emerson's oeuvre—and not the once favored "small canon" of 1836–1844 (as described in the introduction)—contains the core expression of his transcendentalist politics. In these writings, many anthologized in 1995 as *Emerson's Antislavery Writings,* Emerson really emphasizes the *politics* of transcendentalism: that is, how the awakening to one's own inner divinity necessitates first the recognition of everyone else's and then the building of a just nation. His 1844–1863 writings center especially on the recognition of the enslaved as godly, too, and emphasize the tremendous distance between the current slave-supporting United States and a just state. Emerson stated this point earlier in these three sentences spoken by "the man of ideas"—that is, the transcendentalist—in the 1841 "Lecture on the Times": "'If,' he says, 'I am selfish, then is there slavery, or the effort to establish it, wherever I go. But if I am just, then is there no slavery, let the laws say what they will. For if I treat all men as gods, how to me can there be such a thing as a slave?'" (E&L, 164). The 1844–1863 writings all elaborate upon this basic insight: not human laws but justice (that is, treating all men as transcendentally equal, or "treat[ing] all men as gods") necessitates an end to slavery.

In his first major antislavery address, the 1844 "Address on the Emancipation of the Negroes in the British West Indies," Emerson stresses how the abolitionist Granville Sharp cited the principle of transcendental equality in the British court, referring to it as "the God's truth . . . for all the mumbling of the lawyers" (AW, 27). At some point, all of us will recognize that truth, Emerson states, making use of the same arresting image he did in Nature and "The Method of Nature" and "The Over-Soul": "One feels very sensibly [in the British emancipation] . . . that a great heart and soul are behind there, superior to any man, and making use of each, in turn, and infinitely attractive to each person according to the degree of reason in his own mind" (AW, 27). Listening to their "reason," the transcendental faculty, constrains us to recognize this truth of transcendental equality: "Not the least affecting part of the history of abolition, is, the annihilation of the old indecent nonsense about the nature of the negro" (AW, 29). All persons are godly. What Toussaint L'Ouverture and the rebel leaders in Haiti, Jamaica, and the Barbados teach us, Emerson explains, is that "here is man: and if you have man, black or white is an insignificance. The intellect"—a mixed faculty that is partially transcendental and thus proof of the indwelling Creator—"is miraculous!" (AW, 31).[26] The political conclusion of this recognition once again follows: in 1837, "a nation of men will for the first time exist, because each believes himself inspired by the Divine Soul which also inspires all men" (E&L, 71); in 1841, "more and more the surges of everlasting nature enter into me, and I become public and human in my regards and actions" (E&L, 400); and in 1844, "the civility of no race can be perfect whilst another race is degraded. It is a doctrine alike of the oldest, and of the newest philosophy, that man is one, and that you cannot injure any member, without a sympathetic injury to all the members" (AW, 32). This is the core of Emerson's politics. First we must recognize the godly faculty within us, and then in all human beings; and then we proceed to build just states.

Developments through the 1840s aiding the expansion rather than abolition of slavery, culminating in the Fugitive Slave Act of 1850, compelled Emerson to speak even more frankly about the need for transcendental politics. But these developments also led him to wonder privately if all individuals were indeed capable of recognizing "the indwelling of the Creator in man" (E&L, 167). Is the transcendental faculty simply suffocated most of the time by our selfishness? Back in 1842, in "The Transcendentalist," Emerson had been confident that "if . . . I am selfish, then is there slavery . . . [b]ut if I am just, then is there no slavery." In March 1851, though, he suggested to a friend that "it seems we must wait for the Almighty to create a new generation, a little more keenly alive to moral impression" (*AW*, 51). In the May 1851 "Address to the Citizens of Concord," he confessed that "I question the value of our civilization when I see that the public mind had never less hold of the strongest of all truths." "The sense of injustice is blunted,—a sure sign of the shallowness of our intellect" (*AW*, 55–56), intellect again being a mixed faculty, receptive of transcendental truths though sometimes hampered in the construal of them. Acknowledging the United States' industrial advances, Emerson still "cannot think the most judicious tubing a compensation for metaphysical debility" (*AW*, 56). Nonetheless, Emerson then asserts once more his conviction about transcendental equality, hoping to spark the recognition of the same among his auditors, and thus initiate the politics of transcendentalism. Though it is presented dramatically as a moment of doubt, this passage is worth citing at length, for it is an exemplary expression of Emerson's transcendentalist convictions:

> I thought that all men of all conditions had been made sharers of a certain experience, that in certain rare and retired moments they had been made to see how man is man, or what makes the essence of rational beings, namely, that whilst animals have to do with eating the fruits of the ground, men have to do with rectitude, with benefit, with truth, with something which is, independent of appearances: and that this tie [via this essence to one another] makes the substantiality of life, this, and not their ploughing, or sailing, their trade or the breeding of families. I thought that every time a man goes back to his own thoughts, these angels receive him, talk with him, and that, in the best hours, he is uplifted in virtue of this essence, into a peace and into a power which the material world cannot give : that these moments counterbalance the years of drudgery, and that this owning of a law, be it called morals, religion, or godhead, or what you will, constituted the explanation of life, the excuse and indemnity for the errors and calamities which sadden it. In long years consumed in trifles, they remember these moments, and are consoled. I thought it was this fair mystery, whose foundations are hidden in eternity, which made the basis of human society, and of law; and that to pretend anything else, as that the acquisition of property was the end of living, was to confound all distinctions, to make the world a greasy hotel, and, instead of noble motives and inspirations, and a heaven of companions and angels around and before us, to leave us in a grimacing menagerie of monkeys and idiots. All arts, customs, societies, books, and laws, are good as they foster and

concur with this spiritual element: all men are beloved as they raise us to it; hateful as they deny or resist it. The laws especially draw their obligation only from their concurrence with it. (*AW,* 58–59)

The core of Emerson's political philosophy is here. We each have a transcendental faculty that, when heeded, affirms the divine "essence" of "all men of all conditions." Both this faculty and this essence go by many names ("moral, religion, or godhead, or what you will"), but, whatever it is called, this essence is the only true "basis of human society, and of law." Our culture, society, and law must be dedicated to "foster[ing] and concur[ring] with this spiritual element."

While Emerson, especially in the 1850s, sometimes doubted if Americans could acknowledge let alone uphold transcendental equality, Emerson never wavered in his conviction that transcendental equality is real.[27] The problem is that our "atheism" (*E&L,* 269)—our "damnable atheism" (*AW,* 37), our "metaphysical debility" (*AW,* 56)—blinds us to the reality of transcendental equality. The 1855 "Lecture on Slavery" emphasizes this problem of skepticism. Proslavery attitudes, he contended, "rest on skepticism, which is not local, but universal." The tolerance for slavery is a sign of this skepticism: "I call slavery and the tolerance it finds, worst in this,—the stupendous frivolity it betrays in the heart and head of a society without faith, without aims, dying of inanition. An impoverishing skepticism scatters poverty, disease, and cunning through our opinions, then through practice. The Dark Ages did not know that they were dark; and what if it should turn out, that our material civilization has no sun, but only ghastly gas-lights?" (*AW,* 93). This skepticism infects all of American society and culture, including judges who are "skeptics too" and "share the sickness of the time." The slave-supporting United States is in its own dark age, eyes closed to the reality of transcendental equality. "The open secret of the world [is] hid from their [American society's] eyes" (*AW,* 101), Emerson explained, the secret being "the art of subliming a private soul with inspirations from the great and public and divine soul from which we live" (*AW,* 101). When our private souls are "sublimed" or inspired by this divine soul, the United States will be transformed into a just state. This had been his same message long ago in the 1838 "Divinity School Address": leave the church and "be to [other people] a divine man" (*E&L,* 89). Now, in 1855, the message is that we should leave the state—its corrupt proslavery laws—and sublime our private souls with inspiration from the divine soul. Judges and others are obscuring that inspiration; they are "hiding . . . the light." But, when abolitionists and others acted, "the light shone." Emerson then describes the reality of transcendental truths in a way that reveals just how different his philosophy is from that imposed on him by the detranscendentalists: "Truth exists, though all men should deny it" (AW, 102). For detranscendentalists like Rorty, truth is made; for transcendentalists like Emerson, truth is found.[28] In the United States in the 1850s, too few (Emerson concluded) had found the truth of transcendental equality.

One of the few champions of transcendental equality, in Emerson's view, was John Brown, and Emerson's support of Brown reveals a lot about his own commitment to transcendental equality. Brown became Emerson's hero in the second half of the 1850s because Brown had found the truth of transcendental equality and acted upon it. Brown was "a pure idealist," as Emerson put it in his tribute to Brown just prior to Brown's execution in late 1859. Where "the judges rely on the forms"—that is, the corrupt proslavery human-made laws—Brown "see[s] the fact behind the forms": the fact or reality of transcendental equality (AW, 119). After Brown's execution, Emerson announced in a January 1860 speech that God would find new ways to carry on Brown's work. "Our blind statesmen go up and down, with committees of vigilance and safety, hunting for the origin of this new heresy," meaning this belief in transcendental equality that he and Brown both shared. Emerson is being ironic: nothing could be less heretical than transcendental equality, as he makes clear. "They [the blind statesmen]," he continued, "will need a very vigilant committee indeed to find its [this "heresy's"] birthplace, and a very strong force to root it out. For the arch-Abolitionist, older than Brown, and older than the Shenandoah Mountains, is Love, whose other name is Justice, which was before Alfred, before Lycurgus, before Slavery, and will be after it" (AW, 124). Transcendental equality—here labeled as "love," as in the passage from "Experience" cited above (E&L, 485)—is independent of political institutions. But, just as he hoped more than two decades earlier ("a nation of men will for the first time exist"), Emerson still hoped U.S. political institutions might dedicate themselves to transcendental equality. Emerson had hoped Brown would found that new nation, but once Lincoln issued the Emancipation Proclamation (changing the purpose of the war from preserving a proslave Union to ending slavery), Emerson hoped the president might do this instead. In his 1863 "Fortune of the Republic," Emerson explained that "the end of all political struggle, is, to establish morality as the basis of all legislation. 'Tis not free institutions, 'tis not a republic, 'tis not a democracy, that is the end,—no, but only the means: morality is the object of government." Following its political struggle, Emerson envisioned how the United States will indeed become moral: "The height of Reason, the noblest affection, the purest religion will find their house in our institutions, and write our laws for the benefit of men" (AW, 153, 154). The public institutions of the United States will soon be based upon the religion of transcendental equality.

Emerson did not live long enough to witness the failure of Reconstruction, and so in the final stage of his career, from 1864 until he stopped actively writing in 1872, Emerson continued to remain optimistic that transcendental equality would form the basis of the new United States. Perhaps the most powerful of his late political statements is "The Sovereignty of Ethics," an essay written in this last stage and published in 1878. Here, Emerson expresses the permanent truth of transcendental equality with a vocabulary now fitted for the age of Darwin. While recognizing the "scale from the gorilla to the gentleman," Emerson still draws a line between those creatures without the transcendental faculty and those with it. Those without it include the grub, which simply "yield[s] itself to nature," and the earlier hominid ("man down in Nature"), who "occupies himself in guarding, in feeding, in warming and multiplying his body." "[A]s long as he [that earlier hominid] knows no more, we justify him": that is, we excuse his animalistic self-interested behavior. But, "presently a mystic change is wrought," "a new perception opens, and he is made a citizen of the world of souls: he feels what is called duty; he is aware that he owes a higher allegiance to do and live as a good member of this universe. In the measure in which he has this sense he is a man, rises to the universal life. The high intellect is absolutely at one with moral nature" (CW, 10:85). Here, once more, is the conviction that we humans not only contain God within us (as does the whole creation) but can uniquely know this using our transcendental faculty: the "high intellect." Here, also, is the political repercussion: we become "citizens of the world of souls." Remarking on Emerson's entire career in 1870, the sectarian (Methodist) minister Gilbert Haven—disturbed by Emerson's postsectarian transcendentalism for the last four decades—lambasted the philosophy once more. Emerson's philosophy, Haven cried, is simply, "I am

God." But, Haven added, sarcastically but accurately, at least Emerson "was generous. All else were in like condition. Everybody was God."[29]

Dramatizing Belief

As mentioned above, some of the detranscendentalists, particularly Poirier and Cavell, persuasively show how Emerson dramatizes his thought in passages. Less persuasive, though, is their contention that these passage-length dramas are about the loss of belief. The opposite is true. Emerson often dramatically affirms his transcendentalist beliefs by including brief and transitional moments of doubt. Consider a few examples from one of the essays favored by the detranscendentalists, who read it as a drama of lost belief, the 1841 "Circles." "Circles," Poirier contends, is about how we make our own truths: how "an Emersonian 'circle' actively creates truths and knowledge." "It follows," Poirier concludes, "that truths and systems of knowledge are to be viewed as in themselves contingent, like other convenient fictions" (*Poetry and Pragmatism*, 22). But Poirier's strong reading of Emerson as a proto-pragmatist who makes rather than finds his truths requires overlooking all the sentences in "Circles" that urge us to shift from epistemological skepticism to ethical certainty. For example, Poirier points to two sentences describing how the soul can "burst over [a] boundary . . . and expand another orbit on the great deep" and how "the heart refuses to be imprisoned" (23). This means the soul never stays the same, Poirier contends, moving on to examples from other essays. But the drama in "Circles" is not yet over. Following two more paragraphs about "every ultimate fact [being] only the first of a new series" and that "step by step we scale this mysterious ladder," Emerson then explains that men eventually "rest at last on the divine soul" (*E&L*, 405). Later short dramas from "Circles" reach this same affirmation more conclusively. A few pages later, for example, Emerson writes that "there are degrees in idealism": first we "play with it academically"—that is, as epistemological skeptics—but then eventually "[idealism] shows itself ethical and practical." As Emerson summarizes later in the same paragraph: "The idealism of Berkeley is only a crude statement of the idealism of Jesus, and that again is a crude statement of the fact, that all nature is the rapid efflux of goodness executing and organizing itself" (*E&L*, 407). A few pages after that comes Emerson's announcement that he is "only an experimenter" and that "no facts are to me sacred; none are profane; I simply experiment, an endless seeker, with no Past at my back" (*E&L*, 412). But that is not his last word on the subject; Emerson immediately adds: "Yet this incessant movement and progression which all things partake could never become sensible to us but by contrast to some principle of fixture or stability in the soul. Whilst the eternal generation of circles proceeds, the eternal generator abides. That central life is somewhat [i.e., something] superior to creation, superior to knowledge and thought, and contains all its circles" (*E&L*, 412).

There are more formally significant dramas that Emerson created, and these are the focus of this section of the essay: specifically, "Self-Reliance," "Fate," and "Experience." Consider "Self-Reliance" first. Many or even most readers have been too impatient with this essay to grasp its full message, focusing instead on the infamous seventh paragraph, where Emerson most stridently insists that "whoso would be a man must be a nonconformist"; this is the paragraph that includes such Nietzschean utterances as, "Good and bad are but names very readily transferable to that or this," and "the only right is what is after my constitution," and "I would write on the lintels of the door-post, *Whim*," and "are they my poor?" (*E&L*, 262). That paragraph has its own subtleties that complicate the detranscendentalist reading (as Shklar, for one, sees, as explained in the introduction and her essay in this volume), but the main point here is that "Self-Reliance" is not seven paragraphs long; it is fifty paragraphs long, and the essay includes many more "acts" in the drama of Emerson's belief. The first twenty paragraphs are indeed largely occupied with the theme of the seventh paragraph—that is, the impressive way self-reliance circumvents conformity and consistency. But, why are these self-reliant acts so impressive? What exactly are we relying upon when we flout social norms with our own original actions? Emerson explains this in the twenty-first paragraph:

> The magnetism which all original action exerts is explained when we inquire the reason of self-trust. Who is the Trustee? What is the aboriginal Self, on which a universal reliance may be grounded? . . . The inquiry leads us to that source, at once the essence of genius, of virtue, and of life, which we call Spontaneity or Instinct. We denote this primary wisdom as Intuition, whilst all later teachings are tuitions. In that deep force, the last fact behind which analysis cannot go, all things find their common origin. For, the sense of being which in calm hours rises, we know not how, in the soul, is not diverse from

things, from space, from light, from time, from man, but one with them, and proceeds obviously from the same source whence their life and being also proceed. (E&L, 268–69)

As David M. Robinson notes, this paragraph shows how "Emerson gradually reveals reliance on the self to be reliance on God as self becomes 'the aboriginal Self on which a universal reliance may be ground.'"[30] And, while Emerson's treatment here of the complex relationship between our Intuition (that is, the transcendental faculty) and our tuitions (or worldly understanding) is more sophisticated, the message here is ultimately the same as that made more urgently and simply in his 1851 "Address" (as cited above): "I thought that every time a man goes back to his own thoughts, these angels receive him." The 1841 passage continues: "Here [in these moments of Intuition] are the lungs of that inspiration which giveth man wisdom, and which cannot be denied without impiety and atheism. We lie in the lap of immense intelligence, which makes us receivers of its truth and organs of its activity. When we discern justice, when we discern truth, we do nothing of ourselves, but allow a passage to its beams. If we ask whence this comes, if we seek to pry into the soul that causes, all philosophy is at fault. Its presence or its absence is all we can affirm" (E&L, 269). On the one hand, Emerson registers his liberal indifference to whatever name we give this divine source, but on the other hand he absolutely insists that to deny the existence of this divine source is "impiety and atheism." Transcendentalism cannot be proven by philosophy, only affirmed "in calm hours" when we sense we are part of God—or, in this case, "lie in the lap of immense intelligence." The rest of "Self-Reliance" then builds on this equation of self-reliance to God-reliance, referring to "God" specifically thirteen times in the final thirty paragraphs (as opposed to just four times in the opening twenty).[31]

The 1860 essay "Fate" also dramatizes Emerson's belief in transcendentalism, the moment of clarification also coming about midway through the essay: in the thirty-second paragraph, to be exact. As with the fifty-paragraph "Self-Reliance," though, too many readers have been too impatient with this sixty-six-paragraph essay to recognize this. Others do look to later paragraphs of "Fate" but only for utterances to "prove" that Emerson embraced, like Nietzsche, a provisional self. For example, Poirier points to a passage in the middle of the essay where it sounds like Emerson is saying that we constantly refashion ourselves, struggling against our prior selffashionings. "Identity is discernible to [Emerson]," Poirier explains, only "in acts of antagonism directed against the already formulated, against your own previous utterance, 'against ourselves as much as others,' as he says in 'Fate,' if it proves to be in the interests of the Universe" (*Renewal*, 176–77). Poirier alludes to Emerson's words in the thirty-third paragraph, "interests of the Universe," to suggest Emerson meant merely "whim" by the phrase. But is that what Emerson really meant by "interests of the Universe"? Prior to the words cited by Poirier, Emerson does indeed make self-realization sound entirely worldly and pugilistic—as if the Universe was entirely indifferent to our fate. With no one to rely on but ourselves, Emerson explains, let's remember that we, too, are part of fate, and simply "confront fate with fate" (*E&L*, 954). However, Emerson then adds this, the thirty-second and thirty-third paragraphs:

> 1. But Fate against Fate is only parrying and defence: there are, also, the noble creative forces. The revelation of Thought takes man out of servitude into freedom. . . . The day of days, the great day of the feast of life, is that in which the inward eye opens to the Unity in things, to the omnipresence of law;—sees that what is must be, and ought to be, or is the best. This beatitude dips from on high down on us, and we see. It is not in us so much as we are in it. If the air come to our lungs, we breathe and live; if not, we die. If the light come to our eyes, we see; else not. And if truth come to our mind, we suddenly expand to its dimensions, as if we grew to worlds. We are as lawgivers; we speak for Nature; we prophesy and divine.
>
> This insight throws us on the party and interest of the Universe, against all and sundry; against ourselves, as much as others. (*E&L*, 954–55)

In the thirty-second paragraph, numbered "1" by Emerson, he clearly counsels not just pugilism against fate but a trust in "Thought," described here unmistakably as the transcendental faculty: it "opens [us] to the Unity in things, to the omnipresence of law," and so forth. More, Emerson then numbers the thirty-sixth paragraph "2," in which he proposes another transcendental faculty, here called "the moral sentiment" (*E&L*, 956): this, too, we can trust to guide us in how we define ourselves. And so, once again, Emerson counsels us to trust in a transcendental faculty (here actually two such faculties) to teach us that we are part of God. "We are as lawgivers" (Emerson writes) not because we are Nietzschean *Übermenschen* whimsically writing our own laws, but because in receiving "truth" we now "speak for Nature" and act on behalf of "the interest of the Universe."[32] "Interest of the Universe" means the Universe's law; we act as that law's agent so long as we trust in Thought and the moral sentiment.

And so, having made this important turn in the essay at the thirty-second paragraph, Emerson goes on to counsel not a surrender to fate, but rather a sharper awareness of our "double consciousness" (*E&L*, 966), yet another version of Emerson's Reason/Understanding paradigm (as described in the introduction): on the one hand, we enjoy transcendental insight via Reason (here, Thought and the moral sentiment), but on the other hand, we too often rely only upon our Understanding (the "fate" we pit against the larger fate). Nearly two decades before, near the end of the 1842 "The Transcendentalists," Emerson explained that "the worst feature of this double consciousness is, that the two lives, of the understanding and of the soul, which we lead, really show very little relation to each other" (*E&L*, 205–6). However, with "patience, and still patience" (*E&L*, 206), "when we pass, as presently we shall, into some new infinitude, out of this Iceland of negations, it will please us to reflect that . . . we bore with our indigence" (*E&L*, 206). In "Fate," he counsels precisely the same: "So when a man is the victim of his fate [that is, living by the lights only of the Understanding] . . . he is to rally on his relation to the Universe [his Reason], which his [material] ruin benefits. Leaving the daemon who suffers [his Understanding], he is to take sides with the Deity who secures universal benefit by his pain" (*E&L*, 966–67). We are to recall our "relation to the Universe"—our "original relation to the universe" from *Nature* (*E&L*, 7)—and side with the Deity, knowing that even our personal ruin and pain ultimately secures the universal benefit. This trust in universal progress is a hallmark of Emerson's transcendentalism, as the final lines of "Fate" show: "Let us build altars to the Beautiful Necessity . . . which rudely or softly educates him to the perception that there are no contingencies; that Law rules throughout existence, a Law which is not intelligent but intelligence,—not personal nor impersonal,—it disdains words and passes understanding; it dissolves persons; it vivifies nature; yet solicits the pure in heart to draw on all its omnipotence" (*E&L*, 967–68). This supposedly fatalistic essay thus ends here with the same convictions found in the late 1830s lectures and the 1844–1863 political addresses: that we are each part of God or Law, which "educates" us that everything has a reason (and thus "there are no contingencies"), and "*yet*"—importantly—that those who accept this Law become not ethically passive but active: they become "pure in heart," alluding gently (in Emerson's carefully worded postsectarian style) to the Sermon on the Mount: "Blessed are the pure in heart: for they shall see God" (Matthew 5:8). This final sentence fits harmoniously alongside any of the other earlier calls to transcendental action, such as those in "The American Scholar" and "The Over-Soul" as cited above, or this, cited below, from the 1844 "Address on the Emancipation," which refers not to a "Beautiful Necessity" but a "blessed necessity," recognized not by "intelligence" but "Intellect." Little else has changed: "There is progress in human society. There is a blessed necessity by which the interest of men is always driving them to the right; and, again, making all crime mean and ugly. . . . The Intellect, with blazing eye, looking through history from the beginning onward, gazes on this blot [of slavery], and it disappears. The sentiment of Right, once very low and indistinct, but ever more articulate, because it is the voice of the universe, pronounces Freedom" (AW, 33).

Finally, there is the 1844 essay "Experience," which best dramatizes Emerson's struggles with skepticism. This has been the most important essay for those critics determined to prove Emerson's skepticism about "the soul" and other transcendental truths; however, to do so requires, as we have seen in "Self-Reliance" and "Fate," focusing strictly on utterances and overlooking the structure of the whole essay, a structure that Emerson actually explicitly announces in the opening poem and reiterates in the third to last paragraph of the essay. In those two places, Emerson describes various "moods" that man suffers: he calls them the seven "lords of life." These are spectral Wrong/Illusion (the name varies in the two places), Temperament, Succession, Surface, Surprise, Use/Reality, and Dream/Subjectiveness (E&L, 469, 490–91). While Emerson notes in that third-to-last paragraph that "I dare not assume to give their order" (E&L, 491), he does use these seven moods to structure the essay, which he intentionally divides with line breaks into eight sections: first come the seven moods and then a concluding eighth section of three paragraphs. Each of the seven mood sections is written mostly in that mood, excepting some illuminating moments when Emerson dramatically breaks out of the mood, as shown below.[33]

In some of these moods, Emerson is indeed extremely skeptical about transcendental equality; in other moods, his skepticism is much milder, or even nonexistent (as in the section labeled "Reality," which is not surprising given the meaning of this word to Emerson). Moving through these moods,

Emerson dramatizes the many kinds of struggles the transcendentalist must work through. However, to treat "Experience" as proof that Emerson is a skeptic, and by extension that he is advocating detranscendentalism, is to reach exactly the wrong conclusion. Only by focusing on utterances from the skeptical mood sections, or from brief moments of doubt in the nonskeptical mood sections, can one reach this conclusion. This is Cavell's method in the most influential such reading of "Experience," his 1989 essay "Finding as Founding." A brilliant statement of Cavell's own philosophy, this essay has "lost Emerson in the process."

For Cavell, "Experience" is where Emerson renounces his young confidence (expressed in the 1836 *Nature*) that "the issue of skepticism [is] solvable or controllable"; in "Experience," Cavell writes, Emerson "takes [skepticism's] unsolvability to the heart of his thinking."[34] As evidence, Cavell mainly relies on eight or so passages from "Experience," about half of which come from the opening section, "Illusion," the most skeptical and dark of the seven moods. Here, Emerson reflects bitterly on the death of his son: "I cannot get it nearer to me," he writes, and "I grieve that grief can teach me nothing, nor carry me one step into real nature" (*E&L*, 473). Cavell interprets these sentences to mean, respectively, that Emerson is "still recovering from illusions that grief has something to teach, for example that there exists some known and established public source of understanding and consolation, call this religion" (106) and that it is instead possible to imagine "what happens to philosophy if its claim to provide foundations is removed from it—say the founding of morality in reason or in passion" (109). Cavell then translates another sentence from this section—"I take this evanescence and lubricity of all objects, which lets them slip through our fingers then when we clutch hardest, to be the most unhandsome part of our condition" (*E&L*, 473)—as "the unhandsome is . . . what happens when we seek to deny the standoffishness of objects by clutching at them" or "when we conceive thinking . . . as grasping something" (86).

Cavell does indeed show that Emerson in this section of the essay proves to be a connoisseur of skepticism, someone highly attuned to the ways in which epistemological problems can lead us to convictions about "the standoffishness of objects," the lack of "public sources of understanding," and the impossibility of foundations. That Emerson understood skepticism is not all that surprising to learn, given how important an influence David Hume was upon him in his youth.[35] But this first section, "Illusion," is just one of seven moods in this essay. One could choose a half-dozen utterances from another section, say, the next one, "Temperament," and subsequently reach an entirely different conclusion about "Experience": for example, that sternly rejecting illusory dreams is—pace Cavell—not what Emerson is teaching at all, for (as Emerson writes in shifting formally in his essay from "Illusion" to "Temperament") temperament is "the iron wire on which the beads [i.e., illusions] are strung" (E&L, 474). Focusing exclusively on "Temperament," then, one might conclude that Emerson is teaching us not how to deal with skepticism (Cavell's section) but how to deal with temperament (the next section). But both readings would be wrong, for, as Emerson states in the shift to the next section after that, "Succession," "temperament also enters fully into the systems of illusions, and shuts us in a prison of glass which we cannot see" (E&L, 474). Each of these moods is a prison, and we only get our first hint of what Emerson's true philosophy is when he momentarily and dramatically breaks out of the designated mood of the "Temperament" section to renounce it—particularly the pseudo-science of phrenology, which reduces a man to the temperament his skull shape supposedly reveals—as degrading to our transcendental equality: that is, as degrading "the indwelling of the Creator in man" or what Emerson here beautifully calls our "original equity."

> The physicians say, they are not materialists; but they are:—[in their view s]pirit is matter reduced to an extreme thinness: O *so* thin!—But [contra the physicians] the definition of *spiritual* should be, *that which is its own evidence*. What [wrong-headed] notions do they [the physicians] attach to love! what to religion! One would not willingly pronounce these words in their hearing, and give them the occasion to profane them. I saw a gracious gentleman who adapts his conversation to the form of the head of the man he talks with! I had fancied that the value of life lay in its inscrutable possibilities; in the fact that I never know, in addressing myself to a new individual, what may befall me.... Shall I preclude my future, by taking a high seat, and kindly adapting my conversation to the shape of heads?... [Believing only in t]emperament is the veto or limitation-power in the constitution, very justly applied to restrain an opposite excess in the constitution, but absurdly offered as a bar to original equity. (E&L, 475)

As fate ought to be used against fate (as argued in "Fate"), so temperament ought to be used against an "excess in the constitution." However, none of this struggle between our various physiological qualities even touches "*spiritual*" truths, including "original equity," which are not to be proven or disproven by physicians or philosophy but are rather "their own evidence." (Emerson makes the same point in "Self-Reliance" about our transcendental essence: "If we ask whence this comes, if we seek to pry into the soul that causes, all philosophy is at fault. Its presence or its absence is all we can affirm" [E&L, 269].) Keep physicians away from explaining away love or religion! Instead, Emerson continues to earnestly elaborate upon his real convictions during this candid moment within "Temperament": "On this platform [of living according to temperament], one lives in a sty of sensualism, and would soon come to suicide. But it is impossible that the creative power should exclude itself. Into every intelligence there is a door which is never closed, through which the creator passes. The intellect, seeker of absolute truth, or the heart, lover of absolute good, intervenes for our succor, and at one whisper of these higher powers, we awake from ineffectual struggles with this nightmare" (E&L, 476). Emerson's transcendentalist convictions are all here: there are "higher powers" or a "creative power" or just "the creator" who comes to us via our "intelligence" or our "intellect" or our "heart," which then in turn reaches the ethical conclusion to seek "absolute truth" and "absolute good." As he wrote in "The American Scholar," "More and more the surges of everlasting nature enter into me, and I become public and human in my regards and actions."

Two more of Cavell's favored utterances in "Finding as Founding" come from the "Reality" section of "Experience," a section that actually is dedicated to affirming transcendentalism. One would never guess this, however, from Cavell's presentation of the utterances, which refer to "this new yet unapproachable America" and to "skepticisms [being] not gratuitous or lawless." Both utterances come in moments of affirmation of transcendental equality, affirmations Cavell obscures by leaving out the surrounding sentences. Consider just the "unapproachable America" sentence. As in "Fate" and "The Transcendentalist," Emerson reaches the conclusion in "Reality" that we live with a "double consciousness," sometimes dominated by the understanding and worldly forms, sometimes by Reason and spiritual law and religious or transcendental truths: "So is it with us, now skeptical, or without unity, because immersed in forms and effects all seeming to be of equal yet hostile value, and now religious, whilst in the reception of spiritual law. Bear with these distractions, with this coetaneous growth of the parts: they will one day be *members,* and obey one will. On that one will, on that secret cause, they nail our attention and hope. Life is hereby melted into an expectation or a religion. Underneath the inharmonious and trivial particulars, is a musical perfection, the Ideal journeying always with us, the heaven without rent or seam" (E&L, 484).

Emerson then describes how these moments of illumination occur, in a manner quite similar to that of the famously ecstatic passage in *Nature* about the transparent eyeball; it is also where he uses the phrase "new yet unapproachable America": "But every insight from this [transcendental] realm of thought is felt as initial, and promises a sequel. I do not make it; I arrive there, and behold what was there already. I make! O no! I clap my hands in infantine joy and amazement, before the first opening to me of this august magnificence.... And what a future it opens! I feel a new heart beating with the love of the new beauty. I am ready to die out of nature, and be born again into this new yet unapproachable America I have found in the West" (E&L, 485). The unapproachable America stands here for that transcendental realm, always a reality, but also always an aspiration for us to realize, hindered as we are by the habits of worldly understanding. Do we make our truth, as the detranscendentalists would have us believe? No, we "do not make it": "I make! O no!" These truths are found; "I arrive there, and behold what was there already." But the paragraph is not yet over. Emerson then immediately quotes the moment in Sophocles' play *Antigone* when the heroine challenges her uncle Creon for breaking the "unwritten laws" in leaving one of her brothers unburied; Emerson often called these the "higher laws," one of which this essay is calling "transcendental equality." Note how Emerson immediately read these lines from *Antigone* as alluding to the source of our ethical actions:

> "Since neither now nor yesterday began
> These thoughts [the unwritten laws], which have been ever, nor yet can
> A man be found who their first entrance knew."

> If I have described life as a flux of moods [i.e., the seven lords of life], I must now add, that there is that in us which changes not, and which ranks all sensations and states of mind.

Recall here that similar moment in "Circles" when Emerson realizes, "Yet this incessant movement and progression which all things partake could never become sensible to us but by contrast to some principle of fixture or stability in the soul." Do not be distracted by this incessant movement, Emerson cautions us! The passage from "Experience" continues, imagining our consciousness as a scale of experience, the most stable [Reason] connecting us to God, the most chaotic [Understanding] trapped in the flux of experiential moods: "The consciousness in each man is a sliding scale, which identifies him now with the First Cause [Reason], and now with the flesh of his body [Understanding]; life above life, in infinite degrees. The [moral] sentiment from which it sprung determines the dignity of any deed, and the question ever is, not, what you have done or forborne, but, at whose command you have done or forborne it" (E&L, 485). If we act upon the flesh of the body, upon the Understanding, we remain in the flux of moods: our deeds lack dignity. But if we act upon "the First Cause" or Reason, we act as Antigone did, in accordance with the "unwritten laws." How do we know these laws? We know them when we transcend this "flux of moods" by way of "that in us which changes not," a "sentiment" by which Emerson means of course the "moral sentiment" that "command[s]" us. This use of *Antigone* (indeed, these very lines) is echoed in several other places by Emerson.[36] And so, in short, the start of the passage that Cavell used as evidence of Emerson's skepticism ends with yet another affirmation that we must act upon transcendental truths.

In addition to these breakthrough moments of transcendentalist affirmation in "Temperament" and "Reality," there is a final moment of affirmation in the final section of "Experience," the one section outside of the "moods." Yet Cavell treats this as an affirmation of "loss" (114) awaiting the justifications of Heidegger and Wittgenstein (116). This is, again, to ignore the structure of the essay. Emerson sets up this final moment of affirmation by means of a line break, and then an opening sentence that clarifies that he is done dramatizing the experience of the seven lords of life. That first sentence lists the seven lords exactly in the order of his prior sections: "these are threads on the loom of time, these are the lords of life" (490–91). Rather than dwelling any further upon them, Emerson instead describes in three paragraphs how he steps outside the interminable flux of moods. He describes this in the course of presenting three "fruits," for all three paragraphs are mounted in response to an imagined challenge: "Let who will ask, where is the fruit?" (491).

In the first paragraph, Emerson contends, "This is a fruit,—that I should not ask for a rash effect from meditations, counsels, and the hiving of truths" (*E&L*, 491). Effects, and causes too, are "deep and secular," that is, worldly; they "work on [i.e., develop over] periods in which mortal lifetime is lost." One fruit Emerson has, then, is to know that debates about what or who exactly causes this or that are ultimately fruitless. This is a fruit he has shared in other writings. In the 1841 essay "The Method of Nature," Emerson reacts similarly to an overemphasis upon cause and effect: "Away profane philosopher! seekest thou in nature the cause? . . . Known it will not be, but gladly beloved and enjoyed" (*E&L*, 119–20).

His second paragraph announces the second fruit: "Also, that hankering after an overt or practical effect seems to me an apostasy." His use of the word "apostasy" is important, for he thus suggests that to dwell on worldly effects is to renounce a religious belief in transcendental truths. We've heard this before from Emerson, of course: to trust only in the worldly faculty of Understanding is to forsake the transcendental faculty of Reason. Emerson, in the next sentences, announces he will not forsake Reason, even if it requires passing over a lot of "thinking" and "doing," terms that he consistently associates in these paragraphs with the Understanding. "In good earnest," he writes, "I am willing to spare [skip] this most unnecessary deal of doing." Give up all this doing and thinking, and suddenly "life wears to me a visionary face." He defends his turn to the transcendental: "People disparage knowing and the intellectual life," he writes, "and urge doing. I am very content with knowing, if only I could know."

The third paragraph continues to build on this distinction between "thinking," which is the work of the Understanding, and "knowing," which is the work of Reason. He contends that he can indeed know, and act on that knowledge. How can he know? Emerson makes a favorite move of his, one that he makes in a few other places.[37] He explains here that our ability to identify the limitations of thinking—our ability to be skeptics—is in fact proof of our Reason, proof of our ability to transcend those limitations. He puts it this way (the emphasis is his): "I know that the world I converse with in the city and in the farms, is not the world *I think*" (491). Thinking about (i.e., Understanding) the world is hopelessly different from acting in the world; Emerson remembers this, and how those who forget it tend to "foam at the mouth, . . . hate and deny" and so forth. But just *knowing* this "discrepancy"—the frustrating discrepancy between our thoughts about the world and the actual world—is proof that we can leave skepticism behind. Knowing this—standing above the epistemological problem, so to speak—enables us to shift away from these quandaries and the despair they breed, and instead focus on ethical knowledge and action: "far be from me the despair which prejudges the [transcendental] law by a paltry empiricism,—since there never was a right endeavor, but it succeeded" (*E&L*, 492). Right endeavors succeed; the transcendental law cannot be prejudged by empiricism. In the last sentences, Emerson reenacts the same kind of transcendental awakening he does throughout his oeuvre: "We dress our garden, eat our dinners, discuss the household with our wives, and these things make no impression, are forgotten next week; but in the solitude to which every man is always returning, he has a sanity and revelations, which in his passage into new worlds he will carry with him. Never mind the ridicule, never mind the defeat: up again, old heart!—it seems to say,—there is victory yet for all justice; and the true romance which the world exists to realize, will be the transformation of genius into practical power" (*E&L*, 492). We can lose hope in the welter of daily details "but"—and here Emerson once again makes a classic move—"in the solitude to which every man is always returning, he has a sanity and revelations, which in his passage into new worlds he will carry with him." Every person has these moments of insight. The final sentences are entirely assured that "there is victory yet for all justice" so long as we attend to our transcendental faculty—our "genius"—and act upon it. These are Emerson's transcendentalist politics: recognize I am part of God, recognize that others are, too, and transform that insight into practical power.

"Retranscendentalizing" Emerson

This essay has thus far made the case for reading Emerson as a transcendentalist on factual grounds. Set aside the bad interpretive habits of the detranscendentalists (it has argued), and the textual facts are that Emerson was committed to a political principle here called "transcendental equality." For many readers, hopefully, this is reason enough that Emerson's politics ought to be retranscendentalized. This is not to reject out of hand future "strong readings" that take their inspiration from the detranscendentalists; there can and should be strong readings of Emerson that simply reject these facts: that refuse to ask, "Am I getting Emerson right?" and willingly "lose

Emerson in the process." That is one kind of intellectual work. However, for those readers who do a different kind of intellectual work—work where "getting Emerson right" is the first and most important question—these facts are for you.

There's another case to be made for retranscendentalizing Emerson, though, and that is not as a matter of facts but as a matter of values. In the 1980s and 1990s, the detranscendentalists seemed to have concluded that the old transcendentalist Emerson—the Emerson of the 1960s and 1970s, whose master term was the Soul—was no longer valuable. More specifically, they seemed to have sensed that conventional wisdom had turned against this kind of transcendentalism as quaint and embarrassing. The detranscendentalists were probably right about this. Consider as representative of that conventional wisdom a 1984 article in the *New Yorker* by John Updike. "There [is] something dim at the center of [Emerson's] reputation," Updike pronounced, "something fatally faded about the works he has left us." Referring to Bloom and others who were just starting to invent a new detranscendentalist Emerson, Updike mocked this effort as obviously "embarrassed by the Neoplatonic, supernaturalist content of the early essays" and thus scrambling toward the journals and other obscure places for contrary evidence. Despite these desperate efforts, Updike decided, "there is awkwardness in Emerson's present reputation: what we like about him [his rare moments of apparent detranscendentalism] is not what is important, and what is important [his transcendentalism in his major writings] we do not much like."[38]

Faced with the conventional wisdom, then, that Emerson was "fatally faded," all four of the detranscendentalists under scrutiny in this essay seem to have concluded that the best way to save Emerson was not to defend his transcendentalism as philosophically interesting, but to detranscendentalize him: more specifically, to develop a set of interpretive tactics that allowed them to effectively invent a new Emerson to serve now as America's foremost Nietzschean (as Alan Levine shows in his essay) rather than as America's leftover transcendentalist.

In so doing, all four of the detranscendentalists made a value judgment. They concluded with Updike that a religious Emerson of any kind was basically worthless. For example, Cavell, who strenuously objected to Updike's condescending conclusions in a 1985 essay,[39] insisted in 1987 that Emerson never endorsed a transcendental foundation. How did Cavell know this? Because "no grown-up philosophy can secure the permanence of any [foundation]" ("Hope against Hope," 96–97). In 1995, Kateb similarly expressed the assumption that if Emerson is seriously religious, he is not worth our time. "It is a horror to say so," Kateb wrote, "but it may be rather wasteful to study Emerson unless one shares his religiousness" (*Emerson and Self-Reliance*, 65). To make Emerson valuable again, Kateb proposed, meant "provid[ing a] basis for reading him as a secular thinker, or near enough to secularism" (81). Introducing his 1985 collection of Emerson's essays, Bloom also suggested that a religious Emerson was useless; he began by emphatically stating that "Emerson is an experiential critic and essayist, and not a Transcendental philosopher."[40] And, while politely recognizing that there is, of course, a "human desire" to "expect . . . that there really was something waiting to be discovered, something 'inside' that no other creature possessed," Poirier also insisted what Emerson teaches us is to overcome that desire. It is "exactly at this point," Poirier explained, that "pragmatism reveals its tough-mindedness as against the tender-minded who want to bring into the story a necessary God and a necessary soul." For Poirier, "some version of Emerson" simply has to be one of the tough-minded, not the tender-minded: "A pragmatist, by which I mean some version of Emerson, might have to use the words 'God' or 'soul,' but would go on to suppose, as I do, that there was in fact really nothing outside to depend on and nothing inside either, nothing except the desire that there should be more than nothing" (*Renewal*, 14).[41] Religion, foundationalism, transcendentalism: for the four detranscendentalists, as for Updike and the other purveyors of conventional wisdom in the 1980s and 1990s, these had no value, except to the religious, the tender-minded, and children. A political theory for grown-ups—for the tough-minded, for the pragmatic—obviously must be emptied of talk of God and the soul: obviously must be secular.

That is not so obvious anymore. Today, many scholars are reconsidering this ideological secularism as one of the great blind spots of twentieth-century intellectual life. The motivation of many of these "postsecularists" is itself pragmatic, tough-minded even: secularists and believers must live in peace together, they argue, and so, as Jürgen Habermas (one of the most prominent converts to postsecularism) has written, it is "in the constitutional state's own interests to treat with care all cultural sources upon which the consciousness of norms and the solidarity of citizens draw."[42] Treating with care would mean, for one, not describing people of faith as tender-minded children.

But postsecularism doesn't mean treating people of faith with kid gloves, either. Emerson understood this probably better than any intellectual writing today, and he consequently offers our postsecular age at least two important lessons. First, he did not back down from arguments about matters of ultimate faith. Rather than attempt to wall off discussion of religion (as "wasteful," not "grown-up," "tender-minded"), Emerson brought up the subject again and again in his public speaking and writing. He had to. Unlike the detranscendentalists at the end the last century and most academics today, who still speak mainly to captive and like-minded audiences (that is, students and fellow academics), Emerson's primary, even entire, audience at his lectures was sectarian believers, paying customers who could just as easily take their business elsewhere. Yet, while he clearly understood he had to craft his message accordingly (as revealed in his approach to vocabulary, as discussed above), Emerson was hardly gentle in delivering it. In his abolitionist addresses, to take just one example from those discussed above, Emerson lambasted those who clung to the transient interests of sects and parties at the cost of permanent truths such as transcendental equality. His practice as a democratic intellectual is a valuable model for those of us ready to engage our fellow citizens both with Habermasian "care" and candor.

Second, Emerson also understood that equality will not be pursued seriously in the United States or in any democracy unless it is recognized as not just a political good but a religious truth.[43] He recognized that persuading sectarians and partisans to accept equality as a religious truth was the most important challenge he faced as a democratic intellectual. One place Emerson makes this observation is in an April 1840 journal entry. Modern commentators often cite the first sentence, but rarely the second: "In all my lectures, I have taught one doctrine, namely the infinitude of the private man. This the people accept readily enough, and even with loud commendation, as long as I call the lecture Art, or Politics, or Literature, or The Household; but the moment I call it Religion, they are shocked, though it be only the application of the same truth which they receive everywhere else, to a new class of facts" (*JMN*, 5:xvi). Emerson understood that transcendental equality—"the infinitude of the private man"—would be acceptable to people so long as he demonstrated its truth only in the realms of art, literature, and even politics. But, when he emphasized that the worth of the individual was not just an artistic or a political truth but a religious one, his audience knew it really mattered, and had to be dealt with, or absolutely resisted. Sometimes that resistance was violent, as Emerson and his abolitionist colleagues discovered, and as Gougeon describes, for example, in his account of the 1861 "Attempted Speech" (*AW*, xlix–l, 125–28). Emerson courageously persevered.

Liberal intellectuals, who might otherwise be Emerson's true heirs, have arguably done otherwise. Faced with similar sectarian resistance to treating equality or human rights as a religious truth, contemporary liberal theory has backed down, arguing that such rights are merely "political" not "comprehensive" (to recall John Rawls's exemplary statement in the early 1990s). Is political liberalism really the best that can be done? Are human rights not metaphysically true but "just how we do things," to paraphrase a famous argument of Richard Rorty's?[44] Given the miserable state of human rights globally, there seems to be at least room for serious debate here, and Emerson should be allowed to offer his potentially valuable, alternative approach. Rather than flatter our own biases by continuing to secularize Emerson's concepts into those of just another political liberal, we should instead retranscendentalize Emerson's politics, and recover his distinctive defense of transcendental equality: and we should do this not only as a matter of getting the facts right but also in pursuit of a potentially valuable political theory for today.

Notes

1. I am indebted to the exceptions: Albert J. von Frank, *The Trials of Anthony Burns: Freedom and Slavery in Emerson's Boston* (Cambridge: Harvard University Press, 1998), 96–106; Peter S. Field, *Ralph Waldo Emerson: The Making of a Democratic Intellectual* (Lanham, Md.: Rowman and Littlefield, 2002), 105–6; Len Gougeon, "Emerson and the Reinvention of Democracy: A Lesson for the Twenty-first Century," in *New Morning: Emerson in the Twenty-first Century*, ed. Arthur S. Lothstein and Michael Brodrick (Albany: State University of New York Press, 2008), 162–63; and Neal Dolan, *Emerson's Liberalism* (Madison: University of Wisconsin Press, 2009), 6–16, 77–100.

2. Lawrence Buell, "The Emerson Industry in the 1980s: A Survey of Trends and Achievements," *ESQ: A Journal of the American Renaissance* 30, no. 2 (1984): 117–36, hereafter cited parenthetically.

3. In Buell's summary (ibid., 117), the postwar consensus included the work of Ralph Rusk, Stephen Whicher, Vivian Hopkins, Charles Feidelson, Sherman Paul, and Jonathan Bishop. Bishop's 1964 book rightly asserts that the "soul" is Emerson's "master term" but construes it strictly as the "subject of the act of experiencing"; in contrast, this essay looks more broadly at the political significance of the soul for Emerson (see Bishop, *Emerson on the Soul* [London: Oxford University Press, 1964], 4, 8).

4. Richard Poirier, *The Renewal of Literature: Emersonian Reflections* (New Haven: Yale University Press, 1987), 192, hereafter cited parenthetically.

5. Michael Lopez, "De-Transcendentalizing Emerson," *ESQ* 34, no. 1–2 (1988): 77, hereafter cited parenthetically.

6. Stanley Cavell, "Hope against Hope" [Appendix A], *Conditions Handsome and Unhandsome: The Constitution of Emersonian Perfectionism* (Chicago: University of Chicago Press, 1990), 133, hereafter cited parenthetically; Stanley Cavell, *This New Yet Unapproachable America: Lectures after Emerson after Wittgenstein* (Albuquerque: Living Batch Press, 1989), 3–4. Cavell emphasizes Rorty's support in the latter.

7. Lopez still concludes Emerson was an early postmodernist ("De-Transcendentalizing Emerson," 83), but he relies less on Emerson's texts than the detranscendentalists' misleading interpretations of them as explored below. In contrast, Buell's later work has moved away from detranscendentalism, as shown below.

8. Harold Bloom, *Agon: Toward a Theory of Revisionism* (New York: Oxford University Press, 1982), 19–20, hereafter cited parenthetically.

9. George Kateb, *Emerson and Self-Reliance* (1995; new ed., Lanham, Md.: Rowman and Littlefield, 2002), 95, hereafter cited parenthetically.

10. "Transient" and "permanent" are the famous terms of fellow Transcendentalist Theodore Parker (see "A Discourse on the Transient and Permanent in Christianity," May 19, 1841, http://digitalcommons.unl.edu/etas/14/).

11. In addition to the newly published *Journals and Miscellaneous Notebooks*, they also capitalized on Joel Porte's *Emerson in His Journals* (Cambridge: Belknap Press of Harvard University Press, 1982).

12. Richard Poirier, *Poetry and Pragmatism* (Cambridge: Harvard University Press, 1992), 156–57, hereafter cited parenthetically.

13. Kenneth S. Sacks argues Emerson felt "the need, which he noted with disgust in his private journals, to temper his message [in public]" but does not provide an example (see introduction to *Emerson: Political Writings* [New York: Cambridge University Press, 2008], xii). Barbara Packer points out that "both letters and journals were regularly passed around among the circle of friends" and that they wrote there "with an exuberance their sense of decorum kept out of

their published works" (see *The Transcendentalists* [Athens: University of Georgia Press, 2007], 94, 95).

14. Robert D. Richardson, *Emerson: The Mind on Fire* (Berkeley and Los Angeles: University of California Press, 1995), 201.

15. Field, *Ralph Waldo Emerson*, 3, hereafter cited parenthetically. Nearly three decades ago, David Robinson also observed that "however eloquent the private Emerson could be in his journals, no writer ever needed an audience more" (see *Apostle of Culture: Emerson as Preacher and Lecturer* [Philadelphia: University of Pennsylvania Press, 1982], 4).

16. *The Correspondence of Emerson and Carlyle*, ed. Joseph Slater (New York: Columbia University Press, 1964), 185.

17. Matthew Arnold, "Emerson," in *The Complete Prose Works of Matthew Arnold*, ed. R. H. Super, 11 vols. (Ann Arbor: University of Michigan, 1960–1977), 10:172. On the essay's influence from the 1880s to the 1960s, see Sarah Ann Wider, *The Critical Reception of Emerson: Unsettling All Things* (Rochester, N.Y.: Camden House, 2000), 68–70. For more recent examples of otherwise supreme scholars of Emerson relying on this "confession" of Emerson's, note how Buell, in his 1984 article, justifies the detranscendentalists' method: that is, "a fruitful—indeed inevitable—mode of approaching a writer who characterized his sentences as infinitely repellent particles and conceded that his moods did not believe in each other" ("The Emerson Industry in the 1980s," 134). Similarly, in both his 1995 biography and a 2009 book, Richardson rationalizes his contention that "Emerson's essays are collections of great sentences on a single topic" by reference to this same letter to Carlyle. However, in the latter, Richardson recognizes that Emerson finally aimed to write not just sentences but whole masterpieces, as Goethe taught him (see Richardson, *Emerson: The Mind on Fire*, 202; and *First We Read, Then We Write: Emerson on the Creative Process* [Iowa City: University of Iowa Press, 2009], 54, 77–82).

18. Emerson's bardolatry had few rivals; "if the world were on trial," he wrote in 1864, "it is the perfect success of this one man that might justify such expenditure of geology, chemistry, fauna and flora, as the world was. . . . Intellect [that is, God] probably call[s] this planet, not Earth, but the Shakespear" (*JMN*, 15:56).

19. Richard Poirier, "An Approach to Unapproachable America," *Raritan* 26, no. 4 (2007): 13, 2.

20. Certainly, like all artists, Emerson was more formal in some works than others, but Emerson *did* care about form. Buell makes a judicious argument in this vein in "Reading Emerson for the Structures: The Coherence of the Essays," *Quarterly Journal of Speech* 58 (1972): 58–69.

21. See the description in Packer, *The Transcendentalists*, chap. 1:"Unitarian Beginnings"; and Field, who shows the unity of Emerson's religious liberalism

and democratic sympathies in his admiration of the Quakers' "notion of the 'Inner Light' . . . [as] a sufficient basis not only for a religion without ritual, but the foundation for a polity in which 'all men take part'" (*Ralph Waldo Emerson*, 113).

22. Lawrence Buell, *Emerson* (Cambridge: Belknap Press of Harvard University Press, 2003), 177.

23. Cf. Barbara Packer, "Signing Off: Religious Indifference in America," in *There before Us: Religion, Literature, and Culture from Emerson to Wendell Berry* (Grand Rapids, Mich.: Eerdmans, 2007), 1–22, which shows how Emerson became indifferent to church religions but misrepresents this as indifference to religion itself. On the contrary, as Kateb (ruefully) notes, Emerson was "ravenously religious" his entire career (*Emerson and Self-Reliance*, 65).

24. Cf. Cavell's "Aversive Thinking," which shows "The American Scholar" is an essay about thinking for yourself (103) by citing, "A nation of men will for the first time exist" and leaving out "inspired by the Divine Soul which also inspires all men."

25. See also Field's excellent discussion of this essay (*Ralph Waldo Emerson*, 225–26), the political importance of which has otherwise been neglected.

26. In the 1841 "Intellect," Emerson explains how this faculty is transcendental in being "receptive" to "what the great Soul showeth" (*E&L*, 420) but also imperfectly "constructive" of that received (*E&L*, 422).

27. On the limits of Emerson's skepticism, see Alan Levine's essay in this volume.

28. Rorty made this postmodern slogan famous in *Contingency, irony, and solidarity* (New York: Cambridge University Press, 1989), 3.

29. Wesley T. Mott, ed., "'October Satisfaction': Methodist Gilbert Haven Reviews Society and Solitude," *Emerson Society Papers* 19, no. 1 (spring 2008): 7.

30. David M. Robinson, "Margaret Fuller and the Transcendental Ethos: Woman in the Nineteenth Century, *PMLA* 97, no. 1 (January 1982): 85.

31. For other examples of Emerson equating self-reliance and God-reliance, see the introduction as well as the following. Defending self-reliance in 1833, Emerson writes, "mean, sneakingly mean, would be this philosophy . . . if *self* were used in the low sense; but I speak of the universal man" (see James Elliot Cabot, *A Memoir of Ralph Waldo Emerson*, 2 vols. [Boston: Houghton Mifflin, 1887], 1:179). In an 1839 letter counseling a young friend to turn to the light, Emerson explains, "That light I am sure is a greater selfreliance [*sic*],—a thing to be spoken solemnly of and waited for as not one thing but all things, as the uprise and revelation of God" (*Letters*, 2:212–13). And, in an 1854 address against the Fugitive Slave Law, Emerson insists that "we are in this world . . . to know . . . that divine sentiments, which are always soliciting us, are breathed into us from on high and area a counterbalance to an universe of suffering and crime,—that self-reliance, the height and perfection of man, is reliance on God" (*AW*, 84).

32. Like Poirier, Cavell secularizes Emerson's terminology in "Fate," translating "Intellect annuls Fate. So far as a man thinks, he is free" to mean "we have a say in what we mean, [and] our antagonism to fate . . . is a struggle with the language we emit" (see "Emerson, Coleridge, Kant," *Emerson's Transcendental Etudes,* ed. David Justin Hodge [Stanford: Stanford University Press, 2003], 72). One of the few scholars otherwise attuned to Emerson's transcendentalism, Neal Dolan comes to a hasty conclusion about "Fate," I believe, when he cites the twenty-seventh and twenty-eight paragraphs and concludes that while "throughout this study I have resisted the recent tendency to associate Emerson with Nietzsche . . . it is impossible to deny the proto-Nietzschean resonances in these passages" (*Emerson's Liberalism,* 285). There are such resonances there, but just a few paragraphs later Emerson turns instead to transcendentalism. So, Emerson does indeed "link existential freedom, moral volition, and scientific pragmatism as antidotes to determinism in 'Fate'" (288); but in the second part of "Fate," Emerson turns to "Thought" and "the moral sentiment"—the transcendental faculties—as the real antidotes.

33. In *E&L,* the eight sections are clearly separated by line breaks. In addition to Buell, "Reading," two other formal appreciations of "Experience" are Kyle Norwood, "'Somewhat Comes of It All': The Structure of Emerson's 'Experience,'" *ATQ* 9, no. 1 (March 1995); and Dolan, *Emerson's Liberalism,* 138–68. My reading differs from these in emphasizing Emerson's final shift out of the "flux of moods" (471–90) and into the ethics of transcendental equality (490–92). On Emerson's innovative use of form generally, see Robinson, *Apostle of Culture,* 158–74.

34. Stanley Cavell, "Finding as Founding: Taking Steps in Emerson's 'Experience,'" in *This New Yet Unapproachable America,* 77–118, 79. In his acknowledgments, Cavell thanks Poirier most of all (120–21). Poirier reads "Experience" similarly in his two books (*The Renewal of Literature,* 31–33; *Poetry and Pragmatism,* 47–75).

35. While Cavell sees Emerson overcoming Hume by anticipating Heidegger, several recent historians point instead to Emerson's reliance upon Scottish Common Sense (which gave him the idea of the moral sense) and neo-Platonism and German transcendental philosophy (which gave him the idea of Reason). See, for example, Packer, *The Transcendentalists,* 35–37; Field, *Ralph Waldo Emerson,* 53–54; and especially Dolan, *Emerson's Liberalism,* 53–65, who notes that all these sources "made similar turns inward to moral sentiment, moral intuition, and moral knowledge . . . to overcome . . . Cartesian epistemology" (65). Richardson writes that "to a great extent Emerson's life and work—indeed, transcendentalism itself—constitutes a refutation of Hume" (*Emerson: The Mind on Fire,* 31).

36. In his 1871 "Plutarch," Emerson describes these same three lines as "the memorable words of Antigone, in Sophocles, concerning the moral sentiment." See "Plutarch" (*CW,* 10:313). In the 1836 *Nature,* Emerson describes Antigone

as the rare "human being [who] has penetrated the vast masses of nature with an informing soul, and recognized itself in their harmony, that is, seized their law" (*E&L*, 36–37).

37. In addition to the moment in "Circles," cited above, where he shifts from the idealism of Berkeley to that of Jesus to that of nature itself (*E&L*, 407), see, for example, chapter 6. "Idealism," in the 1836 *Nature*, where Emerson notes "the frivolous make themselves merry with the Ideal theory [that is, "whether nature enjoy a substantial existence without, or is only in the apocalypse of the mind," but] God never jests" (*E&L*, 32).

38. John Updike, "Emersonianism," in *Odd Jobs: Essays and Criticism* (New York: Knopf, 1991), 149, 164–65. The essay began as a 1983 address and was republished in the June 4, 1984, *New Yorker*.

39. "Hope against Hope."

40. Harold Bloom, introduction to *Ralph Waldo Emerson* (New York: Chelsea House, 1985), 1.

41. Poirier alludes to William James's terminology from *The Varieties of Religious Experience* (1902) as if James read Emerson as one of the "tough-minded." But, as James Bense shows, James appreciated Emerson's tender-minded transcendentalism (see "At Odds with 'De-Transcendentalizing Emerson': The Case of William James," *New England Quarterly*, 79, no. 3 [September 2006]: 355–86).

42. Jürgen Habermas, "On the Relations between the Secular Liberal State and Religion," *Political Theologies: Public Religions in a Post-Secular World*," ed. Hent de Vries and Lawrence E. Sullivan (New York: Fordham University Press, 2006), 258.

43. On the value today of nonsectarian religious arguments for human rights, see my "Human Rights and a Post-Secular Religion of Humanity," *Journal of Human Rights* 9, no. 2 (April–June 2010): 127–42.

44. John Rawls, *Political Liberalism* (New York: Columbia University Press, 1993); Richard Rorty, "Human Rights, Rationality, and Sentimentality," *On Human Rights: The Oxford Amnesty Lectures, 1993*, ed. Stephen Shute and Susan Hurley (New York: Basic Books, 1993).

CHAPTER 10

Emerson's Transcendental Gaze and the "Disagreeable Particulars" of Slavery: Vision and the Costs of Idealism

Shannon L. Mariotti

EMERSON DESCRIBES IDEALISM as "a manner of looking at things."[1] In a fundamental way, he reminds us of the deep connection between thinking and seeing: the term "theory" derives from the Greek *theoria*, which means to look at, view, or see something but also to contemplate and think about it. For Emerson, transcendental idealism was primarily a mode of perception, and he signals the direction of his concentration of mental and moral efforts with overt visual metaphors. How Emerson looks at things, how he focuses his eye, or often his mind's eye, reflects what he values. But the nature of his gaze also communicates what he wants to move past, overcome, and progress beyond, what he often dismisses or denigrates as less significant, less real, less important. As we will see, his eye tends to travel in consistent patterns: taking one of his own terms, I call this visual practice *focal distancing*.[2] Because of the influence the thinker from Königsberg had on him, Emerson has been called "the American Kant."[3] But the movements of Emerson's eye chart his debt to this earlier transcendentalist in the most meaningful way: Emerson's gaze travels in a tran-scending motion, moving up and out, over and above. Scholars have noted that the "recanonization" of Emerson that began in the 1980s has also been characterized by a "detranscendentalizing" of his thought.[4] But when we study the nature of Emerson's gaze, we can see how fundamental and persistent transcendentalism was to his own constitutional makeup, his ways of being, perceiving, and thinking.[5] Transcendentalism persists as an important key to understanding Emerson in my reading, but is most evident as a visual practice that is continually enacted and encouraged to shape the self.[6]

Throughout his essays and lectures, Emerson dramatizes transitions from the material realm of particulars to the ideal realm of universals in terms of vision. Emerson's carefully cultivated mode of transcending perception, the practice of focal distancing, tends to devalue material particularity as superficial, to be looked past, progressed quickly beyond, whereas he associates experiences of illumination and inspiration with the realm of universal ideals that exists more distantly above and beyond. Emerson tries to encourage and enact a shift in perception, from the realm of material things to the realm of ideals, from particulars to universals, from appearance to reality, from epistemological doubt to ethical clarity, from confusion to illumination, from estrangement to inspiration, and from conformist passivity to self-reliant creative action where we try to project the world we imagine into reality. He sees the world as a hierarchically ordered dualism, where we are surrounded by the confused "buzz and din" of material particularity that surrounds us in the immediate foreground of our lives ("Transcendentalist," 214). Here lies conformity, alienation, and uncertainty, a realm of "disagreeable particulars" and "disagreeable appearances."[7] But there is another realm that exists beyond the material world: this is the ideal realm that, in Emerson's writings, variously goes under the name of Universal Spirit, Universal Mind, Consciousness, Genius, Aboriginal Self, Over-Soul, Spiritual Laws, Reason, or God. When we can see into this realm, we realize the superficiality of the material world, come into contact with a deeper reality, and are inspired to undertake the kind of nonconformist, independent, and truly individual action that embodies Emerson's practice of self-reliance.

In his early writings, Emerson tends to celebrate and confidently encourage the shifts in perception, this practice of focal-distancing, just described above. But 1844 marks a shift in his thought: this is the year that his son Waldo dies, which he writes about in "Experience," and it is also the year that Emerson begins to engage seriously with the antislavery movement. In "Experience," we can see the first moments where Emerson begins to question and measure the costs of his own idealist gaze.[8] But the most unsettling and sustained internal challenges to his theory and practice of transcendentalism come through his involvement with the abolitionist movement, from 1844 to 1855.⁹ As the editors to this volume outline in the introduction, this is Emerson's most intense period of reform. But it is not a period of clearly resolved convictions: as T. Gregory Garvey notes in his introduction to *The Emerson Dilemma,* Emerson comes to us not as the unproblematic "embodiment of transcendental romanticism," but instead "as a representative man struggling with conflicting philosophical and social commitments."¹⁰ These illuminating struggles are starkly apparent in six key antislavery addresses written between 1844 and 1855.¹¹ During these years, the theory and practice of transcendentalism that Emerson has previously celebrated, enacted, and encouraged is fractured. A sincere consideration of slavery antagonizes and challenges his practice of focal distancing and causes him to recognize the costs of his idealism, to realize he has trained himself *too well* to look past the particular things that he now finds himself staring at, focusing on more directly and lingeringly, that he now finds compelling and sometimes even inspiring. When he confronts slavery in a more immediate way, Emerson realizes that moments of illumination can also come through paying attention to particularity and recognizes the costs of his devaluation of the material world in a new way. In his antislavery addresses, in ways that are sometimes fleeting and inconsistent, he experiences scattered moments of illumination and inspiration by *attending* to particularity, instead of dismissing it as something to be quickly transcended, and also fleetingly appreciates the costs of looking past particulars, realizing that they, too, can powerfully stimulate ethical action.¹²

But despite these new experiences, Emerson cannot completely drop his habitual tendency to engage in focal distancing. Ultimately, the years from 1844 to 1855 mark a period of conflict rather than of resolution: Emerson's antislavery addresses seem to experiment with different ways of seeing in ways that are sometimes inconsistent and portray a theory that is more uncertain, in flux, in transition. His antislavery lectures enact his struggle to make sense of this antagonism between his transcendentalism and his abolitionism, but I argue that he is never able to effectively integrate the material world into his vision or into his thinking, to see a horizon that fully takes particularities into account in addition to universals. Despite now recognizing the costs of denigrating the materialist's attention to particulars and lauding the idealist's attention to universals, he still finds it difficult to switch gears and treat those particulars with the attention he now feels they deserve: he does so only inconsistently, often employing his old transcendental rhetoric in ways that do not seem to fit with his changed perspective. Though he comes closest in an 1851 address, he does not fully develop or articulate these new experiences into a reworked political vision that fully integrates both the particular and the universal.[13]

In this way, my essay explores a familiar theme in Emerson scholarship —vision—in a different way, using different texts, and with explicitly political questions in mind. At least since Sherman Paul's 1952 *Emerson's Angle of Vision*, scholars have analyzed the various ways that themes of vision, the eye, and sight figure into Emerson's thought.[14] But whereas others have explored Emerson's eye or his mode of vision as a general metaphor or trope, I analyze the micro-movements of his lines of sight as they play out on the page.[15] In addition, while other scholars have shown how Emerson's eye works to reconcile, synthesize, and unify disparate things into wholes, I highlight the moments of tension, rupture, and conflict in his visual practices.[16] My primary focus throughout, in contrast to previous scholarship, centers on the politics of focal distancing as a visual practice as worked out in the antislavery addresses: I analyze the consequences of what Emerson's eye focuses on as well as what it looks past, and show how his encounters with slavery also stimulate him to appreciate the costs of his idealist gaze, if only fleetingly, and to newly recognize the value of the particularity that his eye has habitually tended to pass over too quickly.

In the first section of this essay, I outline Emerson's transcendental gaze as it generally appears prior to 1844, charting his tendency to experience illumination and draw ethical inspiration from universal ideals. Then I analyze six abolitionist addresses written between 1844 and 1855, to show how Emerson's internal challenges to his idealism play out even in the space of each single address. I try to draw out the nascent lessons that Emerson seems to learn through these struggles and articulate the challenges they pose to his transcendental gaze and practice of focal distancing. The final part of this essay considers how we might draw from Emerson's thought to, borrowing Stanley Cavell's phrase, "amend" the "constitution" of Americans, to rework our own ways of thinking, seeing, and experiencing. Looking at the struggles Emerson enacts, analyzing not just what he *says*, but also what he *does* and what happens *to* him in these addresses, I draw out the larger lessons of the ethical and political importance of attending to material particularities as well as universal ideals.

Focal Distancing and Transcendental Illumination

In an 1842 lecture titled "The Transcendentalist," Emerson outlines his philosophy by distinguishing the materialist from the idealist and ranking them in hierarchical order. The materialist and the idealist perceive in very different ways. The materialist focuses on experience, the "data of the senses," facts, history, "on the force of circumstances and the animal wants of man" ("Transcendentalist," 201). In contrast, the idealist places his faith in consciousness and "perceives that the senses are not final" but are just "representations of things" (201). The idealist focuses "on the power of Thought and of Will, on inspiration, on miracle, on individual culture" (201). Emerson says, "In the order of thought, the materialist takes his departure from the external world, and esteems man as one product of that. The idealist takes his departure from his consciousness, and reckons the world as an appearance" (203). But for Emerson, these are not two equally valuable modes of perceiving and living in the world. Rather, he describes the move from materialism to idealism in terms of intellectual and spiritual progress. As he puts it, "These two modes of thinking are both natural, but the idealist contends that his way of thinking is in higher nature" (201).

Emerson depicts the tension that exists between the world of particulars and the world of universals as a battle: "The worst feature of this double consciousness is, that the two lives, of the understanding and of the soul, which we lead, really show very little relation to each other, never meet and measure each other: one prevails now, all buzz and din; and the other prevails then, all infinitude and paradise; and, with the progress of life, the two discover no greater disposition to reconcile themselves" (214).

These two modes of perception are like oil and water, it seems, and cannot be mixed or integrated into a holistic vision. Emerson sees materialism as a false kind of certainty and counsels an overcoming of this illusory reality, a move toward idealism. Speaking of the materialist, he says, "how easy it is to show him, that he also is a phantom walking and working amid phantoms, and that he need only ask a question or two beyond his daily questions, to find his solid universe growing dim and impalpable before his sense" (202). This less real materialist mode of perception is the part of the self that Emerson encourages his readers (and himself) to progress beyond. But Emerson also counsels patience in cultivating this mode of perception: communion with the ideal realm comes in inspiring flashes that remove him from the world of particularity, but these moments where we come into contact with what Emerson sees as the truer transcendental realm of reality are more fleeting than constant. At the same time, once one has had these flashes of illuminated vision, and has learned to think and see in this idealist mode, there is no going back. For Emerson, the path from materialism to idealism goes in only one direction: "Every materialist will be an idealist; but an idealist can never go backwards to being a materialist" (203).

The move Emerson counsels, from materialism to idealism, or from particulars to universals, pushes us from epistemological doubt and ethical uncertainty, to inspiration and illumination and ultimately also creative action where we remake the world. In this process, Emerson does denigrate the world of immediate particularity, but from his view this is all in service of the larger cause of projecting and realizing the better world that exists in what he variously calls Universal Spirit, Universal Mind, Consciousness, and Genius. Returning to "The Transcendentalist," Emerson notes: "From this transfer of the world into consciousness, this beholding of all things in the mind, follows easily [one's] whole ethics" (204). The Transcendentalist "believes in miracle, in the perpetual openness of the human mind to new influx of light and power; he believes in inspiration and of ecstasy" (204).

But we only get to this point by seeing the world in a certain way, by ceasing to be "near-sighted" and instead projecting our gaze toward more distant universal horizons where there is greater balance, harmony, and compensation.[17] The practice of focal distancing is foundational to Emerson's transcendentalism and underwrites his practice of self-reliance, as well as his theory of compensation and his faith in a "higher law." Otherwise, Emerson asks, "Of what use is genius, if the organ is too convex or too concave, and cannot find a focal distance within the actual horizon of human life?" ("Experience," 30). As we will see, Emerson depicts this horizon as something always in the distance, through images of the cosmos, stars, tranquil landscapes, clouds, and sky. When we engage in this practice of focal distancing and look past what Emerson deems to be superficial, unstable, trivial particular things, we perceive what he considers true reality, the higher law, the "beneficent Supreme power," the "affirmative principle," or the Universal Spirit that unites us across time and space. When we see this way, we can perceive that everything flows from the Universal Mind, that we are all "inlets" to this common universal spirit, that the universal spirit of the ages that flowed through Jesus, Moses, Socrates, and Prometheus flows through us as well.[18] Thus we can overcome our sense of estrangement and insecurity, trust in ourselves, and be confident, even heroic. When we engage in focal distancing, we can abandon ourselves to the inspired, ecstatic, antinomianism of the Universal Spirit and become authentically nonconformist and self-reliant.

Emerson's essays dramatize the practice of focal distancing where we try to perceive the higher law and recognize the more harmonious equilibrium that he thinks characterizes the universe as a whole.[19] Seen from this perspective, as Emerson says in "Compensation," "The world looks like a multiplication table or a mathematical equation, which, turn it how you will, balances itself."[20] When we rely on the "despotism of the senses," the world immediately surrounding us may seem "insane," yet that is only because we are not seeing it with what he elsewhere calls "strong eyes."[21] If we took the long view, the theory of compensation would be a solace, "a star in many dark hours and crooked passages in our journey that would not suffer us to lose our way" ("Compensation," 55). When we experience this illuminated mode of vision, we can appreciate that there is an affirmative, ameliorative, and beneficent force in the universe: "For every thing you have missed, you have gained something else; and for every thing you gain, you lose something" (58). Ultimately, Emerson concludes, "there is always some leveling circumstance that puts down the overbearing, the strong, the rich, the fortunate, substantially on the same ground with all others" (58). Throughout his writings, Emerson encourages and enacts this practice of focal distancing.

But his writings are also peppered with several descriptions of major transcendental moments where he fully achieves the kind of perception toward which he is always striving. These more rare, and more powerful, moments seem to keep Emerson going during the times he finds it harder to leave behind the material realm. The most famous description of one such episode comes in *Nature*. Here, Emerson describes leaving the material realm so fully that he becomes vision itself, at one with the Universal spirit: he has risen above the streets and the village and moved up and over into "blithe air" and uplifted into "infinite space," into the "tranquil landscape," the "distant line of the horizon": "I become a transparent eye-ball. I am nothing. I see all. The current of the Universal Being circulate through me; I am part or particle of God. . . . In the tranquil landscape, and especially in the distant line of the horizon, man beholds somewhat as beautiful as his own nature" (*Nature*, 10). Emerson describes this kind of experience as a moment when "the eye of Reason opens": for Emerson, "The best, the happiest moments of life, are these delicious awakenings of the higher powers" (30). If we cultivate this practice of focal distancing, we can experience this kind of illumination, and, as Emerson famously says, "build" our "own world" (45). We can become inspired, realize new possibilities, and "so shall we come to look at the world with new eyes" (44).

Emerson describes a similar kind of experience in "The Transcendentalist," the same essay where he describes the tension between materialist and idealist modes of perception as a double consciousness. Here, he also alludes to transcendent experiences when we are "but a thought of serenity and independence, an abode in the deep blue sky," yet also notes the fleeting nature of this experience: "Presently the clouds shut down again; yet we retain the belief that this petty web we weave will at last be overshot and reticulated with veins of the blue, and that the moments will characterize the days. Patience, then, is for us, is it not? Patience and still patience" ("Transcendentalist," 214). In this moment, he moves up and over, into a higher realm associated with the clouds and sky, passing into an affirmative infinite: with practice he hopes this kind of transcendent experience will characterize the days and we can pass "into some new infinitude."

Emerson also describes this kind of revelation in "Experience." The flash of illumination experienced here is also associated with this higher realm of universals, with a parting of the clouds, as it were, and a clear view into the distant horizon: "Do but observe the mode of our illumination. . . . I am at first apprised of my vicinity to a new and excellent region of life. By persisting to read or to think, this region gives further sign of itself, as it were, in flashes of light, in sudden discoveries of its profound beauty and repose, as if the clouds that covered it parted at intervals, and showed the approaching traveler the inland mountain, with the tranquil eternal meadows spread at their base, whereon flocks gaze, and shepherds pipe and dance" ("Experience," 41). These passages illustrate the kind of inspiration that Emerson is always striving to reach. But here, given the over-the-top pastoral imagery of pipers and meadows, he may also be lightly mocking the transcending tendencies that he will later, in the antislavery addresses, come to measure most soberly and critically.

As we have seen in all of these pre-1844 examples, given the dualistic hierarchy that structures his thought, Emerson thinks he must look past the material aspects of life, seeing them primarily as things to be overcome on the way toward envisioning the universal. In these pre-1844 years, he thus tends to denigrate, devalue, and even at times despise the realm of immediate material particularity and characterize it, as we have seen, in terms of a messy and confused "buzz and din," a "despotism of the senses." Unlike the materialist, he notes that the idealist "does not respect" particular things such as "sensible masses, Society, Government, social art, and luxury, every establishment, every mass" ("Transcendentalist," 203). Throughout these early writings, Emerson adds to this list of "disagreeable appearances" to be quickly looked past: men and women and their social life, poverty, labor, sleep, fear, fortune, tragedy, moaning women, and hard-eyed husbands, swine, spiders, snakes, pests, mad-houses, prisons, enemies, to name a few.[22] He contrasts "the inharmonious and trivial particulars" with the "musical perfection" of "the Ideal journeying always within us, the heaven without rent or seam" ("Experience," 41). In another passage that highlights the devalued status of particulars, he says, "Every roof is agreeable to the eye, until it is lifted; then we find tragedy and moaning women, and hard-eyed husbands, and deluges of lethe" ("Experience," 28). But when you see past such things and "conform your life to the pure idea in your mind," a "correspondent revolution in things" will occur, and the "temporary," "disagreeable appearances" will "vanish" and "be no more seen (*Nature*, 45). But, as we will see, Emerson comes to question and rethink this attitude toward particularity and his practice of focal distancing during his encounters with slavery as he enters the abolitionist movement.

The Antislavery Addresses, 1844–1855

In the 1844 "Address on the Emancipation of the Negroes in the British West Indies," Emerson presents himself to his audience not as an expert on slavery or an established abolitionist. He comes "from other studies, and without the smallest claim to be a special laborer in this work of humanity" ("Emancipation," 7). Prior to his lecture, he made, for the first time, a wide and extensive study of the history of slavery, digesting historical studies, legal reports, and records. Len Gougeon says this prompted a "conversion" experience that fundamentally changed Emerson's thinking and allied him with the reformers he had previously opposed. As Gougeon notes, "Emerson's extensive study of these sources had a profound effect on his understanding of slavery and changed forever his approach to the eradication of the evil."[23] The term "conversion" may imply too permanent, wholesale, and uncomplicated an attitude given how (as we will see) Emerson still struggles to make sense of his transcendental gaze in light of his new perspective on slavery. However, this whole address certainly marks a significant change and bears the imprint of Emerson's startling encounter with the details and specifics of the peculiar institution. Throughout the 1844–1855 period, as we will see, he will struggle to balance the particular things that he now recognizes as powerful and important, beginning with this address.

Here, Emerson focuses his mind's eye on the particulars of slavery and records them: he relates specific anecdotes that seem designed to bring unsettling images to his audience in a more immediate way. He tells of one slave ship trying to escape from the pursuit of a man-of-war: to lighten its load and speed its flight, the crew "flung five hundred slaves into the sea," like getting rid of so much ballast ("Emancipation," 13). He tells of a boy who "was set to strip and to flog his own mother to blood, for a small offence" and notes that there "is no end to the tragic anecdotes in the municipal records of the colonies" (13). More striking images: "iron collars were riveted on their necks with iron prongs ten inches long; capsicum pepper was rubbed in the eyes of the females" (13). As Emerson says:

> We sympathize very tenderly here with the poor aggrieved planter, of whom so many unpleasant things are said; but *if we saw* the whip applied to old men, to tender women; and, undeniably, though I shrink to say so,—pregnant women set in the treadmill for refusing to work, when, not they, but the eternal law of animal nature refused to work;—*if we saw* men's backs flayed with cowhides, and "hot rum poured on, superinduced with brine or pickle, rubbed in with a cornhusk, in the scorching heat of the sun";—*if we saw* the runaways hunted with blood-hounds into swamps and hills; and, in cases of passion, a planter throwing his negro into a copper of boiling cane-juice,—*if we saw these things with eyes,* we too should wince. They are not pleasant sights. The blood is moral: the blood is anti-slavery: it runs cold in the veins: the stomach rises with disgust and curses slavery. (10, emphasis added)

Emerson's struggle plays out in terms of vision here, and metaphors of sight figure strongly in this passage: Emerson repeats "if we saw" over and again and then notes the horror and sickness we would feel "if we saw these things with eyes." Emerson himself seems to be seeing in a new way, no longer employing an abstracting, distancing, transcending gaze. Instead his eye is lingering on the immediate, particular phenomena that he would normally try to look past. The effect of newly focusing on these unpleasant and disgusting "sights" is clear: Emerson says, "Conscience rolled on its pillow, and could not sleep" ("Emancipation," 9).

As his address turns from the West Indies to the United States, Emerson describes a culture that is "cheap," dominated by a "shopkeeping civility" that finds it more convenient to turn a blind eye to the unpleasant facts of slavery.[24] But this tendency to look away, to look past, can be a problem, as Emerson now appreciates. He does not excuse himself from blame and complicity here, using the term "we," and even seems to be criticizing his own tendency to dismiss particular things, questioning his own previous practice of focal distancing: "We found it very convenient to keep [the slaves] at work, since, by the aid of a little whipping, we could get their work for nothing but their board and the cost of whips. What if it cost a few unpleasant scenes on the coast of Africa? That was a great way off; and the sense could be endured by some sturdy, unscrupulous fellows, who could go for high wages and bring us the men, *and need not trouble our ears with the disagreeable particulars.* If any mention was made of homicide, madness, adultery, and intolerable tortures, we would let the church-bells ring louder, the church organ swell its peal, and drown the hideous sound. The sugar they raised was excellent: nobody tasted blood in it" ("Emancipation," 20, emphasis added). Emerson introduces the term "disagreeable particulars" here, but now it seems that these are phenomena he can no longer look past. He startles us—as he himself was apparently startled—by the powerful image of sugar that ought to be red given its mode of production, that should have the metallic taste of blood. Try as he might, he could not banish these disturbing images from his mind: he speaks of making an effort to keep his imagination filled with more agreeable images, but again and again, he sees these disagreeable particulars. Emerson finds his thoughts drawn back to specific images of slavery, almost against his will: "Whilst I have meditated in my solitary walks on the magnanimity of the English Bench and Senate . . . I have found myself oppressed by other thoughts. . . . *I could not keep my imagination on those agreeable figures, for other images that intruded on me.* . . . No: I see other pictures—of mean men: I see very poor, very ill-clothed, very ignorant men, not surrounded by happy friends,—to be plain,—poor black men of obscure employment as mariners, cooks, or stewards, in ships, yet citizens of this Commonwealth of Massachusetts,—

freeborn as we,—whom the slave-laws of the States of South Carolina, Georgia, and Louisiana, have arrested in the vessels in which they visited those ports" ("Emancipation," 23, emphasis added). In a novel departure from his previous way of seeing, Emerson, at this point in the address, shows how he was inspired to ethical action through these considerations of particular things.[25] Prior to 1844, Emerson associates ethical inspiration and illumination with universal ideals, but here he seems to recognize the value of focusing directly upon particular experiences of pain and suffering. In this address, particular images—pregnant women, runaways, bloodied bodies—stir him, inspire him, and motivate his abolitionism.

But then the address shifts from the particular to the universal, as was his earlier pattern prior to 1844. The lecture ends with an affirmation and appeal to the illumination and inspiration that he had tended to associate with focusing beyond the immediate here-and-now, focusing on universals: "Out it would come, the God's truth, out it came, like a bolt from a cloud, for all the mumbling of the lawyers. One feels very sensibly in all this history that a great heart and soul are behind there, superior to any man, and making use of each, in turn, and infinitely attractive to every person according to the degree of reason in his own mind" ("Emancipation," 27). He says that nature will balance everything out: if men "are rude and foolish, down they must go" (31): "The genius of the Saxon race, friendly to liberty; the enterprise, the very muscular vigor of this nature, are inconsistent with slavery. The Intellect, *with blazing eye,* looking through history from the beginning onward, *gazes on this blot and it disappears.* The sentiment of Right, once very low and indistinct, but ever more articulate, because it is the voice of the Universe, pronounces Freedom" ("Emancipation," 33, emphasis added). In this final section, Emerson seems to revert to his old habit of sharply separating the material from the ideal, and ordering them hierarchically so that idealist universals are again associated with the moments of inspiration. He employs rhetoric we are more familiar with from his earlier writings, invoking clouds, the Universe, the soul, and abstract concepts of Freedom and Right. There is also a reference to the practice of focal distancing, in the image of the Intellect, the Universe, and the strong blazing eye that employ a distancing, abstracting gaze, moving up and over the immediate "blot" of slavery, which from this perspective seems like a temporary blip on the radar screen. Even though Emerson has, at least fleetingly in these addresses, recognized the costs of his idealist gaze and appreciated the value of what he has previously looked past, he picks up his more traditional transcendental language again at the end of this lecture. He does not revise or rework his mode of vision to account for the new experience of illuminating particularity that he captures at the start of the address. But his reaffirmation, in this context, now seems discordant: after all the images he has given us, one does *not* feel very sensibly that there is an affirmative spirit behind all action and his conclusion seems again to look past these particulars without fully taking them into account, drawing on their power, or integrating them into his vision in a way that might allow him to see the realities of slavery and at the same time see past them.

Speaking the following year in his 1845 "Address on the Anniversary of West Indian Emancipation," Emerson seems similarly motivated and stirred by particular images. In the beginning of the address, Emerson worries that the men of New England acquiesce to slavery, and he gives us a startling image of "rowdy boys" and "rowdy men" who "sing Jim Crow and jump Jim Crow in the streets and taverns," shouting the word *"Niggers!"* in the "bar-rooms, in shops, in streets, in kitchens, at musters, and at cattle-shows" in a way that "blows away with a jeer all the efforts of philanthropy, all the expostulations of pity" ("Anniversary," 36). But this address in general treats particulars more briefly and quickly moves past them to universals in a way that is different from the 1844 address just discussed, perhaps because Emerson recognized how dwelling so much on particulars undercut the power of his concluding affirmations. In any case, the "Anniversary" address is a kind of return to traditional form for Emerson after the more radical departure of the 1844 "Emancipation" address discussed above.

After this short opening discussion of particulars, Emerson shifts the focus away from this more immediate realm and begins "looking forward" to a time when emancipation will also be celebrated in America (35). But as we will see, Emerson now seems to find this shift especially difficult. His language echoes other moments where he also seems to have difficulty pulling himself away from the immediate world around him to project the world he imagines in the realm of the Universal. There are instances of this struggle to move past the particular in earlier essays, but he invokes a mantra of patience with even more pathos in the years after 1844.

In the "Anniversary" lecture, for example, he says: "But no, it is not so; the Universe is not bankrupt: still stands the old heart firm in its seat, and knows that, come what will, the right is and shall be. Justice is for ever and ever" (36). He seems to counsel patience out of a sense that there is little else he can do: "The only reply, then, to this poor skeptical ribaldry is the affirming heart. The sentiment of right . . . fights against this damnable atheism" (37). There is a real sense of uncertainty here, a kind of lamenting hopefulness, and it seems as though Emerson is trying to convince himself of the truthfulness of what he says. He speaks similar words in the haunting final passage from "Experience," also invoking the need for patience, the affirming heart, and a faith in justice: "Patience and patience. We shall win at last. . . . Never mind the ridicule, never mind the defeat: up again, old heart!—it seems to say,—there is victory yet for all justice; and the true romance which the world exists to realize, will be the transformation of genius into practical power" ("Experience," 49). These words are spoken with hope, but without great confidence.

The different tone of these two post-1844 invocations of "patience" is even starker when compared with two similar examples from the pre-1844 writings. Emerson calls for patience in "The American Scholar," where he speaks to "young men of promise" who are disgusted, uninspired, and even ready to commit suicide. "What is the remedy?" he asks, answering that the problem has to do with perception and perspective, with a failure to practice focal distancing: "They did not yet see, and thousands of men . . . do not yet see, that if a single man plant himself indomitably upon his instincts, and there abide, the huge world will come round to him. Patience—patience;—with the shades of all the great and good for company; and for solace, the perspective of your own infinite life" ("American Scholar," 69).[26] Even though he speaks to those in despair, there is somehow still an air of sureness, certainty, and optimism in his counsel and a sense that illumination and inspiration will indeed come from looking past particulars and taking up the practice of focal distancing. Emerson's invocation of patience in "The Transcendentalist" has the same sense of assurance, as though he is asking a question for the sake of form but is quite confident of the answer: "Patience, then, is for us, is it not? Patience and still patience" (Transcendentalist," 214). In these two pre-1844 examples, Emerson speaks as though *he* is certain, even if his audience is not. But in the post-1844 address, he seems uncertain as well.

The change in tone that we see especially in the post-1844 antislavery addresses seems rooted in Emerson's nascent recognition of the power and importance of material particularities and in his new sense that they also might function as inspiring motivations to realize a better world. But fully following through on this line of thought would mean rethinking his practice of focal distancing and reshaping his transcendentalism, which he does not ultimately do. Instead, in these lectures, we see Emerson struggling with the hierarchical dualistic attitude toward idealism and materialism that previously was unproblematic for him. The immediate material realities that he explores have clearly struck him deeply and can also inspire action—and Emerson presumably recognizes their power because he shares these specific images with his reader. But in the 1845 "Anniversary" address, too, there is still a jarring jump from the disruptive particulars of slavery to a vision of a more harmonious future. Despite his new experiences, Emerson reverts to old form and, in his affirmation, once again advocates focal distancing and moving beyond the particulars without fully marshaling their power or truly incorporating them into his affirmative vision.

This reversion to form is even more holistic in "Antislavery Remarks at Worcester," an informal talk Emerson gave at an antislavery meeting in Massachusetts in 1849. Whereas the other addresses I analyze in this essay all bear some marks of Emerson's internal struggle with his transcendental gaze given the "disagreeable particulars" of slavery, the 1849 speech is notable and anomalous for its silence on the matter. The address is deeply optimistic, even explicitly celebratory, and from the beginning gives evidence of Emerson's faith that slavery will be inevitably overcome through an unfolding of the higher law. But, as we might expect given its almost complete reversion to pre-1844 form, the speech also does not mention any particular images of slavery and does not engage the realities of the institution in any immediate ways. The speech was also given extempore and delivered without prior preparation: Emerson was called on to speak at an August meeting of the Massachusetts Anti-Slavery Society and, feeling it his duty, obliged by giving a few words. There is no extant manuscript of the speech, which is unsurprising if it was given spontaneously, but the *Liberator* printed the text of Emerson's short speech.[27] But this speech is especially illuminating *because* of its silences regarding "disagreeable particularity" and because Emerson explicitly relies on habit in these off-the-cuff remarks. The address shows how deeply engrained Emerson's practice of focal distancing was, how habitual it was to his own constitution, but it also works as a foil to highlight how unsettled these more traditional transcendental habits were in addresses where Emerson addressed slavery in a more conscious and deliberate way. Because of its anomalies, the "Worcester" speech highlights the complex nature of the process of struggle, revising, and reenvisioning that Emerson was going through in the other deliberately crafted addresses that I analyze.

In his spontaneous 1849 remarks, Emerson's eye is wholly focused on the universal realm. He begins by saying we should greet "the great evil of slavery" with a tone "not of fear but of congratulation" and speaks of "heartfelt joy" ("Worcester," 47). His optimism and joy are rooted in his faith in the ultimate victory of the abolitionist cause, given the power of the higher law: "I think the scope left for human exertion, for individual talent to be very small. I believe that we are to congratulate ourselves, as rational beings, that we are under the control of higher laws than any human will. We may congratulate ourselves on the impotence of the human will. We are to rejoice in the march of events, in the sequence of the centuries, the progress of the great and universal human, and shall I not say, divine, genius, which overpowers all our vices as well as our virtues, and turns our vices to the general benefit" (47). He describes a sense of cosmic balance when we take the correct perspective and refers to the theory of compensation: "The course of history is one everywhere. It is a constant progress of amelioration" (48). He speaks of being able "see the great and beautiful laws to which you and I are all subject" and which he should "be glad to unfold as they should be." But though he describes the overcoming of slavery as inevitable, he certainly doesn't advocate that his audience rest on their laurels; instead he speaks of the need for action: "it is the order of Providence that we should conspire heartily in this work" (49).

Emerson does not question, challenge, or struggle against his transcendentalism in this speech or reckon the costs of his practice of focal distancing, as he does in other speeches from this period. But there is also no explicit imagery of slavery and no engagement with immediate material particulars in this speech. Slavery is only spoken of abstractly, in general terms, and perceived from a distance. The "Worcester" address is an anomaly for this period, but it also acts as an illuminating foil that reveals how the more immediate engagements with material particularity that we see in other addresses work to unsettle and disrupt this habitual transcendental gaze: such moments are absent from these remarks, and thus there is no evidence of internal tension. Emerson himself even seemed to recognize that this speech relies on old habits, unsurprisingly since it was given spontaneously. As he says near the beginning of the speech, "I am accustomed to consider more the men than the abolitionists. It is perhaps the vice of my habit of speculation, that I am prone rather to consider the history of the race, the genius and energy of any nation, than to insist very much upon individual action" (47). Here, Emerson speaks of his practice of focal distancing, his transcendental mode of perception that takes in universals and ideals—here, men in general as opposed to particular kinds of men, the race in general as opposed to particular contexts—as both a "habit," something he is "prone" to, and also, as he will increasingly appreciate in the 1844–1855 period, perhaps also a "vice" that itself has costs. But those are not the struggles or challenges he dwells on or works through in this speech.

We can mark a sharp departure from the traditional form of the "Worcester" remarks in the next two addresses I discuss, however, where Emerson does confront "disagreeable particularity" in the most direct and personal way. In the years after the 1849 address, things changed dramatically in Massachusetts. Slavery came nearer to Concord in the form of the Fugitive Slave Law, which obligated every citizen to uphold the institution of slavery: on September 18, 1850, the Fugitive Slave Law was passed, requiring free states to capture and return escaped slaves, in effect making every citizen a potential slave catcher. The Fugitive Slave Law represents an event in Emerson's life that poses further grave challenges to his practice of focal distancing.

In the 1851 "Address to the Citizens of Concord," Emerson's disgust and anger is palpable, but the circumstances of his outrage also play out in terms of a struggle against his own habitual practice of focal-distancing.[28] Emerson's tendency to try to see past the world immediately around him certainly bolstered his faith, upon joining the abolitionist movement, that slavery would be overcome. But given his repeated discussions of this theme, it also seems like his tendency to look past the events in the immediate foreground of life slowed his engagement with the antislavery movement. Emerson himself seems to recognize how he was most compelled to act when slavery came to his own doorstep and made everyone in Massachusetts a potential slave catcher. At that point, slavery forced itself into his line of sight in the most personal and immediate way he had so far encountered. In the aftermath of the passage of the Fugitive Slave Law, he is powerfully struck by the conditions that surround him and realizes that he can no longer look past this to seek out more harmonious sights. Emerson's sense of unease, anxiety, and agitation is strong: "We do not breathe well. There is infamy in the air. I have a *new experience.* I wake in the morning with a painful sensation, which I carry about all day, and which, when traced home, is the odious remembrance of the ignominy which has fallen on Massachusetts. . . . I have lived all my life in this State, and never had an experience of personal inconvenience from the laws, until now. *They never came near to my discomfort before"* ("Concord," 53, emphasis added). But now, in the same departure from traditional form that we see especially in the 1844 address, Emerson describes a moment of illumination, an experience of revelatory vision that is stimulated by the particular and immediate experiences of life in Massachusetts after the enactment of Fugitive Slave Law: "One intellectual benefit we owe to the late disgraces. The crisis has the *illuminating power* of a sheet of lightening at midnight. It *showed* truth. . . . It *showed* the slightness and unreliableness of our social fabric. . . . It *showed* the shallowness of leaders; the divergence of parties from their alleged grounds; *showed* that men would not stick to what they had said: that the resolutions of public bodies, or the pledges never so often given and put on record of public men, will not bind them" (5, emphasis added). This is a moment of clear vision that illuminates Truth, but in a break with traditional form, it has come to Emerson from keeping his focus trained on what lies "near" instead of trying to see past this immediacy.

In other ways, throughout this lecture, the usual (pre-1844) order of Emerson's world seems to be reversed, turned upside down. First, he now expresses doubts about whether turning inward, to access what he sometimes called the "Aboriginal Self" or the "Universal Mind," will lead us to the same kind of illuminating truth that he has just experienced from attending to the immediate realities that surround him in the foreground of his life: "I thought that every time a man goes back to his own thoughts, these angels receive him, talk with him, and that, in the best hours, he is uplifted in virtue of this essence, into a peace and power which the material world cannot give: that these moments counterbalance the years of drudgery . . . I thought it was this fair mystery, whose foundations are hidden in eternity, which made the basis of human society, and of law" ("Concord,"

58). The language here is familiar: the association of clarity, justice, and virtue with the "higher" realm into which we can be "uplifted." Peace and power are things he thought the "material world cannot give." But now these are things he comes to doubt, and he finds himself reassessing the power of the material world. Whereas earlier he has described the material realm in terms of the "despotism of the senses" and characterized it as a superficial and trivial "buzz and din" that we can move beyond in our best hours, here he seems to appreciate that some valuable power may derive from the material realm itself.

Second, the polarity of his discussion of compensation is reversed in this lecture. Emerson's usual system turns upside down, and every positive thing is compensated for by a negative: "Africa has its malformation; England has its Ireland; Germany its hatred of classes; France its love of gunpowder; Italy, its Pope; and America, the most prosperous country in the universe, has the greatest calamity in the universe, negro slavery" ("Concord," 57). And even though the crisis of the Fugitive Slave Law has spurred some intellectual progress and "has been like a university to the entire people," turning "every dinner table into a debating club" and making "every citizen a student of natural law," even this modest light was also eventually blacked out: "But the Nemesis works underneath again. It is a power that makes noonday dark, and draws us on to our undoing" ("Concord," 64). In this address, Emerson uses some of his traditional formulas and metaphors, but in ways that signal a change in his mode of perception.

In the affirmation Emerson tends to give toward the end of his lectures, there is also a difference. In this 1851 address, in fact, we see perhaps Emerson's most effective integration of particulars *and* universals. His recent "new experiences" and his changed perspective on particularity seem to have an effect on how he tries to rally his audience. There is less of a chasm between his depiction of material realities and the ideal he imagines, which seems a more effective motivational tool because it does not jar the reader from a pessimistic material world to a harmonious universal in a way that seems artificial and hollow. In this lecture, the power he ascribes to the material world seems more integrated into his vision of the universal. We get a few passages of his more traditional rhetoric: "Nothing is impracticable to this nation, which it shall set itself to do. . . . Their power of territory seconded by a genius equal to every work. . . . We are on the brink of more wonders" (69). But, in general, Emerson here seems to set more realistic goals and connects point A to point B, showing his audience how they can respond to immediate conditions to actively foster the universal ideals he hopes to realize. Part of what gives his other antislavery addresses a disjointed and jarring quality is the chasm between the immediate particular images Emerson gives his audience of where they currently are versus the universal images of where they ideally should be, and hopefully one day will be. But the 1851 address does not have that disconnected quality. In answer to the question, "What shall we do?" he says: "First abrogate this law; then proceed to confine slavery to the slave states, and help them effectually to make an end of it" (68). But what of slavery as a whole? "She got Texas, and now will have Cuba, and means to keep her majority. The experience of the past gives us no encouragement to lie by" (69). Ultimately, his answer to the question, "What must we do?" is more humble: keep the "little state" of Massachusetts pure: "One thing is plain, we cannot answer for the Union, but we must keep Massachusetts true. It is of unspeakable importance that she play her honest part. She must follow no vicious examples" (70). At the same time, when he says "Massachusetts" here, he seems to mean the idea of America. We must keep the little state that was the site of the Battle of Lexington and Concord, the cradle of the American Revolution, the exemplar of all that is best in America, pure: "And Massachusetts is little, but, if true to itself, can be the brain that turns around the behemoth. I say Massachusetts, but I mean Massachusetts in all the quarters of her dispersion; Massachusetts, as she is the mother of all New England states, and as she sees her progeny scattered over the face of the land, in the farthest south and in the uttermost west" (70). For "Massachusetts is as strong as the universe" (71). Even though "Massachusetts" here functions as a kind of placeholder for the universal realm, the fact that Emerson chooses something local and "near" highlights how the power of particularity works in this lecture, in small ways, to effectively reshape his attitude toward the practice of focal distancing that he unequivocally celebrated in earlier years. This address is the best example of a reworked mode of perception that takes both immediate material particulars and more distant universal ideals into account to look toward a future horizon in a less hierarchical and less dualistic way.

Emerson seems to continue to build on these lessons regarding particularity and revises his mode of perception along these lines in his 1854 "Fugitive Slave Law" lecture. In this address, he recognizes that illumination and inspiration can also stem from immediate material particularity and employs a gaze that takes these particularities into account while still connecting them with universal ideals. This lecture followed hot on the heels of the Kansas-Nebraska Act, which created new territories for slave states by nullifying the Missouri Compromise, which had excluded slavery from Louisiana Purchase territories. Addressing this piece of legislation, Emerson again begins by emphasizing that, until recently, he had never personally suffered "any known inconvenience from American slavery": "I never saw it; never heard the whip; I never felt the check on my free speech and action; until the other day when Mr. Webster by his personal influence brought the Fugitive Slave law on the country ("Fugitive," 74). On the one hand, this might be a rhetorical strategy to build an alliance with his audience and signal that, however they may have acted in the past, the Fugitive Slave Law has changed things. But on the other hand, Emerson's repeated use of this language seems to signal a recognition that his own practice of focal distancing also tended to separate him from the institution of slavery in ways he now finds problematic and troubling. He seems to reflect critically on his own privileged distance from slavery: "I said I had never in my life suffered before from the slave institution. It was like slavery in Africa or in Japan for me. There was a fugitive slave law, but it had become, or was fast becoming, a dead letter; and, by the genius and laws of Massachusetts inoperative. The new Bill made it operative; required me to hunt slaves; and it found citizens in Massachusetts willing to act as judges and captors" (80). Again, we see how this struggle between his abolitionism and his transcendentalism plays out in terms of vision, though here Emerson speaks of it in explicitly nonliteral terms. He describes slavery as something that "cuts out the moral eyes" and clouds our "moral perception" (85). As Emerson says, "I know that when *seen near, and in detail,* slavery is disheartening" (85, emphasis added. He also issues a call to action based on this experience of having his vision illuminated by something "near" as opposed to something distant. He says: "Nature is not so helpless but it can rid itself at last of every wrong. . . . But the spasms of nature are centuries and ages and will tax the faith of short-lived men. Slowly, slowly, the avenger comes, but comes surely" (85). Hope and faith are not enough, Emerson realizes. We must act; we must cooperate with the Divine Providence that is still at work: "I hope we have come to the end of our unbelief, have come to a belief that there is a Divine Providence in the world which will not save us but through our own cooperation" (89). He persists in thinking that "the inconsistency of slavery with the principles on which the world is built guarantees its downfall," but the situation—which he characterizes as one where we are "disenchanted"—also "seems to demand of us more than mere hoping" (87). Now, instead of devaluing or dismissing what lies in the immediate foreground and drawing inspiration and illumination from the practice of focal distancing, Emerson's call to action is based on the illumination that has come from focusing on this disagreeable particular: "It seemed, as the Turks say, "Fate makes that a man should not believe his own eyes" (89). "But," as he notes, "the Fugitive Slave Law did much to unglue the eyes of men, and now the Nebraska Bill leaves us staring" (89). The eyes of men are unglued from the horizon in the distance and gaze directly on the disruptive, disagreeable particular in ways that now have greater value for Emerson.

By the time of his 1855 "Lecture on Slavery," Emerson's audience had also noticed that something was different. One commentator at the time observed that "Mr. Emerson has given a fine anti-slavery lecture" but noted that it was "full of pith and point" and did not contain "anything of the old Transcendentalism. No more feeling in the skies after the absolute, but sharp observations on human life and manners. Never was such a change, apparently, as from the Emerson of '45 to the Emerson of '55." The commentator notes that Emerson has left the "upper sphere."[29] Though this commentator is right to note that Emerson's addresses have undergone a change related to a greater attention to particularity that began with the 1844 address, as we have seen, Emerson never really leaves the "upper sphere" entirely. During this period, he is instead struggling to renegotiate how he thinks about, sees, and contemplates particularity. This revised mode of perception that attends more seriously to the immediate material realm seems most fully developed in the 1851 address, though we also see it effectively at work in the 1854 address. But as we will see in the discussion below, in contrast to the commentator's sense of things, by the end of the 1855 address, the "upper sphere" figures as prominently in Emerson's thought as ever: he picks up his old habit of focal distancing, leaving behind the new attitude toward particularity that he has been developing, if inconsistently, since the 1844 address.

In this 1855 address, Emerson castigates American citizens for being too focused on their immediate material self-interests, commercial investments, trade concerns, as well as personal comforts—some even underwritten by slavery—to see the universal injustice of this institution. In this address, the *kinds* of material particularity that Emerson identifies are different, having to do not with slavery itself but with men's complicity with and acquiesce to slavery. To overcome this, however, he still issues a call to Americans to engage in the practice of focal distancing, to see past the immediate material realm and focus their gaze on the Universal realm that he thinks would stir them to abolitionism. But in this address, Emerson throws the baby out with the bathwater, so to speak: in his rage against those who acquiesce to slavery out of a selfish pursuit of material interests, he reverts to his strong bias against *all* particularity, without acknowledging the other ways that things in the realm of immediate particularity might also inspire, motivate, and encourage abolitionist activity, as he himself has recognized at other moments. Some particulars, as Emerson appreciates especially in the 1844 address, help one see how slavery is wrong. But in the 1855 address, Emerson reverts to form by reviving the dualistic hierarchical view that tends to denigrate the realm of particularity generally.

Emerson begins this address in a more familiar way that echoes the previous addresses we've just analyzed, by remarking that slavery was difficult to bear when it was distant, "three hundred, five hundred, a thousand miles off" but impossibly "disheartening" when it became our "present grief," when it came home to Concord and Massachusetts ("Slavery," 92): "But to find it here in our sunlight, here in the heart of Puritan traditions in an intellectual country, in the land of schools, of sabbaths and sermons, under the shadow of the White Hills, of Katahdin, and Hoosac; *under the eye* of the most ingenious, industrious, and self-helping men in the world,—staggers our faith in progress" (93, emphasis added). As in his earlier antislavery addresses, Emerson struggles with the nearness and immediacy of the institution. Slavery is presented as something that blocks out the light and makes it hard for us to look past it: slavery and war as "shadows in the vast picture of Providence" (92). Slavery has made it dark in America, like the Dark Ages: "The Dark Ages did not know they were dark; and what if it should turn out, that our material civilization has no sun, but only ghastly gas-lights?" (93). Again, he finds it difficult to turn his eye away from these immediate images of slavery that are deeply unsettling. He finds it hard to engage in the practice of focal distancing now, difficult to look past the immediate foreground of his life. This, so far, is consistent with tendencies in the other post-1844 addresses: Emerson is struggling to come to grips with powerful conditions that seem anything but trivial or superficial, and are not easily transcended.

But then there is a shift. His tone becomes critical, and he calls for Americans to "disdain" the immediate material realm—here populated by different things—and converse with "eternity." Emerson begins to blame Americans for their "skepticism" and "dreary superficiality," for being focused primarily on property, trade, and money in ways that make them unable to see the universal wrong of slavery (96):

> Go into the festooned and tempered brilliance of the drawing rooms, and see the fortunate youth of both sexes, the flower of our society, for whom every favor, every accomplishment, every facility has been secured. Will you find genius and courage expanding those fair and manly forms? Or is their beauty only a mask for an aged cunning? . . . A few cherished their early dreams and resisted to contumacy the soft appliances of fashion. But they tired of resistance and ridicule: they fell into file, and great is the congratulation of the refined companions that these self-willed protestants had settled down into sensible opinions and practices. Time was when a heroic soul conversing with eternity disdained trifles of hard or easy lot, enamored of honor and right. The same career invites us. The method of nature is ever the same. God instructs men through the Imagination. *But the opera-glasses of our young men do not reach to ideas and realities.* (94–95, emphasis added)

He notes the privileged distance from slavery enjoyed by the youth of America, even when they are complicit with it. His use of the metaphor of "opera-glasses" is especially apt. Not only are they an elite accessory, one of the "soft appliances of fashion" he criticizes. But opera glasses would have allowed what was distant—the universal realm—to be clearer and more visible. Because they cannot see past the present, because of the way their immediate interests and comforts hold their eyes fast, he blames these men for having "their eyes over their shoulders," looking at the past instead of the future (95): "What means this desperate grasp on the past, if not that they find no principle, no hope, no future in their own mind? Some foundation we must have and, *if we can see nothing, we cling desperately to those whom we believe can see*" (96, emphasis added). He describes this skepticism in terms of a lack of vision, an inability to see: "I employed false guides and they misled me; shall I therefore put my head in a bag?" (96). He blames his countrymen for being shortsighted and nearsighted in their pursuit of selfish pleasures, in wanting to enjoy the fruits of slavery without being bothered by the injustice of it. Emerson thinks these Americans need to be reminded of ideals, to lift their focus from the "counting-room," the "railroad," and industry and open themselves to the voice of Intellect, "the great imaginative soul," and the "broad cosmopolitan mind," all of which would tell them slavery was wrong (94). Emerson calls for his audience to move beyond the realm of the senses, the realm of immediate material particularity: "What happens after periods of extraordinary prosperity, happened now. *They could not see beyond their eye-lids, they dwell in the senses;—cause being out of sight is out of mind:*—They see meat and wine, steam and machinery, and the career of wealth. I should find the same ebb of thought from all the well alike. . . . Everywhere dreary superficiality, ignorance and disbelief in principles, a civilization magnifying trifles" (97, emphasis added). Concerns with wealth, prosperity, and the immediate material things in the realm of the senses are described as superficial things and trifles that are obstacles that make it harder to see the distant, harmonious, universal realm that Emerson thinks would motivate abolitionist sentiment. Again, the problem is depicted in terms of a problem of vision, a failure to engage in focal distancing: "There are periods of occulation when the light of the mind seems to be partially withdrawn from nations as well as from individuals. This devastation reached its crisis in the acquiescence in slavery in this country. . . . And there are moments of greatest darkness and of total eclipse" (98). "Occulation," also called "occultation," describes a process where one object is concealed or occluded by another object that comes between it and the observer. This describes what happens during an eclipse: for example, when the sun is totally or partially concealed by the occluding object, the moon. The moon blocks out the light from the sun. A more distant celestial object is hidden from the observer by an intermediary object: an object in the foreground occults or covers up an object in the background.

But Emerson also reminds us that the mind's eye, by nature, when it is strong, when it is healthy, when it is not "inflamed," engages in the practice of focal distancing. Emerson describes a man in a calico-printing mill who did not understand why one pattern pleased and another did not: "I asked him, if he had that blue jelly he called his eye, by chance? . . . Everything rests on foundations, alike the globe of the world, the human mind, and the calico print. The calico print pleases, because the arrangements of colors and forms agrees with the imperative requirements of the human eye" (97). It seems significant that Emerson chooses someone working in a textile mill, an industry reliant upon southern cotton and thus dependent upon the products of the institution of slavery: here, he is again implying that this man's failure to see is bound up with his own material self-interest. In these dark times, Emerson says, "the open secret of the world was hid from their eyes" (101). But despite this "hiding of the light," "the light shone, if it was intercepted from us. Truth exists, though all men should deny it. There is a sound healthy universe whatever fires or plagues or desolation transpire in diseased corners. The sky has not lost its azure because your eyes are inflamed" (102). For Emerson, the problem is that men currently do not move beyond the immediate material realm to *envision* the universal truth: the "sound healthy universe" still exists if we could take this more distant view.

But there is still no sense of the ways in which things that are immediate, near, and particular, things that stimulate our senses, can also illuminate and inspire action, as we got in Emerson's previous antislavery lectures. Though his criticism of these superficial young Americans seems well-placed and is motivating, he paints the entire realm of material particularity with the same broad brush and describes it in highly negative tones as "superficial" and "trifling" whereas "genius" and "courage" and everything associated with a positive valence come through focusing on the universal realm. The call to action is to stop being nearsighted. As opposed to the moments when Emerson recognizes how the practice of focal distancing can itself have costs, in this lecture he once again diagnoses the problem simply in terms of a failure to see with the traditional idealist gaze. Reverting to his pre-1844 perspective, Emerson once again lauds the idealist mode of perception and calls for us to try to see past immediate conditions that merely feed data into our senses. Emerson speaks to inspire and reassure. But he also once again invokes a hierarchical dualism that devalues material particularity, thus making it difficult for him to marshal the power of that same material realm. In this passage, he castigates men for dwelling in their senses, whereas in other addresses, as we have seen, he himself describes experiences of inspiration and illumination that also stem from the realm of sensuous material particularity. He also excoriates the "young men" in this essay for struggling with the same thing he himself is battling during these years: Emerson has also been finding it difficult to look to universal truths given the ways different kinds of particularity figure more prominently in his line of sight. Here he reverts to his more traditional call for his audience to look past these immediate conditions, to focus their gaze up and over and regain the healthy mode of vision, to recover their capacity for focal distancing. But this practice of focal distancing is exactly what he has come to question and challenge at several points since the 1844 address.

This reversion to the older transcendental language becomes even stronger toward the end of the 1855 address. He invokes an image of America as a "city upon a hill," a "new order," and exemplar of liberty: "All the mind in America was possessed by that idea" ("Slavery," 104). He presents America as united in the Universal Spirit, sharing a common idea, a common mind: "The Declaration of Independence, the Constitution of the States, the Parties; the newspapers, the songs, the star-spangled banner, land of the brave and home of the free, the very manners of the Americans, all showed them as the receivers and propagandists of this lesson to the world. For this cause were they born and for this cause came they into the world. . . . That is the meaning of our national pride. It is a noble office. For liberty is a very serious thing" (104). In the final paragraph, there is a call to action: nearly every sentence begins, "we will" and "we shall," all toward the aim or eradicating slavery: "We shall one day bring the states shoulder to shoulder, and the citizens man to man, to exterminate slavery" (106). He tries to project the future where America is an example to the world, a beacon of freedom. Whereas at the beginning of this address, Emerson describes how slavery is "disheartening" and even "staggers" us when viewed "near," when it came to rest more immediately "under the eye" of citizens of Massachusetts, at the end of the address he tries to focus his eyes again on the distant harmonious horizon and invokes all that is best in America. But Emerson ends the address with extremely positive images of what America is supposed to represent that are sharply juxtaposed with the current realities discussed earlier. In his struggles to negotiate the immediate material realities of slavery with universal ideals, he moves from one extreme to the other without bridging these two realms. He tends to privilege the universal realm and issues the familiar call to engage in focal distancing in ways that do not advance the process of revising and re-envisioning to recognize the value of particularity that has characterized other addresses during this period.

Amending the Constitution of Americans

The movements of Emerson's eye and his struggles between looking around him versus looking up and over have larger significance for America, in that—as Stanley Cavell argues—Emerson is also trying to found a new America and to amend the constitution of Americans. "Constitution," here, of course, links the political concept with our physical and mental makeup, how we think, feel, and experience: for Cavell, "Emerson identifies his writing, what I am calling his philosophical authorship, as the drafting of the nation's constitution; or, as I have come to say, as amending our constitution."[30] According to Cavell, Emerson, through thinking, writing, and philosophizing, is trying to found a space for the "better possibility" of our nonconformist, thoughtful, self-reliant action, to turn away from loss, from trauma, toward the affirmative. Emerson fantasizes about "becoming pregnant and giving birth to the world, to his writing of the world, which he calls a new America and calls Being."[31] As Cavell says, "The endlessly repeated idea that Emerson was only interested in finding the individual should give way to or make way for the idea that this quest was his way of founding a nation, writing its constitution, constituting its citizens."[32]

But what advice about how to amend our constitutions can we glean from Emerson's own visual practices, looking not just to what he says but to the nature of his own struggles over perception? Though this is not the point that Cavell makes, I would argue that generally, and especially in the years before 1844, Emerson seems to be encouraging Americans to amend their constitution to engage in the practice of focal distancing, to become what he calls "surrendered souls" whose faith in the universal allows them to act in self-reliant ways. But, as we have seen, the antislavery lectures complicate this picture considerably. Beginning with the 1844 address on emancipation in the West Indies, Emerson's attitude toward particularity changes quite dramatically. He begins to appreciate the power of immediate material particularity, to recognize how it can also inspire ethical action and illuminate truth. He recognizes the progressive political potential of attending to particularity in a way that marks a radical shift in his thought. Consequently, he also begins more fully to reckon the costs of his previous practice of focal distancing that treats particularity more dismissively, as something superficial to be quickly transcended and moved beyond. But this new attitude toward particularity is not consistently evident in the later addresses, nor does Emerson ever fully rework his theory and practice of transcendentalism to take particularity more fully into account, though he comes closest to this in the 1851 and 1854 addresses.

In these lectures, however, Emerson does recognize, sometimes in momentary, fleeting, and inconsistent ways, that to engage in focal distancing can also mean problematically turning a blind eye to immediate physical suffering and anguish. To abstract away from the particulars of slavery makes it less real, less immediate—he notes how different it *feels* when slavery comes closer to him, when he turns his gaze directly on it. Emerson recognizes how his practice of focal distancing can also alienate him from the immediate issues that constitute the everyday features of the foreground of his life. When slavery came to Massachusetts and forced itself under Emerson's eye, he realized how his previous mode of perception allowed him to perpetuate a problematic sense of detachment and immunity: it is as though he lived in a different world altogether from the world that the slaves lived in, even the world that the abolitionists lived in. Recognizing the alienating effects of his idealist mode of perception, he wants to connect, to be nearer to the abolitionist movement, to engage with the world immediately around him to work against slavery.

Despite the compelling quality of nearness and immediacy, however, he also never fully loses sight of the seductions of distance. Emerson's transcendental gaze makes slavery less real in ways that are both a cost and a benefit to him. This is the cause of his ongoing struggle. Making slavery seem temporary, transitory, a contradiction that will be balanced out by the law of compensation, is the benefit of focal distancing for Emerson. Though there are costs associated with looking past disagreeable and disruptive particulars, the faith in a higher law also ultimately offers great comfort. Consequently, in illuminating and instructive ways, in these addresses, Emerson enacts a struggle with his own idealism, without ever really developing a coherent new mode of perception that can take both the particulars of the material realm and universal ideals into account, seeing them both as vital paths toward the illumination of ethical imperatives and political action. He never fully moves beyond the hierarchical, dualistic view of the world that he outlines in "The Transcendentalist," though his habit of focal distancing is unsettled, challenged, ruptured, and questioned at many points during the antislavery lectures.

We, however, can try to draw out the lessons of Emerson's struggles more fully and try to piece together that reworked mode of perception that he reaches toward in these antislavery lectures. If we could draw out the lessons of Emerson's own tensions with idealism, and look not just at what he *says*, but at what he *does*, at the struggles he enacts, we might arrive at a different sense of the way his work amends the constitution of Americans. As a representative man, struggling with the tension between his transcendental idealism and his more worldly abolitionism, Emerson can teach us about the importance of focusing our eyes in a way that takes in the material world without losing sight of ideals, a way of seeing that can also draw inspiration and illumination from what is particular, material, and immediate. We might amend our own constitutions by recognizing how material particularity, as well as universal ideals, can inform both our ethical action and our democratic politics. Drawing out the lessons of the constitutional amendments Emerson himself undergoes in his encounter with slavery, paying attention to his struggles and even his failures, we can get a picture of how both material particularity and universal ideals valuably work as paths to illumination, inspiration, and self-reliant action.

Notes

1. Ralph Waldo Emerson, "The Transcendentalist," in *Nature, Addresses, Lectures* (Cambridge: Belknap Press of Harvard University Press, 1971), 202, hereafter cited parenthetically as "Transcendentalist."

2. Emerson uses this term in "Experience": "Of what use is genius, if the organ is too convex or too concave, and cannot find a focal distance within the actual horizon of human life?" (Ralph Waldo Emerson, "Experience," in *Essays: Second Series* [Cambridge: Belknap Press of Harvard University Press, 1983], 30, hereafter cited parenthetically as "Experience").

3. See Robert D. Richardson, *Emerson: The Mind on Fire* (Berkeley and Los Angeles: University of California Press, 1995), 233. Richardson's book also gives a good account of Emerson's sympathies with and departures from Kant (as well as Hegel). On this topic, see also Lawrence Buell, *Emerson* (Cambridge: Belknap Press of Harvard University Press, 2003). See also Emerson's essay "The Transcendentalist" for his own discussion of Kant.

4. T. Gregory Garvey, "Introduction: The Emerson Dilemma," in *The Emerson Dilemma: Essays on Emerson and Social Reform*, ed. Garvey (Athens: University of Georgia Press, 2001), xx, xxi. The term "detranscendentalizing" has been used to describe the work of scholars who focus explicitly on the material, social,

and political context of Emerson's writings but also of those who reconsider his vision of the self outside of or apart from the theory of transcendental idealism. In the introduction to this volume, the editors trace the complete historical context of Emerson's waxing and waning popularity in rich detail: as they show, Emerson was first canonized by being depoliticized, then later by being detranscendentalized. Daniel Malachuk's essay in this volume also analyzes these "detranscendentalists."

5. In addition, as Alan Levine argues in his essay in this volume, Emerson's transcendentalism serves as a valuable limit to his skepticism, distinguishing him from both Montaigne and Nietzsche.

6. In this way, my reading is informed both by traditional readings that emphasize transcendentalism as an essential element in Emerson's thought and by more recent approaches that forefront themes of "becoming," mutability, and reconstitution. Stanley Cavell's important and valuable work on Emerson might be said to have inaugurated this revitalized, if also sometimes detranscendentalized, approach to Emerson. In her recent volume *On Leaving: A Reading in Emerson* (Cambridge: Harvard University Press, 2010), Branka Arsić discusses the pathways that Cavell opened with this new way of thinking about the Emersonian self, describing a literature that also includes Barbara Packer's *Emerson's Fall* (New York: Continuum, 1982); Richard Poirier's *The Renewal of Literature: Emersonian Reflections* (New York: Random House, 1987); George Kateb's *Emerson and Self-Reliance* (1995; new ed., Lanham, Md.: Rowman and Littlefield, 2002); Sharon Cameron's essay "The Way of Life by Abandonment: Emerson's Impersonal"; as well as Arsić's own recent work on Emerson.

7. Emerson uses these terms in several essays, but see especially *Nature* and his "Emancipation" address (Ralph Waldo Emerson, *Nature*, in *Nature, Addresses, and Lectures* [Cambridge: Belknap Press of Harvard University Press, 1971], 45, hereafter cited parenthetically as *Nature*; Ralph Waldo Emerson, "An Address . . . on . . . the Emancipation of the Negroes in the British West Indies [1844]," in *Emerson's Antislavery Writings*, ed. Len Gougeon and Joel Myerson [New Haven: Yale University Press, 1995], 20, hereafter cited parenthetically as "Emancipation").

8. See Shannon Mariotti, "On the Passing of the First-Born Son: Emerson's 'Focal Distancing,' Du Bois' 'Second Sight,' and Disruptive Particularity," *Political Theory* 37, no. 3 (June 2009).

9. Scholars have characterized the relationship between Emerson's philosophy of transcendental idealism, his practice of self-reliance, and his participation in the antislavery movement in many different ways. Some argue that Emerson was motivated to join the abolitionist cause by his idealist principles, finding compatibility between his larger theory of idealism and his abolitionism; in this reading, the ethical principles that spurred Emerson to speak out against slavery stem from his transcendentalism. For example, in his essay in this volume, Jack Turner shows

how the problem of "complicity" is central to Emerson's notion of citizenship: part of the practice of self-reliance is trying to remove oneself from being complicit even in the secondary effects of injustices such as slavery (such as eating food produced through slave labor). In a different way, Michael Strysick argues that Emerson's notion of self-reliance evolved over time to become compatible with his abolitionism (Strysick, "Emerson, Slavery, and the Evolution of the Principle of Self-Reliance," in *The Emerson Dilemma*). But where some scholars find sympathy, others find more tension. James Read, also in this volume, argues that slavery productively highlights the limits of Emerson's thoughts on individual self-reliance. Others argue that Emerson reconsidered the exclusive value of his early commitments to transcendentalism when he "converted" to the abolitionist cause. See, for example, Len Gougeon, "Emerson's Abolition Conversion," in *The Emerson Dilemma*. For a different kind of critical analysis of the idea of Emerson's wholesale conversion, see Amy Earhart, "Representative Men, Slave Revolt, and Emerson's 'Conversion' to Abolitionism," *American Transcendental Quarterly* 13, no. 4 (1999). Still more scholars see Emerson's antislavery activities as a temporary aberration or deviation from his orienting belief in self-reliance and transcendentalism. For an exploration of these incompatibilities, see Kateb, *Emerson and Self-Reliance*.

10. T. Gregory Garvey, introduction to *The Emerson Dilemma*, xxi.

11. Ralph Waldo Emerson, "An Address . . . on . . . the Emancipation of the Negroes in the British West Indies" (1844); "Anniversary of West Indian Emancipation" (1845), hereafter cited parenthetically as "Anniversary"; "Antislavery Remarks at Worcester" (1849), hereafter cited parenthetically as "Worcester"; "Address to the Citizens of Concord" (1851), hereafter cited parenthetically as "Concord"; "Fugitive Slave Law" (1854), hereafter cited parenthetically as "Fugitive"; "Lecture on Slavery" (1855), hereafter cited parenthetically as "Slavery." All of these addresses are in *Emerson's Antislavery Writings*, ed. Len Gougeon and Joel Myerson (New Haven: Yale University Press, 1995).

12. My readings of Emerson are informed by the critical theory of the German social theorist Theodor W. Adorno. Adorno's method of "negative dialectics" is uniquely helpful in analyzing the moments where Emerson questions his own idealism. Adorno combines a critique of transcendental idealism (primarily directed toward Kant and Hegel) with materialist sympathies, and emphasizes the ethical, political, and even democratic value of paying close attention to the dissonant voice of particular things. Adorno's critique of idealism in many ways mirrors Emerson's own nascent challenges to his transcendentalism, helping us characterize these struggles. Further, putting Adorno in conversation with Emerson helps to more fully articulate the argument for the ethical value of focusing on particularity that Emerson himself reaches toward in the antislavery addresses between 1844 and 1855. For a deeper analysis of productive connections between

Adorno, Thoreau, and Emerson, see Shannon Mariotti, *Thoreau's Democratic Withdrawal: Alienation, Participation, and Modernity* (Madison: University of Wisconsin Press, 2010).

13. There are some important sympathies, as well as some key differences, between Daniel Malachuk's readings of Emerson's antislavery addresses—also in this volume—and my own. Both Malachuk and I agree that Emerson's transcendentalism must be taken seriously, but Malachuk focuses primarily on the positive moments where Emerson's abolitionist politics was motivated and driven by his transcendentalism, whereas I focus on how Emerson's habitual transcendental gaze could also hinder his ability to fully perceive the particulars of slavery and obstruct his capacity to fully recognize how particularity itself might also powerfully motivate his abolitionism.

14. In one sense, my reading of Emerson can be seen as exploring the obverse elements of one of the first treatments of Emerson and vision, Sherman Paul's *Emerson's Angle of Vision: Man and Nature in American Experience* (Cambridge: Harvard University Press, 1952). Paul describes Emerson's vision in terms of a synthesis and reconciliation of the "horizontal" or "linear" realms of man and nature with the "vertical" realm of spirit and universe. Paul explores how, "by a process of distant vision," Emerson "affirms" the "correspondence," identity, and analogy of man and the universe, as well as the natural and spiritual universes. "Emerson felt called on," Paul writes, "to raise the vertical axis, to give the universe its spiritual dimension, to reinstate its mystery and wonder by giving scope to the mythic, symbolic, and religious components of human experience: the vertical was the inner and spiritual and 'put nature underfoot' by making nature serve the moral needs of man" (22). In Paul's reading, Emerson's "angle of vision was a religious perspective and correspondence, the prism through which his natural eye spiritualized the facts of life" (230). The ideal angle of vision was a distancing vision that found a "bipolar unity" where everything synthesized into a "sympathetic correspondence" in a faraway horizon, where sea met sky or mountains met clouds. In contrast, my analysis focuses instead on the costs of this distancing angle of vision, and highlights the ways it tends to devalue and dismiss particular things in the immediate foreground of life, with problematic consequences that Emerson himself appreciated, if only in momentary and undeveloped ways. Where Paul finds a mode of vision tending toward affirmation and reconciliation, I highlight tension and struggle, exploring specifically how they play out in Emerson's encounter with slavery.

15. In addition to Sherman Paul's *Emerson's Angle of Vision*, see also F. O. Matthiessen's chapter on Emerson titled "In the Optative Mood," in his *American Renaissance: Art and Expression in the Age of Emerson and Whitman* (New York: Oxford University Press, 1941); Kenneth Burke's "I, Eye, Aye: Emerson's Early Essay on 'Nature,' Thoughts on the Machinery of Transcendence," *Sewanee Review*

74 (1966): 875–93; Tony Tanner's "Emerson: The Unconquered Eye and the Enchanted Circle," in *The Reign of Wonder: Naivety and Reality in American Literature* (New York: Cambridge University Press, 1977); James Cox, "R. W. Emerson: The Circles of the Eye," in *Emerson: Prophecy, Metamorphosis, and Influence* (New York: Columbia University Press, 1975); Richard Poirier's "Is There an I for an Eye?: The Visionary Possession of America," in his *World Elsewhere: The Place of Style in American Literature* (Madison: University of Wisconsin Press, 1985); Barbara Packer's "The Instructed Eye: Emerson's Cosmogony in 'Prospects,'" in *Emerson's Nature: Origin, Growth, Meaning*, ed. Merton Sealts and Alfred Ferguson (Carbondale: Southern Illinois University Press, 1979); and Carolyn Porter's *Seeing and Being: The Plight of the Participant Observer in Emerson, James, Adams, and Faulkner* (Middletown, Conn.: Wesleyan University Press, 1981). See also Cornel West's discussion of Emerson and vision in *The American Evasion of Philosophy: A Genealogy of Pragmatism* (Madison: University of Wisconsin Press, 1989); David Jacobson's *Emerson's Pragmatic Vision: The Dance of the Eye* (University Park: Pennsylvania State University Press, 1993); Shannon Mariotti, "Alienated Existence, Focal Distancing, and Emerson's Transcendental Idealism," in *Thoreau's Democratic Withdrawal: Alienation, Participation, and Modernity*; and Russell Sbriglia's "The Ethics of Eye-dentity: Emerson, Skepticism, Sympathy," *Arizona Quarterly* 66, no. 2 (Summer 2010). Sarah Ann Wider reviews some of this scholarship on Emerson and vision in *The Critical Reception of Emerson: Unsettling All Things* (Rochester, N.Y.: Camden House, 2000).

16. In his recent "The Ethics of Eye-dentity: Emerson, Skepticism, Sympathy," Russell Sbriglia describes Emerson's dialectical "vibration" between "skeptically imbued, performative revisionings of the self and his sympathetic, passionate identifications with others that constitutes his ethics" but sees both of these as motivated and enabled by Emerson's "oculocentrism," here borrowing a term Stephen Esquith uses (4). Ultimately, Sbriglia concludes that "Emerson compares the eye to the sympathetic heart just as often as he compares it to the skeptical head. . . . For Emerson, then, the eye needn't always bathe itself in the blithe air. It can just as easily, and as often, derive equal pleasure from miring itself in 'the lowest trench' and coming face to face with whatever—or whomever—is next at hand" (29). Though the visual themes of the essay are not as central to the argument or as fully developed as the title would suggest, Sbriglia sees Emerson's vision as holistic, unified, and consistent with other aspects of his thought, describing it in terms of reconciliation, sympathy, and identification. In contrast, I show how Emerson focuses his eye in different ways at different times and highlight key moments in his antislavery addresses where he comes to doubt his traditional mode of focal distancing, showing how these moments are marked more by struggle, doubt, questioning, and internal conflict.

17. Emerson uses the metaphor of "near-sightedness," which we might see as the opposite of focal distancing, in the "Divinity School Address": "Life is comic or pitiful, as soon as the high ends of being fade out of sight, and man becomes near-sighted, and can only attend to what addresses the senses" (Emerson, "Divinity School Address," in *Nature, Addresses, Lectures*, 80).

18. As Emerson says: "There is one mind common to all individual men. Every man is an inlet to the same and to all of the same. . . . What Plato has thought, he may think; what a saint has felt, he may feel; what at any time has befallen any man, he can understand. Who hath access to this universal mind, is a party to all that is or can be done, for this is the only and sovereign agent" (Emerson, "History," in *Essays: First Series* [Cambridge: Belknap Press of Harvard University Press, 1979], 3).

19. There are some interesting resonances between my argument concerning "focal distancing" and Sharon Cameron's characterization of Emerson's "impersonality" (though she does not root her argument in Emerson's transcendental idealism). In her analysis of "Experience," she describes Emerson's way of dealing with grief, and also experience generally after Waldo's death, in terms of a process of displacement and "impersonalism"—by setting aside what I would call the immediate particulars of experience, in the margins of life, as a kind of living memento—to be kept alive in this state of displacement. What Cameron calls the "impersonal" and Emerson's air of detachment, I attribute to the devaluing attitude he has toward particularity: what Cameron calls Emerson's "impersonalism" might be seen as a result of his practice of focal distancing. He distances himself from, detaches from, particularity. But, in contrast to Cameron, I would argue that this "impersonalism" is never wholly successful for Emerson: particularity and personal pain and suffering do force their way into Emerson's consciousness at many points in his writings (see Sharon Cameron, "Representing Grief: Emerson's 'Experience,'" *Representations,* no. 15 [Summer 1986]: 15–41). See also her article "The Way of Life by Abandonment: Emerson's Impersonal," *Critical Inquiry* 25, no. 1 (Autumn 1998): 1–31.

20. Ralph Waldo Emerson, "Compensation," in *Essays: First Series*, 60, hereafter cited parenthetically as "Compensation."

21. As Emerson writes, "Yet, in every sane hour, the service of thought appears reasonable, the despotism of the senses insane" (Emerson, "Literary Ethics," in *Nature, Addresses, Lectures*, 100).

22. Emerson lists these particular things in both *Nature* and "Experience."

23. Len Gougeon, "Historical Background," in *Emerson's Antislavery Writings*, xxviii. See also Gougeon's "Emerson's Abolition Conversion," in *The Emerson Dilemma*.

24. As Jack Turner has noted in his reading of this passage, Emerson is

concerned with the ethical problem of "complicity" in slavery (see Turner, "Self-Reliance and Complicity: Emerson's Ethics of Citizenship," in this volume).

25. Russell Sbriglia points to this passage as an example of Emerson's ethics and his tendency toward sympathetic identification (see Sbriglia, "The Ethics of Eye-dentity: Emerson, Skepticism, Sympathy," *Arizona Quarterly* 66, no. 2 [Summer 2010]).

26. Ralph Waldo Emerson, "The American Scholar," *Nature*, in *Nature, Addresses, and Lectures* (Cambridge: Belknap Press of Harvard University Press, 1971).

27. See the textual commentary on "Antislavery Remarks at Worcester," in *Emerson's Antislavery Writings*, 164. The text of the speech is reprinted from the *Liberator*, August 17, 1849, 131.

28. See Barbara L. Packer, *The Transcendentalists* (Athens: University of Georgia Press, 2007), 220–24.

29. This anonymous commentator was cited in an article printed in the *Christian Inquirer*, reprinted in the *National Anti-Slavery Standard* (see Gougeon, "Historical Background," xliii).

30. Stanley Cavell, "Emerson's Constitutional Amending: Reading 'Fate,'" in *Emerson's Transcendental Etudes*, ed. David Justin Hodge (Stanford: Stanford University Press, 2003), 208.

31. Ibid., 203.

32. Stanley Cavell, "Finding as Founding: Taking Steps in Emerson's 'Experience,'" in *Emerson's Transcendental Etudes*, 122.

PART IV

Emerson and Liberal Democracy

CHAPTER 11

Property in Being: Liberalism and the Language of Ownership in Emerson's Writing

Neal Dolan

The Language of Property

AN INTERESTING FAMILY OF words appears at important moments throughout Emerson's writing. Near the beginning of his first major work, *Nature* (1836), Emerson draws on the language of ownership to urge his readers to look afresh at the world around them: "There is a *property* in the horizon which no man has but he whose eye can integrate all the parts" (*E&L*, 9, emphasis added). Later in the same tract he uses similar rhetoric to appeal to moral reason: "We are taught by great actions that the universe is the *property* of every individual in it. . . . Every rational creature has all nature for his *dowry* and *estate*" (*E&L*, 16, emphasis added). In the "Divinity School Address," first delivered in 1838, Emerson uses the language of property to parody what he sees as the unmanning effect of much Unitarian preaching: "You shall not be a man even, you shall not *own* the world" (*E&L*, 81, emphasis added). He spiritualizes ownership in 1841 in "History," when he writes that "Property also holds of the soul" (*E&L*, 248). In "Compensation," also published in 1841, he uses economic terms to formulate nothing less than a sort of existential reality principle: "Thou shall be paid exactly for what thou hast done, no more, no less." "What will you have? quoth God; pay for it and take it" (*E&L*, 293). And in "Experience" (1844), in the most painful sentences he ever wrote, Emerson expresses a state of bereaved numbness by turning yet again to the idiom of property: "In the death of my son, now more than two years ago, I seem to have lost a beautiful *estate*,—no more. I cannot get it nearer to me" (*E&L*, 472).

Examples are no less abundant in Emerson's later work: "Money is of no value," Emerson declares in "The Young American" (1844), "it cannot spend itself. All depends on the skill of the spender" (*E&L*, 224). In *Representative Men* (1850), he approvingly quotes Napoleon saying, "The market-place is the Louvre of the common people" (*E&L*, 736). *English Traits* of 1856 is in substantial part a paean to the commercial ethos of nineteenth-century England, and includes many passages like this one: "Property [there] is so perfect, that it seems the craft of that race, and not to exist elsewhere" (*E&L*, 845). Emerson's last great book, *The Conduct of Life*, published in 1860, contains two essays—"Power" and "Wealth"—which strikingly reprise his by now lifelong tendency to draw moral and spiritual analogies from the world of business and money: "The interest of petty economy is this symbolization of the great economy; the way in which a house, and a private man's methods, tally with the solar system, and the laws of give and take, throughout nature" (*E&L*, 1000). And even the title of Emerson's most serious reflection upon the Civil War—"Fortune of the Republic" (1863)—plays intriguingly upon a term of economic bounty.

I could cite many more examples. But the point should be clear enough already. In all of his writing, Emerson drew repeatedly and in rhetorically rich and complex ways on a large set of terms taken from the sphere of commerce and property—words such as "debt," "credit," "possession," "plantation," "warranty," "deeds," "dominion," "own," "right," "thine," "alienate," "joint-stock company," "trustee," "poverty," "fortune," "compensation," and "wealth." Indeed, this economic idiom is so central and pervasive in Emerson's work as to raise the question of its larger significance. In the pages that follow, I argue that Emerson uses the language of property to symbolically resolve a cultural dilemma—a symbolic resolution that goes to the core of his distinctive liberal vision. On the one hand, Emerson wished throughout his career to honor and extend America's liberal revolution against the European feudal-aristocratic social system—a transformation which he understood to be bound up with an abstract conception of property and with historically unprecedented opportunities in the young United States for substantial material ownership for the general (white male) population. And yet, on the other hand, Emerson wanted to counter the tendency he had observed in this newly emancipated society to reduce all relationships to marketplace calculations, including its relationships to southern slaves and to less-advanced neighboring civilizations, such as those of Mexicans and

Native Americans. In the examples above and in countless other instances, Emerson used the language of property in part to appeal affirmatively to his postrevolutionary audience's hard-won, proudly held legal right to own things. He used words like "own" and "profit" and "pay" at once to recognize and to keep the attention of notoriously busy folk by referring to an intimate and pressing aspect of their ordinary daily experience. But at the same time, Emerson inflected this economic idiom in distinctive ways in an attempt to raise his audience's understanding of their rightful property, and thus of their rightful selves, to a yet higher, more spiritual, and more ecstatic plane. Emerson was uniquely prepared to arrive at this balanced approach by the influence of three contexts: Puritanism, the Scottish Enlightenment, and the full emergence of a market economy in antebellum America.

Puritanism

The first important contextual influence on Emerson's complex attitude toward commerce and property was the ambivalent legacy of Puritanism. Max Weber is only the most well-known among many scholars who have observed that Calvinism, for all its moral severity, indirectly fostered a more affirmative attitude toward bourgeois material success than did Roman Catholicism. As Weber observed, Calvin opened the door to an epochal departure from Roman Catholic antimaterialism by suggesting that hard work in one's profession and concomitant material success could be understood as a sign of God's grace. In an inwardly intense culture for which anxiety about grace was the principal psychic engine, such a possibility was powerful inducement to the whole set of middle-class virtues—disciplined labor, punctuality, perseverance, prudence, thrift, probity, and careful reinvestment of gains—for which Puritans, and, in time, Yankees, became renowned, and which, indeed, often helped to make them rich. Weber acknowledges that many ascetic religious traditions preached the benefits of disciplined work, but he suggests that Puritanism gave this teaching distinctive this-worldly efficacy: "It not only deepened this idea most powerfully, it also created the force which was alone decisive for its effectiveness: the psychological sanction of it through the conception of this labor as a calling, as the best, often in the last analysis the only means of attaining certainty of grace. . . . It is obvious how powerfully the exclusive search for the Kingdom of God only through the fulfillment of duty in the calling, and the strict asceticism which Church discipline naturally imposed, especially on the propertyless classes, was bound to affect the productivity of labour in the capitalistic sense of the word."[1] However far Emerson may have moved from orthodox Calvinist theology by the time he delivered the "Divinity School Address" in 1838 or published "Self-Reliance" in 1841, he never let go of a semi-secularized, residual Calvinist attachment to the notion of disciplined work and middle-class material success as evidence of a kind of higher inner blessedness. Charles Sellers was not off the mark when, in pages sharply critical of Emerson from the point of view of the beleaguered and ultimately doomed subsistence culture of the Jacksonian hinterlands, he remarked that "like Hopkins, Finney, and Bushnell, Emerson preached transcendental grace for bourgeois/middle-class Americans 'born to be rich.'"[2] And William Hedges was similarly on target when he wrote that Emerson preached "the Protestant ethic in a highly exalted form."[3] But Sellers's explicit and Hedges's implicit disapproval, characteristic of a large body of scholarship, which acknowledges many aspects of Emerson's liberalism only to lament them,[4] fails to register the full richness, complexity, and duality of Emerson's language of property.

To fully appreciate this complexity, it helps to remember that Emerson's treatment of work and wealth was significantly influenced by the Puritans in another respect as well. As the scion of generations of New England ministers in the Puritan tradition who was himself trained to be a minister, Emerson inherited a remarkably rich and powerful legacy of what one might call symbolic correlation. Whether it was Thomas Hooker assigning precise salvific significance to the subtlest gradations of feeling, Mary Rowlandson finding an apt line of scripture for every new stage of distress in captivity, Cotton Mather seeing his own baseness reflected in a dog urinating against a fence, or Jonathan Edwards musing upon a spider, the Puritan psyche was superabundantly stocked in symbolic language and imagery derived from the Bible and immensely practiced in fitting the data of its experience and observation into this symbolic framework. There was nothing so trivial or so large that it could not be mapped into the Puritan symbolic system. Indeed, much of the pleasure of reading Puritan literature comes from following the elaborate strategies and extensive reach of its symbolic mediations. Emerson, it may be said, inherited the Puritan habit of symbolization and the hope of coherence implicit within it, but as a young man he lost the

Puritan confidence in the Bible as the ultimate source of all symbols and as the authoritative code for their decipherment.[5] Like his Puritan forebears, Emerson looked for larger symbolic significance in every incident of both inward and outward experience, but without ultimate confidence in the Bible, he found it necessary to fashion his own network of secular symbolic equivalents. For this he turned in part to nature, but also to history and to the marketplace. In the language of property and sale, cost and profit, debt and credit, loss and gain, investment and return, Emerson found a network of vivid, perspicuous, pithy, and coherently interrelated metaphors that could not fail to resonate sharply with the daily concerns of his pragmatic Yankee auditors and readers. The language of the marketplace thus helped Emerson to provide that set of compelling "moral analogies" that Tocqueville found missing in what—in his darker moments—he lamented as the callow culture of democratic America: "The harmony that has always been observed between the feelings and the ideas of mankind appears to be dissolved and all the laws of moral analogy abolished."[6] Though Emerson would not have agreed with Tocqueville that the laws of moral analogy had ever been fully abolished in America, he nonetheless drew upon the language of property to refigure them in a form befitting the distinctive acquisitive energies of his own residually Puritan region and historical moment.

The Scottish Enlightenment

The second important context for understanding Emerson's complex attitude toward commerce cuts counter to the first. After some painful and protracted youthful vacillation between the claim of Christian tradition on the one hand and the claim of scientific rationalism on the other, at the age of twenty-nine Emerson at last gave himself over fully to science and reason as he understood it: "Calvinism suited Ptolemaism. The irresistible effect of Copernican astronomy had been to make the great scheme for the salvation of man absolutely incredible" (*JMN*, 4:26).[7] It was the influence of the Enlightenment, broadly speaking, that undermined the authority of Calvinism and the Bible as a symbolic resource for the young minister: "What has imagination created to compare with the science of Astronomy? What is there in Paradise Lost to elevate and astonish like Herschel & Somerville? ... Who can be a Calvinist or who an Atheist? God has opened this knowledge to us to correct our theology & educate the mind" (*JMN*, 3:24). Not long after writing these words in his journals, Emerson resigned his father's former pulpit at the Second (Unitarian) Church in Boston, and in his first series of secular lectures delivered soon thereafter, on the apt topic of "Science," he declared that "we have come to look at the world in quite another light from any in which our fathers regarded it" (*EL*, 1:28–29). Though Emerson's brilliant and at times extravagant romantic style has made it easy to overlook the foundational role played by Enlightenment rationalism in his thinking, it is crucial to remember that throughout his career he had repeated recourse to this fundamental Enlightenment (and classical) preference for nature/reason/empiricism over custom/tradition/revelation. Wilson Carey McWilliams emphasized Emerson's debt to the Enlightenment in *The Idea of Fraternity in America* (his discussion of Emerson is included in this volume), and I have developed the connection in full in *Emerson's Liberalism* (2009), but this crucial influence has been otherwise insufficiently taken into account.

It is not enough, however, to speak merely generically of the "Enlightenment" context of Emerson's thought. It was largely from the moderate Scots rather than the radical French that Emerson took his instruction in Enlightenment, and the Scottish influence, like that of the Puritans, also contributed significantly to the rich duality of his outlook on property and commerce. The leading figures of the Scottish Enlightenment were all committed to a "conjectural" four-stage narrative of human progress as the product of an evolving conception of property.[8] According to Scottish anthropology, human societies started out with only (1) a "savage" hunter-gatherer's narrow notion of ownership as literal physical possession of what could be held in one's hand. From this they progressed in the next two stages to (2) herding societies' marking of the beasts in a given herd so that strays could be returned to their owners, to (3) the limited conception of alienability (legality of sale) of lands characteristic of agrarian societies. Finally, in the advanced urban centers of the seventeenth- and eighteenth-century West, human societies evolved to (4) a fully abstract conception of property. Under these conditions, a high degree of division of labor led to exponentially increased productivity and prosperity, crucially enabled by the necessarily flexible symbolic mechanisms of frequent, fluid, and unrestricted trade—including instruments such as "credit notes," "paper currency," and "bills of exchange."[9] On this Scottish account, the evolution of an increasingly abstract conception of property was nothing less than the key and principal catalyst of gradual and ultimately universal human material progress.

But this quasi-materialist conception of progress as founded on property did not prevent the Scots, no less rooted in Calvinism than Emerson, from also giving morality its progressive-historical due. It is not incidental that Adam Smith's two major works, both of which Emerson read as a young man, were respectively entitled *The Wealth of Nations* and *A Theory of Moral Sentiments*. Starting with Frances Hutcheson and continuing through major works by David Hume, Thomas Reid, and Smith among others, the Scots argued persistently and systematically that human morality was derived from deep-seated emotional reflexes rather than from any elaborate process of ratiocination. And the Scots also saw material progress, rooted in an evolving conception of property, as at once expressing and facilitating the slow historical maturation and institutionalization of the intuitions of what they called "the moral sense." The Scottish liberals argued that the freedom to advance one's own interests in legally enabled pursuits of commerce would have the effect of liberating individual human beings from a wide array of long-standing, deeply entrenched, and morally inhibiting forms of servitude and dependency—including serfdom, chattel slavery, the subjugation of women, and the basic material and intellectual deprivation endemic to most agrarian existence. They voiced a hope furthermore that as commercial societies grew up around the globe, mutually advantageous relationships of trade would replace mutually destructive relationships of martial rivalry as the principal mode of international interaction. Commercial societies devoted to trade rather than to farming and/or warfare, the Scots suggested, would foster morally improved human personalities—at once gentler, more rational, more tolerant, more prudent, more polite, and more knowledgeable of the world.[10]

The liberal Calvinists in charge of Emerson's education at Harvard were deeply influenced by this Scottish liberal outlook, and they passed its mix of property-based historical progressivism and "moral sentiment" psychology on to their students.[11] Both the concept of innate "moral sentiment" and the entire Scottish-Whig narrative of the history of liberty became axiomatic in Emerson's mature work. One can verily watch Emerson lift the

Scottish-Whig cup to his lips in his earliest journals as he paraphrases his instructors in sweeping summaries of the advance of human freedom and well-being by means of the invention of the printing press, the reformation of religion, the renaissance of scientific inquiry and artistic expression, the rise of towns, and the global spread of commerce. He laments the long history of human religious self-abasement: "What odious vice, what sottish and debasing enormity the degenerate naughtiness of man has never crouch[ed] unto and adored?" He fancies that "the moral sense" must have quietly rebelled even in the most benighted idolater when "he knelt before the false altar, in obedience to a greater idol, Custom" (*JMN*, 1:78). He marvels in special horror at the Catholic "Dark Ages" of the "six centuries 5, 6, 7, 8, 9, 10" (*JMN*, 1:66). But he finds hope in the perception of a "joyful change" when, through reason, "human nature unshackl[es] herself and asserts her divine origin" (*JMN*, 2:18). The Italian Renaissance heralds "the dawn of the restoration of human honour," as philosophy now "extends her influence in a thousand branches," "reviving all that was worthy in Ancient Science" (*JMN*, 1:66, 68). Early modern Italy also "demonstrates better than any other the remarkable and vast effects upon national prosperity of free Commerce and agriculture, which exalted individual character, and filled the public treasury with a boundless wealth" (*JMN*, 1:77–78). The "convulsion" of the Reformation then dealt a decisive blow to lingering papist repression, and the emerging liberty of the press as the crucial medium of civil society "tended to enlighten and emancipate . . . the lower orders of Europe: when at length moral discussions which before were strange and unintelligible to their ears began to be understood and they comprehended the nature of property and government, things were in train for amendment" (*JMN*, 1:344). Having thus arrived at the decisive modern turning point of all Whig history—the (implicitly) Lockean teaching about "property and government"—the young Emerson situates himself finally in the happy midst of an extended "Age of Reason": "The (Roman) bondage was so crafty and so strong that it was long before the mind was hardy enough to break it. But it was finally broken, and thenceforward the Age of Reason commenced. I use a term which has been perverted and abused, but I apply it with propriety to the era of Luther and Calvin, with still more propriety to the advanced reason of Clarke and Newton, and with still more perfect propriety to this latter day when our eyes read with all the added splendour of these great and various lights" (*JMN*, 2:17).

Emerson had not yet read Hegel at this early phase of his intellectual development, but when the time came, this Scottish Enlightenment narrative would render him ideally receptive to the Enlightenment-romantic philosopher's Germanic-Whig definition of history, itself partially informed by the Scots, as "the progress of the consciousness of freedom."[12] The phrase accurately captures both Emerson's mature sense of history and the implicit moral-progressive purpose of all of his work: he sought throughout his career, not least in his relatively late antislavery writings, to put his rhetorical shoulder to the world-historical wheel and to give the "consciousness of freedom" another gigantic turn. Indeed, if the Scottish conception of the "moral sentiment" may be said to supply the nerves of Emerson's outlook, the Scottish conception of the history of liberty may be said to supply its narrative backbone. In much the same way that the Puritans from John Cotton to Jonathan Edwards had recourse to "the history of the work of redemption" as an overarching narrative frame in reference to which the events of their lifetimes could be rendered intelligible and thus meaningful, so Emerson relied upon Scottish "moral sense" psychology and the Scottish-Whig property-based history of liberty as, respectively, the moral and the metahistorical axes of an ambitious liberal-progressive symbolic system.

The Market Revolution: Jacksonian America

The third context in which we must consider Emerson's view of property is his most immediate and pressing one—the economy, society, and politics of the United States in the first half of the nineteenth century. The fledgling nation underwent the first dramatic stages of what was to be a century-long process of transformation from a primarily subsistence-agrarian to a commercial-industrial basis precisely during the years of Emerson's coming-of-age and maturity.[13] From its earliest colonial beginnings, the economic structure of American agrarianism in the Northeast and the West had been different from Europe's. As in Europe, the vast majority of Americans lived by tilling the land in the seventeenth and eighteenth centuries, but unlike in Europe, a high percentage of white males owned the land they tilled, with no attached rents or tithes or debts of work and almost no taxation.[14] "Men were equal in that no one of them should be dependent on the will of another," Gordon Wood writes, "and property made this independence possible. Americans in 1776 therefore concluded that they were naturally fit for republicanism precisely because they were 'a people of property, and almost every man is a freeholder.'"[15] As the eighteenth century turned into the nineteenth, and the nineteenth century advanced through its first six decades, the American yeoman increasingly owned other things as well as land: surplus yields from farms, nonagricultural commodities, crafted artifacts, professional expertise, or simple manual labor were often traded for profit or wages. Towns and cities expanded in size and population as many of these independent owners as well as farmers with surpluses sought markets for what they had to sell. One of the two major American political parties, the Whigs, and a significant faction of the other—the so-called "national" Democrats—were committed to the promotion of all such market activity by means of government-funded improvements in transportation and communication infrastructure—turnpikes, canals, bridges, telegraph wires, and, most significantly, as soon as the technology became available in the early 1830s, railroads. With the increase of commercial exchange came the need for the drawing up and enforcement of contracts and the concomitant rise of lawyers. Banks, uniform currency, and laws of credit were established by (politically highly contentious) fits and starts. As a result, the national economy grew in size substantially and consistently from 1820 to 1860, with only the depression of 1837 causing a temporary dip in a long ascent toward proto-industrial "takeoff" around 1843.[16] And the Marshall Court and its immediate successors authored an epochal body of constitutional jurisprudence securing the legal stability, combinability, and predictable exchangeability of so much amassing property.

Here again, as with Puritanism and the Scottish Enlightenment, Emerson's direct experience of the "market revolution"[17] contributed to the formation of a complex, two-sided outlook on commerce and property. On one hand, there was a seemingly perfect fit between the extraordinary technology-fueled economic expansion Emerson witnessed on the ground in America from the 1820s through 1860 and the property-based progressive historical framework he had derived from the Scottish Enlightenment. This congruence had the dual effect of further reinforcing Emerson's Scottish-Whig orientation even as his Scottish-Whig background helped him to intellectually accommodate what he was observing. Emerson recognized and welcomed most of these market changes as what he understood from the Scots to be inevitable steps in the incipiently global and quasi-providential march of universal human progress.[18] Indeed, the first step toward an accurate placing of Emerson in his immediate historical context is to recognize that almost everything in his Boston-Unitarian-Harvard-Whig background and milieu predisposed him to favor the "market" tendencies of the profound economic and cultural transformation unfolding around him.

On the other hand, however, Emerson did not like everything that he saw in emerging commercial society. Like his friends Thoreau and Carlyle or other observers such as Tocqueville, Emerson was deeply troubled by the tendency of Jacksonian America to all-devouring materialism. "Things are in the saddle, and ride mankind,"[19] is only his most striking formulation of a genuine concern about pervasive market instrumentalism that surfaces frequently in his notebooks, lectures, and published writing. "This is the good and this is the evil of trade," he writes in "The Young American," a lecture largely celebratory of the emancipating effects of commerce, "that it would put everything into market, talent, beauty, virtue, and man himself" (E&L, 221). While largely free of Thoreau's hankering for the simplicity of subsistence living,[20] Emerson grasped, disliked, and deeply feared the moral and psychological impoverishment latent in market society's drive to reduce all relationships—personal, spiritual, and environmental no less than commercial—to an instrumental, means-to-an-end calculus. "At this day amidst the grandeur of Commerce," he says in the "Introductory" remarks to the 1839–1840 lecture series entitled "The Present Age," "the philosopher may well occupy himself with the price of its gifts." "Commerce has no reverence. Prayer and prophecy are irrelevant to its bargain. It encroaches on all sides. 'Business before friends' is its byword." "An admirable servant, it has become the hard master" (EL, 3:190–91). Like Thoreau, Emerson also objected explicitly and vehemently to the politically popular presumption of his era that American society's burgeoning economic strength justified the displacement of Native Americans or the seizure of Mexican lands.[21] And in the 1840s and 1850s, he became bitterly critical of the unholy alliance between northern merchant capital and southern slavery.[22]

Property in Being

Three of Emerson's most important contexts thus overlapped both in attuning him to the importance of commerce and property, and in contributing to an ambivalence or duality at the core of his attitude toward these central values of modern liberalism. The Puritans seemed to valorize bourgeois materialism, but only within a demanding religious mind-set that valued the possession of material property primarily as a sign of spiritual grace. The thinkers of the Scottish Enlightenment saw property as the essential catalyst of human progress, but in keeping with Scotland's Calvinist cultural roots, they conceived a strong link between material and moral improvement. And the market revolution that played out immediately before Emerson's eyes in Jacksonian America brought about remarkable advances in general material well-being the ameliorative benefits of which Emerson fulsomely acknowledged, but the proliferation of goods seemed at the same time to be contributing toward what Emerson saw as a distressing coarsening of moral relations. So when he sat down to compose his moral-political exhortations to his countrymen, Emerson faced a thrice-reinforced dilemma: how to preserve in secular times the strong Calvinist link between material and spiritual property; how like the Scots to somehow fuse together material and moral progress; or, more generally, how to preserve the great material benefits of market liberalism while countering the incipient moral dangers of its tendency toward pervasive instrumentalism. Emerson was, of course, not the only cultural leader of the time thus challenged: a rich and oft-noted variety of utopian ventures and a widespread evangelically driven congeries of reform movements sought to compensate for commercial society's ever-increasing atomization and instrumentalism by the renewal, at times public and frenzied, of communal bonds.[23] But it is a measure of Emerson's commitment to liberalism that where antebellum evangelicals or utopians thus sought to locate communitarian resources to compensate for what they saw as commercial society's atomistic individualism, Emerson looked within, to a nonmaterial intensification and enhancement of a central liberal value—individual ownership. Where evangelicals, utopians, Jacksonians, and Thoreau all hearkened back to subsistence values, Emerson pushed his New England Whig–Scottish liberal education a step further and called for "internal improvements" of a higher order, improvements of consciousness and reception and solitude—expanded property in being.

The precise nature and character of such ontological property may be understood by a perhaps unlikely blend of Stanley Cavell and Hegel. Cavell was drawn to the writing of Emerson and Thoreau, he explained, in part because they articulated a deep intuition of ordinary language philosophy better than Searle or Wittgenstein—an idea of our "intimacy with existence, or intimacy lost": that "our relation to the world's existence is somehow closer than the ideas of believing and knowing are made to convey."[24] Although Cavell does not himself make this connection, I would suggest that Emerson uses the language of property and ownership precisely to evoke this quality of "intimacy with existence." To say we have property in existence, as Emerson finds so many ways of doing, such as "there is a property in the horizon which no man has but he whose eye can integrate all the parts" (*E&L*, 9), or "the universe is the property of every individual in it" (*E&L*, 16) suggests indeed a closer, more familiar, and more ordinary (but not therefore less important) relationship than knowing or believing. (It is one mode of the "democratization of 'being'" that Borden Flanagan so astutely identifies in his contribution to this volume as Emerson's distinctive adaptation of Plato to American circumstances.) And the idiom of ownership had the additional benefit for Emerson of liberal-historical connotations with which Cavell is not explicitly concerned. By affirmatively evoking and elaborating his readers' multidimensional "property" in existence, Emerson manages at once to pay tribute to the genuine emancipation afforded by the liberal right to property, and at the same time to shift the focus of that right away from material things and toward the fluid interior realm of consciousness—the sphere of what George Kateb (also excerpted in this volume) aptly calls the "inner ocean."[25] Emerson thus manages to honor the world-historical significance of the American Declaration of Independence and the Constitution, but also to suggest that Americans have not yet begun to discover the full (inner) wealth, dignity, and happiness that these documents secured for them. Just as a political founder of the previous generation also steeped in Scottish liberalism—James Madison—had proposed in the *Federalist* a "republican remedy for the diseases most incident to republican government,"[26] so Emerson thus employs the language of property as what might be called a liberal remedy to ills—rampant materialism and instrumentalism—peculiar to liberal-commercial society. Ultimately Emerson resolves the thrice-reinforced duality in his outlook on property in the way that great writers most often resolve their value conflicts—by verbally exploiting it as a source of fresh perspectives. Emerson develops a richly multivalent idiom of property even more abstract than the abstract conception that, according to the Scots, made commercial society possible, and in this way hopes to push progress along to a yet higher stage than any the Scots had imagined.

Nature

For illustration, we may now look in more depth at some of the quotations with which I began the essay. The first one came from the first "chapter" of *Nature,* also entitled "Nature": "The charming landscape which I saw this morning, is indubitably made up of some twenty or thirty farms. Miller owns this field, Locke that, and Manning the woodland beyond. But none of them owns the landscape. There is a property in the horizon which no man has but he whose eye can integrate all the parts, that is, the poet. This is the best part of these men's farms, yet to this their warranty-deeds give no title" (*E&L,* 9). The passage plays on a contrast between two types of ownership. The first is the familiar material kind wherein one purchases exclusive rights to occupation and/or use, as represented by a deed or a title. It is perhaps not accidental that Emerson here associates this level with two characters named "Locke" and "Manning," since the right to acquire and hold such material property is the foundation of John Locke's theory of man in society—arguably the philosophical foundation of modern liberalism. Even as Emerson here suggests a different sense of ownership, he characteristically does not seek to undermine, destabilize, or even to criticize the normative liberal idea. He attempts rather to supplement it by evoking a higher, more abstract, less instrumental conception. It is directly analogous to the passage in *Walden* where Thoreau declines to make any profit when he agrees to resell a farm back to a man who changes his mind after having sold it to Thoreau: "I sold him the farm for just what I gave for it. . . . But I retained the landscape, and I have since annually carried off what it yielded without a wheelbarrow."[27] To "own" the landscape in the aesthetic way that Emerson and Thoreau here advocate requires no documentation and no fences. There is a boundary in the horizon, which gives the perception definition and form, and allows the landscape to become a holistic object of cognition and thus possession, but since this object may be spontaneously produced by any human consciousness at any time, its acquisition is non-exclusive, infinitely renewable, requires no wheelbarrow, and thus leaves, as it were, no carbon footprint. Manning, Locke, or Miller will never know that their lands have been thus silently possessed by a sensitive wayfarer, but this does not make the event less real. Emerson also plays here on the quasi-scientific meaning of "property"—a distinctive characteristic of a substance—to suggest that the poet's aesthetic harvest is no less objectively substantive than the farmers' corn or wheat. This progression from specific farms to a generalized abstract-aesthetic consciousness of the landscape at once parallels and steps beyond the evolution from concrete "land" to abstract "market" values globally conjectured by the Scots and played out locally in Jacksonian America.

The next two chapters of *Nature* are entitled, respectively, "Commodity" and "Beauty." Taken together, they reiterate the complementary relationship we just traced between two levels of property, material and spiritual, evoked in the passage above. Under the heading of "Commodity," Emerson places the innumerable material benefits—the "prodigal provision"—available to humankind in nature: "this ocean of air above, this ocean of water beneath, this firmament of earth between . . . , [b]easts, fire, water, stones, and corn . . . the wind sows the seed; the sun evaporates the sea; the wind blows the vapor to the field; . . . the rain feeds the plant; the plant feeds the animal; and thus the endless circulations of the divine charity nourish man" (*E&L*, 12). Emerson also includes in his praise the remarkable technological devices human beings have recently developed to enhance their access to nature's bounty. He celebrates steamships: "He no longer waits for favoring gales, but by means of steam, he realizes the fable of Æolus's bag, and carries the two and thirty winds to the boiler of his boat" (*E&L*, 12). He celebrates railroads: "He paves the road with iron bars, and mounting a coach with a ship-load of men, animals, and merchandise behind him, he darts through the country, from town to town, like an eagle or a swallow through the air" (*E&L*, 12, 13). And he evokes a long arc of progress leading to what he correctly perceives as the relative historical good fortune of even a poor white North American in the early nineteenth century: "By the aggregate of these aids, how is the face of the world changed, from the era of Noah to that of Napoleon! The private poor man hath cities, ships, canals, bridges, built for him. He goes to the post-office, and the human race run on his errands; to the book-shop, and the human race read and write of all that happens, for him; to the court-house, and nations repair his wrongs" (*E&L*. 13). Emerson's particular political sympathies are in evidence here as he selects for approving example many of the projects of federal "improvement"—canals, bridges, roads, a national post office—favored by the American Whigs. But the passage reaches beyond American political debates of the 1830s to celebrate the unprecedented material resources—"commodities"—made newly accessible to ordinary individuals by modern commercial-industrial economies more generally.

But however warmly Emerson welcomes such ameliorating advances in material well-being, for him commodities are never enough. Just as we saw him shift in the farm-landscape passage from a conventional-legal to a spiritual-aesthetic point of view, so in *Nature* as a whole he now shifts from use-value to aesthetic value, from "Commodity" to "Beauty," from the need for food and shelter to a "nobler want." What distinguishes the latter from the former in Emerson's mind is that beauty is an entirely noninstrumental value. We may well derive a palpable relief by stepping away from our desks out of doors into a sunlit afternoon, but Emerson insists that the value of the experience cannot be reduced to a drop in blood pressure: "Nature satisfies by its loveliness, and without any mixture of corporeal benefit. I see the spectacle of morning from the hill-top over against my house, from day-break to sun-rise, with emotions that an angel might share" (*E&L*, 15). As evidence, Emerson includes in this section three extended passages of purely phenomenological nature writing worthy of Thoreau, a surprisingly rare occurrence in Emerson's opus, where natural objects are usually quickly subsumed into metasymbolic or metaphorical nets. "The long slender bars of cloud float like fishes in the sea of crimson light," he writes in one instance. And: "The beauty that shimmers in the yellow afternoons of October, who could ever clutch it? Go forth to find it, and it is gone: 'tis only a mirage as you look from the windows of diligence" (*E&L*, 16). What is "angelic" about such writing, for both writer and reader, is not only the vivid alacrity of the language, but the absence within it of any ulterior practical, symbolic, or ideological aim. Emerson here merely represents and tries to evoke necessarily evanescent moments of pure receptivity, pure beholding, and in this respect the passages run directly and pointedly counter to the massive and manifold instrumentation of commodity extraction and transport celebrated in the previous section. Heidegger might have called these moments of "the memory of Being" in a technological society doomed to "forgetfulness of Being." Cavell calls them moments of "intimacy with existence"—among many valuably recorded in the writings of Emerson and Thoreau. Whatever they might be called, Emerson himself believed that such counterbalancing aesthetic moments were a higher form of property essential to the spiritual health of a liberal-commercial-technological society such as he saw emerging in the United States. Precisely because its pragmatic middle-class people, newly emancipated from deferential dependency and subordination, were so understandably eager to "clutch" the comfort and dignity afforded by unprecedented material plenty, they were in danger of allowing their sensibilities to be swamped and their imaginations to be coarsened by too much attention to commodified objects. Immersed in a world of things, it would be too easy for Americans to begin to conceive of reality in general, or another human being, or themselves, as a thing. Matthew Arnold advocated the similarly counterbalancing influences of what he called "culture" in industrializing mid-nineteenth-century England for similar reasons, and explicitly recognized Emerson as a New World ally in this cause.[28]

Having thus moved from "Commodity" to "Beauty," in the immediately ensuing paragraphs of *Nature,* Emerson raises the property stakes higher still—to morality: "Beauty is the mark God sets upon virtue. Every natural action is graceful. Every heroic act is also decent, and causes the place and the bystanders to shine. We are taught by great actions that the universe is the *property* of every individual in it. Every rational creature has all nature for his *dowry* and *estate.* It is his, if he will. He may *divest* himself of it; he may creep into a corner, and abdicate his kingdom, as most men do, but he is *entitled* to the world by his constitution" (*E&L,* 16, emphasis added). In broadest terms, the conception of virtue Emerson preaches here is entirely consistent with the classical Platonic doctrine: action in accordance with nature. But Emerson here gives this teaching a distinctive modern liberal inflection by recourse to the language of property. For Plato, discerning nature's order is not a simple task: it requires the rigorous use of our powers of reason to override the passions and to pierce through accumulated conventional illusions, and it can be accomplished by few, if any, human beings. But in the Scottish moral-sense tradition to which Emerson ascribed, the discernment of the good is not so hard: every individual knows what is right—and therefore what is in accordance with the nature of things—by almost instantaneous affective intuition. We have, in other words, an immediate attunement to nothing less than the underlying order of the cosmos—a kind of inner highway to virtue. Emerson uses the language of property here to call his readers' attention to the magnitude of this astounding inner gift. When he says, "the universe is the property of every individual in it," the statement is not meant to give encouragement to spoiled children, rapacious adults, or exploitative companies, but, on the contrary, to alert every individual that she carries around with her an instinctive orientation to the world's underlying moral structure, as well as the capacity to act accordingly. It is thus a striking illustration of what Alan Levine means in his essay in this volume when he correctly observes that "Emerson situates his ontology of becoming in a metaphysics of being" (233). It is akin to Kant's statement of awe before "the starry skies above me and the moral law within me."[29] It is meant to proclaim our "intimacy with existence." But although it is significant that Emerson vouchsafes this moral knowledge to individuals apparently regardless of communal or social input, his clever use of legalistic property words such as "dowry," "estate," "will," "divest," "abdicate," "kingdom," "entitle," and, especially, "constitution" ensures that he does not mean to reserve the consciousness of such intimacy to the exaltations of solitude. The pun in the statement that one is "entitled to the world by [one's] constitution" suggests an empowering harmony between the inner moral structure of the self and the official founding legal document of America's liberal polity: both orient us appropriately toward full ownership of our own individual existence. The playful use of "kingdom" also serves to remind the reader of the specific political-historical origins of this felicitous internal and external rightness—that it was hard-won in the recent revolutionary overthrow of a feudal-aristocratic regime which denied such existential ownership to all but a few. Just to be sure, Emerson makes this historical context unmistakable in the long passage immediately following in which he invokes a long line of the heroes and martyrs of the history of liberty from Winkelried to Columbus to Harry Vane and Lord Russell, emphasizing the extent to which the achievement of the right to property is a recent step in a long, inexorable progressive-historical ascent.

Early Lectures

In the years immediately following the publication of *Nature*, Emerson is sometimes said to have inclined toward socialist political radicalism. Stephen Whicher long since authorized this view by breaking Emerson's career as a whole into a bipartite schema in which a youthful utopian (socialist) phase reaches its optimistic apex in the later 1830s and early 1840s, followed by lifelong contraction and "acquiescence" to existential finitude and the liberal-capitalist norm after the death of Waldo Jr. in 1842.[30] Many others have since adopted versions of the Whicher narrative, including Michael

Gilmore, who finds a laudable "anti-market" emphasis in Emerson's writing from 1837–1843, after which he "became an apologist for industrial capitalism."[31] And Sacvan Bercovitch also suggests that Emerson "came to the edge of class analysis" during these years, before regrettably lapsing back into the inescapable American liberal consensus.[32] But this view is directly belied by the several substantial lecture series which underlie Emerson's early publications.

Emerson was pro-market during his supposedly radical phase in two interlocking ways: in his actions and in his thought. In his actions, Emerson successfully marketed himself. Emboldened by his successes on the lyceum circuit from 1833 to 1836, Emerson first went out on his own as a lecturer between 1836 and 1842. He hired out the Masonic Temple in Boston, advertised in newspapers, sold tickets, and then delivered lecture series on broad topics of his own choosing, usually then repeating some or all of the series for paying audiences in neighboring towns. For Emerson as for so many others, such engagement with the market economy proved profitable, yielding a comfortable living for him and his growing family. Lecturing would remain his principal source of income for the rest of his career, as well as providing a valuable testing ground for ideas that arose in his journals and eventually arrived at their most polished expression in his essays and books.

More importantly, Emerson's thought during his early years was equally pro-market. Perhaps not surprisingly, given this favorable market context, and what we have already noted in *Nature,* property is a frequent topic of the several series delivered during these years—"The Philosophy of History" (1836–1837), "Human Culture" (1837–1838), "Human Life" (1838–1839), and "The Present Age" (1839–1840). The most striking case in point is found in the fifth lecture of "The Philosophy of History" series, first delivered on January 12, 1837. It is entitled "Politics," and it stands as one of Emerson's most sustained, if not most coherent, statements on political theory. But the lecture could just as accurately be titled "Politics and Property" since after a brief initial nod to the political role of "persons," Emerson turns his attention for the entire remainder of the piece to the political significance of property, asserting that "if explored in its foundations . . . the philosophy of property would open new mines of practical wisdom which would in the event change the face of the world" (*EL,* 2:79). Emerson makes four main substantive points in the lecture, which I will cite in an order of ascending prominence. The first is the broadly empirical observation, the importance of which we have already touched on in this essay, that "the last ages have been characterized in history by the immense creation of property" (*EL*, 2:80). He draws secondarily the progressive corollary more recently noted by Eric Hobsbawm in his account of the nineteenth century as most fundamentally shaped by a "dual" liberal and industrial "revolution"[33]—that the proliferation of goods had transformative effects on the political structure of Western societies, contributing to the overthrow of feudal-aristocracy by liberal democracy: "With power comes the consciousness of power," Emerson writes, "and therefore indomitable millions have demanded forms of government more suited to the facts" (*EL*, 2:80). Emerson's third point moves into familiar Scottish liberal territory as he evokes the moral education afforded to the millions of new modern proprietors by the empowering experience of ownership—"that the creation of so many new households and so many forcible and propertied citizens, has been the creation of lovers of order, knowledge, and peace and hating war" (*EL*, 2:81). These three points on property are all characteristically Scottish and liberal.

The fourth point is perhaps the most troubling to a twenty-first-century reader, but it is the principal focus of the piece as a whole. Emerson first states the familiar foundational Lockean axiom that government exists for the purposes of "protection," but he then makes a brief sequence of less familiar moves. He emphatically distinguishes two equally worthy "objects" of protection—"1. Persons, and 2. Property" (*EL*, 2:70): "no distinction in politics seems to be so fundamental as this" (*EL*, 2:73). He then asserts that "while the rights of all as persons are equal . . . , their rights in Property are very unequal." He points out that due to differences in "skill and virtue," some people will legitimately acquire more property than others: "One man owns his clothes; another owns a county" (*EL*, 2:71). These proprietors will also legitimately pass their acquired wealth along to their children or other beneficiaries: "As much right as the first owner had in it, so much right had he to bestow it on the second" (*EL*, 2:72). Having thus already arbitrarily established "persons" and "property" as two entities of equal legal-political status, Emerson then infers that since it is likely that there will be fewer proprietors than nonproprietors in a given state, the legitimate interests of property cannot be adequately represented by strictly quantitative democratic methods under the principle of one-person-one-vote. "Property should make the law for property," he concludes, "and persons the law for persons": "the proprietors of the nation should have more elective franchise than non-proprietors."

The proposal as a whole stands no chance of being enacted or even seriously taken up. But it is nonetheless highly significant that Emerson attempted to make this argument in Jacksonian America in 1837. In still residually aristocratic Europe at this time it would not have been unusual. The principle of a property qualification for voting was still staunchly defended by nineteenth-century aristocratic liberals such as Guizot in France. In England, even radical middle-class "Manchester liberals" such as Richard Cobden did not yet contemplate universal manhood suffrage. In mid-nineteenth-century England, John Stuart Mill gave the idea a slightly new twist by proposing to give more votes to people with more education. But the world-historical significance of the Jacksonian revolution in the United States—which had officially started with Jackson's near-election in 1824, arrived in full with his triumphs in 1828 and 1832, and continued apace in 1836 with the election of his designated successor, Martin van Buren—was precisely that it represented the end of the property franchise and the advent of mass (white male) democracy in U.S. federal elections. It was not coincidental that Andrew Jackson, the first national leader in history to be democratically elected by universal (white) manhood suffrage, was also the first U.S. president who was not a member of the Virginia or Massachusetts elite. Emerson here reveals his Massachusetts elite loyalties, about which he was in fact never shy, by proposing in effect to roll back the electoral basis of the Jacksonian revolution. Far from radical or utopian, such a proposal can only be read as starkly conservative in an American context. The fact that it was delivered first and then partially repeated twice during precisely the years designated by Whicher, Gilmore, and others as a time of burgeoning socialist radicalism for Emerson—first in 1837, again in "The Present Age" series in 1840, and again verbatim in the essay "Politics" in *Essays: Second Series* in 1844—casts significant doubt on the accuracy of their claim. But to be conservative in an American context is not to be antiliberal, as Louis Hartz long since showed,[34] and indeed Emerson's position here is in fact perfectly in keeping with the moderate, Scots-based, and eminently realistic aristocratic liberalism he grew up with in Federalist Boston and found duly reinforced at Whig-Unitarian Harvard. Emerson here in effect restates in terms of "Property" and "Persons" a variant of the classic tension between "Liberty" and "Equality" that Tocqueville among others placed at the dynamic center of liberal-democratic culture. And like many liberals both European and American who grew alarmed in the 1830s and 1840s by the emerging socialist prospect of a democratically authorized redistribution of wealth, Emerson here weighs in on the side of liberty and property.

But in these early lectures as we saw him do in *Nature*, Emerson also makes clear that he sees the constitutional protection of material property as only a first step. In "Trades and Professions"—the seventh lecture in the same series that contains "Politics"—he celebrates all kinds of labor as the exercise of an innate human right to a kind of ontological "possession": "What is labor but the act of the individual man going out to take possession of the world which the universal mind has built?" (*EL*, 2:114, 115). In this lecture, he pointedly bridges the emerging cultural gap between "land" and "market" by praising the labors of both the farmer and the merchant for the vast intimacies they establish between human consciousness and the world: "[The farmer's] head is an almanac. . . . No blast that sings in the sky from the freezing January wind to the tuneful south wind of midsummer but he knows them all and what they bring to man" (*EL*, 2:115); while the merchant "stands as the mediator or broker of all the farmers on the earth to exchange for them the products of their labor . . . [h]e learns the riches of each zone and climate, where the cotton, the logwood, the corn, the tea plant, hides, and drugs are to be found and what fruits and wares the owners of these will barter them for" (*EL*, 2:116). And in the extraordinary introductory lecture to the next series, which he delivered the following winter, Emerson explicitly names this capacity for various and intimate interrelationship with the world as the faculty of what he here calls "culture": "The means of culture is the related nature of man: he is so strongly related to everything that he can go nowhere without meeting objects that solicit his senses, and yield him new meanings" (*EL*, 2:220). A growing child steps into maturity and full self-development, Emerson suggests, when she at last learns to distinguish spiritual from material ownership, and thus discovers that she has legitimate property in all of the various things she encounters: "This is the discipline of man in the degrees of Property. He learns that above the merely external rights to the picture, to the park, to the equipage, rights which the law protects,—is a spiritual property which is Insight. The kingdom of the Soul transcendeth all the walls and muniments of possession and taketh higher rights not only in the possession but in the possessor, and with this royal reservation, can very well afford to leave the so-called proprietor undisturbed as its keeper or trustee" (*EL*, 2:223). Thus, for Emerson, consciousness itself comes to be understood as a form of property. To grasp this is to discover great wealth indeed. But rather than drawing on this inner resource for a "radical" quasi-socialist critique of liberalism as Bercovitch, Whicher, and Gilmore suggest, the young Emerson sought rather to offer an expanded account of liberalism that included this capacious and capable inner dimension—a process we saw initiated in *Nature* and extended in these early lectures which was then brought to new artistic heights in the great early essays.

Early Essays

In addition to being (erroneously) seen as a time of incipient socialist radicalism, the period from the publication of *Nature* in 1836 to the publication of "Experience" in 1844 is also often said to contain Emerson's best published writing. Although an Emerson scholar should never accede too quickly to a consensus, it is hard to disagree with this one. Nothing in his subsequent work, and no other moral essays in English that I know of, can compare to the metaphorical richness, associative suddenness, or ecstatic lift and force of Emerson's great prose of these years. Nietzsche loved the lightness and force of Emerson's essays, and it is not implausible to suggest that Emerson carried these qualities directly into his prose from the high spirits and high aims of his young nation. Jefferson wrote in a late letter that "something new under the sun" had been born in the founding of the United States, and in works such as "Self-Reliance," "Divinity School Address," "History," and "Compensation," Emerson seems to successfully mimic America's abrupt departure from its European past in the abrupt and energetic departure of each sharp new sentence from the one before it. And thematically these essays lift to new lyrical-philosophical heights the conception of spiritual property which we have already seen preliminarily established in *Nature* and the early lectures.

A paradox at the heart of this set of essays parallels the paradoxical structure of modern commercial society as described by Adam Smith and Emile Durkheim. While the greater division of labor characteristic of modern life separates the individual from the community—each person hived off in pursuit of her specialty without connection to the larger social whole—industrial-commercial society also generates a greater interdependency. Since no one can acquire all the know-how needed to perform all the specialized functions of ordinary life in an advanced society, each person remains tacitly dependent on a very large number of (mostly anonymous) others. Smith famously cites the example of a day laborer's simple "woolen coat": "The shepherd, the sorter of the wool, the wool-comber or carder, the dyer, the scribbler, the spinner, the weaver, the fuller, the dresser, with many others, must all join their different arts in order to complete even this homely production. How many merchants and carriers, besides, must have been employed in transporting the materials from some of those workmen to others who often live in a very distant part of the country!"[35] Durkheim emphasizes the collective dimension in making the same general point: "Even where society rests wholly upon the division of labor, it does not resolve itself into a myriad of atoms juxtaposed together, between which only external and transitory contact can be established. . . . Each one of the functions that the members exercise is constantly dependent upon others and constitutes with them a solidly linked system."[36] In the rhetoric of Emerson's early essays, the call to solitude and self-reliance also results paradoxically in a deepened consciousness of both social and ontological interdependence. "Go alone" (*E&L*, 272), "insist on yourself" (*E&L*, 278), "shun father and mother and wife and brother" (*E&L*, 262), Emerson recommends in "Self-Reliance." "Obey thyself" (*E&L*, 81), "pierce the deep solitudes of absolute ability and worth" (*E&L*, 89), he urges in the "Divinity School Address." These would seem to be formulae of fragmentation and atomization, but to heed them is paradoxically to discover, as Emerson puts it in "History," that "a man is a bundle of relations, a knot of roots, whose flower and fruitage is the world" (*E&L*, 254).

The theme of paradoxical liberal-individualist interrelatedness and the language of property come together in a striking passage near the end of "Self-Reliance":

> And so the reliance on Property, including the reliance on governments which protect it, is the want of self-reliance. Men have looked away from themselves and at things so long, that they have come to esteem the religious, learned, and civil institutions as guards of property. . . . They measure their esteem of each other by what each has, and not by what each is. But a cultivated man becomes ashamed of his property, out of new respect for his nature.

> Especially he hates what he has, if he sees that it is accidental—came to him by inheritance, or gift, or crime, then he feels that it is not having; it does not belong to him, has no root in him, and merely lies there, because no revolution or robber takes it away. But that which a man is does always by nature acquire, and what the man acquires is *living property*, which does not wait the beck of rulers, or mobs, or revolutions, or fire, or storm, or bankruptcies, but perpetually renews itself when the man breathes. (*E&L*, 281–82)

Most of this passage turns upon an opposition between "being" and "having," in which "being" is strongly privileged. On the side of "being," Emerson places such primary and fundamental terms as "self," "is," and "nature," while secondary terms such as "government," "things," "property," "accident," "inheritance," "gift," and "crime" are linked along a subordinate axis of "having." If Emerson were simply a critic of liberal materialism, he would have maintained this opposition throughout the passage, as Carlyle might have done, even perhaps tapping into the still culturally potent Christian tradition of antimaterialism: "Lay up your stores in heaven." But instead Emerson dissolves his own opposition in the final sentence when he says, "That which a man is does always by nature acquire, and what the man acquires is living property." Now being and having are said to be inherently linked, and the terms "acquire" and "property" are given a somewhat mysterious higher meaning. The passage thus provides excellent illustration of Emerson's self-appointed dual role with respect to liberal culture: he here sharply criticizes its excessive materialism and overreliance on material "things," but this decidedly does not lead him to a rejection of liberal values per se. It leads him instead to something we have seen before: a rhetorical effort to revitalize liberal culture by charging one of its core values—"property"—with a deeper, nonmaterial meaning. Thus what starts out as a new formulation of a long-standing binary opposition between being and having becomes a refiguring of being as inseparable from having and vice versa. "To be is to have property (in being)," Emerson says essentially. It would be hard to imagine a clearer example of his use of the language of property as a means of conveying intimacy with existence. It would also be hard to imagine a more fundamental endorsement of liberalism's construction of the self. C. B. Macpherson's opposition to liberalism did not render him mistaken when he suggested that in liberal theory "the relation of ownership, having become for more men the critically important relation determining their actual freedom and actual prospect of realizing their full potentialities, was *read back* into the nature of the individual."[37] For Emerson here as elsewhere in his writing, property and selfhood are similarly superimposed—not so much as retrospective projection and original text but rather as a kind of imminent and ongoing circular interpenetration. This passage offers, furthermore, a striking example of how for Emerson even the maximal removal of the individual from society—to the level of mere being—does not remove him/her entirely from property and interrelationship. If to be is to acquire, then to be is also to enter into a kind of relationship, potentially even into an elaborate network of relationships.

Where "Self-Reliance" may thus be said to concern itself with freeing the self as far as possible from merely conventional social attachments, the "Divinity School Address," "History," and "Compensation" may be said to each concern itself with a different thread in the deep "bundle of relations" in which this free self then finds itself joined. Taken together, these essays do not preach an antisocial rejection of community; they call instead for a turning away from superficial relationships in order to clear a space for the development of deeper, more authentic and life-giving ones. "When halfgods go," Emerson writes in "Give All to Love," "the gods arrive."[38] And, again, the words Emerson uses in these essays to characterize the deeper relationship to God, to human others, and to existence that the self finds on the other side of solitude are most often words of property and ownership.

In the "Divinity School Address," the relationship in question is with God or the divine. It is not surprising that the authorities at Harvard were offended by this speech, for Emerson suggests herein that the self may climb the rungs of the moral sentiments up to nothing less than ownership of God: "Under the influence of the sentiment of virtue, he learns that his being is without bound . . . that which he venerates is still his *own*, though he has not realized it yet" (*E&L*, 76, emphasis added); "If a man is at heart just, then in so far is he God; the safety of God, the immortality of God; the majesty of God do enter into that man with justice" (*E&L*, 76). In another passage, Emerson offers a verbally audacious alternative to the sacrament of the "Lord's Supper" which again suggests a kind of ownership of the divine: "In how many churches, by how many prophets, tell me, is man made sensible that he is in an infinite soul; that the earth and heavens are passing into his mind, that he is drinking forever the soul of God" (*E&L*, 84). To borrow the terms of Daniel Malachuk's apt critique in this volume, it is hard to see how "detranscendental" readers of Emerson can account for passages such as these, and there are a great many of them throughout these astounding early essays, often voiced in his most brilliant lyrical prose. The shift from ingesting a solid—the Eucharist—in Communion to ingesting a liquid in this passage allows for greater interpenetration of self and God. Where the former occurred in a structured ceremony performed at regulated intervals, this latter is a spontaneous function of consciousness itself perpetually engaged in an act of communion with the (divine) world around it. And throughout the essay, Emerson executes a reversal in the directionality of intracultural borrowing. Where cultural leaders had typically looked to the religious sphere to check or mitigate the excesses of the commercial sphere, Emerson instead draws upon the language of commerce to reinvigorate religion.

"History" celebrates the capacity of the free individual to "possess" through reading nothing less than all of human experience. Indeed, like *Nature*, "History" is in part an effort to reassure the post-Enlightenment, post-Christian self that in the absence of the Bible she will not lack for symbolic resources. On the contrary, Emerson argues that the symbolic record of human experience provided in secular literature—in which he includes history writing–is vast, rich, readily available, and fully intelligible. But one must learn to avail oneself of this resource by the practice of reading as a form of possession—in the senses both of ownership and of allowing one's own consciousness to be temporarily occupied by another: "We as we read must become Greeks, Romans, Turks, priest & king, martyr and executioner, must fasten these images to some reality in our secret experience"; "All that Shakespeare says of the king, yonder slip of boy feels to be true of himself" (*E&L*, 238). As such great twentieth-century readers as Jorge Luis Borges and Harold Bloom have recognized, Emerson was one of the great readers of the nineteenth century, and it is above all in "History" that he expresses his sense of reading as a kind of ordinary ecstasy, a daily inner metamorphosis, an ongoing and infinitely advantageous exchange of being. There are multiple passages in "History" akin to the famous "transparent eyeball" passage in *Nature* where the boundaries of the self are implicitly or explicitly dissolved as it comes into immediate contact with a greater surrounding reality. But where in *Nature* the agent of this dilation is vision, in "History" it is reading. And again the language of property and ownership plays a crucial role in representing this interchange: "The advancing man discovers how deep a property he has in literature,—in all fable as well as in all history" (*E&L*, 250); "Those old worships of Moses, of Zoroaster, of Menu, of Socrates . . . they are mine as much as theirs" (*E&L*, 249); "He that is once admitted to the right of reason is made a freeman of the whole estate" (*E&L*, 238); "Property also holds of the soul, covers great spiritual facts" (*E&L*, 238). In every case, Emerson uses the language of property and possession to mark a commonplace but nonetheless intense, intimate, and perpetually transformative relationship at the heart of print-based liberal culture—that of a solitary consciousness and a text.

Emerson uses economic language somewhat differently in "Compensation" than in the "Divinity School Address" or "History," but his aims in this essay are no less ambitious. Where in the first two pieces Emerson draws on the language of ownership to urge nothing less than the individual's internalization of God and human history, here he uses the language of commercial exchange and acquisition to represent nothing less than what we might call the deep structure of human finitude, and to advocate a particular kind of individual efficacy within this ontological order. Every individual human self, Emerson suggests in this essay, is allotted a finite quantum of time and energy for its lifetime. This allotment may be utilized in an almost infinite variety of ways to pursue or produce an almost infinite variety of goods—material, moral, spiritual, aesthetic, and otherwise. To this extent, existence may and should be gratefully received as pure gift. But there is also a painful, even tragic condition built in to this gift. Because time and energy are limited, and because most goods take substantial amounts of time and energy to bring to fruition, the pursuit of any one good or set of goods will require forgoing the pursuit of all the rest. The fully conscious self will be at once deeply grateful to know that the disciplined pursuit of any good will bring about some form of realization, but it will also be painfully aware of all the alternative goods it must forgo. Everything, as we sometimes say in ordinary language, is a trade-off. The inevitable pain thus associated with all human ambitions caused most of the Eastern sages to whom Emerson looked on these matters to counsel withdrawal and quiescence. By minimizing one's desires and needs, one could minimize the inevitable pains associated with the pursuit of their satisfaction. But in "Compensation," Emerson gives this doctrine a more dynamic and perhaps distinctively American inflection. He counsels choice, the disciplined and determined pursuit of desired goods, and the willing payment of the price in inevitable pain and regret for surrendered alternatives. His message is at once optimistic and entirely realistic within the terms of this economy: If you pay the price in energy and time and forgone alternatives, you cannot fail to get the good you seek. But you must pay! "What will you have? quoth God; pay for it and take it" (*E&L*, 293), he writes at a turning point just a bit more than halfway through, and the rest of the essay is shot through with the frequent repetition of the word "pay," along with "property," "price," "debt," and "tax."

One cannot help but hear traces of Calvinism's punitive Old Testament god in the word "pay" as Emerson repeats it with such relish in these paragraphs. But the echo also provides some measure of the secularizing distance that Emerson has traveled. An inevitable payment must still be made, but the precise degree and character of it has been brought within the sphere of efficacious human choice, and within the span of unredeemed mortal time. In "Compensation," as throughout Emerson's writing, it is the unredeemed consciousness of human finitude that makes existence seem like (precious) property. And this is perhaps why, in "Experience," Emerson found himself turning to property metaphors in grappling with the loss of his son. It had long been true that he "could not get" existence (or its loss) "any closer" to him.

Middle and Later Works

It is true, as the Whicher narrative suggests, that never again after the great early essays did Emerson's prose reach such lyrical heights, but this was not related to any significant change in his political orientation or his attitude toward property. Throughout his career, Emerson remained fully committed to the Scottish-inflected Lockean-libertarian liberalism whose influence we have traced back to his earliest notebooks. Indeed, his turn to more overtly political and historical themes in his writing between 1841 and 1860 is consistent with the Scots' dual interest in both the moral-psychological and the social-institutional history of liberty. Having lavished his lyrical-rhetorical gifts upon the evocation of the astounding inner property of the free liberal individual in works such as *Nature*, "The Philosophy of History," "Human Culture," the "Divinity School Address," "History," "Self-Reliance," and "Compensation," Emerson turned his attention in his later work to the legal and institutional arrangements by which the multifarious properties of such free selves, both inward and outward, were best protected. The political lectures of the early 1840s—"Man the Reformer" (1841), "Lecture on the Times" (1841), "The Conservative" (1842), "The Young American" (1844), "Politics" (1844), and "New England Reformers" (1844)—react skeptically to the emergence of socialist utopianism in both Europe and America, in no small part out of fear of state encroachment on both material and spiritual property. These speeches recognize the ongoing need for reform in American politics and society, but they attempt implicitly to counter the overweening, unrealistic, and potentially tyrannical state envisioned by utopian theorists in favor of organic processes of critique arising from the private moral intuitions of the citizenry.[39] Emerson constructs the English antislavery movement as a success story of precisely such an organically mobilized civil society in his first major antislavery speech—"An Address . . . on . . . the Emancipation of the Negroes in the British West Indies" (1844).[40] And, as Len Gougeon's work has made clear, Emerson continued thereafter to forcefully give voice to his own outraged moral sense at various venues in a substantial sequence of antislavery lectures, letters, and addresses through 1863.[41]

It is consistent with the lifelong ambivalent preoccupation with property that we have been tracing that in these speeches Emerson characterizes the slavery crisis in good part as a problem of the limits of ownership in a society built upon its protection. "It was a question," as Emerson puts it in his 1854 address on "The Fugitive Slave Law," "whether a man shall be treated as leather? Whether the Negroes shall be, as the Indians were in Spanish America, a species of money" (AW, 79). For Emerson, the answer to this question was a self-evident negative. Just as the Quaker John Woolman felt something was gravely amiss when he found himself "writ[ing] a bill of sale of a negro" (AW, 12), so, Emerson argues, does any morally sentient person recoil when he/she reads or hears about "pregnant women set in the treadmill for refusing to work" or "men's backs flayed with cowhides, and hot rum poured on, superinduced with brine or pickle" (AW, 10). Reflexive horror and disgust, Emerson believed, was the intimate action of the moral sense. Such feelings expressed what Emerson saw as humanity's deep innate attunement to a metaphysically subsistent moral law akin to Kant's categorical imperative against treating any human subject as an object. As a younger man, Emerson had assumed that the brazen violation of such fundamental moral principles by the southern slave system had doomed the region not only to moral barbarism but to economic backwardness and would in time give way to both moral and economic imperatives—as it had in the British West Indies. But the passage of the Fugitive Slave Act in 1850 with the support of his former hero Daniel Webster had convinced Emerson of the truth of what more strident abolitionists had long been saying—that the southern "slave power" was not only not receding, it was aggressively advancing. And Emerson was all the more perturbed by his perception that the slave power threatened to morally co-opt northern society, as it had Webster, by recourse to a core liberal idea, which he himself held sacrosanct: it was out of respect for the idea of lawful property, after all, that the Fugitive Slave Act obligated northerners to return runaway slaves. It is thus not surprising that in these speeches Emerson's outrage against slavery's reduction of human beings to things often spills over into some of the harshest strictures anywhere in his writing against the tendency of acquisitive liberal-commercial civilization per se to a morally corrosive instrumentalism. "We peddle, we truck, we sail, we row, we ride in cars, we creep in teams, we go in canals—to market, and for the sale of goods. The national aim and employment streams into our ways of thinking, our laws, our habits, and our manners. The customer is the immediate jewel of our souls. . . . It was or it seemed the dictate of trade, to keep the negro down. . . . We found it very convenient to keep them at work, since, by the aid of a little whipping, we could get their work for nothing but their board and the cost of whips. What if it cost a few unpleasant scenes on the coast of Africa? . . . The sugar they raised was excellent: nobody tasted blood in it" (AW, 20). In another speech, Emerson castigates "dirt-eating" legislators who "represented the property of their constituency. . . . Our merchants do not believe in anything but their trade" (AW, 97). Indeed, in these speeches Emerson repeatedly attacks Webster for a kind of bare-bones Lockeanism that we have seen Emerson himself express in other contexts: "His finely developed understanding only works truly with all its force, when it stands for animal good, that is, for property. He believes, in so many words, that government exists for the protection of property. He looks at the Union as an estate, a large farm" (AW, 66–67).

Yet on the whole, the antislavery addresses are decidedly not simply antiproperty or anticommercial or, to be sure, antiliberal. On a pragmatic level, for one, while advocating abolition Emerson remains sufficiently respectful of the claims of property that he advocates compensating former slave owners for their economic losses due to manumission—as was done in the West Indies (AW, 105). He is quick to stipulate that such a policy does not "concede the right of the planter to own" (*AW*, 105), but rather seeks realistically to address the legitimate practical difficulty faced by slave owners in a time of transition. And on a deeper level the antislavery writings stand together as the works of Emerson which most sharply draw a distinction between material and spiritual property, and which most forcefully counter the former with the latter: "Gentlemen, man is born with intellect, as well as a love of sugar," he writes in the 1844 "Address . . . on . . . the Emancipation of the Negroes in the British West Indies," "and with a sense of justice, as well as a taste for strong drink" (*AW*, 20–21). For even as Emerson sternly asserts the limits of material property in these speeches—it stops at the human body—he simultaneously exalts the progress and power of moral-spiritual property in the form of legally recognized human rights. The most moving passages in the entire antislavery group are those in the first 1844 address on emancipation in the West Indies which poetically reconstruct the solemn and dignified new bearing of former slaves placed abruptly in full possession of their own selfhood: "On the night of the 31st of July, they met everywhere at their churches and chapels, and at midnight, when the clock struck twelve, on their knees, the silent, weeping assembly became men; they rose and embraced each other; they cried, they sung, they prayed, but there was no riot, no feasting. I have never read anything in history more touching than the moderation of the negroes" (*AW*, 15). Emerson constructs the scene as a kind of spontaneous baptism in the secular religion of human rights. These former slaves are born again into full humanity by the joyful assumption of the serious burden of self-ownership. And laced through the rest of the antislavery addresses we find Emerson's clearest and most forceful assertions of natural rights as sacred and intrinsic human property. "A man's right to liberty is as inalienable as his right to life" (*AW*, 57), he writes in 1851 in his first "Address . . . on the Fugitive Slave Law." "The idea of abstract right exists in the human mind, and lays itself out in the equilibrium of nature," he writes in the 1855 "Lecture on Slavery" (*AW*, 98). "Law [is] not an opinion, not an egotism of any king or the will of any mob," he declares in the same speech, "but a transcript of natural right" (*AW*, 100). In his 1859 "Speech at a Meeting to Aid John Brown's Family," Emerson approvingly quotes the martyred abolitionist on the awesome moral responsibility Americans take on with their political birthright: "Better that a whole generation of men, women and children should pass away by a violent death than that one word of either [the Declaration of Independence or The Golden Rule] should be violated in this country" (*AW*, 118). In 1862, in the immediate aftermath of Lincoln's Emancipation Proclamation, Emerson suggests that the cosmic force of the principle of natural rights was carried in the very bones of every northern soldier: "The war existed long before the cannonade of Sumter and could not be postponed. It might have begun otherwise or elsewhere, but war was in the minds and bones of the combatants, it was written on the iron leaf, and you might as easily dodge gravitation" (*AW*, 133). And in perhaps his last prominent published play on the language of property, in the 1863 "Fortune of the Republic," Emerson suggests that America's true wealth derives not from its vast material resources, but rather from its counterfeudal possession of the moral-spiritual principle of natural rights in all its still-unfolding liberating effects: "The politics of Europe are feudal. The six demands of Chartism, are: 1. Universal Suffrage; 2. Vote by ballot; 3. Paid legislation; 4. Annual Parliament; 5. Equality of Electoral District; 6. No property qualification. In England they are all postponed. They have all been granted here to start with." "We are coming,—thanks to the war,—to a nationality" (*AW*, 144). The bloody evidence of the people's immense reserves of spiritual property has, for the moment, caused even this cautious Yankee to clutch the prerogatives of material property a bit less tightly.

Emerson's stark critique of slavery as an excess of material property in the antislavery addresses, however, should not be taken to imply any abandonment of his long-standing commitment to liberal acquisitiveness properly delimited. During the same years that Emerson was delivering most of his significant antislavery speeches, he also traveled to England (1848) and took notes preparatory to the publication of *English Traits* in 1855. The book lavishly praises the commercial instincts and strong work ethic of the English middle class, as well as the long legal tradition of robust protection of property rights that, Emerson argues, secured the abundant fruits of English talent and labor: "The house is a castle which the King cannot enter. The Bank is a strong box to which the King has no key. . . . Vested rights are awful things, and absolute possession gives the smallest freeholder identity of interest with the duke" (*E&L*, 856). And "Wealth," the most well-known essay in Emerson's last great book of essays, *The Conduct of Life* (1860), also contributes an important chapter to what may be called the liberal revaluation of values by its ringing assertion of the moral legitimacy of the pursuit of material self-interest: "It is of no use to argue the wants down: the philosophers have laid the greatness of man in making his wants few; but will a man content himself with a hut and a handful of dried pease? He is born to be rich" (*E&L*, 991). This is only one of many passages that could be cited as representative of the essay's thoroughgoing rejection of both Christian antimaterialism and Jacksonian subsistence culture. And in this work more explicitly than anywhere else in his opus, Emerson adds the marketplace to nature and history as a symbolic resource for postbiblical society: "The counting room maxims liberally expounded are laws of the Universe. The merchant's economy is a coarse symbol of the soul's economy." He first draws eminently practical lessons from these abstract reflections: "The subject of economy mixes itself with morals, inasmuch as it is a peremptory point of virtue that a man's independence be secured. Poverty demoralizes. A man in debt is so far a slave" (*E&L*, 992). But at the close of this essay, Emerson also again takes up a countervailing point that we have seen before and that is the focus of two important essays in this collection, "Culture" and "Worship"—that the securing of a foundation in material property is only the first step in the fulfillment of the free self. Thereafter one must look to spiritual acquisition: "The true thrift is always to spend on the higher plane; to invest and invest, with keener avarice, that he may spend in spiritual creation, and not in augmenting animal existence" (*E&L*, 1010).

The essays "Culture" and "Worship" play an analogous role in relation to "Wealth" and "Power" that we saw the chapter on "Beauty" play in relation to the "Commodity" section of *Nature*. They provide an account of the place of what may be called "counterinstrumental" values in a liberal-commercial culture in which the pragmatic and instrumental values of the marketplace have been given the central role. "A man is a beggar who only lives to the useful," Emerson writes in "Culture," "and however he may serve as a pin or rivet in the social machine, cannot be said to have arrived at self-possession" (*E&L*, 1030). The language is chosen with characteristic playful precision yet again to suggest two levels of property. The use of a "pin" as a metaphor for a narrowly instrumental selfhood alludes ironically to Adam Smith's famous example in *The Wealth of Nations* of the exponential advances in productivity achieved by the application to pin-making of the principle of the division of labor.[42] We know well by now how fulsomely Emerson generally applauds these advances as a means of gradually extending the freedom, dignity, and power associated with property ownership to human beings across the globe, and thus as the material basis for the overthrow of feudal aristocracy. But his use of the term "self-possession" to characterize what is missing from a too narrowly instrumental and materialistic outlook slyly insists yet again on the necessity of a spiritual conception of property as a supplement. For Emerson, to be able to own things is a necessary and important step in self-emancipation, but full ownership of oneself must also include more abstract forms of property: "We only vary the phrase, not the doctrine, when we say, that culture opens the sense of beauty" (*E&L*, 1030); "We call these millions men; but they are not yet men. Half-engaged in the soil, pawing to get free, man needs all the music that can be brought to disengage him" (*E&L*, 1033).

Scholars have noted that liberalism not only grants individuals a right to property, but also grants them property in their rights. In his later-career mix of libertarian political addresses, antislavery speeches, *English Traits*, and *The Conduct of Life*, as in his opus as a whole, Emerson lent his uniquely formidable voice to the defense of both levels of liberal ownership. To borrow a phrase from "The American Scholar," for Emerson the right to property, like all the other liberal rights, was both "a wall of defense and a wreath of joy around all" (*E&L*, 71). It provided an essential "negative" libertarian bulwark against state encroachment on the freedom of the individual—a freedom that thus properly protected would joyously flower in innumerable and unpredictable ways.

Notes

1. Max Weber, *The Protestant Ethic and the Spirit of Capitalism*, trans. Talcott Parsons (London: Unwin Hyman, 1989), 178–79.

2. Charles Sellers, *The Market Revolution: Jacksonian America 1815–1846* (New York: Oxford, 1991), 379.

3. William L. Hedges, "From Franklin to Emerson," in *Ralph Waldo Emerson: A Collection of Critical Essays*, ed. Lawrence Buell (Englewood, N.J.: Prentice Hall, 1993), 42.

4. A large number of otherwise friendly progressively minded readers stretching from John Dewey to Sacvan Bercovitch have found Emerson's approving use of the language of property unsettling to their efforts to construct him as a radical social democrat. They tend to invoke Stephen Whicher's bipartite narrative of Emerson's career and attribute the frequency of economic language in his later work to

encroaching bourgeois conservatism or "acquiescence" (see Stephen E. Whicher, *Freedom and Fate: An Inner Life of Ralph Waldo Emerson* [Philadelphia: University of Pennsylvania Press, 1953]). But this overlooks the no-less-frequent use of economic language in Emerson's earlier writing, which these critics wish to see as expressive of antimarket utopianism. Michael Gilmore's discussion of Emerson in his valuable *American Romanticism and the Marketplace* (Chicago: University of Chicago Press, 1985) typically keeps to the Whicher narrative—claiming that Emerson passed through "an anti-market" stage between 1837 and 1843 before "becoming an apologist for industrial and commercial capitalism." See also John Dewey, "Emerson: The Philosopher of Democracy," *International Journal of Ethics* (July 13, 1903); Sacvan Bercovitch, "Emerson, Individualism, and the Ambiguities of Dissent," in *Ralph Waldo Emerson*, ed. Buell; Sacvan Bercovitch, *The American Jeremiad* (Madison: University of Wisconsin Press, 1978); and Sacvan Bercovitch, *Rites of Assent: Transformations in the Symbolic Construction of America* (New York: Routledge, 1993). For other democratically oriented readings of Emerson, see Vernon Parrington, *Main Currents in American Thought: An Interpretation of American Literature from the Beginnings to 1920* (New York: Harcourt, Brace, 1927); F. O. Matthiessen, *The American Renaissance: Art and Expression in the Age of Emerson and Whitman* (London: Oxford University Press, 1941); and Daniel Aaron, *Men of Good Hope* (New York: Oxford University Press, 1951). A smaller set of hostile critics including George Santayana, the early Van Wyck Brooks, and Quentin Anderson sweepingly deny to all of Emerson's work any serious interest in society, history, or politics, and thus offer no substantial commentary at all on his use of economic terminology (see George Santayana, "The Genteel Tradition in American Philosophy," in *Winds of Doctrine and Platonism and the Spiritual Life* [1913; Gloucester, Mass.: Peter Smith, 1971], 186–215; Van Wyck Brooks, *America's Coming of Age* [New York: R. W. Huebsch, 1915]; and Quentin Anderson, *The Imperial Self: An Essay in American Literary and Cultural History* [New York: Knopf, 1971]). Nor does the most recently influential school of Emerson interpretation—the antifoundationalist or pragmatist strain articulated by Richard Poirier and Cornel West, among others—have much to say about this historically resonant diction, preferring to focus on what they anachronistically and erroneously see as Emerson's proto-deconstructionist linguistic and moral skepticism (see Cornel West, *The American Evasion of Philosophy: A Genealogy of Pragmatism* [Madison: University of Wisconsin Press, 1989]; and Richard Poirier, *The Renewal of Literature: Emersonian Reflections* [New York: Random House, 1987]). I offer a more thorough critique of these approaches in *Emerson's Liberalism* (Madison: University of Wisconsin Press, 2009).

5. For Emerson's crisis of confidence in the sacred authority of the Bible, see Robert Richardson, *The Mind on Fire* (Berkeley and Los Angeles: University of

California Press, 1995), esp. 108–27; for the secularization of biblical discourse in Emerson and other antebellum New England writers, see the chapter "Literary Scripturism" in Lawrence Buell, *New England Literary Culture: From Revolution through Renaissance* (Cambridge: Cambridge University Press, 1986): for example, "The institutionalization of American belles letters was accompanied and facilitated by a shift in biblical studies, led by New England scholars, from something like universal agreement among professing Christians that the canonical Scriptures were inspired, historically accurate writings to something like the present state of controversy, in which the traditional view had to contend against varying shades of liberalization, including the claim that the bible was no more inspired than any other document" (167).

6. From *Democracy in America*, in *The Tocqueville Reader*, ed. Olivier Zunz and Alan S. Kahan (Oxford: Blackwell 2002), 1:71: "I can recall nothing in history more worthy of sorrow and pity than the scenes which are passing before our eyes. It is as if the natural bond that unites the opinion of man to his tastes, and his actions to his principles, was now broken."

7. For a thorough account of Emerson's lifelong creative engagement with natural science, see Laura Dassow Walls, *Emerson's Life in Science: The Culture of Truth* (Ithaca: Cornell University Press, 2003).

8. For an excellent account of the Scottish anthropology of property, see Christopher J. Berry, *Social Theory of the Scottish Enlightenment* (Edinburgh: Edinburgh University Press, 1997).

9. Ibid., 98.

10. The locus classicus of this conception of the greater civility of the self in modern commercial society is Hume's *Essays Moral Political and Literary* (Indianapolis: Liberty Fund, 1985), especially "The Rise of Arts and Sciences," "Of Commerce," and "Of Refinement in the Arts." "Nothing is more favorable to the rise of politeness and learning," he writes in "The Rise of Arts and Sciences," "than a number of neighboring and independent states, connected together by commerce and policy" (119). "Thus *industry, knowledge,* and *humanity*," he writes in "Of Refinement in the Arts, "are linked together by an indissoluble chain, and are found, from experience as well as reason, to be peculiar to the more polished, and, what are commonly denominated, the more luxurious ages" (271).

11. See Daniel Walker Howe, *The Unitarian Conscience: Harvard Moral Philosophy 1805–61* (1970; Middletown, Conn.: Wesleyan University Press, 1988).

12. G. W. F. Hegel, "Introduction to 'Philosophy of History'" in *The Hegel Reader,* ed. Stephen Houlgate (London: Blackwell, 1998), 402.

13. Charles Sellers's powerful and influential *The Market Revolution: Jacksonian America from 1815 to 1846* (New York: Oxford, 1991) describes the changes brought about by the emergence of commercial society during these years in great

breadth and depth—noting its transformative effects on everything from the relative stressfulness of daily life in America's vast rural hinterlands to developments in evangelical spirituality to policy debates and political intrigues in the rarefied arenas of the nation's capital cities. Daniel Walker Howe, in his recent monumental contribution to the *Oxford History of the United States—What Hath God Wrought: The Transformation of America, 1815–1848* (New York: Oxford, 2007), helps to further fill out the picture of this era in part by defusing some of Sellers's binaries. While he does not dispute the transformative impact of rapid economic development, Howe points out, contra Sellers, that the capitalist marketplace did not descend abruptly on America's subsistence farmers starting in 1815. It had evolved gradually over a long time stretching well back into the eighteenth century, and most American farmers had long since made adaptations to it—practicing a "composite" agriculture in which some produce was consumed while some was traded. Howe stresses throughout that the most revolutionary transformations of the era were brought about not by the advent of market capitalism, but rather by astounding technological advances in communication and transportation.

14. Gordon Wood, *The Radicalism of the American Revolution* (New York: Knopf, 1991), 4: "The colonists knew they were freer, more equal, more prosperous, and less burdened with cumbersome feudal and monarchical restraints than any other part of mankind in the eighteenth century."

15. Ibid., 234, quoting from *Philadelphia, Pennsylvania Packet*, November 26, 1776; *Charleston, South Carolina and American Gazette*, November 6, 1777.

16. See Howe, *What Hath God Wrought*.

17. Scholars owe the application of this term to Jacksonian America to Charles Sellers, cited above.

18. Although Emerson's commitment to a Scots-based conception of historical progress is implicit everywhere in this work, it is perhaps made most explicit in his 1844 essay "The Young American." "Gentlemen, there is a sublime and friendly Destiny by which the human race is guided . . . to results affecting masses and ages. Men are narrow and selfish, but the Genius or Destiny is not narrow, but beneficent. . . . The history of commerce is the record of this beneficent tendency. . . . The philosopher and lover of man have much harm to say of trade; but the historian will see that trade was the principle of Liberty; that trade planted America and destroyed Feudalism; that it makes peace and keeps peace, and it will abolish slavery. . . . Trade is an instrument in the hands of that friendly Power which works for us in our own despite" (*E&L*, 213–30). He expresses the same general confidence in progress in the concluding peroration to his great antislavery speech of the same year, "An Address . . . on . . . the Emancipation of the Negroes in the British West Indies": "Seen in masses, it cannot be disputed, there is progress in human society" (*AW*, 32, 33). And he is still thinking in these terms in 1862 in his

address entitled "The President's Proclamation": "Liberty is a slow fruit. It comes, like religion, in short periods and in rare conditions, as if awaiting a culture of the race which shall make it organic and permanent. Such moments of expansion in modern history were, the Confession of Augsburg; the plantation of America; the English Commonwealth of 1648; the Declaration of American Independence in 1776; the British emancipation of slaves in the West Indies; the passage of the Reform Bill; the repeal of the Corn Laws; the magnetic ocean Telegraph; though yet imperfect, the passage of the Homestead Bill in the last Congress; and now, eminently, President Lincoln's Proclamation on the twenty-second of September" (*AW*, 129).

19. Ralph Waldo Emerson, "Ode, Inscribed to W. H. Channing," in *Essays and Poems*, ed. Joel Porte, Harold Bloom, and Paul Kane (New York: Library of America, 1996), 1111–14.

20. Although it must be noted that in *Walden*, Thoreau also deploys the language of property and economics in a complex and multivalent symbolic manner expressive of his own ambivalences. His symbolic return to subsistence simplicities does not necessarily entail a blanket rejection of economic or technological advances.

21. "Sir, does the Government think that the People of the United States have become savage and mad?" Emerson wrote to President van Buren in an 1838 letter protesting the forced removal of the Cherokees from their traditional homelands. "The soul of man, the justice, the mercy, that is the heart's heart in all men, from Maine to Georgia, does abhor this business," he wrote, and "A man with your experience in affairs must have seen cause to appreciate the futility of opposition to the moral sentiment" (*AW*, 3, 4, 5). For Emerson's opposition to the Mexican War, see Len Gougeon, *Virtue's Hero: Emerson, Antislavery, and Reform* (Athens and London: University of Georgia Press, 1990), 111–23, which includes Gougeon's reading of the "Ode Inscribed to W. H. Channing" as a critique of both slavery and the aggression toward Mexico.

22. See Gougeon, *Virtue's Hero*, 86–249.

23. See Robert Abzug, *Cosmos Crumbling: American Reform and the Religious Imagination* (New York: Oxford University Press, 1994).

24. Stanley Cavell, "An Emersonian Mood," in *Emerson's Transcendental Etudes*, ed. David Justin Hodge (Stanford: Stanford University Press, 2003), 22, 23.

25. See George Kateb, *The Inner Ocean: Individualism and Democratic Culture* (Ithaca: Cornell University Press, 1992).

26. Alexander Hamilton, James Madison, and John Jay, *The Federalist*, ed. Max Beloff (1948; New York: Blackwell, 1987), 47–48.

27. Henry David Thoreau, *Walden and Other Writings* (New York: Modern Library, 1981), 74.

28. See "Emerson" in Matthew Arnold, *Discourses in America* (London: Macmillan, 1885).

29. See Immanuel Kant, *Critique of Practical Reason,* trans. Werner S. Pluhar (Indianapolis: Hackett, 2002), 203: "Two things fill the mind with ever new and increasing admiration and reverence, the more frequently and persistently one's meditation deals with them: the starry sky above me and the moral law within me. . . . I see them before me and connect them directly with the consciousness of my existence."

30. Whicher, *Freedom and Fate.*

31. Gilmore, *American Romanticism and the Marketplace,* 21–22, 30.

32. Sacvan Bercovitch, "Emerson, Individualism, and Liberal Descent," in *The Rites of Assent,* 324.

33. Eric Hobsbawm, *The Age of Revolution* (New York: Vintage, 1962), 96.

34. Louis Hartz, *The Liberal Tradition in America* (New York: Harcourt, Brace, 1955).

35. From *The Wealth of Nations,* in *The Essential Adam Smith,* ed. Robert Heilbroner (New York: Norton, 1986), 167.

36. Emile Durkheim, *The Division of Labor in Society* (New York: Simon and Schuster, 1984), 173.

37. C. B. Macpherson, *The Political Theory of Possessive Individualism: Hobbes to Locke* (New York: Oxford, 1962), 3, emphasis added.

38. Emerson, *Essays and Poems* (New York: Library of America, 1983), 1123.

39. See Dolan, *Emerson's Liberalism,* 169–93.

40. See ibid., 194–222.

41. Gougeon, *Virtue's Hero*; Len Gougeon and Joel Myerson, eds. *Emerson's Antislavery Writings* (New Haven: Yale University Press, 1995).

42. See bk. 1, chap. 1, of *Wealth of Nations,* in *The Essential Adam Smith,* ed. Heilbroner, 160–62.

CHAPTER 12

Standing for Others: Reform and Representation in Emerson's Political Thought

Jason Frank

A man may stand outside the prejudices of religion, country, and race; if such a man be king, he is able to achieve surprising revolutions in society. [But] a whole nation could not possibly rise, as it were, above itself.
—Alexis de Tocqueville, *Democracy in America*

I find [the great man] greater, when he can abolish himself and all heroes, by letting in this element of reason, irrespective of persons, this subtilizer, and irresistible upward force, into our thought, destroying individualism.
—Ralph Waldo Emerson, *Representative Men*

WAS RALPH WALDO EMERSON a democratic theorist? And, if so, which aspects of his political thought provide the best resources for thinking through the dilemmas of contemporary democratic theory? In recent years, a scholarly revaluation of Emerson's politics has engaged deeply with these questions, enriching the study of American political thought and offering a more affirmative picture of Emerson as a political thinker. An earlier generation of political theorists often overlooked Emerson's political thought to focus instead on his role as a prophet of the Imperial Self, as a "radical egoistic anarchist" whose theory of self-reliance contributed mightily to America's escapist political culture of "masterlessness."[1] Carey McWilliams, for example, offered an influential view of Emerson the apolitical individualist: "The divinity which Emerson saw in man was a deified self, independent of other individuals and the democratic public alike," McWilliams writes. "Government and politics moved him only to disdain."[2] As the editors of this volume demonstrate in their introduction, this familiar view has recently come under increasing scrutiny. But even as scholars attend more carefully to Emerson's political activism—especially his militant abolitionism in the 1850s—and, doing so, attempt to integrate his practical affirmation of political participation and "social action" into his theory of self-reliance, the familiar view of Emerson persists. George Kateb, for instance, views Emerson's political activism in the 1850s as a "deviation from his theory of self-reliance, not its transformation."[3] Many of Emerson's critics and admirers in contemporary political theory seem to agree on one essential point: Emerson is first and foremost a theorist of radical individualism, and this diminishes the value of his work for thinking affirmatively about political activism generally and about democratic politics in particular.

This essay takes a different approach. Building on the recent scholarship emphasizing the political dimensions of Emerson's thought, I examine an important but underemphasized aspect of Emerson's work: his concept of representation. This element of Emerson's writing both troubles the apolitical individualist reading and provides a theoretical resource for better appreciating Emerson's distinctive approach to political activism. Stanley Cavell has noted "Emerson's incessant attention to representation," and influentially recovered "representativeness" as one of Emerson's "master-tones."[4] Taking orientation from Cavell's moral perfectionist reading of Emerson, defined and elaborated in his contribution to this volume, I reconstruct an Emersonian theory of political representation that moves the concept beyond an unnecessarily narrow focus on formal institutions of electoral accountability. As I argue below, such a theory can contribute to democratic theory's recent "rediscovery of representation" by exposing the limitations of the all-too-familiar opposition between the "mandate" and "independence" theories of representation explored below in section 2.[5] Emerson outlines a theory of representation that is internally related to his perfectionist understanding of "reform." That is, it is a theory of representation centered on how a representative could provoke a perfectionist transformation and self-overcoming in the represented—a dynamic expression of Emerson's general preoccupation with the emergent and the yet-to-come—and that can therefore begin to account for the dilemmas of representing a democratic people never at one with itself, but inscribed within a horizon of unrealized futurity. "The coming only is sacred," Emerson wrote in "Circles" (1841), and the democratic people he envisions—described in "Experience" (1844) as this "new yet unapproachable America"—is a people that is forever not one . . . yet (413, 485).

In contrast to recent attempts to assimilate Emerson's theory of representation to such familiar theoretical categories as political rotation, public sphere theory, or (strangest of all!) communitarianism, I emphasize here the internal relationship between Emerson's accounts of representation and perfectionist reform.[6] I hope to recover an important element of Emerson's theory of representation unexplored in much of the existing scholarship. Emerson's turn to representation and the democratic importance of the "representative man" is not a departure from his theory of self-reliance—it does not entail heteronomous submission to delegated authority—but is instead a more avowedly public and political elaboration of that theory, one that reveals it not to be a theory of radical individuality so much as a theory of transformative impersonalism. Emerson's representatives elicit the transformative capacities of democratic constituencies forever in the midst of a process of, in Cavell's words, "moving to, and from, nexts."[7] They disenthrall their public of routine capitulations "to badges and names, to large societies and dead institutions" (262). Emerson's representative men are not best understood as "individuals who represent the beliefs, values, and ways of life present in their communities."[8] They neither stand in the place of their constituencies (as the independence view would dictate) nor merely reflect their preferences (as the mandate view demands), but rather reveal the "irresistible upward force" and "capacity" found in all. Emerson's theory of representation does not simply replace one notion of representation with another—that is, it does not establish a more accurate correspondence between the representative and the represented—but instead supplements the insufficiencies of existing theories by revealing a productive dynamic between representative and represented that can better account for the recurring democratic encounter with the emergence and revelation of the new.[9] For Emerson, this emergence is, of course, oriented by the moral horizon of "Spirit," "Over Soul," or "Nature," even though he never gives these aspirational ideals fixed content or philosophical articulation; they do not serve as categorical imperatives or principles of justice that improve their public through an unfolding process of reflective equilibrium. A fixed moral teleology would diminish the very sacredness Emerson identified with the emergent, and unjustifiably narrow his repeated preoccupations with divinity, beauty, character, and genius. Emerson's work is not so easily domesticated by the prevailing concerns of contemporary democratic theory. "The one thing which we seek with insatiable desire is to forget ourselves," Emerson writes in "Circles," "to be surprised out of propriety, to lose our sempiternal memory, and to do something without knowing how or why. . . . Nothing great was ever achieved without enthusiasm. The way of life is wonderful: it is by abandonment" (414). Emerson's representative men—far from being inspiring personifications of legible moral law or from simply reflecting the interests of constituents—facilitate such transformative surprise, loss, and abandonment.

Emerson's representative elicits or inspires capacities that had remained latent or virtual among the represented. By enabling the actualization of these formerly latent capacities (of self-reliance), Emerson's representative inspires transformation (self-overcoming) among the represented. As such, representation is an important category of Emerson's political theory of democratic perfectionism. Although he does not preclude the representative politician, Emerson's representative men are neither heroes nor kings, congressmen nor party leaders, but poetic public mediators who offer a perpetual exhibition of—and provocation toward—new possibilities. Emerson's representatives do not "reveal the community to itself," much less give "public expression to the particular range of qualities that give the community and its members their identity."[10] They act instead as catalysts of conversion capable of spurring a nation, in Tocqueville's words, to "rise *above* itself" without a fateful compromise of democratic autonomy.

The essay proceeds in three parts. In the first, I examine the impact of Emerson's developing conception of representativeness in the 1840s on his evaluation of reform and reformers. I am particularly interested in how Emerson's understanding of the representative reformer comes to conceptually underpin and explain his own increasingly radical political activism on behalf of abolition. In the second section, I offer a conceptual elaboration of his theory of representation and its departure from the governing terms of "mandate-independence controversy" in democratic theory. This section emphasizes the centrality of the "representative man" to Emerson's account of democratic perfectionism. In the concluding section, I sketch some of the political consequences of Emerson's account through the troubling case of John Brown, who more than any other public figure in the 1850s seemed to exemplify for Emerson the radical reformer as representative man. Brown appeared to Emerson as a paradoxical personification of the transformative impersonal.

1844: Radicalism and Reform

"Perhaps no other American intellectual in the nineteenth century," Peter S. Field writes, "so consciously and effectively endeavored to have an impact upon both contemporary thought and public behavior as Emerson."[11] Yet we know that Emerson also took a dismal view of many of the reformers of his time, those "miscellaneous popular charities . . . and thousand-fold Relief Societies" that proliferated in antebellum America, as he wrote in the 1841 "Self-Reliance" (263). Emerson's writing on reform provides a good point of entry into his thinking on representation. It does so, first, because it brings into initial focus some of the most novel elements of his theory, in particular those elements centered on the provocation and elevation of "the whole of our social structure" (146), as he put it in the 1841 "Man the Reformer," or the ability to "revolutionize the entire system of human pursuits" (408), from "Circles" in the same year; and, second, because the development of his theory of representation in the essays of the 1840s— beginning especially with *Essays: Second Series* (1844) and culminating with *Representative Men* (1850)—also provided the conceptual underpinnings of his increasingly outspoken political activism on behalf of abolition. Representation was the concept that united commitments that appeared in tension, if not contradiction, in Emerson's earlier work; representation was a way of navigating the competing imperatives of self-reliance and self-culture, on the one hand—"the doctrine of the independence and inspiration of the individual"—and the practical exaltation of public reform and "social action," on the other.[12] Emerson's developing conception of representation—and its internal relation to his conception of reform—provides an important framework for understanding how Emerson translated his theory of self-reliance into an emphatic theory of democratic perfectionism in his more avowedly political addresses of the late 1840s and 1850s.

Emerson was notoriously critical of the myriad reform movements that proliferated in the United States during the antebellum years—which one historian describes as "the most fervent and diverse outburst of reform energy in American history"—disdaining their heavy-handed moralism, their single-issue partiality, their love of association, and, which these all add up to, their rejection of individual self-reliance.[13] "The superior mind will find itself equally at odds with the evils of society," Emerson writes in "Montaigne," "and with the projects that are offered to relieve them" (702). In undertaking the direction of others, in "meddling in other people's affairs," reformers too often put themselves into what Emerson called, in the 1844 "Politics," "false relations" with those they would direct (567). In obsessively pursuing particular causes—abolition, temperance, charity, moral uplift—"the movement party" of reformers exhibited what Emerson, referring to the abolitionist Wendell Phillips, derided as a merely "platform existence." They were "mere mouthpieces of a party" aimed at reforming a mere fraction of man rather than regenerating the whole "personality."[14] In much of his writing on reform, Emerson expressed a sentiment vividly echoed by Thoreau in *Walden:* "If I knew for a certainty that a man was coming to my house with the conscious design of doing me good, I should run for my life . . . for fear I should get some of his good done to me,—some of his virus mingled with my blood."[15]

As persistent as Emerson's antireform sentiments are in such prominent earlier essays as "The Protest" (1839) and "Self-Reliance" (1841), his thoughts on reform in general, and on abolitionist reformers in particular, assumed a different character in later essays, perhaps especially in two prominent essays from 1844: "New England Reformers" and "Address . . . on . . . the Emancipation of the Negroes in the British West Indies." While Emerson derided the abolitionist reformer as an "angry bigot" in "Self-Reliance," and ridiculed his "incredible tenderness for black folk a thousand miles off," in later essays abolitionists became shining exemplars of Reform itself, the very cynosure of transformative inspiration (262). Many Emerson scholars, therefore, consider 1844 a watershed year in the development of both Emerson's thinking and his political activism, and rightly place the intensifying crisis around slavery at the heart of both of these developments. By 1844, as Gary Collison writes, Emerson had become the authoritative "spokesman for American idealism," and, as such, it had become increasingly difficult if not impossible for Emerson "to be silent without appearing to condone the continuation of slavery."[16] Len Gougeon has gone so far as to describe 1844 as the year of Emerson's "conversion" from moral suasion to radical abolition. Emphasizing the significance of the "Emancipation" address in particular, Gougeon writes that "there can be little doubt that on 1 August 1844 [the date of the address], Ralph Waldo Emerson made the transition from philosophical antislavery to active abolitionism."[17] This conversion, Gougeon argues, was sustained "throughout the remainder of the decade [as Emerson] drew closer to the abolitionist movement and its leading figures."[18]

In the "Emancipation" address, Emerson radically revised his earlier estimation of abolitionist reformers as partial, single-issue bigots and fanatics. The British abolitionists Emerson celebrates there—Granville Sharp, William Wilberforce, Lord Stanley, and others—are taken as regenerative exemplars of idealism, who through their tireless antislavery campaigning exercised a powerful moral force not only on the British public, but on the broader world. "We are indebted to this movement and to the continuers of it," Emerson wrote, "for the popular discussion of every point of practical ethics, and a reference of every question to the absolute standard" (AW, 28). In his stirring outline of the history of English abolition, Emerson looked beyond the heroic figureheads of the abolitionist movement to also celebrate the "plain men, working not under a leader, but under a sentiment" (AW, 26); Emerson, moreover, elevated black abolitionists and leaders of slave insurrections above the prophetic status of their American and British counterparts. "The arrival in the world of Toussaint, and the Haytian heroes," he wrote, and "the leaders of their race in Barbadoes and Jamaica, outweighs in good omen all the English and American humanity" (AW, 31). Beginning with the "Emancipation" address, Emerson proclaims that antislavery fanatics, zealots, and enthusiasts illuminate a broadly patterned moral arc of history: "One feels very sensibly in all this history that a great heart and soul are behind there, superior to any man, and making use of each, in turn, and infinitely attractive to every person according to the degree of reason in his own mind" (AW, 27). The defenders of slavery, on the other hand, demonstrated for Emerson their own compromised humanity in the nature of their defense of the institution. They "appeal only to cold prudence, barefaced selfishness, and silent votes," Emerson wrote (AW, 12). They are partial, "built on the narrow ground of interest," whereas the abolitionist radicals stand for Nature itself. Slavery, Emerson argues, is not based merely in the human-all-too-human love of "luxury" and material well-being, but instead is animated by a dark lower layer of human motivation: beyond covetousness lurks "the love of power, the voluptuousness of holding a human being in absolute control" (AW, 17).

Emerson's elevation of the abolitionist reformer to the status of representative in the "Emancipation" address is tied to a concomitant shift in his evaluation of slavery itself. In order to embrace the abolitionist reformer as a universal exemplar—as what will later be developed in terms of the representative man—Emerson views slavery itself as a form of universal crime. While the pervasive theme of "complicity," as Jack Turner has insightfully described it, "hovers in the background" of many of Emerson's works, and is explicitly associated with the lessons abolitionists taught the American public, this theme takes on a new salience in his antislavery addresses beginning in 1844.[19] The most moving passages in the "Emancipation" address, for example, demonstrate civilization's complex implication in the barbarism of slavery and reveal slavery as a question of universal responsibility. Emerson's focus on complicity and implication resoundingly rejects the self-proclaimed innocence of those not directly involved in the institution of slavery (i.e., his New England neighbors) and those who comfort themselves by the distance of slavery from their own sensuous experience. Indeed, the very pleasures of sense, Emerson suggests, anesthetize civilized subjects and disguise the barbarism that lurks hidden within their own experience: "If any mention was made of homicide, madness, adultery, and intolerable tortures, we would let the church-bells ring louder, the church organ swell its peal, and drown the hideous sound. The sugar [the slaves] raised was excellent: nobody tasted blood in it. The coffee was fragrant; the tobacco was incense; the brandy made nations happy; the cotton clothed the world" (AW, 20). This theme of personal complicity and sensuous captivation is reiterated in a number of Emerson's antislavery speeches, and seems to mandate and help explain both his increasing political activism over the issue and his emphasis on the difficulties of public disenthrallment. Complicity emerges not just from commerce and the commodity's hidden and bloody origins, but from democracy itself, insofar as individuals are taken to be responsible for actions carried out in their name. As Emerson wrote in his journal: "It is impossible to disengage/extricate oneself from the questions in which your age is involved. You can no more keep out of politics than you can keep out of the frost."[20]

In recovering the forgotten importance of such essays as the "Emancipation" address, Gougeon and other authors of what the introduction of this volume calls "the new history" have definitively revived an older understanding of the activist Emerson obscured by the more familiar portrait of him as radical individualist, withdrawn scholar, or mystical romantic. But there has been less emphasis in this literature on whether Emerson's increasing political activism was accompanied by a similar conversion in his political thinking beyond what some have characterized as the pronounced deflation of his otherworldly transcendentalism. As one of Emerson's contemporaries put this point, in his antislavery addresses there is "no more feeling in the skies, after the absolute, but sharp observation on human life and manners."[21] In *Virtue's Hero,* Gougeon carefully excavates the proliferation of Emerson's explicit and increasingly radical antislavery statements in the late 1840s and 1850s without situating them in relation to any broader conceptual changes in Emerson's thought. By contrast, Amy E. Earhart's examination of Emerson's 1844 "conversion" emphasizes intellectual over political causality, and argues that the conceptual revaluation of reform occasioned by Emerson's growing preoccupation with representativeness explained his growing abolitionist activism and underwrote his understanding of abolitionist reformers in the "Emancipation" address. Earhart argues that Emerson's conversion was not just to becoming more active in the abolitionist cause, in other words, "but to a new understanding of the representative man."[22] The abolition movement was "merely Emerson's site of communication and connection rather than the *form* of change itself."[23] We need not take sides in this methodological dispute over historical causality to benefit from the perspective Earhart's analysis opens up—that is, from her demonstration that Emerson's growing political activism was accompanied and supported by (as opposed to caused by) his developing conception of representativeness and its relation to reform. Whereas Emerson's August "Address . . . on . . . the Emancipation of the Negroes in the British West Indies" is the centerpiece of Gougeon's account of Emerson's growing political activism, Earhart focuses on his earlier "New England Reformers," delivered on March 3 of that year. If the abolitionist reformer appears for the first time as a representative man in Emerson's August "Emancipation" address, it is only because Emerson's conception of representativeness—which, despite Earhart's claims, is already invoked in outline form in such influential essays as "The American Scholar" (1837) and "The Poet" (1844)—had been extended beyond the withdrawn scholar and poet to encompass more explicitly political activity in "New England Reformers."[24]

In "New England Reformers," Emerson develops a distinction between legitimate and illegitimate reform that can be productively translated into representative versus unrepresentative reform. Echoing earlier critical comments on the partiality of reform, Emerson writes that "every project in the history of reform, no matter how violent and surprising, is good, when it is the dictate of man's genius and constitution, but very dull and suspicious when adopted from another" (592). This would seem to be but another articulation of the credo of self-reliance—"trust thyself" or "what I must do is all that concerns me" (260, 263)—but the force of the essay is to articulate an approach to reform that can stimulate "fertile forms of antinomianism" and a "spirit of protest and detachment" without being captivated by the narrow partialities that have marred previous reform efforts (592). Emerson writes that the reformer has typically "become tediously good in some particular," but has failed to recognize that "the wave of evil washes all our institutions alike" (596–97). For Emerson, then, the reformer has failed to exemplify a promise of total regeneration.

In contrast to these partial scolds, Emerson invokes a reformer capable of uniting a public without diminishing individual self-reliance—indeed, a type of reformer who can stimulate self-reliance. Such a representative reformer, for Emerson, works to inspire enactment primarily through the informal mechanisms of a public space of appearances rather than through political organizations, civic associations, and electoral institutions. The idea of the representative reformer is important to several of the essays that immediately follow "New England Reformers," particularly those that make up *Representative Men* (1850). Emerson celebrates the power of a reformer who is "a powerful and stimulating intellect, a man of great heart and mind," who can by example disenthrall the public and elevate them above their captive partialities: "Very quickly . . . frozen conservators will yield to the friendly influence [of these reformers], these hopeless will begin to hope, these haters will begin to love, these immovable statues will begin to spin and revolve" (602). This representative reformer does not flatter people but "exposes" them, reveals them to be men "instead of ghosts and phantoms."[25] In this essay, Emerson portrays a representative reformer who resonates with and helps to reveal in the public the "general doctrine of the latent but ever soliciting Spirit" (605). The representative reformer elicits what is latent in the public, and this revelation, as we will see, involves a dynamic of transformation and self-overcoming central to his account of the "Uses of Great Men," the remarkable essay that opens *Representative Men*.

Emerson's increasing political activism, then, was also accompanied by a conceptual change in his account of the reformer as representative, but this conception of representation must be brought into sharper conceptual focus. Earhart still sees Emerson as "teetering between social reform and individualism" in the essays from 1844, whereas I argue that his developing conception of representation becomes a more deliberate means of navigating, if not definitively resolving, this animating tension in his work. Doing so requires looking beyond the essays of 1844. The representative man stimulates a public ethos of self-reliance on which Emerson believed democracy was necessarily based. While the view of the representative reformer who is free of partial attachments and can elicit a transformative and critical capacity in those he represents—the public who see themselves represented in him—is elaborated in "New England Reformers," the essay with which *Essays: Second Series* ends, it is important to note that these issues are most clearly conceptualized in "The Poet," the essay with which *Essays: Second Series* begins. In order to understand what is most distinctive about Emerson's theory of representation—and how it shaped his approach to politics and public life—it is not enough to show that he extended this theory to include reformers and political activists in and around 1844. We first need a clearer conceptualization of what that theory of representation entailed in the first place. Before we understand Emerson's contributions to a theory of political representation, we must first see how this theory developed in his influential essay on the public role of the poet.

Representation: Beyond Principles and Persons

Emerson's concept of the representative poet is, as Robert Richardson observes, "the cornerstone of the democratic aesthetic Emerson was to work out over the next ten years."[26] It also powerfully prefigures Emerson's later conception of the representative reformer, and some of the most distinctive elements of this conception. "The poet is representative," Emerson writes, because "he stands among partial men for the complete man, and apprises us not of his wealth, but of the commonwealth" (448). By connecting the poet's representation with "the commonwealth," and with the abandonment of "his privacy of power as an individual man" in favor of "a great public power" (459), Emerson signals that the representative poet he envisions does not stand above and against but rather stands with and for some kind of political constituency (an implication famously elaborated by Walt Whitman in *Leaves of Grass*).[27] However, this constituency is not best described as a "community," or an existing collectivity "contented with a civil and conformed manner of living" (447). Indeed, Emerson's poet is "isolated among his contemporaries," passes for "a fool and a churl for a long season," and might be accurately characterized as untimely in Nietzsche's sense: out of step with the settled doxa and conformities of the present (448). While Emerson emphasizes the capacity of the poet to speak for—to "express," "publish," "utter"—he also insists that what is being expressed, published, and uttered is a "secret" held by all, a democratically distributed capacity to converse with Nature. Even if "the great majority of men seem to be minors . . . or mutes, who cannot report the conversation they have had with nature," the poet's words, his "meter-making argument" and "freer speech," make such a report. The poet thus reveals that "nature has a higher end, in the production of new individuals, than security, namely *ascension*, or the passage of the soul into higher forms," an insight at the heart of Emersonian perfectionism (458).

Emerson's representative poet is a productive mediator through which the represented of the "commonwealth" come to an elevated apprehension of themselves and their capacities. This apprehension is more than mere understanding or conception and marks a conversion or transfiguration of subjectivity: through it the representative poet sparks an aversion to the "settled" selves they have become. Emerson insists on this transformative arousal and provocation throughout "The Poet." Through the poet, "new passages are opened for us in nature . . . and metamorphosis is possible"; poets are "liberating gods. . . . They are free, and they make free"; "We love the poet, the inventor, who in any form, whether in an ode, or in an action, or in looks and behavior, has yielded us a new thought. He unlocks our chains, and admits us to a new scene" (463). The representative poet—whom Emerson broadly associates with inventors in many forms, actions as well as odes—frees the public from the privations of a private existence, and thereby enables self-reliance, the "reliance of the attained on the unattained/attainable" self, in Cavell's words.[28] This transformative provocation does not compromise the self-reliance of the represented, because the poet is "more himself than he is" (448). Even though Emerson describes the poet in familiar romantic terms as "the sayer, the namer," even as "a sovereign" who "stands at the center" (449), the representative poet is not Shelley's heroic "unacknowledged legislator of the world," "the influence which is moved not, but moves," because the power of Emerson's representative poet derives only from the fact that "through better perception, he stands one step nearer to things, and sees the flowing or metamorphosis" (456).[29] Only through the poet's impersonal "abandonment to the nature of things," Emerson writes, is his speech "thunder" and his thought "law." He is only "representative of man, in virtue of being the largest power to receive and to impart" what is already there for all to see and to be (448).

In *Representative Men*, Emerson generalizes the characteristics of the representative poet to other regions of cultural and political life—religion and philosophy, statesmanship and war—and in doing so further emphasizes this theme of dynamic interdependence and receptivity. Emerson's continual preoccupation in *Representative Men* is, as Andrew Delbanco writes, the "dependency of the great on the common."[30] It is widely recognized that Emerson envisioned *Representative Men* in part as a response to Thomas Carlyle's *Heroes, Hero-Worship and the Heroic in History* (1841), and the contrast between Carlyle's heroes and Emerson's representative men further illuminates what is distinctive and avowedly political in Emerson's conception. Carlyle argued that "Universal History . . . is at bottom the History of the Great Men who have worked here,"[31] and that the recognition of heroic authority was "inexpressibly precious" in a disenchanted modern world where a leveling materialism had reduced human life to the insignificant statistical aggregates of a "machine universe." For Carlyle, the hero marked the very possibility of significance in an age of entropic mediocrity. "The voice of the world's Maker" speaks only through singular heroic examples, he wrote, and this voice commands first and foremost an obedience and hierarchical authority that "extends from divine adoration down to the lowest practical regions of life."[32] Because the heroic is about the centrality of authority and subordination in human life, for Carlyle the "most important of Great Men" is the king, the one to whom he dedicates the longest and concluding chapter of his book. Carlyle's king is "he to whose will our wills are to be subordinated, and loyally surrender themselves, and find their welfare in doing so."[33] Of course, the political consequences of the ordering authority of the king directly contradicted the democratic tendencies of the age, which Carlyle emphasized throughout: "Find in any country the Ablest Man that exists there; raise him to the supreme place, and loyally reverence him; you have a perfect government for that country; no ballot-box, parliamentary eloquence, voting, or constitution-building, or other machinery whatsoever can improve it a whit. It is the perfect state; an ideal country."[34]

Emerson's engagement with Carlyle's *Heroes* drew out the more explicitly political dimensions of his theory of representation and provoked him to more clearly reconcile his affirmation of the importance of extraordinary individuals with his committed democratic egalitarianism. Judith Shklar is surely right that *Representative Men* was an elaboration of Emerson's worry about "the impact of greatness on the rest of us," and an attempt to navigate "the tension between the sense of the apartness of the great and the claims of humanity."[35] Emerson was preoccupied with acknowledging both the vital importance and use of "great men" within a democracy, and the alluring danger of worshipful submission that lurks in this acknowledgment. In "Emerson and the Inhibitions of Democracy," Shklar brilliantly demonstrates that Emerson navigates this tension in the very movement of his argument in "Uses of Great Men," as it "zig-zags" between affirmations of the inspiring exceptions of the great, and their ultimate dependence on the general and the common for their greatness.[36]

But the novelty of Emerson's emphasis on the democratic importance of representative men in general and representative reformers in particular goes beyond Shklar's emphasis on the "inhibitions of democracy" or what Robert Richardson similarly describes as Emerson's attempt to "reconcile the reality of the unequal distribution of talent with a democratic belief in the fundamental equality of all persons."[37] Emerson was clearly concerned with elaborating how greatness and heroic individuality—traits most clearly associated with an aristocratic culture—could be made not only compatible with democracy but vitally essential to it. However, bracketing the more esoteric dimensions of Emerson's account of representation—either by assimilating the representative's provocation of "ascension" and "metamorphosis" to the practical considerations of change and "rotation" in representative government, as Shklar has done, or by reducing the representative's exemplary ability to "surprise us out of our propriety" to a more capacious model of "deliberative justice" or "public reason" than provided by contemporary political liberals like John Rawls, as Rautenfeld has done—obscures much of what is most provocative about his work and too quickly assimilates it within familiar rubrics of representation.[38] To fully grasp Emerson's contribution to an idea of political representation beyond the formal institutions of electoral politics, we must see the political salience without losing sight of mystical provocations of earlier essays like "The Poet." The question of what it is that the representative represents—neither principles, I will argue, nor persons—returns us to Emerson's perfectionism, while giving it a much more avowedly public or political dimension than do familiar interpretations that focus primarily on dynamics of individual self-culture.

What most clearly distinguishes Emerson's representative men from Carlyle's heroes is the distinctive way Emerson envisions the dynamic and productive *relation* between representatives and the represented, and how this relation stimulates perfectionist transformation. The great man "must be *related* to us," Emerson writes, and our life receive from him some promise of explanation" (617). Reversing Carlyle's insistence on the ordering authority and causal power of the hero, Emerson's representative does not impose form and meaning upon a public world, but is instead—like Shakespeare as described in that chapter—characterized by "being altogether receptive" to this public (711). "The greatest genius is the most indebted man," Emerson declares. "He will not have any genius great, except through the general" (710). "It is easy to see that what is best written or done by genius in the world was not man's work," he continues, "but came by wide social labor, when a thousand wrought like one, sharing the same impulse" (715). Emerson reverses Carlyle's focus on the self-sufficient singularity of the hero, which he deems superficial in its attention to appearances of greatness, and instead reveals how the power and the truth of the "great man" is actually an emanation of the too often hidden influences of the common and the low, the ordinary and the general. Rather than being captivated, for example, by "the learned member of the legislature at Westminster or at Washington" who "speaks and votes for thousands," Emerson demands that readers look for the myriad and subtle influences that sustain and animate that greatness. "Show us [instead] the constituency, and the now invisible channels by which the senator is made aware of their wishes. The crowd of practical and knowing men, who, by correspondence or conversation, are feeding him with evidence, anecdotes, and estimates." The effect of this changed preoccupation will "bereave" the "fine attitude and resistance" of the great of "something of their impressiveness" (715). The effect of this changed orientation is to disenthrall the public of their dangerous tendencies of worshipful reverence, to cultivate a sense of "the speedy limit to the use of heroes," and the realization that "every benefactor becomes so easily a malefactor" (628).

Emerson urged that we come to see the great men in a new light, not to diminish their greatness but to apprehend it as a catalyst for better appreciating and realizing our own. As he wrote in "Experience" (1844): "Instead of feeling a poverty when we encounter a great man, let us treat the new comer as a travelling geologist, who passes through our estate, and shows us good slate, or limestone, or anthracite," who reveals the riches within us (489). The distance between the great man and the common man merely simulates an internal distance between the selves we are and those we have yet to become, between our "attained" and "unattained/attainable selves," as Cavell puts it. "True genius will not impoverish, but will liberate, add new sense" (623). Rather than inspiring ascent, the inherited discourses of heroism and genius frame the "masses" as "food for knives and powder," passive recipients of noble beneficence, "sacks and stomachs" (616). These discourses diminish the significance of the common; they thus not only contradict a commitment to democratic equality, but sustain fundamental misunderstandings of the nature of the relation between the great and the common, framing it as one of simple hierarchy and subordination. From Emerson's perspective, such discourses preserve the narrow partiality of the hero—emphasize his "wealth" over the "commonwealth"—and deny the hero the very power of representativeness that Emerson wants to recover: "The power which [great men] communicate," in short, "is not theirs" (624). What "entitles" those in the "position of leaders and lawgivers" is that they "teach the qualities of primary nature,—admit us to the constitution of things" (624). Great men, for Emerson, rely on those they represent because their greatness resides in this representativeness. "Great men exist so that there may be greater men" (632).

Although this theme is most pronounced in *Representative Men*, it does not originate there. Already in "Self-Reliance" (1841), for example, Emerson describes the common phenomenon of reverence for the great and the heroic—"the joyful loyalty with which men have everywhere suffered the king, the noble, or the great proprietor to walk among them by a law of his own"—as "the hieroglyphic" through which common men "obscurely signified of their own right and comeliness, the right of every man" (268). Here, too, Emerson counsels looking beyond the evidence of merely empirical observation, to a more careful attentiveness to the significance communicated beyond the appearance of surface hieroglyphics. However, in the later work Emerson places much stronger emphasis on the importance of the decentering relationship between representative and represented as a catalyst for disseminating a broader *public* ethos of transformative self-reliance, giving individual cultivation ("self-culture") a more pronounced political dimension. Like the poet, Emerson's representatives enable a transformative act of recognition, an act that defines their very representativeness. "Man is endogenous," Emerson writes in "The Uses of Great Men," but his "unfolding" is facilitated through encounters with "other men," and the great man, the man of "genius," is, Emerson writes, "the *otherist*" (616). The representative will not reduce the represented to "underlings and intellectual suicides," but awaken an unrealized latent capacity. "Each philosopher, each bard, each actor," Emerson writes, "has only done for me, as by delegate, what one day I can do for myself" (67).

The emphasis in *Representative Men* is therefore on the productive rather than the passive or merely mimetic nature of the relationship between representative and represented, which clearly distinguishes Emerson's conception of representation from the two most familiar views of representation in democratic theory, which together make up the so-called "mandate-independence controversy."[39] Hanna Pitkin describes the "mandate-independence controversy" as the "central classic controversy in the literature on political representation," and she succinctly summarizes the debate as follows: "Should (must) a representative do what his constituents want, and be bound by mandates or instructions from them; or should (must) he be free to act as seems best to him in pursuit of their welfare?"[40] The mandate view, taken to its fullest extent, reduces the representative to a mere agent of the represented, acting only on the basis of their explicit instructions. This position reduces the representative to a servant of the represented, a passive instrument of their interests or preferences. Because the mandate view is anchored in the express wishes of voting and petitioning constituencies, it is often associated with the highly localist "actual" view of representation that came to dominate American politics in the wake of the American revolutionaries' critique of the British Parliament's claim of "virtual representation."[41] In the terms of contemporary democratic theory, the descriptive literalism of the mandate view makes it broadly compatible with "aggregative" conceptions of democracy, which "take expressed preferences as the privileged or primary material for democratic decision making" rather than decisions based in moral justification and reasoned deliberation.[42]

The independence view, by contrast, emphasizes the normative importance of independent deliberation and judgment on the part of the representative. It is not the explicitly articulated preferences of the represented that are essential but the broader, more objective, and "unattached" interests of the constituency taken as a whole. Edmund Burke gave the canonical expression of this view in a 1774 speech to the electors of Bristol: "Your representative owes to you, not his industry only, but his judgment; and he betrays, instead of serving you, if he sacrifices it to your opinion."[43] James Madison provided the canonical American articulation when he wrote in the *Federalist* no. 10 that rather than merely reflecting the partial views of constituents representatives will "refine and enlarge" them, and that "the public voice pronounced by the representatives of the people, will be more consonant to the public good, than if pronounced by the people themselves."[44] Representation is not evaluated here on the basis of how accurately it corresponds with the stated interests or preferences of the represented (whether articulated through votes or opinion polls), but with an ability to judge independently of them. If the mandate view risks reducing the representative to a passive instrument, the independence view seems to undermine accountability and undemocratically to inflate the wisdom, expertise, or superior rationality of the representative. The eighteenth-century language of a "natural aristocracy" captures an important aspect of this view, and, in the terms of contemporary democratic theory, it is typically associated with deliberative conceptions of democratic politics.

Because Emerson emphasizes the broadening and transformative dimensions of representation, his view is sometimes compared with an independence theory of representation. Jay Grossman, for example, argues that Emerson, like Madison, endorses a view of representation that "filters" out the narrowly parochial views of the represented, and attains an "enlarged" perspective that can take a better view of the whole.[45] From Grossman's perspective, Emerson is engaged in an ongoing discursive battle over whether the political (and the poetic) project of representation in the United States was to represent an elevated and purified version of "the will of the people," or whether it was instead to convey that will in a more directly correspondent, mandated form. There are passages in Emerson's work that would seem to accord with this view, as when he writes that political representatives who truly represent "do not need to inquire of their constituents what they should say, but are themselves the country they represent" (496). However, the independence theory ultimately too closely resembles the heroic ideal that Emerson contrasted to the democratic uses of great men. At the same time, Emerson's view is far indeed from the opposing mandate theory of representation, which, at its most radical, goes beyond the mere reflection of interests of constituents to the actual resemblance of them.[46] Some have tried to read Emerson in this way, and there are scattered passages that can confirm this view as well, as when, for example, Emerson writes, "the reason he knows about them is that he is of them" (617).[47] However, the "receptivity" of Emerson's representative is poorly conceived in the terms of instruction or even shared beliefs, values, or ways of life.

Notice that both the independence and mandate theories of representation correspond to something objectively given, "ontic," often an "interest." In the case of the independence theory, this is generally thought of in terms of what Pitkin calls an "unattached interest." This interest is a more or less objective, fixed, public interest which can be discovered through the reasoned reflection and deliberation of elite representatives; it might be construed as the representation of a principle rather than empirical persons. The mandate theory of representation, by contrast, anchors representation in persons, in the explicitly stated interests or preferences of the represented. If the former view of representation is untethered from responsiveness to the mandate of the represented, the latter is never more than a pale copy of the original. The stage is thereby set for a familiar argument: "It just isn't really representation," the mandate theorist will say, "if the [representative] doesn't do what the constituents want." "It just isn't really representation," the independence theorist responds, "if the representative isn't free to decide on the basis of his own independent judgment."[48] Both of these familiar views leave the commonwealth as it is and neglect what I take to be a central component of Emerson's theory of representation as a theory of democratic perfectionism: its productive and transformative capacity, its ability to provoke transformations in individual and collective selves.

The key to understanding the radicalism of Emerson's distinctive theory of representation as a dynamic relation between representative and represented—and its direct challenge to the mandate and independence views—is its grounding in what Sharon Cameron has identified as Emerson's "impersonal." Emerson's representative men do not represent interests—neither unattached objective interests nor subjective preferences—but that is because neither do they represent *persons*. "Persons are poor empirical pretensions," Emerson writes in "Nominalist and Realist" (1844), and representatives at once reveal and provoke the overcoming of such partial pretensions (576). The impersonal is Emerson's "antidote for the egotistical, the subjective, the solipsistic."[49] As Emerson declares in the "Over-Soul" (1841): "What we commonly call man, the eating, drinking, planting, counting man does not, as we know him, represent himself, but misrepresents himself. Him we do not respect, but the soul, whose organ he is, would he let it appear through his action, would make our knees bend" (387). The "commonwealth" and "public power" of the representative, then, is not made up of "what we commonly call man." Indeed, Emerson's representatives provoke an abandonment of such personhood, an ascension beyond confining (and conforming) individualism.

Emerson's representatives are a "collyrium to clear out our eyes from egotism." They "enable us to see other people and their works" (626). They do so by way of tapping into a "sympathy and likeness" that is common although inarticulate, public but obscured by convention, virtual yet resonant. The tapping of this latent commonality is an important aspect of Emerson's account of how the privations of private existence are overcome: "All that respects the individual is temporary and prospective, like the individual himself, who is ascending out of his limits into a catholic existence" (631). Emerson uses many different terms, with differently textured connotations, for this underlying impersonal commonality: universal mind, Nature, Over-Soul, Whole, Power. As already noted above, in "New England Reformers," he calls it "the general doctrine of the latent but ever soliciting Spirit" (605). Although the influence of German Idealism on this doctrine is clear, it should not be overstated, and can lead to a misunderstanding or domestication of Emerson's thought on these points. Emerson's representatives don't represent persons, but neither do they represent or exemplify a principle or law, at least not one that can be given a clearly articulate and universally accessible determination. Emerson does not attribute a philosophically articulate principle to this commonality, and it is not based in a universally law-conferring transcendental subjectivity, as it is for Kant. Neither, however, is it accurately described as shared values or as an ascriptive identity. Emerson goes out of his way both to insist on the universal circulation of this "divine fire" of commonality and to proclaim its resistance to a final legibility, articulation, or representation. This ambiguity has enabled both theists and immanent vitalists to find inspiration in Emerson's work. Emerson can be read as a "geographer" of the infrasensible and immanent as well as the supersensible and transcendent regions—that is, the regions of sensation and affect prior to being organized as experience as well the regions of inspiration and faith.[50] This is not a controversy that Emerson's work definitively settles, but his appeal to "the general doctrine of the latent but ever soliciting Spirit" operates on both the infrasensible and transcendental levels to dissolve sedimented certainties of ontic particularity. Emerson insists on such productive ambiguities: "I unsettle all things" and "break the chain of habits" (412), he writes in "Circles"; in "Montaigne" he declares, "The philosophy we want is one of fluxions and mobility, we are but volitant stabilities, houses founded on the sea" (696).

In spite of these bold proclamations, Emerson recognized how difficult the practical realization of these insights must be, due to the powerful inertia woven into being, or what Emerson calls the "perpetual tendency to the set mode" (582). Social conspiracies against such transfigurations and self-overcomings are countless, as Emerson writes in "Self-Reliance," because of "one fact the world hates, that the soul becomes" (271). Legislated consistencies and imperative conformities define social life, as individuals are mandated through countless daily interactions to remain the individuals they have always been. The greatest single obstacle to transformative becoming is an ossification of the very self one is said to rely upon. "Each man is a tyrant of tendency," he writes in "Self-Reliance," and no tendency is more captivating than the partialities of personhood (582). The representative encounter with transformative impersonality oriented by the "doctrine of the ever-soliciting Spirit" works to liberate the represented from what Cameron calls "the tyranny of egotistical self-enclosure."[51] Emerson's representatives take us outside of ourselves and enable us to forget ourselves, to be "surprised out of our propriety." As Emerson writes of Napoleon, by "transcending the ordinary limits of human ability," he "appeals to the imagination" and "wonderfully encourages and liberates us" (739).

The words that Emerson uses to describe this transformation emphasize the radicalism of the transformation he envisions—it is not merely a change of view or a shift of opinion, but of conversion and transfiguration. As Emerson writes in the concluding paragraph of "Circles" (1841): "The one thing which we seek with insatiable desire is to forget ourselves, to be surprised out of our propriety, to lose our sempiternal memory, and to do something without knowing how or why; in short, to draw a new circle" (414). For Emerson, the representative who can elicit such transformative circle drawing, or assist us in the endogenous "unfolding" previously discussed, little resembles the political representatives of his time, if by that term we mean the formal representatives of the state (but neither does he necessarily exclude these figures). The fact that Emerson's representatives are *not* American politicians—indeed, not American at all, and, with the qualified exception of Napoleon, not politicians either!—should not obscure their avowedly public and political character. They are a key component of Emerson's theory of democratic perfectionism. It may well be that *Representative Men* has not received the attention it deserves from some of Emerson's more politically oriented readers because it seems to be less obviously political than are, for example, his writings on slavery and abolition. I have tried to demonstrate the continuities rather than the differences across these works. As recent scholarship has emphasized, in the late 1840s and 1850s Emerson became more politically active and also more radically critical of the formal politics of (representative) state institutions. This simultaneous development in Emerson's thinking and practice—growing political activism and growing disgust with institutions of electoral politics—often revolved around the question of representation and misrepresentation. Emerson's developing conception of the representative reformer was invested in envisioning a new form of politics, one where competing claims of representation were central, and where the representative reformer was explicitly contrasted with the (misrepresentative) claims of elected officials. Emerson's controversial attack on the famed Massachusetts Senator Daniel Webster, contrasted with his even more controversial celebration of John Brown, exemplifies Emerson's distinctive negotiation of this problem in some of his antislavery writings.

John Brown, Representative Man

"I have little esteem for government," Emerson wrote in 1856. "I esteem them good only in the moment they were established" (*AW,* 113). What Emerson disdained in established rather than inaugural government was what he called "the blunder which stands in colossal ugliness in the governments of the world": "undertaking for another" (567). According to

Emerson, there is no governance of others in inaugural moments of political self-constitution like 1776, when each is "his own governor" and stands "on his own feet."[52] The dim view of established political institutions, however, including the institutions of representative government, is reiterated in many of Emerson's essays and has helped sustain his image as an apolitical individualist. "Leave governments to clerks and desks," Emerson disdainfully wrote in "American Scholar" (67). He loathed partisan politics that demanded loyalty to platform ideologies and political institutions built around bureaucratic hierarchies. He rejected the idea that political participation was a good in itself. "The end of all political struggle is to establish morality as the basis for all legislation," he wrote. "'Tis not free institutions, 'tis not a republic, 'tis not a democracy, that is the end,—no but only the means" (*AW*, 153). "At the heart of Emerson's idealism," Larry Reynolds summarily writes, "is the call for spiritual redemption, for new men, not new social orders."[53]

Emerson's disparaging view of formal political institutions often translated into a similar view of the political representatives—"senators and sovereigns"—elected through them. At one point in the *Conduct of Life* (1860), Emerson suggests that elections should be decided by weighing candidates on hay scales, and in his journals he wrote contemptuously of a neighbor who busied himself with "teaching his little circle of villagers their political lessons": "Here thought I is one who loves what I hate. I hate numbers, he cares for nothing but numbers and persons."[54] Emerson occasionally made an exception for the great Massachusetts Senator Daniel Webster, in whose law office Emerson's younger brother Edward had begun his career.[55] Webster was seen by many contemporaries as the "one eminent American of our time, whom we could produce as a finished work of nature" (*AW*, 66). However, Webster's decisive support for the Compromise of 1850—and especially its strengthened Fugitive Slave Law, requiring the capture and return of escaped slaves in the North—occasioned perhaps the most vitriolic public attack Emerson ever delivered, driven by a pervasive sense of outrage and betrayal. "The fairest American fame ends in this filthy law," Emerson announced (*AW*, 65). In his celebrated embrace of "Union," Webster had presented himself "as the representative of the American continent," as "the most American man in America," but his actions in 1850 revealed him to be far from representative in Emerson's sense. Webster was sullied in compromise. "Union" for him was merely the authority of existing legal contracts which assured that "government exists for the preservation of property" alone. He "lives by his memory," Emerson declared; "he adheres to the letter." Webster was not representative because only "what he finds *already written* will he defend. For he has no faith in the power of self-government; none whatever in *extemporizing a government*" (AW, 66–67). Webster and other political representatives merely stood for the given, for existing law, existing interests, existing persons. Making the connection with political self-constitution explicit, Emerson writes that Webster was "happily born late—after independence had been declared." "In Massachusetts, in 1776, he would . . . have been a refugee" (67). Emerson elaborated on Webster's misrepresentation in a revealing journal entry from 1851: "Webster truly represents the American people just as they are, with their vast material interests, materialized intellect, & low morals. Heretofore, their great men have led them, have been better than they, as Washington, Hamilton, & Madison. But Webster's absence of moral faculty is degrading to the country."[56] Far from raising the nation above itself, Webster's example left the represented further diminished and degraded.

The Compromise of 1850 radicalized Emerson beyond this critique of Webster, and led him to more broadly conclude that the United States "has ceased to be a Representative Government." Again, the appeal was to inaugurate or to enact a reformative politics through channels outside electoral institutions. "Nothing remains but to begin at the beginning to call every man in American to counsel," Emerson wrote. "Representatives do not represent, we must (now) take new order and see how to make representatives represent us."[57] The crisis in representation Emerson declared in 1850 only intensified in the following years, and involved a crisis of both political institutions and of language itself. Writing in 1856, Emerson declared: "Language has lost its meaning in the universal cant. *Representative Government* is really misrepresentative" (AW, 113). Emerson responded to this crisis with increasingly strident calls for "a spontaneous expression of the injured people; in fault of their leaders creating their own, and shaking off from their back these degenerate and unworthy riders."[58] The people as they could be had no representative in government in the 1850s, and their spontaneous expression was hindered by the lack of inspiring example.

Much to the discomfort of some of his liberal admirers, no man seemed to better exemplify the ideal of exemplary representativeness in the crisis period of the 1850s than "the hero of Harpers Ferry," John Brown. Emerson met Brown during the latter's fund-raising visit to Concord in 1857, and was deeply impressed by Brown's unwavering commitment to higher principle and to action. Emerson affirmed Brown's own belief in the superior importance of a single "good, believing, strong-minded man" who might "give a permanent direction to the fortunes of a State."[59] After Brown's failed 1859 raid on Harpers Ferry, Emerson delivered two remarkable speeches, both of which were subsequently reprinted and circulated. These lectures, as David Reynolds writes, "helped open the floodgates of Northern appreciation of Brown."[60] They are remarkable not only for their courageous eloquence in defense of Brown—whose execution, Emerson declared, "will make the gallows glorious, like the cross"—but for the justifications that he provides.[61] Emerson celebrated Brown alongside some of history's most luminary moral heroes and affirmed him as a true "representative of the American public" (*AW*, 117). Connecting this provocative claim with his own distinct conception of representation, Emerson roundly rejected the "easy effrontery" of "political gentlemen" who asserted that Brown was not in fact representative and that there are "not a thousand men in the North who sympathize with him." "It would be far safer and nearer the truth," Emerson responds, "to say that all people, in proportion to their sensibility and self-respect, sympathize with him" (*AW*, 123). Indeed, "nothing can resist the sympathy which all elevated minds must feel with Brown" (*AW*, 118). To sympathize with Brown appeared to be both the outcome and the potential cause of such elevation insofar as Emerson's lectures were meant to provoke this sympathetic conversion in his public. For Emerson, Brown appeared as a collyrium for the morally clouded eyes of the nation, a prophetic voice awakening the nation from its trance of complicity and corruption.

For Emerson, Brown was a glowing example of the abolitionist crusader who was not partial or interested, but spoke for the regeneration of the whole. If Emerson had come to see the abolitionist reformer in representative terms by 1844, Brown in 1857 became the purest exemplification of this ideal. He was "the rarest of heroes, a pure idealist, with no by-ends of his own" (*AW*, 118). Echoing the arguments of his "Emancipation" lecture, Emerson wrote that it was a mistake to treat abolitionists like Brown as engaged in a "personal affair." Brown was not a heroic *person* fighting against slavery, but a representative of a universal resistance to enslavement: "No matter how many Browns [the slaveholder] can catch and kill, he does not make their numbers less, for the air breeds them"; "The air this man breathes is liberty, & is breathed by thousands and millions."[62] Brown was Emerson's paradoxical personification of the impersonal. "He was of no agent of party or persons, he saw through the "idolatry of forms," and "believed in his ideas to put them all into action" (AW, 119). Indeed, Emerson celebrated the fact that in his raid at Harpers Ferry, Brown demonstrated that he "did not believe in moral suasion;—he believed in putting the thing through." As Thoreau would say in his own remarkable address "A Plea for Captain John Brown" (1859), Brown was an enthusiast who "did not set up even a political graven image between him and his God."[63]

In both Brown addresses, Emerson emphasized the captivating mystifications of "forms" as a brand of "idolatry," and celebrated Brown's violent acts as having the power to disenthrall the public of such forms. "Rather than recoil from Brown's violence," Reynolds writes, "Emerson dwelt on it."[64] But why? Emerson's simultaneous affirmation of Brown's violent immediatism—his appeal to the spirit beyond the letter of the Law—and his representativeness brings us back to the heart of what is most novel and provocative about Emerson's theory of representation and its relation to reform. Brown exemplifies the more radical dimensions of Emerson's democratic perfectionism and what Aletta Norval has described as his vision of aversive citizenship.[65] He does so because Emerson envisions Brown's spectacular acts as catalysts for converting the public they elicit into a more elevated form. Emerson's controversial celebration of Brown was a continuation of this conversion. Both Brown's acts and Emerson's celebration of them are attempts to elicit and enact what Emerson described as a "new public." The "arid forms which states incrust themselves with," Emerson would later write in response to Lincoln's Emancipation Proclamation (1863), are occasionally interrupted by "a poetic act and record." Such poetic acts and records "provoke no noisy joy, but are received into a sympathy so deep as to apprise us that mankind are greater and better than we know. At such times, it appears as if a new public were created to greet the new event."[66]

Some of his recent admirers have explained Emerson's account of representative reformers through the concepts and preoccupations of contemporary public sphere theory and the norms of democratic deliberation. The account I have given here challenges that interpretation. Much that is distinctive and provocative about Emerson's understanding of the dynamics of representativeness is lost if we read him as a "precursor" to contemporary deliberative democrats.[67] Emerson certainly did envision transformation, conversion, and regeneration occurring primarily through an informal public rather than the formal institutions of representative democracy, but the public he envisioned was not the deliberative space of public reason endorsed by contemporary advocates of political liberalism. As the representative example of John Brown suggests, the converted public envisioned by Emerson was neither coolly deliberative nor even free of spectacular violence.

The public Emerson envisioned and addressed—and the representative figures the public was built around—had the capacity to convert and regenerate, not just persuade or convince. This formulation resonates with Rousseau's famous description of the lawgiver in the *Social Contract*, and it may not go too far to say that Emerson's representative men, especially the representative reformers exemplified by Brown, confronted a speech situation similar to that modeled by Rousseau's lawgiver: how to inspire a public to see their own latent capacities exemplified in speech and deed, and thereby convert that public to its unattained ascendant self without denying their own self-reliance. The lawgiver, like the representative reformer, may aspire to (re)found a people and to elicit their ascendant self, "but in the end it is up to the people themselves to accept or reject his advances."[68] Emerson's representative men were not Carlyle's heroes; their greatness instead depended on creating a public that would affirm their representativeness, and that affirmation was the very sign of representativeness.

Like Thoreau, Emerson seems to have conceived this question of popular acceptance or rejection as a problem of arousal or awakening. The representative reformer enacts what Cavell calls "a seduction from our seductions (conformities, heteronomies)."[69] Emerson believed the poetry of Brown's acts could rouse and startle a nation to "rise above itself." As such, Emerson's vision of the representative reformer was a productive mediator of collective self-overcoming, a figure of transformative disenthrallment and conversion. The ultimate demonstration of Emerson's commitment to a public of transcendent reformation and conversion rather than reasoned deliberation and moral uplift comes not only in what he explicitly says so much as what his writing continually does. What Rousseau said of the speech of his lawgiver can perhaps be equally said of Emerson's prose: it "compels without violence and persuades without convincing." Similarly, Emerson's Reason—"this subtilizer, and irresistible upward force"—is closer to the lawgiver's "sublime reason" than to the "public reason" celebrated by contemporary deliberative democrats. Emerson's representative reformers do not just change opinions; they trigger new ways of seeing, of perceiving, and they reorient passionate commitments to another frame of reference. That John Brown attempted to do so through an inspiring act of antislavery violence is troubling, but also revealing. It may be tempting to translate the moralizing influence of representatives into the imperatives of a politics of deliberative engagement, but this would be a domestication of Emerson's thought, and a misunderstanding of its profound but deeply ambiguous legacy for democratic politics and democratic theory.

Notes

Epigraphs are from Alexis de Tocqueville, *Democracy in America* (New York: Penguin, 2003), 418; Ralph Waldo Emerson, "The Uses of Great Men," in *Essays and Lectures* (New York: Library of America, 1983), 615–32, 625. Unless otherwise noted, all subsequent Emerson citations refer to this volume and are cited parenthetically.

1. Quentin Anderson, *The Imperial Self: An Essay in American Literary and Cultural History* (New York: Knopf, 1971); Stephen E. Whicher, *Freedom and Fate: An Inner Life of Ralph Waldo Emerson* (Philadelphia: University of Pennsylvania Press, 1957), 49; D. H. Lawrence, *Studies in Classic American Literature* (New York: Penguin, 1990), 3.

2. Wilson Carey McWilliams, "Emerson: The All and the One," in this volume, 48.

3. George Kateb, "Self-Reliance, Politics, and Society," in this volume, 73.

4. Stanley Cavell, *Conditions Handsome and Unhandsome: The Constitution of Emersonian Perfectionism* (Chicago: University of Chicago Press, 1990), 11, 53 (see also Cavell, "Aversive Thinking: Emersonian Representations in Heidegger and Nietzsche," in this volume, 110).

5. Nadia Urbinati, *Representative Democracy: Principles & Genealogy* (Chicago: University of Chicago Press, 2006), 5.

6. On rotation, see Judith Shklar, "Emerson and the Inhibitions of Democracy," in this volume, 61–62; on both public sphere theory and communitarianism, see Hans von Rautenfeld, "Thinking for Thousands: Emerson's Theory of Political Representation in the Public Sphere," *American Journal of Political Science* 49, no. 1 (2005): 184–97.

7. Cavell, *Conditions Handsome and Unhandsome*, 12.

8. Rautenfeld, "Thinking for Thousands," 184.

9. I intend this to be analogous to Cavell's argument that Emerson's moral perfectionism does not offer an alternative and self-sufficient "theory of the moral life," but rather addresses itself to "the possibility or necessity of the transforming of oneself and of one's society"—Emerson's thematic of "reform"—that is a part of any moral, and I would add democratic, theory (see Cavell, *Conditions Handsome and Unhandsome*, 2).

10. Rautenfeld, "Thinking for Thousands," 187.

11. Peter S. Field, *Ralph Waldo Emerson: The Making of a Democratic Individual* (Lanham, Md.: Rowman and Littlefield, 2002), 210.

12. Emerson, "Lecture on Slavery, 25 January, 1855," in *Emerson's Antislavery Writings*, ed. Len Gougeon and Joel Myerson (New Haven: Yale University Press, 1995), 91–106, hereafter cited parenthetically as *AW*.

13. Ronald G. Walters, *American Reformers, 1815–1860* (New York: Hill and Wang, 1978), ix.

14. Ralph Waldo Emerson, *Selected Journals, 1841–1877* (New York: Library of America, 2010), 625.

15. Henry David Thoreau, *Walden and Civil Disobedience* (New York: Penguin, 1986), 118.

16. Gary Collison, "Emerson and Antislavery," in *A Historical Guide to Ralph Waldo Emerson*, ed. Joel Myerson (New York: Oxford University Press, 2000), 179–210, 189.

17. Len Gougeon, "Historical Background," *AW*, xi–lvi, xxx. See also Len Gougeon, *Virtue's Hero: Emerson, Antislavery, and Reform* (Athens: University Press of Georgia, 1990).

18. Gougeon, "Historical Background," xxxvii.

19. See the opening of Jack Turner's essay in this volume; see "Man the Reformer," 135–50, 137.

20. Emerson, *Selected Journals, 1841–1877*, 779.

21. Cited in Gougeon, "Historical Background," xliii.

22. Amy E. Earhart, "Representative Men, Slave Revolt, and Emerson's 'Conversion' to Abolitionism," *American Transcendental Quarterly* 13, no. 4 (1999): 287–303.

23. Ibid., 290.

24. I argue below for the importance of "The Poet" to Emerson's theory of representation, but his turn to representation as a way of navigating the tension between self-reliance and public reform can already be found in "The American Scholar." Collison recognizes this tension in "The American Scholar," if not the importance of representation to engaging it, when he writes, "The tension between

the conflicting demands of Emerson's creative genius for isolation and disengagement and the demands of his public role as guide and preceptor to his community and to humanity would continue to define and plague Emerson throughout his career" (Collison, "Emerson and Antislavery," 188).

25. Ibid., 602–3.

26. Robert D. Richardson Jr., *Emerson: The Mind on Fire* (Berkeley and Los Angeles: University of California Press, 1995), 372.

27. On Whitman's development of this theme, see my essay "Aesthetic Democracy: Walt Whitman and the Poetry of the People," *Review of Politics* 69, no. 3 (2007): 402–30.

28. Cavell, *Conditions Handsome and Unhandsome*, 12.

29. Shelley, *A Defense of Poetry*, ed. Albert S. Cook (New York: Ginn, 1890), 84.

30. Andrew Delbanco, introduction to *Representative Men: Seven Lectures* (Cambridge: Harvard University Press, 1996), vii–xiv, xii.

31. Thomas Carlyle, *On Heroes, Hero-Worship, and the Heroic in History* (Lincoln: University of Nebraska Press, 1966), 1.

32. Ibid., 203.

33. Ibid., 196.

34. Ibid., 197.

35. Shklar, "Emerson and the Inhibitions of Democracy," 60.

36. Ibid., 58.

37. Richardson, *Emerson*, 414.

38. Rautenfeld, "Thinking for Thousands," 184.

39. Hanna Fenichel Pitkin, *The Concept of Representation* (Berkeley and Los Angeles: University of California Press, 1972), 144–67.

40. Ibid., 145.

41. See, for example, Gordon S. Wood, *The Creation of the American Republic, 1776–1787* (New York: Norton, 1969), 162–88.

42. See, for example, Amy Gutman and Dennis Thompson, *Why Deliberative Democracy?* (Princeton: Princeton University Press, 2004), 13–21, 15.

43. Edmund Burke, *On Empire, Liberty, and Reform: Speeches and Letters*, ed. David Bromwich (New Haven: Yale University Press, 2000), 55.

44. Jacob E. Cooke, ed., *The Federalist* (Middletown: Wesleyan University Press, 1961), 62.

45. Jay Grossman, *Reconstituting the American Renaissance: Emerson, Whitman, and the Politics of Representation* (Durham, N.C.: Duke University Press, 2003), 128.

46. This view was given a classic American articulation during the debates over constitutional ratification by the Anti-Federalist Brutus: "The very term, representative, implies, that the person or body chosen for this purpose, should

resemble those who appoint them—a representation of the people of America, if it be a true one, must be like the people. It ought to be so constituted that a person, who is a stranger to the country, might be able to form a just idea of their character, by knowing that of their representatives. They are the sign—the people are the thing signified" ("Brutus III," in *The Anti-Federalist: Writings by the Opponents of the Constitution,* ed. Herbert J. Storing [Chicago: University of Chicago Press, 1981], 122–27, 124).

47. See, for example, Rautenfeld, "Thinking for Thousands," 184.

48. Pitkin, *The Concept of Representation,* 150.

49. Sharon Cameron, "The Way of Life by Abandonment: Emerson's Impersonal," in *Impersonality: Seven Essays,* by Cameron (Chicago: University of Chicago Press, 2007), 79–107, 80.

50. I take the term "infrasensible" from William Connolly, *Neuropolitics: Thinking, Culture, Speed* (Minneapolis: University of Minnesota Press, 2002), 85. For the immanent vitalist Emerson, see George J. Stack, *Nietzsche and Emerson: An Elective Affinity* (Athens: Ohio University Press, 1992); for a good example of the theistic Emerson, see Daniel S. Malachuk's contribution in this volume.

51. Cameron, "The Way of Life by Abandonment," 83.

52. Cited in Richardson, *Emerson,* 535.

53. Larry Reynolds, *European Revolutions and the American Literary Renaissance* (New Haven: Yale University Press, 1995), 42.

54. Ralph Waldo Emerson, *Selected Journals, 1820–1842* (New York: Library of America, 2010), 642.

55. Richardson, *Emerson,* 177.

56. Emerson, *Selected Journals, 1841–1877,* 552.

57. Ibid., 423.

58. Ibid., 538.

59. Ralph Waldo Emerson, "Courage," in *Society and Solitude: Twelve Chapters* (Cambridge: Fields, Osgood, and Co., 1870), 225–50, 242.

60. David S. Reynolds, *John Brown, Abolitionist: The Man Who Killed Slavery, Sparked the Civil War, and Seeded Civil Rights* (New York: Knopf, 2005), 369.

61. Ibid., 366.

62. Emerson, *Selected Journals, 1841–1877,* 725.

63. Henry David Thoreau, "A Plea for Captain John Brown," in *Civil Disobedience and Other Essays* (New York: Dover, 1993), 31–48, 37.

64. Reynolds, *John Brown, Abolitionist,* 223.

65. In addition to Cavell, see Aletta J. Norval, *Aversive Democracy: Inheritance and Originality in the Democratic Tradition* (New York: Cambridge University Press, 2007).

66. Ralph Waldo Emerson, "On the President's Proclamation," *Atlantic*, November 1862, 638–42, 638.

67. Alex Zakaras, *Individuality and Mass Democracy; Mill, Emerson, and the Burdens of Citizenship* (New York: Oxford University Press, 2009), 10.

68. Honig, "Between Decision and Deliberation," 6.

69. Cavell, "Aversive Thinking," in this volume, 117.

CHAPTER 13

Emerson's Democratic Platonism in *Representative Men*

G. Borden Flanagan

THIS VOLUME HAS SOUGHT to correct two trends in Emerson scholarship—the underappreciation of Emerson's political thought, and the tendency to read doctrines and positions into Emerson that belong more to ourselves (or to our enemies) than to him. Scholars tend to assimilate Emerson to what is familiar and useful. His works ask for this mistreatment by virtue of their complexity, subtlety, and charm, all of which can be either off-putting to those who want action and political utility in their authors, or beguiling to those seeking authoritative allies. In the face of Emerson's poetic obscurity, it can be difficult not to bend him to suit our instincts. Postmodernists seek to marshal his charm on their behalf, libertarians on theirs, communitarians on theirs, and so on, each with real but partial textual backing.

The tendency to assimilate Emerson to what is familiar in contemporary political thought is clear in the scholarship on *Representative Men*. Judith Shklar argues (rightly, I believe) that Emerson was caught between his respect for equality and his recognition of the simple superiority of great individuals such as Shakespeare. Shklar's thesis is that this tension is resolved for Emerson not so much by an argument, but by his moral commitment to democratic decency, a commitment she shared. Emerson's commitment to equality was more recognizable to Shklar than his argument for it, and that is where she took her stand. Neal Dolan, our fellow contributor, laid the ground for my essay by arguing in his *Emerson's Liberalism* that *Representative Men* is an attempt to counteract certain drawbacks of modern rationalism by means of advancing a new kind of spirituality. He interprets *Representative Men* through the lens of Ernst Gellner, Emile Durkheim, and modern epistemology, and sees it as both an example of modern empiricism (in the mode of Gellner) and an attempt to overcome it. Hans von Rautenfeld uses Emerson's book to advance a Habermasian argument about representative participation in the mediated discourse of the public sphere. Each of these arguments has its advantages and disadvantages, but what is striking is their tendency to read Emerson through the lens of what is most recognizable, and perhaps most appealing, to contemporary political theorists.[1]

I wish to argue that the key to *Representative Men* is what is least familiar and least intuitive for contemporary readers, namely its Platonism. In Platonic (and Aristotelian) fashion, Emerson begins *Representative Men* by characterizing the cultivation of excellence as the purpose or *telos* of society. Social relations exist, ideally, in order to serve that cultivation. The cardinal excellence for Emerson, as for Plato, is wisdom. Five of the six representative men are distinguished, and treated by Emerson, as knowers (as George Kateb points out);[2] each represents a type of human wisdom. Emerson's typology of greatness is really a typology of knowledge. The structure of this typology gives Plato the highest ranking. The first four representative men form an account of intellectual greatness as available in all times and places, while the last two represent peculiarly modern dangers (Napoleon) and opportunities (Goethe). Among the first four, Plato stands as the comprehensive figure who incorporates the partial genius of the other three; Emerson describes Plato as mystic (Swedenborg's role, *E&L*, 634), poet (Shakespeare's, 635), and skeptic (Montaigne's, 641, 643–44, 655–56), all in his capacity as the most "balanced soul," or philosopher.[3] Of the six representative types of greatness, Plato and philosophy stand supreme. The goal of wisdom for Emerson, as for Plato, is knowledge of being, or the comprehensive totality and character of existence. The basic framework that Emerson lays out for his argument in the first two chapters, and elaborates through the rest, then, is a formula from ancient Greek political philosophy: excellence is the purpose of politics, the highest excellence is wisdom, the goal of wisdom is knowledge of being.

Representative Men is not primarily about politics, at least as we moderns think of it. Emerson's two great subjects here are wisdom and the relation between wisdom and society. His political teaching is mostly implied by those discussions. The political ideal that emerges from Emerson's account of wisdom and being is a democracy of intellectually self-reliant, wisdom-seeking individuals, or a kind of universal "aristocracy," in the ancient sense of "most virtuous."

The political implications of Emerson's opening framework are not obviously democratic, given their ancient Greek provenance; on the surface, Plato's *Republic* advocates a philosopher-king, and Aristotle's *Politics* describes the best regime as one that distributes power and honor undemocratically on the basis of virtue.[4] Yet we know that *Representative Men* was intended as a defense of democracy in response to Thomas Carlyle's neo-aristocratic *Heroes and Hero-Worship*.[5] The genius of Emerson's response to Carlyle (and to others contemptuous of equality) is to defend liberal democracy before the bar of excellence. Emerson answers those who associate democracy with the leveling of human possibilities by articulating an understanding of excellence, showing how it is friendly to democratic equality, and suggesting how the characteristic features of democracy suit or can be made to suit the cultivation of excellence. In doing so, Emerson also defends excellence before the bar of democracy, encouraging citizens who were already committed to equality and democracy to love excellence as well. He encourages readers to view democratic citizenship as a means to higher, suprapolitical ends for themselves. It is in this regard that Emerson draws on the Greeks, and on Plato in particular.

Central to this dual defense of excellence and democracy is Emerson's marriage of ancient political teleology to his own very liberal and democratic ontology. Emerson's ontology democratizes "being," which is Emerson's word for the totality of existence when comprehended as a whole. What we experience when we glimpse being, according to Emerson, is the fundamental unity of all things. When viewed in this light, all individual distinction disappears. As Shklar argued, Emerson is not altogether convincing when he claims that equal wisdom is available to all. (Shklar goes so far as to call this notion "ridiculous.")[6] But if all are ultimately one, the highest wisdom (which is the highest excellence) reveals the deepest equality. Emerson's ontology reconciles excellence with equality.

Besides democratizing being, Emerson "liberalizes" the transcendence we achieve when we glimpse being by making transcendence exclusively the product of the individual's free inquiry and intellectual self-discovery; transcendence is available to each without being a mass phenomenon. In

Representative Men, the manner in which the highest wisdom is achieved is thus consistent with the individuality Emerson advocates in "Self-Reliance." Transcendence does not require absorption of the self into a social whole, such as a state or party or church, as a stepping-stone to the universal; in fact, it requires that the individual avoid such absorption. In *Representative Men*, the path to transcendence that Emerson emphasizes is philosophic or scientific investigation, which is individual in character.

Emerson makes clear, however, that reality falls short of his ideal. He suggests that grave political dangers lie in the character of modern rationalism in the West. In Emerson's account, modern Western rationalism forgets "being" for the sake of "nature," which is Emerson's word for existence as viewed in its concrete particulars (639–40). Modern rationalism cultivates natural science, or the art of making distinctions and definitions that capture the articulation of nature into many heterogeneous parts. The political advantage of the focus on distinctions and parts is an appreciation of diversity that fosters democracy and individuality. The disadvantage is that, rather than seeking a unifying or highest end, modern Western rationalism concentrates on means, and therefore ends up pursuing technology, wealth, and power. The political consequences of the concentration on means, according to Emerson, are class hierarchy, imperialism, and soul-killing materialism. Modernity's focus is mastery of heterogeneous nature rather than contemplation of nature's unity, or being.

It is the danger of Western modernity that elicits Emerson's account of excellence and society. Emerson's political thought aims to bring together what he deems best in ancient and modern thought: attention to being, on the one hand, and equality and liberty on the other. His political ideal counters modern instrumental rationalism with ancient political theory; where modern instrumental rationalism emphasizes heterogeneous means (various kinds of power, and wealth) as ends in themselves, Emerson's classically inflected political ideal urges that attention be paid to unifying ends instead. In this manner Emerson seeks to influence politics by affecting what people take to be the highest purpose of their societies. *Representative Men* is therefore a political act in being an attempt at spiritual or cultural leadership. In his chapter on Goethe, Emerson gives readers reason to hope for writers who can push back against the suffocating materialism of modernity, and reason to fear that such writers may not be able to break free of modern Western presuppositions about the nature of excellence and the purpose of political life.

Though Emerson's use of Platonic ideas in *Representative Men* has not been explored, his treatment of the relation of excellence to democracy, and his common ground (construed broadly) with Plato, have both been addressed before. Stanley Cavell compares the two thinkers in *Conditions Handsome and Unhandsome: The Constitution of Emersonian Perfectionism*. By "perfectionism," Cavell understands an account of human life that addresses the grounds and conditions of individual flourishing and locates these in the quest for self-development and self-knowledge. Perfectionism refers therefore to Emerson's notion of self-reliance, as well as to the importance of self-reliance in Emerson's thought as a whole. The "perfection" implied by perfectionism plays the role in Cavell's argument that "excellence" does in mine. Although Cavell notes similarities of theme between Plato and Emerson, and connects them as outstanding thinkers in a perfectionist tradition, his comparison asserts three fundamental differences between the two thinkers, differences that depend on a misreading of Emerson that this chapter rebuts. First, Cavell asserts that Emerson differs from Plato by denying any metaphysical basis for or essence of the self.[7] Second, Cavell's Emerson differs from Plato by understanding self-perfection without reference to a "Good," that is, to a goal outside the self, by which the self's progress may be assessed; Cavell's Emerson therefore understands self-perfection as having, strictly speaking, no path that can be externally discerned or recommended, because self-perfection means "individuation."[8] Cavell claims, presumably for this reason, that Emerson offers no model or representative of the self-perfecting life in the way that Plato offers the example of Socrates.[9] These claims serve as the basis of a third, that (contrary to Plato) Emerson's version of self-perfection results in no hierarchical judgments of other selves (let alone political coercion to morality), but is compatible rather with all moral systems. Cavell uses this third claim to reconcile Emersonian self-perfection to Rawlsian democracy. That is, Cavell's Emerson reconciles excellence with democracy by replacing excellence or Platonic virtue with "individuation."

Contrary to Cavell's three points, this chapter shows, first, that Emerson's view of the self is emphatically metaphysical. Second, this chapter demonstrates that Emerson understands the self to be oriented properly, even essentially, toward transcendence, and that this directedness of the self establishes a fundamental path that Emerson exhorts us to follow. (Contrary to Cavell's claim that Emerson offers us no representative to exemplify virtue, as Plato offers Socrates, Emerson offers his five exemplary knowers as a carefully articulated typology of intellectual excellence from which we are clearly meant to draw guidance. The peak type, Plato, serves as Emerson's Socrates.) Third, this chapter shows that Emerson's account of excellence necessitates certain hierarchical judgments implicit in the distinction Emerson makes between more and less thoughtful, more and less self-reliant, or more and less materialistic modes of life—though I agree that Emerson does not provide a basis for political hierarchy (for example, on moral grounds). But Emerson makes and advocates hierarchical judgments about a host of issues, from ways of life to imperialism and Western political economy. The relation of *Representative Men*, or of Emerson's thought more broadly addressed, to Rawls's *A Theory of Justice* is outside the scope of this chapter. But as Emerson's argument unfolds in *Representative Men*, he explicitly contradicts each of Cavell's assertions about Emerson's differences from Plato and reconciles excellence with democracy on an entirely different basis than Cavell claims.[10] This basis is Emerson's combination of transcendentalist metaphysics with ancient political theory.

Emerson's Ancient Political Theory

Emerson begins *Representative Men* with a remarkable teleological claim so counterintuitive to modern and postmodern tastes that the scholarship has yet to recognize, let alone digest it: Human social life has human virtue as its natural end or purpose. More specifically, Emerson claims that being guided by examples and standards of excellence is necessary for human happiness, and in practice societies and individuals orient themselves by such examples and standards: "Nature seems to exist for the excellent. The world is upheld by the veracity of good men: they make the world wholesome. They who lived with them found life glad and nutritious. Life is sweet and tolerable only in our belief in such society; and actually, or ideally, we manage to live with superiors. We call our children and our lands by their names. Their names are wrought into the verbs of language, their works and effigies are in our houses, and every circumstance of the day recalls an anecdote of them" (615). The human mind naturally gravitates to ideas and examples of excellence, our quotidian social life is permeated and made worthwhile by our reverence for them, and (later) even our great religions are expressions of them (616).

Emerson goes so far as to say that human populations bereft of excellence, those that are "beggars" in the sense of lacking reverence for standards higher than their material subsistence, "are disgusting, like moving cheese, like hills of ants, or of fleas—the more, the worse" (615). In *Representative Men*, Emerson uses the word "society" only in reference to groups of people oriented toward notions of excellence (614–15, cf. 675, 677, 694–95); in this opening chapter, groups without such orientation are mere "populations" (615). Like ancient political philosophers such as Plato and Aristotle (and contrary to Cavell's third claim), Emerson uses a notion of virtue and the good life to distinguish between better and worse types of human organization (and implicitly, between better and worse individuals, as becomes clear in the Napoleon chapter). Populations not directed toward the cultivation of human excellence are likened by Emerson to less-than-human kinds of life for having contracted the horizon of human possibility.

Emerson's opening treatment of the relation between excellence and society is very reminiscent of Aristotle's definition of politics. For Aristotle, the difference between a mere village and a city (a *polis*) is that the former only serves self-preservation, while the latter makes a life of full flourishing, a life of excellence, possible. Cities emerge when several villages unite for the sake of physical self-sufficiency, and "while coming into being for the sake of living, it exists for the sake of living well" (*Politics*, 1252b27–30, cf. 1323a15–1324a4). Plato suggests a similar argument in the *Republic*.[11] In like fashion, Emerson suggests that populations may exist for mere life, but society, like the *polis*, exists properly for the good life, which means a life lived virtuously, which means a life lived in emulation of the great (*E&L*, 615–16). (The similarities between Plato and Aristotle are more relevant to Emerson's argument in *Representative Men* than their differences, and Aristotle's accounts of these similarities are often more direct and concise, so for the sake of elucidating the most basic ideas I will refer to them both under the rubric of "ancient.")

To live well, for Plato and Aristotle, is to fulfill one's potential as a human being. Each kind of organism has its own characteristic activity, the doing of which fulfills or actualizes its potential. Plants are fully actualized through the uptake of nutrition and growth, animals are fully actualized on the level of sentience, while the activity peculiar to man is reasoning.[12] If an organism is doing its characteristic activity well, that is to say, excellently, then the organism is fulfilling its nature. Virtuous life for the ancients means the full flourishing or actualization of potential, and is the definition of happiness (Aristotle, *Nicomachean Ethics*, 1097b21–1098a17; Plato, *Republic*, 444d–445b, 580b–587a, 588c–592c). Living well, or flourishing, is the highest human goal for Plato and Aristotle. It is the end that all our endeavors seek. All our other goals, when properly understood, turn out to be mere means to this highest goal. Plato's Socrates argues (as Emerson points out [*E&L*, 657]) that receiving punishment may even be choice-worthy on these grounds, if it contributes to virtue, and so to happiness.

For both Plato and Aristotle, political life is a necessary condition of fulfilling our potential. Excellence or flourishing is something of a collective endeavor because, for most people, excellence requires good laws and influences, such as teachers, friends, and the peace and prosperity that make flourishing possible. Moreover, according to Plato and Aristotle, it is only on the political level that issues of good and bad, justice and injustice emerge, which are necessary for rational deliberation to be fully developed. Human reasoning comes into its own in reflecting on its own conditions and purposes, as these come to sight in deliberation over what the community and its citizens should do and be.

Readers of Emerson may object that the importance of engaging in political life for full human flourishing is something that Emerson appears to deny. The ancients may have thought that virtue is perfected in citizenship, but the Emerson of "Self Reliance" appears to argue that, as our highest duty is to our inner genius, we should avoid the chains of social duties. But both sides of this comparison—the picture of Emerson as antipolitical and of the ancients as thoroughly political—need refinement.

As the introduction to this volume and several of the chapters (especially Gougeon's) amply demonstrate, Emerson is more political than has been assumed. In *Representative Men*, Emerson's account of Goethe, explored below, articulates a public—and at times, explicitly political—role for the Emersonian intellectual, and a cultural project that Emerson himself wishes to undertake. The Emersonian is not a joiner, but this is not the same as disengagement or indifference to the public weal. Emerson is not above recognizing the banality that being true to oneself may require political action; the source of obligation for Emerson need not be social to issue in recognition of one's involvement in society, and therefore potential complicity in injustice.

Just as social engagement is likely to follow self-reliance as a consequence, social engagement is identified by Emerson as an important condition of intellectual self-discovery, and therewith self-reliance. He warns that when thinking of how to benefit from great men, we "must not deny the substantial existence of other people. I know not what would happen to us. We have social strengths. Our affection towards others creates a vantage or purchase which nothing will supply. I can do that by another which I cannot do alone. I can say to another what I cannot first say to myself" (616). That last sentence is fundamental, and sets the stage logically for the one before: we discover who we are through our social discourse with others, and our cooperation with others makes it possible to pursue the principles and interests we are thus in the process of discovering.[13]

Like Plato and Aristotle, Emerson emphasizes human flourishing and the necessity of political life to enable such flourishing. He opens *Representative Men* with an account of communities (not isolated individuals) revering and being influenced by the excellent. Reverence and emulation, fostered in social settings, are important conditions of the pursuit of excellence. Emerson expresses doubt that pursuit of excellence can be undertaken or even understood apart from the social context. The acquisition of excellence requires and begins in the community.

The crux of the argument shared by Plato, Aristotle, and Emerson is that the highest human ends must be the highest ends of political society, a position that is debatable, of course. One could respond with Weber, for example, that even if political life does serve the cultivation of excellence, politics can conceivably serve, and historically has served, every kind of end, and therefore cannot be defined in relation to any goal or end. But according to Plato and Aristotle, if excellence and flourishing are the highest good and if they require political life, then politics must be understood as a means to that good above all. To put the same point another way, if happiness and excellence are the goals of all our rational actions, then they must be the goals of our rational political actions as well. As individuals who form, maintain, or reform political societies, our natures are still directed toward our own flourishing. Politics, as a species of human choice and action, has happiness or the good as its overriding purpose. Emerson implies the same view with his remark that only social life lived in light of examples of greatness is "sweet and tolerable" (615). If life is only tolerable, for Emerson, when lived in pursuit of excellence, and this pursuit requires social life, then social life is only choice-worthy when oriented toward excellence. (And as we have seen, societies that ignore excellence are not real societies in his view, but disgusting accumulations of population.) This is not to say that society always is directed to excellence—Plato, Aristotle, and Emerson make clear that societies in reality almost never understand excellence or pursue it very well. But for all three thinkers, society has a rational purpose that follows from human nature, whether people understand it or not.

When Plato and Aristotle think about the good society, then, they think about it in terms of what sort of human being this or that regime will produce, rather than what package of rights this or that regime protects. The connection between excellence and politics is emphatic for Plato and Aristotle because the community we live in determines the spectrum of acceptable behavior, and exercises tremendous influence over what we want to do. The great question for Plato and Aristotle is whether all the civic virtues that communities tend to require of their citizens (courage in defense of the city, for example, or reverence for the gods or for the law) are compatible with the excellence that suits human nature. Emerson begins *Representative Men* by encouraging the reader to view social life the same way, and to ask the same question. Emerson's subsequent pantheon of great men asks the reader to consider what sort of human type society should revere and seek to encourage.

Just as Emerson's political or socially engaged side must be appreciated for his use of the ancients to be properly understood, the fact that the ancients looked beyond and above politics, to the perfection of the individual's soul, must also be appreciated. Political life is a necessary but by no means a sufficient condition of excellence for the ancients. For Emerson, for Plato, and for Aristotle, the virtue that gives social life its end is not strictly a political excellence, such as prudent statesmanship, but wisdom broadly understood. Plato and Aristotle both assert explicitly that the activity through which human beings come into their own is reasoning. For Aristotle, philosophy represents the full flourishing of human potential (*Nicomachean Ethics*, 1097b21–1098a17, 1177a12–b25, 1178a2–8). Likewise in the account of virtue in Plato's *Republic*, the most virtuous man is the philosopher (442c–d, 443c–e, 444d–e, 485d–486c, 492a; cf. Aristotle, *Politics*, 1323a14–1325b31, esp. 1325b16–31). Consequently, most of the institutions of the ideal regime laid out in Plato's *Republic* are educational in intention, and the highest goal of this education is the cultivation of the philosopher-king (381b–382c, 401d–402d, 411e–412b, 473d, 497b–d, 520b–540c). Plato goes so far as to call the value of justice into question (even the justice of the best regime), by reference to perfection of the soul. Justice in Socrates' ideal city requires minding one's role and accepting the city's religious myth that explains and justifies that role (433a–434c). But justice in the soul, which turns out to be the basis of the just man's superior happiness, requires something quite different, namely that the soul be led by reason, which has its fulfillment in philosophy, and therewith in the questioning of myth (442c–444a, 514a–520a, 619c–e). The philosopher-king knows that the religious myth upon which the city is founded is a lie, even if a noble lie, which is to say that the philosopher-king sees through the basis of political obligation as understood by the citizen. In the most important respect, the philosopher, even if made to be king, is not a citizen, for he does not inhabit the same community of assumptions, and has a completely different relation to the claims the city makes. The philosopher understands the superiority of justice of the soul to citizen-justice, and considers himself obligated to the former (591c–592b). Or, to put it another way, the philosopher's justice is to seek the elaboration and flourishing of his inner genius, which means pursuing wisdom rather than his duty as citizen and ruler. Plato makes clear that the philosopher would not want to be king (517d, 519d–e). For the ancients, most emphatically for Plato, the highest virtue requires us at some point to look beyond and above politics, which brings the ancients much closer to Emerson than might otherwise be assumed.

As for Emerson, wisdom takes different forms in *Representative Men*, so perhaps for him wisdom is a group of virtues, but apart from the (not uncritical) chapter on Napoleon, all of Emerson's examples of greatness are knowers. Even the literary artists discussed in *Representative Men* are worthy of being representative for Emerson by virtue of the wisdom they display or seek. The first representative man is the philosopher, the philosopher Emerson chooses as philosophy's peak embodiment is Plato—not Kant, not Hegel, not Locke, not Rousseau, not any modern thinker (not even Montaigne)—and in his chapter on Plato, Emerson endorses Plato's famous formulation that virtue is knowledge (*E&L*, 657).

Instead of advocating the reform of political institutions to turn them into educational ones along the lines of the *Republic,* Emerson offers us five representative thinkers to inspire admiration and emulation. When Emerson speaks of representative men, his primary meaning of "representative" is therefore not political but intellectual; the great represent things or ideas to us in the sense of explaining those things or ideas to us. "Men have a pictorial or representative quality," Emerson says, "and serve us in the intellect. Behman and Swedenborg saw that things were representative. Men are also representative; first, of things, and secondly, of ideas" (618). Emerson explains what he means by representation in the next paragraph, saying that "each man is, by secret liking, connected to some district of nature, whose agent and interpreter he is, as Linnaeus, of plants; Huber, of bees . . . Newton, of fluxions" (618). The relation of representation Emerson uses is not political, as between one individual and other aggregates of individuals, but philosophic, between the knower and the things known. In explaining nature, the great also represent the virtue of wisdom to their (actual and potential) students.

Just as excellence is the highest end of society, and wisdom is the highest excellence, knowledge of being is the highest wisdom for Emerson. Because knowledge of being is therefore the highest excellence and the purpose of society in Emerson's account, it deserves some discussion, for what Emerson means by knowledge of being determines his view of human flourishing, and of how politics can serve it. In his chapter on Plato, Emerson gives his most extensive account of the character and limits of human wisdom and of the longing for being that drives our pursuit of it. In his view, wisdom has two sides that must be united: "Philosophy is the account which the human mind gives to itself of the constitution of the world. Two cardinal facts lie forever at the base; the one, and the two; 1. Unity, or Identity; and, 2. Variety. We unite all things, by perceiving the law which pervades them; by perceiving the superficial differences, and the profound resemblances. But this very mental act, this very perception of identity or oneness, recognizes the differences of things. Oneness and otherness. It is impossible to speak, or to think, without embracing both" (637). Human thought is torn between contemplating the unity of being, and describing and defining the articulation of being into heterogeneous particulars. According to Emerson, neither side is fully intelligible on its own. We do not fully understand the various parts of the natural world until we understand how they are parts of a unified whole. Likewise we cannot know the unifying principle of nature without knowing how this principle unifies heterogeneous parts. Each side of this duality seems to require, and to deny, the other. The perspective within which all things are one is the perspective of being, in Emerson's usage, while the perspective that sees all things in their heterogeneity is that of "nature." Nature is composed of discrete parts whose connection to every other part is mostly unknown, whereas the whole that explains their "partness," and so resolves them into a unity, is being. Complete wisdom would require capturing both sides. According to Emerson, this accomplishment is Plato's alone, in whom "a balanced soul was born, perceptive of the two elements" (641).

Emerson treats knowledge of being as the highest wisdom, higher than knowledge of nature, because being is prior to nature logically, in the sense that a whole is prior logically to its parts. These two kinds of wisdom must be combined, but they are not equal in rank. Knowledge of being can explain heterogeneous nature only if it incorporates knowledge of heterogeneous nature, but knowledge of being is higher than knowledge of heterogeneity, because parts are intelligible only in light of the whole they comprise. The meaning and essence of heterogeneous nature is therefore the unity of being. Nature is the expression of being in the dimensions of time and space ("the surfaces and extremities of matter"); being is nature's final cause.[14] As regards science or philosophy, then, knowledge of being unifies and gives direction to all the other inquiries and bodies of knowledge. For society to serve the highest wisdom, it must value the quest for knowledge of being as the highest end.

Emerson's approving use of Platonic ontology extends to Platonic psychology. Knowledge of being is the highest end of human endeavor not just because of its explanatory power, but because for Emerson it is the object of the deepest human longing: "That which the soul seeks is resolution into being, above form, out of Tartarus, and out of heaven,—liberation from nature" (639). Citing Plato's *Symposium* (or *The Banquet*), Emerson applauds Plato for the teaching that the deepest longing of the soul is to become aware of being. As discussed below, the essence or "substance" or principle of being is reason for Emerson, and therefore to have knowledge of being is, however partially, to join with being. Physical erotic longing "is initial; and symbolizes, at a distance, the passion of the soul for that immense lake of beauty it exists to seek" (649). Contrary to Cavell, Emerson's account of the soul's quest for perfection is both explicitly metaphysical and asserts a highest good, or goal, for self-perfection. Whatever practical needs society must address in its daily functioning (such as the acquisition of wealth and security) must be understood to be directed to, and limited by, the project to satisfy this deepest human need.

How society can operate as a philosophic project is suggested in *Representative Men*'s first chapter, "Uses of Great Men," where Emerson describes three kinds of relation: our social relations with our fellows; our relation to the great; and our relation to being. These three kinds of relation form a ladder; each kind of relation is a rung that serves our ascent to the next. As mentioned above, active relations with our fellow citizens form the first rung on the ladder to wisdom. Conversation with our fellows helps us to learn what we ourselves think. Yet our fellows may not lead us very far, or may mislead us altogether, a shortcoming supplemented by the influence of the great, which for Emerson means the wise: the great writers, thinkers, and scientists that illuminate the path to knowledge of being. If we learn from Emerson how properly to revere and emulate the great, our relation to them (the second rung) will lead us much further along the road to wisdom. From the great we receive training in the use of our faculties, as well as knowledge. In turning us to the pursuit of knowledge, the great point us in the direction of being. The relation to being is the third rung, the highest and most satisfying relation we can achieve in Emerson's account. The first two kinds of relation serve our ascent to the third.

Yet organizing society around virtue seems to imply antidemocratic consequences, even (or especially) if the highest virtue is wisdom. One might imagine Emerson's arguments inspiring some alarm today. However disappointing Emerson's advocacy of self-reliance might be for some communitarians, advancing virtue as the principle of social organization seems even more antidemocratic and strangely un-Emersonian, at least to modern ears. It would seem to militate against self-reliance and nonconformity, as well as against respect for equality. The ideal regime in Plato's *Republic* is run by a philosopher-king, and radically restricts all manner of freedom for the sake of producing virtuous citizens and future philosopher kings (377c–424e, 449c–464e). The ideal regime has a strict class structure (414d–415c). Similarly Aristotle's distributive justice requires giving unequal position and power to citizens unequal in virtue (*Politics* 1280b5–8; 1280b39–1281a8; 1284b23–34). Regardless of how one ultimately interprets these features of ancient political theory, they seem to offer a prima facie case against democracy to Carlyle and his followers.

The antidemocratic implications of Emerson's emphasis on wisdom must be dealt with forthrightly; the problem of how to reconcile virtue-seeking with respect for equality cannot be solved by assimilating Emerson's position to a pluralism more comfortable for contemporary democratic tastes. Emerson is just not a pluralist in the late- or postmodern sense, for three evident reasons. First, though the late- or postmodern reader may wish to relativize notions of virtue as mere artifacts of time and place, Emerson argues that the major theologies that express these notions are "the necessary and structural action of the human mind," and that "our theism is the purification of the human mind" (*E&L*, 616). A contemporary response to these assertions could be that, though the *emergence* of notions of virtue may be necessary, as consequences of the structure of human thought, Emerson must still regard their *content* as contingent. But, second, he claims that the virtues that history has sifted out and embodied in the great monotheistic traditions are uniform, and therefore, implicitly, not arbitrary historical artifacts. These religions "run all our vessels into *one* mold" (616, emphasis added). The late- or postmodern reader could interpret Emerson to mean that, however strong the human tendency is to arrive at fundamentally similar standards of excellence, nevertheless those standards cannot be considered true. But, third, Emerson presents his examples as revelatory of the truth about human flourishing throughout *Representative Men*. He identifies the great as those who "hold of nature and transcend fashions, by their fidelity to universal ideas" (627). Greatness in Emerson's view is therefore not culturally contingent. Emerson concedes that the great have historical contexts that provide opportunities and source material, but he makes clear that their genius is not itself socially constructed. Finally, the great in *Representative Men* are for the most part great discoverers and describers of truth. Emerson does not historicize truth, which means that knowing the truth stands as a measure by which individuals may be ranked. Again, historical contexts comprise necessary but not sufficient conditions of greatness: "The river makes its own shores, and each legitimate idea makes its own channels and welcome,—harvests for food, institutions for expression, weapons to fight with, and disciples to explain it" (617). Contrary to Cavell, the great are not great by virtue of their individuation.[15] The greatness of the great is according to nature, and results in the apprehension of, and fidelity to universal ideas—ideas not apprehended or upheld by the "fashions" of their fellows. There is no way to avoid the fact that Emerson asserts a universal standard of excellence, and that not everyone can be a genius. The fact that Emerson's emphasis on virtue, and on wisdom in particular, is problematic for egalitarian democracy must be acknowledged before a genuine resolution can be found.

It is not immediately clear how democratic citizens can maintain their respect for equality in the face of great superiority, especially if society makes admiration for the great one of its fundamental principles. One would expect those admired for superiority in virtue to have greater social power by virtue of that admiration, and therefore, to have greater political power. And if society exists to foster virtue, it is unclear how equality and liberty can continue to be justified or respected as social goods in their own right. If virtue is the end of society, then equality is not, and freedom is merely one means among many, valuable insofar as it fosters virtue and dispensable when and where it does not. From the beginning of *Representative Men*, Emerson presents us with the question of how to square his Platonic claims about the ends of the self and of society with his intention to defend democratic liberty and equality against Carlyle's aristocratic contempt.

Wisdom, Self-Reliance, and Equality

To reconcile the dedication of society to wisdom with democratic liberty and equality, Emerson must show that each needs the other—and he does this in three ways. First, excellence is reconciled with respect for equality by virtue of the fact that the highest excellence, which is the highest wisdom, is awareness of the unity of being, which reveals that all distinctions between individuals are illusory. Second, excellence needs liberty because freedom of speech and thought, and the liberal social relations that they make possible, greatly advance the development of wisdom. Third, the admiration for the great that naturally follows from dedication to excellence supports liberal democracy because proper admiration, in Emerson's rendering, cultivates self-reliant, independent-minded citizens; proper admiration treats the great the way citizens of a democracy should treat authority, with interrogative self-reliance.

The first way that Emerson's account of excellence works as a defense of democracy is by reconciling the quest for wisdom with respect for equality. Emerson's transcendental ontology, to which he subordinates his view of excellence, proves to be the key to this argument, for individuality, and therefore individual distinctions, are illusory when viewed in light of the unity of being. The insight into this ultimate unity is the highest knowledge, which in turn is the highest excellence. The truth about hierarchy, and about all individuality, is a unity in which hierarchy and individual personality are dissolved. This insight may or may not be available to all to the same degree in practice, but it is perhaps the most urgent lesson Emerson seeks to convey in *Representative Men*. Emerson's argument for the equal wisdom and virtue of all individuals is weak when viewed from ground level, as Shklar makes clear (58–59). But from the standpoint of being, all souls are equal. Both resentment and pride must give way before the truth, Emerson writes, for "even more swiftly the seeming injustice [of disparities of talent and position] disappears, when we ascend to the central identity of all the individuals, and know that they are made of the substance which ordaineth and doeth" (*E&L*, 631). The highest virtue reveals the highest egalitarianism.

This argument from the standpoint of being is quite the reverse of the argument Cavell attributes to Emerson; rather than ground an egalitarian perfectionism or notion of virtue in a denial of metaphysics, Emerson reconciles virtue and equality by embracing metaphysics. For Cavell, Emersonian perfectionism is democratic/egalitarian because there is no essence to the self, nor any objective goal that stands as the end of the self's path of perfection, and hence no metaphysical basis for political hierarchy between selves. It is worth asking whether the rejection of metaphysics, in destroying the philosophical grounds for oppression, does not also destroy the grounds for opposing oppression in the same breath. (What about the self ought to be inviolable if the self is, itself, groundless?) But however one answers this question, Emerson's text is emphatically metaphysical. Far from denying a metaphysical basis for the self, Emerson declares that the self is made "of the substance which ordaineth and doeth"; the self is continuous somehow with the divine. Far from denying a goal that gives a direction for the self's perfection—far from describing this perfection as a matter of mere individuation—Emerson specifies knowledge of being as the soul's culmination. He goes so far as to describe the experience of knowledge of being in metaphysical terms, as a kind of union with, or dissolution into being. The individual pursuing self-perfection or excellence "is ascending out of his limits, into a catholic existence. We have never come at the true and best benefit of any genius, so long as we believe him an original force.

In the moment when he ceases to help us as a cause, he begins to help us more as an effect. Then he appears as an exponent of a vaster mind and will. The opaque self becomes transparent with the light of the First Cause" (631). Cavell denies that for Emerson the soul has the transcendence of its partiality as a goal, yet Emerson quite clearly asserts that it does. For Emerson, it is the standpoint of being that dissolves all distinction between individuals, and renders everyone equal.[16]

The second way that Emerson reconciles democracy and the dedication of society to wisdom is by arguing that the cultivation of wisdom draws irreplaceable support from liberal-democratic liberty and the social relations it makes possible. Emerson makes this argument by calling attention to the importance of social relations to the development of our faculties. Just as knowledge is the end of society, social relations are necessary for the development of knowledge—especially of knowledge of human excellence. As cited above, Emerson writes that "we have social strengths. Our affection towards others creates a sort of vantage or purchase which nothing will supply. I can do that by another which I cannot do alone. I can say to you what I cannot first say to myself. Other men are lenses through which we read our own minds" (616). Conversing with our fellow citizens draws us into forming judgments, and therefore helps us to elucidate our minds to ourselves; we discover ourselves through our discursive relations with others. By implication, liberal democratic society, in which freedom of thought and discussion are legally protected, and which calls on individuals to deliberate as a matter of citizenship, is the regime most conducive to intellectual self-reliance—assuming individuals take up the challenge to participate in deliberation. Man is the philosophical animal by virtue of being the political animal, and liberal democracy best knits the philosophical and the political together.

George Kateb offers a different but related account of how democratic citizenship supports intellectual self-reliance in *Emerson and Self-Reliance*. Kateb makes a persuasive case that for Emerson self-reliance means the sympathetic thinking-through, even to the point of (sympathetic) exaggeration, of every alternative point of view (to the extent possible).[17] Liberal democratic freedom of thought is both the most suitable precondition and the logical consequence of the equality of voices implied by self-reliance construed as this kind of "receptivity" to differing positions. This interpretation does not quite apply to *Representative Men* (though Kateb's view of self-reliance is not incompatible with it). As cited above, the benefit of discourse with my fellow citizens is not primarily receptivity to their views but the discovery of my own (though receptivity to alternatives may be a precondition of the most thorough self-discovery). Intellectual independence consists more in self-clarity than in openness, which means it is more conducive to judgment than Kateb allows. For example, the role of the writer in *Representative Men* is in part to correct the divergent follies of most men, and to return them to the proper perspective. The writer does not sympathetically elaborate and entertain the various swings of perspective in a democracy, but engages them to provide a center of calm rationality (748). (Similarly, Emerson does not set the views of his great men uncritically side by side, but provides critical comparisons that draw attention to each figure's partiality, and that point therefore in the direction of synthesis rather than open-ended multiplicity.)[18] But Kateb is right that self-reliance is fostered in active engagement with the views of fellow citizens, and that this requires and mandates democracy. As Kateb writes, self-reliance (intellectual primarily, but also active) "is a democratically-inspired doctrine, a doctrine unthinkable outside democracy and that also signifies the culmination and spiritual reason for the being of democracy."[19] To return to the issue of virtue and democracy: If intellectual self-reliance is necessary for the excellence of wisdom, and democracy is necessary (or optimal) for intellectual self-reliance, then democracy is necessary (or optimal) for the pursuit of wisdom. Virtue may not be the same as citizenship simply, but democratic citizenship is nevertheless good for us.

This manner of reconciling democracy with the elevation of wisdom as the leading social good takes a page from Tocqueville's argument about "self-interest properly understood." In Tocqueville, the materialism that equality of conditions, large-scale democracy, and liberty breed can foster the egoistic self-isolation that he calls "individualism," as people neglect the public sphere for the sake of private gains.[20] The danger is that by neglecting the public sphere, citizens lose the habits of self-government that guard against creeping statism, political apathy, and loss of liberty. The solution for Tocqueville lies in the American propensity to see the private advantages of involvement in public affairs; self-interest properly understood leads Americans to active political participation, and trains them in the habits and virtues of self-government (*Democracy in America*, 2.2.8). Emerson's argument follows a similar path by urging the benefits of self-reliance on his democratic readers, and connecting those benefits to discursive involvement with their fellow citizens. Emerson's emphasis on the value of seeking out intellectual diversity is especially relevant here. Our intellectual liberty depends on stepping outside our accustomed circles of thought.[21] Our profoundest self-interest, properly understood as the pursuit of wisdom, is born and maintained in active exploration of the realm of public discourse.

The value of intellectual self-reliance—and therefore of democratic liberty, which protects and fosters intellectual self-reliance—to the pursuit of wisdom depends on Emerson's transcendentalist ontology, which casts the inner genius as the individual's only route to knowledge of being. Without this ontology intellectual self-reliance could be seen to lead as easily to folly, stubbornness, or eccentric dogmatism as to wisdom. In Emerson's system self-reliance, or attending to one's inner genius, puts the individual in contact with being because the inner genius is the individual's representative or "portion" of being. Emerson conceives of being as universal mind or universal genius, which in some works he calls the Over-Soul. In *Representative Men*, Emerson identifies following one's genius with following one's reason, and to the extent individuals engage their reason, they participate in this larger rational principle. Wisdom is therefore not a private possession, like property, but is more like a distributed substance that exists in everyone. However superior the great genius is to the rest of us, he or she remains merely "an exponent of a vaster mind and will" (*E&L*, 631). Everyone can be interpenetrated by this mind, because everyone is an extension or piece of this mind. The reason genius or mind is not the same in everyone, but is precisely the thing that makes us individuals, is that being is articulated into heterogeneous parts. The relation between universal genius and individual genius is the same as the relation between the whole of being and its instantiation in the many particulars of nature. Universal and particular cannot be separated. As individuals we live in the realm of heterogeneity (nature), and so our only access to being is through the portion of being that we are (our nature). Individuals have to follow the diverse paths dictated by their portion of genius. It is not surprising, then, that to follow our nature means to attend to some portion of external nature: "Each man is, by secret liking, connected with some district of nature, whose agent and interpreter he is. . . . Each plant has its parasite, and each created thing its lover and poet" (618). Emerson's use of scientific inquiry as the model of intellectual self-reliance is telling; the paths of inquiry are infinite, but have the same end in knowledge of some portion of truth (and ultimately, the totality of truth, or being). It is of the utmost importance to Emerson to emphasize that the self is not isolated or self-subsistent, but intimately connected and directed to what is beyond it. Contrary to Cavell, following one's genius is not a matter of free idiosyncrasy or individuation, and contrary to Kateb, self-reliance is not the ascetic, judgment-withholding discipline of maximal receptivity. Both of these interpretations sever the link Emerson is careful to describe between the self and nature/being, or between self-reliance and discovery of (first) nature and (ultimately) being. Kateb's view of self-reliance as maximal receptivity to all views is an overstatement that operates as part of a more general exaggeration (with Cavell) of Emerson's perspectivism; for Kateb's Emerson, truth looks something like the universal aggregate of all actual and possible perspectives.[22] But such an interpretation cannot make sense of Emerson's use of science as a model, for science is in the business of rejecting most actual and possible perspectives in favor of truth. Kateb's view also obscures Emerson's widespread emphasis on transcendence of the realm of heterogeneity to the level of unity, elaborated above. Human inquiry extends outward in every direction; "Life is girt all round with a zodiac of sciences" (620) but has its logical conclusion in unity. It is the nature or essence of the self in its relation to nature and being that makes the freedom to follow one's endogenous path of inquiry a necessary condition of the highest wisdom. Emerson's ontology is the deepest ground for reconciling the pursuit of wisdom with liberty-loving liberal democracy, just as it was the deepest ground for reconciling the pursuit of wisdom with equality.

However beneficial liberal democracy may be for the cultivation of wisdom, Emerson's reader may still have doubts about whether the cultivation of wisdom, as a social goal, is good for liberal democracy. One could argue along with Shklar that liberal democracy and respect for equality are undermined by admiration for great geniuses, which can prevent people from finding their own voices (603–9). Emerson himself warns us that the wrong kind of admiration can turn students into disciples and, by implication, turn self-governing citizens into mindless followers of demagogues: "Our delight in reason degenerates into the idolatry of the herald. Especially when a mind of powerful method has instructed men, we find the examples of oppression. . . . Alas! every man is such a victim. The imbecility of men is always inviting the impudence of power. It is the delight of vulgar talent to dazzle and to bind the beholder" (623). The bad kind of relation of the individual to the great is like the bad kind of relation of the liberal democratic citizen to authority: passive, worshipful, dogmatic.

The third way that Emerson demonstrates an affinity between liberal democracy and the pursuit of wisdom is by showing that the proper kind of admiration for genius requires and cultivates intellectual self-reliance, which implicitly supports an independent, "undazzled" citizen body. Our relation to the great, like our relations to our fellows, must be active, dialectical. The alternative to "idolatry of the herald" is the kind of devotion to the genius's arguments that allows one to discover the genius's insights for oneself, or reject them in favor of one's own. It is "delight in reason" rather than attachment to the individual genius: "The best discovery the discoverer makes for himself. It has something unreal for his companion, until he too has substantiated it" (628). The remedy for the wrong kind of reverence is the right kind of devotion—which can also mean seeking out and thinking through "other great men, new qualities, counterweights and checks on each other" (627). Our relations with the great are then like our relations with our fellow citizens in offering us the opportunity to learn our own minds. The great thinker is "he that should marshal us the way we were going" (626). With the proper kind of active, exploratory devotion, Emerson argues, we need not fear excessive devotion to the thought of great geniuses, for our individuality will inevitably assert itself (629).

Relations to great geniuses, in turn, offer needed support for self-reliance in liberal democratic social (and political) relations because an active relation with great minds is even more conducive to self-reliance than our relations with our fellows. The reason for this is that the danger of conformity is greater in the latter case. A few may become unthinking devotees of a genius, but nearly everyone falls blithely into step with their time and place.

> Men resemble their contemporaries, even more than their progenitors. . . . [T]he ideas of the time are in the air, and infect all who breathe it. . . . Again; it is very easy to be as wise and good as your companions. We learn of our contemporaries what they know, without effort, and almost through the pores of the skin. We catch it by sympathy. . . . But we stop where they stop. Very hardly can we take another step. The great, or such as hold of nature, and

transcend fashions, by their fidelity to universal ideas, are saviors from these federal errors, and defend us from our contemporaries. They are the exceptions which we want, where all grows alike. A foreign greatness is the antidote for cabalism. (627)

Great thinkers teach us how to think for ourselves. "True genius seeks to defend us from itself. True genius will not impoverish, but will liberate, and add new senses" (623). Conversing with our fellows is the good and necessary foundation of intellectual self-reliance and wisdom, but conversing with the great is the next step, because it is more challenging of our assumptions ("a *foreign* greatness"), and therefore more invigorating of our reason. Intellectual relations with great geniuses are by implication supremely beneficial to self-government in Emerson's account. In his description, in the chapter on Goethe, of how intellectuals benefit democracy, Emerson writes that "society has, at all times, the same want, namely, of one sane man with adequate powers of expression to hold up each object of monomania in its right relations" (748). The danger Emerson addresses is that the ambitious can dazzle a multitude with a slogan, but "let one man have the comprehensive eye" and "the illusion vanishes, and the returning of reason of the community thanks the reason of the monitor" (748). Attention to geniuses brings reason back to a community, and with reason comes independence from the "mumbo-jumbo" of the "ambitious and mercenary" (748).

Emerson's transcendental ontology is again the ground for why admiration for the great is compatible with democratic liberty. Admiration for excellence is a ladder to self-reliance, because to recognize another's genius is to see, however opaquely, the presence of the universal (reason) in the individual admired: "When we are exalted by his ideas, we do not owe this to Plato, but to the idea, to which, also, Plato was debtor" (623). Therefore admiration is or can be a means to self-respect, a recognition of one's own participation, through the action of questioning and learning, in the greatness that animated the thoughts of the one admired. This recognition would remain true even when the superiority of the great puts them beyond imitation, for one's own participation in reason is undiminished. A moralistic egalitarianism that dreads or denies superiority is implicitly an obstacle to self-reliance. To deny the superiority of the genius would be to cut ourselves off from the interrogative relationship that develops our own genius. The great genius leads and spurs us to find our path to being. This path is our true individuality for Emerson, just as being is the true ground for equality. Emerson wishes to show in *Representative Men* that the choices between virtue and equality, and between admiration and self-reliance, are false ones. Both individuality and intellectual hierarchy are, on the one hand, indispensable means to enlightenment, and on the other, illusions to be discarded once the ultimate enlightenment has been achieved.

The political ideal that emerges from Emerson's account of excellence is, in contrast to Plato and Aristotle, a liberal democracy composed of a diverse group of self-reliant wisdom-seekers. If cultivation of excellence is the principle of the political community, and the highest excellence must be cultivated in a self-reliant manner, the most important principle of the regime is liberty. If the highest insight is equally available to all persons in theory, and reveals the unity of all persons, then liberty must be paired with respect for equality. The ideal regime would be a liberal democracy composed of citizens who (properly) admire and emulate the ideal types of knowers Emerson describes.

The basic principle of such a society is that the relationship that provides the deepest satisfactions for human beings, and corresponds to our fundamental nature, is our relationship with being. Our social relations (and our relation to ourselves) are echoes or adumbrations of this primary relation, and properly serve to cultivate and sustain it. The purpose of political life is to serve the longing for being that gives rise to the virtues of knowledge. Politics surely requires taking care of more urgent needs, such as internal and external security, some minimum of prosperity, etc., but Emerson understands his mission to be to warn us against confusing requirements with purposes, and makes liberty and equality indispensible to the latter. To the extent that we take our political and economic relations seriously as their own ends, we misunderstand them. Political ambition or ideology that is not directed to the suprapolitical aims of Emersonian transcendence, then, must be seen as an incomplete or misdirected expression of the soul's fundamental longing for being, or as unacceptably base.

The political purpose of Emerson's account of excellence, and of the political ideal it implies, is to provide cultural ballast to the tendency he sees in modernity toward materialism. Emerson makes amply clear that he does not expect a society devoted to his principles to be a real possibility. Though he expresses faith in the historical necessity of political progress, he sees politics itself as directed to selfish, even criminal ends (709). *Representative Men* is an attempt to raise citizens' sights, and to alert them to the dangers that Emerson regarded as inherent to the modern West.

Emerson's Critique of Western Modernity

Emerson's critique of the modern West is that it has elevated the pursuit of means, such as wealth and power, over considerations of ends, such as excellence, wisdom, or oneness with being. Western materialism, and its characteristic social ills of economic and imperial exploitation, arise as the logical consequence of the West's intellectual orientation toward mastery of heterogeneous nature and its forgetting the unity of being. This section will first examine Emerson's account of this intellectual orientation and how it can turn into a soul-killing preoccupation with power and wealth. Then it will examine Emerson's avatars of modernity, Napoleon and Goethe, the only moderns among Emerson's representative men. Their chapters form one concluding section of *Representative Men* about the character and potential of two peculiarly modern kinds of greatness, both inferior to what has gone before, and fully intelligible only in light of the Platonic-transcendentalist argument that precedes it. The virtues Napoleon and Goethe inspire and the dangers they represent are not the most important at all times but the ones most urgent for us to examine. Napoleon represents the great danger of bourgeois materialism, while Goethe represents a powerful but insufficient modern attempt (insufficient because it is still too modern) to revive spiritual and intellectual seriousness. This section examines Emerson's account of these last two representative men in order to clarify his critique of modernity and his project to respond to it.

Emerson's critique of Western modernity follows from his account of the two sides of wisdom—knowledge of unity (being) and knowledge of heterogeneity (nature in its diversity). All thinkers other than Plato, and all civilizations, tend excessively in the direction of either unity or heterogeneity: "A too rapid unification, and an excessive appliance to particulars, are the twin dangers of speculation" (639–40). The East overemphasizes unity or being: "The raptures of prayer and ecstasy of devotion lose all being in one Being. This tendency finds its highest expression in the religious writings of the East" (638). The negative social consequences of this focus take the form of caste and oppressive authority. "A too rapid unification" of nature under doctrines of being obscures the reality of heterogeneous individuals and their choices. As trees are lost for the forest, individuality and freedom are occluded: "The country of unity, of immovable institutions, the seat of a philosophy delighting in abstractions, of men faithful in doctrine and in practice to the idea of a deaf, unimplorable, immense fate, is Asia; and it realizes this faith in the social institution of caste" (640). The West, on the other hand, overemphasizes heterogeneity, definition, the systematic accounting of the particulars in nature and in human life. The advantages of this tendency are the arts and sciences, and freedom in politics, culture, and economics. Europe "is a land of arts, inventions, trade, freedom. If the East loved infinity, the West delighted in boundaries" that define and situate things in relation to one another (640).

Focus on particulars and on variation goes with liberalism, for Emerson; the West sees the individual as individual, embraces multiplicity, rather than seeking, as a kind of intellectual instinct, the subordination of multiplicity to static unity. The focus of "defining, result-loving, machine-making, surface-seeking, opera-going Europe" gives rise ultimately to "the town meeting, the ballot-box, the news-paper and cheap press" (640). The downside of the focus on heterogeneity for Emerson has three steps. First, the focus on heterogeneity leads to a focus on means in exclusion of consideration of ends. To seek ends is to seek principles of unification; every end is an organizing principle that unifies the means subordinate to it. The movement of the intellect away from unity is a movement away from unifying ends. The focus on heterogeneity can look at means (architecture, navigation, finance, etc.) only on their own terms, in light of their immediate and heterogeneous ends (buildings, travel, wealth), cut off from consideration of higher unifying ends: What are buildings, travel, and wealth for? This truncated view of the world replaces comprehensive meaning with particularized success. Second, the focus on means leads ultimately to a societywide obsession with power and wealth. All means are modes of power; to orient the mind, and therefore society, toward the advancement and perfection of means is to devote these to the acquisition of power and resources, and to define progress accordingly. To cultivate the various sciences of means is to organize the multiplicity of nature to make it subject to human control. In a word, the Western intellectual focus for Emerson is technological rather than contemplative. In a manner that foreshadows Heidegger's critique of the technological West, Emerson summarizes the differences between the focus on unity and the focus on heterogeneity: "One is being; the other, intellect: one is necessity; the other, freedom: one, rest; the other, motion . . . one, caste; the other, culture: one, king; the other, democracy: and, if we dare carry these generalizations a step higher, and name the last tendency of both, we might say, that the end of the one is escape from organization,—pure science; and the end of the other is the highest instrumentality, or use of means, or executive deity" (639). The phrase "executive deity" suggests that in the modern West the science of means has obscured and replaced the divine, or knowledge of ends. The phrase suggests the pursuit of godlike power without godlike wisdom. This leads to the third step in Emerson's critique: the pursuit of means (power) leads to "sinister political economy," the "pitiless subdivision of classes" consequent to the rise of capitalism, the slums of Paris and London, and the imperial exploitation of Ireland and India (640). The more the West focuses on means in exclusion of consideration of ends, the more it elevates power as its own end. But for Emerson the pursuit of power for its own sake is infinite, becomes all-consuming, and produces tremendous oppression and suffering.

The exemplar of Western modernity emerges in the form of Napoleon. He represents for Emerson the maximum excellence and depravity of the man without longing for being, the purely materialistic man. Contrary to Stendhal, Balzac, and Nietzsche, for whom Napoleon is the antithesis of bourgeois timidity and smallness, Emerson views Napoleon as the bourgeois par excellence by virtue of the baseness of his ends. "Napoleon is its [the modern middle class's] representative," Emerson asserts; "He had their virtues and their vices; above all, he had their spirit or aim. . . . subordinating all intellectual and spiritual forces into means to a material success. To be the rich man, is the end" (727–28). Like modernity, Napoleon's strength and weakness is his dissociation of means from consideration of higher ends: "Bonaparte wrought, in common with that great [modern middle] class he represented, for power and wealth,—but Bonaparte, specially, without any scruple as to the means. All the sentiments which embarrass men's pursuit of these objects, he set aside" (729). Weak in modernity, these sentiments are absent in Napoleon. Unburdened by higher concerns, Napoleon could devote his considerable energies to the tasks most advantageous to his material elevation: "Men found that his absorbing egotism was deadly to all other men" (745). He "would steal, slander, assassinate, drown, and poison, as his interest dictated" (743). His project led only to ruin, however, in spite of his mastery of means. The logic of modernity is self-defeating in Emerson's account because the pursuit of power and wealth, unlimited by a higher end, necessarily burns itself out. Through imperialism, exploitation, and war, the pursuit of power consumes its own material basis; Napoleon "squandered treasures, immolated millions of men," and "demoralized Europe" (744–45). But Emerson does not blame Napoleon: "It was not Bonaparte's fault" that his egoistic materialism led to disaster, but the consequence of "the eternal law of man and of the world" (745). Napoleon represented "an experiment, under the most favorable conditions, of the powers of intellect without conscience" (744). The experiment "came to no result. . . . He left France smaller, poorer, feebler, than he found it; and the whole contest for freedom was to be begun again. The attempt was, in principle, suicidal" (745). Napoleon's career illustrates the potential consequences of a persistent human type, the soul without longing for being, elevated in modernity to social and political dominance. Emerson's response is to try to inspire this longing, and to raise the sights of social life to the limited extent he thought he could.

Emerson's account of Napoleon suggests that Carlyle's hero worship should be rejected because, among other reasons (such as the stunting effect of worship), heroes in the modern age are likely to be soulless and grasping men of executive genius. Emerson reminds readers that great power is likely to be concentrated in the hands of mediocre souls.

As Napoleon exemplifies the problem posed by modernity—radical materialism—Goethe exemplifies the best strictly modern response to that problem: the elevation of culture as its own purpose. Goethe is therefore superior to his fellow moderns, and yet, by being modern, is unable to see and address the problem of modernity fully. It is in Goethe's capacity as modern counterweight to modernity that Emerson uses him to exemplify the role of "The Writer," who uses his or her cultural authority to pull against modern materialism by defending the life of thought, and by countering the political excesses of the public. As previously mentioned, Emerson presents the writer as supplying a permanent need of society: "Society has, at all times, the same want, namely, of one sane man with adequate powers of expression to hold up each object of monomania in its right relations" (748). The examples Emerson gives all point to the special role of the writer in a modern democracy (America, specifically), to counterbalance the folly of the multitude. "The ambitious and mercenary bring their last new mumbo-jumbo, whether tariff, Texas, railroad, Romanism, mesmerism, or California . . . and a multitude go mad about it, and they are not to be reproved or cured by the opposite multitude, who are kept from this particular insanity by an equal frenzy on another crotchet" (748). Once the sane observer uses his or her powers of expression to show the mumbo-jumbo in its true light, "the illusion vanishes, and the returning of reason of the community thanks the reason of the monitor" (748). The writer's role is not to reflect or represent the views of his time and place, but to monitor and, where possible, correct them.

The proper role of the writer in democratic modernity, then, is to engage the issues of the day from an independent and superior vantage point. Emerson faults writers for having lost their authority through pandering to "the giddy opinion of a reckless public," and urges them to oppose the tastes of the time. The elitism of these passages is interesting not least in being at odds with what he says in "Uses of Great Men" against those who would look down on the "multitude": "there are no common men. All men are at last of a size; and true art is only possible, on the conviction that every talent has its apotheosis somewhere" (630). When speaking about the pursuit of wisdom Emerson is more willing to grant the common citizen his or her individuality than when speaking about democratic politics. This discontinuity in Emerson's treatment of the common man implies that in his view people are more likely to conform to the enthusiasms of their fellows in political matters than in intellectual ones. Perhaps we are more likely to cling to the herd when our material interests are in play. Geniuses playing the role of "the writer" have the job of transposing the independence cultivated by intellectual pursuits to the political sphere. Through them, intellectual self-reliance can be a model for political self-reliance. At the very least, the intellectually self-reliant can check the irrationality of political monomania.

In particular, Emerson urges scholarly writers to oppose the American tendency of contempt for the theoretical life. "In this country, the emphasis of conversation, and of public opinion, commends the practical man. . . . Our people are of Bonaparte's opinion concerning ideologists. Ideas are subversive of social order and comfort, and at last make a fool of the possessor" (748). The writer should take a stand against this, for "Mankind have such a deep stake in inward illumination" (749).

Goethe is Emerson's example of the writer who occupies a superior and independent vantage point, due, not surprisingly, to his attention to questions of higher ends. "No more instructive name occurs than that of Goethe," Emerson explains, "to represent the powers and duties of the scholar or writer" (750). His superiority and independence come from a magnification of German seriousness; as Napoleon is the bourgeois intensified, Goethe is the German reading public intensified. German seriousness consists in the demand that writers create art with a philosophic purpose. According to Emerson, Germans are distinguished from the French, the English, and the Americans by their "habitual reference to interior truth" (756). The French, English, and American reading publics are satisfied by talent in expression. By contrast, Emerson asserts: "The German intellect wants the French sprightliness, the fine practical understanding of the English, and the American adventure; but it has a certain probity, which never rests in a superficial performance, but asks steadily, *To what end?* . . . Here is activity of thought; but what is it for? What does the man mean? Whence, whence all these thoughts?" (756). Where other authors entertained, Goethe "wishes more to know the history and destiny of man; whilst the clouds of egotists drifting about him are only interested in a low success" (759). Goethe fits Emerson's role of the author whose attention to questions of ends lifted him above his public and made him both an advocate and a representative of the life of the mind.

Goethe's great limitation, according to Emerson, was that the purpose of all his endeavors was mere culture, by which Emerson seems to mean the typically modern cultivation of the various sciences and arts without reference to the higher purpose—knowledge of being—that unifies them and gives them meaning. "He has not worshipped the highest unity," Emerson laments, "His is not even the devotion to pure truth; but to truth for the sake of culture" (758). Devotion to culture is better than devotion to "low success" (759). But once culture is severed from the wisdom it is meant to serve, it ceases to address the deepest longing of the soul. To seek culture for its own sake is typically modern in treating a means as if it were an end. Emerson illustrates the meaning and superficiality of Goethe's pursuit of culture for its own sake by citing Goethe on religion: "'Piety itself is no aim, but only a means, whereby, through purest inward peace, we may attain to highest culture'" (758). Goethe makes religion, which Emerson described as the efforts of the soul to lose itself in being, as something subordinate to the individual's self-development. Goethe implicitly treats being as likewise an instrument for self-development. But this confuses the relation of self and being; self is subordinate to being, not the other way around. For Emerson, the zenith of self-development is precisely loss of self in union with being: "All that respects the individual is temporary and prospective, like the individual himself, who is ascending out of his limits, into a catholic existence" (631). By subordinating his quest for wisdom to a foreshortened view of the individual's perfection, Goethe guarantees that he will not understand any purpose larger than the individual. As much as Goethe's superiority to his contemporaries lay in "this aim of culture," the "idea of absolute, eternal truth, without reference to my own enlargement by it, is higher" (760). Goethe rises above the immediate, low aims of technological modernity, but views being in technological terms. He was deeper than his contemporaries in thinking about ends, but his thinking about ends was not itself sufficiently deep.

Goethe represents the possibility that superior, self-reliant writers can emerge from within modernity, and the danger that even geniuses will be limited by the modern focus on means and heterogeneous nature. Emerson's account of Goethe suggests that a radical break with Western modernity is needed to liberate future geniuses from instrumental rationality. Goethe's flaws explain the importance of Emerson's use of Plato and transcendentalism to his goal of ameliorating modernity's excesses.

Emerson's praise and criticism of Goethe clarifies his own response to modernity, and his vision of himself as a political-cultural actor. I have argued above that Emerson's defense of democracy consists in the elevation of wisdom as the purpose of political life and of being as the object of wisdom. If the danger of modernity is a materialistic focus on means, the solution is a countervailing focus on wisdom about ends. In seeking to affect the ends sought by Western polities, *Representative Men* is a political act. By fostering admiration for Plato, Swedenborg, Montaigne, Shakespeare, and Goethe, Emerson makes admiration for Napoleon impossible (however encouraged we may be by the spectacle of his efficient virtues [731, 739]).

In Emerson's critique of the technological West, it is the forgetting of being (understood metaphysically), and so of questions of ends, that prepares the way for obsession with wealth and power. This critique suggests the possibility that the dominant mode of interpreting Emerson which this volume seeks to contest[22]—Emerson as antimetaphysical, quasi-Nietzschean champion of self-creation—walks the very path Emerson criticizes. The rejection of metaphysics, the denial of an essence to the self and of an end to self-perfection, the consequent turn from the question of the soul's purpose or goal to the question of the soul's autonomy or self-command, are all prominent in the work of Cavell and Kateb, among others treated earlier in this volume, and speak to the focus on the contingent realm in which man seeks mastery. Like Goethe, current antifoundationalist interpreters of Emerson for the most part reject looking beyond or above the horizon of culture. That is, in the chapter on Goethe, Emerson inadvertently explains his own misinterpretation at the same time that he clarifies his chief aims and concerns as a writer. To the extent that Emerson's critique of the West's forgetting of ultimate ends can be applied to postmodernism, the possibility emerges that postmodernism aids and abets precisely the technological, all-consuming engine of commercial and political domination so many postmodern thinkers seek to oppose. Perhaps by telling us that we have no access to being, and that higher ends are mere constructions—that is to say, products, to be compared to other products, hence offering no alternative to the realm of production and consumption—postmodern thought may close the door on considerations that pull against devotion to wealth and power. Or to put it another way, denying the possibility of the high may end up confirming the self-satisfaction of the low.

Representative Men ends by reminding readers of the good to be taken from the examples of Napoleon and Goethe, which Emerson summarizes as vigorous opposition to dead tradition. But dead tradition must be replaced by new spiritual efforts. Emerson praises Goethe's role as a champion of seriousness. He also makes clear that what is needed to supplement Goethe's failings is someone to take up the writer's role in the service of more truly philosophic and spiritual purposes. Emerson obliquely nominates himself.

By attempting to reconcile excellence and equality, Emerson acts as a democratic citizen, at the point of juncture between culture and politics. By presenting an account of greatness that anchors an understanding of excellence in a belief in ultimate unity, Emerson teaches democratic citizens how to be virtue-loving while also being engaged citizens committed to equality. The pursuit of wisdom, properly understood, requires intellectual self-reliance, and therefore freedom of speech and thought. The character of being, properly understood—as popularized by Emerson—teaches the unity of all things, and therefore supports respect for equality. As a resource for citizens, Emerson's book demonstrates the political import possible for cultural endeavors. It rebuts the claim that Emerson's advocacy of intellectual and moral self-reliance removes him from politics or consideration of the common good.

Notes

1. Judith N. Shklar, "Emerson and the Inhibitions of Democracy," in this volume, 53–68; Neal Dolan, "Empiricism," in *Emerson's Liberalism* (Madison: University of Wisconsin Press, 2009), 224–25, 229–30, 241; Hans von Rautenfeld, "Thinking for Thousands: Emerson's Theory of Political Representation in the Public Sphere," *American Journal of Political Science* 49, no. 1 (January 2005): 184–85. Dolan offers an account of Emerson's critique of modernity, modern science in particular, but does not mention Emerson's teleological claims, and in my view does not do justice to how radical Emerson's critique is. In Dolan's treatment, Emerson plays the role of an early Ernst Gellner/Emile Durkheim, that is, as a kind of positivist who is much more skeptical of metaphysics than Emerson was. Rautenfeld reads Emerson's use of the term "representative" exclusively politically, that is to say, in very literal fashion, even when context makes it clear that Emerson is using a political term as a metaphor for something else. (I urge Rautenfeld's readers to compare his citations at 185, 187–190 with their original contexts, to take just a few examples.) The meaning of "representation" is deeply tied to science, which for Emerson is directed toward being. Rautenfeld cuts representation off from its Emersonian end by interpreting it solely in terms of political discourse.

2. George Kateb, *Emerson and Self-Reliance* (1995; new ed., Lanham, Md.: Rowman and Littlefield, 2002), 25.

3. Ralph Waldo Emerson, *Essays and Lectures* (New York: Library of America, 1983), hereafter cited parenthetically.

4. Plato, *The Republic of Plato*, trans. Allan Bloom (New York: Basic Books, 1991), 473d; Aristotle, *Politics,* trans. Carnes Lord (Chicago: University of Chicago Press, 1985), 1280b5–10, 1280b40–1281a8, 1284b23–34, hereafter cited parenthetically.

5. Thomas Carlyle, "Heroes and Hero-Worship," in *Complete Works of Thomas Carlyle* (New York: Collier and Son, 1901).

6. Shklar, "Emerson and the Inhibitions of Democracy," in this volume, 58–59.

7. Cavell, *Conditions Handsome and Unhandsome: The Constitution of Emersonian Perfectionism* (La Salle: Open Court Press, 1990), xxxi.

8. Ibid., xxxiv, 9–10, 12.

9. Ibid., 9.

10. Kateb also briefly compares Emerson to Plato at various points, citing as their greatest similarity the style or "method" of impersonation, that is, the textual practice of presenting explorations of divergent, even antagonistic views in a manner that deliberately abstains from offering clear resolutions. I agree, though, as I argue below, Kateb overstates the extent to which Emerson is aporetic in order to divest him of the metaphysics that I think is unavoidably central to him. In my view, Cavell and, to a lesser extent, Kateb misinterpret Plato as well as Emerson. Where Cavell makes Emerson the shape-shifting skeptic and Plato the metaphysician, I would argue something like the reverse. My view of Plato is not at issue here, but I demonstrate Emerson's commitment to metaphysics below.

11. Compare in Plato, *Republic*, the account of the "city of sows" and its expansion at 372a–376d to Socrates' assertions regarding the virtue of the city at 441c–445b, for example.

12. Aristotle, *Nicomachean Ethics*, trans. H. Rackham (Cambridge: Harvard University Press, 1982), 1097b21–1098a18, hereafter cited parenthetically.

13. For a different account of how citizenship supports intellectual self-reliance for Emerson, see Kateb, *Emerson and Self-Reliance*, chap. 1.

14. Emerson, *E&L*, 638–39.

15. Contrary to Kateb, the great are not great by virtue of their openness (see Kateb, *Emerson and Self-Reliance*, chap. 1, and my discussion of him below).

16. Cavell, *Conditions Handsome and Unhandsome*, xxxi, xxxiv.

17. Kateb, *Emerson and Self-Reliance*, 3–16.

18. As suggested in my opening account of the relation of Plato to the other figures treated by Emerson, the structure Emerson gives *Representative Men* suggests a synthesis of his exemplars as well. If Plato is the synthesis of the first four, and the last two represent peculiarly modern dangers and opportunities, then the figure to synthesize the lessons of all six exemplars would be one who sees the modern opportunity to bring a Platonic response to modern dangers, or Emerson.

19. Kateb, "Self-Reliance, Politics, and Society," in this volume, 74.

20. Alexis de Tocqueville, *Democracy in America*, trans. Harvey C. Mansfield and Delba Winthrop (Chicago: University of Chicago Press, 2000), 2.2.2, hereafter cited parenthetically.

21. Kateb, *Emerson and Self-Reliance*, chap. 1. One might add that by emphasizing the fundamental importance of social interaction to intellectual develop-

ment, Emerson quietly underlines the stake that intellectuals have in the character of their societies, especially regarding what their societies value and respect. Freedom of speech and thought is the all-important premise of the statement that "I can say to you what I cannot first say to myself" (616). The more freedom of speech and thought is valued, the more vigorously it will be defended.

22. Ibid., 3–4. See especially Levine's and Malachuk's essays in this volume.

Selected Bibliography

Works by Ralph Waldo Emerson

The Collected Works of Ralph Waldo Emerson. Edited by Robert E. Spiller, Alfred R. Ferguson, Joseph Slater, Jean Ferguson Carr, Wallace E. Williams, and Douglas Emory Wilson. 7 vols. to date. Cambridge: Harvard University Press, 1971–.

The Complete Sermons of Ralph Waldo Emerson. Edited by Albert J. von Frank et al. 4 vols. Columbia: University of Missouri Pres, 1989–1992.

The Complete Works of Ralph Waldo Emerson. Edited by Edward Waldo Emerson. 12 vols. Boston: Houghton Mifflin, 1903–1904.

The Early Lectures of Ralph Waldo Emerson. Edited by Robert E. Spiller, Stephen E. Whicher, and Wallace E. Williams. 3 vols. Cambridge: Harvard University Press, 1959–1972.

Emerson: Political Writings. Edited by Kenneth Sacks. Cambridge: Cambridge University Press, 2008.

Emerson's Antislavery Writings. Edited by Len Gougeon and Joel Myerson. New Haven: Yale University Press, 1995.

Essays and Lectures. Edited by Joel Porte. New York: Library of America, 1983.

The Journals and Miscellaneous Notebooks of Ralph Waldo Emerson. Edited by William H. Gilman et al. 16 vols. Cambridge: Harvard University Press, 1960–1982.

The Later Lectures of Ralph Waldo Emerson: 1843–1871. Edited by Ronald Bosco and Joel Myerson. 2 vols. Athens: University of Georgia Press, 2001.

The Letters of Ralph Waldo Emerson. 1939. Edited by Ralph L. Rusk and Eleanor M. Tilton. 10 vols. New York: Columbia University Press, 1990–1995.

The Political Emerson: Essential Writings on Politics and Social Reform. Edited by David Robinson. Boston: Beacon Press, 2004.

Uncollected Lectures by Ralph Waldo Emerson. Edited by Clarence Gohdes Jr. New York: William Edwin Rudge, 1932.

Biographies of Emerson

Allen, Gay Wilson. *Waldo Emerson: A Biography*. New York: Viking, 1981.
Buell, Lawrence. *Emerson*. Cambridge: Harvard University Press, 2003.
Cabot, James Elliot. *A Memoir of Ralph Waldo Emerson*. 2 vols. Boston: Houghton Mifflin, 1887.
Conway, Moncure. *Emerson at Home and Abroad*. Boston: James R. Osgood, 1882.
Cooke, George Willis. *Ralph Waldo Emerson: His Life, Writings, and Philosophy*. Boston: James R. Osgood, 1881.
Field, Peter. *Ralph Waldo Emerson: The Making of a Democratic Intellectual*. Lanham, Md.: Rowman and Littlefield, 2002.
Ireland, Alexander. *Ralph Waldo Emerson: His Life, Genius, and Writings*. London: Simpkin, Marshall and Company, 1882.
Richardson, Robert D. *Emerson: The Mind on Fire*. Berkeley and Los Angeles: University of California Press, 1995.
Rusk, Ralph L. *The Life of Ralph Waldo Emerson*. New York: Scribner's Sons, 1949.

Works on Emerson's Politics

Aaron, Daniel. "Emerson and the Progressive Tradition." In *Emerson: A Collection of Critical Essays*, edited by Milton R. Konvitz and Stephen E. Whicher, 85–99. Englewood Cliffs, N.J.: Prentice Hall, 1962.
———. *Men of Good Hope: A Story of American Progressives*. New York: Oxford University Press, 1951.
Anderson, Douglass R. "Emerson's Natures: Origins of and Possibilities for American Environmental Thought." In *New Morning: Emerson in the Twenty-first Century*, edited by Arthur S. Lothstein and Michael Brodrick. Albany: State University of New York Press, 2008.
Anderson, Quentin. *The Imperial Self: An Essay in Literary and Cultural History*. New York: Knopf, 1971.
Arvin, Newton. "The House of Pain: Emerson and the Tragic Sense." In *Emerson: A Collection of Critical Essays*, edited by Milton R. Konvitz and Stephen E. Whicher. Englewood Cliffs, N.J.: Prentice Hall, 1962.
Augst, Thomas. "Composing the Moral Senses: Emerson and the Politics of

Character in Nineteenth-Century America." *Political Theory* 27, no. 1 (1999): 85–120.

Bercovitch, Sacvan. "Emerson, Individualism, and the Ambiguities of Dissent." In *The Rites of Assent: Transformations in the Symbolic Construction of America*. New York: Routledge, 1993.

Berry, Edmund G. *Emerson's Plutarch*. Cambridge: Harvard University Press, 1961.

Bishop, Jonathan. *Emerson on the Soul*. Cambridge: Harvard University Press, 1964.

Bloom, Harold. *Agon: Toward a Theory of Revisionism*. Oxford: Oxford University Press, 1982.

———, ed. *Emerson's Essays: Modern Critical Interpretations*. New York: Chelsea House, 2006.

———. "Emerson: The American Religion." In *Ralph Waldo Emerson: A Collection of Critical Essays*. Englewood, N.J.: Prentice Hall, 1993.

———. *A Map of Misreading*. Oxford: Oxford University Press, 1975.

———. "Mr. America." *New York Review of Books*, November 22, 1984, 19–24.

Boller, Paul. *American Transcendentalism, 1830–1860: An Intellectual Inquiry*. New York: Putnam's Sons, 1974.

Buell, Lawrence. "The Emerson Industry in the 1980s: A Survey of Trends and Achievements." *ESQ: A Journal of the American Renaissance*, 30, no. 2 (1984): 117–36.

———. "Individualism, Natural Law, Human Rights: Emerson on 'The Scholar' vis-à-vis Emerson on Reform." In *New Morning: Emerson in the Twenty-first Century*, edited by Arthur S. Lothstein and Michael Brodrick. Albany: State University of New York Press, 2008.

———, ed. *Ralph Waldo Emerson: A Collection of Critical Essays*. Englewood, N.J.: Prentice Hall, 1993.

———. "Reading Emerson for the Structures: The Coherence of the Essays." In *Emerson's Essays: Modern Critical Interpretations*, edited by Harold Bloom. New York: Chelsea House, 2006.

———. "Transcendentalism, Manifest Destiny, and the Question of the Moral Absolute." In *The Oxford Handbook to Transcendentalism*, edited by Joel Myerson, Sandra Harbert Petrulionis, and Laura Dassow Walls. Oxford: Oxford University Press, 2010.

Burkholder, Robert, and Joel Myerson, eds. *Critical Essays on Ralph Waldo Emerson*. Boston: G. K. Hall, 1983.

Bush, Harold K. "Emerson, John Brown, and 'Doing the Word': The Enactment of Political Religion at Harpers Ferry, 1859." In *The Emerson Dilemma: Essays on Emerson and Social Reform, edited by Gregory T. Garvey. Athens: University of Georgia Press, 2001.

Cadava, Eduardo. *Emerson and the Climates of History.* Stanford: Stanford University Press, 1997.

Cameron, Sharon. "The Way of Life by Abandonment: Emerson's Impersonal." In *Impersonality: Seven Essays.* Chicago: University of Chicago Press, 2007.

Capper, Charles. "'A Little Beyond': Transcendentalism in American History." In *Transient and Permanent: The Transcendentalist Movement and Its Contexts,* edited by Capper and Conrad Edick Wright. Boston: Massachusetts Historical Society, 1999.

Cavell, Stanley. *Conditions Handsome and Unhandsome: The Constitution of Emersonian Perfectionism.* Chicago: University of Chicago, 1990.

———. *Emerson's Transcendental Etudes.* Edited by David Justin Hodge. Stanford: Stanford University Press, 2003.

———. *This New Yet Unapproachable America: Lectures after Emerson after Wittgenstein.* Albuquerque, N.M.: Living Batch Press, 1989.

———. "What's the Use of Calling Emerson a Pragmatist?" In *The Revival of Pragmatism: New Essays on Social Thought, Law, and Culture,* edited by Morris Dickstein. Durham, N.C.: Duke University Press, 1998.

Cayton, Mary Kupiec. *Emerson's Emergence: Self and Society in the Transformation of New England, 1800–1845.* Chapel Hill: University of North Carolina Press, 1989.

Cole, Phyllis. *Mary Moody Emerson and the Origins of Transcendentalism.* New York: Oxford University Press, 1998.

———. "Pain and Protest in the Emerson Family." In *The Emerson Dilemma: Essays on Emerson and Social Reform,* edited by Gregory T. Garvey. Athens: University of Georgia Press, 2001.

———. "Women's Rights and Feminism." In *The Oxford Handbook to Transcendentalism,* edited by Joel Myerson, Sandra Harbert Petrulionis, and Laura Dassow Walls. Oxford: Oxford University Press, 2010.

Collison, Gary. "Emerson and Antislavery." In *A Historical Guide to Ralph Waldo Emerson,* edited by Joel Myerson. New York: Oxford University Press, 2000.

Crane, Gregg D. *Race, Citizenship, and Law in American Literature.* New York: Cambridge University Press, 2002.

Cromphout, Gustaaf von. "Emerson and the Dialectics of History." *PMLA* 91, no. 1 (1976): 54–65.

———. *Emerson's Ethics.* Columbia: University of Missouri Press, 1999.

Davis, Merrell R. "Emerson's 'Reason' and the Scottish Philosophers." *New England Quarterly* 17, no. 2 (1944): 209–28.

Delano, Sterling F. "Transcendentalist Communities." In *The Oxford Handbook to Transcendentalism*, edited by Joel Myerson, Sandra Harbert Petrulionis, and Laura Dassow Walls. Oxford: Oxford University Press, 2010.

Dewey, John. "Emerson: The Philosopher of Democracy." 1903. In *Emerson: A Collection of Critical Essays*, edited by Milton R. Konvitz and Stephen E. Whicher, 24–30. Englewood Cliffs, N.J.: Prentice Hall, 1962.

Diggins, John Patrick. *The Lost Soul of American Politics: Virtue, Self-Interest, and the Foundations of Liberalism*. Chicago: University of Chicago Press, 1984.

Dolan, Neal. *Emerson's Liberalism*. Madison: University of Wisconsin Press, 2009.

Earhart, Amy E. "Representative Men, Slave Revolt, and Emerson's 'Conversion' to Abolitionism." *American Transcendental Quarterly* 13, no. 4 (1999): 287–303.

Esquith, Stephen L. "Emerson Reconsidered." In *Intimacy and Spectacle: Liberal Theory as Political Education*. Ithaca: Cornell University Press, 1994.

———. "Power, Poise, and Place: Toward an Emersonian Theory of Democratic Citizenship." In *The Emerson Dilemma: Essays on Emerson and Social Reform*, edited by Gregory T. Garvey. Athens: University of Georgia Press, 2001.

Fanuzzi, Robert. *Abolitionism's Public Sphere*. Minneapolis: University of Minnesota Press, 2003.

Frost, Bryan-Paul, "Religion, Nature, and Disobedience in the Thought of Ralph Waldo Emerson and Henry David Thoreau." In *History of American Political Thought*, edited by Bryan-Paul Frost and Jeffrey Sikkenga. Lanham, Md.: Lexington Books, 2003.

Garvey, T. Gregory. *Creating the Culture of Reform in Antebellum America*. Athens: University of Georgia Press, 2006.

———, ed. *The Emerson Dilemma: Essays on Emerson and Social Reform*. Athens: University of Georgia Press, 2001.

———. "Emerson's Political Spirit and the Problem of Language." In *The Emerson Dilemma*, ed. Garvey. Athens: University of Georgia Press, 2001.

Gilbert, Armida. "Emerson in the Context of the Woman's Rights Movement." In *A Historical Guide to Ralph Waldo Emerson*, edited by Joel Myerson. New York: Oxford University Press, 2000.

Goodman, Russell B. *American Philosophy and the Romantic Tradition*. New York: Cambridge University Press, 1990.

———. "Moral Perfectionism and Democracy: Emerson, Nietzsche, Cavell." In "Emerson/Nietzsche," edited by Michael Lopez. Special issue, *ESQ: A Journal of the American Renaissance* 43, no. 1–4 (1997).

Gougeon, Len. *Emerson and Eros: The Making of a Cultural Hero*. Albany: State University of New York Press, 2007.

——. "Emerson and Great Britain: Challenging the Limits of Liberty." In *REAL—Yearbook of Research in English and American Literature*, edited by Brook Thomas. Tübingen: Gunter Narr Verlag, 2006.

——. "Emerson and the Reinvention of Democracy: A Lesson for the Twenty-first Century." In *New Morning: Emerson in the Twenty-first Century*, edited by Arthur S. Lothstein and Michael Brodrick. Albany: State University of New York Press, 2008.

——. "Emerson and the Woman Question: The Evolution of His Thought." *New England Quarterly* 71, no. 4 (December 1998): 570–92.

——. "Emerson's Abolition Conversion." In *The Emerson Dilemma: Essays on Emerson and Social Reform*, edited by Gregory T. Garvey. Athens: University of Georgia Press, 2001.

——. "'Fortune of the Republic': Emerson, Lincoln, and Transcendental Warfare." *ESQ: A Journal of the American Renaissance* 65 (1999): 263–78.

——. "'Only Justice Satisfies All': Emerson's Militant Transcendentalism." In *Emerson for the Twenty-first Century: Global Perspectives on an American Icon*, edited by Barry Tharaud. Wilmington: University of Delaware Press, 2010.

——. "Transcendental Politics and Economics." In *The Oxford Handbook to Transcendentalism*, edited by Joel Myerson, Sandra Harbert Petrulionis, and Laura Dassow Walls. Oxford: Oxford University Press, 2010.

——. *Virtue's Hero: Emerson, Antislavery, and Reform*. Athens: University of Georgia Press, 1990.

Grossman, Jay. *Reconstituting the American Renaissance: Emerson, Whitman, and the Politics of Representation*. Durham, N.C.: Duke University Press, 2003.

Gura, Philip F. *American Transcendentalism, A History*. New York: Hill and Wang, 2007.

Habich, Robert D. *Building Their Own Waldos: Emerson's First Biographers and the Politics of Life Writing in the Gilded Age*. Iowa City: University of Iowa Press, 2011.

Harrison, John S. *The Teachers of Emerson*. New York: Sturgis and Walton, 1910.

Howe, Daniel Walker. *The Political Culture of the American Whigs*. Chicago: University of Chicago Press, 1979.

——. *The Unitarian Conscience: Harvard Moral Philosophy, 1805–61*. Middletown, Conn.: Wesleyan University Press, 1988.

Howe, Irving. *The American Newness: Culture and Politics in the Age of Emerson*. Cambridge: Harvard University Press, 1986.

James, William. "Address at the Emerson Centenary." In *Emerson: A Collection of Critical Essays*, edited by Milton R. Konvitz and Stephen E. Whicher. Englewood Cliffs, N.J.: Prentice Hall, 1962.

Kateb, George. "Democratic Individuality and the Meaning of Rights." In *Liberalism and the Moral Life*, edited by Nancy Rosenblum. Cambridge: Harvard University Press, 1984.

———. *Emerson and Self-Reliance*. 1995. New ed., Lanham, Md.: Rowman and Littlefield, 2002.

———. *The Inner Ocean: Individualism and Democratic Culture*. Ithaca: Cornell University Press, 1992.

Konvitz, Milton R., and Stephen E. Whicher, eds. *Emerson: A Collection of Critical Essays*. Englewood Cliffs, N.J.: Prentice Hall, 1962.

Ladu, Arthur. "Emerson: Whig or Democrat?" *New England Quarterly* 13, no. 3 (1940): 419–41.

Lange, Lou Ann. *The Riddle of Liberty: Emerson on Alienation, Freedom, and Obedience*. Athens: University of Georgia Press, 1986.

Lasch, Christopher. *The True and Only Heaven: Progress and Its Critics*. New York: Norton, 1991.

Lopez, Michael. "*Conduct of Life:* The Anatomy of Power." In *Cambridge Companion to Ralph Waldo Emerson*, edited by Joel Porte and Saundra Morris. New York: Cambridge University Press, 1999.

———. "De-Transcendentalizing Emerson." *ESQ* 34, no. 1–2 (1988): 77–139.

———. "Emerson and Nietzsche: An Introduction." In "Emerson/Nietzsche," edited by Lopez. Special issue, *ESQ: A Journal of the American Renaissance* 43, no. 1–4 (1997).

———, ed. "Emerson/Nietzsche." Special issue, *ESQ: A Journal of the American Renaissance* 43, no. 1–4 (1997).

———. *Emerson and Power: Creative Antagonism in the Nineteenth Century*. DeKalb: Northern Illinois University Press, 1996.

Lothstein, Arthur S., and Michael Brodrick, eds. *New Morning: Emerson in the Twenty-first Century*. Albany: State University of New York Press, 2008.

Malachuk, Daniel S. *Perfection, the State, and Victorian Liberalism*. New York: Palgrave Macmillan, 2005.

———. "The Republican Philosophy of Emerson's Early Lectures." *New England Quarterly* 71, no. 3 (September 1998): 404–28.

Mariotti, Shannon. "Alienated Existence, Focal Distancing, and Emerson's Transcendental Idealism." In *Thoreau's Democratic Withdrawal: Alienation, Participation, and Modernity*. Madison: University of Wisconsin Press, 2010.

———. "On the Passing of the First-Born Son: Emerson's 'Focal Distancing,' Du Bois' 'Second Sight,' and Disruptive Particularity." *Political Theory* 37, no. 3 (June 2009): 351–74.

Marr, David. *American Worlds since Emerson*. Amherst: University of Massachusetts Press, 1988.

Matthiessen, F. O. *American Renaissance: Art and Expression in the Age of Emerson and Whitman*. Oxford: Oxford University Press, 1941.

McClay, Wilfred M. *The Masterless: Self and Society in Modern America*. Chapel Hill: University of North Carolina Press, 1994.

———. "Mr. Emerson's Tombstone." *First Things* 83 (May 1998): 16–22.

McWilliams, Wilson Carey. *The Idea of Fraternity in America*. Berkeley and Los Angeles: University of California Press, 1973.

Milder, Robert. "The Radical Emerson?" In *Cambridge Companion to Ralph Waldo Emerson*, edited by Joel Porte and Saundra Morris. New York: Cambridge University Press, 1999.

Miller, Perry. "Emersonian Genius and the American Democracy." In *Emerson: A Collection of Critical Essays*, edited by Milton R. Konvitz and Stephen E. Whicher. Englewood Cliffs, N.J.: Prentice Hall, 1962.

———. "From Edwards to Emerson." In *Ralph Waldo Emerson: A Collection of Critical Essays*, edited by Lawrence Buell. Englewood, N.J.: Prentice Hall, 1993.

Mitchell, Charles. *Individualism and Its Discontents: Appropriations of Emerson, 1880–1950*. Amherst: University of Massachusetts Press, 1997.

Mott, Wesley T. "'The Age of the First Person Singular': Emerson and Individualism." In *A Historical Guide to Ralph Waldo Emerson*, edited by Joel Myerson. New York: Oxford University Press, 2000.

Myerson, Joel, ed. *Emerson Centenary Essays*. Carbondale: Southern Illinois University Press, 1982.

———, ed. *A Historical Guide to Ralph Waldo Emerson*. New York: Oxford University Press, 2000.

Myerson, Joel, Sandra Harbert Petrulionis, and Laura Dassow Walls, eds. *The Oxford Handbook to Transcendentalism*. Oxford: Oxford University Press, 2010.

Newfield, Christopher. *The Emerson Effect: Individualism and Submission in America*. Chicago: University of Chicago Press, 1996.

Nicoloff, Philip L. *Emerson on Race and History: An Examination of "English Traits."* New York: Columbia University Press, 1961.

Packer, Barbara. *Emerson's Fall: A New Interpretation of the Major Essays*. New York: Continuum, 1982.

———. "Signing Off: Religious Indifference in America." In *There before Us: Religion, Literature, and Culture from Emerson to Wendell Berry*, edited by Roger Lundin. Grand Rapids: Eerdmans, 2007.

———. *The Transcendentalists*. Athens: University of Georgia Press, 2007.

Painter, Nell Irvin. *The History of White People.* New York: Norton, 2010.
Parrington, Vernon Louis. *Main Currents in American Thought.* Vol. 2, *An Interpretation of American Literature from the Beginnings to 1920.* New York: Harcourt, Brace and World, 1954.
Patterson, Anita Haya. *From Emerson to King: Democracy, Race, and the Politics of Protest.* Oxford: Oxford University Press, 1997.
Paul, Sherman. *Emerson's Angle of Vision: Man and Nature in American Experience.* Cambridge: Harvard University Press, 1952.
Petrulionis, Sandra Harbert. "Transcendentalism and Antislavery." In *The Oxford Handbook to Transcendentalism,* edited by Joel Myerson, Petrulionis, and Laura Dassow Walls. Oxford: Oxford University Press, 2010.
Poirier, Richard. "An Approach to Unapproachable America." *Raritan* 26, no. 4 (2007): 1–13.
———. *Poetry and Pragmatism.* Cambridge: Harvard University Press, 1992.
———. *The Renewal of Literature: Emersonian Reflections.* New Haven: Yale University Press, 1987.
Porte, Joel, ed. *Emerson: Prospect and Retrospect.* Cambridge: Harvard University Press, 1982.
———. *Representative Man: Ralph Waldo Emerson in His Time.* New York: Oxford University Press, 1979.
Porte, Joel, and Saundra Morris, eds. *Cambridge Companion to Ralph Waldo Emerson.* New York: Cambridge University Press, 1999.
Rautenfeld, Hans von. "Charitable Interpretations: Emerson, Rawls, and Cavell on the Use of Public Reason." *Political Theory* 32, no. 1 (February 2004): 61–84.
———. "Thinking for Thousands: Emerson's Theory of Political Representation in the Public Sphere." *American Journal of Political Science* 49, no. 1 (2005): 184–97.
Reynolds, David S. *John Brown, Abolitionist: The Man Who Killed Slavery, Sparked the Civil War, and Seeded Civil Rights.* New York: Knopf, 2005.
Reynolds, Larry. *European Revolutions and the American Literary Renaissance.* New Haven: Yale University Press, 1995.
Richardson, Robert D. "Emerson and Nature." In *Cambridge Companion to Ralph Waldo Emerson,* edited by Joel Porte and Saundra Morris. New York: Cambridge University Press, 1999.
———. "Liberal Platonism and Transcendentalism: Shaftesbury, Schleiermacher, Emerson." *Symbiosis* 1 (1997): 1–20.
Robinson, David M. *Apostle of Culture: Emerson as Preacher and Lecturer.* Philadelphia: University of Pennsylvania Press, 1982.
———. *Emerson and the Conduct of Life: Pragmatism and Ethical Purpose in the Later Work.* New York: Cambridge University Press, 1993.

———. "Emerson and Religion." In *A Historical Guide to Ralph Waldo Emerson*, edited by Joel Myerson. New York: Oxford University Press, 2000.

———. "Emerson's 'American Civilization': Emancipation and the National Destiny." In *The Emerson Dilemma: Essays on Emerson and Social Reform*, edited by Gregory T. Garvey. Athens: University of Georgia Press, 2001.

———. "Introduction: Emerson as a Political Thinker." In *The Political Emerson: Essential Writings on Politics and Social Reform*, edited by David Robinson. Boston: Beacon Press, 2004.

Rowe, John Carlos. *At Emerson's Tomb: The Politics of Classic American Literature*. New York: Columbia University Press, 1997.

Rubin, Charles T. "The Mystery of Nature and Culture: Ralph Waldo Emerson." In *Conservation Reconsidered: Nature, Virtue, and American Liberal Democracy*, edited by Charles T. Rubin. Lanham, Md.: Rowman and Littlefield, 2000.

Sacks, Kenneth S. Introduction to *Emerson: Political Writings*, edited by Sacks. Cambridge: Cambridge University Press, 2008.

Santayana, George. "The Genteel Tradition in American Philosophy." In *Winds of Doctrine and Platonism and the Spiritual Life*. Gloucester, Mass.: Peter Smith, 1971.

Sbriglia, Russell. "Revision and Identification: Emerson and the Ethics of Skepticism and Sympathy." *Arizona Quarterly* 66, no. 2 (Summer 2010): 1–34.

Schlesinger, Arthur, Jr. *The Age of Jackson*. Boston: Little, Brown, 1945.

Shklar, Judith. "Emerson and the Inhibitions of Democracy." *Political Theory* 18, no. 4 (November 1990): 601–14.

Smith, Henry Nash. "Emerson's Problem of Vocation." In *Emerson: A Collection of Critical Essays*, edited by Milton R. Konvitz and Stephen E. Whicher. Englewood Cliffs, N.J.: Prentice Hall, 1962.

Stack, George J. *Nietzsche and Emerson: An Elective Affinity*. Athens: Ohio University Press, 1992.

Stoehr, Taylor. *Nay-Saying in Concord: Emerson, Alcott, and Thoreau*. Hamden, Conn.: Archon Books, 1979.

Strysick, Michael. "Emerson, Slavery, and the Evolution of the Principle of Self-Reliance." In *The Emerson Dilemma: Essays on Emerson and Social Reform*, edited by Gregory T. Garvey. Athens: University of Georgia Press, 2001.

Teichgraeber, Richard F., III. "'Our National Glory': Emerson in American Culture." In *Transient and Permanent: The Transcendentalist Movement and Its Contexts*, edited by Charles Capper and Conrad Edick Wright. Boston: Massachusetts Historical Society, 1999.

———. *Sublime Thoughts/Penny Wisdom: Situating Emerson and Thoreau in the American Market*. Baltimore: Johns Hopkins University Press, 1995.

Updike, John. "Emersonianism." In *Odd Jobs: Essays and Criticism.* New York: Knopf, 1991.
von Frank, Albert J. *The Trials of Anthony Burns: Freedom and Slavery in Emerson's Boston.* Cambridge: Harvard University Press, 1998.
Walls, Laura Dassow. *Emerson's Life in Science: The Culture of Truth.* Ithaca: Cornell University Press, 2003.
Weisbuch, Robert. "Post-Colonial Emerson and the Erasure of Europe." In *Cambridge Companion to Ralph Waldo Emerson,* edited by Joel Porte and Saundra Morris. New York: Cambridge University Press, 1999.
Wellek, Rene. "Emerson and German Philosophy." *New England Quarterly* 16, no. 1 (1943): 41–62.
West, Cornel. *The American Evasion of Philosophy: A Genealogy of Pragmatism.* Madison: University of Wisconsin Press, 1989.
Whicher, Stephen. "Emerson's Tragic Sense." In *Emerson: A Collection of Critical Essays,* edited by Milton R. Konvitz and Whicher. Englewood Cliffs, N.J.: Prentice Hall, 1962.
———. *Freedom and Fate: An Inner Life of Ralph Waldo Emerson.* Philadelphia: University of Pennsylvania Press, 1953.
Wider, Sarah Ann. *The Critical Reception of Emerson: Unsettling All Things.* Rochester, N.Y.: Camden House, 2000.
Wolfe, Cary. "Alone in America: Cavell, Emerson, and the Politics of Individualism." *New Literary History* 25 (1994): 137–57.
Zakaras, Alex. *Individuality and Mass Democracy: Mill, Emerson, and the Burdens of Citizenship.* New York: Oxford University Press, 2009.
Ziser, Michael. "Emersonian Terrorism: John Brown, Islam, and Postsecular Violence." *American Literature* 82, no. 2 (2010): 333–60.
———. "Transcendentalism and World Revolutions." In *The Oxford Handbook to Transcendentalism,* edited by Joel Myerson, Sandra Harbert Petrulionis, and Laura Dassow Walls. Oxford: Oxford University Press, 2010.

Contributors

Stanley Cavell is Walter M. Cabot Professor of Aesthetics and the General Theory of Value, Emeritus, at Harvard University. In addition to his work on Emerson, collected in *Emerson's Transcendental Etudes,* he is the author of many books, including *The Senses of Walden, The Claim of Reason: Wittgenstein, Skepticism, Morality, and Tragedy,* and most recently, *Philosophy the Day after Tomorrow.*

Neal Dolan is associate professor of English at the University of Toronto. In addition to *Emerson's Liberalism,* he has published articles in *Raritan* and elsewhere. He is also the author of the introduction and chronology for *The Cambridge History of American Literature: Nineteenth-Century Poetry 1800–1910.*

G. Borden Flanagan is assistant professor of political theory in the Department of Government at American University. He is writing a book on Thucydides' political psychology.

Jason Frank is associate professor of government at Cornell University. He is the author of *Constituent Moments: Enacting the People in Postrevolutionary America* and of a forthcoming work titled *Publius and Political Imagination.* He is the coeditor of *Vocations of Political Theory* and of a special double issue of the journal *Diacritics.* He is currently editing *A Political Companion to Herman Melville.*

Len Gougeon is professor of American literature and Distinguished University Fellow at the University of Scranton. He is the author of *Virtue's Hero: Emerson, Antislavery, and Reform; Emerson & Eros: The Making of a Cultural Hero*; and coeditor, with Joel Myerson, of *Emerson's Antislavery Writings*. He has published a number of articles in such journals as *New England Quarterly, American Literature, American Transcendental Quarterly, South Atlantic Review, Walt Whitman Quarterly Review, Modern Language Studies, Emerson Society Papers, Thoreau Society Bulletin, Studies in the American Renaissance, College Language Association Journal, ESQ: A Journal of the American Renaissance*, and others.

George Kateb is William Nelson Cromwell Professor of Politics, Emeritus, at Princeton University. His books include *The Inner Ocean: Individualism and Democratic Culture; Emerson and Self-Reliance; Patriotism and Other Mistakes*; and, most recently, *Human Dignity*.

Alan M. Levine is associate professor of political theory in the Department of Government at American University. He is the author of *Sensual Philosophy: Toleration, Skepticism, and Montaigne's Politics of the Self*, and the editor of *Early Modern Skepticism and the Origins of Toleration*. He has also published articles and book chapters on Montaigne, Machiavelli, Nietzsche, Chinua Achebe, Judith Shklar, and European views of America. He is currently working on a book about the idea of America in European political thought from 1492 to 9/11.

Daniel S. Malachuk is associate professor of English at Western Illinois University–Quad Cities. He is the author of *Perfection, the State, and Victorian Liberalism* and numerous articles and chapters on Thoreau, Mill, William James, and other nineteenth-century figures. He is working on a book on higher law in the political theory of American transcendentalism.

Shannon L. Mariotti is assistant professor of political science at Southwestern University. She is the author of *Thoreau's Democratic Withdrawal: Alienation, Participation, and Modernity*. She has published articles on Thoreau, Adorno, Emerson, and Du Bois. She also contributed an essay to *A Political Companion to Henry David Thoreau*.

Wilson Carey McWilliams (1933–2005) was professor of political science at Rutgers University. In addition to his influential *The Idea of Fraternity in America,* he was the author of many essays, including those on American elections collected as *The Politics of Disappointment* and *Beyond the Politics of Disappointment* as well two new collections from University Press of Kentucky, *Redeeming Democracy in America* and *The Democratic Soul: A Wilson Carey McWilliams Reader.*

James H. Read is professor of political science at the College of St. Benedict and St. John's University. He is the author of *Power versus Liberty: Madison, Hamilton, Wilson, and Jefferson*; *Doorstep Democracy: Face-to-Face Politics in the Heartland*; and *Majority Rule versus Consensus: The Political Thought of John C. Calhoun.*

Judith N. Shklar (1928–1992) was John Cowles Professor of Government at Harvard University. In additions to her many books, including *Men and Citizens: A Study of Rousseau's Social Theory*; *After Utopia: The Decline of Political Faith*; and *Ordinary Vices,* she is also the author of the classic essay "The Liberalism of Fear."

Jack Turner is assistant professor of political science at the University of Washington. His book *Awakening to Race: Individualism and Social Consciousness in America* is forthcoming. His articles have also appeared in *Political Theory, Raritan, Modern Intellectual History,* and *Polity.* He is the editor of *A Political Companion to Henry David Thoreau* and a contributor to *A Political Companion to Walt Whitman.*

Index

Aaron, Daniel, 37n45, 46, 378n4
Abolition. *See* Antislavery
Action, 25, 50, 94, 127–28, 136–37, 140–43, 150n96, 155, 177, 187, 190, 202, 211, 233, 254, 256, 277–78, 284, 291–92, 295, 307, 316–17, 319–20, 325–26, 330–34, 343, 359, 361, 372, 379n6, 384, 387, 394, 402, 407–8, 429
   collective, 5, 168, 195, 202–3
   economic, 126
   individual, 5, 49, 153, 175–77, 192, 306, 321
   political, 27, 66, 128, 141, 159, 161, 163, 166, 172, 192, 258, 333, 422–23
   public, 23
Adams, John, 103, 204
Admiration, 31, 56, 59, 64, 80, 83, 107, 169, 173, 176, 182n37, 302n22, 182n39, 426, 430, 435–38, 445
   See also Emulation; Reverence
Africa, 131, 315, 323, 325
Alaric, 237
Alcott, Amos Bronson, 79
America, 17–18, 20, 43–44, 50–51, 65, 76, 83, 86, 98, 101, 117, 136, 139, 200, 207–9, 211–12, 264n52, 324, 328, 331–32, 344–45, 351–52, 365, 372, 375, 380–81n18, 387, 405, 413n46
   democratic, 5, 8, 11, 54, 77, 153, 188, 195, 210, 347, 443

Jacksonian, 61, 65, 346, 353–54, 357, 363, 376, 380n17
   and slavery, 82, 132–33, 147n36, 153, 162, 169, 174, 180, 195–96, 317, 323, 327
   "unapproachable," 291–92, 385
American Whigs. *See* Whigs
Anarchism, 60, 84–85, 152, 165, 250–51, 383–84
Ancient Mariner, 102
Ancient thinkers, 8, 228, 245, 416–18, 421–22, 424–25
Anderson, Quentin, 19, 378n4
Anglo-Saxons, 166, 182n41
   See also Race
Antigone (Sophocles), 292–93
Antigone, 292–93, 303–4n37
Antipolitics, 74
Antislavery, 34n19, 146n30, 148n13, 150n93, 181n25, 183n44, 212
   Emerson's support of, 3–16, 26–28, 39n62, 65, 72–73, 81, 127–43, 148n67, 153–80, 180nn6–7, 182n34, 185, 192–200, 205, 217–18n34, 274, 277–81, 298–99, 306–8, 312–21, 324–34, 335–36n9, 337n13, 338n16, 351, 372–74, 377, 380–81n18, 384–91, 404–7, 410
   Emerson's supposed indifference to, 19, 22–26, 46
   See also Reparations for slavery

467

Apolitical individualism. *See* Individualism
Aristocracy, 20–21, 25, 56, 60, 75–76, 90, 114, 208, 211, 250–53, 258, 344, 360–63, 377, 396, 416–17
  natural, 103, 400
  neo-aristocracy, 417, 430
Aristotle, 19, 31, 43, 85, 114, 417, 421–24, 428, 438
Arnold, Matthew, 31, 112, 271, 359
Asia, 87, 440
Association. *See* Conventions: political
Austin, J. L., 93
Authority, 20, 77, 139, 164, 188, 234, 258, 347, 385, 395, 397, 405–6, 430, 436, 442
  rejection of, 44, 154
  religious, 347, 378n5
Awakening, 132, 141, 277, 295, 312, 407, 409
  See also Wakefulness

Babbitt, Irving, 17, 20, 22
Balzac, Honoré de, 441
Barbados, 157, 197, 278, 389
Beauty, 17, 59, 88, 90, 187, 238, 242, 249, 273, 292, 312, 328, 353, 358–59, 377, 385, 427
Being, 45, 59–60, 70, 74, 90, 187, 232–33, 246–49, 257, 284, 311, 332, 354–55, 358, 367–69, 403, 416–18, 426–28, 430–35, 437–42, 444–47, 447n1
  See also God
Bercovitch, Sacvan, 32n3, 361, 365, 377n4, 382n32
Bible, 228, 346–47, 369, 378–79n5
  "dead Bible society," 23, 55
Bishop, Jonathan, 300n3
Blacks, 150, 167, 169, 189, 195–97, 211, 217n31, 315
Bleeding Kansas. *See* Kansas; Kansas-Nebraska Act
Bloom, Harold, 20, 29, 114, 226–27, 232, 258, 266–70, 296–97, 369
Bonaparte, Napoleon, 24, 57, 80, 237, 344, 357, 403–4, 416, 421, 425, 439, 441–42, 444–46

Borges, Jorge Luis, 369
Boston, 76, 77, 128, 133, 146n31, 153, 198, 200, 348, 353, 361, 363
Boston Vigilance Committee, 198, 218n38
Brook Farm, 70, 173
Brooks, Preston, 181n12
Brooks, Van Wyck, 17, 378n4
Brown, John, 11, 13–14, 28, 31, 35n24, 80, 82, 155, 160, 165–66, 175–76, 178, 182n29, 182n37, 205, 211–12, 220n56, 281, 374, 386, 404, 406–10
Buell, Lawrence, 18, 28, 32n4, 38n52, 206, 220n59, 266–67, 274, 300n3, 300n7, 301n18, 301n21, 303n24, 379n5
Burns, Anthony, 3, 128
Butcher, Phillip, 35n26

Cabot, James Elliot, 16, 36n32, 302n32
Cadava, Eduardo, 129, 143
Calhoun, John C., 147n43, 181n24, 194
California, 84, 165, 443
Calverton, V. F., 18–19
Calvin, John, 245, 350
Calvinism, 4, 45, 245, 345–47, 349, 354, 371
Cape Cod, 84, 89
Capitalism, 146n32, 361, 378n4, 380n13, 441
Capper, Charles, 19, 35n27, 36n35, 36n39, 37n45, 37n47, 37n50
Carlyle, Thomas, 23, 31, 57, 62, 137, 257, 271, 301n18, 353, 367, 395–97, 409, 417, 428, 430, 442
Cartesian thought, 96, 105, 117, 303n36
Caste, 54, 77, 252, 439–41
Catholicism, 45, 345, 350
Cavell, Stanley, 21, 25–26, 31, 39n61, 125, 224–26, 251, 253, 261n16, 263n36, 266–67, 271, 283, 289–91, 293, 296–97, 300n6, 302n25, 303n33, 303n36, 308, 332, 335n6, 354–55, 358, 384–85, 394, 398, 409, 411n9, 419–21, 427, 429, 431–32, 435, 446, 448n10
Chaos, 238, 242, 248, 293
Character, 12, 22, 47, 49–50, 56, 58, 69,

71, 74, 77, 83–84, 92, 99, 114, 129, 139, 142, 171, 177, 204, 235, 238, 244, 275, 350, 385, 413n46, 439
Charity, 88–89, 212, 357, 388
Chartists, 199–200, 218n36
Cherokee Indians, 8, 80, 381n21
Christianity, 6, 55, 72, 112, 126, 183n47, 228, 245, 249–53, 256, 263n50, 300n11, 347, 367, 376, 379n5
  post-Christian characteristic, 232, 369
Citizen, individual, 1, 5, 11, 28, 54, 83, 114, 139, 161, 164, 201–3, 282, 321, 323, 425, 436, 443, 446
Citizenry, 139, 216n23, 372
  See also Democracy
Citizens, bad, 64, 67
Citizenship, 4, 73–81, 86, 125–51, 175, 191, 198, 213, 336n9, 408, 417, 422, 432–33, 448n13
  second-class, 210
Civic motivation, 125, 128, 143
  See also Action: public
Civic virtue, 19, 79–80, 424
"Civil Disobedience" (Thoreau), 85, 135, 139
Civil disobedience, 20, 34n16, 138–40, 149n90, 202
Civility, 131, 168, 278, 315, 379n10
Civil War, 4, 14–16, 35n25, 75, 77, 81–82, 141, 150n93, 150n96, 153, 155–56, 174, 185–86, 190, 206–14, 216n15, 217n24, 219n51, 281, 344, 375
Cobden, Richard, 363
Coleridge, Samuel Taylor, 97, 187, 215n9, 303n33
Collison, Gary, 388, 411–12n24
Commager, Henry Steele, 185
Commerce, 30, 39n65, 50, 129–30, 134, 136, 245, 344–50, 353–54, 369, 380n18, 390
  See also Capitalism; Markets; Trade
Communitarians, 19, 23, 354, 385, 410n6, 415, 428
Complicity, 27–28, 33n10, 125–43, 148n56, 162, 168, 181n9, 315, 327, 336n9, 340n24, 390, 407, 423

Compromise, moral, 56, 70, 72, 88, 114, 142–43, 164, 189, 192, 212, 214, 386, 389, 394, 405–6
Compromise of 1850, 137, 405–6
  See also Fugitive Slave Law
Commodities, 130, 134, 352, 358, 390
Community, 10, 13, 65, 91, 111, 152, 158, 186, 205, 217n26, 219n52, 258, 365, 368, 386, 394, 412n24, 422–25, 437–38, 443
Concord, Massachusetts, 37n49, 43, 77, 138, 185, 194, 197, 201, 205, 217n26, 219n52, 220n56, 266, 268, 321, 324, 327, 407
Conformity, 4, 8, 10–11, 25, 54, 66, 70, 86, 95, 103–5, 116–17, 120, 127, 257–58, 275, 284, 306, 436
  See also Nonconformity
Congress, U.S., 11, 60, 79, 137–38, 150, 161–62, 165, 191, 194–95, 201, 203, 217n28, 219n51, 381n18
"Congress of nations," 232–33
Conjectural history, 94, 348
Conscience, 28, 50–51, 66, 82, 133, 140, 154, 190, 198, 251, 256, 315, 442
Constitution, U.S., 11, 13–15, 135, 138, 154, 161, 188, 197, 331
Constitutional amendments, 197, 334
  First, 162
  Thirteenth, 213
  Fourteenth, 162, 213
  Fifteenth, 162, 213
Contemplation, 135, 418
Conventions
  moral and social, 64, 225, 244, 296–97, 358–59, 368, 402
  political, 26, 54, 140, 156, 172
Copperheads, 208
Cotton, John, 351
Craft, Ellen and William, 218n38
Crane, Gregg D., 35n30, 188, 216n15, 216n23
Cuba, 130, 146–47n36, 324
Cultivation. See Self-culture
Culture, 15, 17, 20, 25, 61, 208, 230, 266–67, 315, 345–47, 370, 383, 396

Culture (*continued*)
  Emerson's moral conception of, 31, 35, 44, 50, 106–13, 118, 173, 213, 245, 280, 309, 359, 364, 367, 376–77, 380n18, 440–41
  See also Self-culture
Culture war, 15, 19
Custom, 63, 82, 120, 152, 154, 187, 225, 279, 348, 350

Dalton, John, 60
Dark Ages, 47, 280, 327, 350
Declaration of Independence, 11, 13–14, 75, 188–89, 202, 210, 214, 216n14, 219n49, 331, 355, 374–75, 381n18
Deconstruction, 227, 232, 271, 378n4
  See also Postmodernism
Deistic vision, 250
Deity, 44, 248, 275, 287, 441
  See also God
Deliberation, 8, 400–401, 408, 422
Democracy, 2–11, 14–15, 23–31, 34n19, 48–50, 53–68, 74–87, 90, 103, 107–9, 113–14, 117, 125–28, 137–39, 142, 144n6, 149n90, 150n100, 152–53, 156, 168, 177–80, 186–93, 200–210, 213–14, 225–27, 251–53, 257, 262, 270, 274, 282, 298, 302n22, 334, 336n12, 347, 362–64, 378n4, 383–87, 390, 394–401, 404–5, 408–10, 411n9, 415–20, 428–46
  See also Liberalism
Descartes, René, 105
  See also Cartesian thought
Detranscendentalism, 28–29, 265–73, 281, 283–84, 289, 292, 295–99, 300n7, 301n18, 305, 334n4, 335n6, 368–69
  See also Retranscendentalism; Transcendentalism
Devil, 225, 236
Dewey, John, 98, 377n4
Dial, The, 7, 205
Diggins, John Patrick, 19–20
Dignity, 62, 74, 126, 189, 210, 257, 293, 355, 359, 377
Disagreeable particularity, 131, 305–40
Disengagement, civic. *See* Individualism

District of Columbia, 150n93, 161
"Ditto heads," 214
Divine, the, 5–6, 113, 186, 188–89, 227, 239–41, 245, 248–49, 273, 285, 368–69, 431, 441
  essence, 273, 275, 280
  fact, 240–41
  fire, 402
  spark, 257
  See also God; Intuition
Division of labor, 131, 136, 348, 365–66, 376
Docility, 74, 88, 127, 240, 244
Dolan, Neal, 3, 30–31, 35n25, 38n57, 39n63, 148n57, 188, 261n15, 261n20, 264n52, 303n33, 303n36, 415, 447n1
Domination, 230, 253, 446
  See also Will
Douglass, Frederick, 155, 162–63
Duberman, Martin, 217n29
Dumm, Thomas, 148n59, 150n103
Durkheim, Emile, 365–66, 415, 447n1
Duty, 5–6, 28, 79–80, 106, 108, 134–35, 139, 152, 154–56, 161, 164–65, 167, 177, 180, 201, 282, 319, 345, 422, 425, 444

Earhart, Amy, 336n9, 391, 393, 411n22
East, the, 212, 439–40
Ecstasy, 292, 311, 345, 365
  See also Emerson's politics; Liberalism: ecstatic; Liberalism: sober
Edwards, Jonathan, 18, 45, 346, 351
Egalitarianism, 13, 126, 144n7, 168, 251, 253, 256–57, 259, 396, 430–31, 437
  See also Equality
Eliot, Charles, 16
Elkins, Stanley, 19
Emancipation, 14, 35n25, 75, 164, 167, 196–97, 200, 205, 207–10, 212, 278, 332, 355, 374, 318n18
  compensated, 28, 81–82, 127, 140–42, 150n93, 150nn95–96, 155, 166
Emancipation Proclamation of 1863, 10, 14–15, 141, 150n96, 207, 277, 281, 375, 381n18, 408
Emerson, Lidian, 199

Emerson, Waldo (son), 97–98, 271, 289, 306, 335n8, 339n19, 343, 360, 371
"Emerson Industry in the 1980s, The" (Buell), 18, 28, 37n45, 266, 301n18
Emerson's politics
  before Civil War, 4–14, 125–84, 190–206, 274–82, 305–40
  during and after Civil War, 14–15, 206–14, 281–83
  classic interpretations of, 21–26
  and complicity, 125–51
  democratic, 60–65, 75–89, 136–43, 154–56, 172–73, 185–220, 251, 256–57, 383–414, 417–20
  and human excellence, 415–49
  misinterpretations of, 16–21, 185–86, 223–27, 257–59, 265–73, 295–99
  new interpretations of, 26–32
  and nonparticipation, 16–21, 46–49, 74–75, 153, 163, 177–79, 182n29, 185, 383–84
  physiological basis of, 178, 236, 290–91
  and property, 343–82
  and representation, 382–414
  and self-reliance, 1–13, 15, 18, 54–56, 69–71, 73–74, 77–83, 86–87, 89–90, 125–28, 132, 135, 137, 139–43, 152–60, 164, 166–80, 185–90, 192–93, 195–97, 202, 212, 239, 240, 269–70, 284–85, 302n32, 306, 383–84, 387–88
  and transcendentalism, 186–214, 223–340
  and violence, 14, 28, 73, 80–86, 96–97, 105, 109, 136, 155, 158, 162, 165–69, 175–79, 205, 299, 374–75, 392, 408–10
  See also Antislavery; Brown, John; Civil disobedience; Complicity; Democracy; Emancipation; Excellence; Individualism; Individuality; Liberalism; Representation; Self-reliance; Transcendentalism; Wisdom
Emerson's writings
  "Address . . . on . . . the Emancipation of the Negroes in the British West Indies" (1844), 10, 11, 34n21, 131, 167–70, 194, 277–78, 313–15, 372, 374, 380n18, 388, 391
  "Address to the Citizens of Concord [on the Fugitive Slave Law]" (1851), 13, 79–82, 138, 145n18, 159–60, 164, 181n9, 183n45, 201, 279, 321–23, 374
  "American Politics" (1863), 207–8
  "American Scholar, The" (1837), 8, 10, 90, 94–95, 99–120, 142, 256, 275–76, 288, 291, 318, 377, 391, 405
  "Anniversary of West Indian Emancipation" (1845), 149n72, 317–19
  "Antislavery Remarks at Worcester" (1849), 149n72, 319–21
  "Antislavery Speech at Dedham" (1846), 147n48, 149n72
  "Aristocracy" (1883), 75
  "Art and Criticism" (1893), 76
  "Assault on Charles Sumner" (1856), 205–6
  "Attempted Speech" (1861), 181n12, 299
  "Beauty" (1860), 88, 357–59, 376
  "Boston" (1893), 75, 76
  "Boston Hymn" (1863), 141, 150n95
  "Celebration of the Intellect" (1861), 206–7
  "Cherokee Removal Letter" (1838) (*see* "Letter to Martin Van Buren")
  "Circles" (1841), 8, 13, 283–84, 292, 304n38, 384, 386, 387, 403
  "Compensation" (1841), 135, 242, 311, 343, 365, 368, 370–71
  Conduct of Life (1860), 3, 87, 88, 90, 155, 171–75, 177–78, 344, 375, 377, 405
  "Conservative, The" (1842), 372
  "Considerations by the Way" (1860), 88, 89
  "Country Life" (1858), 272
  "Courage" (1870), 69
  "Culture" (1860), 245, 276
  "Divinity School Address" (1838), 8, 84, 96, 112, 154, 216n11, 275, 280, 339n17, 343, 346, 365–71, 383
  English Traits (1856), 39n66, 182n41, 344, 375, 377
  Essays (1841), 8, 224

Emerson's writings (*continued*)
  Essays (1844), 8, 224, 387, 393
    "Experience" (1844), 8, 29, 30, 36n33, 39n61, 96–98, 113, 144n8, 228, 234, 243–49, 265, 274, 281, 284, 288–93, 303nn34–35, 306, 310, 312–13, 318, 334n2, 339n19, 339n22, 343, 365, 371, 384
    "Fate" (1860), 29, 30, 36n33, 39n61, 87, 89, 128–30, 171–78, 184n70, 234, 235–38, 241–43, 248–49, 265, 284–88, 290–91, 303n33
    "Fortune of the Republic" (1863), 10, 14, 76–79, 207–12, 218n36, 281, 344, 375
    "Fortune of the Republic" (1878), 213–14, 217n24
    "Fugitive Slave Law, The" (1854), 132, 138, 190, 202, 216n20, 302n32, 324, 372
    "Historical Discourse at Concord" (1835), 7, 77–79, 83
    "History" (1841), 339n18, 343, 365–66, 368–71
    "Human Culture" (1837–38), 361, 371
    "Human Life" (1838–39), 361
    "Illusions" (1860), 88, 90
    "Individual, The" (1837), 86
    "Intellect" (1841), 230, 302n27
    "Introductory" (to "Human Culture") (1837), 75
    "John Brown" (1860), 13, 407–8
    Journals, 3, 6, 14, 15, 19, 39n66, 58, 80, 81, 148n67, 149n92, 159, 160, 163, 167, 170, 181n12, 183n45, 189, 217n26, 269–70, 272, 296, 298, 300–301n14, 301n16, 348, 361, 390, 405–6
    "Kansas Relief Meeting" (1856), 83–85, 164–65, 404, 406
    "Lecture on Slavery" (1855), 29, 128, 140, 203, 280, 326
    "Lecture on the Times" (1841), 71, 372
    "Letter to Martin Van Buren" (1838), 8, 11, 80, 381n21
    "Literary Ethics" (1838), 228, 339n21
    "Love" (1841), 263n40
    "Manners" (1844), 70
  "Man the Reformer" (1841), 9, 27, 72, 129, 130, 134, 136, 138, 191, 372
  "Method of Nature, The" (1841), 9, 71, 88, 276, 278, 294
  "Montaigne; or, the Skeptic," 225, 229, 388, 403
  "Moral Forces" (1862), 207
  Nature (1836), 8, 98, 231, 263n40, 263n44, 264n52, 265, 275, 276, 278, 287, 289, 292, 303–4n37, 304n38, 311–13, 335n7, 343, 356–61, 364–69, 371, 376
  "New England Reformers" (1844), 70–73, 158, 192, 372, 388, 391–93, 402
  "Nominalist and Realist" (1844), 402
  "Ode Inscribed to W. H. Channing" (1847), 381n19, 381n21
  "Over-Soul, The" (1841), 6, 29, 76, 186, 187, 199, 227, 257–58, 273, 276–77, 287, 306, 402, 434
  "Perpetual Forces" (1862), 207
  "Philosophy of History, The" (1837), 361
  "Plutarch" (1883), 87, 303n37
  "Poet, The" (1844), 190, 231, 272, 291, 393, 394, 397, 411–12n24
  "Politics" (1837), 361–64
  "Politics" (1844), 11, 22, 74, 83–85, 188, 372, 388
  "Power" (1860), 172, 173, 175–78, 344, 376
  "Present Age, The" (1840), 361, 363
  "President's Proclamation, The" (1862), 14
  "Progress of Culture, The" (1875), 76, 77
  "Reforms" (1840), 192–93
  Representative Men (1850), 23, 31, 36n33, 57, 58, 65, 80, 87, 209, 237, 249, 344, 382–83, 387, 395–96, 398–99, 415–22, 425, 428–29, 431–34, 438–39, 445–46, 448n18
  "Self-Reliance" (1841), 8, 19, 23, 29–30, 39n61, 53–58, 65, 94–95, 102, 105, 110, 113–15, 148n52, 154, 157–60, 167–68, 171–73, 189, 193, 195, 225, 228, 234–36, 238, 240–43, 247–49, 265, 284–85, 288, 291, 346, 365–68, 371, 387–88, 398, 403, 418

Sermons, 3, 5–7, 9, 263n40, 274–75, 327
"Society" (1837), 72, 79
"Speech at a Meeting to Aid John Brown's Family" (November 1859), 11, 13, 374, 407–8
"Spiritual Laws" (1841), 263n40
"Transcendentalist, The" (1842), 191, 274, 278, 287, 291, 309–10, 318, 333
"Uses of Great Men," 58, 87, 392–93, 396, 428, 443
"Wealth" (1860), 344, 376
"West Indian Emancipation Address" (1844) (*see* "Address . . . on . . . the Emancipation of the Negroes in the British West Indies")
"Worship" (1860), 2, 263n40, 376
"Young American, The" (1844), 75–76, 344, 353, 380n18
Empiricism, 295, 348
Emulation, 421, 423, 426
  See also Admiration; Reverence
Ends, 9, 13, 75, 80, 84, 116, 229, 339n17, 423, 430, 438–41, 444–46
  ideal, 210
  moral, 141
  in ourselves, 26, 103–4, 417–18
  public, 85
  universal, 237
England, 75, 166–67, 183n45, 195, 199, 323, 344, 359, 363, 375
Enlightenment, personal, 27, 92, 169
Enlightenment, the, 5, 44, 45, 51, 92, 264n52, 369
  See also Scottish Enlightenment; Scottish liberalism
Epistemology, 33n13, 303n36, 416
Equality, 46, 49, 54, 58, 61–62, 77, 78, 153–54, 186, 189, 204, 206, 208, 211, 218–19n47, 219n49, 277, 299, 351, 362, 415, 417–18, 435, 438, 443
  democratic, 24, 54, 179, 204–5, 207–8, 364, 398, 417, 430
  legal, 190
  moral, 76, 126, 132
  principle of, 186
  respect for, 428–30
  social, 200

  transcendental, 30, 212, 265, 273–78, 280–82, 288, 290–91, 295, 298, 303n34
  universal, 6, 13, 28, 188, 199, 210, 213, 257, 362, 396, 431–32
  for women, 213
  See also Egalitarianism
Essence (of self, life, cosmos), 231, 235, 238, 246, 255, 263n41, 265, 273, 279, 284, 291, 322, 419, 422, 431, 435, 446
  See also God
Eternal, the, 248
  Cause, 65, 241
  generator, 284
  law of, 241, 314, 442
  See also God; Transcendentalism
Eucharist, 9, 269, 369
  Lord's Supper, 268
Europe, 16, 20, 44, 47, 75–76, 80, 98, 99, 117, 199, 211, 267, 344, 350–51, 363–65, 372, 375, 440, 442
European revolutions of 1848, 199
Excellence, 26, 30, 31, 58, 83, 104, 108, 109, 416–24, 426, 429–31, 434, 437–39, 441–46
  See also Wisdom
Existentialism, 92, 99
Existential passion, Emerson's, 27, 82
Exploitation, 126, 129–30, 132–33, 135, 147n40, 238, 439, 441–42

Faculties
  of culture, 364
  divine, 273, 275
  of intellect, 278–80, 302n27
  of moral perception, 188, 237, 406
  of Reason, 5–6, 187, 273–75, 278–80, 282, 285–86, 294–95
  of understanding, 294
  See also Culture; Intellect; Intuition; Moral sentiment; Reason; Soul; Transcendentalism
Faith, 19, 29, 45, 276, 280, 298, 325
  Emerson's in higher law of equality and justice, 196, 199, 263n45, 276, 310, 318–21, 332–33

Faith (*continued*)
   Emerson's in the individual, 50, 174
   Emerson's in progress, 22, 45, 65, 264, 327, 438
   Emerson's in Providence, 179
   good and bad, 132–33, 140, 258
Fallibilism, 126, 144n8
Fatalism, 45, 287
Fate. *See* Emerson's writings: "Fate"
Federalist Papers, The, 355, 400, 412n46
   See also Hamilton, Alexander; Madison, James; Publius
Feidelson, Charles, 300n3
Few, the, 87–88, 235, 257
   See also Many, the; Multitude, the
Field, Peter, 4, 10, 33n9, 33n13, 34nn17–19, 39n65, 145n13, 145n23, 147n44, 148n67, 149n72, 150–51n104, 183n44, 270, 275, 299n1, 301n16, 301n22, 302n26, 303n36, 387, 411n11
First Cause, 249, 293, 432
   See also God
Flanagan, G. Borden, 31, 257, 355
Flourishing, 126, 419, 421–26, 429
Focal distancing, 184, 304–13, 315–16, 318–19, 321, 325–27, 329–33, 338n16, 339n17, 339n19
Fortune, 240, 245, 274, 313, 344, 407
   See also Emerson's writings: "Fortune of the Republic" (1863), "Fortune of the Republic" (1878)
Fourier, François Marie Charles, 65, 70
France, 199, 323, 363, 442
Frank, Jason, 31, 182n37, 257
Frank, Waldo, 17
Franklin, Benjamin, 61
Fraternity, 23, 47, 49, 51
Freedom, 6, 27, 66, 77, 79, 105–6, 120, 126–29, 135, 138, 146n32, 152–54, 157, 171–79, 186–91, 196, 199–202, 206–8, 211–13, 218n31, 236–37, 286–88, 303n33, 316, 331, 349–51, 367, 377, 428–32, 435, 440–42
   of speech, 447, 449n20
   See also Liberty

Free Soil Party, 138, 155, 163–64, 177–78, 201
Freud, Sigmund, 100, 114–16
Friendship, 22, 47, 70–71, 114, 116
Frothingham, Octavius Brooks, 44
Fugitive Slave Law (1850), 11, 66, 73, 79–81, 127–28, 137–39, 153–55, 159–60, 163–64, 166, 170–71, 173, 175, 182n39, 200, 302n32, 321–23, 325–36, 405
Fugitive slaves, 13, 27, 128, 138, 139, 154, 159, 162, 167, 170–71, 179
   See also Antislavery; Blacks; Fugitive Slave Law

Gag rule, congressional, 133, 158, 162, 205
Gandhi, Mahatma, 5
Garrison, William Lloyd, 155, 157, 159–60, 162–64, 177–78, 195, 200
Garvey, T. Gregory, 3, 8, 19, 32n1, 37n47, 186, 189–90, 307
Gellner, Ernst, 415–16, 447n1
Genius, 17, 43, 55–59, 62, 80, 102, 106, 110–14, 139, 158, 197, 211–13, 228, 231, 234, 239–40, 246, 256–57, 273–74, 284, 295, 306, 310, 316–18, 320–25, 328–30, 334n2, 380n18, 385–86, 392, 397–99, 412n24, 416, 422, 425, 429–31, 434–37, 442–45
Georgia, 159, 161, 316, 381n24
Germans, 129, 323
German thought, 5, 15, 44, 187, 215n9, 303n26, 402, 444
   See also Romanticism
Gerry, Elbridge, 150n93
Giamatti, A. Bartlett, 20, 24
God, 5–6, 9, 13, 21, 29–30, 33n15, 43–44, 59, 78, 195, 207, 212, 215n9, 231–33, 240–41, 248–50, 253, 256–57, 265–66, 273–75, 281–83, 286–88, 293–97, 301n19, 304n38, 306, 311, 343, 347, 359, 368–71, 408
   death of, 270
Godhead, 241, 248–49, 274, 279, 280
God-reliance, 239, 240, 247, 270, 285, 302n32

Kingdom of (of heaven, of the Soul), 113, 345, 364
Son of, 108
See also Being; Divine, the; First Cause; Ideal, the; Infinitude; Metaphysics; One, the; Over-Soul, the; Providence; Soul; Spirit; Spiritual life and thought; Transcendentalism; Universals
Goethe, Johann Wolfgang von, 57, 215n9, 272, 301n18, 416, 418, 422, 437, 439, 442, 444–46
Golden Rule, the, 14, 375
See also Law
Good, the, 44, 45, 104, 106–8, 192, 206, 250, 254, 256, 359, 271, 421, 423–24, 437, 446
Goodman, Russell, 225, 261n19
Gougeon, Len, 3, 5, 11, 15–16, 28, 33n14, 34n17, 146n31, 180n6, 181n12, 181n25, 182n29, 183n44, 216n14, 217n27, 217n33, 218n35, 219nn52–53, 220n56, 256–57, 263nn42–43, 299, 313, 336n9, 340n29, 372, 381n21, 388–91, 422
Government, 5, 7, 11–4, 20, 48, 54, 65, 76–78, 81–85, 89, 112, 161–65, 178, 189, 194, 201, 204, 217n32, 219, 245, 256, 282, 313, 350–52, 355, 362–67, 373, 381–84, 396, 404–6, 433, 437
Graber, Mark, 181n24
Great men, 23, 56, 58–59, 61, 67, 107, 257, 295–96, 398, 401, 406, 423–24, 433, 436
See also Emerson's writings: *Representative Men*
Greatness, 23–24, 35n25, 48, 55–59, 62–63, 111, 144n7, 211, 253, 376, 396–98, 409, 416, 424–25, 429, 437, 439, 446
Greeks, ancient, 228, 252, 305, 369, 416–17
Guizot, François, 363
Gura, Phillip, 215n10, 216n16, 218n43, 220n56

Habermas, Jürgen, 297–98, 416
Habich, Robert, 36n32

Habit, 19, 29, 43, 54, 127, 132, 134, 139, 225, 244, 265–66, 276, 292, 295, 307–8, 316, 319–21, 326, 333, 337n13, 346, 373, 403, 433, 444
Haiti, 169, 197, 278, 389
Hamilton, Alexander, 406
See also Federalist Papers, The; Madison, James; Publius
Hamlet, 101
Happiness, 210, 355, 420, 422, 423, 425
Harmony, 45, 187, 238, 242, 258, 304n37, 310, 347
Harpers Ferry, 13, 35n24, 155, 165–66, 220n56, 408
Harvard University, 16, 82, 95, 96, 145n23, 213, 349, 353, 363, 368
Hawthorne, Julian, 43
Hedges, William, 346
Hegel, Georg Wilhelm Friedrich, 258, 334n3, 336n12, 351, 354, 425
Heidegger, Martin, 25, 91, 94–99, 101, 119, 243, 261n16, 293, 303n36, 358, 441
Hertz, Neil, 114
Heterogeneity, 418, 426–27, 434–35, 439–41, 445
Hicks, Granville, 18
Hierarchy, 76, 312, 398, 418, 420, 431, 438
Higginson, Thomas Wentworth, 16, 212, 220n56
Higher law. *See* God; Law; Transcendentalism; Truth
Hindus, 90
Historical context. *See* Interpretive context
Hoar, Samuel, 205
Hobbes, Thomas, 251
Hobsbawm, Eric, 362
Holmes, Oliver Wendell, Jr., 15–16, 36n32
Holmes, Oliver Wendell, Sr., 16
Holy Ghost, 245, 274
Home, 104, 112, 118, 120, 128, 138, 157, 165, 182n34, 199, 203, 217n26, 223–24, 240, 254–55, 257, 259n4, 322, 327, 331
Honesty, 5, 44, 64–65, 127, 132, 163, 204, 223, 258
Hooker, Thomas, 346

Hopkins, Vivian, 300n3
Horizon, 246, 307, 310–12, 324, 326, 331, 334n2, 337n14, 343, 355–56, 384–85, 421
Howe, Daniel Walker, 380n13
Howe, Irving, 38n56
Human nature, Emerson on, 8–9, 49, 126, 152, 171, 187–91, 225, 230, 239, 275, 312, 367–68, 389, 424
Hume, David, 45, 98, 225, 261n20, 289, 303n36, 349, 379n10
Hurka, Thomas, 113
Hutcheson, Frances, 349

Ideal, the, 119–20, 186, 219n49, 248–49, 292, 306, 309, 313
  See also God
Ignorance, 79, 134–35, 329
Immorality, 65, 83–84, 105, 126
  See also Morality
Immoral laws, 80, 133, 139, 200–201
Imperialism, 418, 420, 442
Inaction. *See* Action
Individualism, 1–3, 6, 22, 32n3, 44, 47, 56, 70, 80–81, 90, 143, 174, 190, 194, 204, 250, 354, 383–84, 393, 402, 433
  apolitical, 15, 17–21, 23–24, 31, 38n51, 38n56
Individuality, 2, 21–26, 32n3, 54, 70–71, 80, 85–86, 139, 149n90, 181n9, 190, 193, 212, 251, 279, 327, 329, 336n9, 385, 396, 418, 422–23, 430–31, 436, 438, 440, 443
Infinitude, 126, 144n8, 174, 287, 298, 309, 312
  See also God
Injustice, 80, 126, 134–35, 142, 176
  See also Justice
Instinct, 22, 44, 50, 75, 100–101, 118, 206, 209, 224, 239, 284, 318, 360, 375, 415, 440
Instrumentalism, 30–31, 353–58, 373, 376–78, 418, 441, 445
  counterinstrumental values, 376
Intellect, 61, 99, 116, 120, 137, 142, 167, 172, 176, 206, 230, 235–37, 241, 244, 278–79, 282, 288, 291, 301n19, 302n27, 303n33, 316, 329, 374, 392, 406, 442–44
  See also Faculties
Intellectual life, 60, 86, 93, 95, 97–98, 102, 132–34, 153, 168, 178, 231, 247, 259, 269, 294, 296–97, 309, 323, 423, 432–34, 436–37, 439–41, 443, 447
Intellectuals, 15, 63, 191, 299, 327, 437
  Emerson as one, 4, 5, 39n66, 44, 213–14, 220n59, 224, 265, 270, 298, 351, 387
  Emerson defends, 50, 126–27, 416–17, 420, 422, 426, 448–49n21
Interpretive context, 23, 37, 95, 103, 142, 167, 236, 271, 317, 335n4, 345, 347, 351, 353, 360, 363, 423, 447n1
Intuition, 5–6, 18, 28, 45, 51, 91, 94, 97, 100, 112, 187–88, 216n11, 216n15, 239, 243, 273, 284–85, 303n36, 349, 354, 359, 372
  See also Faculties; Reason
Irish, the, 129
Italy, 323, 350

Jackson, Andrew, 37n49, 185, 363
Jacksonian America, 61, 65, 346, 351, 353–54, 357, 363, 376, 380n17
Jamaica, 197, 278, 389
James, William, 16, 304n42
Japan, 252, 325
Jaspers, Karl, 92
Jefferson, Thomas, 55, 61, 103, 204, 365
  Jeffersonian, Emerson as, 36n39, 37n45
Jesus, 84, 112, 245, 274, 283, 304n38, 310
Jim Crow, 197, 317
Joy, 10, 223, 238, 242, 275, 292, 320, 350, 374, 377, 398, 408
Judgment, 47, 50, 53, 64, 71, 77, 83, 87, 89, 112, 133, 139, 154, 223, 226, 244, 260n14, 296, 400–401, 419–20, 432–33, 435
Justice, 5, 8, 11–14, 25, 57, 77–80, 84, 87, 99–100, 107, 111–14, 118, 125, 142–43, 152, 165, 186, 189, 198–202, 207–9, 212, 257, 277, 281, 285, 295, 318, 323, 368, 374, 381n21, 385, 396, 422, 425, 428, 447n1
  See also Injustice

Kansas, 83–85, 155, 164–66, 182n34, 205, 325
Kansas-Nebraska Act (1854), 164, 325–26
Kant, Immanuel, 45, 94, 97–98, 100, 102–6, 108, 114–19, 187, 215n9, 305, 334n3, 336n12, 360, 372, 382n29, 402, 425
   categorical imperative of, 372, 385
Kateb, George, 21, 24–27, 29, 39n61, 126–28, 135, 137, 140, 144n7, 145n15, 149n71, 149n90, 153, 174–76, 180n7, 225–26, 251, 266, 268–69, 271, 297, 302n24, 335n6, 336n9, 355, 384, 416, 432–33, 435, 446, 448n10, 448n13, 448n15
Kaufmann, Walter, 224, 260n14
Knowledge, 45, 50, 59, 91–92, 97–99, 119, 131, 135, 165, 241–45, 267, 273–75, 283–84, 294–95, 303n36, 349, 360–62, 379n10, 416, 425–28, 431–35, 438, 441, 444
Knox, Robert, 166

Language, 24–25, 30, 47, 51, 60, 63, 65, 92–93, 95–97, 143, 179, 226–27, 230, 233, 241, 246, 248, 303n33, 317, 323, 325, 331, 343–47, 354–55, 358–59, 366–67, 369–70, 375–76, 377n4, 381n20, 400, 406, 420
   ideal, 232
   picturesque, 231
Lasch, Christopher, 38n58
Law, 8–9, 12, 50, 55, 61, 75, 80, 84, 89, 103–16, 133, 138–39, 160, 165, 176–79, 188–90, 193, 200–204, 213, 225, 239–43, 250, 262n35, 279–80, 286–87, 291, 304n37, 314, 322, 363–64, 374, 395, 398, 402, 405–8, 424–26
   of compensation, 333
   higher (eternal, God's), 13, 15–16, 29, 33n15, 154, 166, 188, 201, 215n9, 227, 241, 249, 251, 256, 263n45, 287, 291, 292, 295, 310–11, 314, 319–20, 333, 442
   immoral, 80, 133, 139, 200, 201
   lack of, 9, 291
   moral, 15, 67, 102, 104–5, 116, 119, 198, 360, 372, 382n29, 386
   natural, 139, 201, 323
   of nature, 13, 61
   rule of, 12
   See also Civil disobedience; Constitution, U.S.; Fugitive Slave Law; God; Natural rights
Levine, Alan, 29, 30, 39n58, 260n11, 262n28, 263n48, 296, 302n28, 335n5, 360, 449n21
Lewis, C. I., 96–97
Liberalism, 3, 30, 33n8, 44, 252–53, 255, 299, 301n22, 343, 355–56, 377, 409, 440
   ecstatic, 9–15, 242, 259, 263n49
   Emerson's critique of, 10, 346, 365
   Emerson's defense of, 354, 364, 367, 371
   sober, 9, 14
   See also Democracy; Ecstasy; Emerson's politics
Liberator, The, 135, 157, 219
Liberia, 164
   See also Emancipation
Libertarians, 371, 377, 415
Liberty, 10–11, 14, 54, 76, 105, 119–20, 129, 142, 162, 172, 188, 200–201, 206–7, 210–12, 218n35, 219n49, 316, 331, 349–51, 360, 364, 371, 374, 380–81n18, 408, 418, 430–38
   versus equality, 364
   See also Freedom
Lincoln, Abraham, 4, 14, 35n25, 81, 149n86, 150n93, 150n96, 207–10, 212, 219n49, 219n51, 281, 375, 381n18, 408
Locke, John, 33n13, 44, 261n20, 356, 425
   Lockean views, 5, 37n45, 350, 362, 371, 373
Lopez, Michael, 38–39n58, 226, 230, 232, 261n15, 266–68, 300n7
"Lords of life," 288–93
Louisiana, 198, 316
Love, 10–14, 20, 46–48, 71, 79, 87, 101, 110–14, 117, 133, 157–58, 161, 187, 190, 246, 274–76, 280–81, 290–94, 368, 380n18, 388, 392–94, 405, 417, 434, 440

Lovejoy, Elijah P., 8, 133
Lycurgus, 13, 281
Lynd, Staughton, 37n45

Machiavellianism, 203, 237, 250
Macpherson, C. B., 367
Madison, James, 23, 54, 150n93, 355, 400, 406
See also *Federalist Papers, The*; Hamilton, Alexander; Publius
Magee, Michael, 129, 146n31
Maine, 381n21
Malachuk, Daniel S., 29–30, 33n8, 34nn15–16, 38n57, 256, 263n40, 263nn42–43, 264nn60–61, 335n4, 337n13, 368, 413n50, 449n21
Many, the, 87, 253, 257
See also Few, the; Multitude, the
Mariotti, Shannon, 30, 182n29, 184n79, 335n8, 336–37n12, 338n15
Markets, 131, 146n32, 344–45, 347, 351–54, 357, 361, 364, 373, 376, 378n4, 380n13
See also Capitalism; Commerce; Trade
Marr, David, 38n51
Martineau, Harriet, 133
Marx, Karl, 12, 57, 103, 258
Marxist critics, 18
Massachusetts, 7, 13–14, 70, 77, 84, 128, 138–39, 150n93, 158, 160–61, 165, 181n12, 181n21, 194–95, 197, 200, 205, 211, 315–16, 319, 321–22, 324–25, 327, 331, 333, 404–6
Masses, 60, 62, 74, 84, 87–90, 141, 190, 192, 203, 209–10, 275, 304n37, 313, 380n18, 398
"Massification," 25, 86–87, 90
Materialism, 17, 31, 64, 189, 245–46, 309–10, 319, 353–55, 367, 395, 418, 433, 438–39, 442
Mates, Benson, 93
Mather, Cotton, 346
Matthiessen, F. O., 18
McClay, Wilfred M., 38n54
McWilliams, Wilson Carey, 21–24, 39n61, 125, 348, 383
Melville, Herman, 1

Menand, Louis, 15
Metaphysics, 20, 88, 126, 226, 232–35, 238–43, 247, 249–51, 253, 256, 258–60, 263n41, 279–80, 299, 372, 419–20, 427, 431, 446, 447n1, 448n10
See also God; Transcendentalism
Mexican War, 194, 198, 217n29, 381n21
Mill, John Stuart, 2, 10, 31, 54, 119–20, 363
Miller, Perry, 18, 19, 356
Milton, John, 187, 215n9
Paradise Lost, 215n9, 347
Mind, 5, 11, 44, 57, 59, 65–68, 73–75, 78, 88, 94, 109, 119–20, 131–32, 136, 140, 146n36, 158–59, 165, 173, 195, 201, 205, 208, 212–14, 228–31, 235–36, 241, 244, 249, 254–55, 259, 267, 270, 275–79, 286, 292, 297–98, 304n38, 305–10, 313–16, 322, 328–29, 331, 339n18, 348–50, 354, 358, 364, 368, 374–75, 377n4, 382n29, 388–89, 392, 402, 407, 420, 425–26, 429–36, 440–44
Minerva, 245, 274
Minkins, Shadrach, 218n38
Missouri Compromise, 194, 325
Mitchell, Charles, 16–17
Modernity, 418, 438–39, 441–45, 447n1
Modern life and thought, 5, 8, 29, 31, 74–76, 87, 104, 118, 130–31, 136, 169, 196, 220n59, 225–26, 229, 253, 264n51, 264n52, 274, 298, 350, 354, 356–59, 362, 365–66, 379n10, 381n18, 395, 415–16, 418–20, 425, 428, 438–39, 448n18
Monism, 268
Montaigne, Michel de, 12, 29, 34n23, 57, 59, 63–65, 223–34, 243–59, 259n1, 259n6, 260n7, 260n9, 260n11, 262–63n35, 263n48, 263n50, 264n51, 335n5, 388, 403, 416, 425, 445
See also Emerson's writings: "Montaigne; or, the Skeptic," *Representative Men*
Montesquieu, Baron de, 8, 34n21
Moral abomination, slavery as, 35n25, 81, 128, 139, 186, 201

Moral absolutism, 14
Moral complacency, 133
Moral duty, 165
  See also Duty
Moral equality, 76, 126, 132
  See also Equality: transcendental
Moral faculty, 406
Moral flaws, 141–42, 349, 373, 407
Moral force, 195, 389
Moral genius, 59, 197
Moral imperative, 74, 134, 191
Moral intuition, 303n36
Morality, 12, 14, 44, 49–50, 70, 77, 104, 118, 120, 135, 168–69, 188–89, 202, 205, 226, 241, 250–54, 256, 264n58, 282, 289, 349, 359, 405, 419
  See also Immorality; Virtue
Moral judgment, 139
Moral law, 15, 67, 102, 104–5, 116, 119, 198, 360, 372, 382n29, 386
Moral life, 102–5, 109, 120, 411n9
Moral motive (drive, zeal), 69–70, 79, 87, 174, 303n33
Moral principles, 13, 204, 210, 372
Moral progress, 191, 195, 351, 354
Moral purpose of state, 14, 24, 28, 65, 77
Morals, 49, 241, 274, 279, 376, 406
Moral sense, 5, 64, 66, 131, 160, 167, 169, 188, 201, 215n9, 252, 257, 273, 303n36, 325, 349–51, 359, 372
  See also Faculties; Reason
Moral sentiment, 64, 188, 195, 202, 204, 207, 216n11, 237, 286–87, 293, 303n33, 303n36, 349, 351, 368, 381n21
  See also Faculties; Reason
Moral suasion, 4, 6–8, 34n16, 34n17, 34n19, 160–66, 191, 205, 388, 408
Moral uplift, 388, 409
Moral worth, 6, 104
More, Paul Elmer, 22, 49
Morton, Samuel, 166
Moses, 84, 310, 370
Mott, Wesley T., 5, 190
Mozart, Wolfgang Amadeus, 58–59, 62, 272
Multitude, the, 443
  See also Many, the

Muse, the, 48, 245, 274
Mystical qualities, 37n47, 37n49, 65, 282, 391, 397
Mystics, 18, 416

Natural rights, 374–75
  See also under Law
Nature, 11, 98, 116, 118, 210
  Emerson on, 9, 45–47, 50, 55–58, 60–65, 109–13, 128, 136, 156, 168, 170, 172–73, 196–98, 231, 236, 238, 240, 242–45, 248, 250, 272, 277, 282, 286–87, 289–94, 303–4n37, 304n38, 309–16, 325, 337n14, 344, 347–48, 356–60, 374–76, 389, 394, 398, 402, 418, 420, 426–29, 434–36, 439–40
  See also Emerson's writings: "Method of Nature, The," Nature
Necessity, 59, 74, 76, 89, 103, 115, 172, 176, 179, 202, 237, 238–39, 242, 245, 287–88, 377, 411n9, 423, 438, 441
  blessed, 242, 288
Neo-Platonism, 5, 60, 303n36
  See also Platonism
New England, 7, 15–17, 24, 44, 65–67, 70–73, 77, 128–36, 146n31, 147n50, 158, 163, 167, 183n45, 192, 195, 199, 205, 223, 317, 324, 346, 354, 372, 379n5, 388, 390–93, 402
Newfield, Christopher, 127–28
New Hampshire, 55, 153
"New history," 1–6, 8–9, 14–15, 21, 24, 26–28, 31, 32n1, 32n4, 33n8, 33n15, 38n56, 270, 390
New Zealander, 157
Nicoloff, Phillip L., 145n23, 183n44
Nietzsche, Friedrich, 20–29, 39n63, 47, 53–54, 92–94, 98–100, 104–11, 113–14, 117, 175, 223–43, 246–47, 249–54, 256–59, 259n1, 259n4, 259n6, 260n7, 260n10, 260–61n14, 261nn15–16, 261n18, 262nn29–30, 263nn40–41, 263n45, 264n58, 267, 270, 284–86, 296, 303n33, 335n5, 365, 394, 441
Noncomplicity, 134, 142
  See also Complicity

Nonconformity, 26, 428
    See also Conformity
Norwood, Kyle, 303n34

Ohio, 208
One, the, 49
    See also God
Ontology, 233–34, 247, 360, 417, 427, 430, 434–35, 437
Oppression, 60, 132, 196, 431, 435, 441
Optimism, 12, 45–46, 200, 318, 320
Over-Soul, the, 18, 186–87, 199, 227, 257–58, 273, 276–77, 306, 434
    See also God
Owen, Robert, 70

Packer, Barbara, 33n13, 267, 300n14, 302n24, 335n6, 338n15
Painter, Nell Irvin, 39n66, 146n23, 183n44
Palfrey, John Gorham, 73, 138, 201
Parrington, Vernon Louis, 36n39, 37n45, 44
Participation, 26, 108–9, 143, 191, 384, 405, 416, 433, 437
Pascal, Blaise, 230
Patriotism, 11, 173, 203
Patterson, Anita Haya, 145n23
Paul, Sherman, 300n3, 308, 337nn14–15
Perfection, 18, 25–26, 142, 216n11, 244, 248, 292, 303n32, 313, 424–25, 427, 441, 445–46
Perfectionism, 94–95, 104, 106–7, 110, 112–14, 116–17, 119–20, 225, 251, 253, 261n16, 384–86, 394, 397, 401, 404, 408, 411n9, 419, 431
Performativity, 229
Perry, Ralph Barton, 47
Perspective, 78, 87, 91, 102, 114, 175, 177–79, 216n23, 229, 260n7, 262n29, 311, 318, 320, 330, 337n14n, 355, 398, 400, 427, 433
Perspectivism, 435
Perspectivity, 228
Phillips, Wendell, 155, 157, 159–60, 162–64, 177–78, 195, 388
Philosopher-king, Plato's, 12, 39n66, 103, 417, 425, 428

Philosophers, 1, 19, 21–23, 29, 43, 48–50, 53, 56, 91–95, 98–99, 111–12, 117–20, 154, 187, 224, 260n14, 265, 294, 297, 351, 356, 376, 380n18, 399, 416, 421, 424
    See also specific philosophers
Philosophy
    analytical, 92
    Continental, 29
    modern, 104
    ordinary language, 92–93, 354
    twentieth-century, 226
    Western, 92, 99
    See also Emerson's politics; Philosophers; *and specific philosophers*
Pippen, Robert, 224, 259n1, 259n4, 260n7
Plato, 8, 12, 31, 57, 59, 63, 88, 114, 116, 118, 250, 339n18, 355, 359, 416–17, 419–28, 430, 437–39, 445, 448nn10–11, 448n18
Platonism, 249–50, 416
    See also Neo-Platonism
Pluralism, 429
Plutarch, 87
    See also Emerson's writings: "Plutarch"
Poet, the, 111, 231–32, 251, 356–57, 393–95, 399
    See also Emerson's writings: "Poet, The"
Poirier, Richard, 20–21, 29, 226, 229, 266–68, 270–72, 283, 285–86, 297, 303n35, 304n42, 378n4
Polis, 421
Political acts, 2, 4, 26, 66, 137, 141, 159, 161, 172, 192, 333, 384, 388, 390–91, 393, 422–24
Political complicity, 125–28, 138–43, 203
Political economy, 420, 441
Political ideal, 46, 418, 438
Political life, 10, 73, 81, 84, 395, 419, 422, 445
Political philosophy and thought, 1, 3, 6, 19, 21, 23, 27, 29, 32, 74–75, 166, 177, 207, 223, 226, 270, 280, 383, 415, 421
    See also Emerson's politics
Political science, 7, 176
Political teaching, 8, 17, 83, 416

Political theory, 31, 77, 224, 269, 297, 361, 386, 420, 428
Political virtue, 24, 49
Politics. *See* Emerson's politics
Poor, the, 23, 55, 66, 77–78, 90, 111, 148n52, 211–12, 284, 314–15, 357, 442
Postmodernism, 20, 31, 38n58, 258, 262n35, 266–67, 300n7, 302n29, 415, 420, 429, 446
  See also Deconstruction
Postsectarianism. *See* Sectarianism
Postsecularism, 297–98
  See also Secularism
Potential, 6, 54, 81, 112, 125, 134, 187, 257, 368, 421–22, 424, 439
Pragmatism, 15, 21, 267, 297, 303n33
Principle, 11–13, 35n26, 55, 70–74, 80, 85, 106–7, 114, 126, 156–58, 163–64, 170, 175, 186–92, 195–96, 201, 204, 207–10, 213–14, 273–77, 284, 292, 295, 310, 326–29, 335n9, 343, 362–63, 372, 375–76, 379n6, 380n18, 385, 393, 397, 401–2, 407, 423, 426–30, 434, 438–42
Private character, 12, 22, 49
Private consumption and property, 131, 135, 433, 434
Private life and thought, 11, 17, 19, 20, 23, 25, 34n23, 41, 48–49, 66–67, 79, 83–85, 96, 101–4, 108, 111, 125, 131, 134–35, 159, 166, 170, 173–76, 181n12, 190–92, 244, 255–56, 266–71, 278–81, 298, 300n14, 301n16, 344, 357, 372, 394, 402, 433–34
Progress, moral, 191, 195, 351, 354
Prometheus, 55, 310
Protestantism, 4, 33n13, 37n45, 66
  See also Puritans
Protestant work ethic, 346
Power. *See* Emerson's politics: and violence; Emerson's writings: "Power"; Faculties; God
Providence, 128, 131, 156, 172, 179, 190, 226–27, 234, 241, 320, 325–27, 352–53
  See also God

Public, the, 44, 48, 125, 202, 279, 383
  American, 35n25, 165, 191, 206, 390, 409
  British, 389
Public good (ends, interest, necessity, weal), 79, 85, 89, 209, 212, 400–401, 422
Public life, 12, 23, 28, 31, 49, 53, 61, 64, 65, 67, 72, 101–3, 106, 109, 126, 133, 135, 143, 159, 162, 195–96, 198, 213–14, 220n59, 255, 265, 274, 276–77, 280, 287, 289, 291, 298, 322, 350, 383–410, 433, 442–44, 447n1
  Emerson's career in, 4–7, 15, 31, 39n66, 49, 67, 73, 104, 128, 162, 170, 190–91, 194, 198, 213, 270, 273
Public opinion, 54, 61, 203, 443
"Public reason," 396, 409–10
Publius, 8, 12
  See also *Federalist Papers, The*; Hamilton, Alexander; Madison, James
Puritanism, 15, 345, 352
Puritans, 18, 66, 76, 327, 345–48, 351, 354

Race, 14, 39n66, 48–49, 70, 77, 85, 128–30, 132, 145n23, 153–54, 164, 166–71, 177–79, 182n40, 186, 196–97, 207, 211–13, 217n31, 219n51, 257, 278, 316, 321, 344, 357, 381n18, 383, 389
Rationalization, moral, 127, 132, 186
Rautenfeld, Hans von, 144n3, 396, 410n6, 411n8, 411n10, 412n38, 413n47, 416, 447n1
Rawls, John, 25, 105–9, 111, 114, 299, 396, 419–20
Read, James H., 27–28, 151n106, 181n24, 257, 336n9
Reality, Emerson on. *See* Transcendentalism
Reason, 5–6, 15, 28, 33n14, 72, 94, 187–89, 273, 282, 287, 291, 293–94, 306, 312, 350, 409
  See also Faculties; God
Reciprocity, 126, 135
Reconstruction, 15, 207, 282
Reform
  self-, 4–5, 71, 133–34, 192

Reform (*continued*)
　social, 5, 32n4, 65, 133–34, 158, 174, 185–86, 189, 191–92, 393
　See also Culture
Reid, Thomas, 349
Relativism. *See* Truth
Religion, 5, 9, 12, 15, 19, 44, 47, 56, 63, 65, 74, 79, 94, 106, 118, 152, 154, 173, 191, 245, 249, 263n50, 268–70, 274–75, 279–80, 282, 289–92, 297–98, 302n22, 350, 369, 374, 381n18, 383, 395, 421, 429, 445
Renaissance, 350
Reparations for slavery, 141, 150n96
　See also Antislavery
Representation, 3, 23–24, 26, 30–31, 60, 110, 387, 408, 411n24, 426, 447n1
Representative democracy, 4, 31, 53, 81, 195, 203–5, 208, 214, 362–63, 384–86, 404, 409, 412–13n46
　See also Democracy
Representative men, 57–58, 60, 62, 63, 165–66, 257, 334, 386–87, 391–402, 404–10, 416, 425–26, 439, 441–42, 444–45
　See also Emerson's writings: *Representative Men*
Republicanism, civic, 37n45, 54, 142, 352, 355
Republican Party, 15, 155, 160–61, 163–66, 169, 177–78
Resistance, 23, 79–80, 127, 139, 154–55, 159–60, 172, 183n56, 196, 198–99, 201, 205, 209, 217n29, 236, 299, 328, 397, 402, 407
"Resistance to Civil Government." *See* Thoreau, Henry David: "Civil Disobedience"
Respect, 10, 13, 27, 54, 59, 65, 73, 76–77, 84, 126, 132, 140–42, 144n7, 154–55, 162, 166, 169, 195–96, 204, 209, 214, 256–57, 276, 313, 366, 373, 402, 407, 415, 428–30, 435–38, 445–47, 449n20
Responsibility, 19, 37n49, 65, 105, 112, 125, 131, 134, 201, 374

Retranscendentalism, 28, 265, 273–304
　See also Detranscendentalism; Transcendentalism
Reverence (for others), 144n7, 353, 382n29, 395–98, 421, 424, 428, 436
　See also Admiration; Emulation
Reynolds, David S., 35n24, 35n28, 200n56, 407, 413n60, 413n63
Reynolds, Larry J., 218n35, 405, 413n53
Richardson, Robert D., 3, 33n15, 206, 270, 301n18, 303n36, 334n3, 378n5, 393, 396
Rights, 11, 13–15, 27–28, 30–31, 126, 142, 144n7, 167, 188–90, 197–99, 204, 208, 211, 213, 216n15, 253, 256–57, 299, 304n44, 356, 362, 364–65, 374–75, 377
Ripley, George, 218n40
Robinson, David M., 3, 33n11, 33n15, 34n19, 39n62, 184n70, 186, 215n3, 285, 301n16, 303n34
Romans, 86, 252, 350, 369
Romanticism, 5, 57, 59, 92, 108, 110, 119, 125, 307, 351, 391
　romantic views, 19, 62, 76, 93, 110, 348, 394
Rorty, Richard, 242, 263n46, 266–68, 281, 299, 300n6, 302n29
Rousseau, Jean-Jacques, 57, 78–79, 105, 409, 425
Rowe, John Carlos, 185, 215n4
Rowlandson, Mary, 346
Rusk, Ralph, 215n9, 300n3

Sacks, Kenneth, 33n7, 33n13, 182n40, 184n66, 300n14
Saint-Simon, Henri de, 70
Sale, Maggie, 217n31
Sandel, Michael, 151n105
Sandy Hook, New Jersey, 89
Santayana, George, 17, 44, 378n4
Schlesinger, Arthur M., 37n49, 185
Scholars. *See* Emerson's writings: "American Scholar, The"
Scholarship. *See* Emerson's politics: classic interpretations of, misinterpretations

of, new interpretations of; "New history"
Schopenhauer, Arthur, 107, 109–11, 223
Science and the scientific, 102, 106, 118, 173, 177–78, 182n41, 183n44, 191, 243, 245–46, 264nn51–52, 290, 303n33, 347, 350, 356, 379n7, 418, 427, 434–35, 440–41, 444, 447n1
Scottish Enlightenment, 5, 345, 348–52, 354, 362, 382
See also Enlightenment, the
Scottish liberalism, 355
Secession, 28, 160–61, 155, 163, 177, 182n12
Sectarianism, 9, 66, 273–74, 282–83, 288, 298–99, 304n44
Secularism, 21, 29–30, 112, 253, 268–74, 294, 297–99, 303n33, 346–48, 354, 369, 371, 374, 379n5
Self
  aboriginal, 239, 284–85, 306, 322
  good of, 225
  as internally divided, 232–33
  internal motion of, 234, 236
Self-absolution, 137
Self-articulation, 242
Self-authorship, 135
Self-awareness, 133, 256
Self-creation, 53, 55, 232, 254, 261n18, 446
Self-culture, 25, 95, 186, 211–12, 387, 397, 399, 442–46
Self-deception, 127, 132–33, 234
Self-development, 225, 234, 364, 419, 445
Self-discovery, 417, 423, 433
Self-examination, 128
Self-interest
  animalistic, 282
  and concern for others, 226, 256
  enlightened, 169
  material, 326, 330, 376
  and morality, 256
  of party politics, 209
  properly understood, 27, 433
  and toleration, 256
  and wisdom, 434

Self-interrogation, 134
Self-knowledge, 49, 109, 256, 419
Self-mastery, 141
Self-overcoming, 252, 386, 392, 403, 409
Self-perfection, 419, 427, 431, 446
  See also Perfectionism
Self-realization, 85, 132, 286
Self-reform, 4–5, 71, 133–34, 192
Self-reliance, 15, 56, 70–71, 77–79, 81, 86–87, 126, 132, 135, 148n56
  definition of, 1, 2, 4, 55, 126
  active, 70–71, 77–79, 81, 86–87, 126, 132, 135, 148n56
  and complicity, 126–42
  and conformity, 8, 10, 70, 127–43, 428
  critics and, 15–26, 55, 69, 73, 185–86, 269–70, 383–84, 419
  and democracy, 2–8, 10–11, 15, 30, 34n19, 56, 74–90, 127–43, 152–80, 185–214, 385–88, 392–94, 399, 409, 423, 430–38, 443
  and equality, 28
  and great men, 56, 430–38, 443, 447
  and interdependence, 366
  and justice, 142–43, 185–214
  limits of, 28, 69–90, 152–80
  mental, 26, 86, 126, 132, 135, 159
  and moral suasion, 4
  as a political practice, 3, 5–9, 11–12, 27–28, 70–71, 74–90, 127–43, 152–80, 185–214, 385–88, 392–94, 399
  properly understood, 27, 447
  and Reason, 6
  and slavery, 4, 10, 27–28, 34n21, 39n62, 73, 127–43, 152–80, 185–214, 335n9
  and toleration, 126
  transcendental basis of, 6, 26–28, 187–214, 239–43, 247–49, 285, 302n32, 306, 310
  See also Emerson's writings: "Self-Reliance"; Individualism; Individuality
Self-seeking, 47, 239
Self-sufficiency, 136, 397, 411n9, 421
Self-trust, 92, 127, 139, 239, 247, 284
  subjective, 227
  See also Individuality

Sellers, Charles, 346, 379–80n13, 380n17
Sermon on the Mount, 288
Shakespeare, William, 57–58, 93, 223, 271, 369, 387, 415–16, 445
　See also Emerson's writings: *Representative Men*
Sharp, Granville, 277, 389
Shklar, Judith, 21–25, 31, 39n61, 127, 128, 142, 153, 180n7, 182n37, 224–25, 257, 260n11, 261n18, 261n23, 284, 396, 410n6, 415, 417, 431, 435, 447n1
Sims, Thomas, 145n18, 200, 218n38
Skepticism, 23–24, 71, 93, 118–19, 127, 156, 192, 209, 231, 245–46, 261n20, 263n40, 266, 280, 283, 288–94, 302n28, 328, 335n5
Skeptics, 8, 27, 29–30, 32n33, 63–67, 151n106, 166, 223, 225, 227, 229, 232–34, 243–44, 247–48, 251, 257, 263n48, 318, 338n16, 372, 378n4, 416
Slavery. See Antislavery; Reparations for slavery
"Small canon," 2, 8, 16, 18–19, 21–23, 26, 30, 36n33, 37m45, 39n61, 277
Smith, Adam, 349, 365, 376
Smith, Gerrit, 150n93
Social action, 190, 202–3, 384, 387
Social activism, 7, 215n3
Social conditions, 12, 156
Social conformity, 8, 25, 54, 78, 87, 257
Social goods, 433
Social life, 190, 209, 313, 403, 420–24, 428, 442
Social norms, 258, 284
Social progress, 191, 212
Social realm, 3, 11, 17, 19, 55–56, 59, 62–64, 84, 126–27, 129, 142, 156, 168, 179, 199, 233, 258, 307, 322, 360, 366, 376, 418
Social reform, 5, 32n4, 65, 133–34, 158, 174, 185–86, 189, 191–92, 393
Social relations, 416, 428, 430, 432, 436, 438
Social world, 152, 157, 159
Society. See Citizenship; Communitarians; Democracy; Individualism; Individuality; Social life; Social norms; Social realm; Social relations; Social world
Socrates, 223, 310, 370, 419–20, 422, 425, 448n11
Solipsism, 24, 402
Sophocles, 292, 303n37
Soul, 2, 5–6, 8–10, 18, 29, 44, 46–49, 96, 99, 112, 142, 187, 193–94, 203, 216n11, 223–24, 233–36, 239–44, 248, 252, 256, 263n43, 270, 273–87, 291–93, 296–97, 300n3, 302n25, 304n37, 309, 316, 328–29, 332, 343, 364, 368–70, 373, 376, 381n21, 389, 394, 403, 416–18, 424–27, 431–32, 438–39, 442–46
　See also God; Reason
South Carolina, 161, 181n12, 205, 212, 219n52, 316, 380n15
Spinozistic vision, 250
Spirit, 9, 15–17, 27–28, 44–48, 66, 75, 79, 144, 155, 161, 190, 195, 197, 199–200, 203, 208, 224, 237, 239–41, 247, 259n1, 267, 272, 276, 310–11, 317, 331, 337n14, 392, 402–3, 408, 441
　See also God
Spiritual life and thought, 4, 18–20, 49, 55, 57, 74, 95, 112, 187–89, 204, 231–32, 234–35, 238, 241, 249, 259, 264n52, 274, 280, 290–91, 309, 337n14, 343–45, 353–54, 357–58, 364–65, 370, 374–77, 380n13, 415, 418, 433, 439, 441, 446
　See also God; Reason; Soul
Spontaneity, 22, 50, 239, 284
Stanley, Edward George Geoffrey Smith, 389
State, the, 7, 11–12, 22, 49, 61–62, 84–85, 91, 110–11, 120, 136, 138–39, 144n7, 191, 206, 255, 263n49, 277, 280, 362, 372, 377, 396, 404, 418
statism, 433
　See also Union (American); United States
Stendhal, 441
Stewart, James B., 181n25
Stoehr, Taylor, 38n51
Stoics, 86

Stout, Jeffrey, 150n100
Stroud, Barry, 93
Strysick, Michael, 39n62, 336n9
Suffrage, 76, 190, 213, 363
Sugar, 130–31, 146n30, 147n36, 169, 315, 373–74, 390
Sumner, Charles, 163, 181n12, 205
Superiority, 50, 57, 187, 415, 425, 430, 437, 444–45
Supreme Cause, 240
 See also God
Swedenborg, Emanuel, 57, 416, 426, 445
 See also Emerson's writings: *Representative Men*

Tate, Allen, 18
Taylor, Charles, 19, 38n52
Technology and the technological, 352, 358, 380n13, 381n20, 418, 440–41, 445–46
Teichgraeber, Richard F., III, 35n27
Teleology, 385, 417
Telos of society, 416
Temperance movement, 65, 192, 388
Texas, 194, 217n28, 217n29, 324, 443
Thinking, 91–121, 125–26, 134, 142, 157, 159, 171, 174–76, 244, 289, 294, 302n25, 305, 307–9, 332, 373, 432, 436, 445
Thompson, C. Bradley, 34n16
Thoreau, Henry David, 1, 32, 37n45, 72, 79–80, 85, 114–15, 118, 135–36, 139, 148n59, 162–63, 182n29, 337n13, 353–56, 358, 381n29, 388, 408–9
 "Civil Disobedience," 85, 135, 139
 "A Plea for Captain John Brown," 408
Tocqueville, Alexis de, 1–3, 7, 9–10, 20, 24, 27, 42, 54, 347, 364, 383, 386, 433
 Democracy in America, 7, 27, 43, 379n6, 383, 433
Totality, 416–17, 435
Toussaint L'Ouverture, François-Dominique, 169, 278
Town meeting, 7–8, 11, 24–25, 77–79, 84, 440
Trade, 50, 66, 76, 129–31, 136, 138, 147n36, 191–92, 199, 213, 279, 327–28, 348–49, 352–53, 373, 380n13, 440
 See also Capitalism; Commerce; Markets
Tradition, 4, 33n13, 39n64, 43, 45, 49, 149n90, 152, 154, 172, 214, 225, 268, 327, 345–48, 359, 367, 375, 419, 429, 446
Transcendence, 16, 59, 126, 268, 417–18, 420, 432, 435, 438
"Transcendental Club," 7
Transcendental equality, 30, 212, 265, 273–78, 280–82, 288, 290–92, 295, 298–99, 303n34
Transcendental gaze, 30, 305, 308, 314, 320
Transcendental idealism, 30, 305, 334, 335n4, 335n9, 336n12
Transcendentalism, 3, 15, 28–30, 186–87, 207–8, 212, 216n14, 219n49, 219n53, 220n56, 223–40, 391, 445
 See also Detranscendentalism; God; Retranscendentalism; Truth
Transcendental reality, 28–29, 226, 230–36, 240–42, 247, 249–51, 256–57, 269, 274, 276, 280, 281, 288–89, 291–93, 306, 309–31
Truth, 6, 16, 29, 51, 63, 67, 117, 152, 189–95, 202, 206, 227, 257, 259, 278–79, 285–86, 322, 332, 397, 407, 429, 431, 435, 444
 absolute (spiritual, transcendental), 19, 20, 29, 189, 237–40, 247–50, 256, 263n41, 274, 281, 291–92, 298–99, 302n29, 316, 322, 330, 444–45
 relative, 46, 50, 58, 227–32, 237–39, 263n41, 281, 282, 285, 292, 299, 302n29
 See also God; Skepticism; Transcendentalism
Turner, Jack, 27, 28, 33n10, 181n9, 183n56, 257, 335–36n9, 339–40n24, 390, 411n19

Übermenschen, 257, 286

Unifying ends, 418, 426, 440
Union (American), 5, 11, 13–14, 28, 84, 150n93, 155, 161–64, 175, 177–78, 181n12, 186, 190, 194, 196, 206, 208, 211–12, 217nn28–29, 219n51, 281, 324, 373, 405
  See also State, the
Union, of men, 10, 22, 48, 71, 144n7, 193–94, 246, 431, 445
Unitarianism, 7, 34n17, 44, 205, 245, 269, 275, 343, 348, 353, 363
United States, 11
  free, 82, 140, 154, 159, 160–63, 178, 195, 200, 203, 321
  northern, 1, 14–15, 162, 166, 171, 205, 208, 212, 274, 405, 407
  slave, 139, 150n93, 158, 191, 164, 167, 194, 217n29, 324–25
  southern, 1, 15, 35n26, 133, 139, 146n31, 158, 166, 168, 183n45, 205, 211–12, 274
Unity, 43–46, 87, 91–92, 162, 187–88, 204, 236, 241–43, 248, 254–55, 268, 286, 291, 301n22, 337n14, 417–18, 426–27, 430–31, 435, 438–41, 444, 446–47
  blessed, 238, 242
  See also Necessity: blessed
Universal divine, 186, 187, 227, 239, 248–49
Universal ends, 237, 242
Universal force, 237
Universal fraternity, 10, 47, 49, 171
Universal laws, 187
Universal principles and standards, 112, 173, 187–88, 196, 201, 204, 206–7, 209–10, 237, 274, 330
Universal progress, 287, 349, 353
Universal rights and freedom, 13, 31, 186, 188–89, 196, 208, 212, 216n23, 253
Universals, 102, 112, 255, 277, 282, 302n32, 306–13, 316–17, 320–34, 339n18, 349, 353, 364, 390, 402, 418, 429–30, 434, 437
  See also God; Reason; Soul; Transcendentalism; Truth

Universal soul, 47, 263
Universal whole, 240, 242
Updike, John, 20, 296, 297, 304n39
Utopianism, 12, 13, 65, 66, 173, 186, 360, 372, 378n4

Vallandigham, Clement L., 208
Van Buren, Martin, 8, 11, 80, 363, 381n21
Vermont, 55, 153
Vietnam War, 19
Vikings, 252
Virginia, 128, 159, 363
Virtue, 8, 20, 24, 31, 37n49, 99, 171, 185, 188, 214, 240, 247, 275, 279, 284, 322–23, 353, 359, 362, 368, 376, 417, 419–33, 438, 447, 448n11
  civic, 19, 79–80, 424
  public, 49, 67
  skepticism as, 64
  "wild," 157
  See also Morality
Vision, 305–40, 369
Von Frank, Albert, 3, 32n6, 33n15, 145n13, 145n18, 181n21, 214n3, 219n52, 299n1

Wakefulness, 127, 133
  See also Awakening
Wall Street, 133, 174
Walzer, Michael, 150n102
War, 87, 136, 179, 239, 251, 264n52, 327, 362, 395, 442
  See also Civil War; Kansas; Kansas-Nebraska Act; Mexican War; Vietnam War
Washington, George, 59, 61, 204, 406
Wealth, 61, 77, 85, 128, 136, 141, 173, 213, 329, 344, 346, 350, 355, 362, 364–65, 375, 393, 398, 418, 428, 439–42, 446
Weber, Max, 345, 421
Webster, Daniel, 166, 173, 182n39, 204, 325, 373, 404–6
Weiskell, Thomas, 114
West, Cornel, 145n23, 338n15, 378n4
West, the, 118, 139, 146, 165, 268, 292, 351, 418, 439–41, 446

West Indies, 130, 140, 196–97, 315, 373–74
  abolition of slavery in, 131, 141, 169–70, 196–97, 200, 332, 374, 381n18
Whicher, Stephen, 18, 19, 174, 180n2, 360, 363, 365, 371, 377–78n4
Whigs, 178, 349–54, 357, 363
Whites, 81, 167, 169, 196
Whitman, Walt, 44, 394, 412n27
Whittier, John Greenleaf, 217–18n34
Whole, the, 231, 407, 427, 434
Wider, Sarah, 18, 36n41, 37n47, 38n51, 39nn63–64, 301n18, 338n15
Wilberforce, William, 389
Will
  collective, 71, 78, 83, 90, 208, 212, 400–401
  divine, 241, 248, 291, 320, 434
  of the great, 57, 80
  individual, 20, 49, 51, 53, 67, 69, 78, 90, 176, 186, 233–43, 247–49, 251–59, 263n41, 328
  limits of, 174
  to power, 235–36, 238–39, 242, 249, 251, 253, 258, 263n41
  world as, 49
Willey, Basil, 215n9
Wills, Gary, 219n49
Winters, Yvor, 18, 20
Wisdom, 31, 47, 49–50, 79, 241, 284–85, 296–97, 361, 400, 416–17
Wise men, 12, 61, 192, 203, 207, 231, 428
Wittgenstein, Ludwig, 93, 101, 118–19, 293, 355
Wolfe, Cary, 19, 38n51
Wood, Fernando, 208
Wood, Gordon, 351, 380n14
Writers, 25, 98, 108, 111, 161, 224, 229, 270–71, 301n16, 355, 358, 379n5, 418, 428, 433, 442–46

Yankees, 55–57, 67, 345, 347, 375

Zakaras, Alex, 33n8, 143, 144nn5–7, 149n71, 414n67

www.ingramcontent.com/pod-product-compliance
Lightning Source LLC
Chambersburg PA
CBHW020631230426
43665CB00008B/128